THE
BEETHOVEN
COMPENDIUM

THE BEETHOVEN COMPENDIUM

A GUIDE TO BEETHOVEN'S LIFE AND MUSIC

*BARRY COOPER, ANNE-LOUISE COLDICOTT,
NICHOLAS MARSTON AND WILLIAM DRABKIN*

EDITED BY BARRY COOPER

THAMES AND HUDSON

Managing Editor BARRY MILLINGTON

FRONTISPIECE: Detail from oil painting of Beethoven by Joseph Willibrord Mähler, 1815

Designed by Liz Rudderham

© 1991 Thames and Hudson Ltd, London

First paperback edition with corrections 1996

ISBN 0-500-27871-7

Printed in the USA Print on Demand Edition

CONTENTS

Section 13   *BEETHOVEN LITERATURE*

Reader's Guide

THE AIM OF THIS BOOK is to provide a compendium of information on every significant aspect of Beethoven and his music. The entire range of subject matter has been covered: a chronological survey of his life; his friends and acquaintances; the musical and historical background; his character and personality; the sources from which our knowledge about him is derived; a full listing and discussion of the works; his musical style; problems of performance practice; and his impact on others, ranging from early reviews of his music to the whole Beethoven research 'industry' that exists today. The book thus incorporates within a single volume many of the best features of most of the major Beethoven reference books, including Theodor Frimmel's *Beethoven-Handbuch*, Georg Kinsky and Hans Halm's thematic catalogue of his works, *Thayer's Life of Beethoven*, the genre-by-genre discussion of his works in *The Beethoven Companion*, the Beethoven entry in *The New Grove Dictionary of Music and Musicians* (and its separately published revision), and the recent monumental survey of his sketchbooks by Douglas Johnson, Alan Tyson and Robert Winter (Frimmel, 1926; Kinsky, 1955; Thayer, 1967; Arnold, 1971; Kerman, 1983; Johnson, 1985. Here and elsewhere bibliographical references are cited in abbreviated form; see the Select Bibliography for the full citation).

Throughout, the emphasis has been on presenting hard, factual data in concise form, rather than lengthy and eloquent commentary, the assumption being that the book is likely to be regarded more as a handy reference tool than a work of literature. But commentaries also have their place, and they have been designed for the most part to be easily understood by all musicians. Thus each section is intended to offer a clearly presented, accessible and thoroughly up-to-date summary of the most authoritative writing on the subject. Non-specialists will find in the book virtually any information they are likely to want about Beethoven and his music, while Beethoven specialists should find it a convenient reference work for checking facts and figures, dates and places. Bibliographical references have been minimized, being omitted where a fact or opinion is generally accepted. They have been used mainly to indicate controversial opinions or recently discovered and little-known facts.

Each section of the book is written by one or other of the four co-authors, but all four have had opportunities to comment on each other's work, while the General Editor has had overall responsibility for designing the layout of the contents and coordinating the various contributions. There should therefore be no inconsistencies of fact between the various sections. There may, however, be differences of style, emphasis and opinion. These have been allowed to stand, so as to illustrate something of the variety of responses to Beethoven's music that can legitimately be made by scholars. The identity of the author of each section is indicated in the list of contents.

It is hoped that this list of contents will lead the reader swiftly to the desired information. Cross-references have therefore been kept to a minimum. In particular it should be noted that information about dates and events is concentrated in Section 1; additional details about individuals referred to anywhere in the book can normally be found in Sections 2 and 3; and information about the music can be found in the genre-by-genre lists of works and commentary in Section 10. If the opus number of a work is known but not its genre, the work can be traced through the numerical list of works at the beginning of Section 10.

Many of Beethoven's works have a popular title. Where this stems from Beethoven himself and is therefore in a sense part of the composition, it is given in italics, as in the *Pastoral* Symphony; but where it is merely a whimsical nickname coined later, it is given in quotation marks, as in the so-called 'Moonlight' Sonata (quotation marks are also used for the first words or titles of arias etc. in longer works). With sets of variations on the work of another composer, that composer's name is given without italics or quotation marks, as in the Diabelli Variations. References to Beethoven's letters use the numbers allocated in the standard English edition by Emily Anderson: *The Letters of Beethoven* (London, 1961).

I should like to express my warmest thanks to each of my colleagues for their readiness to contribute to the volume, and for their friendly and helpful cooperation throughout its preparation. Also I should like to thank Barry Millington, formerly of Thames and Hudson, for inviting me to oversee the project, and for his useful editorial advice at each stage of it.

Barry Cooper
UNIVERSITY OF MANCHESTER 1990

Section 1
CALENDAR OF BEETHOVEN'S LIFE, WORKS AND RELATED EVENTS

CALENDAR OF BEETHOVEN'S LIFE, WORKS AND RELATED EVENTS

THE FOLLOWING CALENDAR CONTAINS all the most important events in Beethoven's life, many of the less important ones, and a few significant events from outwith his immediate environment. Not included are many of his less important compositions (see Section 10), his numerous changes of residence (see Section 6) and the dates of his Conversation Books and sketchbooks. Where there is a mixture of precise and approximate dates within a single year, they are listed in the following order: precise day; approximate day; precise month (if day uncertain); approximate month; precise year (if month uncertain); approximate year. Approximate dates are marked **c.** (*circa*). Details about most individuals mentioned are given in Section 3.

c. 1740
Beethoven's father Johann born in Bonn.

1746
19 Dec. Beethoven's mother Maria Magdalena born in Ehrenbreitstein.

1752
Beethoven's father enters court chapel as treble.

1761
6 Apr. Maximilian Friedrich, Beethoven's first patron, appointed Elector of Cologne.

1763
30 Jan. Beethoven's mother's first marriage.

1764
24 Apr. Beethoven's father appointed as court musician in Bonn.

1765
28 Nov. Beethoven's mother widowed.

1767
12 Nov. Marriage of Beethoven's parents.

1769
2 Apr. Beethoven's older brother, Ludwig Maria, baptized (died six days later).

1770
c. Mar. Beethoven's life begins.
16 Dec. Beethoven born (there is still slight doubt about the precise date).

17 Dec. Beethoven baptized in the church of St Remigius.

1773
24 Dec. Beethoven's beloved grandfather Ludwig dies.

1774
8 Apr. Beethoven's brother Caspar Anton Carl baptized.
c. 1774 Beethoven begins learning music (taught initially by his father).

1775
30 Sep. Beethoven's grandmother Maria Josepha dies.

1776
2 Oct. Beethoven's brother Nikolaus Johann baptized.

1778
26 Mar. Beethoven's first known public performance, in Cologne, playing 'various concertos and trios'.

1779
23 Feb. Beethoven's sister Anna Maria Franziska baptized (died four days later).
Oct. Neefe arrives in Bonn, and shortly after begins giving Beethoven musical instruction.

1781
17 Jan. Beethoven's brother Franz Georg baptized.

16 Mar. Mozart moves to Vienna.
Summer (?) Beethoven leaves school.

1782
Beethoven's first published work appears – the Dressler Variations (WoO 63).

1783
2 Mar. Neefe publishes commendatory notice about Beethoven in Cramer's *Magazin der Musik*.
16 Aug. Beethoven's two-year-old brother Franz Georg dies.
14 Oct. Three 'Kurfürsten' Sonatas (WoO 47) published.
c. Nov. Beethoven and his mother visit Rotterdam (travelling by ship down the Rhine).
1783 *Schilderung eines Mädchens* (WoO 107) and Rondo in C (WoO 48) published.
c. 1783 Organ fugue (WoO 31) composed. Beethoven becomes acquainted with Wegeler and Stephan von Breuning, two lifelong friends, and deputizes for Neefe as cembalist in court orchestra.

1784
Feb. Bonn flooded.
15 Apr. Elector Max Friedrich dies, succeeded by Maximilian Franz.
Jun. Beethoven appointed court organist (alongside Neefe), at a salary of 150 fl. (100 thalers).
1784 Two more compositions published (Rondo, WoO 49, and *An einen Säugling*, WoO 108).
c. 1784 Piano Concerto in E♭ (WoO 4) composed.

1785
Three piano quartets (WoO 36) composed. Anton Reicha arrives in Bonn and becomes closely acquainted with Beethoven.

1786
5 May Beethoven's sister Maria Margaretha Josepha baptized.
20 Nov. Bonn University inaugurated.
1786 Trio for piano and wind (WoO 37) composed.

1787
Mar.–May Beethoven visits Vienna to study with Mozart, remaining there about two weeks. During his journey he stops at Munich (1 and 25 Apr.) and Augsburg, amongst other places.
17 Jul. Beethoven's mother dies of consumption.
25 Nov. Beethoven's one-year-old sister Maria Margaretha dies.
c. 1787 Earliest version of Second Piano Concerto composed.

1788
c. 30 Jan. Count Waldstein arrives in Bonn.

1789
3 Jan. Opera theatre opens at Bonn court. Beethoven plays viola in several operas during the next few months, including Mozart's *Die Entführung aus dem Serail*.
13 Oct.–23 Feb. 1790 Second season of operas in Bonn, including Mozart's *Nozze di Figaro* and *Don Giovanni*.
20 Nov. Beethoven's father retires and his 200-reichsthaler salary is halved, the other 100 thalers being awarded thenceforth to Beethoven for the upkeep of his brothers. (In order to maintain their public image, however, these 100 thalers in fact continued to be paid to the father, who made them over privately to Beethoven.)
1789 (?) Two preludes (op. 39) composed.

1790
20 Feb. Emperor Joseph II dies.
24 Feb. News of Joseph II's death reaches Bonn.
28 Feb. Text of a cantata on Joseph's death is presented in Bonn for setting to music, and plans are made to perform it on 19 Mar. Beethoven is asked to make the setting.
17 Mar. Plans to perform Beethoven's setting of the cantata (WoO 87) abandoned.
30 Sep. Leopold II elected emperor.
c. Sep.–Oct. Cantata on the Elevation of Leopold II (WoO 88) composed.
9 Oct. Coronation of Leopold II.
23 Oct. Start of third opera season in Bonn (including works by Paisiello, Dalayrac, Umlauf and others).
25 Dec. Haydn and Salomon, travelling from Vienna to London, arrive in Bonn.
26 Dec. Haydn and Salomon dine with several Bonn musicians, perhaps including Beethoven.

1791
6 Mar. Beethoven's newly composed *Ritterballett* (WoO 1) first performed.
c. Jul.–Aug. Righini Variations (WoO 65) published.
c. 30 Aug. Bonn court musicians, including Beethoven, depart for Mergentheim, where Elector Max Franz is to attend a meeting of the Teutonic Order (18 Sep.–20 Oct.).
Sep. At Aschaffenburg Beethoven hears the virtuoso pianist Sterkel, and then plays some of his Righini Variations to him, improvising some additional variations in Sterkel's style.
5 Dec. Mozart dies in Vienna.
28 Dec. Start of fourth opera season in Bonn (including Mozart's *Die Entführung* and works by Dittersdorf, Paisiello, Dalayrac and others).
c. 1791 Two bass arias (WoO 89–90), soprano aria (WoO 92), the Swiss Variations (WoO 64), Violin Concerto in C (WoO 5), a Piano Trio (WoO 38) and a few minor works composed.

1792

Jul.   Haydn stops at Bonn during his return journey to Vienna.

Early Oct.   French troops in Rhine area, invading Mainz and other cities; Elector Max Franz temporarily leaves Bonn on 22 Oct.

24 Oct.   First farewell entry in Beethoven's album (see 'Diaries and other documents', p. 169) as he prepares to depart for Vienna to study with Haydn.

c. 2 Nov.   Beethoven leaves Bonn for Vienna with a companion, passing through Remagen, Andernach, Coblenz, Montebaur, Limburg, Würges. Here his companion leaves him, and he travels on via Nuremberg, Regensburg, Passau and Linz.

c. 10 Nov.   Beethoven arrives in Vienna and begins equipping himself for his new life ('wood, wig, coffee...overcoat, boots, shoes, piano-desk...'). His study with Haydn commences shortly after arrival.

18 Dec.   Beethoven's father dies.

c. 1792   Oboe Concerto (Hess 12), sets of variations (op. 44; WoO 40, 66, 67), Octet (op. 103), several songs (see p. 264) and some minor works composed.

1793

Jul.   'Se vuol ballare' Variations (WoO 40) published.

c. 24 Oct.   Beethoven dines at Van Swieten's.

Oct.   Beethoven buys coffee and chocolate for Haydn and himself.

c. Oct.   Dittersdorf Variations (WoO 66) published.

1793   Octet (op. 103) and Second Piano Concerto revised (the latter probably with the Rondo WoO 6 as finale).

1794

19 Jan.   Haydn departs for England. Beethoven thenceforth continues his musical studies with Albrechtsberger (three times a week).

Mar.   Termination of Beethoven's salary payments from Elector Max Franz.

c. May   Beethoven's brother Carl moves to Vienna.

c. Aug.   Waldstein Variations (WoO 67) published.

Oct.   Wegeler arrives in Vienna and renews his friendship with Beethoven.

1794   Beethoven begins composing what became his first major publication – the Piano Trios op. 1. Also composes many fugues for the tutorials with Albrechtsberger, several other minor works, and ideas for the Piano Sonatas op. 2. Lorenz von Breuning moves to Vienna.

1794–early 1795   Second Piano Concerto revised again, probably with a new slow movement and finale.

1795

29 Mar.   Beethoven's first public performance in Vienna, at the Burgtheater, when he probably premiered the First Piano Concerto (according to an alternative hypothesis, he played the Second Piano Concerto at this concert and premiered the First at the one on 18 Dec.). Wegeler reports that Beethoven wrote the Rondo of this concerto only two days before the performance, while feeling unwell, and at the rehearsal next day Beethoven had to play his part in C♯ major as the piano was a semitone flat!

30 Mar.   Second concert at the Burgtheater, at which Beethoven also takes part.

May   Invitations for subscriptions to Beethoven's Trios op. 1 appear in the *Wiener Zeitung*.

c. Jul.   Conclusion of Beethoven's studies with Albrechtsberger.

Jul.–Aug.   Trios op. 1 published.

20 Aug.   Haydn arrives back in Vienna. On hearing Beethoven's Trios op. 1 he advised against the publication of no. 3 in C minor, according to Ries; but if the story is correct the advice must have been given after the event.

c. Sep.–Oct.   Beethoven's recently completed sonatas op. 2 are performed before Haydn, their dedicatee, at one of Lichnowsky's concerts.

22 Nov.   Grand ball of the Gesellschaft der bildenden Künstler, for which Beethoven composes two sets of dances (WoO 7–8).

18 Dec.   Beethoven performs his First or Second Piano Concerto at a concert given by Haydn.

26 Dec.   Beethoven's brother Johann arrives in Vienna.

1795   Unfinished symphony in C begun; final version of Trio op. 3 completed; Quintet op. 4, Variations (WoO 68–70), Minuets (WoO 10) composed.

c. 1795   Beethoven allegedly proposes marriage to Magdalena Willmann, a singer from Bonn resident at that time in Vienna, but is refused. Sextet op. 81b, Trio op. 87, Variations (WoO 28 and 72), arias (WoO 91), songs and minor works composed.

1796

8 Jan.   Beethoven plays a piano concerto at a concert in the Redoutensaal.

19 Feb.   Beethoven writes (to brother Johann) from Prague, where he had recently arrived with Prince Lichnowsky for the start of a concert tour.

Feb.–Apr.   Beethoven composes *Ah! perfido* (op. 65) and mandolin music (WoO 43–4) for Countess Josephine de Clary in Prague; Six German Dances (WoO 42) for the Countesses Thun; the Piano Sonata op. 49 no. 2; and the Wind Sextet op. 71.

11 Mar.   Beethoven gives a concert in Prague.

Mar.   Piano Sonatas op. 2 published.

23 Apr. Beethoven arrives in Dresden.
29 Apr. Beethoven performs in Dresden before the Elector of Saxony, before leaving the city shortly afterwards for Leipzig and Berlin.
c. **May** Trio op. 3 and Quintet op. 4 published.
c. **May–Jul.** Beethoven in Berlin. While there he composes the Cello Sonatas op. 5 (for the court cellist Jean-Louis Duport), the *Judas Maccabaeus* Variations (WoO 45), part of the Quintet op. 16, ideas for the Third Piano Concerto, and part of the soon-to-be-abandoned Symphony in C.
c. **Jul. (?)** Beethoven returns to Vienna.
Nov. Beethoven visits Pressburg (Bratislava) and Pest (Budapest), giving a concert in the former on 23 Nov.
c. **Nov.** Variations (WoO 71) composed.
c. **1796** *Adelaide* (op. 46) and Variations (op. 66) composed; Sonata op. 10 no. 1 begun.

1797
Jan. Beethoven performs in a concert given by Andreas and Bernhard Romberg of Bonn, who were temporarily in Vienna.
Feb. Cello Sonatas (op. 5) and *Adelaide* (op. 46) published.
c. **early 1797** Sonatas opp. 6 and 7, Serenade op. 8 composed.
6 Apr. First performance of Quintet op. 16.
Apr. Variations (WoO 71) published, dedicated to Countess Browne; in return the Count presents Beethoven with a horse, which, however, the composer rode only a few times.
Summer Beethoven's activities during this period are undocumented. From this time (alternatively from summer 1796) may date a serious illness which perhaps gave rise to the onset of his deafness.
1 Oct. Beethoven bids farewell to Lorenz von Breuning.
Oct. Opp. 6–8 published.
Nov. Beethoven's dances (WoO 7–8) written for the grand ball two years earlier are reused by the Gesellschaft der bildenden Künstler.
23 Dec. 'La ci darem' Variations (WoO 28) performed.
c. **1797** Piano Sonata op. 49 no. 1 composed.

1798
c. **early 1798** Piano Sonatas op. 10 completed; Trios op. 9 composed (publication contract dated 16 Mar.); Trio op. 11, Violin Sonatas op. 12, composed.
5 Feb. General Bernadotte arrives in Vienna.
29 Mar. Beethoven and Schuppanzigh perform a violin sonata (probably one from op. 12).
c. **Apr.–Jul.** Piano Sonata op. 14 no. 1 composed.
21 Jul. Publication announcement for Trios op. 9. (Works tended to appear a few days before the publication announcement, which is the most

accurate indication of their exact publication date.)
c. **Jul.–Aug.** Beethoven begins using sketchbooks instead of just loose sketch leaves.
c. **Aug.** Quartets op. 18 begun.
22 Sep. Publication announcement for Cello Variations op. 66.
26 Sep. Publication announcement for Piano Sonatas op. 10.
c. **Sep.–Oct.** Second Piano Concerto revised and a new score written out.
3 Oct. Publication announcement for Trio op.
11. First issue of the Leipzig *Allgemeine Musikalische Zeitung*, edited by Rochlitz.
c. **mid-Oct. (?)** Beethoven visits Prague and performs both First and Second Piano Concertos.
27 Oct. Beethoven performs a concerto in Vienna.
Dec. (or Jan. 1799) Violin Sonatas op. 12 published.
1798 Septet op. 20 begun: *Pathétique* Sonata op. 13 and various minor works composed.

1799
c. **early 1799** Dragonetti visits Vienna and probably meets Beethoven. Beethoven probably begins instruction with Salieri about this time.
Feb. Salieri Variations (WoO 73) published.
25 Jun. Quartet op. 18 no. 1 (first version) given to Beethoven's close friend Amenda, who leaves Vienna a few weeks later.
Sep. J. B. Cramer visits Vienna, becoming closely acquainted with Beethoven and remaining until the following spring.
c. **Oct.** *Pathétique* Sonata (op. 13) published.
21 Dec. Publication announcement for Piano Sonatas op. 14 and Variations WoO 75.
1799 Extensive work on String Quartets op. 18; First Symphony begun.

1800
c. **early 1800** Third Piano Concerto sketched (?), perhaps intended for Beethoven's Apr. benefit concert.
2 Apr. Beethoven's first benefit concert in Vienna, including the premieres of his newly completed Septet and First Symphony, plus works by Haydn and Mozart and a piano concerto (No. 1?) by Beethoven (see 'Beethoven's musical environment', p. 90 for complete programme).
18 Apr. First performance of the Horn Sonata (op. 17), specially written for the visiting virtuoso Johann Stich (alias Punto), who had recently arrived in Vienna.
7 May Beethoven and Stich appear together again in a concert, in Budapest, where Beethoven probably remained until early Jul.
4 Aug. Beethoven sends a copy of his setting of Matthisson's *Adelaide* to the poet, thanking him for the pleasure that his poetry has provided.

1800 *(cont.)*
c. Dec. The composer and music publisher
Franz Anton Hoffmeister moves from Vienna to
Leipzig to set up a publishing house (Hoffmeister
& Kühnel). In response to his enquiries
Beethoven offers him four works (opp. 19–22) on
15 Dec.
Late 1800 Violin Sonata op. 23 composed;
Second Symphony begun.

1801
30 Jan. Beethoven and Stich perform the Horn
Sonata at a charity concert.
c. Jan. Beethoven commissioned to write the
music for Vigano's ballet *Die Geschöpfe des
Prometheus*; other compositions are temporarily set
aside.
21 Mar. Publication announcement for First
Piano Concerto, Quintet, and Horn Sonata (opp.
15–17).
28 Mar. Premiere of the ballet *Die Geschöpfe des
Prometheus*. (It was performed thirteen more times
that year and nine times the next.)
Apr. Piano part of Second Piano Concerto
written out for the first time and sent to
Hoffmeister for publication.
c. Apr.–Jun. Piano Sonata op. 26 composed.
Mid-Jun. Stephan von Breuning moves to
Vienna.
29 Jun. Beethoven writes a long letter to
Wegeler revealing for the first time his hearing
deficiency.
c. Jun. Three Quartets op. 18 nos 1–3
published.
1 Jul. Beethoven writes a long letter to
Amenda, similar in tone to one to Wegeler two
days earlier; he also asks Amenda not to lend the
Quartet op. 18 no. 1 to anyone as he has 'only
just learned to write quartets' properly and has
made a new version.
26 Jul. Elector Max Franz dies at Hetzendorf,
Vienna; the intended dedication of the First
Symphony to him is subsequently changed in
favour of Van Swieten.
28 Oct. Publication announcement for three
Quartets (op. 18 nos 4–6) and two Violin
Sonatas (opp. 23–4).
Oct. Ries arrives in Vienna and is immediately
welcomed by Beethoven, who starts giving him
piano lessons.
16 Nov. Beethoven writes to Wegeler
mentioning a 'dear charming girl' with whom he
is in love – probably Countess Guicciardi. He
starts giving the Countess piano lessons about this
time.
Dec. Second Piano Concerto (op. 19) and First
Symphony (op. 21) published.
1801 Piano Sonatas opp. 27–8 and Quintet op.
29 composed.
c. 1801 Serenade op. 25, Violin Romance op.

40, and Gellert Lieder (op. 48) composed.
Czerny begins receiving piano lessons from
Beethoven.

1802
c. early 1802 Anton Reicha, Beethoven's old
friend from Bonn, arrives in Vienna and renews
their friendship.
c. Feb. Second Symphony completed.
3 Mar. Publication announcement for Piano
Sonatas opp. 26 and 27.
23 Mar. First Viennese performance of
Cherubini's *Lodoïska* (produced by Schikaneder),
which meets with great success.
Mar. Piano Sonata op. 22 published.
c. Mar. *Tremate* (op. 116) composed; Serenade
(op. 25) published.
c. Mar.–May Violin Sonatas op. 30 composed.
Early Apr. Beethoven's anticipated benefit
concert is not permitted by the Court Theatre
director Baron Braun.
Apr. Beethovens moves to Heiligenstadt in an
attempt to relieve his ears.
c. May Piano Variations opp. 34–5 begun.
c. Jun.–Sep. Piano Sonatas op. 31 composed.
c. late Jun. Septet op. 20 published
(publication announced 24 Jul.).
13 Aug. First Viennese performance of
Cherubini's *Les Deux Journées* (*Der Wasserträger*).
14 Aug. Publication announcement for Piano
Sonata op. 28.
6 Oct. Beethoven writes the Heiligenstadt
Testament (see pp. 169–72).
10 Oct. Beethoven writes an addendum to the
Heiligenstadt Testament; shortly afterwards he
returns to Vienna.
18 Oct. Piano Variations opp. 34–5 offered to
Breitkopf & Härtel of Leipzig.
9 Nov. Beethoven learns of publication
problems over his Quintet op. 29. Having sold a
copy to Count Fries for his private use, and sold
the work to Breitkopf & Härtel for publication,
he discovers that Fries has passed on his copy to
Artaria for publication.
12 Nov. Beethoven obtains from Artaria an
undertaking not to publish their edition of op. 29
until fourteen days after Breitkopf's has
circulated in Vienna.
13 Nov. Beethoven, having obtained proof
copies of Artaria's edition of op. 29 and made
numerous corrections (apparently with the aid of
Ries, who was instructed to correct them so
heavily as to render them useless), writes to
Breitkopf explaining the problem, exonerating
himself and observing that his brother Carl, who
had been helping him sort out the situation, lost
his favourite dog in the confusion.
23 Nov. Brother Carl offers Beethoven's Second
Symphony and Third Piano Concerto to the
publisher André, stating that Beethoven now

composes 'only oratorios, operas, etc.'. This is the first indication of Beethoven's intention to write the oratorio *Christus am Oelberge*.
Dec. Quintet op. 29 published by Breitkopf & Härtel, followed in due course by Artaria's edition.
1802 Bagatelles op. 33 composed.

1803
22 Jan. Beethoven places an announcement in the *Wiener Zeitung* attacking Artaria's edition of op. 29 as 'very faulty, incorrect, and utterly useless to players'.
c. **Jan.** Beethoven appointed composer at the Theater an der Wien, and shortly afterwards takes up residence there, along with his brother Carl.
14 Feb. Artaria file Court petition demanding Beethoven retract his statement; the Court supported Artaria over the matter, but Beethoven never published a full retraction.
c. **Feb.–Mar.** *Christus am Oelberge* composed; Third Piano Concerto completed.
5 Apr. Beethoven's benefit concert in the Theater an der Wien: premieres of Second Symphony, Third Piano Concerto and *Christus am Oelberge*; First Symphony also performed. Beethoven gains receipts of about 1800 fl.
c. **early Apr.** The violinist George Bridgetower arrives in Vienna.
Apr. Sonatas op. 31 nos 1–2, Variations op. 34, published.
24 May Recital by Bridgetower, who performs Beethoven's newly written violin sonata (later dedicated to Kreutzer) with the composer. The recital was postponed from 22 May, perhaps because the sonata was still not ready.
28 May Publication announcement for Violin Sonatas op. 30 and Bagatelles op. 33; but op. 30 nos 2–3 were apparently delayed until Jun.
c. **Jun.** Beethoven and Schikaneder plan a new opera, *Vestas Feuer*.
c. **Jun.–Oct.** *Eroica* Symphony composed.
20 Jul. First letter from the Scottish publisher George Thomson to Beethoven (who replied on 5 Oct.).
4 Aug. *Christus am Oelberge* given second performance.
6 Aug. Piano maker Sebastien Erard of Paris sends Beethoven a new piano, with extended compass up to high c'''', as a gift. The instrument still survives.
Aug. *Prometheus* (or 'Eroica') Variations op. 35, Gellert Lieder op. 48, published.
c. **Aug.** Three Marches for piano duet, op. 45, composed. A letter (Letter 61) mentioning two of them, which also refers to Beethoven being at Heiligenstadt, was formerly taken to indicate that the marches were written in 1802; but the sketches prove that they belong to 1803, and it

seems probable that his reference to Heiligenstadt denoted his 1803 lodgings in Oberdöbling, which were less than a mile from Heiligenstadt.
Sep. Beethoven assigns six works (opp. 39–44) to the publisher Hoffmeister & Kühnel for 50 ducats; the works are all published in Dec. and Jan.
c. **Nov.–Dec.** 'Waldstein' Sonata composed (with WoO 57 as second movement).
c. **Dec.** *Vestas Feuer* abandoned; *Leonore* taken up.

1804
4 Jan. Beethoven returns a libretto by Rochlitz to the author, since he is starting to work on *Leonore*.
14 Feb. Sonnleithner, who is adapting the libretto of *Leonore*, is appointed Secretary of the Court Theatre.
c. **Feb.** Earliest ideas sketched for the Fifth Symphony and Fourth Piano Concerto.
10 Mar. Publication announcement for Second Symphony and Marches op. 45.
27 Mar. *Christus am Oelberge* performed in a revised version.
c. **Apr.** Beethoven's contract at the Theater an der Wien is terminated. He moves out of his rooms there and the plans to perform *Leonore* are abandoned. Schikaneder is also dismissed.
c. **Apr.–Sep.** Triple Concerto, Piano Sonata op. 54 composed.
20 May Napoleon proclaimed Emperor. The news reaches Vienna a few days later and on hearing it Beethoven tears up the title page of the *Eroica* bearing the dedication to Napoleon (cf. 'Symphonies', pp. 214–15; Beethoven's action may not have taken place until after the actual coronation on 2 Dec. – see Beahrs, 1989).
c. **May–Jun.** Piano Sonata op. 31 no. 3 published.
Early Jul. Beethoven and Breuning, who had for a short time been sharing lodgings, have a serious disagreement and Beethoven leaves. Friendship is restored a few months later.
19 Jul. Ries performs Beethoven's Third Piano Concerto at one of the Thursday concerts at the Augarten, with Beethoven conducting. (Ries had composed his own cadenza, which included a very difficult passage; Beethoven was opposed to him attempting the passage at the concert, but Ries did so successfully and Beethoven was delighted.)
c. **late Aug.** Schikaneder and Beethoven are reinstated at the Theater an der Wien, and the *Leonore* project is revived.
c. **Oct.** Beethoven becomes closely acquainted with the Brunsvik sisters, and begins giving Josephine piano lessons.
c. **Dec.** The song *An die Hoffnung* (op. 32) composed.

1805

c. **Jan.–Feb.** Beethoven presents Josephine Deym-Brunsvik with *An die Hoffnung* (op. 32), and their relationship becomes very close. Schuppanzigh gives a series of recitals of chamber music by Beethoven and others, including quartets by him and his Sextet op. 71.

13 Feb. Earliest review of the *Eroica* in the *Allgemeine Musikalische Zeitung*, after its performance at a concert organized by the banker Würth.

7 Apr. The *Eroica*, already performed several times at Lobkowitz's palace, receives its first public performance at Franz Clement's benefit concert, with Beethoven conducting.

Apr. Violin Sonata op. 47 ('Kreutzer') published.

15 May Publication announcement for Violin Romance op. 50 and 'Waldstein' Sonata op. 53.

c. **spring** 'Appassionata' Sonata composed. An anecdote by Ries seems to place the composition in summer 1804, but the sketches clearly suggest 1805 for the main period of written work.

26 Jun. Publication announcement for Eight Songs, op. 52.

Jul. Beethoven's first meeting with Cherubini.

c. **Jul.** Aria *Ah! perfido* (op. 65) published.

18 Sep. Publication announcement for *An die Hoffnung* (op. 32).

30 Sep. Projected performance of *Leonore* banned by the censor.

c. **Sep.** *Leonore* completed (first version, with overture *Leonore* No. 2). Ries leaves Vienna. *Andante favori* (WoO 57) published.

5 Oct. Censor's ban on *Leonore* lifted after a petition from Sonnleithner.

13 Nov. French army occupies Vienna. Napoleon shortly thereafter establishes his headquarters at Schönbrunn Palace.

20 Nov. Premiere of *Leonore* (postponed from 15 Oct.).

21–22 Nov. Repeat performances of *Leonore*.

Late 1805 Count Razumovsky commissions three string quartets.

1806

Jan.–Mar. *Leonore* revised, with the text altered by Stephan von Breuning.

c. **late 1805 to mid-1806** Fourth Piano Concerto composed.

29 Mar. *Leonore* (2nd version, with overture *Leonore* No. 3) performed.

9 Apr. Publication announcement for Piano Sonata op. 54.

10 Apr. *Leonore* repeated (last public performance of this version).

12 Apr. Publication announcement for Trio op. 87.

4 May Plans being made for a performance of *Leonore* at Prince Lobkowitz's palace (see Letter

131). It is not known whether these plans materialized.

25 May Beethoven's brother Caspar Carl marries; about the same time he effectively ceases his role as Beethoven's secretary.

26 May Beethoven begins writing out the score of the first 'Razumovsky' Quartet (op. 59 no. 1), which was probably completed the following month.

c. **late Aug.** Beethoven travels with Prince Lichnowsky to stay at the Prince's castle at Grätz, near Troppau, Silesia.

c. **summer** Fourth Symphony composed.

4 Sep. Beethoven's nephew Karl is born.

c. **Sep.** Beethoven and Lichnowsky visit Count Oppersdorff's castle near Ober-Glogau, Upper Silesia. During the visit the Second Symphony is performed.

19 Oct. Publication announcement for the *Eroica* Symphony.

Late Oct. Beethoven has a quarrel with Lichnowsky and returns rapidly to Vienna. The rain from a storm on the journey damages the score of the 'Appassionata' Sonata and, apparently, part of the score and sketches for the 'Razumovsky' Quartets (Tyson, 1982a). On reaching Vienna he reportedly destroys his bust of Lichnowsky.

c. **Oct.** Fourth Symphony completed, and the score sold to Count Oppersdorff for 500 fl. for six months' private use (receipt is dated 3 Feb. 1807).

c. **Nov.** 'Razumovsky' Quartets completed; Piano Variations WoO 80 composed.

23 Dec. First performance of Beethoven's newly composed Violin Concerto, given by Franz Clement at his benefit concert.

1807

Early 1807 *Coriolan* Overture composed.

c. **early 1807** Prince Nikolaus Esterházy commissions a mass from Beethoven to be performed in September.

3 Feb. Count Oppersdorff pays Beethoven 500 fl. for the Fourth Symphony, which had been composed for him.

21 Feb. Publication announcement for 'Appassionata' Sonata, op. 57.

4–5 Mar. Beethoven's invitation to Marie Bigot to take her and her child for a drive in the fine weather is misunderstood by her husband, causing a strain in their relationship, although the friendship continued (Letters 137–9).

8 Mar. Review of a recent concert given by Prince Lichnowsky at which Beethoven's newly written *Coriolan* Overture received its first performance.

Mar. Beethoven gives two concerts at the house of 'Prince L' (Lobkowitz according to Thayer; Lichnowsky according to Kinsky; if the latter is correct, one of the concerts may be the same as the one reviewed on 8 Mar.). All the works are by Beethoven and include his first four symphonies, the Fourth Piano Concerto, the *Coriolan* Overture and some arias from *Leonore*.

Mar.–Apr. Beethoven's promised benefit concert is prevented by various obstacles from taking place.

20 Apr. Clementi, recently arrived in Vienna on his way to Rome, has established a friendship with Beethoven, and they now conclude an important contract: Clementi is to pay £200 for the right to publish in Great Britain the three 'Razumovsky' Quartets, the Fourth Symphony, the *Coriolan* Overture, the Fourth Piano Concerto, the Violin Concerto, and an adaptation (yet to be made) of the Violin Concerto as a piano concerto. Beethoven is also commissioned to write three piano sonatas or (as it turned out) two sonatas and a fantasia, for £60; these three works later appeared as opp. 77–9.

c. **May** Beethoven evidently concludes a contract for 1500 fl. with the Bureau des Arts et d'Industrie for the continental publication rights for the six works recently sold to Clementi.

Jun. Baron Gleichenstein and Beethoven's brother Johann are now acting as Beethoven's secretary in place of his brother Carl, who had married the previous year. Count Oppersdorff, evidently well pleased with Beethoven's Fourth Symphony, commissions the Fifth for 500 fl. BZ, and pays the first instalment of 200 fl.

1 (or 25) Jul. Publication announcement for the Triple Concerto, op. 56.

10 Sep. Beethoven travels to Eisenstadt in preparation for the first performance of the Mass in C.

13 Sep. Mass in C performed at Prince Esterházy's castle chapel in Eisenstadt. With little rehearsal, the event was not a success and Beethoven left Eisenstadt shortly afterwards, returning to his summer lodgings at Heiligenstadt.

Autumn Several letters to Josephine Deym-Brunsvik reflect her cool response to Beethoven's expressions of affection. Beethoven unsuccessfully petitions the new theatre directors for regular employment as an opera composer. Meanwhile a winter series of 'Concerts of Music-Lovers' is set up, run by Häring (later by Clement), at which major orchestral works (including Beethoven's Symphonies 2–4 and the *Prometheus* and *Coriolan* Overtures) are performed to semi-private audiences. The overture *Leonore* no. 1 and parts of the Fifth Symphony are composed.

1808

9 Jan. Publication announcement for the 'Razumovsky' quartets and the *Coriolan* Overture.

c. **early 1808** Four settings of Goethe's *Sehnsucht*

(WoO 134) composed; Cello Sonata op. 69 completed.

13 Mar. Beethoven's brother Johann buys an apothecary shop in Linz, and takes up residence there shortly afterwards.

Mid-Mar. A serious infection to Beethoven's finger nearly causes its loss.

27 Mar. Beethoven attends the final event in the 'Concerts of Music-Lovers' series – a performance of Haydn's *Creation* (in Italian) in honour of its composer, who is also present.

13 Apr. Beethoven directs his Fourth Symphony, Third Piano Concerto (with Friedrich Stein as soloist) and *Coriolan* Overture at a charity concert.

May First known public performance of the Triple Concerto, at the Augartensaal.

Spring–summer *Pastoral* Symphony and Trio op. 70 no. 1 composed.

Jul. Beethoven plans to compose an opera *Macbeth*, with Collin adapting the libretto from Shakespeare.

10 Aug. Publication announcement for the Fourth Piano Concerto and Violin Concerto.

27 Aug. Ries arrives back in Vienna.

c. **Aug.** Count Razumovsky sets up a string quartet led by Schuppanzigh, with Mayseder or the Count himself as second violin, Franz Weiss as viola and Joseph Linke (recently arrived from Breslau) as cello.

14 Sep. Beethoven is paid 100 ducats by Breitkopf & Härtel for the Fifth and Sixth Symphonies, the Cello Sonata op. 69 and the two Piano Trios op. 70.

c. **Oct.** Beethoven is invited to become Kapellmeister to the King of Westphalia in Kassel for a salary of 600 ducats.

1 Nov. Beethoven writes to Count Oppersdorff apologizing for the delay in handing over the score of the Fifth Symphony; it may have been handed over a few weeks later, in exchange for Oppersdorff's final payment, but no record of this exchange survives.

15 Nov. Beethoven takes part in a charity concert in the Theater an der Wien, conducting *Coriolan* and other works.

24 Nov. Johann Friedrich Reichardt, Kapellmeister at Kassel, arrives in Vienna, and is surprised when he hears of Beethoven's invitation to Kassel.

Autumn Trio op. 70 no. 2 composed.

Early to mid-Dec. Choral Fantasia composed for forthcoming benefit concert.

22 Dec. Beethoven gives his long-awaited benefit concert at the Theater an der Wien. Programme – Part I: Sixth Symphony; Aria *Ah! perfido* (op. 65); Gloria from the Mass in C; Fourth Piano Concerto; Part II: Fifth Symphony; Sanctus from the Mass in C; Piano Fantasia (improvised by Beethoven, but probably using

1808 (*cont.*)

ideas later incorporated into his Fantasia op. 77);
Choral Fantasia. The concert lasted from 6.30 to
10.30 on a very cold evening. The performance
was far from perfect, and in the Choral Fantasia
it broke down altogether at one point. The same
evening Haydn's *Ritorno di Tobia* was performed
elsewhere in Vienna at a charity concert for the
Widows and Orphans Fund.

23 Dec. Repeat performance of Haydn's *Ritorno
di Tobia*, preceded by a Beethoven piano concerto
(No. 3?).

1808 Fourth Symphony published (perhaps as
early as Mar.; more likely about Sep.).

1809

7 Jan. Beethoven accepts the offer of an
appointment as Kapellmeister at Kassel. Shortly
afterwards, however, he begins negotiating with
Viennese aristocrats for a contract that would
keep him in Vienna.

c. Jan. Work begun on the Fifth Piano
Concerto.

26 Feb. Beethoven receives an annuity contract
granting him an annual salary of 4000 fl. BZ,
made up of 1500 fl. (from Archduke Rudolph),
700 fl. (Prince Lobkowitz) and 1800 fl. (Prince
Kinsky), inducing him to stay in Vienna and
abandon plans to move to Kassel.

1 Mar. Annuity contract ratified.

5 Mar. First public performance of the Cello
Sonata op. 69, played by Nikolaus Kraft and
Baroness Ertmann.

c. 14 Mar. With a secure income, Beethoven's
thoughts turn to marriage, and he writes to
Gleichenstein (temporarily in Freiburg) asking
him to help find a wife.

28 Mar. Beethoven sends Breitkopf & Härtel a
list of alterations for the Fifth and Sixth
Symphonies – alterations he claimed to have
made during their performance the previous Dec.

9 Apr. Austria declares war on France.

Apr. Cello Sonata op. 69 published with a
dedication to Gleichenstein – perhaps in token of
the latter's secretarial assistance. Fifth Symphony
published without Beethoven's alterations, but is
reprinted shortly afterwards with them.

c. Apr. Fifth Piano Concerto completed;
introduction to the Choral Fantasia composed (it
had been improvised at the performance of the
work the previous Dec.).

4 May Archduke Rudolph and other members
of the imperial family depart from Vienna
because of the military threat. To mark
Rudolph's departure Beethoven composes the
first movement (*Das Lebewohl* [The Farewell]) of
his Sonata op. 81a. Later in the year the
remaining two movements are composed in
anticipation of his return.

10 May French army surrounds Vienna.

11–12 May French bombard and capture
Vienna. During the bombardment Beethoven
takes refuge in his brother's cellar, according to
Ries, and covers his head with pillows because of
the noise.

31 May Haydn dies.

May *Pastoral* Symphony published.

c. May–Sep. Quartet op. 74, Piano Variations
op. 76, and Piano Sonata op. 79 composed.

Jun. Piano Trio op. 70 no. 1 ('Ghost')
published.

c. Jun.–Jul. Beethoven prepares theoretical
material from treatises for the purpose of
instructing Archduke Rudolph.

Aug. Piano Trio op. 70 no. 2 published.

8 Sep. Beethoven directs the *Eroica* at a charity
concert.

Oct. Piano Fantasia and Sonata, opp. 77–8,
completed.

23 Nov. Beethoven writes to Thomson of
Edinburgh agreeing to set forty-three folksongs,
adding that he has already begun.

Dec. Beethoven ill for most of the month.

c. late 1809 Two new productions are planned
for the theatre – Schiller's *Wilhelm Tell* and
Goethe's *Egmont*. Music for them is commissioned
from Gyrowetz and Beethoven respectively.

1809 Songs from op. 75, op. 82 and WoO
136–9 composed.

c. 1809 Beethoven begins instruction of
Archduke Rudolph in piano and composition
(the piano instruction may have begun as far
back as 1803–4, but the theory and composition
instruction probably started only shortly before
the Archduke's exile or even after his return).
Beethoven also composes cadenzas for his first
four piano concertos, apparently for Rudolph's
use.

1810

30 Jan. Archduke Rudolph returns to Vienna.

c. early 1810 Beethoven is at last paid for the
six works sold to Clementi three years earlier.
Sextet op. 81b published.

27 Apr. *Für Elise* is presented to Therese
Malfatti (date is on autograph score, though year
not specified and open to question).

Apr. Sextet op. 71 published.

2 May Beethoven asks for a copy of his
baptismal certificate, in a letter to Wegeler in
Koblenz. This request was evidently in
preparation for his possible marriage to Therese
Malfatti, to whom he is reported to have
proposed unsuccessfully about this time.

May Beethoven becomes acquainted with
Bettine, Franz and Antonie Brentano.

6 Jun. Goethe writes to Bettine Brentano
suggesting that he and Beethoven might be able
to meet in Karlsbad, where Goethe usually went
in the summer (Beethoven approved of the idea

and met Goethe in Teplitz, near Karlsbad, in 1812).

15 (or 18) Jun. First performance of Beethoven's newly completed *Egmont* music; it had not been ready in time for the performance of the play on 24 May.

4–11 Jul. E. T. A. Hoffmann's famous review of Beethoven's Fifth Symphony is published in the *Allgemeine Musikalische Zeitung*.

17 Jul. Beethoven sends his first fifty-three folksong arrangements to Thomson in Edinburgh.

18 Aug. Clementi's edition of Piano Variations op. 76 is entered at Stationers Hall (such entry dates normally denote the work has just been or is just about to be published).

25 Aug. Two Marches (WoO 18 and 19, the latter newly composed) performed at the tournament at Laxenburg held in honour of the Empress's birthday.

31 Aug. Clementi's editions of five songs (op. 75 nos 1–5), the Piano Fantasia (op. 77) and two Piano Sonatas (opp. 78–9) are entered at Stationers Hall.

1 Sep. Clementi's edition of the Quartet op. 74 is entered at Stationers Hall.

31 Oct. Clementi's editions of the song op. 75 no. 6 and Choral Fantasia op. 80 entered at Stationers Hall.

Oct. Quartet op. 95 completed (according to the date on the autograph, which, however, is unreliable). Breitkopf's editions of the songs op. 75 and Piano Variations op. 76 published.

***c.* Oct.–Dec.** Three Goethe Songs op. 83 composed; 'Archduke' Trio begun. Gleichenstein gradually ceases to act as Beethoven's secretary; before long Franz Oliva is filling the role.

1 Nov. Clementi's edition of the Fifth Piano Concerto is entered at Stationers Hall.

Nov. Breitkopf & Härtel's edition of the Quartet op. 74, the Piano Fantasia op. 77 and the Piano Sonatas opp. 78–9 published.

Dec. *Egmont* Overture published.

1811

28 Jan. Clementi's edition of the Sonata op. 81a ('Les Adieux') is entered at Stationers Hall.

1 Feb. Clementi's edition of the Italian songs op. 82 is entered at Stationers Hall.

Feb. Breitkopf & Härtel's edition of the Fifth Piano Concerto published.

3 Mar. Autograph score of the 'Archduke' Trio begun.

15 Mar. A *Finanz-Patent* devalues the currency fivefold; a table is issued from which the new value of Beethoven's annuity contract could be calculated (see 'Economics', p. 69). Archduke Rudolph, however, increases his portion of the annuity fivefold to compensate for the devaluation.

26 Mar. 'Archduke' Trio apparently completed (although it was probably rewritten somewhat later: see 'Chamber music for piano and strings', pp. 230, 232).

12 Apr. Beethoven writes to Goethe for the first time, mentioning their mutual friend Bettine Brentano and informing him that he is to receive a copy of the *Egmont* music (presumably the piano reduction, which was published in May 1812) direct from Breitkopf & Härtel. Beethoven's letter was delivered personally by Oliva.

8 Jun. The poet Heinrich Collin, who had previously been considering collaborating with Beethoven on an operatic project, dies.

25 Jun. Goethe replies to Beethoven's letter of 12 April.

***c.* Jun.** After a period of relatively poor health Beethoven decides, on the advice of his doctor, to recuperate at the spa of Teplitz.

Jul. Breitkopf & Härtel's edition of the Choral Fantasia, the sonata 'Les Adieux' (or *Das Lebewohl* as Beethoven preferred it called) and the Italian songs op. 82 published.

***c.* 1 Aug.** Beethoven departs for Teplitz. Shortly before departure he receives a commission for two dramatic works (*König Stephan* and *Die Ruinen von Athen*) to celebrate the opening of a new theatre at Pest (Budapest), which was due to take place at the beginning of Oct.

Aug.–Sep. While at Teplitz Beethoven meets several old or new friends including Prince Kinsky, Oliva, Varnhagen, Tiedge, Varena and Amalie Sebald.

13 Sep. Beethoven despatches the complete music of *König Stephan* and *Die Ruinen von Athen*, only to learn afterwards that the planned opening of the new theatre at Pest had been postponed. A Court Decree establishes the rate for Beethoven's annuity contract as payable by Lobkowitz and Kinsky. About this time, however, financial problems force Lobkowitz to suspend payments altogether (they were not renewed until 1815).

18 Sep. Beethoven leaves Teplitz for Prague, two days after Oliva and Varnhagen had left.

Late Sep. Beethoven visits Prince Lichnowsky at his estate at Grätz near Troppau, where the Mass in C is performed successfully after three days of rehearsals. Subsequently Beethoven returns to Vienna.

9 Oct. Beethoven writes a long letter to Breitkopf & Härtel mentioning amongst other things that they have published some copies of his Sonata op. 81a with a French title 'Les Adieux' instead of the German *Das Lebewohl*, which he considers is not an exact equivalent.

Oct. Three Goethe songs (op. 83) and *Christus am Oelberge* published.

***c.* Oct.** Seventh Symphony begun.

1811 (*cont.*)

Early Dec. Beethoven sends copies of *Christus am Oelberge*, the Choral Fantasia and an overture to Varena, the Graz musician whom he had met at Teplitz that summer, for use at a charity concert.

22 Dec. Varena puts on a very successful charity concert at Graz, using Beethoven's music.

Dec. The song *An die Geliebte* (WoO 140) composed.

1811 During a long period of illness, Antonie Brentano is regularly visited by Beethoven, who comforts her by improvising at the piano.

1812

Jan. Incidental music to *Egmont* published.

9, 10, 11 Feb. First performances of *König Stephan* and *Die Ruinen von Athen* at the new theatre at Pest, where they are well received.

11 Feb. Czerny gives the first Viennese performance of the Fifth Piano Concerto.

2 Mar. Autograph score of *An die Geliebte* [To the Beloved] presented to Antonie Brentano at her request.

29 Mar. (Easter Day) Varena gives another charity concert at Graz, having obtained unpublished music (from *König Stephan* and *Die Ruinen von Athen*) from Beethoven for the purpose.

13 Apr. Autograph score of the Seventh Symphony begun (not 13 May as given in Kinsky, 1955; see Johnson, 1985, p. 212).

5 May *Prometheus* Overture and Fifth Symphony performed by Schuppanzigh at the Augarten.

c. May Eighth Symphony begun.

8 Jun. Varnhagen, acting on Beethoven's behalf at the request of Oliva, obtains from Prince Kinsky a verbal assurance that the full value of Kinsky's portion of Beethoven's annuity will be paid thereafter.

26 Jun. Autograph score of the newly written Piano Trio WoO 39 presented to Maximiliane Brentano, daughter of Antonie and Franz.

28 or 29 Jun. Beethoven leaves Vienna for Teplitz.

1 Jul. Beethoven arrives in Prague *en route* for Teplitz.

2 Jul. Beethoven meets Varnhagen in Prague.

c. 2 Jul. Beethoven sees Prince Kinsky concerning the revaluation of his annuity, and receives an interim payment of 60 ducats.

3 Jul. The Brentano family arrive in Prague *en route* for Karlsbad. Beethoven fails to attend a prearranged meeting with Varnhagen that evening.

4 Jul. Beethoven leaves Prague for Teplitz.

5 Jul. Beethoven arrives at Teplitz in the early morning; the Brentanos arrive in Karlsbad.

6 Jul. Beethoven writes a passionate letter to an unnamed woman, known as the Immortal Beloved, in Karlsbad. Today most scholars believe this to be Antonie Brentano, although a few maintain it was Josephine Deym-Brunsvik.

7 Jul. Beethoven adds a postscript to his letter of 6 July, but evidently does not send the letter.

14 or 15 Jul. Goethe arrives in Teplitz.

19 Jul. Goethe and Beethoven meet; thereafter they are in daily contact for about a week.

c. 25 Jul. Beethoven leaves Teplitz for Karlsbad, where he stays in the same guest house as the Brentanos.

26 Jul. Much of Baden destroyed by fire.

6 Aug. Beethoven and the violinist–composer Giovanni Battista Polledro give a concert in Karlsbad for the benefit of the Baden inhabitants. The programme includes a violin sonata by Beethoven and an improvisation by him.

7 or 8 Aug. Beethoven and the Brentanos move from Karlsbad to Franzensbad.

7–8 Sep. Beethoven returns to Karlsbad, where Goethe is now staying.

12 Sep. Goethe leaves Karlsbad.

c. 15 Sep. Beethoven returns to Teplitz.

c. Sep. The Brentanos return to Vienna.

5 Oct. Beethoven arrives in Linz (probably direct from Teplitz, via Prague) to visit his brother Johann. A prime object of the visit was evidently to end the relationship between Johann and Therese Obermeyer, his 'housekeeper'. Within the next weeks Beethoven remonstrates with his brother, sees the bishop and the civil authorities about the matter and eventually obtains an order to have Therese Obermeyer removed from his brother's house.

Oct. Mass in C published; autograph score of the Eighth Symphony written out.

c. Oct. Beethoven becomes closely acquainted with Franz Glöggl, the Kapellmeister at Linz Cathedral, and writes three Equali for trombones for him.

2 or 3 Nov. Prince Kinsky dies after being thrown from his horse near Prague.

8 Nov. Beethoven's brother Johann and Therese Obermeyer respond to Beethoven's interference by marrying. Beethoven returns to Vienna shortly thereafter.

c. Nov. The Brentanos finally leave Vienna and return to settle in Frankfurt.

c. Nov.–Dec. Beethoven begins his *Tagebuch* entries.

c. 1 Dec. Spohr arrives in Vienna (he becomes acquainted with Beethoven about two months later).

Early Dec. The celebrated violinist Pierre Rode arrives in Vienna on a concert tour.

29 Dec. Beethoven's last Violin Sonata (op. 96), newly written for Rode, is performed by the violinist and Archduke Rudolph at a concert given by Prince Lobkowitz.

30 Dec. Beethoven petitions Princess Kinsky for payment of his annuity at the new rate which Prince Kinsky had agreed before his death.

1812 Beethoven's new friend Friedrich Starke, having been to breakfast with Beethoven, hears him improvise and then plays the Horn Sonata with him; the piano being a semitone lower than the horn, Starke offers to play his part in E instead of F, but Beethoven prefers to transpose the piano part to F♯.

1813

12 Feb. Beethoven again petitions Princess Kinsky for a settlement of his annuity.

3 Mar. Trios op. 70 favourably reviewed in the *Allgemeine Musikalische Zeitung*. Earliest sketches for *Meeresstille und glückliche Fahrt* (op. 112) perhaps made on or just after this date.

26 Mar. Premiere of Beethoven's newly written March for Christoph Kuffner's tragedy *Tarpeja*, at the Burgtheater.

11 Apr. *Christus am Oelberge* performed again by Varena at Graz.

12 Apr. Beethoven's brother Carl, having become very ill with consumption, makes a declaration that in the event of his death Beethoven should become guardian of Carl's son Karl.

Early Apr. Beethoven applies to give a benefit concert at the University, but is refused; subsequent efforts to arrange one elsewhere are also unsuccessful.

1 May Schuppanzigh performs the March from *Tarpeja* and the Fifth Symphony at the Augarten.

27 May Beethoven sends more music to Varena in Graz.

21 Jun. The Duke of Wellington wins the Battle of Vittoria. When news reaches Vienna, Maelzel persuades Beethoven to write a commemorative piece for Maelzel's mechanical instrument the panharmonicon. The piece (op. 91) is composed during the summer and early autumn, and arranged for orchestra.

13 Oct. The *Wiener Vaterländische Blätter* publishes an article announcing Maelzel's invention of the chronometer (the immediate predecessor of the metronome), and of its approval by several leading composers including Beethoven.

22 Oct. The music publisher Steiner lends Beethoven 1500 fl. to support his sick brother Carl and his wife Johanna. The loan was evidently repaid only indirectly, through Steiner acquiring publishing rights to certain of Beethoven's compositions.

8 Dec. Charity concert given by Maelzel and Beethoven, including the premiere of *Wellingtons Sieg* (op. 91), the first public performance of the Seventh Symphony, and music played by Maelzel's Mechanical Trumpeter.

12 Dec. Repeat performance of the highly successful concert of 8 Dec.; the two concerts together raised net receipts of 4006 fl. for the war wounded.

1814

2 Jan. *Wellingtons Sieg* and parts of *Die Ruinen von Athen* performed at a benefit concert awarded to Beethoven. Most of the musicians were those who had performed at the concerts of 8 and 12 Dec., but Maelzel was not involved this time.

24 Jan. Beethoven publicly thanks all the performers who had taken part in his concert of 2 Jan., by placing a notice to this effect in the *Wiener Zeitung*.

Jan.–Feb. The success of Beethoven's concerts induces the theatre directors to revive *Leonore/Fidelio*. Beethoven agrees on condition that he is able to revise it. Treitschke is called upon to assist in making the necessary changes to the libretto.

27 Feb. Another successful benefit concert for Beethoven, consisting of the Seventh Symphony, the premieres of the trio *Tremate* op. 116 (sketched many years earlier) and the Eighth Symphony, and *Wellingtons Sieg*.

16–17 Mar. Maelzel, having left Vienna after a disagreement with Beethoven over *Wellingtons Sieg*, performs the work twice in Munich. On hearing of these performances Beethoven institutes legal action against Maelzel for having stolen the work, but the litigation is eventually dropped.

25 Mar. Beethoven conducts the *Egmont* Overture and *Wellingtons Sieg* at a charity concert.

11 Apr. Beethoven gives the first public performance of the 'Archduke' Trio (with Schuppanzigh on the violin); according to Spohr, Beethoven's deafness results in an unsatisfactory performance, with some of the notes too loud and others inaudible. Schindler claims to have made the acquaintance of Beethoven shortly before this concert and to have met him again at the concert. The same day Treitschke's Singspiel *Die gute Nachricht*, written to celebrate the defeat of Napoleon and containing movements by several composers including Beethoven (WoO 94), receives its first performance (it is performed seven more times before the middle of Jun.).

15 Apr. Beethoven's old patron Prince Karl Lichnowsky dies.

Mid-Apr. Rehearsals for *Fidelio* begin.

Apr. Beethoven sends a score of *Wellingtons Sieg* to the Prince Regent in London, with a dedication to him, evidently hoping thereby to forestall a performance of the work in London by Maelzel (who did not in the end take the work to London).

1814 (*cont.*)

c. Apr.   Thomson publishes his first volume of Beethoven folksong arrangements.

23 May   First performance of the newly revised *Fidelio* (but with a different overture since the new one was not ready), with Beethoven and Umlauf conducting.

26 May   *Fidelio* repeated, now with the new overture. Several more performances follow in the ensuing weeks.

c. May   Beethoven again performs the 'Archduke' Trio, at one of Schuppanzigh's morning concerts. This was one of Beethoven's last public performances as a pianist.

24 Jun.   Beethoven's cantata *Un lieto brindisi*, newly written for the name-day of Giovanni Malfatti (St John's Day), is performed in his honour.

c. Jun.   Moscheles accepts the task of making the piano reduction of *Fidelio*; his work is checked and occasionally improved by Beethoven. Piano Sonata op. 90 begun.

18 Jul.   Beethoven's benefit performance of *Fidelio* – the first performance of the opera in its final form with a newly revised version of Rocco's aria and Leonore's recitative and aria (sung by Anna Milder-Hauptmann).

c. Jul.   *Elegischer Gesang* (op. 118) composed for performance on 5 Aug.

16 Aug.   Autograph score of Piano Sonata op. 90 written out.

Aug.   Piano score of *Fidelio* (arranged by Moscheles) published.

26 Sep.   *Fidelio* performed before several foreign heads of state assembled for the Congress of Vienna.

1 Oct.   Autograph score of *Namensfeier* Overture begun (it is then set aside and finished the following Mar.).

Oct.–Nov.   Cantata *Der glorreiche Augenblick* composed.

29 Nov.   Beethoven gives a concert including the Seventh Symphony, the premiere of *Der glorreiche Augenblick*, and *Wellingtons Sieg*, before a large and enthusiastic audience that includes several heads of state.

2 Dec.   Repeat performance of Beethoven's concert of 29 Nov.

25 Dec.   Another repetition of Beethoven's concert of 29 Nov.

31 Dec.   Count Razumovsky's magnificent palace destroyed by fire.

c. Dec.   Polonaise op. 89 composed for the Empress of Russia, who is in Vienna for the Congress. Beethoven plans to collaborate with Treitschke on a new opera, *Romulus und Remus*.

1815

18 Jan.   The Kinsky heirs finally agree a settlement of Beethoven's annuity. The compromise reached is that Beethoven should from 1812 receive 1200 fl. WW – more than the 726 fl. he was legally entitled to but less than the 1800 fl. he had claimed. The arrears are eventually paid on 26 Mar., and thereafter payments are made regularly.

25 Jan.   At a grand concert in honour of the Empress of Russia's birthday, Beethoven accompanies the singer Franz Wild in a performance of *Adelaide*.

c. Jan.   Unfinished Sixth Piano Concerto begun.

10 Feb.   *Wellingtons Sieg* is performed in London under Sir George Smart (repeated on 13 Feb.).

27 Feb.   Publication announcement for Polonaise op. 89 (see Johnson, 1985, p. 234).

c. Feb.   Beethoven's earliest known sizeable pocket sketchbook (Mendelssohn 1) begun.

c. early Mar.   *Namensfeier* Overture completed.

16–19 Mar.   Beethoven and Häring write to Sir George Smart in London asking him to find an English publisher for a long list of works. Eventually Robert Birchall takes four of them (piano arrangements of *Wellingtons Sieg* and the Seventh Symphony, plus the Violin Sonata op. 96 and the 'Archduke' Trio) for 130 ducats or £65.

c. Mar.   Music for *Leonore Prohaska* (WoO 96) composed.

c. 1 Apr.   Beethoven receives the opera libretto *Bacchus*, by Rudolph von Berge, from his friend Amenda; a few sketches from later this year may relate to this.

19 Apr.   Prince Lobkowitz agrees to pay his share of Beethoven's annuity plus arrears at the new rate of 700 fl. WW – the full amount demanded by Beethoven.

29 Apr.   Beethoven sells a large number of works to the publisher Steiner (partly, apparently, to repay a loan made in October 1813). These include *Wellingtons Sieg*, the Seventh and Eighth Symphonies, the Quartet op. 95, the Violin Sonata op. 96 and the 'Archduke' Trio, all of which were published within two years; also three overtures (opp. 113, 115 and 117) and the vocal trio *Tremate*, published in the 1820s; *Der glorreiche Augenblick* (published by Steiner's successor Haslinger in the 1830s); and a full score of *Fidelio* (not published by Steiner) and twelve 'English songs with German text' – some Irish folksong arrangements from WoO 152–3.

c. May   Unfinished Sixth Piano Concerto abandoned; Cello Sonatas op. 102 begun.

c. 1 Jun.   Charles Neate is introduced to Beethoven by Häring and becomes well acquainted with him. He brings an order from the Philharmonic Society of London for three overtures for 75 guineas, and Beethoven gives him his overtures opp. 113, 115 and 117 in July.

9 Jun. Publication announcement for the Piano Sonata op. 90 – the first of many Beethoven works published by Steiner.

15 Jul. Premiere of Beethoven's newly composed music for Treitschke's Singspiel *Die Ehrenpforten* (WoO 97); the work is repeated on 16 and 23 Jul.

Late Jul. Cello sonata op. 102 no. 1 completed.

Early Aug. Autograph score of Cello Sonata op. 102 no. 2 begun.

14 Nov. Beethoven's brother Carl, mortally ill, makes his will, appointing his wife Johanna and Beethoven co-guardians of his son Karl. Beethoven then has Johanna's name deleted, 'since I did not wish to be bound up in this with such a bad woman' (Thayer, 1967). In a codicil allegedly added under pressure from Johanna in Beethoven's absence, Carl then reinstates her as co-guardian, stipulating that his son Karl should continue to live with her.

15 Nov. Beethoven's brother Carl dies of consumption.

22 Nov. Johanna appointed guardian of Karl, Beethoven appointed associate guardian.

28 Nov. Beethoven appeals to the Landrecht to exclude Johanna from Karl's guardianship. The appointed tribunal meets several times before the end of the year to assess the evidence, without reaching a verdict.

25 Dec. Beethoven takes part in a charity concert in the Redoutensaal; the programme includes the premieres of the *Namensfeier* Overture and *Meeresstille*, and a performance of *Christus am Oelberge*.

Late 1815 The Gesellschaft der Musikfreunde asks Beethoven to compose an oratorio, which he agrees to do when a suitable text is found.

1816

9 Jan. The Landrecht tribunal settles Karl's guardianship in Beethoven's favour.

19 Jan. Beethoven legally appointed sole guardian of Karl.

24 Jan. Beethoven writes two farewell canons (WoO 168) for Neate, who departs for London.

2 Feb. Karl is removed from his mother and placed in a boarding school run by Giannatasio del Rio.

11 Feb. Schuppanzigh gives a farewell concert (including Beethoven's third 'Razumovsky' quartet, Quintet op. 16, and Septet op. 20), with Beethoven present, before departing for Russia.

18 Feb. The cellist Linke gives a farewell concert (including Beethoven's Cello Sonata op. 69 and 'a new piano sonata' – probably op. 90 or one of the new Cello Sonatas op. 102).

Feb. *Wellingtons Sieg* published in score and parts – his first orchestral work to be published in this manner. Birchall receives the four works he had agreed to publish.

22 Apr. Publication announcement for the song *An die Hoffnung* (op. 94).

c. Apr. *An die ferne Geliebte* composed. Piano Sonata op. 101 begun.

2 May First eighteen of Beethoven's continental folksong settings completed.

c. May Unfinished Piano Trio in F minor sketched.

29 Jul. Publication announcement for the Violin Sonata op. 96.

Jul. Beethoven deposits 10,000 fl. WW, earned from his recent concerts and publications, with Steiner at 8% interest.

18 Sep. Karl undergoes a hernia operation. During his recuperation the Giannatasios take him to stay with Beethoven in Baden.

Sep. Quartet op. 95 and 'Archduke' Trio op. 97 published.

c. Sep. Beethoven begins making plans to have Karl live with him, and consults Zmeskall and later Nanette Streicher about domestic arrangements.

14 Oct. Beethoven, back in Vienna, falls ill and remains indoors until early Nov.

Oct. *An die ferne Geliebte* published.

Nov. Seventh Symphony published (score and parts); Piano Sonata op. 101 completed.

15 Dec. Prince Lobkowitz dies; his contributions to Beethoven's annuity, however, are continued by his successors.

1816 Czerny begins giving Karl piano lessons. He also begins giving musical entertainments each Sunday, at which Beethoven is usually present and sometimes improvises.

1817

2 Jan. First issue of a Viennese music journal, the *Allgemeine Musik Zeitung*, published by Steiner (editor initially unnamed; later Mosel in 1819–20 and Kanne in 1821–4).

23 Feb. Beethoven sends dedicatory copy of his newly published Piano Sonata op. 101 to Baroness Ertmann. A month earlier he had decided that the term 'pianoforte' should be replaced by the German 'Hammer-Klavier', and he uses this term for the first time in this sonata.

Early 1817. Persistent ill-health combined with domestic problems greatly impedes Beethoven's creativity throughout this period.

Mar. Cello Sonatas op. 102 published.

c. Apr. Eighth Symphony published.

3 May Beethoven composes *Gesang der Mönche* (WoO 104) in memory of his friend Krumpholz, who died the previous day.

10 May Beethoven's sister-in-law Johanna signs a contract agreeing to make substantial payments towards her son's upkeep.

9 Jun. Ries writes a long letter to Beethoven on behalf of the Philharmonic Society of London, inviting him to visit London the next winter and

1817 (*cont.*)
to compose two new symphonies for the society. The fee offered is 300 guineas.

7 Jul. Beethoven asks Streicher to prepare as loud as possible a piano to try to overcome his increasingly weak hearing.

9 Jul. Beethoven replies to Ries accepting his invitation to visit England but proposing some additional conditions.

15 Jul. Value of paper currency fixed at 2.5 fl. WW = 1 fl. CM. Beethoven's annuity of 3400 fl. thus becomes fixed at 1360 fl. CM thenceforth.

14 Aug. Beethoven completes the quintet arrangement op. 104 of his Piano Trio op. 1 no. 3 – an arrangement based on an earlier, rather incompetent attempt by one Herr Kaufmann (see Tyson, 1974).

10 Sep. Beethoven receives a reply from the Philharmonic Society rejecting his additional proposals and reiterating the original offer, which he then accepts. About this time a few sketches are made for the Ninth Symphony.

c. autumn Cipriani Potter and Heinrich Marschner visit Beethoven, who recommends Potter to go to Förster for composition lessons. Maelzel returns to Vienna and settles his differences with Beethoven. 'Hammerklavier' Sonata begun.

28 Nov. Fugue in D for string quintet op. 137 completed.

17 Dec. *Allgemeine Musikalische Zeitung* (Leipzig) publishes Beethoven's metronome marks for his first eight symphonies.

25 Dec. Beethoven conducts the Eighth Symphony at a charity concert.

27 Dec. Broadwood & Sons (London), piano manufacturers, send Beethoven a new six-octave grand piano (the instrument is today in the National Museum in Budapest).

1818
24 Jan. Karl leaves Giannatasio's boarding school and begins living with Beethoven, studying with a private tutor.

Jan. Beethoven's planned trip to London is abandoned, Beethoven later blaming poor health for the cancellation.

3 Feb. Beethoven thanks Broadwood for the gift of the piano, which had not at that time arrived.

14 Feb. Beethoven and Salieri recommend the use of the metronome, in a public statement in the Viennese press.

Feb. Beethoven's increasing deafness finally forces him to use conversation books (see pp. 164–7).

c. Feb.–Mar. Part of the first movement of the Ninth Symphony sketched.

Early 1818 Beethoven composes the theme *O Hoffnung* (WoO 200) for Archduke Rudolph to use for a set of variations.

Early Apr. First two movements of the 'Hammerklavier' Sonata completed (in preparation for Archduke Rudolph's name-day, 17 Apr.).

19 May Beethoven and Karl move to Mödling for the summer months; Karl is taught for a month by the village priest.

May The Gesellschaft der Musikfreunde again asks Beethoven to write an oratorio, and he replies that he is ready to do so.

22 Jun. Thomson commissions twelve sets of folksong variations.

Jun. Twenty-five folksong settings op. 108 published in Edinburgh.

c. Aug. 'Hammerklavier' Sonata completed.

18 Sep. A new petition by sister-in-law Johanna, aided by Hotschevar, to obtain guardianship of Karl, is rejected by the Landrecht.

c. Sep. More sketches are made for the first movement of the Ninth Symphony.

3 Oct. Another appeal by Johanna is also dismissed.

18 Nov. Twelve sets of variations (from opp. 105 and 107) completed and sent to Thomson; four additional sets are composed a few months later.

c. Nov. Archduke Rudolph completes his Forty Variations on a Theme by Beethoven. Beethoven sends his Quintet op. 104 and the 'Hammerklavier' Sonata to Ries for publication in London.

3 Dec. Karl runs away to his mother; Beethoven enlists the help of the police to bring him back. Karl then spends the next few weeks at Giannatasio's school again.

7 Dec. Johanna uses the fact of Karl's having run away as justification for a further attempt to remove the boy from Beethoven's control, and she again petitions the Landrecht.

11 Dec. The Landrecht court hearing takes place; Beethoven, his nephew and the boy's mother are all interviewed separately (detailed account in Thayer, 1967). Beethoven, who is accompanied by Karl Bernard, admits he has no documentary proof of his nobility.

18 Dec. The Landrecht transfers Beethoven's case to the lower court, the Magistrat, since he is not of noble birth.

1818 Final entries in Beethoven's *Tagebuch*.

1819
11 Jan. The Magistrat hears the case concerning Beethoven's nephew. As a result of the hearing Beethoven is forced to relinquish the guardianship and find another guardian, while Karl temporarily returns to his mother's, receiving instruction at an institute run by Johann Kudlich.

17 Jan. Beethoven conducts the *Prometheus*

Overture and the Seventh Symphony at a charity concert.

6 Feb. Anna Giannatasio and Leopold Schmerling marry; for the occasion Beethoven writes his Hochzeitslied (WoO 105), one version of which is dated 14 Jan. 1819.

18 Feb. Publication announcement for the Quintet op. 104.

26 Mar. Tuscher appointed guardian of Karl.

c. Mar. Diabelli invites all the leading composers in Vienna to write a variation on his waltz theme. Beethoven begins a whole set of variations almost immediately; the earliest dated variation by another composer is Czerny's of 7 May 1819.

c. early Apr. *Missa Solemnis* begun.

16 Apr. Beethoven sends Ries an additional bar to be inserted at the start of the slow movement of the 'Hammerklavier' Sonata.

Apr. Beethoven and Tuscher propose to send Karl out of the country to Landshut, but there is opposition and a passport is eventually refused (7 May).

12 and 27 May Nine of Beethoven's sets of folksong variations (opp. 105 and 107) sent to Thomson are entered at Stationers Hall.

c. May Beethoven's Diabelli Variations are set aside half-finished; the *Missa Solemnis* is sketched intensively during the following months.

4 Jun. Archduke Rudolph appointed Archbishop of Olmütz, with the enthronement ceremony, including the *Missa Solemnis*, to take place the following year. Plans for this appointment had, however, probably been known some months before Jun.

15 Jun. Beethoven receives 400 fl. WW advance payment from the Gesellschaft der Musikfreunde for an oratorio he had agreed to compose.

22 Jun. Karl enters Blöchlinger's institute.

5 Jul. Tuscher asks to resign as Karl's guardian; Beethoven unofficially assumes the role again.

13 Jul. Beethoven withdraws the money invested with Steiner since 1816, by now worth 4000 fl. CM, and buys eight bank shares as an intended legacy for Karl.

2 Aug. Beethoven's brother Johann purchases a large estate at Gneixendorf.

Summer Beethoven writes several long letters to Bernard and Blöchlinger concerning Karl.

6 Sep. Publication announcement for the Viennese edition of the folksong variations op. 105.

15 Sep. Publication announcement for the Viennese edition of the 'Hammerklavier' Sonata.

17 Sep. Tuscher relieved of Karl's guardianship, which is transferred to Leopold Nussböck and Johanna.

1 Oct. English edition of the 'Hammerklavier' Sonata, published by the Regent's Harmonic Institution, entered at Stationers Hall. Gebauer begins a series of Concerts Spirituels, at which major choral and orchestral works are performed at sight; this season and the following one (1820–21) together included all eight Beethoven symphonies plus the Mass in C, *Christus*, and the still unpublished *Meeresstille*.

13 Oct. Beethoven unsuccessfully attempts to purchase a house.

31 Oct. Beethoven protests to the Magistrat concerning Karl's guardianship, but his protest is rejected on 4 Nov. and again on 20 Dec.

c. Nov. Main sketches for the Gloria of the *Missa Solemnis* completed; Beethoven moves on to detailed work on the Credo.

Dec. Archduke Rudolph's Forty Variations on a Theme by Beethoven published.

1820

7 Jan. Beethoven petitions the Court of Appeal about Karl's guardianship.

10 Feb. Beethoven offers four works (the Variations op. 107, Folksongs op. 108, Diabelli Variations and *Missa Solemnis*) to Simrock of Bonn, who eventually receives only op. 107.

18 Feb. Beethoven drafts a very lengthy memorandum (Anderson, 1961, pp. 1388–1408) in preparation for its submission to the Court of Appeal. It includes information about Johanna, the Magistrat, Karl, his school reports, Beethoven's activity on his behalf, and Karl's property.

4 Mar. *Abendlied*, one of Beethoven's last songs, completed.

9 Mar. Enthronement of Archduke Rudolph as Cardinal Archbishop of Olmütz; the *Missa Solemnis* written for the occasion was still unfinished, with Beethoven still only sketching the Credo in detail. Some authorities give the date 20 Mar. for the enthronement ceremony, but this seems to be incorrect (see Köhler, 1968, i.482).

8 Apr. The Court of Appeal rules in Beethoven's favour concerning Karl's guardianship; Beethoven and Karl Peters are appointed co-guardians. Johanna subsequently appeals unsuccessfully to the Emperor.

c. early Apr. First movement of Piano Sonata op. 109 composed (probably intended as a single piece for Friedrich Starke's piano method). Beethoven then reverts to composing the *Missa Solemnis*.

22 Apr. Folksong Variations op. 107 despatched to Simrock for publication.

31 May Beethoven agrees to write three piano sonatas (opp. 109–11) for Schlesinger for 90 ducats. The Mass is again set aside while the rest of the first sonata is composed during the summer.

29 Aug. Beethoven is unwell for a few days.

1820 (*cont.*)

Late Sep. Folksong arrangements op. 108 sent to Schlesinger in Berlin.

***c.* Sep.** German edition of Variations op. 107 published (Simrock).

Autumn Beethoven continues writing the *Missa Solemnis*; his precise speed of progress, however, is unclear – he may have had almost all of the work sketched by about Oct. or alternatively not until the following spring/summer. Sonata op. 109 completed and sent to Schlesinger.

Dec. Oliva, who had been assisting Beethoven for several years, departs for St Petersburg.

1821

1 Jan. Five newly completed bagatelles (op. 119 nos 7–11) presented to Starke for his piano method. They are published by him later in the year.

Jan. After a brief recovery, Beethoven falls ill again for a long time, spending six weeks in bed with rheumatic fever.

31 Mar. Josephine Deym-Brunsvik-Stackelberg dies after prolonged ill health.

***c.* spring/summer** Piano Sonata op. 110 begun.

***c.* early Jul.** After feeling poorly for several months, Beethoven develops jaundice, which persists until the end of Aug.

10 Sep. Beethoven sends Haslinger a canon (WoO 182) which he says occurred to him in a dream the previous day (and which he had since modified).

Early Nov. Piano Sonata op. 109 published.

12 Nov. Beethoven informs Franz Brentano that he has at last recovered his health; he also implies that a score of the *Missa Solemnis* had by then been completed.

6 Dec. Beethoven sends dedicatory copy of Sonata op. 109 to Maximiliane Brentano.

12 Dec. Beethoven offers the *Missa Solemnis* to Adolf Schlesinger for 1000 fl. CM.

25 Dec. Sonata op. 110 completed (but with an early version of the finale).

***c.* Dec.** Sketches for Sonata op. 111 begun.

1822

13 Jan. Autograph score of Sonata op. 111 begun.

***c.* Jan.** Beethoven again becomes unwell, suffering till May or Jun. with 'gout in the chest'.

Feb. *Fidelio* Overture and *Meeresstille* published.

***c.* Feb.** Two sonatas (opp. 110 and 111) sent to Schlesinger in Berlin.

9 Apr. Beethoven agrees to sell Schlesinger the Mass for 650 reichsthaler (975 fl. CM), despite the fact that he had already promised it to Simrock.

***c.* 10 Apr.** Revised version of the finale of op. 111 sent to Schlesinger.

Apr. Schubert's piano duet variations op. 10 (D 624) published, dedicated to Beethoven. Schubert is said to have delivered a copy personally to Beethoven's lodgings.

***c.* Apr.** Rossini visits Vienna; his brief encounter with Beethoven is hampered by language barriers and Beethoven's deafness.

18 May The publisher C. F. Peters of Leipzig writes to Beethoven asking for compositions.

19 May Beethoven writes that he had retrieved a score of the *Missa Solemnis* from Archduke Rudolph three days earlier; how long the score had been in existence is unclear, but it was to be recopied and undergo further revision.

21 May Goethe receives from Beethoven a dedicatory copy of *Meeresstille* (a setting of his own poems).

24 May Rochlitz, editor of the *Allgemeine Musikalische Zeitung*, arrives in Vienna.

5 Jun. Beethoven offers Peters the Mass, the Diabelli Variations, various songs, military marches, a Wind Trio (WoO 28) and piano bagatelles, all of which are 'ready', and a piano sonata and string quartet which could be made available 'soon'.

Jun.–Sep. A rapid series of letters is exchanged between Beethoven and Peters, in which Beethoven agrees to sell him the Mass (despite having promised it elsewhere), the marches, some songs, and bagatelles. In anticipation of receiving them, Peters sends 360 fl. CM in advance, while Beethoven begins preparing fresh versions of the marches, songs and bagatelles.

31 Jul. Beethoven, already in debt to Steiner, Artaria, Brentano, and his brother Johann, asks the last for a further loan.

Jul. Beethoven's health has improved but he is still taking various medicaments. Piano Sonata op. 110 and the German edition of the folksong arrangements op. 108 are published.

2 Aug. Rochlitz leaves Vienna; later he claims to have met Beethoven several times during his visit, but this is very doubtful.

22 Aug. Beethoven offers the *Missa Solemnis* to yet another publisher, Artaria; by this time he had decided not to sell it to Schlesinger.

***c.* 2 Sep.** Karl Hensler informs Beethoven he is planning to open the Josephstadt Theatre in Vienna with Carl Meisl's adaptation of Beethoven's *Die Ruinen von Athen* as *Die Weihe des Hauses*; as a result Beethoven spends the month composing a chorus ('Wo sich die Pulse') and then a new overture (op. 124) for the occasion.

3 Oct. *Die Weihe des Hauses* performed, complete with the new overture and chorus, with Beethoven directing from the piano.

4, 5, 6 Oct. Repeat performances of *Die Weihe des Hauses*.

Oct. Beethoven makes sketches for the Ninth and Tenth Symphonies and composes the *Gratulations-Menuett* (WoO 3). Piano version of a chorus (op. 114) from *Die Weihe des Hauses* is published.

3 Nov. *Gratulations-Menuett* is performed at a private serenade in honour of Karl Hensler. The same day *Fidelio* is revived at the Kärntnertor Theatre; Beethoven was to have conducted, with Umlauf, but after the rehearsals it was decided he should not because of his poor hearing.

4 Nov. Hensler holds a dinner party for Beethoven and others at 3 pm; Beethoven sits by a musical clock which plays the theme from his *Fidelio* Overture, and comments that the clock plays it better than the theatre orchestra! During the dinner Schindler makes several entries in Beethoven's Conversation Book – his earliest genuine entries known. *Fidelio* is repeated that evening, with Beethoven present, and is performed five more times during the winter season.

9 Nov. Prince Galitzin writes to Beethoven asking for one, two or three quartets at a price to be named by Beethoven, who as it happened was already contemplating composing something in this genre.

10 Nov. The Philharmonic Society of London, in response to an enquiry from Beethoven, resolves to offer him £50 for a new symphony; Ries communicates the offer in a letter of 15 Nov.

22 Nov. Beethoven informs Peters that he now has two masses, one of which is 'not yet finished'; Peters can expect to receive one of them.

Late Nov. Bagatelles op. 119 nos 1–6 completed; all but the last (which is entirely new) had been drafted many years earlier.

Nov.–Dec. Beethoven works on the material for Peters, revises a few passages in the *Missa Solemnis*, and turns his attention to the half-finished Diabelli Variations.

20 Dec. Beethoven replies to Ries, accepting the Philharmonic Society's offer for a new symphony.

23 Dec. First performance of newly completed *Opferlied*, in Pressburg (Bratislava).

Dec. *Der Kuss* (op. 128) and probably *Bundeslied* (op. 122) completed.

1823

c. **1 Jan.** Beethoven applies to become Imperial and Royal Chamber Music Composer in succession to Anton Teyber (1754–1822); the post, however, is abolished.

7 Jan. First mention (in a letter to Griesinger) of Beethoven's plan to offer manuscript copies of the *Missa Solemnis* to all the great European courts, instead of publishing it.

23 Jan. First subscription invitations for manuscript copies of the Mass are sent out; others are sent shortly afterwards, and in some cases Beethoven also writes to a personal contact

to seek support for the scheme. Eventually there are ten subscribers (see 'Choral music', p. 256).

25 Jan. Beethoven agrees to write quartets for Galitzin at 50 ducats apiece and promises to have the first ready by mid-Mar.

8 Feb. Beethoven writes to Goethe about the *Missa Solemnis*. He also sends Peters some long-awaited scores – three songs (opp. 121b, 122 and 128); Six Bagatelles (op. 119 nos 1–6); and one of the Four Marches (WoO 18–20, 24).

15 Feb. The remaining three Marches are sent to Peters.

25 Feb. Beethoven sends scores of the overture *Die Weihe des Hauses* and the Bagatelles op. 119 to Ries to sell in London, which he plans to visit in spring 1824.

28 Feb. Publication announcement for overture *Die Ruinen von Athen*.

Feb. Beethoven's debts have accumulated so much that he is forced to sell one of his eight bank shares to avoid a lawsuit from Steiner.

4 Mar. Peters returns to Beethoven the music recently sent, saying it was uncharacteristic of the composer and that he wanted something better.

6 Mar. Beethoven nominates his nephew legal heir to all his property.

19 Mar. Beethoven delivers a presentation copy of the *Missa Solemnis* to Archduke Rudolph.

Mar. Diabelli offers Beethoven 1000 fl. CM for the Mass but wishes to publish it immediately, which would interfere with the plans for manuscript subscriptions.

Winter–spring After the recent success of *Fidelio* Beethoven is encouraged to plan another opera, and several subjects are considered (see 'Unfinished and projected works', p. 277).

10 Apr. Weber receives the score of *Fidelio* in Dresden for performance there (the performances are very successful).

12 Apr. Beethoven composes a Cantata (WoO 106) for the birthday of Prince Ferdinand Lobkowitz.

13 Apr. Liszt (aged eleven) gives a recital, probably attended by Beethoven.

25 Apr. Clementi's edition of the Sonata op. 111, which Beethoven had earlier sent to Ries, is entered at Stationers Hall. The same day Beethoven writes to Ries telling him to ensure the sonata is published immediately.

26 Apr. Beethoven sends a musical greeting (WoO 184) to Schuppanzigh, newly returned from Russia.

Apr. Diabelli Variations completed (the copy for Ries is dated 30 Apr.).

c. **Apr.** Sonata op. 111 published by Schlesinger (the date is not certain – there is some evidence it may have been several months earlier).

c. **May** Beethoven begins intensive work on Ninth Symphony, which occupies him until early 1824.

1823 (*cont.*)

3 Jun. Clementi's edition of the Bagatelles op. 119 is entered at Stationers Hall (this is the earliest edition of the first six bagatelles).

14 Jun. Schuppanzigh resumes his quartet recitals (with Holz, Weiss and Linke).

16 Jun. Publication announcement for the Diabelli Variations.

c. late Jun. Diabelli reprints the Sonata op. 111 with numerous corrections supplied by Beethoven.

Jun.–Sep. Beethoven suffers from trouble with his eyes, which is cured only gradually.

6 Aug. Wenzel Schlemmer, Beethoven's chief copyist for many years, dies.

29 Aug. Karl leaves Blöchlinger's institute and spends the rest of the summer with Beethoven in Baden.

28 Sep. Schultz visits Beethoven in Baden.

5 Oct. Weber visits Beethoven in Baden, along with Haslinger, Piringer and Sir Julius Benedict.

Oct. Beethoven returns to Vienna and Karl enters the University, but continues living with Beethoven.

Late Oct. Bernard provides Beethoven with the long-awaited oratorio text *Der Sieg des Kreuzes*, but Beethoven is dissatisfied with it.

Autumn Further discussion with Grillparzer about a proposed opera comes to nothing. Moritz Schlesinger publishes the Bagatelles op. 119 in an edition copied from Clementi's, thus depriving Beethoven the chance of selling nos 1–6 to a continental publisher.

1824

25 Feb. Beethoven offers the *Missa Solemnis*, the overture *Die Weihe des Hauses*, the Ninth Symphony and some as yet unwritten quartets to Moritz Schlesinger.

Feb. Beethoven is presented with a petition (published in two local journals) from many leading Viennese music-lovers, including Count Lichnowsky, Artaria, Streicher, Stadler, Diabelli, Fries, Kuffner, Dietrichstein, Czerny and Steiner, asking him to perform his Mass and Ninth Symphony in Vienna.

c. Feb. Ninth Symphony completed. Schott's Sons, of Mainz, write asking Beethoven to contribute an article for their journal *Caecilia*, and to send them compositions for publication.

Feb.–Mar. Plans for a concert containing the new symphony are made, with several people offering their assistance. Count Palffy, director of the Theater an der Wien, agrees to make the place available, but Clement is the leader of the theatre orchestra and Beethoven wants Schuppanzigh. Dates proposed are 22, 23 or 24 Mar.

10 Mar. Beethoven writes to Schott's refusing to write an article for their journal but offering

them the Mass, the Ninth Symphony and his next quartet.

7 Apr. Galitzin gives the premiere of the *Missa Solemnis* in St Petersburg, having obtained a score through his subscription.

c. 23 Apr. Venue for Beethoven's concert fixed as the Kärntnertor Theatre (run by Duport).

27 Apr. Copy of Ninth Symphony sent to the Philharmonic Society in London.

c. end Apr. Date for Beethoven's concert fixed as 7 May.

2 May Rehearsal schedule fixed: choral rehearsal on 3 May, full rehearsals on 4, 5 and 6 May (one of these is later cancelled).

7 May Publication announcement for 'Kakadu' Variations op. 121a. In the evening a 'Grand Musical Concert' in the Kärntnertor Theatre, with Sontag (soprano), Unger (alto), Haitzinger (tenor), Seipelt (bass – a last-minute replacement for Preisinger), Schuppanzigh (leader) and Umlauf (director); Beethoven assists in the direction, mainly by setting the tempi. Programme: overture *Die Weihe des Hauses*; Kyrie, Credo, Agnus Dei from *Missa Solemnis*; Ninth Symphony. The theatre is full (apart from the imperial box) and the audience very enthusiastic; at the end of the concert (or after the Scherzo of the Symphony), Caroline Unger turns Beethoven to face the applause, which he had not noticed because of his deafness. The gross receipts, however, are only 2200 fl. WW, leaving 420 fl. net – well below Beethoven's expectations.

23 May Beethoven's concert repeated in the Redoutensaal, omitting the Credo and Agnus Dei but including the trio *Tremate* and a Rossini aria. The hall is half-empty and the concert makes a net loss, underwritten by Duport. After the concert Schindler and Beethoven part company for a lengthy period.

c. May–Jun. Bagatelles op. 126 composed.

c. Jun. Quartet op. 127 begun.

c. 20 Jun. Karl, who is still studying philology at the University, informs Beethoven of his desire for a military career – a desire fulfilled in 1826.

3 Jul. Beethoven agrees to sell the Mass and the Ninth Symphony to Schott's for 1000 fl. and 600 fl. CM respectively.

9 Jul. Publication announcement for Diabelli's *Vaterländischer Künstlerverein*, a collection of variations on his waltz theme by fifty different composers.

24 Aug. Beethoven agrees to write a piano duet sonata for Diabelli for 80 ducats, but the intention is never fulfilled.

Late Sep. Stumpff visits Beethoven; on hearing of his love for Handel, Stumpff secretly resolves to send him Arnold's forty-volume Handel edition.

Nov. Beethoven offers the overture *Die Weihe des Hauses*, the Bagatelles op. 126 and the three songs rejected by Peters, to Schott's for 130 ducats (having already offered the same works to Probst for 100 ducats). The fee is to go to his brother Johann to repay a debt.

c. 15 Dec. Beethoven's last known composition lesson to Archduke Rudolph.

Mid-Dec. Schott's having accepted Beethoven's latest offer, he and Johann decide to send the works to them rather than Probst.

20 Dec. The Philharmonic Society, through Neate, again invite Beethoven to London.

c. Dec. Quartet op. 132 begun.

1825
16 Jan. Beethoven at last sends the Mass and Ninth Symphony to Schott's.

22 Jan. Beethoven sends two canons (WoO 180 and 187) to Schott's for their journal *Caecilia* and, as a joke, he adds a 'romantic biography' of Tobias Haslinger; the joke later backfires when Schott's publish the 'biography'.

c. Jan. Quartet op. 127 completed.

4 Feb. Overture *Die Weihe des Hauses* sent to Schott's; the other works, including the new quartet, are sent in Mar.–Apr.

6 Mar. Schuppanzigh gives premiere of the Quartet op. 127, but neither the audience nor the players are pleased with the result.

19 Mar. Beethoven informs Neate that he has decided not to visit London for the present.

c. 20 Mar. Joseph Böhm performs op. 127, which is very well received; it is played twice more by him on 23 Mar.

21 Mar. First London performance of the Ninth Symphony, directed by Sir George Smart (the finale was evidently sung in Italian!).

c. mid-Apr. Beethoven falls ill with a serious abdominal complaint; he is attended by Dr Braunhofer, who prescribes a strict diet.

Mid–late Apr. *Namensfeier* Overture published.

Apr. Karl leaves the University and enters the Polytechnic Institute to study commerce. The deputy director Reisser is appointed Karl's co-guardian in place of Peters, and Karl lodges with Matthias Schlemmer.

c. Apr. Bagatelles op. 126 and *Der Kuss* op. 128 published.

7 May Beethoven moves to Baden, Karl remaining in Vienna and visiting his uncle on Sundays.

13 May Beethoven sends Dr Braunhofer a humorous canon (WoO 189) composed two days earlier, informing him he is still feeling very weak.

Mid-May Beethoven begins composing the 'Heiliger Dankgesang' for the Quartet op. 132, to mark his recovery.

c. Jun. Quartet op. 130 begun.

Jul. Two songs (op. 121b and 122) published.

Late Jul. Two overtures (opp. 115 and 124) are sent to Prince Galitzin, the latter with a dedication to him.

c. Jul. Quartet op. 132 completed; Holz becomes a close associate of Beethoven.

c. 23 Aug. *Grosse Fuge* (op. 133) begun, as the finale for op. 130 (for date see Cooper, 1990, p. 209).

2 Sep. Danish composer Kuhlau visits Beethoven and they have a merry dinner party with Holz, Haslinger and others, at which much champagne is drunk; Beethoven composes a canon (WoO 191) on Kuhlau's name, using the B–A–C–H motif.

3 Sep. Beethoven writes out the Kuhlau canon and sends it to him.

4 Sep. Moritz Schlesinger visits Beethoven to try to obtain publishing rights for his latest quartets and perhaps other works.

7 Sep. Quartet op. 132 is given its first rehearsal; it is performed privately two days later to an audience of about fourteen people.

10 Sep. Moritz Schlesinger buys op. 132 for 80 ducats.

11 Sep. Op. 132 is performed privately to a larger audience than on the 9th; Smart, who is in Vienna to visit Beethoven, is present on both occasions, and after the second one he dines with Beethoven, his nephew, the four performers (Schuppanzigh, Holz, Weiss and Linke), Czerny, Schlesinger and the flautist Jean Sedlatzek. After dinner Beethoven improvises for about twenty minutes.

16 Sep. Smart visits Beethoven in Baden, and Karl tries unsuccessfully to persuade Beethoven to go to London. On Smart's departure Beethoven composes for him a canon (WoO 192).

15 Oct. Beethoven moves from Baden to his final lodgings in Vienna, the Schwarzspanierhaus.

6 Nov. First public performance of op. 132, at Linke's benefit concert, which also includes the 'Archduke' Trio.

25 Nov. Beethoven writes to Peters offering to return his 360 fl. payment of 1822 or alternatively to send a quartet for that price (Peters opted for the repayment).

29 Nov. Beethoven elected honorary member of the Gesellschaft der Musikfreunde.

c. 15 Dec. Quartet op. 131 begun.

Dec. Overture *Die Weihe des Hauses* published.

1826
9 Jan. Newly completed Quartet op. 130 (with *Grosse Fuge* finale) handed to Mathias Artaria for publication.

Late Jan. Beethoven unwell with eye and abdominal complaints.

Feb. Quartet op. 132 sent to Galitzin; trio *Tremate* op. 116 published.

1826 (*cont.*)

21 Mar.   First performance of the Quartet op. 130/133, by the Schuppanzigh Quartet.

Mar.   Quartet op. 127 published.

Late Mar.   Anton Halm asked to arrange the *Grosse Fuge* for piano duet.

c. Mar.   Quartet op. 130/133 sent to Galitzin.

6 Apr.   Schott's offer 80 ducats for the Quartet op. 131 – an offer accepted by Beethoven.

25 Apr.   Halm delivers his arrangement of the *Grosse Fuge* to Beethoven; the composer is dissatisfied, however, and decides to make one of his own.

Apr.   Bernard's oratorio text *Der Sieg des Kreuzes* is finally set aside in favour of Kuffner's proposal for a text on Saul.

Jul.   Beethoven's last quartet, op. 135, begun. Overture *König Stephan* and *Elegischer Gesang* published.

c. 3 Aug.   Karl, having resolved to commit suicide, buys a pistol. His intentions become known and the pistol is discovered by Matthias Schlemmer.

5 Aug.   Karl pawns his watch, buys another pistol and drives to Baden without returning to his lodgings.

6 Aug.   Karl shoots himself in the head; the first bullet misses and the second only injures him; he is taken to his mother and his injury treated there.

7 Aug.   Karl is admitted to hospital for further treatment.

12 Aug.   Quartet op. 131 sent to Schott's; Beethoven had already described it as 'finished' on 20 May.

Aug.   Beethoven's piano duet arrangement of the *Grosse Fuge* completed (Mathias Artaria pays him 12 ducats for it on 5 Sep.).

Late Aug.   Ninth Symphony published.

c. Aug.   Steiner retires; his assistant Haslinger takes full control of the publishing house.

Late Sep.   Manuscript copy of the Ninth Symphony, with a dedicatory letter, is sent to the King of Prussia (the work was to have been dedicated to the Emperor of Russia, who had died on 1 Dec. 1825).

25 Sep.   Karl leaves hospital.

28–9 Sep.   Beethoven and Karl travel to Gneixendorf to stay with Johann.

c. Sep.   New finale for Quartet op. 130 begun.

13 Oct.   Beethoven informs Haslinger that the Quartet op. 135 is finished. He also sends metronome marks for the Ninth Symphony to Schott's.

30 Oct.   Quartet op. 135 sent to Schlesinger, Beethoven having written out the instrumental parts himself for lack of a copyist in Gneixendorf.

22 Nov.   New finale for Quartet op. 130 sent to Mathias Artaria.

c. Nov.   String Quintet WoO 62 begun –

Beethoven's last major compositional undertaking.

1–2 Dec.   Beethoven and Karl travel back to Vienna, spending the night of 1 Dec. in a cold village tavern where Beethoven falls ill.

4 or 5 Dec.   The canon *Wir irren allesamt* (WoO 198), Beethoven's last completed work, composed.

5 Dec.   Drs Braunhofer and Staudenheim having been unable to come, Beethoven is at length attended to by Dr Wawruch, whom Holz had summoned.

9 Dec.   Beethoven feels considerably better and is able to get out of bed, read and write.

10 Dec.   Beethoven's health takes a turn for the worse; from this time onwards virtually no work is done as dropsy and jaundice set in.

14 Dec.   Beethoven receives Stumpff's gift of Arnold's forty-volume edition of Handel from London (cf. Sep. 1824).

20 Dec.   Beethoven undergoes an operation to reduce his abdominal swelling.

1827

2 Jan.   Karl departs for military service in Iglau.

8 Jan.   Beethoven undergoes a second operation and another large quantity of fluid is drained off.

2 Feb.   Beethoven's third operation.

8 Feb.   Beethoven thanks Stumpff by letter for his 'glorious gift' of the Handel scores, expressing the great joy they have given him and informing Stumpff of his illness. By this time Schindler is acting as his amanuensis for his correspondence.

22 Feb.   Beethoven dictates a letter for Schott's asking for some Rhine or Mosel wine.

27 Feb.   Beethoven's fourth operation. ·

28 Feb.   The Philharmonic Society of London resolves to send Beethoven £100 to provide comforts during his illness.

4 Mar.   Karl's last letter to Beethoven from Iglau.

18 Mar.   Beethoven thanks the Philharmonic Society for their gift and offers to compose for them a new symphony (already sketched), a new overture or something else.

c. 22 Mar.   Beethoven receives the last rites.

24 Mar.   The wine from Schott's arrives. 'Pity, pity, too late,' says Beethoven – reportedly his last words. Later he lapses into unconsciousness.

26 Mar.   A storm arises in the late afternoon. According to Hüttenbrenner, at about 5 pm there was a flash of lightning and a violent clap of thunder. 'After this unexpected phenomenon of nature, which startled me greatly, Beethoven opened his eyes, lifted his right hand and looked up for several seconds with his fist clenched and a very serious, threatening expression.... When he let the raised hand sink to the bed, his eyes closed half-way... Not another breath, not a heartbeat more.' (Thayer, 1967). Another report says Beethoven died at about 5.45 pm.

29 Mar. Beethoven's funeral. The oration is written by Grillparzer and delivered by the actor Heinrich Anschütz (complete text in Thayer, 1967).

Early Apr. *Missa Solemnis* published.

7 May Publication announcement for Quartet op. 130.

10 May Publication announcement for *Grosse Fuge* (quartet and piano duet versions).

4 Jun. Stephan von Breuning dies.

Jun. Quartet op. 131 published.

16 Aug. Inventory of Beethoven's musical effects completed in preparation for an auction.

Sep. Quartets opp. 132 and 135 published.

4 Oct. Record of Beethoven's estate completed.

5 Nov. Auction of Beethoven's musical effects.

BARRY COOPER

Section 2

BEETHOVEN'S FAMILY TREE

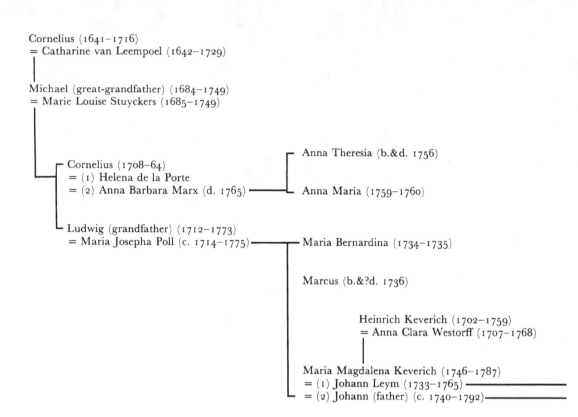

BEETHOVEN'S FAMILY TREE

Beethoven's ancestors lived in the area of Mechelen (Malines), Belgium, and his name indicates that at some stage they lived at or near a beet farm. His family tree has been traced back about 200 years (see Schmidt–Görg, 1964); its principal members are shown here. Note that Karl was the only member of the family in the generation after the composer, but his line survives through his eldest daughter.

Compiled by BARRY COOPER

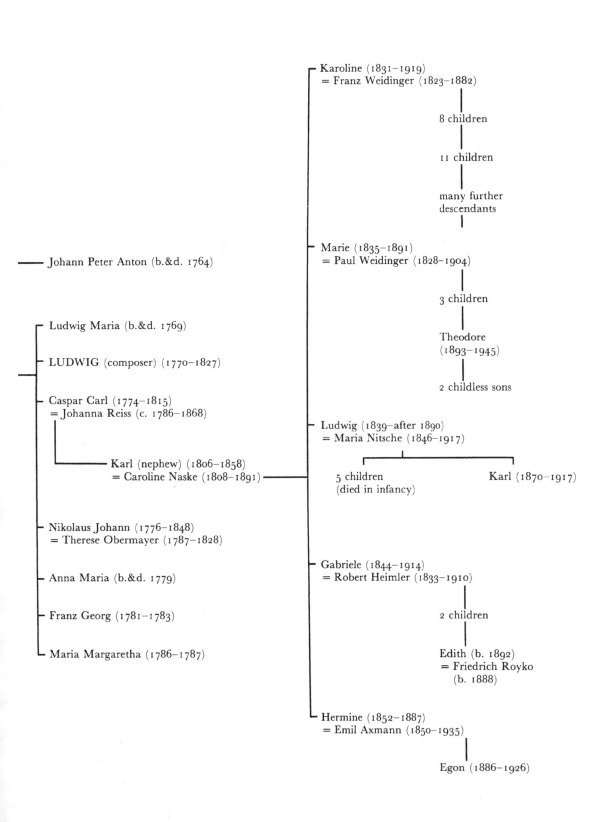

Section 3

WHO'S WHO OF BEETHOVEN'S CONTEMPORARIES

WHO'S WHO OF BEETHOVEN'S CONTEMPORARIES

THE PERSONS LISTED IN THIS SECTION are the most important among the many hundreds who are known to have had some connection with Beethoven in the course of his life. His publishers (see 'First editions and publishers', pp. 192–4) are generally omitted here unless they had some close personal contact with him (for example Steiner). Also omitted are composers who had little or no connection with him (such as Paganini and Field) or whom he knew only through their music (such as Gluck). Further information on both publishers and composers can be found in *The New Grove Dictionary*. The information in this section is derived chiefly from Frimmel, 1926; Kinsky, 1955; Anderson, 1961; Thayer, 1967; Köhler, 1968; Solomon, 1977; and *The New Grove Dictionary*.

Adamberger, Antonie (1790–1867?). Actress who sang and played the part of Klärchen at the first performance of Beethoven's *Egmont* music in 1810.

Albrechtsberger, Johann Georg (1736–1809). Theorist and composer. He was a renowned contrapuntist and leading composer of the old style, and when Haydn left Vienna for London in January 1794 Beethoven turned to Albrechtsberger for tuition in counterpoint, fugue and canon. Lessons continued for a period of about one and a half years. (See also 'Influences on Beethoven's style', p. 79).

Alexander I, Emperor of Russia (1777–1825). Dedicatee of the op. 30 violin sonatas, the Emperor met Beethoven at the Congress of Vienna in 1814 and was later one of the ten subscribers to the *Missa Solemnis*. His wife, Empress Elisabeth Alexiewna, also met Beethoven in 1814 and received the dedication of the Polonaise, op. 89.

Amenda, Karl (1771–1836). Theologian and violinist. He became a close friend of Beethoven during his short spell in Vienna (1798–9). Beethoven gave him the early version of his Quartet op. 18 no. 1, but after revising the work asked him not to show the early version to anyone. Amenda complied.

Anschütz, Heinrich (1785–1865). Tragedian and actor who delivered Beethoven's funeral oration.

He had come to Vienna in 1821 and became acquainted with Beethoven during the following years.

Arnim, Bettine von. See Brentano.

Averdonk, Severin Anton (1768–?). Author of the texts of two of Beethoven's Bonn cantatas (WoO 87 and 88) in 1790. His sister Johanna Helena, a contralto, was taught by Beethoven's father for a time.

Bach, Johann Baptist (1779–1847). Eminent lawyer. He advised Beethoven in many legal matters from 1816 onwards and was of particular assistance in 1819–20 in connection with Beethoven's appeal concerning the guardianship of nephew Karl. He made entries in several of the Conversation Books and is mentioned in many others.

Beethoven, Caspar Anton Carl van (*b* 1774; *d* 15 Nov. 1815). Elder of the composer's two surviving brothers and father of Karl. He followed Beethoven to Vienna in 1794 and for a while was active as a musician, teaching, assisting Beethoven and occasionally composing himself. In 1800 he became a clerk in the Department of Finance, but continued to assist Beethoven in dealings with publishers until at least 1806, the year of his marriage and of Karl's birth.

Beethoven, Johann van (*b* 1739 or 1740; *d* 18 Dec. 1792). Father. He was for many years a tenor at the Electoral court at Bonn, taught singing and keyboard and could also play the violin. He taught Beethoven music from an early age, but as a father was very harsh and severe. In later life he became an alcoholic and was eventually dismissed from active service at the Court in 1789.

Beethoven, Johanna van, *née* Reiss (*c.*1784–1868). Wife of Caspar Carl and mother of Karl. Daughter of an upholsterer, she married Caspar Carl on 25 May 1806 and gave birth to their only child less than four months later. In 1811 she was convicted of stealing from her husband; this offence and her lax morals were cited as evidence by Beethoven during their struggle for the guardianship of Karl, and he sometimes referred to her as 'the Queen of the Night' (a character in Mozart's *Magic Flute*); but his descriptions of her evil nature are grossly exaggerated.

Beethoven, Karl van (*b* 4 Sep. 1806; *d* 13 Apr. 1858). Nephew. With the death of Beethoven's brother Caspar Carl on 15 November 1815, Beethoven assumed guardianship of Karl. He wished to exclude the boy's mother Johanna from co-guardianship, and a lengthy legal battle ensued. At first Beethoven was successful, being declared legal guardian in January 1816, and Karl was placed in a private boarding school (the Giannatasio Institute) in February. In January 1818 Beethoven moved the boy to his own house – an action that led to renewed efforts by Johanna to win back her son. In December, during the legal hearing, Beethoven unintentionally revealed that he was not of noble birth as had been assumed, and the case was consequently transferred from the Landrecht to a lower court, the Magistrat. This court was much less sympathetic to the composer, and the boy was returned to his mother early in 1819. She and Leopold Nussböck were appointed co-guardians in September that year. Beethoven's protests to the Magistrat were ineffective and he appealed to the Court of Appeal, who eventually ruled in his favour on 8 April 1820, with him and Karl Peters being appointed co-guardians. The boy meanwhile had been placed in a series of schools (from which he had run away to his mother on more than one occasion), the last being Joseph Blöchlinger's, where he remained from June 1819 to August 1823. He then lived with Beethoven for a time and attended Vienna University before transferring to the Polytechnic Institute in 1825. Beethoven's overbearing love meanwhile placed increasingly intolerable pressure on Karl, and eventually in desperation he shot himself on 6 August 1826. He survived the suicide attempt, however, and later that year was fit enough to join the army. He left it in 1832, the year of his marriage,

and from then on lived as a private citizen. (See also 'Personal relationships', pp. 108–10.)

Beethoven, Ludwig van (1712–73). Grandfather. Born in Malines, the son of a master baker, he moved to Bonn in 1733, where he became court musician and in 1761 Kapellmeister. Although he died when Beethoven was just three, the composer retained fond memories of him and regarded him as his true spiritual forbear.

Beethoven, Maria Magdalena van, *née* Keverich (*b* 19 Dec. 1746; *d* 17 Jul. 1787). Mother. Daughter of the kitchen overseer at the palace of Ehrenbreitstein, she married one Johann Leym in 1763. He died less than two years later and the young widow married Johann van Beethoven on 12 November 1767. She bore one son (who died in infancy) by her first marriage and seven children by her second, of whom four died in infancy: Ludwig Maria (*b* and *d* 1769); Anna Maria Franziska (*b* and *d* 1779); Franz Georg (1781–3); and Maria Margaretha Josepha (1786–7). She was a quiet, serious woman but Beethoven was very fond of her and often spoke highly of her in later years. 'She was such a good, kind mother to me and indeed my best friend.' (Letter 1)

Beethoven, Nikolaus Johann van (1776–1848). Younger of the composer's two surviving brothers. He followed Beethoven to Vienna in December 1795 and was a pharmacist's assistant until 1808, when he moved to Linz to run his own pharmacy. From this he became very wealthy and in 1819 he purchased a large estate at Gneixendorf (near Krems), where Beethoven stayed from 29 September to 1 December 1826.

Beethoven, Therese van, *née* Obermayer (1787–1828). Sister-in-law. She became the mistress of Beethoven's brother Johann in Linz in 1812, and when the composer arrived to try to end the relationship the couple responded by marrying, on 8 November 1812. The marriage turned out to be an unhappy one, however, and they had no children.

Bernadotte, Jean Baptiste Jules (1764–1844). General in Napoleon's army, he was briefly French Ambassador in Vienna in 1798, when he became acquainted with Beethoven. He later became King Karl XIV of Sweden, and was in 1823 invited to subscribe to the *Missa Solemnis*, but he declined. The story that he suggested the idea for the *Eroica* Symphony is without foundation.

Bernard, Carl Joseph (Joseph Karl) (1780–1850). Writer and librettist. He came to Vienna in 1800, and in 1819 became editor of the *Wiener Zeitung*. His first connection with Beethoven was probably as author of the text of the *Chor auf die verbündeten Fürsten* (WoO 95) of 1814. During the next few years he became one of Beethoven's closest friends, and made numerous entries in the Conversation Books. In 1823 he completed the text for the oratorio *Der Sieg des Kreuzes*, which Beethoven was to compose for the Gesellschaft der Musikfreunde, but the project never materialized.

Bertolini, Dr Andreas. Friend and medical adviser of Beethoven from 1806 to 1816. In 1814 he organized an evening in honour of his friend Johann Malfatti for which Beethoven wrote *Un lieto brindisi* (WoO 103).

Bigot, Marie, *née* Kiene (1786–1820). Pianist. She moved to Vienna in 1804, and she and her husband (Count Razumovsky's librarian) formed a friendship with Beethoven. In 1806 she played the then unpublished 'Appassionata' Sonata at sight from Beethoven's autograph score, which was later given to her. She moved to Paris in 1809.

Birkenstock, Johann Melchior von (1738–1809). Art- and music-lover, scholar and statesman in Vienna, and father of Beethoven's friend Antonie Brentano. It seems, however, that he was never personally acquainted with Beethoven.

Blöchlinger von Bannholz, Joseph (1788–1855). Originally from Grobelingen, Switzerland, he came to Vienna in 1804, and in 1814 opened a boarding school there. Beethoven's nephew Karl attended it from 1819 to 1823, during which time Beethoven and Blöchlinger were often in close contact, as is evident from correspondence and the Conversation Books.

Böhm, Joseph Michael (1795–1876). Violinist. Professor at the Conservatory in Vienna from 1819 and member of the imperial orchestra from 1821, he was leader at the second performance of Beethoven's Quartet op. 127 in March 1825 and gave a much better rendition than Schuppanzigh had done at the first performance. Another Böhm, Joseph Daniel (1794–1864), was a medal-maker who in 1820 was intending to make a Beethoven medal.

Boldrini, Carlo (*c.*1780–1850?). Assistant and later (1807–24) partner at the music publisher Artaria & Co. His name (spelt 'Poldrini') is also found at the front of a (now lost) Beethoven sketchbook of 1817.

Bonaparte, Jerome (1784–1860). Youngest brother of Napoleon. He resided in Kassel during 1807–13 as 'King of Westphalia', and in 1808 invited Beethoven to become Kapellmeister there. This led to a counter-offer in 1809 from some Viennese noblemen (Princes Kinsky and Lobko-witz, and Archduke Rudolph) inducing Beethoven to remain in Vienna.

Bonaparte, Napoleon (1769–1821). French dictator and emperor. Beethoven's admiration for him as champion of freedom from oppression was an important factor leading to the composition of the *Eroica* Symphony, which was originally entitled *Bonaparte*. Although Beethoven suppressed this title after Napoleon had proclaimed himself emperor (see pp. 144 and 215), he retained an ambivalent attitude towards him in later years.

Brauchle, Joseph Xaver. Friend of Beethoven and amateur musician. He was tutor to the Erdödy family from about 1803 and left Vienna with them in 1815. The following year one of the children died, and Brauchle was suspected of having caused the child's death (by beating).

Braun, Baron Peter von (1758–1819). Businessman, music-lover and theatre director. In this last capacity he angered Beethoven in 1802 by not permitting use of the theatre for a benefit concert, but as director of the Theater an der Wien in 1804–5 he played a major role in setting up the first performances of *Leonore*. His wife Josephine (1765–1838) received dedications of the Piano Sonatas op. 14 and the Horn Sonata op. 17 in 1799 and 1801 respectively.

Braunhofer, Dr Anton. Physician and professor at the University of Vienna. He attended Beethoven during the period 1820–26 – chiefly during the illness of spring 1825. For him Beethoven wrote two canons (WoO 189 and 190) that year.

Brentano, Antonie, *née* Birkenstock (*b* 28 May 1780; *d* 12 May 1869). Friend of Beethoven and the probable intended recipient of Beethoven's famous letter to the 'Immortal Beloved' in July 1812 (see 'Personal Relationships', p. 107). Born in Vienna, she married Franz Brentano (1765–1844), a merchant from Frankfurt, on 23 July 1798 and moved with him to that city. In 1809 she returned to Vienna on hearing that her father was dying, and remained there until 1812. During this period she came to know Beethoven intimately and developed a great admiration and (probably) love for him. In 1812 she and Franz holidayed in Karlsbad while Beethoven went first to Teplitz and then joined them in Karlsbad. After a brief return to Vienna the Brentanos went back to Frankfurt for good, but continued to correspond with Beethoven occasionally, and remained among his most loyal friends at least until 1823. Franz lent him considerable sums of money without ever demanding repayment, and in 1823 Beethoven dedicated to Antonie the Diabelli Variations. The Brentanos had six children: Mathilda (1799–1800); Georg (1801–52);

Maximiliane (1802–61); Josefa (1804–75); Francisca (1806–37) and Karl (1813–50). For Maximiliane Beethoven wrote a simple Piano Trio (WoO 39) in 1812, dated only ten days before his letter to the Immortal Beloved. Assuming the latter was Antonie, it is possible, albeit unlikely, that Beethoven was the father of her youngest child.

Brentano, Bettine (1785–1859). Half-sister of Franz Brentano and friend of Goethe, she married the poet Achim von Arnim on 3 March 1811. She had met Beethoven a year earlier in Vienna and formed a brief friendship with him. She had a very strange imagination which frequently played havoc with her memory. Of the three letters Beethoven is supposed to have written to her, one is genuine but the other two, both rather romantic and rambling, are probably her own invention.

Brentano, Clemens (1778–1842). Poet and half-brother of Franz Brentano. In early 1811 he sent Beethoven, through Antonie Brentano, the text of a cantata, but Beethoven dismissed its subject as not important enough. The two men may have met in Teplitz in 1811.

Brentano, Franz Dominik Maria Joseph. See Brentano, Antonie.

Breuning, Dr Gerhard von (1813–92). Son of Beethoven's friend Stephan von Breuning by his second marriage, Gerhard became a frequent visitor to the composer's lodgings in 1825–7, and in 1874 published his recollections of Beethoven in *Aus dem Schwarzspanierhause.*

Breuning, Stephan von (*b* 17 Aug. 1774; *d* 4 Jun. 1827). Member of a prominent Bonn family who were closely connected to the Beethovens. His sister Eleonore Brigitte (1771–1841) married Franz Gerhard Wegeler (*q.v.*) in 1802, and his elder brother Christoph (1773–1841) went into law; his younger brother Lorenz or Lenz (1777–98) was a pupil and close associate of Beethoven while in Vienna (1794–7). Stephan himself moved to Vienna in 1801 and immediately renewed his childhood friendship with Beethoven, which lasted a lifetime (though with interruptions, including a complete break between 1815 and 1825). In 1806 he revised Sonnleithner's original text of *Leonore* for the second version of the opera, and (perhaps as a sign of gratitude) Beethoven in 1808 dedicated to him the Violin Concerto. The piano arrangement of this work was dedicated to his first wife Julie (*née* Vering), who died in 1809. Stephan then married Constanze Ruschowitz (mother of Gerhard von Breuning).

Bridgetower, George Augustus Polgreen (1779–1860). Mulatto violinist from Poland. He emigrated to London in 1790, but visited the continent on a concert tour in 1802 and reached Vienna the following year. Prince Lichnowsky introduced him to Beethoven, who rapidly wrote for him the 'Kreutzer' Sonata, op. 47; the work was first performed by the composer and Bridgetower on 24 May 1803.

Broadwood, Thomas. Member of a well-known firm of piano makers. In 1817–18 he sent Beethoven as a gift from the firm a magnificent six-octave piano, now in the National Museum, Budapest.

Browne (Browne-Camus), Count Johann Georg von (1767–1827). Officer (of Irish extraction) in the Russian Army. During Beethoven's early years in Vienna, Browne was one of his chief patrons, and besides providing financial support, once presented him with a horse (which was evidently not kept for long). He received the dedications of opp. 9, 22, 48 and WoO 46, and he commissioned the three Marches op. 45; his wife, Countess Anna Margarete (*d* 1803) received op. 10, WoO 71 and WoO 76. He was described by one acquaintance as 'one of the strangest men' with many talents but also many weaknesses (Thayer, 1967, p. 212).

Brunsvik (Brunswick), family. Count Anatol Brunsvik (1745–93) and his wife Anna (1752–1830) were Hungarian aristocrats. They had five children: (Maria) Therese (1775–1861), Franz (1777–1849), Josephine (1779–1821), Charlotte (1782–1843) and Julietta. The three eldest were very musical and became intimately acquainted with Beethoven in the early 1800s after the two girls had visited Vienna with their mother in 1799. Franz, a cellist, corresponded with Beethoven from Budapest until at least 1814 and received the dedications of opp. 57 and 77. Therese, who never married, was taught the piano briefly by Beethoven, and to her was dedicated the Sonata op. 78. Her memoirs and correspondence provide much information about Beethoven's relationship with the family (see La Mara, 1920). For Therese and Josephine, Beethoven wrote the song *Ich denke dein* (WoO 74) with variations for piano duet. Josephine married Count Deym in 1799 (see entry for her under Deym).

Castelli, Ignaz Franz (1781–1862). Poet and playwright. During 1811–14 he worked at the Court Theatre in Vienna, and for a time it seemed Beethoven might write an opera based on one of his libretti. His memoirs, which include many references to Beethoven, were published in 1861–2.

Cherubini, Luigi (*b* Sep. 1760; *d* 15 Mar. 1842). Italian composer who settled in Paris in 1788. He is best known for his operas and sacred music but he wrote in many other genres, and Beethoven greatly admired his music (see 'Influences on Beethoven's style', pp. 84–5). The two composers met when Cherubini visited Vienna in 1805, and he apparently attended the premiere of *Leonore*. In 1823 Beethoven wrote to him in connection with the *Missa Solemnis* but the letter seems never to have arrived.

Clement, Franz (1780–1842). Viennese violinist, who made his début at the age of nine. Beethoven knew him by 1794, and in 1805 the first public performance of the *Eroica* Symphony was at Clement's benefit concert. The following year Beethoven wrote the Violin Concerto for him. Clement was often away on concert tours, but was back in Vienna as the orchestral leader at the Theater an der Wien during 1818–24. In 1824 he would have been leader at the first performance of the Ninth Symphony, but Beethoven insisted on having Schuppanzigh, and so the venue was switched from the Theater an der Wien to the Kärntnertor Theatre.

Clementi, Muzio (*b* 23 Jan. 1752; *d* 10 Mar. 1832). Pianist, composer, music publisher and piano maker. Italian by birth, he moved to England at an early age and remained there till his death, apart from some extended concert tours. On one of these he visited Vienna in 1807 and met Beethoven. Beethoven seems initially to have been suspicious of this famous pianist whose piano works he greatly admired (see 'Influences on Beethoven's style', pp. 83–4), but before long they had become friends and done a very successful business deal: Clementi agreed to publish several completed works, and commissioned some new ones including opp. 77–9 and a piano arrangement of the solo part of the Violin Concerto. (See also 'First editions and publishers', p. 194.)

Collin, Heinrich Joseph (1772–1811). Viennese poet and playwright. His tragedy *Coriolan* (first produced in 1802) inspired Beethoven to compose an overture for it in 1807, though Beethoven seems not to have written it for any particular production. The following year the two men decided to collaborate on a new opera; among the topics proposed were *Bradamante* and *Macbeth*, but nothing came of the plans.

Cramer, Johann Baptist (*b* 24 Feb. 1771; *d* 16 Apr. 1858). Pianist, composer and music publisher. Born in Mannheim, he moved to London with his family in 1772. In 1799 he visited Vienna, where he remained until the following spring. During this time he became well acquainted with Beethoven, who afterwards occasionally imitated certain aspects of Cramer's style in his own compositions (see 'Influences on Beethoven's style', p. 84).

Czerny, Carl (*b* 21 Feb. 1791; *d* 15 Jul. 1857). Viennese pianist and composer. He received piano lessons from Beethoven from 1801 to 1803, and he in turn taught Beethoven's nephew from 1816 to 1818. He was thoroughly acquainted with practically all Beethoven's piano works (which he knew from memory), as well as with the composer himself. He published numerous compositions (especially piano studies), and in Volume 4 of his *Complete Theoretical and Practical Piano Forte School*, op. 500, he gave detailed instructions on how to perform each of Beethoven's major piano works. In addition, in his memoirs (1842) he gives many fascinating details about Beethoven.

Czerny, Joseph (1785–1842). Viennese pianist and composer, unrelated to Carl Czerny. He was piano tutor of Beethoven's nephew in 1820, and made several entries in Beethoven's Conversation Books. In 1824 he became a partner in the music publishing firm Cappi & Co. (from 1826 Cappi & Czerny).

Dembscher, Ignaz. Official at the imperial court in the 1820s, and a wealthy music-lover. Karl Holz relates that when Dembscher failed to attend Schuppanzigh's performance of the op. 130 Quartet in March 1826, Beethoven insisted that Dembscher send Schuppanzigh the price of the subscription. Dembscher asked, 'Must it be?', to which Beethoven sent in reply the canon *Es muss sein* ('It must be', WoO 196), the theme of which was later borrowed for the op. 135 String Quartet.

Deym, Countess Josephine, *née* Brunsvik (*b* 1779; *d* 31 Mar. 1821). A member of the Brunsvik family (see separate entry), she married Count Joseph Deym (*c.* 1752–Jan. 1804) in 1799. After her husband's death she was in close contact with Beethoven and before long he was in love with her. Altogether fourteen letters survive from Beethoven to her from the period 1804–7; in some of them he expresses his love quite openly, referring to her as his 'only beloved' (Letter 151), and he also wrote for her the song *An die Hoffnung* (op. 32). How far his feelings were reciprocated is uncertain but undoubtedly Josephine was very fond of him for a time. By 1807 the relationship had cooled, and after that year there is no further definitely known meeting between them. In 1810 she married Baron Christoph von Stackelberg, but the marriage was unsuccessful and the couple separated for good in 1813. The relationship between Beethoven and her in 1804–7 has led some people to believe she was Beethoven's 'Immortal Beloved' of 1812 (Tellenbach, 1983) and even that her daughter Minona, born 1813, was his child. The supporting evidence is flimsy but the hypothesis has not yet been disproved (see 'Personal relationships', p. 107).

Diabelli, Antonio (1781–1858). Composer and music publisher. He settled in Vienna in 1803 as a teacher of piano and guitar. Later he worked in Steiner's publishing firm before forming a partnership with Pietro Cappi (nephew of the publisher Giovanni Cappi) in 1818. In 1819 he invited fifty Viennese composers to write a variation each on a waltz of his. Beethoven responded by writing not one but thirty-three variations (op. 120), which Diabelli published in 1823. The collection of variations by fifty other composers (including Czerny, Schubert and the boy Liszt) appeared the following year.

Dietrichstein, Count Moritz von. (1774–1864). Composer, friend of Beethoven and for a time (1821–6) court theatre director. His sixteen Goethe songs (1811) were the first significant Viennese settings of Goethe apart from Beethoven's. Beethoven's song *Merkenstein* (op. 100) was dedicated (by the poet) not to Moritz but to Count Joseph Karl von Dietrichstein (1763–1825).

Doležalek, Johann Nepomuk Emanuel (1780–1858). Pianist, cellist and composer. He first met Beethoven in 1800 and many years later gave Otto Jahn his recollections of the composer. Their reliability, however, has been questioned (Webster, 1984).

Dragonetti, Domenico (1763–1846). Virtuoso double-bass player. As a travelling performer he occasionally visited Vienna, and first met Beethoven in 1799, when he reportedly revealed hidden possibilities in his instrument by performing the Cello Sonata op. 5 no. 2 with Beethoven. On another visit, in 1813, he took part in the first performance of *Wellingtons Sieg* (op. 91).

Duncker, Johann Friedrich Leopold (*d* 1842). Cabinet secretary to the King of Prussia. He accompanied the King to Vienna for the Congress of 1814 and wrote the play *Leonore Prohaska*, for which Beethoven composed incidental music (WoO 96). In 1823 Beethoven wrote asking him to persuade the King to subscribe to the *Missa Solemnis*, which the King did.

Duport, Jean-Louis (1749–1819) and Jean-Pierre (1741–1818). Brothers who were prominent cellists, working in Berlin when Beethoven visited the city in 1796. The Cello Sonatas op. 5 were evidently composed for Jean-Louis (Johnson, 1980b, p. 39).

Duport, Louis Antoine (1783–1853). Ballet dancer who as director of the Kärntnertor Theatre was closely involved in the first performance of Beethoven's Ninth Symphony.

Eeden (Eden), Heinrich Gilles van den (der) (*c.* 1710–1782). Bonn organist and probably one of Beethoven's earliest teachers.

Elisabeth Alexiewna, Empress of Russia (1779–1826). See Alexander I.

Erdödy, Countess Anna Marie, *née* Niczky (1779–1837). Friend of Beethoven from about 1803. She had married Count Peter Erdödy in 1796 and for a short time in 1808 Beethoven actually lived with them. She was an excellent pianist and an admirer of Beethoven's compositions, and he dedicated to her the Trios op. 70 and the Vienna edition of the Cello Sonatas op. 102. She had two daughters and one son – Marie (Mimi), Friederike (Fritzi) and August (Gusti). In 1815 the family left Vienna but the Countess still corresponded with Beethoven, who intended to express his affection for the children in a Piano Trio (F minor). Her son August, however, died in 1816 and the Trio was left unfinished. The Countess was back in Vienna in 1819–20 but eventually settled in Munich in 1824.

Ertmann, Baroness Dorothea von, *née* Graumann (1781–1849). Friend of Beethoven and an outstanding pianist. She married Peter von Ertmann in 1798 and by 1804 knew Beethoven well. She studied the piano with him for a time and became one of the greatest Beethoven exponents of the day. The Sonata in A (op. 101) was dedicated to her in 1817.

Esterházy, Prince Nikolaus (1765–1833). Grandson of Haydn's patron of the same name who had died in 1790, the Prince (also Haydn's patron) subscribed to Beethoven's op. 1 Trios and later commissioned a Mass from him to celebrate the name-day of his wife (Maria Josepha) in 1807. The Mass in C was duly performed at Eisenstadt on 13 September but did not please the Prince.

Fischer, Gottfried (1780–1864). Ninth and youngest child of a prominent Bonn family, and a close acquaintance of the young Beethoven. With the help of his sister Cäcilia (1762–1845) he began writing down reminiscences of Beethoven in 1838, gradually adding to his manuscript (now in the Beethoven-Archiv) for many years (see Schmidt-Görg, 1971).

Förster, Emanuel Aloys (1748–1823). Austrian composer and theorist who settled in Vienna in the 1780s. He is particularly noted for his quartets. Beethoven met him at Prince Lichnowsky's during the 1790s and may have studied with him briefly. In 1802 Beethoven was giving piano lessons to Förster's young son.

Forti, Anton (1790–1859). Viennese baritone. He sang the part of Pizarro in *Fidelio* in 1814 and in later revivals, but was passed over for the Ninth Symphony.

Frank, Dr Joseph (1771–1842). Viennese physician and amateur composer. In the 1790s he organized musical soirées, at which Christine Gerhardi (who married him in 1798) and Beethoven were among the participants.

Franz I, Emperor of Austria (1768–1835). Holy Roman Emperor Franz II from 1792, he established himself as Austrian Emperor in 1804 (see 'Politics', p. 59). He was a great music-lover but never seems to have shown much interest in Beethoven. His second wife was Maria Theresia.

Friedrich Wilhelm III, King of Prussia (reigned 1797–1840). Successor to Friedrich Wilhelm II, who had been a keen cellist and was for a time absurdly rumoured to be Beethoven's father. Wilhelm III was in Vienna for the Congress in 1814 and probably met Beethoven then. He later subscribed to the *Missa Solemnis* and in 1826 received the dedication of the Ninth Symphony.

Fries, Count Moritz von (1777–1826). Wealthy music-lover and head of the banking firm Fries & Co., which acted for a time as intermediary in Beethoven's dealings with the Scottish publisher George Thomson. Fries himself commissioned the Quintet op. 29 and probably also the Violin Sonatas opp. 23 and 24, all of which were dedicated to him. He also received the dedication of the Seventh Symphony.

Galitzin (Golitsïn, Golizyn), Prince Nikolas Borissovich (1794–1866). Russian prince, gifted cellist and great admirer of Beethoven's music. He began corresponding with Beethoven in 1822 and commissioned three Quartets (opp. 127, 132 and 130) which were dedicated to him, as was the overture *Die Weihe des Hauses*. The Prince also subscribed to the *Missa Solemnis* and organized its first performance, in St Petersburg.

Gallenberg, Count Wenzel Robert von (1783–1839). Viennese composer. He married Beethoven's friend Countess Giulietta Guicciardi in 1803 and the couple emigrated to Italy, returning to Vienna in 1822.

Gebauer, Franz Xaver (1784–1822). Austrian music teacher and choirmaster who established a series of Concerts Spirituels in 1819, at which many of Beethoven's major works were performed. He knew Beethoven well and made several entries in his Conversation Books.

Gelinek, Abbé Joseph (1758–1825). Czech priest and composer, active in Vienna from about 1790.

Shortly after Beethoven's arrival there, Gelinek was outshone by him in an improvisation contest. Relations later deteriorated and Gelinek reportedly could not appreciate many of Beethoven's later works, but he published a piano arrangement of the First Symphony in 1804 and some variations on the second movement of the Seventh Symphony in 1816.

George IV, King of Great Britain (1762–1830; reigned 1820–30). Beethoven's admiration for England led him to send George (then Prince Regent) a score of *Wellingtons Sieg* (op. 91), which he also dedicated to him. The Prince allowed the work to be performed in London but never sent acknowledgment or thanks to Beethoven, who consequently always spoke ill of him thereafter.

Giannatasio del Rio, Cajetan (1764–1828). Owner of a boarding school which Beethoven's nephew attended in 1816–18. His elder daughter Fanny (1790–c.1876) kept a diary which reveals many details about Beethoven's relations with the family during 1816–20. Her sister Anna or Nanni (1792–c.1866) married Leopold Schmerling in 1819 and for the occasion Beethoven wrote a *Hochzeitslied* (WoO 105).

Gläser, Peter (1776–1849). One of Beethoven's chief copyists after the death of Wenzel Schlemmer in 1823. His son Franz Joseph (1798–1861) was a composer and conductor, who helped direct the performances of *Die Weihe des Hauses* in 1822.

Gleichenstein, Baron Ignaz von (1778–1828). One of Beethoven's closest friends, acquainted with him from at least as early as 1797. A gifted cellist, he received the dedication of the Cello Sonata op. 69. In 1811 he married Anna Malfatti, younger sister of Beethoven's friend Therese, and he left Vienna a few years later, returning briefly in 1824 and 1828.

Glöggl, Franz Xaver (1764–1839). Musical director at Linz Cathedral. When Beethoven visited his brother Johann in Linz in 1812, Glöggl became well acquainted with him and asked him to compose the Equali (WoO 30) for four trombones.

Goethe, Johann Wolfgang von (1749–1832). World-renowned poet and playwright. Beethoven came to know and love Goethe's poetry in his youth, and set several of his texts (see 'Songs', pp. 262–7), culminating in the incidental music to *Egmont* (1810). In July 1812 the two great men finally met while on holiday in Teplitz, and for a time they were in daily company. Not long afterwards Beethoven began setting Goethe's *Meeresstille und glückliche Fahrt* (op. 112), completed in 1815. The work was published in 1822 with a dedication to Goethe, who received a copy of the score, and the following year Beethoven wrote to him expressing his continuing admiration of his works: 'The admiration, the love and the esteem which already in my youth I cherished for the one and only immortal Goethe have persisted' (Letter 1136). That year he also revealed that his greatest musical ambition was to provide music for Goethe's *Faust*; but the project was never realized. Goethe's view of Beethoven was somewhat different. He was amazed by his ability and was very impressed by the *Egmont* music, but he considered settings such as *Kennst du das Land* (op. 75 no. 1) over-elaborate and found Beethoven's personality rather rough.

Golitsïn or Golizyn: see Galitzin.

Griesinger, Georg August von (1769–1845). Saxon Minister in Vienna, and author of a Haydn biography (published 1810). He was acquainted with Beethoven from 1802 or earlier and acted as intermediary for the King of Saxony's subscription to the *Missa Solemnis*.

Grillparzer, Franz (1791–1872). Well-known dramatic poet. He had strong musical interests and first met Beethoven in about 1805. In 1823 the two men made plans to collaborate on an opera, and two subjects were suggested – *Drahomira* and *Melusine*. Beethoven claimed to have begun work on the latter but no sketches for it have been positively identified. In 1827 Grillparzer wrote Beethoven's funeral oration.

Guicciardi, Countess Giulietta (1784–1856). Piano pupil of Beethoven in about 1801, she fell in love with him for a time, and in 1802 he dedicated to her the 'Moonlight' Sonata, but in 1803 she married Count Gallenberg (*q.v.*). In 1823 Beethoven recalled his relationship with the Countess in a conversation with Schindler (Köhler, 1968, ii.365–6).

Halm, Anton (1789–1872). Composer, pianist and teacher who settled in Vienna in 1815. In 1816 he dedicated a sonata to Beethoven and in April 1826 he made a piano duet arrangement of the *Grosse Fuge* (op. 133); Beethoven, however, was not satisfied with the arrangement and subsequently made his own (op. 134).

Häring, Johann Baptist von (*d.* 1818). Viennese businessman and gifted violinist. Fluent in English, he assisted Beethoven in his correspondence with several English speakers such as Neate, Smart and Thomson.

Haslinger, Tobias (1787–1842). Austrian composer and music publisher. He settled in Vienna in 1810 and worked for many years at Anton Steiner's music publishing company, taking it over in 1826. He became a close friend of Beethoven and always seems to have brought out the humorous side of the composer. With Steiner they set up an imaginary army in which Beethoven was 'Generalissimo', Steiner 'Lieutenant-General' and Haslinger 'Adjutant', while ducats were 'armed men'. Beethoven wrote a humorous scenario for an imaginary biography of Haslinger (Letter 1345) and several little musical settings of his name (WoO 205 g–k and WoO 182, the latter a complete canon that originated in a dream!).

Hauschka, Vicenz (1766–1840). Composer, cellist and finance officer. He was a friend of Beethoven, who wrote for him a short canon (WoO 172) and another fragment (WoO 201). As a founder member of the Gesellschaft der Musikfreunde in Wien, Hauschka tried to arrange for Beethoven to write an oratorio for the society, but the plan never materialized.

Haydn, Franz Joseph (1732–1809). Beethoven left Bonn for Vienna in 1792 principally to study with Haydn, generally regarded then as the greatest living composer. Tuition in counterpoint lasted until the beginning of 1794, when Haydn left for England. After his return, relations between the two men were variable. There was disagreement over the worth of Beethoven's Trio op. 1 no. 3, and Beethoven claimed once that he had 'never learned anything' from Haydn (Wegeler, 1987, p. 75); moreover, Beethoven evidently did not regard Haydn's music as highly as that of Handel, Mozart or Bach. Yet there was no general falling-out between them; Beethoven dedicated his first three piano sonatas (op. 2) to Haydn and always held his former teacher in a place of respect and honour (see Solomon, 1977, pp. 67–77, and Webster, 1984).

Hensler, Karl Friedrich (1761–1825). Playwright and impresario who settled in Vienna in 1784. He became manager of the Josephstadt Theatre in 1821 and rebuilt it. At its reopening on 3 October 1822 a new version of Beethoven's *Die Ruinen von Athen* was performed, entitled *Die Weihe des Hauses*, for which Beethoven wrote a new overture and chorus (op. 124 and WoO 98). For a Hensler celebration a month later Beethoven wrote his *Gratulations-Menuett* (WoO 3).

Hoffmann, Ernst Theodor Amadeus (1776–1822). Famous German poet, writer, composer and music critic. He wrote several reviews of Beethoven's works, including a well-known one of the Fifth Symphony in 1810 (Forbes, 1971). In 1820 Beethoven wrote a canon on Hoffmann's name and also sent him a letter.

Holz, Karl (1798–1868). Official in the Chancellery of Lower Austria and a gifted violinist. He became second violinist in Schuppanzigh's quartet in 1824 and in the following summer became a close friend of Beethoven. For about a year he was the composer's chief assistant and unpaid secretary (as Schindler had been) and Beethoven seems to have been very fond of him. Two canons were written for Holz in 1826 (WoO 197 and 198). Meetings between the two were less frequent during Beethoven's final illness, by which time Holz had married, but their mutual affection was undiminished. Holz's reminiscences of Beethoven seem generally reliable.

Hotschevar, Jakob. Court secretary. As husband of the stepsister of the mother of Beethoven's sister-in-law Johanna, Hotschevar opposed Beethoven and supported Johanna in their dispute over nephew Karl in 1818. In 1827 Hotschevar himself became Karl's guardian.

Huber, Franz Xaver (1760–1810). Librettist who wrote the text of Beethoven's oratorio *Christus am Oelberge* in 1802–3.

Hummel, Johann Nepomuk (1778–1837). Composer and pianist. After touring as a youth he settled in Vienna in 1795 and was from time to time in contact with Beethoven. He conducted the percussion in one or more performances of *Wellingtons Sieg* (op. 91) in 1814, and on his departure from Vienna in 1816 Beethoven wrote for him a canon (WoO 170). During Beethoven's final illness Hummel returned to Vienna to visit him and was present at his funeral.

Hüttenbrenner, Anselm (1794–1868). Composer and friend of Schubert. He first met Beethoven in 1816 but is chiefly noted for his detailed account of Beethoven's death, at which he was one of only two witnesses present.

Jeitteles, Alois (1794–1858). Physician and poet from Brno. As a young medical student he wrote the text of Beethoven's song cycle *An die ferne Geliebte* early in 1816. His cousin Ignaz (1783–1843) associated with Beethoven in the 1820s.

Joseph II, Emperor of Austria (reigned 1780–90). A great reforming emperor (see 'Politics', pp. 58–9). Beethoven evidently admired him and as a nineteen-year-old composed a remarkable cantata on his death (WoO 87).

Kanka, Johann Nepomuk (1772–1865). Lawyer and composer from Prague. Beethoven met him there in 1796, and after Prince Kinsky's death in 1812 Kanka was instrumental in arranging that the annuity that Kinsky had awarded Beethoven in 1809 continued to be paid.

Kanne, August Friedrich (1778–1833). Composer, poet and writer. He came to Vienna in 1808 and later became a friend of Beethoven, making several entries in the Conversation Books. He was a highly talented man with an encyclopaedic knowledge.

Karl XIV, King of Sweden. See Bernadotte.

Kinsky, Prince Ferdinand Johann Nepomuk (1781–1812). One of three aristocratic patrons who contributed to Beethoven's annuity of 4000 florins from 1809 (the others were Prince Lobkowitz and Archduke Rudolph). Beethoven dedicated to him the Mass in C, and to Princess Caroline Kinsky some songs (opp. 75, 83 and 94). The Prince died in November 1812 after falling from his horse and for a time Beethoven was unable to obtain any further payments of his annuity from the Kinsky estate.

Kirchhoffer, Franz Christian. Accountant and acquaintance of Beethoven. He acted as intermediary in several of Beethoven's dealings with England, including the despatch of the Ninth Symphony to the Philharmonic Society.

Koch, family. During his last years in Bonn Beethoven frequented an inn run by a widow Koch. Her daughter Barbara (Babette) was widely admired, including by Beethoven, who wrote to her at least twice after leaving Bonn.

Kotzebue, August von (1761–1819). Writer who had a chequered career in Germany, Vienna and Russia, before eventually being assassinated on suspicion of being a Russian spy. For a time he edited the magazine *Der Freimütige*, for which he wrote reviews of several Beethoven compositions. In 1811 he wrote for the opening of a new theatre in Pest two stage works for which Beethoven provided the music – the prologue *König Stephan* and epilogue *Die Ruinen von Athen* (opp. 117 and 113). Beethoven was evidently pleased with the texts, for in 1812 he asked Kotzebue for an opera libretto to set, although nothing came of the idea.

Kozeluch, Leopold (1747–1818). Prolific composer and pianist who settled in Vienna in 1778. In 1792 he became Imperial Chamber Composer in succession to Mozart, and he occasionally came into contact with Beethoven, but there seems to have been more animosity than friendship between them.

Kraft, Anton (1752–1820). Prominent cellist. He played in the orchestra of Prince Esterházy and later Prince Lobkowitz, and sometimes in Schup-

WHO'S WHO OF BEETHOVEN'S CONTEMPORARIES

panzigh's quartet. His son Nikolaus (1778–1853) was also a cellist and gave the first performance of Beethoven's Cello Sonata op. 69 in March 1809.

Kreutzer, Konradin (1780–1849). Composer and conductor. He probably met Beethoven during his spell in Vienna in 1804–12, and again after his return in 1822. In 1824 he took part in the first performance of the Ninth Symphony.

Kreutzer, Rodolphe (1766–1831). Famous French violinist. He visited Vienna in 1798 and Beethoven later described him as a 'dear kind fellow who during his stay in Vienna gave me a great deal of pleasure' (Letter 99). Beethoven dedicated to him the Violin Sonata op. 47 in 1805.

Krumpholz, Wenzel (1750–1817). Violinist and mandolinist. He settled in Vienna in about 1795 and rapidly became a friend and great admirer of Beethoven (and a close friend of Carl Czerny). On his sudden death in 1817 Beethoven wrote the *Gesang der Mönche* (WoO 104).

Kuffner, Christoph (1780–1846). Viennese writer. He probably wrote the text for Beethoven's Choral Fantasia of 1808, and Beethoven wrote a March and Entr'acte (WoO 2) for his tragedy *Tarpeja* in 1813. Kuffner made many entries in the Conversation Books in 1826, when Beethoven planned to set his oratorio libretto *Saul*.

Kuhlau, Friedrich (1786–1832). Composer. He visited Beethoven in September 1825, when Beethoven at a very merry dinner party composed a canon on his name (WoO 191), using the B–A–C–H motif.

Lichnowsky, Prince Karl (1756–1814). Older brother of Count Moritz and one of Beethoven's leading patrons, especially during the composer's early years in Vienna. For a time in *c.*1793–5 Beethoven actually lived in Lichnowsky's house. Each Friday a concert took place at Lichnowsky's, and several of Beethoven's compositions were first performed at these occasions. Among them were the three Trios op. 1, dedicated to the Prince, who helped subsidize their publication. Also dedicated to him were the Piano Sonatas opp. 13 and 26, the Second Symphony and a set of variations (WoO 69). In 1806 relations between the two men became very strained for a while.

Lichnowsky, Count Moritz (1771–1837). Younger brother of Prince Karl and friend of Beethoven. Beethoven dedicated to him the *Prometheus* Variations (op. 35) and the Piano Sonata op. 90, and in 1823 wrote a short canon for him (WoO 183).

Linke, Joseph (1783–1837). Cellist and composer. He settled in Vienna in 1808 (possibly earlier) and played in quartets for Count Razumovsky until 1815. In 1823 he became the cellist in Schuppanzigh's quartet (see Schuppanzigh).

Liszt, Franz (1811–86). Composer and pianist. He lived in Vienna from 1821 and in 1823 met Beethoven, who was evidently very impressed by the eleven-year-old's abilities. Liszt left the city later that year.

Lobkowitz, Prince Franz Joseph Maximilian von (1772–1816). One of Beethoven's leading patrons, a great music-lover and enthusiastic violinist. From 1796 he had a private orchestra at his palace and allowed Beethoven to make use of it for private performances of his symphonies – notably the *Eroica*, which was tried several times before its first public performance. From 1809 he contributed (along with Prince Kinsky and Archduke Rudolph) to Beethoven's annuity of 4000 florins. He received dedications of the op. 18 Quartets, the Triple Concerto, the Third, Fifth and Sixth Symphonies, the op. 74 Quartet and the song cycle *An die ferne Geliebte*. For his son Ferdinand (*b* 1797) Beethoven composed a short Birthday Cantata (WoO 106) in 1823.

Maelzel, Johann Nepomuk (1772–1838). Inventor. He settled in Vienna in 1792 and was in close contact with Beethoven during the latter part of 1813. Of his many inventions three concerned Beethoven: the panharmonicon – a mechanical orchestra for which Beethoven wrote *Wellingtons Sieg* in 1813; the metronome, which Beethoven was the first major composer to make use of; and several designs of ear trumpet to help Beethoven's bad hearing. The Canon (WoO 162) said by Schindler to have been written in Maelzel's honour is spurious.

Malfatti, Dr Giovanni (Johann) (1775–1859). Italian physician who settled in Vienna in 1795. He became a friend of Beethoven in 1808 through their mutual friend Gleichenstein, and he treated Beethoven (after a lengthy rift) during his final illness in 1827. Malfatti's brother had two daughters: Therese (1792–1851), who married Baron von Drosdick in 1816 and to whom Beethoven is said to have proposed marriage in 1810; and her younger sister Anna (also born 1792), who married Gleichenstein in 1811. For the doctor Beethoven composed a short cantata *Un lieto brindisi* (WoO 103) in 1814; and the well-known piano piece *Für Elise* was probably written for Therese, since the autograph score was at one time in her possession.

Matthisson, Friedrich von (1761–1831). Poet. The setting of his *Adelaide* (op. 46) gave Beethoven

49

particular delight, as he stated in a letter to the poet (Letter 40); so too did Matthisson's *Opferlied*, which was set four times. Beethoven also set his *An Laura* (WoO 112) and *Andenken* (WoO 136).

Maximilian Franz, Elector of Cologne (1756–1801; ruled 1784–94). Beethoven's patron in Bonn. The Elector paid for Beethoven's visits to Vienna in 1787 and 1792, and generally supported and encouraged him and other musicians.

Mayer (Meyer, Meier), Friedrich Sebastian (1773–1835). Actor and singer. He created the role of Pizarro in *Leonore* (1805) and at the time was in close contact with Beethoven.

Mayseder, Joseph (1789–1863). Viennese violinist and composer. A pupil of Schuppanzigh, he sometimes took part in Beethoven's concerts and his name appears in several Conversation Books.

Meisl, Carl (1775–1853). Playwright. In 1822 he wrote the text for *Die Weihe des Hauses*, performed with Beethoven's music at the reopening of the Josephstadt Theatre in Vienna.

Milder-Hauptmann, Anna Pauline (1785–1838). Outstanding soprano who took the title role in the first performances of *Leonore*. She married Peter Hauptmann in 1810 but continued her singing career. Beethoven greatly admired her ability and was also very fond of her as a person, sending her a canon with the words 'I kiss you' (WoO 169) in 1816.

Moscheles, Ignaz (1794–1870). Composer and pianist from Prague. He settled in Vienna in 1808 (though he was often away on concert tours) and was in contact with Beethoven from then until 1820. In 1814 he prepared the piano version of *Fidelio* and later made piano arrangements of several other Beethoven works. He moved to London in 1825 and Beethoven wrote to him three times during his final illness. In 1841 Moscheles published an annotated English translation of Schindler's biography of Beethoven.

Mozart, Wolfgang Amadeus (1756–91). Beethoven evidently met Mozart during his visit to Vienna in 1787, but there are conflicting reports about whether he ever heard him play. Mozart's music was of course one of the main influences on Beethoven (see 'Influences on Beethoven's style', p. 83).

Napoleon. See Bonaparte.

Neate, Charles (1784–1877). Pianist, composer and founder member of the Philharmonic Society. He visited Vienna for eight months in 1815–16 and

became a friend of Beethoven, who wrote two canons for him (WoO 168) when he departed. Beethoven also gave him several scores to take to London for publication, but no publisher would accept them and Beethoven blamed Neate. The rift was soon healed, however, and they corresponded several times in later years.

Neefe, Christian Gottlob (1748–98). Composer and one of Beethoven's first music teachers. He settled in Bonn in 1779 and taught Beethoven piano, figured bass and composition. He quickly appreciated the boy's talents, stating prophetically in Cramer's *Magazin der Musik* in 1783: 'He would surely become a second Wolfgang Amadeus Mozart were he to continue as he has begun' (Thayer, 1967, p. 66). Beethoven was aware of his debt to his teacher, as is seen from his own prophecy: 'Should I ever become a great man, you too will have a share in my success.' (Letter 6)

Niemetz, Joseph (1808–?). Close friend of Beethoven's nephew Karl, who met him at Blöchlinger's Institute in about 1820. Beethoven strongly disapproved of him but Karl refused to abandon him.

Oliva, Franz (1786–1848). Banking clerk and close friend of Beethoven. From about 1809 he frequently acted as Beethoven's unpaid secretary in dealings with publishers etc. – a role performed earlier by Beethoven's brother Carl and later by Schindler and Holz. He made numerous entries in the Conversation Books up to 1820, but in December that year he departed for St Petersburg, where he settled as a language teacher. In 1810 he received the dedication of the Piano Variations op. 76.

Oppersdorff, Count Franz von (1778–1818). Music-lover who had a private orchestra in Upper Silesia. Beethoven visited him (with Prince Lichnowsky) in 1806 and the Count commissioned two symphonies – the Fourth and Fifth, the former of which was eventually dedicated to him.

Pachler, Marie Leopoldine, *née* Koschak (1794–1855). Pianist. She met Beethoven in 1817 and again in 1823. Beethoven once told her: 'I have not found anyone who performs my compositions as well as you do.' (Letter 815); in 1823 he wrote a two-bar farewell for her (WoO 202).

Palffy von Erdöd, Count Ferdinand (1774–1840). Theatre director. He became a director of the Court Theatre in 1806 and bought the Theater an der Wien in 1813. Although he was at times in contact with Beethoven, Palffy was evidently not one of his supporters.

Pasqualati, Baron Johann Baptist von (1777–1830). Music-lover and art collector. From 1804 to 1815 Beethoven frequently lived in Pasqualati's house on the Mölkerbastei in Vienna (the rooms are now kept as a Beethoven memorial). In 1814 Beethoven composed an elegy (op. 118) for the third anniversary of the death of the baron's wife Eleonore, and the following year he gave him a canon (WoO 165) as a New Year gift. During Beethoven's final illness Pasqualati sent him several gifts of food, which were greatly appreciated.

Peters, Karl. Court councillor and tutor to the Lobkowitz children. He became a friend of Beethoven around 1815 and assisted him in the struggle over the guardianship of Beethoven's nephew; from 1820 to 1825 Peters was a co-guardian himself, with Beethoven. Another Peters, Carl Friedrich of Leipzig, was a music publisher who in 1822 invited Beethoven to send him some works for publication.

Piringer, Ferdinand (1780–1829). Viennese official and violinist. He was assistant conductor to Gebauer at the Concerts Spirituels, and after the latter's death he became a director. He became a friend of Beethoven in about 1821, and from 1823 made many entries in the Conversation Books. The first known connection between the two is Beethoven's piano piece WoO 61, dated 18 February 1821 (could it be a misdating for 1822?).

Pleyel, Ignaz Joseph (1757–1831). Composer, publisher and piano maker. Born in Austria, he travelled widely before settling in Paris in 1795. In 1805 he visited Vienna with his son Camille (1788–1855), where they met Beethoven.

Punto, Giovanni. See Stich.

Radziwill, Prince Anton Heinrich (1775–1833). Amateur composer who met Beethoven in 1814 while in Vienna for the Congress. He later subscribed to the *Missa Solemnis*, and Beethoven dedicated to him the *Namensfeier* Overture (op. 115) and the 25 Scottish Songs (op. 108).

Razumovsky, Count Andreas Kirillovich (1752–1836). Art collector, music-lover and Russian Ambassador in Vienna. He commissioned the three 'Razumovsky' Quartets (op. 59) in 1806, and for a time (1808–16) supported a permanent string quartet led by Schuppanzigh, in which Razumovsky himself sometimes played second violin. A disastrous fire at his palace on 31 December 1814 greatly reduced his enormous wealth, but he continued to live in Vienna in retirement. The op. 59 Quartets were dedicated to him (after some vacillation by Beethoven), and the Fifth and Sixth Symphonies were dedicated jointly to him and Prince Lobkowitz.

Reicha, Anton (1770–1836). Czech composer who moved to Bonn in 1785 and became a close friend of Beethoven until the latter's departure for Vienna in 1792. The friendship was renewed in 1802, however, when Reicha also moved to Vienna; he settled in Paris in 1808.

Reisser, Franz de Paula Michael (1769–1835). Deputy director at the Polytechnic in Vienna. When Beethoven's nephew Karl entered it in 1825, Reisser became his co-guardian in place of Peters.

Reissig, Christian Ludwig (*c.*1783–1847). Poet. He was wounded in battle in 1809 and discharged from the army. He persuaded several composers to set his poems to music, including Beethoven, who set seven of them.

Ries, Ferdinand (1784–1838). Composer and pianist. Beethoven studied violin with Ries's father Franz (1755–1846) in Bonn, and readily welcomed Ferdinand when the latter came to Vienna in October 1801. Ries studied the piano with Beethoven for four years and became intimately acquainted with him, being greatly helped in various ways by his teacher. Ries in turn assisted Beethoven, for example by making arrangements of several of his works. In 1805 he left Vienna and apart from a brief visit in 1808–9 did not return. He settled in London in 1813 but continued to promote Beethoven's interests there and tried hard to persuade Beethoven to visit England. In 1824 he returned to the Rhineland, where he performed the Ninth Symphony in 1825 (i.e. before publication). Shortly before his death he collaborated with Wegeler on an important and generally reliable collection of reminiscences about Beethoven, published in 1838 (Wegeler, 1987).

Rio. See Giannatasio del Rio.

Rochlitz, Johann Friedrich (1769–1842). Editor of the important Leipzig journal *Allgemeine Musikalische Zeitung* from 1798 to 1818 and contributor to it thereafter. He visited Vienna in 1822, and claimed after Beethoven's death to have met the composer three times; but his oft-cited descriptions of the meetings probably contain much fabrication and it must be doubted whether he even met Beethoven at all (see Solomon, 1980b).

Röckel, Josef August (1783–1870). Tenor. He came to Vienna from Salzburg in 1805 and sang the part of Florestan in the 1806 version of *Leonore*, at which time he was in close contact with Beethoven.

Rode, Jacques Pierre Joseph (1774–1830). Famous French violinist. Pierre Rode visited Vienna on a concert tour in December 1812 and Beethoven wrote his last violin sonata (op. 96) for him to perform there, deliberately making the music suit Rode's style of playing.

Rossini, Gioachino (Giacomo) Antonio (1792–1868). Opera composer. His music was extremely popular in Vienna during Beethoven's later life, although Beethoven considered it to be of limited merit. Rossini visited Vienna in 1822 and met Beethoven briefly, but problems of language and Beethoven's deafness made communication difficult.

Rudolph, Archduke of Austria (1788–1831). Youngest son of Leopold II and brother of Emperor Franz. He was an excellent pianist, occasional composer and fervent admirer of Beethoven's music. For many years he was both a close friend and the leading patron of Beethoven, as well as being his only composition pupil. In 1809 he combined with the Princes Kinsky and Lobkowitz to provide Beethoven with an annuity of 4000 florins to induce him to remain in Vienna. His compositions include a set of forty variations (on a theme of Beethoven, WoO 200) which Beethoven described as 'masterly' (Letters 933 and 948). Beethoven dedicated far more compositions to Rudolph than to anyone else; they include the Fourth and Fifth Piano Concertos, the 'Les Adieux', 'Hammerklavier' and op. 111 Sonatas, the Violin Sonata op. 96, the 'Archduke' Trio (the nickname is from the dedicatee), the *Missa Solemnis*, the *Grosse Fuge* (and its arrangement for piano duet), and lesser works. Several works have particularly close connections with the Archduke: 'Les Adieux' portrays his departure, absence and return to Vienna in 1809–10; the Violin Sonata was written for him to perform with Rode; the first two movements of the 'Hammerklavier' were written for his name-day; and the *Missa Solemnis* was written for his enthronement as Archbishop and Cardinal of Olmütz in March 1820, although the work was not ready in time for the ceremony.

Rupprecht, Johann Baptist (1776–1846). Writer, poet and botanist. His poem *Merkenstein* was twice set by Beethoven (op. 100 and WoO 144) after he became acquainted with the poet in 1814. Rupprecht's name appears several times in the Conversation Books.

Salieri, Antonio (1750–1825). Composer and (from 1788) Kapellmeister at the Viennese court. In early 1799 Beethoven published a set of variations (WoO 73) on a theme of Salieri and also dedicated to him the Violin Sonatas op. 12. From about 1800 to 1802 Beethoven studied Italian vocal and operatic style with him, but after that there was little contact between the two composers.

Salomon, Johann Peter (1745–1815). Violinist, concert impresario and composer. Born in Bonn,

he had settled in London by the time of Beethoven's birth, although some of the family remained in Bonn. He returned there for a brief visit in 1790, when he met Beethoven, who occasionally corresponded with him in later years. He is renowned for having brought Haydn to England.

Schenk, Johann Baptist (1753–1836). Viennese operatic composer. In his autobiography he claimed that he had taught Beethoven counterpoint for a time, giving him secret instruction to supplement Haydn's inadequate teaching. But there are errors in his account and it cannot be confirmed (Webster, 1984, pp. 10–14); nor can the lasting friendship he claimed to have formed with Beethoven.

Schickh, Johann (1770–1835). Founder and editor of the important *Wiener Zeitschrift für Kunst, Literatur, Theater und Mode* (*Viennese Journal for Art, Literature, Theatre and Fashion*), also known as the *Wiener Modenzeitung*. The journal included musical supplements, occasionally by Beethoven. In the 1820s Schickh was in close contact with Beethoven, making several entries in the Conversation Books.

Schikaneder, Emanuel Johann Joseph (1751–1812). Theatre manager, playwright and librettist, famous as author of *The Magic Flute*. In 1803 he collaborated with Beethoven on a projected opera *Vestas Feuer*; Beethoven actually set some numbers before deciding the text was too weak.

Schiller, Johann Christoph Friedrich von (1759–1805). Famous poet and playwright, author of *An die Freude*, portions of which were used in Beethoven's Ninth Symphony. Although Beethoven never met him he greatly admired his writings and often quoted from them (see 'Literature', pp. 148–50).

Schindler, Anton Felix (1795–1864). Violinist and biographer of Beethoven (see 'Biography and biographers', pp. 308–10). Although he was for a time in very close contact with Beethoven, his propensity for inaccuracy and fabrication was so great that virtually nothing he has recorded can be relied on unless it is supported by other evidence, as has become increasingly clear in recent years. He claimed to be a close friend of Beethoven from 1814 to 1827 but the evidence indicates close contact (as Beethoven's unpaid secretary) only from 1822 to May 1824 and from late 1826 to Beethoven's death the following March. After Beethoven's death Schindler acquired (stole?) many Beethoven manuscripts, including about 140 Conversation Books, into which he inserted many spurious entries, giving the impression he was in Beethoven's inner circle much earlier than he was (the first genuine entry is from November 1822). Beethoven greatly appreciated his assistance but evidently did not think highly of him as a man.

Schlemmer, Matthias. Viennese official with whom nephew Karl resided in 1825–6. During this period Beethoven corresponded with Schlemmer, and the latter also made entries in the Conversation Books. He was probably not related to Beethoven's copyist Wenzel Schlemmer (see 'Corrected copies and copyists', p. 190).

Schlösser, Louis (1800–86). Composer. He met Beethoven in 1822, and before he departed for Paris in 1823 Beethoven gave him a canon (WoO 185) and letters to take to Cherubini and Moritz Schlesinger. His well-known description of his meeting with Beethoven, however, written in 1885, is probably largely fabricated (see Solomon, 1980b).

Schmidt, Dr Johann Adam (1759–1809). Physician, music-lover and professor of anatomy. Beethoven, who was his patient for a time in 1802 and 1807, had a high regard for him and dedicated to him the piano trio arrangement (op. 38) of his Septet.

Schubert, Franz Peter (1797–1828). There is no absolute proof that Schubert ever met Beethoven, despite living in the same city, but several accounts indicate that he did, and the two men probably knew each other at least by sight. It seems, however, that the shy young Schubert was mostly content to admire Beethoven from a distance.

Schultz, J. R. (probably Johann Reinhold). Musician from England who visited Beethoven on 28 September 1823 and published a detailed account the following January. The account is sometimes wrongly attributed to Edward Schulz.

Schuppanzigh, Ignaz (1776–1830). Famous Viennese violinist. He became leader of a string quartet (with Sina, Weiss and Kraft) at Prince Lichnowsky's in the mid-1790s, by which time he had met Beethoven, who may have studied violin with him. In 1808 Count Razumovsky engaged him as leader of a permanent quartet at the Count's palace, but the quartet was disbanded in 1816. Schuppanzigh then moved to St Petersburg, but returned in 1823 and was leader in performances of Beethoven's Ninth Symphony and the late Quartets (except op. 131). Beethoven often made fun of Schuppanzigh's corpulence, calling him 'Falstaff' and in 1801 writing for him the humorous choral piece *Lob auf den Dicken* (*Praise to Fatness*). Schuppanzigh's return in 1823 was greeted with a canon (WoO 184).

Sebald, Amalie (1787–1846). Singer from Berlin. She met Beethoven at Teplitz (Bohemia) in 1811 and 1812, and he became very fond of her during that time, as is evident from several letters to her.

Seyfried, Ignaz Xaver, Ritter von (1776–1841). Composer. From 1797 to 1825 he was Kapellmeister at the Theater an der Wien, and he came into frequent contact with Beethoven – for example, he turned pages for him at the premiere of the Third Piano Concerto, and later left an amusing account of the problems (Thayer, 1967, pp. 329–30). After Beethoven's death he published a rather garbled and inaccurate account of Beethoven's studies in theory (*Beethovens Studien im Generalbass*, 1832), which however includes some interesting reminiscences.

Simrock, Nikolaus (1752–1833). Music publisher. He knew Beethoven in Bonn and later published several of his works (see 'First editions and publishers', p. 193). His son Peter Joseph (1792–1868), who later took over the business, visited Vienna in 1816 and was in close contact with Beethoven for a time.

Smart, Sir George Thomas (1776–1867). English conductor and founder member of the Philharmonic Society. He conducted the first English performance of Beethoven's Ninth Symphony in March 1825 and later that year visited Vienna, where he met Beethoven several times. Beethoven gave him a canon (WoO 192) and Smart later left a detailed account of their meetings.

Smetana, Dr Karl von (1774–1827). Prominent Viennese surgeon. He performed a hernia operation on Beethoven's nephew Karl in 1816, and later treated Beethoven himself.

Sonnleithner, Joseph Ferdinand (1766–1835). Viennese musician and lawyer. In about 1801 he was co-founder of the Bureau des Arts et d'Industrie, which published many of Beethoven's works (see 'First editions and publishers', pp. 192–3). In 1804 he prepared the libretto of *Leonore*, and about the same time became Secretary of the Court Theatre. His brother Ignaz (1770–1831) and Ignaz's son Leopold (1797–1873) also knew Beethoven.

Sontag, Henriette Gertrud Walpurgis (1806–54). Soprano. She lived in Vienna from 1823 to 1825 and sang the soprano solo in the first performances of Beethoven's Ninth Symphony in 1824.

Spohr, Louis (1784–1859). Famous composer and violinist. He was in Vienna during the period 1812–15, when he was leader at the Theater an der Wien, and he became well acquainted with Beethoven. He included a lengthy description of their association in his autobiography.

Stadler, Abbé Maximilian (1748–1833). Priest and composer. He lived in Vienna during 1796–

1803 and again from 1815, and occasionally came into contact with Beethoven. The canon *Signor Abate* (WoO 178) was probably written for him.

Starke, Friedrich (1774–1835). Composer and horn player. He was a friend of Beethoven and taught his nephew piano for a time. In 1820 he asked Beethoven for a contribution to a piano tutor he was publishing (*Wiener Pianoforte Schule*) and was presented with five Bagatelles (op. 119 nos 7–11).

Stein, family. Johann Andreas Stein (1728–92) was a famous piano maker in Augsburg. After his death three of his children became prominent in Vienna: Nanette (see Streicher); Matthäus Andreas (1776–1842), also a piano maker, who was a friend of Beethoven and made several entries in the Conversation Books; and Friedrich (1784–1809), a pianist who made arrangements of Beethoven's Fourth Symphony and *Coriolan* Overture. Matthäus's son Karl Andreas (1797–1863) later joined his father's firm. An unrelated Stein, Anton Joseph (1759–1844), was a Classics professor at Vienna University from 1806 to 1825; he wrote the text of Beethoven's *Hochzeitslied* (WoO 105) and is occasionally mentioned in the Conversation Books.

Steiner, Sigmund Anton (1773–1838). Publisher who issued first editions of many Beethoven works from 1815 onwards (see 'First editions and publishers', pp. 192–3). His retail outlet was in the Paternostergasse in Vienna and it became a common meeting place for Beethoven and his friends (see Tyson, 1962). In Beethoven's dealings with the firm he used military terminology: Beethoven was 'Generalissimo', Steiner 'Lieutenant-General' and his assistant Haslinger (*q.v.*) 'Adjutant'.

Stich, Johann Wenzel, alias **Punto,** Giovanni (1748–1803). Celebrated horn player from Bohemia. He visited Vienna on a concert tour in 1800 and met Beethoven, who wrote for him the Horn Sonata op. 17.

Streicher, Johann Andreas (1761–1833) and Anna Maria (Nanette), *née* Stein (1769–1833). Piano makers and close friends of Beethoven. Andreas, from Stuttgart, one-time friend of Schiller, married Nanette, daughter of a famous piano maker (see Stein) in Augsburg in 1794. The couple then moved to Vienna, where they set up their own piano making business. Beethoven thought very highly of their pianos and for a time preferred them to any other kind. In 1817–18 he frequently turned to Nanette, who he seems to have regarded almost as a kind of mother-figure, for domestic advice after he had become guardian of his nephew, and over sixty letters to her are known. Both Streichers made entries in the Conversation Books.

Stumpff, Johann Andreas (1769–1846). Thuringian harp-maker who lived in London from about 1790. He visited Beethoven in September 1824 and, learning of the composer's admiration for Handel, he resolved to give him a copy of Handel's works. After returning to England he sent a copy of Samuel Arnold's forty-volume edition of all Handel's major works; the gift arrived on 14 December 1826, and Beethoven was absolutely overjoyed.

Swieten, Baron Gottfried van (1733–1803). Friend of Mozart and great admirer of the works of Bach and Handel. He was one of Beethoven's earliest patrons in Vienna, and the First Symphony was dedicated to him in 1800.

Tiedge, Christoph August (1752–1841). Poet. Beethoven set his *An die Hoffnung* (op. 32) in 1804–5 and met Tiedge himself in Teplitz in 1811. A warm friendship quickly developed, but they soon had to go their separate ways. Both were in Teplitz again the following year, but probably not at the same time. In 1813 Beethoven made another setting of *An die Hoffnung* (op. 94).

Tomášek, Václav Jan Křtitel (Thomaschek, Johann Wenzel) (1774–1850). Czech composer. In his autobiography (1845–50) he reports having heard Beethoven perform his first two piano concertos in Prague in 1798, and gives an account of his visits to Beethoven in Vienna in 1814.

Treitschke, Georg Friedrich (1776–1842). Playwright and poet from Leipzig. He settled in Vienna in 1800 and was active as dramatist, actor and stage manager, chiefly at the Kärntnertor Theatre. He seems to have known Beethoven from about 1811, and when *Fidelio* was revived in 1814, Beethoven asked him to rewrite the libretto. This he did very skilfully and Beethoven was extremely grateful. Beethoven also composed two choruses for Singspiels by Treitschke (WoO 94 and 97) and set one of his poems (WoO 147).

Tuscher, Matthias von (1775–?). Councillor in Vienna. He was a friend of Beethoven and guardian of his nephew from March to July 1819.

Umlauf, Michael (1781–1842). Viennese conductor, son of the famous composer Ignaz (1746–96). His most notable performances include the premieres of *Fidelio* (1814 version) and the Ninth Symphony (1824); on both occasions Beethoven also conducted but because of his deafness could do little more than indicate the speeds and some of the expression, while it was Umlauf who held everything together.

Unger, Caroline (*c.*1803–1877). Contralto. She was at the Kärntnertor Theatre from 1819 to

1825, and sang the contralto solo in the first two performances of Beethoven's Ninth Symphony. She made several entries in the Conversation Books.

Varena, Joseph von (1769–1843). Musician in Graz. He met Beethoven at Teplitz in 1811 and later that year Beethoven sent him several scores for use at charity concerts in Graz.

Varnhagen von Ense, Karl August (1785–1858). Writer and diplomat. He met Beethoven in 1811, 1812 and 1814, and tried to assist him in obtaining the full value of Prince Kinsky's annuity after devaluation, while living in Prague (he later moved to Paris and Berlin). His reminiscences contain interesting references to Beethoven.

Vering, Dr Gerhard von (1755–1823). Physician. In 1801 he treated Beethoven for deafness and an abdominal complaint. The treatment was partially successful but Beethoven became dissatisfied and turned to Dr Schmidt (*q.v.*). Vering's daughter Julie, a pianist, married Stephan von Breuning in 1808 and received the dedication of Beethoven's piano version of his Violin Concerto, but she died in March 1809.

Vigano, Salvatore (1769–1821). Dancer, choreographer and composer. He was in Vienna during 1793–5 and again from 1799 and his ballets there were highly successful. One of them was *Die Geschöpfe des Prometheus* of 1801, for which Beethoven provided music that proved to be one of his first great public successes. Vigano and his wife Maria Medina, an outstanding ballerina, both took part in the first production.

Vogler, Abbé Georg Joseph (1749–1814). Composer and theorist. He was in Vienna from 1802 to 1805, and on one occasion is reported to have had an improvisation contest with Beethoven in which, unusually, one listener described Beethoven's attempt as less impressive than his rival's.

Waldstein, Count Ferdinand Ernst von (1762–1823). Music-lover and one of Beethoven's leading patrons in Bonn (i.e. up to 1792). He is said by Wegeler to have been the first fully to appreciate Beethoven's genius, and he received the dedication of the 'Waldstein' Sonata (op. 53) in 1805. Although he was in Vienna in his later years he no longer associated with Beethoven.

Wawruch, Dr Andreas Ignaz (*d* 1842). Physician. His date of birth is given variously as 1771, 1772 and 1782. He had no connection with Beethoven until December 1826, but became his principal doctor during the composer's final illness and wrote a detailed report on it.

Weber, Carl Maria von (1786–1826). Composer. At first opposed to much of Beethoven's music, he later became a great admirer. Beethoven in turn was apparently very impressed by *Der Freischütz*. Weber directed Beethoven's *Fidelio* in Prague in 1814 and in Dresden in 1823, and paid him a visit in October that year.

Wegeler, Dr Franz Gerhard (1765–1848). Physician from Bonn. He was a close friend of Beethoven until the latter's departure for Vienna in 1792, and they renewed their friendship when Wegeler himself was in Vienna from October 1794 until 1796. Thereafter they occasionally corresponded. In 1802 he married Eleonore von Breuning, Stephan's sister (see Breuning). Then in 1838 he published, with Ferdinand Ries, an important and generally reliable collection of reminiscences about Beethoven, to which he added a supplement in 1845 (Wegeler, 1987).

Weigl, Joseph (1766–1846). Composer and conductor, working chiefly at the Kärntnertor Theatre in Vienna. A theme of his was used in the finale of Beethoven's Clarinet Trio op. 11, and in 1804–5 he set Schikaneder's libretto *Vestas Feuer* after Beethoven had abandoned it. His name occasionally appears in the Conversation Books but he had little personal contact with Beethoven.

Weissenbach, Dr Aloys (1766–1821). Poet and surgeon who lived in Salzburg from 1804. In 1814 during a visit to Vienna he wrote the text for Beethoven's cantata *Der glorreiche Augenblick* and became acquainted with the composer. Two years later he published an account of his visit. Like Beethoven, he had a hearing deficiency.

Wölffl, Joseph (1772–1812). Pianist and composer. For a time around 1799 he was in Vienna, where he proved a serious rival to Beethoven as a pianist; he had the advantage of possessing enormous hands.

Wolfmayer, Johann Nepomuk. Businessman and music-lover. He was a great admirer of Beethoven and apparently asked him for a Requiem in about 1818. He was to have received the dedication of the Quartet op. 131 in return for his help, but Beethoven changed his mind at the last minute.

Zelter, Carl Friedrich (1758–1832). Berlin musician and friend of Goethe. He may have met Beethoven in 1796 during the latter's visit to Berlin, and they definitely met briefly in Vienna in 1819. They also corresponded about the *Missa Solemnis* in 1823, and seem to have had a warm regard for each other.

Zizius, Dr Johann Nepomuk (1772–1824). Lawyer and music-lover. He sometimes held musical soirées at his house and was a prominent member of the Gesellschaft der Musikfreunde.

Zmeskall von Domanovecz, Nikolaus (1759–1833). Official in the Hungarian Chancellery, long-standing friend of Beethoven and a capable cellist. A large number of letters and short notes from Beethoven to Zmeskall have survived, the earliest dating from *c.*1795. Zmeskall often helped Beethoven in practical matters such as finding a suitable servant or lending him small sums of money. By the 1820s he was bedridden and unable to associate with Beethoven (his name rarely appears in the Conversation Books) but managed to attend the first performance of the Ninth Symphony. Beethoven's final letter to him was written only a month before the composer's death.

BARRY COOPER

Section 4
HISTORICAL BACKGROUND

HISTORICAL BACKGROUND

Politics

The general situation in Central Europe

THE GERMANY OF THE 18TH CENTURY was very different from that
of today, consisting of a loose association of sovereignties governed
by secular and ecclesiastical princes. These together formed the
Holy Roman Empire, established by Charlemagne in 800, and
given papal blessing in 962, which since the mid-15th century
had been overseen by emperors from the house of Habsburg.

The states embraced by the Empire varied considerably in size
and character, as did the status and the political and military
aspirations of their rulers. The large measure of independence
which they displayed was reflected in their cultural life. Many
courts became centres of artistic entertainment, providing a
thriving atmosphere for composers and performing musicians
alike.

To the south and east of the Holy Roman Empire lay the
Archduchy of Austria and the Kingdom of Hungary, which since
the 16th century had formed the eastern arm of the Habsburg
domains that once stretched from the Straits of Gibraltar to the
Carpathians. From 1438 it became customary for the head of the
house of Habsburg, the Emperor of Austria, to be elected Holy
Roman Emperor. His role was to protect the Empire from its
enemies and to arbitrate between the local rulers in order to
maintain a balance of power.

Maria Theresa's accession to the Habsburg throne in 1740
coincided with a new spirit of Enlightenment permeating Europe
and penetrating Vienna, the seat of the Habsburgs. Although she
was not actively interested in the new philosophical ideas, she
chose able and farsighted counsellors, and took many important
practical measures to reform and strengthen the lands under her
control; but her reforming influence on the Holy Roman Empire
was limited.

Maria Theresa's son Joseph II, however, who reigned with her
from 1765 and was sole ruler from 1780 to 1790, was an outspoken
and firm exponent of enlightened rationalism. History regards
him as a radical reformer because of the vigour and speed with
which he enforced many measures. He wanted uniformity and
centralization, one result of which was that Germanization
became a deliberate policy, whereas under Maria Theresa it had
been incidental.

Joseph attempted to extend his reforming influence to the non-
Habsburg parts of the Holy Roman Empire and to Habsburg

Italy through his two brothers in Milan and Bonn. In Italy the success of Leopold (later Emperor Leopold II) is attested by Milan becoming a prominent Italian centre. Meanwhile Maximilian Franz, the Archbishop Elector of Cologne and, like the Emperor, an enthusiastic supporter of the arts, was responsible for Bonn becoming an example of Enlightenment within the Empire. Joseph felt shortly before his death that he had failed in all his enterprises; but although most of his reforms foundered through bitter opposition, he had changed the character of the lands he controlled, and he and Maria Theresa had achieved a measure of unity between their disparate parts.

Leopold II (1790–92) proceeded to effect compromises of his brother's reforms in order to bring peace at home, and was a skilled diplomat. He might have made a useful contribution but for his untimely death, which also ended the period of reform of the Habsburg Empire.

Joseph II had not been unduly troubled by the French Revolution in 1789, seeing it not as the start of a general European uprising but as an event which would keep France preoccupied by internal affairs for some time. His brother took much the same attitude. But Leopold had been dead only a few weeks when France declared war on 'the King of Hungary and Bohemia' (i.e. on the Habsburgs, not the German Empire or its people). This marked the start of the French Revolutionary and Napoleonic Wars. By now the Holy Roman Empire was nearing the end of its turbulent thousand-year history. It was Napoleon Bonaparte, the apostle of the French Revolution, who was its final destroyer. Franz II, the Habsburg King of Hungary and Bohemia on whom war was declared, had none of his father's or uncle's enlightened outlook and the people of his empire felt no affinity with the French Revolution.

Austria was one of the staunchest and most consistent members of the anti-French coalitions which came together and fell apart repeatedly during the period of French aggression. With the Holy Roman Empire on the point of dissolution, its emperor, Franz II, foresaw himself without the status of the other European leaders, and in 1804 established himself as Franz I, hereditary Emperor of Austria. At each ensuing peace congress the map of Europe was redrawn. After the humiliation of two French occupations of Vienna in 1805 and 1809 Austria was the main sufferer territorially. The last coalition to combat the French invasion of Russia, during which time Metternich came to the fore as the Austrian foreign minister, ended with the defeat of Napoleon in 1814. At the Congress of Vienna, 1814–15, Austria triumphed politically and territorially because of her part in Napoleon's downfall. Many of the lands she had held up to 1792 were restored, but there was no attempt to revive the Holy Roman Empire. A German Confederation, chaired by Franz I, was founded, and a similar scheme was worked out for Italy. The three hundred and more German states had already been reduced to thirty-nine larger ones, under French pressure and influence, making possible a far more viable federal organization; but the prospect of a united Germany was still far off as the new system prevented any focussing of national power.

After the Congress of Vienna, Franz I sought to re-establish the power of the Habsburg Empire. In the post-war depression he was ably guided by Metternich, now prime minister, who worked to achieve a balance of power in international affairs and exercised an uncompromising suppression of democratic movements at home.

Bonn

From 1257 Bonn, Beethoven's birthplace, had been the official seat of the Archbishop of Cologne and the capital of the electorate, and remained so until the French invasion in 1794. When Maximilian Friedrich became Archbishop Elector in 1761, a period of financial retrenchment was required to counter the excesses of his extravagant predecessor. Nevertheless, cultural activities, particularly opera and theatre, were allowed to flourish at court, and the enlightened literature of Rousseau, Klopstock, Herder, Schiller and Goethe was widely disseminated in the ensuing decades.

Influence from Vienna had been nominal until 1784. In that year Maximilian Franz became Elector. His attempts to emulate the achievements of his brother, the Emperor, had bearings on many aspects of life in Bonn – political, social, intellectual and artistic – and the new ideas were readily welcomed. In 1785 the Bonn Academy received university status, with scientists and philosophers – many with strong Enlightenment views – particularly encouraged. The court library offered a collection of enlightened literature and political newspapers. As a consequence, Beethoven's formative years were spent in an environment which could hardly have failed to stimulate his future political and intellectual thinking, and this was to have an indirect influence on his composition in works such as *Fidelio*, *Egmont* and the Ninth Symphony.

Vienna

Vienna, where Beethoven settled in 1792, had recently lost Joseph II. The intellectual leaders still valued his theories of enlightenment; but not so his successors, Leopold and Franz. The revolutionary ideas and ideals emanating from France instilled in them the notion that if human endeavour could achieve anything, it could certainly achieve the overthrow of a régime such as theirs. Consequently they resorted to repression, and liberal movements were stifled at birth by a secret police force.

That there was little resistance to this was in part due to the *laissez faire* nature of Viennese society and the fact that the business classes found a common cause with imperial interests. A 'bread and circuses' approach to domestic problems sufficed to pacify the Viennese: the population could afford to eat and drink, and the nobility kept sumptuous houses and threw lavish parties. Theatre, opera and all types of music flourished. There was a general laxity of morals – dance halls and brothels abounded – and there was little literary and philosophical discussion. The 19th-century image of Viennese society as gay and superficial has its origins here.

Viennese fortunes varied throughout the twenty years of war to which Austria was subjected. The lowest troughs were the two occupations in 1805 and 1809. The setbacks of the first were seemingly shortlived. By 1806, there was, in spite of financial stringencies, a return to entertainment and an indifference to critical political events. The 1809 occupation, however, saw a mass departure, leaving a beleaguered city to suffer shortages of food and an increasingly serious financial situation.

With the defeat of Napoleon the spotlight of Europe fell on Vienna, after Metternich announced that the Peace Congress would convene there on 14 August 1814. It was to last nearly a year, during which time Vienna played host to some 10,000 foreigners, amongst them all the dignitaries of Europe and their entourages. Vienna rapidly resumed its role as a city of lavish entertainment. There was a prolonged carnival atmosphere as balls, receptions, firework displays and concerts were organized to impress the international gathering. As a leading composer Beethoven figured prominently. He was asked to compose suitable pieces, the best known being the cantata *Der glorreiche Augenblick*, which exhorted Vienna to rise to the occasion and honour the assembled potentates. His opera *Fidelio* was the first to be performed during this period; each of its twenty repeats was greeted enthusiastically by full houses, and he was much honoured and feted.

By the time the Congress ended, Vienna was a changed city: impoverished, with some of its nobility irreparably bankrupt. For example, Count Razumovsky's palace had been accidently burnt down during the festivities and he was never able to rebuild it; he gave up his social life and disbanded his string quartet. Money lenders and bankers assumed a new importance, and there was a general increase in the power of the business classes, who were to be the patrons of artistic and musical life in the future.

Although Austria's political importance was destined to decline, and the social climate had already started to change, Vienna's long reputation as an outstanding international cultural centre has remained strong.

ANNE-LOUISE COLDICOTT

Intellectual currents: philosophy and aesthetics

THE VIEW OF THE 19TH CENTURY as an 'age of Romanticism' that counteracted an 18th-century 'age of reason' is still very much with us. In terms of musical history, the usual distinction is between 'Classic' and 'Romantic'. It is by no means entirely without truth; but we should resist the temptation to give too much credence to such broad generalizations when dealing with the history of ideas. True, the appeal to rationality in the 18th century – the ascendancy of scientific method and secularism over older superstitious and religious beliefs, for instance – was very strong. And the related generalization, an 'age of Enlightenment', is unthinkable without it. Throughout late 18th-century Europe, Enlightenment was recognized as a real phenomenon or movement that brought social and educational reform, religious toleration and the wider dissemination of intellectual thought and writing in its wake: Mozart's *The Magic Flute* of 1791 and Haydn's *The Creation* of 1796–8 (particularly the celebration of light in the opening chorus) are two of the best-known musical embodiments of Enlightenment ideals.

But the origins of the Romantic movement also lie in the 18th century: indeed, in his *A Philosophical Enquiry into the Origin of our Ideas of the Sublime and the Beautiful*, published in 1757 (see Le Huray, 1981, pp. 69–74), Edmund Burke already writes of the 'sublime' in essentially the same terms that E.T.A. Hoffmann would use to characterize Beethoven's Fifth Symphony in his famous review of 1810. One also needs to come to terms with other middle and late 18th-century trends such as *Empfindsamkeit* and *Sturm und Drang* (see 'Evolution of the Classical style', p. 72), concepts which overlap to some extent and which may plausibly be viewed as 'Romantic' rather than 'Classical'. Distinctions become even more blurred when we realize that all these movements or trends not only had different national and even local manifestations but also cannot be applied with equal ease to all the arts. In particular, 'use of the literary term [*Sturm und Drang*] for music...is potentially confusing' (Rushton, 1986, p. 25).

To attempt to sketch the general intellectual background to Beethoven's life and work, spanning as they do the last quarter of the 18th century and the first of the 19th, is thus a peculiarly frustrating exercise. A few major landmarks in German literature and philosophy will serve at least to indicate the richness of the cultural and artistic terrain. In 1771, the year after Beethoven was born, Johann Georg Sulzer published his *Allgemeine Theorie der schönen Künste* (*General Theory of the Fine Arts*), a work whose comprehensiveness and contents reflected those of the great French *Encyclopédie*, edited by d'Alembert and Diderot and begun in 1751 although not completed until 1772; Goethe's influential novel *Die Leiden des jungen Werthers* (*The Sorrows of Young Werther*) appeared in 1774; Kant's *Kritik der Urteilskraft* (*Critique of Judgment*), an aesthetic treatise of fundamental importance to later writers, was published in 1790; around the turn of the century writers such as Herder, Tieck, Wackenroder and the Schlegel brothers produced some of the cornerstones of early Romantic literary criticism; finally, the publication of Schopenhauer's *Die Welt als Wille und Vorstellung* (*The World as Will and Idea*) in 1819, before Beethoven had written the last three piano sonatas or the late string quartets, brings us firmly in sight of mid-century Romanticism and in particular the music of Wagner, who was to be so influenced by Schopenhauer's thought.

However difficult it may be to make hard and fast distinctions between intellectual trends in this period, however, there is one broad shift in musical aesthetics – and it is crucial to contemporary and later responses to Beethoven's music – that can be clearly perceived, if not traced in detail. Throughout the 18th century the Aristotelian doctrine of art as an imitation of nature was paramount, particularly in French aesthetic writings. That music was less capable of such imitation than, say, painting led to the alternative idea that it was well suited to expressing the passions or emotions, and likewise could arouse similar emotions in the hearer (thus Sulzer in Le Huray, 1981, p. 135: 'music's aim is to arouse the emotions; this it does by means of sequences of sounds that are appropriate to the natural expression of the emotion'). Thus a doctrine of expression largely replaced that of imitation where music was concerned. However, the low specificity of musical representation, and more particularly the inability of music to express moral concepts (for the arts were valued as a powerful means of inculcating morality) led many writers to place a low value on purely instrumental music; it needed to be allied to words, as in opera, in order to be meaningful. Rousseau launched a particularly hostile attack in the article 'Sonate' in his *Dictionnaire de musique* of 1767, where he compared instrumental music very unfavourably with vocal and quoted Fontenelle's famous quip 'Sonate, que me veux-tu?'. Kant's position in 1790 was more equivocal: while he considered that of all the arts music was the closest to poetry and even that it 'moves us in more ways and with greater intensity than poetry does', he also felt that 'music is least amongst the fine arts, because it plays merely with emotions' (Le Huray, 1981, pp. 221–2).

The Romantic view was quite different. Ideals of universality, rationality and clarity yielded to a way of thinking that placed the highest value on individuality, irrationality and obscurity. In place of the belief that absolute truth and knowledge were attainable came the opposite belief, that these concepts could never be attained. The Romantic artist strove towards the infinite, which he would never reach; and the struggle gradually became more important than the goal itself. The sense that ultimate reality was unattainable, that its essence remained forever vague, even affected the form in which some of the early Romantic critics, such as the Schlegels and Jean-Paul, expressed their ideas: the fragment became an important literary form; texts were left intentionally incomplete or incomprehensible so as to force the reader to reflect actively on them and thereby to contribute to the creation of meaning within them. Thus no. 20 of Friedrich Schlegel's *Kritische Fragmente* (*Critical Fragments*) of 1797 reads: 'A Classical text must never be entirely comprehensible. But those who are cultivated and who cultivate themselves must always want to learn more from it.'

In such a climate, it was inevitable that instrumental music should come to be seen not as the least but as the greatest of the arts. Precisely because of its lack of precise referentiality it was the truest and most pregnant with meaning, so much so that Schopenhauer claimed ultimately that 'music is thus in no sense, like the other arts, the image of ideas, but the image of the *Will itself*' and even that music is 'a uniquely universal language, even exceeding in clarity that of the phenomenal world itself' (Le Huray, 1981, pp. 324–5).

That Beethoven was aware of these shifting theoretical positions is doubtful. Yet certain qualities in his later music do seem to correspond rather closely with some of the literary ideals encouraged by the Schlegels and others. The opening of the first movement of the Piano Sonata in A op. 101, for example, is deliberately vague; it is as if we have come upon the work some way past its true beginning. And the return of the opening bars prior to the beginning of the finale creates an impression of fragmentation. The sense of the work as a series of discrete, closed movements is weakened (this weakening reaches its peak in the seven-section String Quartet in C♯ minor op. 131). And in pieces like the finale of the 'Hammerklavier' Sonata or the *Grosse Fuge* the sense of strain or difficulty placed on performer and listener alike appears almost to be a calculated part of the aesthetic effect; the music seems at times to court incomprehensibility.

Whatever the effect of Romantic aesthetics on Beethoven, there is no doubt that he quickly became seen as the quintessential Romantic composer, and his music as the supreme example of the special Romantic qualities of instrumental music. The classic statement is E.T.A. Hoffmann's review of the Fifth Symphony (quotations are taken from Forbes, 1971, pp. 151–2). For Hoffmann, 'only instrumental music...can express with purity music's peculiar nature.... Music is the most Romantic of all the arts'. Hoffmann stresses that Beethoven's instrumental music opens 'the realm of the colossal and the immeasurable', thereby recalling Burke's (and others') distinction between the 'sublime' and the 'beautiful': 'sublime objects are vast in their dimensions, beautiful ones comparatively small' (Le Huray, 1981, p. 70). Again, in Hoffmann 'Beethoven's music induces terror, fright, horror and pain and awakens that endless longing which is the essence of Romanticism', just as Burke noted that 'the passion caused by the great and sublime in nature...is astonishment;...that state of the soul in which all its motions are suspended with some degree of horror' (Le Huray, 1981, p. 71). Hoffmann repeatedly stresses the arch-Romantic feelings of 'endless longing', 'presentiment of the unknown' and 'foreboding, indescribable longing' that persist throughout the symphony; through music, 'precisely that which we have felt in life leads us out from life into the realm of the infinite'.

The difficulty of distinguishing an 18th-century 'age of reason' from a 19th-century 'age of feeling' is compounded when we reflect further on this great shift in musical aesthetics. For it was precisely the 18th century's that was an aesthetic of 'feeling', with its emphasis on the effect that music had on the listener, while that typified by Hoffmann and Schopenhauer is better thought of as a metaphysical aesthetic. Nor is it coincidental that the latter view is contemporaneous with the beginnings of modern analytical thought about music, distinguished as it is by a 'rationalizing' approach to matters of musical structure. In fact Hoffmann's review is simultaneously a classic expression of the metaphysical aesthetic and one of the first examples of analysis of this kind (see 'Analytical studies', p. 318).

The major legacy of the early 19th-century metaphysical view of instrumental music was the notion that the musical work can be an entirely autonomous and self-justifying object. That is, music (specifically, instrumental music) need serve no extramusical end whatsoever; we can listen to and contemplate a symphony or string quartet for no other reason than that it is 'there'. And the importance of Beethoven's music in establishing that notion must not be underestimated: 'the new insight that Beethoven thrust upon the aesthetic consciousness of his age was that a musical text, like a literary or a philosophical text, harbors a meaning which is made manifest but not entirely subsumed in its acoustic presentation – that a musical creation can exist as an "art work of ideas" transcending its various interpretations' (Dahlhaus, 1989, p. 10).

NICHOLAS MARSTON

Patronage and the place of the artist in society

The undersigned have decided to place Herr Ludwig van Beethoven in a position where the necessaries of life shall not cause him embarrassment or clog his powerful genius.

THESE WORDS COME FROM the contract made in 1809 between Beethoven and his patrons the Archduke Rudolph, Prince Lobkowitz and Prince Kinsky (the complete document is translated in Thayer, 1967, p. 457). It was an extraordinary, perhaps unique agreement that was being made: essentially, Beethoven was to be paid a lifelong annuity to compose what he wanted, when he wanted, how he wanted. And although the value of his annuity was to be considerably diminished due to subsequent economic circumstances in Austria, it effectively relieved Beethoven of serious financial worries.

What is so special about the annuity agreement is the extent to which it recognizes Beethoven as an artist, someone holding a privileged position in society and deserving of special consideration because of his extraordinary gifts. Throughout much of the preceding century, however, musicians of all kinds had been regarded more as artisans than as artists. An independent, freelance existence was largely unknown to them (except, perhaps, in England): composers and performers (although the modern distinction between the two professions hardly applied) were generally employed by the church, the nobility, or in some municipal establishment. They were no more than servants, employees with specific tasks to perform. They wore uniform, received (often poor) wages, and lived their highly circumscribed lives under the threat of immediate and unexplained dismissal. Thus, during his employment as Kapellmeister at Eszterháza in the years 1761–90 Haydn was required to dress and behave in the required manner, to compose music as required by the Prince, and was responsible for the music and musical instruments of the household. A telling condition of his post (and those of most musicians similarly employed) was that he was forbidden to compose for other people without permission.

Such terms and conditions of employment are likely to strike the modern musician as unbearably oppressive and demeaning. Nor was it by any means wholly acceptable to those of the 18th century: Mozart's hatred of his servitude under Archbishop Colloredo of Salzburg is well known, as is his anger at being placed, according to his status, below the valets but above the cooks at table. Much must have depended on the personalities of employer and employee, and on the particular working conditions that obtained. In contrast to Mozart, Haydn clearly enjoyed a very favourable relationship with Prince Esterházy and managed to achieve a position of relative independence and power (the finale of the 'Farewell' Symphony must surely stand as history's most effective and aesthetically rewarding piece of negotiation on behalf of workers' rights).

However unpalatable the régime may have been, it provided musicians with more security than they were likely to find if they tried to establish an independent career (witness Mozart's increasingly difficult circumstances following his departure from the Archbishop's service): at least they were clothed, fed, paid and accommodated in return for their pains. The alternatives were daunting, particularly for composers: writing music was a precarious business in a world where no copyright existed and where one's agent was oneself; concerts could be difficult and costly to arrange; the steadiest source of income was probably from teaching – but that, like everything else, was time-consuming and required good health. Beethoven himself persistently hankered after the security of a permanent post; indeed, it was his threat to take up the offer of appointment as Kapellmeister at Kassel that led to the signing of the annuity agreement in 1809.

During the 18th century various social, economic and other developments gradually effected a change in musicians' circumstances. Chief among these changes was the emergence of a middle class with an insatiable appetite for music, and the concomitant decline in importance of the church and court as institutional employer–patrons. Public concerts grew in number, a development that hastened the rise of the travelling instrumental virtuoso: Beethoven, of course, initially made his name in Vienna as a brilliant pianist rather than as a composer. But music was also cultivated privately in the home, and this decisive development created a huge demand for new compositions. Music publishing expanded accordingly, as did the manufacture of instruments, and a new market was created for composers. Institutional patronage gave way to personal patronage by wealthy individuals or groups of the same; but even that system broke down due to the declining fortunes of the aristocracy in the aftermath of the Napoleonic Wars. What eventually emerged (and remains) as pre-eminent was the patronage of a paying public. During his life Beethoven encountered and benefited from all three types of patronage: institutional (as in his court position at Bonn), personal and public.

There were other, more subtle factors which contributed to the emergence of the musician as an artist, and two of these are particularly relevant to Beethoven. One was the enhanced status gradually accorded to instrumental music (see 'Intellectual currents', pp. 64–5); Beethoven's *oeuvre* is unthinkable without this, as is the concept of the travelling instrumental virtuoso (as opposed to the internationally acclaimed opera singer). Allied to this new status for instrumental music is the emergence of the work of art as an autonomous aesthetic object (again, see 'Intellectual currents') as opposed to a functional one. This development contributed to a split between the professions of composer and performer: from now on it was thinkable for a composer to devote himself to creating 'works', without necessarily having to bring them before the public in performance himself. 'Composers now no longer presented their works to a class in which they served as members; instead, . . . they faced an amorphous multitude that they were to raise to their own sphere' (Blume, 1970, p. 91). Beethoven's deafness eventually shut him off from professional performing and other public music-making, so the possibility of being taken seriously as a full-time composer was of immense consequence to his career. Alternatively, it may have been his enforced career as a full-time composer that blazed a trail for others.

The second important extra factor is the late 18th-century and early 19th-century cult of genius, itself fostered by a growing interest in psychology. The artistic prodigy, whether performer (Paganini, Liszt) or composer, was accorded a status above that of the ordinary man, and 'the musical servant was by now an anachronism' (Rushton, 1986, p. 163). It was Beethoven's evident genius, his 'otherness', that assured him the personal patronage he received from the Viennese music-loving aristocracy. Indeed, the distinction between patron and beneficiary becomes blurred in his case, for aristocratic pride such as that of Lichnowsky needed the fuel of a close acquaintance with Beethoven just as much as Beethoven needed the former's financial support. Those who sought to stifle Beethoven with patronage and protection were apt to arouse him to considerable anger; his desire for security was balanced by an equal loathing of social enslavement. And whereas such rebelliousness was simply unthinkable under the *ancien régime*, the rift between Beethoven and Lichnowsky in 1806, which resulted in Beethoven smashing his cherished bust of the latter, presents us with the interesting picture of the fully-fledged and basically independent artist effectively dismissing the patron.

NICHOLAS MARSTON

Economics

THE ECONOMIC SITUATION IN Vienna in Beethoven's day was extremely complicated, and Beethoven's own financial affairs (see 'Financial affairs', pp. 110–23) have to be seen against a background of steep inflation, currency changes, a bewildering variety of currency units, and prices that tended to rise in real terms.

The two currency units used most often by Beethoven were the silver florin or gulden and the gold ducat. Their value evidently did not alter substantially during Beethoven's thirty-five years in Vienna, although the silver florin was for a time (1809–18) unavailable. There were $4\frac{1}{2}$ florins in a ducat, and the florin was in turn divided into 60 kreuzer. In his transactions Beethoven sometimes specified florins 'at the rate of 20'; this was because Viennese silver florins were of a particular size – 20 to a quantity of silver known as a Cologne mark – whereas some cities had smaller florins or gulden, with correspondingly lower value.

Alongside these coins the imperial government issued paper money in the form of banknotes (Bankozettel) which were meant to be, and for a long time in the 18th century actually were, equal in value to the silver florins they represented. From the end of the 18th century, however, inflation set in, mainly through the government printing far too many banknotes (which was done partly to finance the war against Napoleon). Although the banknote florin remained officially the same value as the silver florin, in reality its value declined, at first gradually and then much more sharply, until in 1809 all silver coins were withdrawn from circulation. By this time one silver florin was worth approximately three banknote florins.

Inflation persisted, however, and by March 1811 the ratio of 1:3 had risen to 1:5. At this point the government by means of a *Finanz-Patent* replaced the banknote florins with new ones known as *Einlösungsscheine* (redemption bonds) at the rate of 5:1, so that the new florin was officially (and also in practice for a short time) worth one (theoretical) silver florin. All prices were ordered to be reduced by $\frac{4}{5}$ to reflect the value of the new currency. A court decree was also issued which showed the number of paper florins in one silver florin (i.e. the amount of inflation) for every month from January 1799 to March 1811. The figures for January and February each year are given below (from Thayer, 1967, p. 523).

	1799	1800	1801	1802	1803	1804	1805	1806	1807	1808	1809	1810	1811
Jan.	1.03	1.13	1.16	1.19	1.30	1.34	1.33	1.47	1.90	2.04	2.21	4.69	5.00
Feb.	1.05	1.14	1.14	1.18	1.27	1.34	1.29	1.49	2.06	2.10	2.48	3.31	5.00

All contracts made prior to 1811 were decreed to return to their original value. Thus Beethoven's annuity of 4000 fl. (banknotes), which had been agreed in February 1809 (and dated 1 March 1809), and which would have become 800 fl. *Einlösungsschein* had the contract been made immediately prior to the change in currency, was instead held to be worth 4000 ÷ 2.48, i.e. 1612.9 fl. Beethoven was thus automatically compensated for inflation in the period 1809–11 but not for inflation prior to the date of the contract nor for any subsequent inflation, and he had to negotiate with his three patrons to try to restore what he thought should be the true value of the annuity.

Einlösungsschein was replaced by *Anticipationsschein* in 1813, but this was a change in name rather than value; both came to be known as Wiener Währung (Viennese Currency). Meanwhile inflation was still not brought under control, so that the new florins WW were for a time worth less than a third of the (still theoretical) silver florin. Eventually in 1818 inflation was halted and silver florins were gradually reintroduced. This currency was known as Conventionsmünze (CM, i.e. assimilated coinage), and its ratio to WW was fixed at 1:2½. Both currencies then ran side by side at this rate until after Beethoven's death, although the price of certain items, notably accommodation in the city, continued to rise gradually.

It is impossible to make a realistic conversion of prices in Beethoven's day into modern currencies, since the relative costs of different commodities were so different from those of today. Instead it is preferable to give a few examples of prices and incomes at the time. In 1804 it was calculated that an average middle-class bachelor living in Vienna would need 967 fl. (banknotes?), excluding any luxuries, entertainment, etc.; including these extras he would need 1200 fl. When Beethoven first arrived in Vienna he was paying 14 fl. a month for a fairly small apartment near the city centre. In 1827 it was still possible to rent a city-centre room for under 100 fl. CM per year, but a larger, family-sized apartment might cost nearly 500 fl. CM a year (Hanson,

1983, pp. 175–6). In 1793 a main midday meal (presumably at a restaurant) cost Beethoven 33–39 kreuzer, whereas in 1824 he was actually able to buy a reasonable meal for less than that – 1 fl. WW or 24 kreuzer CM (Köhler, 1968, vi. 310).

Some of Beethoven's dealings were with foreign publishers, for whom various other currencies were sometimes used. When dealing with British publishers, prices were often stated in pounds sterling or guineas; there were 20 shillings in the pound and 21 in the guinea. The pound was worth about 10 fl. CM; thus the Viennese silver florin was roughly equivalent to the English florin or two-shilling piece that was introduced later in the 19th century, and the Philharmonic Society's gift of £100 to Beethoven in 1827 translated into 1000 fl. CM. The reichsthaler, which Beethoven had known in Bonn, was worth 1 fl. 30 kr., and the kronenthaler 2 fl. 45 kr. Another unit of currency was the louis d'or; this fluctuated in value, but in 1820 Beethoven regarded it as worth 2 ducats, i.e. 9 fl. CM. Other units referred to included the carolin, the friedrich d'or, the groschen and the zecchino; the latter was an Italian coin worth about 5 fl. CM, but was simply used by Beethoven as the Italian word for 'ducat'. A summary of the various currency units is given below. Although it is possible to compile a price index to show fluctuating purchasing power (Moore, 1987), it is easier to regard the main currency unit, the silver florin, as fixed in value, and to express other units in terms of this.

> 1795:   1 fl. BZ   =   1 fl. CM
>
> *Depreciating to:*
> March 1811:   5 fl. BZ   =   1 fl. CM (theoretical)
> BZ replaced by WW
> at rate of 5 to 1:   1 fl. WW   =   1 fl. CM (theoretical)
>
> *Depreciating to:*
> 1818: $2\frac{1}{2}$ fl. WW   =   1 fl. CM

> 1 ducat   = $4\frac{1}{2}$ fl CM
> £1 sterling   =   *c.*10 fl. CM
> 1 guinea sterling   =   *c.*$10\frac{1}{2}$ fl. CM
> 1 louis d'or   =   *c.*9 or 10 fl. CM (variable)
> 1 reichsthaler   = $1\frac{1}{2}$ fl. CM
> 1 kronenthaler   = $2\frac{3}{4}$ fl. CM
> 1 carolin   =   9 fl. CM
> 1 zecchino   =   *c.*5 fl. CM (or $4\frac{1}{2}$ fl. CM)

> 60 kreuzer CM, BZ or WW   =   1 fl. CM, BZ or WW
> 1 groschen   =   3 kreuzer

CM: Conventionsmünze (assimilated coinage)
BZ: Bankozettel (banknote: up to March 1811)
WW: Wiener Währung (Viennese currency: from March 1811)
fl: florin or gulden

BARRY COOPER

Section 5
MUSICAL BACKGROUND

MUSICAL BACKGROUND

Evolution of the Classical style, 1750–1800

Pre-Classical

THE MIDDLE YEARS OF the 18th century saw the transition from the polyphonic style of the Baroque period to a more simple concept based on melody with harmonic accompaniment, which prepared the ground for the emergence of the great Viennese Classical style of Haydn, Mozart and Beethoven. This pre-Classical period lasted until approximately 1775, encompassing Rococo and *style galant*, *Empfindsamkeit* (sentimentality) and *Sturm und Drang* (literally 'storm and stress'). These terms give some idea of the variety within the style. The first two apply specifically to the Viennese/Italian manifestation; *Empfindsamkeit* to the North German expressive style of C.P.E. Bach; and *Sturm und Drang* was a more pervasive influence towards the end of the period, which came to music via an earlier movement in German literature.

In spite of the colossal genius of J.S. Bach, Italy had remained the foremost artistic centre during the Baroque period. In the middle of the 18th century Vienna became the musical capital of Europe, although Italian influence remained strong. Symptomatic of a growing German culture was the rise to prominence of Berlin under Frederick the Great, and to a lesser extent, Mannheim, Leipzig and Dresden. France and England made their contributions in more general ways as international cultural centres.

The period saw a conscious reaction against the excesses, grandeur and complexity of Baroque style and a move towards a simpler and more directly appealing one. There were disparities between the different centres, but certain features were common to all. With the exception of the development of opera, instrumental music took precedence over vocal music: the sonata and concerto were intensively developed, and the symphony and string quartet were established. Simplicity is apparent in all aspects: form, tonality and harmony, melody and thematic development, and the treatment of instruments.

Regarding form, the basis of the Classical genres was established. The trio sonata, contrapuntal in conception, gave way to the accompanied sonata, and the harpsichord or fortepiano sonata replaced polyphonic keyboard works. The multi-movement orchestral suite was superseded by the three-movement symphony, which increasingly adopted sonata form as an organizing factor. The concerto retained elements of ritornello style, but it too began to incorporate features of sonata form, emphasizing the move from textural to harmonic principles. Melodic invention, harmonic organization and new textures were the essential ingredients of the new style. All too often, however, the first two elements particularly were not sufficiently well-handled to ensure lasting fame for the early works the style engendered.

Melody was forced to the fore as the basic sustaining element, generating form and character. Invention in this respect did not come naturally, and as Friedrich Blume (1970, p. 48) said, composers faithfully followed the simple metric layout of the eight-bar phase, producing melodies of very short sections lacking individual impetus, and 'wearing themselves out in small-jointed articulation'. Thematic development was difficult both because of the nature of the themes and the composers' lack of experience in development without recourse to counterpoint.

The role of the orchestra changed dramatically from Baroque practices. There, all parts contributed equally to the contrapuntal content of the music, and there was often little attempt to write for specific instruments. In the pre-Classical period the weight of the melodic line was given to the first violins, the harmonic, non-thematic bass to the cellos and basses, and the inner string parts were reduced to a simple accompanying role. Woodwind instruments at first merely doubled the string parts in *forte* passages, then were gradually used as sustaining instruments. It was not until later that they were to be treated as soloists or their individual colours were fully exploited.

Particularly notable is the change in keyboard music. The organ was ousted by the harpsichord and fortepiano, where most of the interest was confined to the right hand. The left rarely shared in thematic or virtuosic activity but provided a harmonic accompaniment, either in simple chords or in 'Alberti bass' style, which creates an impression of activity whilst remaining harmonically quite static. The melody line would be decorated by a variety of ornaments; thus ceaseless but all too often undirectional movement was a prominent characteristic.

The chief limitation of the pre-Classical composers was that they seldom brought together simultaneously all the vital elements. For example, the symphony developed out of the Italian overture; it was taken to Vienna by Italian composers such as Sammartini, and was cultivated further by Dittersdorf, Michael Haydn, Monn and Wagenseil as public concerts grew in number and popularity. At this stage it was a three- or four-movement form with a quick, slight, dance-like finale. It spread to Mannheim where it underwent further development. Johann Stamitz realized that to achieve longer works, larger-scale contrasts were needed. He accomplished this by establishing longer, tonally stable sections which contrasted harmonically with each other. To prevent monotony he increased the rhythmic and dynamic momentum, attempted to link phrases to give more continuity, and made greater use of orchestral colour. Inherent weaknesses in the form, the lack of a sufficiently weighty recapitulation and a relatively weak ending, were resolved only by Joseph Haydn in his symphonies of *c.*1766–74, ones which incorporated the sentiments of *Sturm und Drang*. Mozart's early symphonies were modelled on the Italian-influenced 'London' Bach, Johann Christian, and retained the three-movement plan. Although the finales were still slender and the second movements very simple, there were advances in the area of orchestral writing, especially in his use of the wind.

The concerto had evolved during the Baroque period as a form based firmly on the ritornello principle. In the mid-18th century it underwent modifications to absorb some elements of sonata form, the violin was replaced by keyboard instruments as the most popular soloists, being better suited to the new style, and the balance shifted from the orchestral to the solo sections. The four main centres of concerto composition were Berlin (C.P.E. Bach), Mannheim (the Stamitz family and Vanhal), London (J.C. Bach) and Vienna (Monn, Wagenseil, M. Haydn, and the Italians Sammartini, Leo and Boccherini). In each centre different aspects of the evolving style were developed: in Berlin, experimentation with harmony, expression and (with respect to the recapitulation of material) form; in Mannheim, a preoccupation with melody and the handling of a wider variety of solo instruments; in London J.C. Bach aimed for greater thematic differentiation; and the Viennese composers were primarily interested in formal problems and brilliant writing for the soloist.

Classical style of Haydn and Mozart

Although the simplicity and grace of the 'galant' style succeeded in cutting the ties with what had gone before, it proved self-limiting, and was ripe for further development. The impetus of the *Sturm und Drang* movement allowed a wider range of emotions. The framework of sonata form was sufficiently established to permit greater harmonic and thematic complexity, and it pervaded all the major genres. The minuet–finale of the early symphony was now followed by a weightier fourth movement in sonata form.

Haydn started composing at a time when Baroque ideas still held fast in some quarters. His earliest works were 'galant' in style, but from about 1780 his mature works, and all but the earliest of Mozart's, display a synthesis of what had gone before, producing the fully-fledged Viennese Classical style which Beethoven was to inherit.

Haydn's symphonies of the late 1760s became hesitant and experimental, minor keys were more prevalent and the finales were longer, as if he was consciously attempting to break away from the charm of the 'galant'. Throughout the 1770s to mid-1780s there was more progress. The first and fourth movements are more dynamic, using wide melodic leaps, counterpoint and syncopation to produce tension. Slow movements are longer and more intense, with richer orchestration, and the third (minuet and trio) movements also lengthened as sonata form influenced their essentially binary form structure. Generally, grace and elegance are balanced by power and grandeur. The new weight came from a synthesis of continuity and articulation, dependent on the pace of harmonic change, cadence and thematic development, unlike the uniform rhythmic movement of the Baroque style. The last group, nos. 93–104 ('Salomon'), are the summit of Haydn's achievement in the form. They demonstrate a new breadth, allowing bold modulations and harmonies, contrasts of mood, and more use of counterpoint. Brilliance is displayed in the orchestration: clarinets are introduced, and solo writing is assimilated.

Mozart's last three symphonies (nos. 39–41) were written in the summer of 1788, before Haydn's last group. Although conceived within a short space of time, they differ greatly in character. The opening Allegro of no. 39 (K.543) is preceded by a long, imposing, slow introduction which creates ever-increasing tension, resolved only by the direct character and the preponderance of the tonic in the Allegro. No. 40 in G minor (K.550) is a passionate work anticipating 'Romantic' features. The change from the original scoring for oboes to clarinets produced a more modern sound, the *piano* opening was unusual, and the whole work is permeated by chromaticism and dissonance. This is particularly apparent in the development section of the first movement, and contributes to the intensity of the second. The third movement is an unusual minuet: it has unprecedented strength, minor tonality, three-bar phrases, and counterpoint between the treble and bass produces effective cross-rhythms. The finale is intensively worked out, balancing the first movement with its dissonance and wide harmonic range. In no. 41 (the 'Jupiter') the sonata-form structure of the finale incorporates a fugue; thus a Baroque form finds a place within the new style.

Chamber music developed rapidly during the second half of the 18th century, and there was a great diversity in the combinations deployed. As the harpsichord was superseded by the fortepiano and its former continuo role became superfluous to the new style, keyboard instruments were either omitted from ensembles, leaving self-sufficient groups of string, wind instruments or combinations of both, or were admitted on new terms. The fortepiano, when present, dominated because, in order to compensate for its mechanical shortcomings, until about 1790 there was a tendency to reinforce the bass line with the cello and to double the melody.

Haydn excelled in the area of the string quartet. Mozart's achievements there are also outstanding, but his string quintets, richer in sonority from the presence of two violas, perhaps outshine them. His Clarinet Quintet (K.581) and other works for mixed combinations, such as the Piano Quartet in G minor, K.478, are of an equally high standard. Both composers wrote numerous piano trios. The earliest were really keyboard sonatas with the violin and cello in accompanying roles. The later examples, however, such as Haydn's Piano Trio in E♭ (H.30) and Mozart's

K.542, allow the string parts true independence. They laid the groundwork for Beethoven, for whom a set of three Piano Trios, op. 1, constituted the first works which he felt worthy of publication with an opus number. Benefitting from the developments in piano manufacturing and advances in technique, he elevated the form to one which could stand alongside any other, as exemplified by the 'Archduke' Trio, op. 97, of 1811.

Haydn was not the first composer to write for four string parts, and it is unclear whether he was not still thinking in terms of the four-part *orchestra* which performed divertimentos when he wrote his first two sets of String Quartets, opp. 1 and 2, in the 1750s. These retain elements of the divertimento: its character (simple, with folklike melodies); its form (five movements: the outer two fast and a slow middle movement flanked by minuets); and its style (dominated by the first violin). The quartets from op. 9 onwards are undoubtedly conceived for four *solo* instruments, and in these and opp. 17 and 20 there is much more elaborate writing for the lower parts.

Ten years elapsed before the op. 33 set, which Haydn described as 'written in an entirely new and special way'. (Did Beethoven know of this in about 1801 when he said '...From today I will take a new path'?) These are known as the 'Scherzi' Quartets because the minuet and trio movements take on the title of 'Scherzo', like so many of Beethoven's. The set was to inspire Mozart's first six mature quartets, which he dedicated to Haydn, and which were in turn to influence him.

Haydn wrote twelve quartets for the violinist Tost. The six of op. 64 are probably the best known, and no. 5, the 'Lark', is possibly the most outstanding. Its nickname comes from the wonderful, soaring first-violin melody of the opening; the eloquence of the second-movement theme is emphasized by alternating major and minor variations. Opp. 76 and 77 are Haydn's crowning achievement in the form. The instrumental handling is supremely confident and fluent, the works display a wide variety of form, and the harmonic style is forward-looking. Variation form provides the framework not only for slow movements, such as op. 76 no. 3 (the 'Emperor'), but also for the first movement of op. 76 no. 6. The second movement of this same quartet is unusual too. The key of the quartet is E♭; the second movement begins without a key signature, but is nonetheless clearly in B. Whereas Beethoven would have had no qualms about announcing this, Haydn seemed to find it necessary to range through a number of other keys before returning to B and bestowing a key signature halfway through the movement. The slow movement of op. 76 no. 5 in D is in the key of F♯. Although this is a relatively 'bright' key, it is also a relatively difficult one for strings, and this brings to the *largo cantabile e mesto* a quality of intensity. The finale of op. 77 no. 2 is a concentrated, monothematic sonata-form movement; its forceful, dance-like character anticipates the dynamism of Beethoven's writing.

For Haydn and Mozart, works for solo keyboard were not as central to their output, in spite of their large number of works for the medium, as the piano sonata was to be to Beethoven. Haydn wrote fifty-one sonatas and Mozart twenty, and they also produced other types such as sets of variations, rondos and fantasias. That only a few are well known may be due to a certain unevenness of quality. Perhaps more significant is the fact that composers writing for solo keyboard had to address two major changes simultaneously: the evolving forms and the developing potential of constantly improving instruments. It is difficult to evaluate accurately works written for instruments which no longer exist.

In the words of Arthur Hutchings (1948, p. 28), the pre-Classical composers 'took the concerto through the weakness and distempers of childhood to the youth, which Mozart nurtured to such glorious manhood'. Building on what had gone before, he made the piano concerto more complex and dramatic. The first-movement form was already the most advanced. In the Baroque period the orchestral tutti or ritornello sections were the pillars of the movement; the solo sections provided contrast and effected the modulations. In the early Classical works, interest was focused disproportionately on the solos. Sonata form influenced the structure, particularly as regards key, so that H.C. Robbins Landon (1956, p. 238) described the form loosely as:

Exposition:
- Tutti 1 (I)
- Solo 1 (I–V) using material from Tutti 1
- Tutti 2 (V) shortened version of Tutti 1

Development:
- Solo 2 (V, modulating) less of a development, rather the repetition of the main theme in remote keys

Varied recapitulation:
- Tutti 3 (I) shortened recapitulation of Tutti 1
- Solo 3 (I) and cadenza
- Tutti 4 (I) partial repetition of Tutti 1 or 2

Mozart's approach cannot be stereotyped, but certain features are characteristic of how he produced a more integrated form. Solo and tutti sections are less clearly delineated: Solo 1 usually consists of new material presented by the soloist, followed by a joint presentation of some or all of the main ideas; the development section too is shared by the soloist and orchestra and is truly developmental, so that the recapitulation feels like a vital point of resolution. The distinctions within this section are less clear-cut, with exposition material presented jointly, often with further variation.

The greater thematic content of the first movement is balanced by variety of form and content in the other two movements. The second may be in variation, simple ABA, rondo or sonata-rondo forms, and a wide variety of moods is found. The finales become longer and more substantial; they are usually in sonata or sonata-rondo form, with the initial presentation of the main theme by the soloist alone before it is taken up by the orchestra.

Such a brief summary can only hint at the wealth of variety to be found amongst Mozart's piano concertos: the variation-form finale of no. 17 (K.453) with its hints of *opera buffa*, the Romantic and dramatic style of the first movement of no. 20 (K.466), which contrasts with its tender rondo-form slow movement, or the intensity of the sonata-rondo structure of the finale of the last concerto, in B♭, K.595, where virtually every idea is interrelated.

ANNE-LOUISE COLDICOTT

Influences on Beethoven's style

BEETHOVEN'S STYLE WAS SHAPED by a number of factors. First there was the common musical language shared by all composers of the day, which he was bound to absorb from an early age – a language based on the major–minor tonal system, standard patterns and figurations such as 'Alberti bass', certain characteristic forms, chord progressions and cadences, and similar features. Then there was Beethoven's formal musical instruction and the influence of theory and pedagogy. And thirdly there were several composers who had particular idiosyncrasies of style which he adopted and developed. Many features of the 'common language' were outlined in the previous section; Beethoven's musical education and the individual influences on his style provide the focus for the present section.

Early instruction

Beethoven's formal instruction began at an early age with lessons from his father, but it was CHRISTIAN GOTTLOB NEEFE who was his principal teacher during the 1780s. Although it is not known exactly what was taught, Neefe did give Beethoven instruction in the basic principles of composition and thoroughbass and also introduced him to Bach's *Well-Tempered Clavier*, which was itself to be a significant influence. When Beethoven moved to Vienna to study with HAYDN he had already composed a substantial number of works, and so it might be supposed that his next composition lessons would consist of exercises in larger forms. But the surviving sources show nothing so advanced. Instead they reveal that during some of this period Beethoven worked nearly three hundred elementary exercises in strict species counterpoint in two, three and four parts – exercises derived by Haydn from Fux's *Gradus ad Parnassum*, first published as far back as 1725.

Despite his earlier training and his general musical sense, Beethoven made quite a number of mistakes in these exercises; but Haydn's corrections left little impression on Beethoven's style in free composition. Indeed in some cases what was technically a 'mistake' in strict counterpoint (for example, sounding a suspension simultaneously with its resolution) became a characteristic feature of his style. Thus when Beethoven told Ferdinand Ries in later years that he had 'never learned anything' from Haydn he was in a sense telling the truth: he did not learn how to compose large-scale works from such counterpoint lessons, and the instruction did not significantly alter his general style. This surely is one reason why he refused, despite Haydn's insistence, to put the words 'pupil of Haydn' on the title-page of works he published at the time. He may have done more advanced exercises for Haydn that are now lost (the surviving ones probably took no more than three to four months at most, judging by the uniformity of ink); but from Haydn's instruction he seems to have learnt only how to teach counterpoint – his own lessons to Archduke Rudolph many years later were closely based on Haydn's methods. (What he learnt from Haydn's actual music, however, is quite another matter.)

When Haydn left for London in early 1794 Beethoven continued his formal instruction with ALBRECHTSBERGER. His lack of progress with Haydn is confirmed by the fact that he did further work on species counterpoint with Albrechtsberger before progressing to fugue, invertible counterpoint at the octave, 10th and 12th, canon, and double fugue (see Nottebohm, 1873). How much immediate effect this more advanced counterpoint study had on his composition is uncertain, but it has been suggested that works of c.1795 may contain more interesting polyphony than they would otherwise have done (Johnson, 1982). Beethoven's interest in fugal techniques and canon only really blossomed during his final ten years; but the instruction did mean that he had an additional compositional resource at his disposal, and as well as ordinary fugal writing he did occasionally resort to contrapuntal tricks of the sort he had learnt with Albrechtsberger. For example, in the first movement of the Violin Sonata op. 30 no. 1 the development section includes a passage in which the second subject is developed imitatively in invertible counterpoint at the 10th and 5th, apparently reflecting the influence of Albrechtsberger's instruction.

By the end of his course with Albrechtsberger Beethoven was already over twenty-four, but he still felt that his musical education was incomplete. He appears to have studied string quartet composition with Emanuel Förster, and only fully mastered the genre in 1800–01. Another deficiency was in vocal writing, particularly in the Italian style. Since he was keen to establish himself in the operatic field and also to master every musical genre, he turned to the leading Italian opera composer in Vienna – SALIERI – in 1799 (Kramer, 1974). For Salieri he produced over a period of about two years a number of exercises in unaccompanied vocal writing in up to four parts in order to gain more experience of Italian vocal style and to clarify problems about Italian wordsetting. The first exercises were short (less than twenty-five bars each on average) and almost entirely homophonic, but Beethoven followed them up with some larger works. The first was the recitative and aria *No, non turbarti* (WoO 92a) for soprano and strings, the autograph of which bears numerous corrections apparently by Salieri. This may have been the last work submitted to Salieri, but Beethoven did write three more large-scale Italian pieces in 1801–2 which he may have shown to him as well – the trio *Tremate, empi, tremate* (op. 116), the unfinished *Grazie al'inganni* and a duet *Nei giorni tuoi felici* (WoO 93). These were immediately followed by a large-scale work in the Italian operatic style – *Christus am Oelberge*. This oratorio forms a natural continuation from the Salieri studies: it contains a soprano aria, like *No, non turbarti*, a duet for soprano and tenor, like *Nei giorni tuoi felici*, and a trio for soprano, tenor and bass, like *Tremate*. The two trios are actually in the same key and even have almost the same opening, although they continue quite differently.

Further theoretical study

After his Salieri instruction Beethoven undertook no more lessons in composition, but he continued self-instruction throughout his life, partly by studying theoretical writings. He always maintained a lively interest in music theory, for its own sake and as an aid to composition, and its influence appears in various forms. As regards harmonic theory, Beethoven was one of the first major composers to be brought up under the influence of Rameau's theories of chord inversion, which had become known in Germany largely through Marpurg's 1757 translation of the *Eléments de musique* by D'Alembert, a disciple of Rameau; previously chords had been described in terms of figured bass notation. Rameau's ideas were also a strong influence on the theorist Johann Kirnberger, whose main work, *Die Kunst des reines Satzes* (1771), was known and used by Beethoven. In his chapter on chords Kirnberger stresses from the start that there are three ways of constructing a chord, which correspond to what are now known as root position, first and second inversions; he discusses dominant sevenths in a similar way. Such an approach regards the 6-4 chord as a variant of the 5-3 chord, whereas pre-Rameau theorists had considered it as a dissonance requiring resolution. Beethoven used the 6-4 chord much more freely than did his predecessors, sometimes treating it virtually on a par with its root position: the second movements of both the Seventh Symphony and the 'Hammerklavier' Sonata actually end on a 6-4 chord! Nevertheless Beethoven thought of chords primarily in terms of their figured bass notation and not the Roman numeral system of today, which first appeared in Gottfried Weber's *Versuch einer geordneten Theorie der Tonsetzkunst* (1817–21).

By Beethoven's day modern key theory was firmly established, but the influence of the old modes, though minimal, had not completely disappeared, particularly in Austria. The subdomin-ant-orientated endings of certain of his minor-key pieces, such as the Sonata op. 10 no. 1 and the Bagatelle op. 119 no. 1, are clearly relics of the Phrygian mode – the most distinctive of the modes and therefore the last to disappear. Beethoven became closely acquainted with the modal system during his exercises under Haydn, which, being based on Fux's *Gradus*, were all in the old modes. He became increasingly interested in the modes in his later years, and during 1819–20 he sought out Zarlino's *Istitutioni harmoniche* (1558) with the intention of making practical use of them. He wrote the 'Et incarnatus' from the *Missa Solemnis* in the Dorian mode and the 'Heiliger Dankgesang' from the op. 132 Quartet in the Lydian, perhaps because each mode traditionally had a particular character that made it suitable for certain ideas and moods.

Beethoven apparently believed the same to be true of modern keys, with each possessing a unique character. This view is implicit in the way he repeatedly selected certain keys for certain ideas – C minor for intense anguish, E major for starry skies – and he is said to have upheld the view forcefully in conversations with Kanne. The idea of key association actually goes back in Germany as far as Johann Mattheson, but Beethoven's precise key associations do not coincide with those of Mattheson, nor of any other theorist.

Theories of form were much less well developed in the 18th century than theories of chords and keys, and the first substantial discussion of such matters as sonata form appeared in Koch's *Versuch einer Anleitung zur Composition*, vol. 3 (1793). Here Koch divides sonata-form movements into two 'parts', of which the first consists of a single 'period' and the second of two 'periods'. He does not mention the coda but does say that the exposition can conclude with an 'appendix', i.e. a codetta. For Beethoven, sonata form consisted of Koch's two 'parts' but really fell into four sections (Koch's three 'periods' plus the coda) and his sketches tend to reflect this. His concepts of form in general, however, were very much derived from practical experience rather than from any fixed theoretical notions.

One special form where Beethoven was assisted by theorists, however, was the 'Heiliger Dankgesang' of the op. 132 Quartet; here not only the form but also some of the melodic and harmonic features were derived from treatises he possessed on chorale improvisation, such as Vogler's *Choral-System* and Türk's *Von den wichtigsten Pflichten eines Organisten* (see Brandenburg, 1982). He also made occasional use of writings by a number of other theorists including C.P.E. Bach, Marpurg and Schulz, and another treatise of significance was Johann Sulzer's *Allgemeine Theorie der schönen Künste* (*General Theory of the Fine Arts*), where amongst other topics of possible relevance can be found views on musical pictorialism that were very similar to Beethoven's own (see Jander, 1987).

Other composers

The main influences on Beethoven's style, however, were neither his teachers nor theorists but the works of other composers, which he studied assiduously. Like Bach, he learnt to compose partly by actually copying out the works of others, and during his life he copied extracts from a wide variety of composers including C.P.E. Bach, J.S. Bach, W.F. Bach, Cherubini, C.H. Graun, Handel, Haydn, Mozart, Georg Muffat, Palestrina and Salieri. In some cases these copies were made for a fairly immediate purpose: extracts from recitatives by Graun were copied in preparation for recitatives of his own in *Christus am Oelberge*; passages from the Act I finale of Mozart's *Don Giovanni* were copied in about 1803, shortly before Beethoven embarked on *Leonore* – presumably to make him better acquainted with the flow of dialogue and interaction between characters in an ensemble, since it is just the ensembles, and just the voice parts, that are copied. Extracts from other operas were also copied at about the same time. Many passages by other composers which Beethoven copied out were fugal, for he was deeply concerned with the problems of voice-leading in a contrapuntal texture. Again the copying was often done while he was working on a specific related composition.

Of course Beethoven was influenced by far more works than just those he copied out, and the list of all composers who may have influenced him would be a very long one. In fact he seems to have set out to master all the various styles in use, which meant having to acquaint himself with all the best music of the day, though in later years he became primarily influenced by earlier composers rather than younger ones such as Rossini and Spohr. Identifying each influence can be difficult: since all composers of the day shared many stylistic features, it is insufficient merely to find passages in Beethoven that are vaguely similar to ones in other composers. The real question is: would he have written something different if he had not known the music that is allegedly influencing him? Obviously this question cannot always be answered with certainty, even where a theme or passage in Beethoven closely resembles one in another composer.

Among the earliest influences on Beethoven's music was that of his teacher Neefe – probably most apparent in the field of song. Neefe's songs, though modelled more on the folklike North German style, show several Italian features in such matters as more elaborate accompaniments, and are therefore much closer to the later German Lied. Beethoven's songs mostly follow this pattern too.

Another composer writing songs of a similar type was C.P.E. BACH, whose influence may have been transmitted partly through Neefe and whose songs include, like Beethoven's, some on religious texts by Gellert. Bach also influenced Beethoven's piano music, partly through his *Versuch über die wahre Art das Clavier zu spielen*, a treatise Beethoven used extensively, and partly through his own sonatas, some of which Beethoven knew and admired (see 'Other composers', p. 154). And although Bach's sonatas are very different from Beethoven's, they foreshadow them in being unusually adventurous and irregular, with strange harmonic digressions, remote keys, rhapsodic passages and other experiments.

The two composers who were the prime influences on Beethoven's music were, inevitably, HAYDN and MOZART. The extent to which Beethoven regarded himself as the heir to these two can perhaps best be seen in the fact that, when he first put on a major concert in Vienna in 1800 all the music performed was by Haydn, Mozart or himself. Haydn's influence can be seen in all manner of ways – in genres chosen, form, melodic style, rhythm, chord progressions, key relationships, dynamics and instrumentation. The very fact that Beethoven wrote so many symphonies and quartets is a measure of Haydn's influence, for Haydn had done more than anyone to raise these two genres to a position of pre-eminence. And Beethoven's oratorio *Christus am Oelberge* would probably not have been written had it not been for the recent success of Haydn's two late oratorios, *The Creation* and *The Seasons*. Many of the regular forms Beethoven used were derived primarily from Haydn (such as sonata-rondo form and even the scherzo); so too were many irregular formal procedures, such as the return, in the coda of a first movement, of music from its slow introduction (Haydn's Symphony no. 103 and Beethoven's *Pathétique* Sonata).

Mozart's influence was equally important (see 'A Conspectus of Beethoven's Style', p. 200–01). When Beethoven was about to depart for Vienna in 1792 Count Waldstein wrote prophetically: 'With the help of assiduous labour you shall receive *Mozart's spirit from Haydn's hands*'. The influence began as early as the 1780s, when Beethoven composed three Piano Quartets (WoO 36) closely modelled on works by Mozart; and the chance thematic similarities between the two composers, such as the opening themes of the *Eroica* and Mozart's *Bastien et Bastienne*, are not cases of borrowing but show how deeply Mozart's spirit had permeated Beethoven's way of thinking. The two Piano Concertos in C minor (Mozart's K. 491 and Beethoven's no. 3) are particularly close, both opening in a similar way with a unison theme initially stated *piano* but later *forte*. Beethoven's concerto is also his first to feature the piano in the first-movement coda – a further feature adapted from K. 491, the only Mozart concerto where this happens.

Another composer who influenced Beethoven from an early age was CLEMENTI. According to Schindler, Beethoven had the greatest admiration for Clementi's sonatas and possessed nearly all of them in his otherwise meagre collection of music. Although Clementi was based in London he visited Vienna several times and some of his sonatas were actually published there; during the 1780s he was 'the pianist with the greatest international reputation' (Plantinga, 1976, p. 310) and so it is natural that

Beethoven should absorb ideas from him. Indeed Beethoven's sonatas are on the whole much closer to Clementi's than to those of Haydn or Mozart. Such features as the high level of virtuosity required, the typically pianistic idioms, and the way the dramatic climaxes are built were among the things that Beethoven took over from Clementi.

Clementi's success as a pianist–composer placed him at the head of what has been termed the 'London Pianoforte School', and several other members of this group may have influenced Beethoven's piano style. Chief among them are Jan Ladislav Dussek, who was in London during the 1790s, and Johann Baptist Cramer, who spent most of his life in London but also visited Beethoven in Vienna. Dussek's sonatas are often very forward-looking, and although similarities between his and Beethoven's may sometimes be just chance resemblance, it is probable that Beethoven knew many of them and was at times influenced by them. A notable example is Dussek's sonata *The Farewell*, op. 44, published in 1800. It is in the same key as Beethoven's sonata of the same name (op. 81a, written in 1809) and there are several resemblances of detail between the two works (Ringer, 1970, pp. 752–3). Of various Cramer-like passages in Beethoven's music the one most often cited is the finale of the Sonata in A♭, op. 26, which was composed shortly after Cramer had published in Vienna three sonatas dedicated to Haydn. According to Czerny, the movement is 'in that uniform, perpetually moving style, as are many of the Sonatas by Cramer, whose sojourn at Vienna prompted Beethoven to the composition of this work' (Czerny, 1970, p. 38/48).

Later influences

A number of other minor influences can be found from Beethoven's early and middle periods (for example Knecht's symphony *Le Portrait musical de la nature*, published in about 1784, provided most of the programmatic content for Beethoven's *Pastoral* Symphony), but the next important influence came in March 1802 with the arrival in Vienna of CHERUBINI's French opera *Lodoïska*, which was so successful that it was followed later that year by three more French operas by him (*Les Deux Journées*, *Médée* and *Elisa*) and eventually in 1805 by a visit from Cherubini himself. Beethoven was profoundly affected by this encounter with Cherubini's music, and in later life he regarded Cherubini as the greatest composer amongst his contemporaries.

Beethoven was impressed amongst other things by the libretti used in French opera, especially *Les Deux Journées* and Spontini's *La Vestale*. The author of the former was Bouilly, and so it was natural that Beethoven should turn to Bouilly's *Léonore* for the source for his own opera. Elements of heroism, too, were prominent in French opera, and they quickly found their way into Beethoven's music – not only his opera but also his oratorio and instrumental music, especially his overtures, where his gradual absorption of the French style of heroic grandeur is perhaps seen at its clearest. It is significant that Beethoven entered what has been termed his 'heroic phase' shortly after his first encounters with Cherubini's music. Other ways in which the French style influenced him are in the type of recitative (Beethoven's are rarely perfunctory in the manner of Italian *secco* recitative) and in his imaginative and varied orchestration. There are also a number of more detailed parallels between Cherubini and Beethoven, of which one example will suffice. The overture to *Médée*, a copy of which Beethoven owned, is in F minor, like Beethoven's *Egmont* Overture, and the two movements are so close that in places Beethoven's sounds almost like a triple-time variation of Cherubini's.

Other composers working in France who seem to have impressed Beethoven include GLUCK, SPONTINI, GRÉTRY (Beethoven wrote a set of variations, WoO 72, on a theme of Grétry) and the Parisian school of violinist composers. Among the latter were such as Viotti and Pierre Rode, and it was to their examples that Beethoven turned when writing his own Violin Concerto, since there were very few good Viennese models.

In later life Beethoven turned increasingly to earlier composers for new ideas – chiefly BACH and HANDEL. Bach's music he always held in high regard (see 'Other composers', p. 154), but his early attempts to follow Bach were not particularly successful: in imitation of Bach's preludes and fugues in every key, he composed two Preludes (op. 39), each of which passes through all twelve major keys. Such a naive attempt to out-do Bach reveals little other than Beethoven's admiration for the composer. But it is in the music of his last dozen years – particularly the fugues – that the Bach influence is most conspicuous. Although these late fugues sound quite un-Bachian, Bach was probably never far from his mind while he was working on them. Moreover it is not just Beethoven's fugues which display Bach influence. His numerous vocal canons, also from the latter part of his life, likewise betray his interest in counterpoint, and one of them incorporates the B–A–C–H motif (WoO 191). Similarly the A major Sonata (op. 101) is very Bach-orientated in several ways, and ultimately Beethoven appropriated Bachian textures, figuration and his obbligato contrapuntal style in general (Zenck, 1986). Beethoven at one stage even began composing an overture on B–A–C–H, but in the end he apparently felt that the best monument to Bach would be a great fugue, which materialized in the *Grosse Fuge*.

Beethoven's admiration for Handel was even greater (see 'Other composers', p. 153). There is actually surprisingly little Handelian influence in most of his work; but there is some. One feature of Handel's style that Beethoven especially admired was his ability to create great music out of very little material: Seyfried was told, 'Go to him and learn how, with such modest means, such great effects may be produced.' (MacArdle, 1960, p. 34) A good example of this technique is the 'Dead March' from Handel's *Saul*, where Handel constructs virtually the entire movement out of a three-note motif. (The March itself was so admired by Beethoven that in 1820 he considered writing a set of orchestral variations on it, and in 1826 was planning to compose a *Saul* of his own.) This technique of building a movement out of a small rhythmic cell is found in many of Beethoven's own works, the most notable example being of course the first movement of the Fifth Symphony. The work most obviously indebted to Handel, however, is the overture *Die Weihe des Hauses* of 1822. Beethoven 'had long cherished the plan to write an overture in the strict, expressly in the Handelian, style', according to Schindler (Thayer, 1967, p. 807). The Handel work that seems to have been uppermost in Beethoven's mind at the time is *Alexander's Feast*, a work he certainly knew and admired; its overture and final chorus show many similarities to Beethoven's overture, such as the use of a dactylic rhythm set against a descending sequence of suspensions. Beethoven's overture also echoes *Alexander's Feast* in bars 37–53, which consist entirely of noisy tonic and dominant chords, similar to the chorus 'Break his Bands', and the rather absurd bassoon runs which accompany this section of the overture also have their counterpart in this chorus.

Beethoven's interest in Bach and Handel and his growing interest in religious music eventually led him to explore even further back in history – to Palestrina and even Gregorian chant. 'In order to write true church music go through all the plainchants of the monks', he wrote in 1818 (Solomon, 1982, no. 168). He came to regard Palestrina as the best composer of church music, partly because his music was written *a cappella*, 'the only true church style' (Letter 1161), and partly because it used the old modes. Palestrina's influence is certainly present, albeit not conspicuous, in the *Missa Solemnis*, which Beethoven once remarked could with slight alterations be performed by voices alone!

The influences on Beethoven's style were, then, very varied, and attest to his very wide knowledge of music. He deliberately sought out all the best music of his predecessors and older contemporaries and regarded this as his starting-point. To some extent the influences came by genre – he tended to follow whoever was best at each genre: for the symphony it was mainly Haydn; the piano concerto, Mozart; the violin concerto, Viotti; chamber music, Haydn and Mozart; the piano sonata, Clementi; opera, Mozart and Cherubini; song, C.P.E. Bach and others; fugue (for whatever medium), J.S. Bach. He was always looking for fresh ideas from other composers, and once remarked that he derived the greatest pleasure from playing works he had never or seldom seen before (Letter 220). In the same letter he asked Breitkopf & Härtel for scores of various works, 'in short, all the scores you have', which he wanted for 'real enjoyment' and also 'the purpose of study'. His appetite for good music was never satisfied and he complained in 1817 that he had not studied composition enough. The music acted as a stimulus to his own creativity, serving both as a model to be followed and a challenge to be taken up.

BARRY COOPER

Beethoven's musical environment

BEETHOVEN'S LIFE WAS SPENT in two centres. His formative years were in his birthplace Bonn, in the German Rhineland, and his years of attainment in faraway Vienna, the capital of the Austrian Empire and the musical capital of Europe. In Bonn he had few opportunities to travel. From Vienna, which he made his home in 1792, he undertook two concert tours in 1796 – the first to Prague, Dresden and Berlin, and the second to Pressburg (Bratislava) – and in 1798 he made a further visit to Prague. Thereafter he left the city only for summer holidays in the countryside.

The Electoral court at Bonn had a long musical tradition, and Ludwig van Beethoven was the third generation of his family for whom it provided employment. His various posts, assistant court organist, cembalist and violist in the court and theatre orchestras, afforded him a wide musical background. Latterly he played alongside some distinguished musicians, amongst them Franz Ries, the Rombergs, Simrock and Reicha, who became lasting friends and influenced his career in various ways.

Electors Maximilian Friedrich (1761–84) and particularly Maximilian Franz (1784–1801) did much to foster musical tradition at court. Consequently Beethoven was exposed to almost all types of music, including operas by Gluck, Grétry, Salieri, Mozart and others; orchestral music by composers of the pre-Classical school, such as J.C. Bach and the two outstanding contemporary composers Haydn and Mozart; and chamber music by C.P.E. Bach, Stamitz, Pleyel, and again Haydn and Mozart. From 1779 Beethoven had the benefit of being taught by the court organist, Christian Gottlob Neefe, who not only provided him with a more systematic approach to his keyboard-playing than hitherto, but also tutored him in composition, using the works of J.S. Bach as a grounding. He sought to foster in his pupil a wide and general interest, in literature and philosophy as well as in music.

Maximilian Franz financed both Beethoven's first visit to Vienna to meet Mozart in 1787, sadly aborted by the death of Beethoven's mother, and his second and final journey there in 1792. He also introduced him to his close friend Count Waldstein, who moved to Bonn in 1788 and became Beethoven's first major patron.

Whatever Bonn's limitations, Beethoven's service in the musical establishment at court gave him a wide range of musical experience, and whilst there he mixed with an extensive circle of cultured people who broadened his intellectual horizon.

The Vienna in which Beethoven found himself in 1792 was without doubt the leading musical city in Europe. All types of music flourished, and opera was probably the most popular. French operas, particularly those by Cherubini (Italian by birth but French by adoption) and Méhul, were the most enthusiastically received. Their popular revolutionary themes appealed to Beethoven and inspired him to attempt an opera of his own, first *Vestas Feuer*, which was not completed, and then *Fidelio*.

A high standard of orchestral and chamber music was attained by the private orchestras and ensembles maintained by the imperial court and members of the nobility. The wealthiest nobles, such as the Princes Lobkowitz and Lichnowsky and Count Razumovsky, had concert halls within their palaces. First-class recitals could be heard in salons both in their palaces and in private houses whose wealthy owners patronized individual performers. Touring virtuosi were much sought after, and these occasions also provided excellent opportunities for aspiring newcomers to establish themselves.

One of the leading exponents of chamber music was the violinist and conductor Ignaz Schuppanzigh. He led several string quartets in Vienna over a long period. The first, dating from 1796, performed once a week at Prince Lichnowsky's palace, presenting works by Förster, Haydn and Mozart. Schuppanzigh quickly established a lasting and productive friendship with Beethoven, and was to play an important role in introducing his chamber music in Vienna, initially with the first performance of the op. 18 String Quartets. In 1804 he formed another quartet which gave the first *public* string quartet recitals. In 1808 Count Razumovsky engaged Schuppanzigh to form a resident quartet, which performed the three op. 59 String Quartets that the Count had commissioned from Beethoven. This quartet was abandoned only in 1816 following the destruction of Razumovsky's palace, whereupon Schuppanzigh left Vienna. Earlier travels had taken him all over Europe; this time he travelled to Russia, where he promoted the music of Haydn, Mozart, Beethoven and Schubert. His return to Vienna in 1823 may have had some influence on the composition of Beethoven's late quartets.

Virtuoso performers who visited Vienna were not only popular with their audiences, but served as inspirations to native musicians. In Beethoven's case the stimulus was two-fold. The effect of the arrival of the pianists Wölffl and Cramer in 1798/9 was to raise the standard of his own playing to new heights. Other instrumentalists inspired him as a composer. For example, he wrote his Mandolin Sonata (WoO 43) for Wenzel Krumpholz, the Horn Sonata op. 17 for Johann Wenzel Stich (who preferred to be known as Punto), and the Violin Sonata op. 47 ('Kreutzer') for George Bridgetower. Less specifically the playing of his Cello Sonata op. 5 no. 2 by the virtuoso double-bassist Dragonetti alerted Beethoven to that instrument's potential and influenced his orchestral treatment of it.

Public orchestral concerts had begun to be a feature of Viennese musical life since the 1770s. The Tonkünstlergesellschaft, founded by Gassmann in 1772, was the first independent body to promote concerts, with four annual performances at Lent and Christmas for the benefit of musicians' widows and orphans. In 1812 the Gesellschaft der Musikfreunde was founded by Joseph Sonnleithner, and in 1819 Franz Xaver Gebauer, an early member of the Gesellschaft der Musikfreunde, founded and became the first conductor of the Concerts Spirituels, modelled on the French series of the same name. Besides these there were a few subscription concerts (that is, concerts where the audience had guaranteed to subscribe in advance) given by both resident musicians and visiting virtuosi.

There were no purpose-built concert halls until 1831, when the Gesellschaft der Musikfreunde acquired its own premises. Theatres and halls primarily intended for other purposes were therefore used. Beethoven presented Akademien (concerts) in the two court theatres, the Burgtheater and the Kärntnertor Theatre, within the Hoftheater. The most important private theatre was the Theater an der Wien, the venue of the first public performance of a number of Beethoven's major works. Amongst a number of other private theatres may be cited the Josephstadt Theatre, to celebrate the reconstruction of which Beethoven wrote the overture *Die Weihe des Hauses* (*The Consecration of the House*), op. 124.

Of the halls, three were most frequently used: the Zur Mehlgrube (literally 'At the Sign of the Flour Shop'), the Jahnischer Saal and the Augarten. All three were primarily restaurants where slightly less formal concerts took place, usually during the daytime. Other possible concert venues were to be found within the imperial castle. These were the two Redoutensäle, the Rittersaal and the Zeremoniensaal. Most used was the Grosser Redoutensaal, a ballroom which could accommodate particularly large concerts. One further venue, which was the scene of many Beethoven performances, was the University's Festsaal, which was used by the Gesellschaft der Musikfreunde before they had their own hall.

The Burgtheater had its own resident orchestra which could be hired for concerts at other venues, but it was more usual for orchestras to consist of *ad hoc* collections of good amateur players, sometimes augmented by a few professionals. Public concerts were usually organized and financed by individual promoters, generally composers, conductors or virtuoso instrumentalists, who assumed control of the entire event: the programmes, the performers, the publicity and the sale of tickets. A translation of a programme prepared in advance by Beethoven may be reproduced here:

Today, Wednesday April 2 1800 Herr Ludwig van Beethoven will have the honour to give a grand concert for his benefit in the Royal Imperial Court Theatre beside the Burg. The pieces which will be performed are the following:

1. A Grand Symphony by the late Kapellmeister Mozart.
2. An aria from 'The Creation' by the Princely Kapellmeister Herr Haydn, sung by Mlle Saal.
3. A Grand Concerto for the pianoforte, played and composed by Herr Ludwig van Beethoven.
4. A Septet, most humbly and obediently dedicated to Her Majesty the Empress, and composed by Herr Ludwig van Beethoven for four stringed and three wind instruments, played by Herren Schuppanzigh, Schreiber, Schindlecker, Bär, Nickel, Matauschen and Dietzel.
5. A Duet from Haydn's 'Creation' sung by Herr and Mlle Saal.
6. Herr Ludwig van Beethoven will improvise on the pianoforte.
7. A new Grand Symphony with complete orchestra, composed by Herr Ludwig van Beethoven

---

Tickets for boxes and stalls are to be had of Herr van Beethoven at his lodgings in the Tiefen Graben No. 241, third floor, and of the box-keeper.

The admission prices are as usual

The start is at half past 6

The length of the above concert would not have been considered out of the ordinary at the time, but a programme consisting of the works of just these three composers was unusual.

After the Congress of Vienna the pattern of cultural life changed. Musicians were not supported to the degree they had previously enjoyed, and with less money about there were fewer commissions. Tastes changed too. Italian opera of a very light kind became all the rage with the Viennese public, who clamoured for greater spectacular effects at the expense of the drama and music. This was perhaps an understandable reaction after years of war, but it satisfied only on a superficial level. Beethoven felt himself out of sympathy with the wider public at this time. This and the torment of his current domestic affairs saw a stagnant period as far as his composition was concerned. Gradually it became apparent that more enlightened people were also not satisfied with the trivial nature of the music in fashion. The later works of Mozart seemed to satisfy their deeper feelings, and previously neglected works of Haydn enjoyed a new-found popularity. From around 1818 Beethoven's compositional inspiration was rekindled and his music displayed a new intensity. He was now seized on as the true artistic apostle of the age, with his music assuming the new values which emerged from the turmoil of war and destruction.

ANNE-LOUISE COLDICOTT

Music copying and publishing

IN BEETHOVEN'S DAY far more music circulated only in manuscript than is the case today. In Vienna, as in most large cities, there were several professional music copyists, and some publishers and music shops actually sold manuscripts as well as printed music. When a new work was written the composer often hired a professional copyist, either to write out a clear, legible version in preparation for publication, or to produce a set of individual parts for performance if it was a work for several voices or instruments. Beethoven employed the services of a number of copyists at various times (see 'Corrected copies and copyists', pp. 190–92), and usually it was a copyist's score, corrected by Beethoven, that was sent to publishers, rather than the autograph.

During his lifetime, however, the amount of music being printed, both in Vienna and elsewhere, increased enormously. Printing costs became lower, publishers more numerous, and the amount of music circulating in manuscript proportionately very much less. Thus although not all his works were published immediately after composition, in the end most of his major ones appeared in print while he was still alive or immediately after his death, whereas Bach, less than a century earlier, had published very little. How rapidly the situation was changing is well illustrated by Beethoven's experience with his two Masses: the one in C (1807) he had great difficulty in publishing because, according to Breitkopf & Härtel (the eventual publishers), there was 'no demand for church works', whereas with the *Missa Solemnis* (1819–23) at least four publishers were willing to offer up to 1000 fl. for the work. Even at this date, however, he was unable to have certain works published, especially stage and vocal works. Works offered to publishers during the 1820s without success include *Die Ruinen von Athen* and *König Stephan*, opp. 113 and 117 (in both cases only the overture was published during his lifetime), and also op. 136, WoO 2a, 3, 19–20, 24, 28, 89 and 90.

Then, as now, publishers were generally prepared to print only what they believed would sell well and quickly. There was no system of royalties, and publishers would offer the composer a single fee, after which the work effectively became their property: its purchase implied an exclusive privilege to print the first edition, and so a composer could not normally sell the same work to two different publishers. There was some form of copyright law within many countries, thus preventing piracy of this first edition; but the law did not then extend beyond national boundaries, and so publishers from other countries were liable to produce pirate copies, perhaps even selling them at a lower price in the original country in competition with the first edition.

In the case of British publishers, however, the position was different. They did not generally export their pirated editions to the continent, and conversely continental publishers would not export to Britain (transport costs evidently made such a practice uneconomical). The two markets were therefore quite separate, and so Beethoven, like Haydn before him, exploited the situation by selling a number of works to both a British and a continental publisher; each paid him a fee and in return owned the work and its sales rights within their territory. Ideally a day had to be fixed for the simultaneous appearance of both the British and the continental edition, thereby preventing any possibility of anyone exporting either edition to a rival publisher ahead of the legitimate one. Complete simultaneity, however, was not really essential and was rarely achieved. For example, Beethoven's 25 Scottish Songs, op. 108, were published in Britain in about August 1818, but the edition was so little known elsewhere that he was able to sell the same songs to Adolf Schlesinger nearly two years later for a German edition that did not appear until July 1822.

Altogether over two dozen works were sold to both a British and a continental publisher (Tyson, 1963a), but occasionally the system broke down, as with the Bagatelles op. 119. The last five of these were published in Vienna and then all eleven were sold to Clementi for publication in England. But the intended continental publisher for the first six (Peters) withdrew, and before Beethoven had found another one the English edition had been pirated, first by Moritz Schlesinger in Paris and then by Sauer & Leidesdorf in Vienna, thus depriving Beethoven of a much-needed fee (Tyson, 1963b).

In Britain, copyright was controlled through a register at Stationers Hall, London. When a work was published it was entered in the register beside a date; the entry normally indicated either that the work had just been published or was about to be published, and such entries are extremely useful for establishing precisely when a work appeared. No such register existed in Vienna, and so for the dates of Beethoven's Viennese publications one has to rely mainly on publication announcements in local newspapers; works tended to appear a few days before the announcement.

Music was generally printed by engraving on metal plates, though other types of printing such as lithography and movable type were occasionally employed. Once the plates had been engraved and corrected, a limited number of copies was printed (most often about a hundred), and the plates then stored for reprinting further batches should additional copies be required (Tyson, 1971b, pp. 474–5). If errors were noticed after the first 'impression' (batch of copies) had been published, it was possible to amend the plates before the second impression. It was even possible to make improvements to the music at this stage, as happened with the Fifth Symphony, where the only surviving copy of the first impression is significantly different from all later copies. Thus although the first edition of a work is the most sought after by collectors today, it is not always the one with the best text (Tyson, 1962). On the other hand, the metal plates became worn after repeated printings and were sometimes replaced, in which case new errors might be introduced, so that no single impression will necessarily convey the best text throughout.

BARRY COOPER

Beethoven's patrons and commissions

THE MAJORITY OF BEETHOVEN'S PATRONS were wealthy noblemen whose patronage manifested itself either in the specific commissioning of works for financial return or in more general ways, such as the giving of gratuitous financial support. This more general type of patronage gives some indication of the respect which Beethoven's talents commanded, and which enabled and led him to expect to be treated on an equal footing with his 'superiors' by dint of his ability. The commissioning of works was not confined to individuals: publishers, musical societies and theatres were also responsible. Outstanding performers (e.g. Bridgetower, Rode, Stich) sometimes inspired Beethoven to write specifically for them (see 'Beethoven's musical environment', pp. 88–9), but they do not qualify as patrons inasmuch as there were no financial arrangements; nor do many of the people to whom he dedicated works, although some dedications were to patrons in the true sense.

Bonn

Beethoven's early years in Bonn raise the problem of the borderline between employment and patronage. They were spent in the employment of the Electoral court, but ELECTOR MAXIMILIAN FRANZ surely exceeded the duties of an employer when in 1787 he financed Beethoven's trip to Vienna to study with Mozart, and in 1792 when he again sent Beethoven to Vienna, this time to study with Haydn.

As a boy Beethoven was befriended by the VON BREUNING family. Although the relationship was to become one of lasting friendship, there was an element of patronage in its broadest sense in the way such a distinguished family welcomed Beethoven as both piano teacher and friend. Later COUNT WALDSTEIN arrived in Bonn and became a firm friend of the Elector. An able musician, he immediately recognized Beethoven's gifts and became an important and influential patron.

Beethoven received his first commission in Bonn. The Lesegesellschaft (Literary Society) planned to mark the death of Emperor

Joseph II in 1790, and Beethoven was invited to set the *Cantata on the Death of Joseph II* (WoO 87). A second cantata, *On the Accession of Leopold II* (WoO 88), was *possibly* commissioned by the Elector. Another commission testifies to Beethoven's friendship with Waldstein. He wrote the music for a ballet the Count was producing, *Ritterballett* (WoO 1) in 1790/91, and allowed it to be passed off under the Count's name. The Variations for piano, four hands, on a theme by Count Waldstein (WoO 67) indicates his respect for him, and although the two later became estranged, as late as 1805 Beethoven was to dedicate the Piano Sonata op. 53 to him.

Vienna

When Beethoven moved to Vienna in 1792, the financial problems posed by the move were softened by the continued payment of his salary from Bonn until March 1794. Thereafter he never again held a secure position, but relied on patronage, income from the publication of compositions, concerts and what little piano teaching he could be persuaded to do. Contradictions occur in several aspects of Beethoven's character. This is certainly true of his attitude towards employment and patronage. Ironically, the man who wanted to be master of his own destiny nonetheless nurtured a desire to hold an important post. 'In the last analysis, Beethoven's desire to be his own master remained in perpetual and irreconcilable conflict with his desire for status and financial stability.' (Solomon, 1977, p. 66) This same conflict was to be apparent in his relationships with those whose patronage he received.

Beethoven's arrival in Vienna was fortunate in many ways. The close connection between the courts at Bonn and Vienna meant that he was not entirely unknown to the Viennese aristocracy; he arrived with letters of introduction from Count Waldstein, who was related to most of the noble families, and he was a pupil of the highly-esteemed Haydn. He was able to gain access to all the important salons, virtually guaranteeing his success as a virtuoso pianist and improviser. Samuel Johnson's somewhat embittered remark in a letter to Lord Chesterfield (7 February 1755) – 'Is not a Patron, my Lord, one who looks with unconcern on a man struggling for life in the water, and, when he has reached ground, encumbers him with help?' – could hardly have been further from the truth as regards Beethoven. From the outset, enlightened and music-loving members of the Viennese aristocracy recognized his genius and were prepared to offer him help which enabled him to work unfettered, in a way impossible had he held an official position.

The list of important individuals who could be described as *general* patrons is a long one. The nature and extent of their help varied, but show a readiness to come to Beethoven's aid when he required assistance, whether of a practical or financial kind.

Biographical details of these principal patrons (below) are given in the 'Who's Who of Beethoven's Contemporaries' (pp. 40–56).

Brentano family	Prince Lobkowitz
Count Browne	Count Oppersdorff
Count and Countess Erdödy	Baron Pasqualati
Count Fries	Count Razumovsky
Prince Galitzin	Archduke Rudolph
Baron Gleichenstein	Baron van Swieten
Prince Kinsky	Nikolaus Zmeskall
Lichnowsky family	

From the LICHNOWSKY family, Prince Karl was a very influential and important patron. He understood Beethoven well, particularly his need for independence, and in 1800 settled an annuity of 600 fl. per year to be paid until he found a suitable appointment. This was paid until 1806. He also donated four valuable Italian string instruments. He, in turn, was the recipient of the dedications of a number of important works. So too were his wife, Princess Christiane (op. 43 and WoO 45), his sister, Countess Henriette (op. 51 no. 2), and Christiane's mother, Countess Thun (op. 11). Count Moritz, the Prince's younger brother, was a patron and dedicatee in his own right.

In 1808 Jerome Bonaparte, the youngest brother of Napoleon, established a court in Kassel, styling himself 'King of Westphalia', and offered Beethoven the position of Kapellmeister. The salary was to be 600 ducats a year, and his duties were to consist only of conducting the King's concerts (apparently short and infrequent), with unlimited access to the orchestra. It is most likely that Beethoven never intended nor wished to leave Vienna, and when news of his impending appointment became known there, he took advantage of the desire of his many benefactors for him to remain. It was apparently Countess Erdödy who originally suggested that a formal contract should be arranged enabling Beethoven to remain in Vienna, financially secure and artistically free. This was arranged by Gleichenstein, and resulted in an agreement that annually he would be paid 1500 fl. by ARCHDUKE RUDOLPH, 700 by PRINCE LOBKOWITZ and 1800 by PRINCE KINSKY, on condition only that he remain in Vienna. Sadly, by February 1811 the sum of 4000 fl. had become worth only about 1600, in September of that year Lobkowitz was forced by his own financial straits to cease payments for nearly four years, and in 1812 Kinsky died suddenly. But with the help of Kanka, Kinsky's heirs eventually agreed to backdate the payments to November 1812 (see p. 24), and by 1815 Beethoven was receiving 3400 fl. WW per annum.

Apart from those individuals already listed, there were a few others who, although not closely acquainted with Beethoven, acted generously towards him. In 1803 the French piano maker Sébastien Erard presented him with a square piano, and in 1818 he received a six-octave grand piano from Thomas Broadwood of London. At the end of 1826 Johann Stumpff sent from London all forty volumes of Arnold's edition of Handel's works. This gift gave Beethoven great pleasure, which he expressed in a letter the following February (Letter 1550), in which he also asked Stumpff to encourage George Smart to promote a concert by the Philharmonic Society of London for his benefit. It was probably due to Stumpff's intervention that the Society almost immediately despatched £100 (1000 fl.), a particularly generous act.

Commissions

A substantial proportion of Beethoven's income resulted from writing works which had been commissioned. The following major works are notable examples:

op. 23 Violin Sonata
Count Fries

op. 24 Violin Sonata
Count Fries

op. 29 String Quintet
Count Fries

op. 31 3 Piano Sonatas
Nägeli (publisher)

op. 43 *Die Geschöpfe des Prometheus*
Vigano?

op. 45 3 Marches for piano, 4 hands
Count Browne

op. 59 3 String Quartets
Count Razumovsky

op. 60 Symphony no. 4
Count Oppersdorff

op. 61 Piano arrangement of the Violin Concerto
Clementi (publisher)

op. 67 Symphony no. 5
Count Oppersdorff

op. 72 *Fidelio*
Theater an der Wien

op. 77 Piano Fantasia
Clementi

op. 78 Piano Sonata
Clementi

op. 79 Piano Sonata
Clementi

op. 84 *Egmont*: Overture and incidental music
J.H. von Luchsenstein, director of the Court Theatre

op. 86   Mass in C
Prince Esterházy

opp. 105 & 107   16 themes with variations for piano and flute
Thomson (publisher)

op. 108   25 Scottish Songs
Thomson

opp. 109–11   3 Piano Sonatas
A. Schlesinger (publisher)

op. 113   *Die Ruinen von Athen*
Hungarian Theatre at Pest

op. 114   March from op. 113 revised for *Die Weihe des Hauses*
Hensler (Josephstadt Theatre)

op. 117   *König Stephan*
Hungarian Theatre at Pest

op. 124   *Die Weihe des Hauses*: Overture
see op. 114

op. 125   Symphony no. 9
Philharmonic Society, London

op. 127   String Quartet
Prince Galitzin

op. 130   String Quartet
Prince Galitzin

op. 131   String Quartet
Schott (publisher)

op. 132   String Quartet
Prince Galitzin

op. 134   Arrangement of *Grosse Fuge* (op. 133)
M. Artaria (publisher)

op. 135   String Quartet
M. Schlesinger (publisher)

WoO 1   *Ritterballett*
Count Waldstein

WoO 30   3 Equali
Glöggl

WoO 87–8   2 Cantatas
(see above)

WoO 91   2 Arias
Umlauf, author of Singspiel *Die schöne Schüsterin*

WoO 94   'Germania'
Treitschke, author of Singspiel *Die gute Nachricht*

WoO 96   *Leonore Prohaska*
Duncker

WoO 97   'Es ist vollbracht'
(see WoO 94)

WoO 102 *Abschiedsgesang*
M. Tuscher, to mark the departure of Leopold Weiss

WoO 106 Lobkowitz Cantata
K. Peters

WoO 152–8 Folksongs
Thomson

Beethoven's relationship with the Philharmonic Society of London deserves mention, particularly with regard to three overtures: *Die Ruinen von Athen* (op. 113), *Namensfeier* (op. 115) and *König Stephan* (op. 117). These were purchased by the Society in 1815 for 75 guineas as unpublished works, although they had been written for other purposes. They were evidently something of a disappointment but nevertheless the Society later commissioned two symphonies, of which they received one – the Ninth. (They also belatedly received a version of one movement of the Tenth, in a completion by Barry Cooper, in 1988.)

Other commissions known to have been made but not fulfilled include:

1795 A string quartet commissioned by Count Apponyi (according to Wegeler).

1803 The librettist Schikaneder asked Beethoven to set the opera *Vestas Feuer* (Hess 115), but only a fragment was completed.

1803 George Thomson asked Beethoven to write six sonatas incorporating Scottish themes.

1809 Thomson asked for a string quartet incorporating a Scottish folktune.

1811 In a letter to Thomson, Beethoven accepted a commission for three sonatas and three quintets. There was also mention of 12 English songs, a cantata *The Battle of the Baltic Sea*, and a possible oratorio. None of these works materialized.

1815 Beethoven was approached by the Gesellschaft der Musikfreunde to write a major work. In 1819 he was paid a fee for an oratorio, *Der Sieg des Kreuzes*. He received the complete text (by Karl Bernard) only in 1823 and despite many promises was never able to come to terms with it.

1824 Diabelli commissioned a 'grand sonata for four hands' and agreed to Beethoven's fee of 80 ducats, but the commission was not fulfilled.

Sometimes Beethoven would seek permission to dedicate works to important figures in the hope that he would receive a retrospective reward. Into this category fall the following:

op. 5 2 Cello Sonatas dedicated to Prince Friedrich Wilhelm II, for which he was rewarded with an expensive present.

op. 20 Septet was dedicated to Empress Maria Theresia, second wife of Emperor Franz. The subsequent commission to write the music for *Die Geschöpfe des Prometheus* (op. 43) may have resulted from this.

op. 30 3 Violin Sonatas were dedicated to Alexander I, Emperor of Russia. These were not acknowledged at the time, although unreliable evidence refers to the donation of a diamond ring.

op. 89 Polonaise for Piano: in 1814 this was written for and dedicated to the Empress of Russia on the advice of Beethoven's friend Bertolini, who thought it might lead to an acknowledgment of op. 30. This proved to be the case, with the Empress giving Beethoven 50 ducats for this work and an extra 100 when it came to her attention that he had received nothing for the Violin Sonatas.

op. 91 *Wellingtons Sieg* ('Battle Symphony') was dedicated to the Prince Regent, later King George IV, of England. Although the Prince had neither commissioned it nor given permission for the dedication, Beethoven held a lasting resentment that it remained unacknowledged and he even referred to it in a letter to the King in 1823 (Letter 1142).

ANNE-LOUISE COLDICOTT

Section 6
BEETHOVEN AS AN INDIVIDUAL

BEETHOVEN AS AN INDIVIDUAL

Appearance and manner

FROM AROUND 1800, Beethoven's fame made him a popular subject with artists. Numerous portraits, drawings, engravings, busts and a life mask, together with contemporary descriptions, have left posterity with a fairly accurate impression of his physique, physiognomy, dress and manner.

Beethoven was short, but broad-framed. Until his early thirties he was slim, as seen in the full-length painting by Mähler of 1804 or 1805 and the engraving by Neidl, *c.*1801 (see plates 1 and 2). These, and the miniature of 1803 by Hornemann (plate 3), are remarkably similar in their portrayal of his facial features, showing penetrating brown eyes beneath a broad forehead and thick eyebrows. His ruddy complexion bears the scars of childhood smallpox, his mouth is shapely, and his chin has a cleft which became more marked in later years. At this time Beethoven dressed elegantly and fashionably, as is further borne out by Neugass's portrait of *c.*1806 (plate 4).

In his later thirties Beethoven became stockier. The change in his physique and manner of dress was recorded by Grillparzer, writing in 1823: 'I first saw Beethoven in my boyhood years – which may have been 1804 or 5.... Beethoven in those days was still lean, dark, and contrary to the habit in later years, very elegantly dressed.... One or two years later I was living with my parents in Heiligenstadt, near Vienna. Our dwelling fronted on the garden, and Beethoven had rented the rooms facing the street.... My brothers and I took little heed of the odd man who in the meanwhile had grown more robust, and went about dressed in a most negligent, indeed even slovenly way.' (Sonneck, 1967, p. 155) Röckel, who sang Florestan in *Fidelio* in 1806, writing of a visit to Beethoven at that time, also testifies to the impression of strength: '...was placed the mighty bathing apparatus in which the Master was laving his powerful chest...and I had the opportunity of admiring his muscular system and sturdy bodily construction. To judge by the latter the composer might look forward to growing as old as Methuselah, and it must have taken a most powerful inimical influence to bring this strong column to so untimely a fall.' (Sonneck, 1967, pp. 64–5)

Beethoven was apparently always clumsy in manner. Amongst many accounts is one by Ries: 'Beethoven was most awkward and bungling in his behaviour; his clumsy movements lacked all grace. He rarely picked up anything without dropping or breaking it.... Everything was knocked over, soiled, or destroyed. How he ever managed to shave himself at all remains difficult to understand, even considering the frequent cuts on his cheeks. – He never learned to dance in time with the music.' (Wegeler, 1987, pp. 106–7)

Important records are the life mask and bust made in 1812 by Franz Klein (plate 5). The facial proportions verify the accuracy of the earlier portraits by Hornemann and Mähler, but now maturity has added strength to the visage. That same strength of character is seen in the engraving by Höfel in 1814 of a sketch by Letronne (plate 6). Beethoven was not handsome, but his appearance was undoubtedly striking, and that was surely due to the expressiveness of his eyes. This characteristic is absent in Mähler's second portrait (1815), whereas Heckel's less accurate likeness captures something of Beethoven's determination and rebelliousness (plates 7 and 8). His eyes were frequently mentioned. Sir John Russell wrote: 'his eye is full of rude energy' (Russell, 1828, II, p. 273); Rossini recorded 'but what no etcher's needle could express was the indefinable sadness spread over his features – while from under heavy eyebrows his eyes shone out as from caverns, and though small, seemed to pierce one.' (Sonneck, 1967, p. 117); and Amenda's friend Dr Carl von Bursy wrote in his diary: 'fiery eyes, which, though small, are deep-set and unbelievably full of life.' (Landon, 1974, p. 153)

Two famous portraits date from around 1819: one by Schimon, and another, somewhat idealized, by Stieler (plates 9 and 10). Both capture something of the essence of greatness and defiance in the face of adversity. A number of sketches, by Böhm, Hoechle, Weidner and Lyser, of Beethoven out walking (plates 11–16), also date from around this time. Their spontaneous character depicts the stocky figure, stalking with his coat collar turned up, either wielding a walking stick or clasping his hands determinedly behind his back. Gerhard von Breuning wrote that Beethoven was a conspicuous figure outdoors, 'usually lost in thought and humming to himself, he often gesticulated with his arms when walking by himself'. (Landon, 1974, p. 170) It is well known that he was never without a pocket sketchbook and would stop to record ideas as they came to him.

One of the last portraits was by the renowned artist Waldmüller in 1823 (plate 17). Here Beethoven is grim-faced, the brightness has gone from his eyes, his hair is completely grey; years of illness have taken a visible toll. The two drawings Teltscher made of Beethoven on his deathbed, depicting his swollen body and pain-wracked, sunken face, seem like intrusions of privacy (plates 18 and 19). In contrast the sketch of him in death by Danhauser is somewhat detached and idealized (plate 20), but his death mask is perhaps one of the saddest and most pathetic memorials.

Character and behaviour

BEETHOVEN'S CHARACTER AND PERSONALITY were a mass of contradictions. A certain immaturity deprived him of tact and too often countered his basic kindheartedness, and his good intentions were frequently belied by his uncontrollable temper. Throughout his life his mood would vacillate wildly; he could be extremely kind, then suddenly hard and cold; morose and then high-spirited, his immaturity allowing him to indulge in a childish sense of humour; argumentative then conciliatory. On consecutive days he wrote letters to Hummel: 'Don't come to me anymore! You are a false dog and may the hangman do away with all false dogs'; followed by 'Dear little Ignaz of my Heart! You are an honest fellow and I now realize that you were right.... Kisses from your Beethoven, also called dumpling.' (Letters 33 and 34)

As a young man Beethoven was frank to the point of rudeness. Headstrong and proud, he was never willing to conform in his behaviour if it did not suit him. As Ries wrote, 'Beethoven was a stranger to the rules of etiquette and all that they imply; he never concerned himself about such things.' (Wegeler, 1987, p. 99) The claim has been made that after a quarrel in 1806 Beethoven wrote to Prince Lichnowsky: 'Prince, what you are, you are by an accident of birth; what I am, I am through my own efforts. There have been thousands of princes and there will be thousands more; there is only one Beethoven!' (Kerst, 1964, p. 73) It is not difficult to reconcile this with other accounts of Beethoven's pride. It was another facet of this characteristic which led him to adopt a high-minded, moralizing attitude. This was often expressed in his dealings regarding his sister-in-law Johanna and his nephew Karl, and is also apparent in his stormy relationships with his patrons.

As he grew older and deafness overtook him, the negative aspects of Beethoven's character came to the fore. He was increasingly given to bouts of despair, the difficulties of communication made him more reserved, and he became more suspicious and distrustful of others. It is impossible to overestimate the devastating effect his disability must have had not only on Beethoven the musician, but also on the man, who valued companionship and the opportunity to exchange ideas. It is hardly surprising that he became progressively dependent on correspondence and grew depressed if he did not receive letters for several days.

That Beethoven presents a contradictory figure is reflected in the impression formed by those who met him. Varnhagen, who met Beethoven in Teplitz in 1811, wrote of him in a letter: 'I made the acquaintance of Beethoven and found this reputedly savage and unsociable man to be the most magnificent artist with a heart of gold, a glorious spirit and a friendly disposition.' (Landon, 1974, p. 142) Goethe, on the other hand, described him as 'an utterly untamed personality'. But Ries, who knew Beethoven well and over a long period of time, gives a balanced view. He refers to his kindness to those in need, his temper and irritability, and the haste with which he was given to suspicion even of his closest friends.

Beethoven's behaviour was as erratic as his complex personality would lead one to expect. He rarely stayed in one abode for long (see 'Residences and travel', pp. 123–9); domestic comforts were apparently unimportant to him and he lived in a state of disorderliness which shocked many observers; he was unable to exercise control over his household affairs; and he became increasingly negligent over his dress. But the disorder was only outward, and he in fact maintained an essentially disciplined routine, as will be discussed below.

The Baron de Trémont's description of his visit to Beethoven in 1809 runs as follows: 'Picture to yourself the dirtiest, most disorderly place imaginable – blotches of moisture covered the ceiling, an oldish grand piano, on which dust disputed the place with various pieces of engraved and manuscript music; under the piano (I do not exaggerate) an unemptied pot de nuit; ... the chairs, mostly cane-seated, were covered with plates bearing the remains of last night's supper and with wearing apparel etc.' (Sonneck, 1967, p. 70) Ignaz von Seyfried and Bettine von Arnim furnish similar descriptions.

Beethoven was persistently beset by domestic problems regarding servants (see 'Personal environment', p. 151). Not only was he unduly suspicious that all were out to cheat him in some way, but he was also inordinately fussy in certain respects. For example, according to Seyfried, he would himself break and examine eggs, and if any were found to be less than fresh would not hesitate to throw them at his housekeeper. Schindler gave an insight into these problems when he reproduced notes Beethoven had made in 1819 and 1820 relating to household matters. One is struck by the regularity with which domestic staff either left of their own accord or were given notice.

Beethoven's negligence regarding dress bordered on eccentricity. Count von Keglevics, nephew of Beethoven's pupil Barbara, wrote: 'He had the whim – one of many – since he lived across from her, of coming to give her lessons clad in a dressing gown, slippers and a peaked nightcap.' (Landon, 1974, p. 62) Writing of a later time, the composer Schlösser recalled having remarked to Mayseder of his surprise at having seen Beethoven unusually elegantly dressed, only to be told that it was not uncommon for his friends to replace his old clothes with new ones overnight. Beethoven would apparently dress the next day completely unaware of the exchange.

Paradoxically he had an almost obsessional attitude towards washing. This ritual would be the cue for him to sing (or howl) at the top of his voice, much to the amusement of his servants or passers-by who were in a position to overlook his apartment. Whether this denoted a particular concern for his personal hygiene, or was essential to his thought processes, is open to question. What is certain is that the overflow from the buckets of water he emptied over himself often leaked through the floor, causing Beethoven to be unpopular with landlords.

As Beethoven grew older there are fewer accounts depicting him as the practical joker of his youth. Burdened by years of ill-health and the problems relating to his nephew, he was seen as an increasingly eccentric figure. Inwardly he became more distrustful and obsessively convinced that he was in a bad pecuniary state, and outwardly his appearance grew more neglected as his hair was allowed to grow unrestrained and he became more bad-tempered.

Personal relationships

THE CONTRADICTIONS IN BEETHOVEN'S CHARACTER and behaviour noted in the previous section are reflected in his personal relationships. Rarely was he able to sustain a friendship; most were marred either by trivial misunderstandings or by bitter quarrels.

Beethoven had a series of close friendships with men of his own age, and he also enjoyed the company of younger men, most notably FERDINAND RIES near the beginning of his career and KARL HOLZ at the end. Into the first category fall STEPHAN VON BREUNING, WEGELER, AMENDA and GLEICHENSTEIN. His friendships with Wegeler and Amenda remained undiminished, probably because both left Vienna early on and the friendships were continued by letter. Beethoven's reaction to a violent quarrel with Breuning in 1806 was totally out of proportion to the quarrel itself, and the subsequent break in friendship was healed only by the generous behaviour of Breuning. This was only one of many incidents when Beethoven's friends overlooked his shortcomings. Whatever his faults, he certainly engendered a sense of loyalty born out of recognition of his genius.

Beethoven was on friendly terms with a number of people whom he evidently did not regard as true friends (see 'Personal environment', pp. 150–51). He wrote of ZMESKALL and SCHUPPANZIGH in 1801 that he regarded them 'merely as instruments on which to play when I feel inclined .... I value them merely for what they can do for me.' (Letter 53) To this group, so cynically described, doubtless belong some of his patrons and SCHINDLER. Something deeper, however, existed between Beethoven and two of his patrons: PRINCE LICHNOWSKY and ARCHDUKE RUDOLPH. The intensity of the relationship with Lichnowsky could not be sustained, but he seems to have had real respect for Rudolph throughout his life (Kagan, 1988).

At least in the early years, Beethoven was attracted to women both as genuine friends and as objects of love. Wegeler recorded that 'Beethoven was never out of love and was normally involved to a high degree'; and Ries that he 'very much enjoyed looking at women; he was very frequently in love, but usually only for a short time' (Wegeler, 1987, pp. 42, 104). But in spite of this he did not marry, and appears never to have had an intimate relationship with a woman. In fact his attitude towards love and marriage was ambivalent, and it can be no coincidence that his female friends were usually of a higher social position and invariably attached to someone else, making marriage out of the question. By putting them beyond his reach he could reconcile the idea of love and marriage with the need to devote his emotional energy to music.

In 1801 Beethoven wrote of 'a dear, charming girl who loves me and whom I love.... and for the first time I feel that marriage might bring me happiness.' (Letter 54) It is perhaps significant that he immediately qualified this by saying that she was not of his class, and besides which, he was very busy. In late 1804 he deepened his friendship with JOSEPHINE DEYM (*née* Brunsvik). Although it developed into love on his part, he quickly agreed to a platonic relationship when it became clear that he had misinterpreted her feelings for him.

Apart from a very early proposal to the singer MAGDALENA WILLMANN, Beethoven mentioned marriage only in connection with GIULIETTA GUICCIARDI and THERESE MALFATTI, both unattainable. But after his death a love letter of 1812 addressed to 'my Angel' and 'my Immortal Beloved' was found amongst his papers. It is a passionate outpouring to a woman who evidently returned his love unequivocally (Letter 373; see plate 30). Her identity is open to question; it was probably ANTONIE BRENTANO (Solomon, 1977), although Josephine is a possibility (Gold schmidt, 1977). The letter was written in three instalments over two days, and appears to be in response to the woman's desire for total commitment. In the first part Beethoven expresses his deep love but is unable to give that commitment; in the second his resistance to the idea of union is lowered. But the final section, written the following morning, is more restrained. He renounces the opportunity, not only for the present, but for ever. The love is not diminished. He still needs her love, but he is forced to acknowledge that he cannot marry. The letter probably remained undelivered, and it is likely that the resolution of his thoughts here were as much for himself as for the intended recipient. There is evidence that the strong emotions aroused remained for some time. According to Fanny Giannatasio he told her father in 1816 that 'Five years ago he had made the acquaintance of a person, a union with whom he would have considered the greatest happiness of his life. It was not to be thought of, almost an impossibility, a chimera – "nevertheless it is now as on the first day".' (Thayer, 1967, p. 646)

The only woman who figured in Beethoven's life in a positive way after he adopted Karl in 1815 was NANETTE STREICHER. He seemed to look on her as something of a mother figure, and consulted her repeatedly for advice on housekeeping matters. From this time his relationship with his nephew became his sole emotional outlet, perhaps even a substitute for marriage, and his hostile feelings towards his sister-in-law Johanna influenced his feelings about women in general.

It is in his relationships with members of his family that Beethoven's lack of insight is most apparent; and it is here too that his inner conflicts led him to cause the most distress both to them and to himself. He took responsibility for his brothers CARL and JOHANN as boys, and this continued until they were established in Vienna. It is widely believed that he did not get on well with them and that they bore bad intentions towards him; there are even two accounts of violence. But a pattern of violent quarrels followed by passionate reconciliations was very much in line with Beethoven's other relationships (here it was probably intensified by family ties), and on balance the evidence suggests he was genuinely attached to his brothers, particularly Carl; he certainly involved them in his affairs.

Beethoven bitterly opposed Carl's marriage to JOHANNA REISS in 1806. In appointing Beethoven and Johanna joint guardians of his son KARL before he died, Carl expressed the wish that they should act 'harmoniously'. This was not to be fulfilled. Beethoven at once sought sole guardianship and entered four and a half years of legal wrangling to prove that he was the more suitable 'parent'. Johanna was subjected to separation from her son and public denigration of her character, penalties out of all proportion to her wrongdoings. That Beethoven could inflict so much suffering and yet remain convinced that he was right cannot be sufficiently explained either by his lack of regard for other people's feelings or by his own conviction that his actions were dictated by duty. The degree of obsession he displayed suggests he was motivated by a more powerful, probably subconscious, force. One possibility is that he believed he could channel into a close relationship with Karl all the pent-up emotions he had expressed in the letter to the 'Immortal Beloved'. He may have seen in Karl the son that he never had; and if he were to assume the role of a father he could not tolerate Johanna's presence. Or his actions could have been prompted by unacknowledged ambivalent feelings towards Johanna.

Beethoven's relationship with Johann was less close than that with Carl. The two had less in common and Beethoven mocked his brother's pretentiousness. When Johann announced himself 'Landowner', Beethoven is said to have signed himself 'Brain-owner' in reply. When news reached Beethoven in 1812 that Johann was having an affair with someone unsuitable, Therese Obermayer, he went to Linz to put an end to it. He went so far as to apply to church, civil authorities and the police, but Johann thwarted him by marrying Therese. This behaviour occurred soon after the emotional turmoil of his letter to the 'Immortal Beloved': in the face of that disappointment, was Beethoven uncontrollably jealous of his brother's happiness? By 1822 the old intimacy was renewed. He wrote: 'Peace, let us have peace. God grant that the most natural bond, the bond between brothers, may not again be broken in any unnatural way' (Letter 1078); soon Johann was helping him in business matters and lending him money.

As for nephew Karl, Beethoven apparently treated him very inconsistently, alternately over-indulging him and punishing him, and showing no understanding of the boy's emotional needs. Beethoven was overjoyed at 'rescuing' his nephew and becoming 'a father'. In his correspondence he wrote of his 'great effort to save my nephew from his depraved mother', and that 'I am now the real and true father [lit. true bodily father] of my deceased brother's child' (Letters 633, 654).

Possession of Karl did not guarantee his affection; the boy continued to love his mother in spite of the criticisms of her. Beethoven temporarily lost the guardianship in 1819 and this brought to the surface his conflicting feelings about Karl: disappointment and rejection, and deep love, expressed by his denial of it. He called him 'callous and ungrateful' and contemplated returning a letter which he claimed was 'without the slightest indication of any affection or sympathy'. He wrote remarks such as: 'My love for him is gone – He needed my love. I do not need his', and 'as long as I live he shall never see me again, for he is a monster' (Letters 956, 960). But ultimately he transferred the blame: 'All this confusion has made him stray from the right path and I even suspect that his mother may have made him swear to show me no marks of affection and love.' (Letter 967)

Following the resolution of the litigation the relationship stabilized until Karl left school in 1823. He had already been undertaking secretarial duties; now he was also entrusted with financial transactions and given responsibility for housekeeping arrangements. This was time-consuming; but the emotional demands on him were even more of a burden. Beethoven's love was tempered by possessiveness and jealousy which made him over-strict and suspicious. He sought to limit Karl's freedom in every way possible, and not surprisingly bitter quarrels occurred.

During 1825 Beethoven spent several months in Baden while Karl remained in Vienna, but he did his best to maintain his hold over his nephew by writing frequently, demanding visits and even asking his friends to report on Karl's movements. In the thirty-eight letters from this period there are many requests to run errands and an abundance of advice on such matters as money, clothes, early rising and the importance of hard work. But it was the assault on Karl's feelings which must have been more difficult to bear: endless criticisms and accusations, attempts to make him feel guilty, and expressions of great affection conflicting with harsh rejection. All the letters were addressed to the 'Son' and signed by the 'Father', as if in a desperate attempt to believe in the relationship.

Karl remained in lodgings, and during 1826 he no longer visited Beethoven as often as before. From the Conversation Books it is clear that he could no longer withstand the perpetual arguments. Here was the clearest example of Beethoven's inability to comprehend another person's feelings: he continued to exert such pressure that finally Karl felt that his only means of escape was to attempt suicide. The attempt failed. Karl said afterwards that he was 'tired of life', 'weary of imprisonment', and that Beethoven had tortured him too much; but he now found the strength to stand up to him. Beethoven himself was devastated, his illusion of a father-and-son relationship shattered. Although they remained on good terms, it was a blow from which he never recovered.

Financial affairs

THE COMPLICATED ECONOMIC SITUATION in Vienna against which Beethoven's financial affairs must be assessed is described under 'Economics' (pp. 68–70). Also of interest is his often inaccurate perception of his position: as the years passed he believed himself to be increasingly badly off, even though he received a generous annuity; and he was invariably suspicious that he was being cheated. His expenses were always high but were not reflected in his lifestyle; as Ries wrote: 'Beethoven needed a good deal of money, even though he enjoyed very little benefit from it for he lived modestly' (Wegeler, 1987, p. 100).

Beethoven was brought up in modest but not the 'very straitened circumstances' to which Wegeler referred. In 1789, with his father unable to support the family, Beethoven took over as head of the household, receiving half his father's salary in addition to his own, and assuming responsibility for his two brothers. This arrangement continued when Beethoven moved to Vienna at the end of 1792. By March 1794, when the salary from Bonn ceased, he would have had a reasonable income from teaching, performing and publications. After 1795 his brothers were no longer dependent on him, and by 1796 he was able to employ a servant.

In 1800 Beethoven began to receive an annuity of 600 fl. from Prince Lichnowsky (which continued until 1806) and he gained considerably from his first benefit concert. The year 1801 saw the publication of several major works (see 'Calendar of Beethoven's Life, Works and Related Events', p. 16). The income from these would have been substantial: he was asking 20 ducats (90 fl.) for a symphony or sonata (Letter 44). He wrote to Wegeler: 'My compositions bring me in a good deal.... People no longer come to an arrangement with me. I state my price and they pay.' (Letter 51) Given that his brother Carl's civil service salary was 250 fl. p.a., his financial success becomes apparent.

By 1803 Beethoven's financial position had improved further. At a time when the average yearly salary was under 1000 fl. he reaped profits of 1800 fl. from a benefit concert, and could expect 30 ducats for a major work (Letter 89), a sum reflecting his growing prestige as a composer. He enjoyed being in a position to be generous; he wrote to Ries: 'Not one of my friends is to be short of money as long as I have some' (Letter 71).

Plates 1–21

THE PORTRAITS

1   Joseph Willibrord Mähler, first of four portraits of Beethoven, oil painting, 1804 or 1805

3   Christian Horneman,
miniature on ivory, 1803

2   Johann Neidl, engraving, published Vienna,
c. 1801, from a drawing by Gandolph Stainhauser

4   Isidor Neugass,
oil painting, c. 1806

5 Franz Klein, bronze bust, modelled
from the mask of 1812

6 Blasius Höfel, engraving from a pencil drawing
by Louis Letronne, 1814

7 Joseph Willibrord Mähler,
oil painting, 1815

8 Johann Christoph Heckel,
oil painting, 1815

9 Ferdinand Schimon,
oil painting, 1818 or 1819

10   Joseph Carl Stieler, oil painting, 1819–20

11, 12   Joseph Daniel Böhm, two drawings, made as studies
for engraved silver plates, *c*. 1819–20

13   Johann Nepomuk Hoechle,
water-coloured pen and ink drawing, *c*. 1823

14   Joseph Weidner,
water-coloured pencil drawing, *c*. 1820?

15 Johann Peter Theodor Lyser,
pencil drawing, *c.* 1823

1υ Johann Peter Theodor Lyser, drawing,
published in the periodical, *Caecilia*, Hamburg, 1833

17 Ferdinand Waldmüller,
oil painting, 1823

18, 19 Joseph Eduard Teltscher,
Beethoven in a coma, two drawings, 1827

20 Joseph Danhauser, Beethoven on his
deathbed, lithograph from his own
drawing, 1827

21 Memorial statue of Beethoven, Bonn,
1845

In 1807 he sold the English publishing rights for six new works, opp. 58–62, to Clementi for £200. He also obtained 1600 fl. from the Bureau des Arts et d'Industrie for the Viennese rights, and the Fourth Symphony brought him a further 500 fl. from Count Oppersdorff, who had commissioned it.

In 1808 Beethoven was invited to become Kapellmeister at Kassel for a salary of 600 ducats. The indirect result was an annuity of 4000 fl. from three patrons (see 'Beethoven's patrons and commissions', p. 95). Although he was also receiving substantial fees from Breitkopf & Härtel, Beethoven began to complain of being short of money, probably on account of the rapidly rising inflation.

In 1811 the devaluation of the banknote florin to $\frac{1}{5}$ the notional value of a silver florin (these had been withdrawn in 1809), and the decree that all contracts be considered as having been made in banknotes, meant that Beethoven's annuity was drastically reduced. Although compensation was made for inflation between 1809 and 1811 (see 'Economics', pp. 68–9), the new figure of 1612.9 fl. (WW) was considerably less than his three benefactors had intended. Archduke Rudolph agreed immediately to make up the difference, but Prince Lobkowitz was unable to make any payments for four years; Prince Kinsky intended his share to be paid in full, but he died in 1812, and it was not until 1815 that his heirs agreed to resume payments.

Throughout 1813 Beethoven complained repeatedly about his financial situation. Although he received a proportion of his annuity, the long delayed £200 from Clementi, over 250 ducats from Thomson (1811–13) and a number of payments from Breitkopf & Härtel, he found himself without ready funds, and equated this with genuine poverty. An initial loan of 1100 fl. from Franz Brentano increased to over 2000 fl., and in order to help his brother Carl he had to secure a loan of 1500 fl. from the publisher Steiner.

Beethoven's finances improved drastically in 1814. At the end of 1813 his *Wellingtons Sieg* (op. 91) had been performed twice. Its great popularity enabled him to repeat it for his own benefit on 2 January, and he gave a further concert in February. During the Congress of Vienna, Beethoven was acclaimed as never before and received appropriate financial rewards, including 4000 florins which he deposited with Steiner in 1816, collecting interest at 8%; in 1819 he invested it in eight bank shares as a legacy for his nephew.

The improvement continued in 1815 when all aspects of the annuity were resolved: a large sum of arrears (nearly 5000 fl.) was received, and henceforward he was paid 3400 fl. WW per year. Nevertheless Beethoven soon began to complain of financial problems. He wrote to Ries: 'I have just lost 600 gulden a year from my salary...and had to face hardship for several years as well as complete loss of my salary....My poor unfortunate brother has just died...I must have given him 10,000 gulden', and the following year, 'My income amounts to 3400 gulden in paper money. I pay 1100 for rent, and my servant and his wife cost me about 900 gulden. Moreover I have to support my little nephew entirely. Until now he has been at boarding school. That costs up to 1100 gulden...' (Letters 572, 632). Beethoven was convinced of the truth of what he said; yet he had never been entirely without his annuity, the money he had given his brother had accumulated over a number of years, and he was not compelled to support Karl alone.

During the next few years the litigation over Karl's guardianship was a considerable drain on his resources, his income declined through lack of productivity, and debts built up. By 1820 he owed 2420 fl. to Steiner, which he arranged to repay in instalments over two years, and 750 fl. to Artaria. Desperately worried about his financial position, he entered into a series of negotiations to sell the *Missa Solemnis* in which his conduct was extremely questionable.

In 1820 he agreed to sell it to Simrock for 900 fl. CM, the money to be deposited with Brentano until the work was completed. Beethoven repeatedly assured both Simrock and Brentano that completion was imminent, and on this understanding persuaded the latter to forward him the money. Even when he wrote, 'The Mass will be with you at the end of next month at the latest' (Letter 1076), he was secretly negotiating with other publishers, including Peters and Artaria.

By 1822 Beethoven's failure to deliver was finding him in trouble from all quarters. He wrote to Simrock that he could have the work at once if he were prepared to pay a further 100 fl.; and to Brentano to reassure him that his debt would soon be discharged. In November he attempted to extricate himself by claiming to Peters that he was writing two masses, only one of which was finished, and that he was undecided which one Peters was to receive. The following February he referred to no fewer than three masses.

Meanwhile he tried to placate Simrock with offers of other works and yet another promise of a mass. But Beethoven was in no hurry for publication because he was busy inviting heads of state to subscribe to manuscript copies of the work at 50 ducats each. This proved a time-consuming exercise, but it realized about 1600 fl. CM. He continued to negotiate with more publishers, but had no further dealings with Simrock. In 1825 he sold both the Mass and the Ninth Symphony to Schott's for 1000 and 600 fl. CM respectively.

Early in 1823 Beethoven's financial problems became so serious that he was forced to sell one of his bank shares. From now on his correspondence is dominated by references to money. He wrote to Franz Stockhausen: 'For my income in Vienna is without substance', and to Schott's: 'Yet I cannot live on my income' (Letters 1321, 1503). There was some justification for his complaints. Although he had entered a period of staggering creativity he did not reap immediate benefits. In 1823 Prince Galitzin commissioned three string quartets for 50 ducats each, but works of the complexity of the *Missa Solemnis*, the Ninth Symphony and the late quartets could not be composed quickly; furthermore, a benefit concert in 1824 proved a major disappointment when the profits yielded only 420 fl.

By the end of 1826 Beethoven was seriously ill and unable to do much work. In 1827, in response to a letter to Sir George Smart revealing that 'my income is so meagre that with it I can hardly meet the half-yearly rent of my rooms' (Letter 1555), the Philharmonic Society of London sent him a gift of £100 (1000 fl. CM). He died convinced that he was poverty-stricken, and in conditions which reflected such a state. After the realization of his bank shares, the sale of his effects, and the collection of outstanding subsidies, he was found to have left 9885 fl. 13 kr. CM and 600 fl. WW, but his liquid assets at the time of his death were extremely low.

Seyfried described Beethoven as having little understanding of money, but generous. He observed that 'only during his last years did he show signs of a worried thriftiness, without, however, ever allowing it to interfere with his inborn propensity for doing good' (Sonneck, 1967, p. 46). This is evidenced by the fact that in 1823, when he was least able to, Beethoven offered financial help to his sister-in-law Johanna.

It was one of Beethoven's tragedies that although he acquired a good deal of money, various factors, such as the financial climate of the day and his innate carelessness, meant that he had very little to show for it; and his inability to see his position realistically led him to believe that he was worse off than he in fact was, and to suffer accordingly.

Residences and travel

Bonn

BEETHOVEN WAS BORN IN LODGINGS in no. 515 Bonngasse (now no. 20, the Beethovenhaus). By 1774 the family had moved to Dreieckplatz. Two years later they were living in rooms in the Fischerhaus (named after its owner) in Rheingasse. They were to spend three periods there in all, and this was the place where Beethoven essentially grew up and felt most at home. He enjoyed the views it afforded, over the Rhine in one direction and towards the Seven Mountains in another, and he was accepted as part of the Fischer household. In 1776 and 1785 the family spent brief periods at Neugasse and Wenzelgasse. In 1787 they left the Fischerhaus for the last time and returned to Wenzelgasse. Beethoven lived there until he finally left Bonn in 1792, but spent much of his time in the home of the Von Breuning family.

Beethoven travelled little while he was in Bonn. In 1783 he accompanied his mother to Holland; and in the spring of 1787 he made his first visit to Vienna, regrettably aborted by the death of his mother. A happy interlude occurred in 1791 when Elector Maximilian Franz, in his capacity of Grand Master of the Teutonic Order, took up residence in his palace at Mergentheim for a few months. He took his orchestra with him, and Beethoven enjoyed both the journey along the Rivers Rhine and Main and the brief stop at Aschaffenburg, where he met the pianist Sterkel.

Vienna

The list of Beethoven's addresses in Vienna (see below and Smolle, 1970) runs to at least thirty, excluding the many lodgings he rented during the summer months either in rural villages on the outskirts of the city or slightly further afield. In forty-three years he moved more than seventy times. Seyfried wrote: 'One of Beethoven's curious manias was his passion for changing his lodgings; although moving with all his possessions always greatly incommoded him, and was always accompanied by a loss of belongings. No sooner had he taken possession of a new dwelling place than he would find something objectionable about it, and would then run his feet sore trying to discover another.' (Sonneck, 1967, p. 45) Although Beethoven lived in a state of disorder he was surprisingly fussy about his lodgings. He preferred them to face south with a good view, and did not like to be overheard. He complained constantly to landlords regarding deficiencies and frequently entered into altercations with neighbouring tenants, seemingly oblivious to his own shortcomings.

Beethoven began life in Vienna in November 1792 in an attic flat in the Alsergrund district. After only a couple of months he moved to a ground floor flat in the same house, and a year and a half later he was living on the first floor as a guest of Prince Lichnowsky, who had his city residence there. Within six or seven months he had moved again; thus the pattern for his nomadic life-style, spurning the comforts of domesticity, was established.

The place for which Beethoven seems to have had most affection was a fourth floor flat in a house belonging to Baron Pasqualati in Mölkerbastei, near the city walls. (It was originally found for him by Ries, and afforded an excellent view.) He first moved there in autumn 1804 and finally left in spring 1815. During this period, however, there were two breaks in his tenancy: from autumn 1808 to the end of 1810, and from February to June 1814. Whilst renting this apartment he frequently lived elsewhere. For example, during the period 1804–8 he had an official residence within the Theater an der Wien for a year, he had no fewer than six stays outside the city, and also spent a few months as the guest of Countess Erdödy in her city apartments.

Stories regarding Beethoven renting two or even three lodgings simultaneously arise from the fact that he would invariably retain his city flat while he was absent during the summer, and on at least two occasions, the winters of 1816–17 and 1819–20, he also took up temporary accommodation elsewhere. On the first occasion it was an inn ('Zum römischen Kaiser'), so it can probably be concluded that this was for comfort and convenience. So frequent were his changes of address that from 1820 Beethoven told correspondents that it would be sufficient to address his mail: 'Ludwig van Beethoven, Vienna', and to Adolf Schlesinger in Berlin he wrote: 'The only address you need put is: 'To Ludwig van Beethoven'! (Letter 1060)

Ironically, Beethoven's last lodgings, in the now famous Schwarzspanierhaus, were in the district in which he had first lived. On 17 October 1825 he wrote to his nephew Karl that he had arrived there from Baden 'vorgestern Abend wie ein Schiffbrüchiger' ('the evening of the day before yesterday like a shipwrecked mariner'). In retrospect there was surely something prophetic in this remark.

Holidays and concert tours

In common with most Viennese, Beethoven adopted the habit of moving out of the city during the summer months. The villages of Unterdöbling, Oberdöbling, Hetzendorf, Mödling, Heiligenstadt, Nussdorf and Penzing have long since been engulfed by the expanding city, but at that time they were charming rural spots where Beethoven could indulge his passion for long country walks. These periods were not holidays in the accepted sense of the word, for it was often at these times, when he felt most at peace, that he was at his most productive as a composer.

Beethoven often went farther afield, usually to Baden, just outside Vienna. There he was able to improve his health by taking the waters. In the summers of 1811 and 1812 he made more extensive trips to visit the spas of Teplitz and Karlsbad in Bohemia. In 1793 Haydn had taken Beethoven to Prince Esterházy's summer residence in Eisenstadt, and he went there again in 1807. He was a fairly frequent visitor to Prince Lichnowsky's palace at Grätz near Troppau, and would occasionally be the guest of the Brunsvik family in Hungary. In 1812 he visited his brother Johann in Linz, and shortly before his death he spent two months at Gneixendorf, near Krems, on the estate which his brother had bought in Lower Austria.

It was not uncommon in the 18th and 19th centuries for notable musicians to travel extensively. Beethoven, however, made only three concert tours, although until quite shortly before his death he frequently talked of possible journeys, particularly to England. In the early part of 1796 he went with Prince Lichnowsky to Prague, and from there went on to Berlin by way of Dresden and Leipzig. Later in the year he visited Pressburg (now Bratislava) and Pest (now Budapest). In 1798 he made another trip to Prague. It is most probable that his increasing deafness from 1801 onwards and his consequent withdrawal from performing deterred him from further journeys.

Addresses in and around Vienna

Nov. 1792–Dec. 1792/Jan. 1793	Attic flat, 45 Alstergasse, Alsergrund (now 30 Alserstrasse)
Dec. 1792/Jan. 1793–late summer 1794	Ground floor flat in same house
Summer 1794–May 1795	1st floor flat in same house
May 1795–Feb. 1796	1st floor, Ogylyisches Haus, 35 Kreuzgasse (now 6 Löwelstrasse)
Feb.–Jul. 1796	Absent from Vienna
Jul. 1796–May 1799	Address(es) unknown
May 1799–Dec. 1799/Jan. 1800	3rd floor, 650 St Petersplatz (now 11 Petersplatz)
Summer 1799	Mödling: address unknown
Jan. 1800–spring 1801	3rd floor, Greinersches Haus, 241 Tiefer Graben (now no. 10)
Apr.–Jun. 1800	Absent from Vienna (visiting Pest)
Summer 1800	Unterdöbling: address unknown
Spring 1801–May 1802	Hambergsches Haus, 1275 Wasserkunstbastei (now on site of 15 Seilerstätte)
Summer 1801	Hetzendorf: address unknown
May–Oct. 1802	Heiligenstadt: 13 Herrengasse (now 6 Probusgasse)
Oct. 1802–Apr. 1803	2nd or 3rd floor flat, 'Zum silbernen Vogel', 649 St Petersplatz (now 11 Petersplatz); also temporary stays with Countess Erdödy at 58 Augasse, Jedelsee (now 17 Jeneweingasse)
Apr. 1803–beg. 1804	Theater an der Wien, 26 An der Wien, Laimgrube (now 6 Linke Wienzeile)
Summer 1803	Baden: address unknown
	Oberdöbling: 4 Hofzeile (now 92 Döblinger Hauptstrasse)
May–Jun. 1804	Rothes Haus, 173 Alservorstädter Glacis, Alsergrund (now between Garnisongasse, Frankgasse and Rotenhausgasse), at first in a single flat then with Stephan von Breuning

Jul. 1804	Baden: address unknown
Aug.–Sep. 1804	Oberdöbling: possibly 4 Hofzeile (as 1803)
Oct. 1804–summer 1808	4th floor flat, Pasqualatihaus, 1239 Mölkerbastei (now no. 8)
End 1804–autumn 1805	Theater an der Wien
Summer 1805	Hetzendorf: address unknown
Summer 1806	To Hungary
Sep.–Oct. 1806	To Grätz
Early summer 1807	Baden: Johanneshof (now Johannesgasse)
Late summer 1807	Heiligenstadt: address unknown
Sep. 1807	To Eisenstadt
Winter 1807–8	Possibly guest of Countess Erdödy at 1074 Krugerstrasse (now no. 10); kept lodgings at Pasqualatihaus
Summer 1808	Heiligenstadt: 8 Kirchengasse (now 64 Grinzingerstrasse)
Autumn 1808	Baden: 'Alter Sauerhof' (now Weilburgstrasse)
Autumn 1808–early 1809	1074 Krugerstrasse (Countess Erdödy)
Early 1809(?)	Brief return to Pasqualatihaus
Early 1809–Jul.	2nd floor, 1087 Walfischgasse (probably now on site of 11 Walfischgasse and 22a Akademiestrasse)
Summer 1809	To Hungary
	Baden: 'Alter Sauerhof'
Aug. 1809–early 1810	3rd floor, 82 Klepperstall (now on site of 1 Schreyvogelgasse)
Early 1810–Feb./Mar. 1814	Return to Pasqualatihaus
Summer 1810	Baden: Johanneshof(?)
Summer 1811	To Teplitz and Grätz
Summer 1812	Baden: 'Alter Sauerhof'
Jul.–Nov. 1812	To Teplitz, Karlsbad, Franzensbrunn and Linz
May–Sep. 1813	Baden: 'Alter Sauerhof'
Feb.–Jun. 1814	1st floor, Bartensteinsches Haus, 94 Mölkerbastei (now no. 10)

Jun.–Sep. 1814	Baden: Johanneshof(?)
Sep.–Oct. 1814	Address unknown
Nov. 1814–spring 1815	Last return to Pasqualatihaus
Spring 1815–Apr. 1817	3rd floor, Gräfl. Lambertisches Haus, 1055–6 Auf der Seilerstadt (now site of 21 Seilerstätte)
Summer 1815	Baden: Johanneshof(?)
Autumn 1815	Unterdöbling: 33–4 An der Steige (now 4 Silbergasse and 2 Nusswaldgasse)
Jul.–Oct. 1816	Baden: Ossolynskisches Schloss, 9 Alandgasse (now 26 Braitnerstrasse)
Winter 1816–17	Temporarily in guesthouse 'Zum römischen Kaiser', 145 Renngasse (now no. 1)
Apr.–Oct. 1817	2nd floor, Haus zum grünen Kranz, 268 Landstrasse (now 26 Landstrasser Hauptstrasse)
Early summer 1817	Heiligenstadt: Schlöglisches Haus, 66 Am Platz (now 2 Pfarrplatz)
Jul.–Aug. 1817	Nussdorf: Greinischeres Haus (now 26 Kahlenbergerstrasse)
Oct. 1817–Apr. 1818	Either Haus zum grünen Kranz; or Haus zum grünen Baum, 26 Gärtnergasse, Landstrasse (now site of 5 Gärtnergasse)
Apr. 1818–May 1819	Haus zum grünen Baum
May–Sep. 1818 *May–Oct. 1819* }	Mödling: Hafner-Haus, 76 Herrengasse (now 79 Hauptstrasse)
Oct. 1819–May 1820	3rd floor, Fingerlingsches Haus, 6 Schwibbogengasse, Josefstadt Glacis (now 3 Auerspergstrasse)
Winter 1819–20	Temporarily at 'Zum alten Blumenstock', 986 Ballgasse (now no. 6)
Summer 1820	Mödling: 'Christhof', 116 Aschenaugasse (now no. 6)
Before 26 Oct. 1820	'Zu den zwei Wachsstocken', 8 Kaiserstrasse, Altlerchenfeld (now 57 Josefstädterstrasse)

Winter 1820–21	Either 391 Ungargasse, Landstrasse; or 2nd floor, Grosses Haus der Augustiner, 244 Landstrasse (now 60 Hauptstrasse)
(?)1821–Aug. 1822	Grosses Haus der Augustiner
Jun.–Sep. 1821	Unterdöbling: 11 An der Winterzeil (now 9 Silbergasse)
Sep.–Oct. 1821	Baden: 94 Rathausgasse (now no. 10)
May–Jun. 1822	Oberdöbling: 135 Alleegasse (now 13 Pyrkegasse)
Jul.–Aug. 1822	(?) Grosses Haus der Augustiner
Sep. 1822	Baden: 'Zum goldenen Schwan', 23 Weinergasse (now 4 Antongasse)
Oct. 1822	Baden: Magdalenahof, 85 Frauengasse (now no. 10)
Nov. 1822–May 1823	1st floor, 60 Obere Pfarrgasse, Windmühle (now 22 Laimgrubengasse)
May–Aug. 1823	Hetzendorf: Villa Prónay, 32 Hetzendorfer Hauptstrasse (now 75a Hetzendorferstrasse)
Aug.–Oct. 1823	Baden: 94 Rathausgasse
Oct. 1823–May 1824	3rd floor, Haus 'zur schönen Sklavin', 323 Landstrasse (now 5 Ungargasse)
May 1824	Penzing: 'Hadikschlössel', 43 Parkstrasse (now 62 Hadikgasse)
May–Nov. 1824	Baden: 'Schloss Gutenbrunn' Hermitage (now Gutenbrunn Sanatorium, Peregrinstrasse)
Nov. 1824–Apr. 1825	4th floor, 969 Johannesgasse (now corner of no. 1 and Kärntnerstrasse)
Apr.–May 1825	1009 Krugerstrasse (now no. 13)
May–Oct. 1825	Baden: Schloss Gutenbrunn
Oct. 1825–death	2nd floor, Altes Schwarzspanierhaus, 200 am Glacis Alsergrund (now 15 Schwarzspanierstrasse)
Oct.–Nov. 1826	Gneixendorf

Daily routine and composing habits

BEETHOVEN'S CHAOTIC LIFESTYLE, as seen from the accommodation and housekeeping problems which beset him, the trouble he had managing his financial affairs, and his negligence as regards his appearance, did not impinge on his approach to his work. Although he worked amidst great untidiness and produced many rough and apparently illegible sketches, the disorder was only external, and he maintained a disciplined working routine.

While he was in Vienna, as opposed to his long summer sojourns away from the city, his daily routine varied little. Schindler (1966, pp. 385–6) wrote: 'Beethoven rose every morning the year round at dawn and went directly to his desk. There he would work until two or three o'clock, his habitual dinner hour. In the course of the morning he would usually go out of doors once or even twice, but would continue to work as he walked.... His afternoons were regularly spent in long walks. Late in the afternoon he would go to a favourite tavern to read the papers.... Beethoven always spent his winter evenings at home reading serious works of literature. Only very rarely did he work with musical scores during the evening for the strain on his eyes was too great.... He would go to bed at ten o'clock at the latest.'

Seyfried, who described Beethoven's working day in much the same way, recalled that the morning consisted of 'mechanical work, actual note-writing', which would certainly include the writing out of autographs, and the latter part of the day was 'dedicated to thought and to the arrangement of his ideas'. Much of the 'thinking' occurred while Beethoven was out walking: 'he would twice make the circuit of the city in double-quick time' (Sonneck, 1967, pp. 43–4). Those who saw him recall that on these occasions he would appear engrossed in thought and would stop every now and then to write in a notebook. According to Seyfried, Beethoven was rarely seen without a little notebook in which he jotted down ideas as they occurred to him. When this was mentioned 'he would parody the words of Joan of Arc: I dare not come without my banner!' When Beethoven spent an evening from home he enjoyed talking, eating and drinking with friends. Although it was not his habit to work in the evenings, exceptions would be made if he felt particularly inspired or if it was imperative that a composition be finished for a specific occasion.

During the summer months Beethoven would take lodgings in the countryside and spend much of his time outdoors. If time spent out walking helped his creativity while he was in the city, it was even more true in the country. As the years passed he looked forward increasingly to these periods of tranquillity when his deafness troubled him least and his productivity was at its richest. In 1818 the artist Kloeber wrote: 'I encountered Beethoven several times on my walks in Mödling, and it was most interesting to see him, a sheet of music paper and a stump of pencil in his hand, stop often as though listening, and then write a few notes on the paper' (Landon, 1974, p. 160), and in 1823 J.R. Schultz accompanied Beethoven on a walk and recorded afterwards: 'On our way to the valley he often stopped short and pointed out to me its most beautiful spots, or noticed the defects of the new buildings. At other times he seemed quite lost in himself, and only hummed in an unintelligible manner. I understood, however, that this was the way he composed...' (Sonneck, 1967, p. 152).

The jotting down and subsequent working out of his ideas in desk and pocket sketchbooks and on loose leaves were essential parts of Beethoven's compositional process. Something of a mystique surrounding the sketches has grown up, partly because of the importance Beethoven himself attached to them and partly due to the difficulties of deciphering them. He told Gerhard von Breuning: 'I always carry a notebook about me, and when an idea occurs to me, at once note it down. I even rise at night when something happens to occur to me, since otherwise I might forget the idea.' (Sonneck, 1967, p. 207) Tomášek visited Beethoven while he was working on the cantata *Der glorreiche Augenblick* and saw a single sheet containing 'a number of the most divergent ideas, jotted down without any connection, the most heterogeneous individual details elbowing each other, just as they might have come to his mind.' (Sonneck, 1967, pp. 100–01) Sir John Russell, writing in 1821, showed some understanding of the nature of the sketches: 'These notes would be absolutely unintelligible even to another musician, for they thus have no comparative value; he alone has in his mind the thread by which he brings out of the labyrinth of dots and circles the richest and most astounding harmonies.' (Russell, 1828, II, p. 274)

In some quarters the sketches have been interpreted as an indication that composition did not come easily to Beethoven. This view has been strengthened by contemporary accounts purporting to demonstrate this, the most well known being Schindler's over-inflated reference to 'a life and death struggle with the whole army of contrapunctists, his everlasting enemies' (Schindler, 1966, p. 229). In fact both the initial recording of ideas and the more detailed drafting are reflections of the wealth of Beethoven's inspiration. This is not to deny that they testify to the great effort that his compositions required, an effort without which works of such complexity and intensity could hardly have been produced.

If further proof of Beethoven's creativity is required, one need not look beyond the accounts of his skill at improvisation (see also 'Beethoven as pianist, conductor and teacher', p. 133). They all refer to his imagination and to the variety of his approach. The most analytical account comes from Czerny: 'Beethoven could improvise in several ways, whether on a theme of his own choosing or on a suggested theme. 1. In the form of a first movement or rondo finale of a sonata. He would play a normal first section, introducing a second melody, etc., in a related key.

In the second section, however, he gave free rein to his inspiration, while retaining the original motive, which he used in all possible ways. Allegros were enlivened by bravura passages, many of which were even more difficult than those found in his sonatas. 2. In free variation forms somewhat like the Choral Fantasy, op. 80, or the choral finale of the Ninth Symphony; both these pieces give a true picture of his improvising in this manner. 3. In a mixed form, one idea following the other as in a potpourri, like his solo Fantasy op. 77.' (Czerny, 1970, p. 15) The improvising and the sketchbooks reveal two aspects of the composer: the inventor and the craftsman.

The use of the piano while composing was important to Beethoven. Ries recalled the composition of the finale of the 'Appassionata' Sonata: 'During a similar walk we went so far astray that we did not get back to Döbling, where Beethoven lived, until nearly eight o'clock. The entire way he hummed, or sometimes even howled, to himself – up and down, up and down, without singing any definite notes. When I asked what this was, he replied: "A theme for the last Allegro of the sonata has occurred to me" (in F minor, op. 57). When we entered the room he rushed to the piano without taking off his hat. I took a seat in the corner and he soon forgot all about me. He stormed on for at least an hour with the new finale of the sonata, which is so beautiful. Finally he got up, was surprised to see me still there, and said: "I cannot give you a lesson today. I still have work to do."' (Wegeler, 1987, p. 87) Schindler (1966, p. 270) wrote that 'while composing music for the pianoforte the master would often go to the instrument and try certain passages, especially those that might present difficulties in performance', and Tomášek's account (see above) also refers to Beethoven working at the piano. This is scarcely surprising in the light of his early career as a virtuoso pianist and his outstanding ability to improvise.

Beethoven as pianist, conductor and teacher

Pianist

BEETHOVEN WAS TO FIND lasting fame as a composer, but initially it was as a virtuoso pianist that he was acclaimed. In this capacity he was immediately welcome in the salons of the Viennese nobility, and as his fame spread he appeared in public concerts playing concertos, chamber music and improvising. Of his sightreading Czerny remarked: 'He was the greatest sight-reader of his day, even of orchestral scores.'

Beethoven had established himself as a pianist while still in Bonn. By 1782 he was already deputizing for the court organist, Neefe, and the following year, still only twelve, he was appointed cembalist in the court orchestra. In 1791 he met the pianist Sterkel. Wegeler recalled the meeting: 'Because he had not yet heard any great or celebrated pianists, Beethoven knew nothing of the finer nuances of handling the instrument; his playing was rough and hard.' After hearing Sterkel, Beethoven was encouraged to play, which he did 'in precisely the same pleasant manner with which Sterkel had impressed him' (Wegeler, 1987, p. 23). At this time the composer and writer Junker heard Beethoven extemporize, and he admired his wealth of ideas, technique and powers of expression. He remarked: 'His style of treating his instrument is so different from that usually adopted, that it impresses one with the idea that by a path of his own discovery he has attained that height of excellence whereon he now stands' (Thayer, 1967, pp. 104–5).

When Beethoven arrived in Vienna he quickly made his mark. The virtuoso Joseph Gelinek, who sought to measure himself against the young man, said of him: 'Ah, he is no man, he is a devil. He will play me and all of us to death. And how he improvises!' (Thayer, 1967, p. 139). Around 1800 Beethoven's position of pre-eminence was challenged by Wölffl and Cramer. The differences between them were of style or taste rather than ability. Beethoven's playing was noted for its power, brilliance and expressiveness, but compared with certain other pianists he lacked accuracy, clarity of tone and elegance. Tomášek, who called him 'a giant among pianists', wrote after hearing him in Prague in 1798: 'Beethoven's magnificent playing and particularly the daring flights of his improvisation, stirred me strangely to the depths of my soul.' (Sonneck, 1967, p. 22) Czerny was later to write of Beethoven drawing 'entirely new and daring passages from the pianoforte by the use of the pedal', and of the 'singing tone and hitherto unimagined effects' from his legato tone (Landon, 1974, p. 44).

It was in 1805 that Cherubini described Beethoven's playing as 'rough', and in 1807 Clementi noted that it was 'not polished, and frequently impetuous, like himself, yet always full of spirit.' By this time he was severely hampered by deafness and had already abandoned his career as a virtuoso pianist. As an improviser he had no equal, and that skill remained undiminished for some time (see also 'Daily routine and composing habits', pp. 131–2). In 1805 he was present at the first performance of a quartet by Pleyel at Prince Lobkowitz's house. He was prevailed upon to improvise, and as he went to the piano Beethoven picked up the second violin part and then used it as a basis. 'He had never been heard to improvise more brilliantly, with more originality and splendour than on this evening! But through the entire improvisation there ran through the middle voices like a thread or cantus firmus the notes, in themselves utterly insignificant, which he had found on the accidentally opened page of the quartet, upon which he built up the most daring melodies and harmonies in the most brilliant concerto style.' (Thayer, 1967, p. 377)

The first performance of his Fourth Piano Concerto at the end of 1808 was the last time Beethoven played a concerto, but in

1814 he was still able to take part in a performance of the 'Archduke' Trio. He made his final public appearance accompanying the song *Adelaide* on 25 January 1815.

Conductor

Even allowing for his hearing problems, Beethoven's conducting appears to have been somewhat idiosyncratic and not very clear. Ries recalls an occasion when he was conducting his *Eroica* Symphony and threw the orchestra out so badly in the first movement that it was necessary to restart it (Wegeler, 1987, pp. 68–9). As Seyfried suggests, Beethoven's involvement in his compositions, and his desire to express their meaning, prevented him from conducting accurately:

> Our master could not be presented as a model in respect of conducting, and the orchestra always had to have a care in order not to be led astray by its mentor; for he had ears only for his composition and was ceaselessly occupied by manifold gesticulations to indicate the desired expression. He often made a downbeat for an accent on a weak beat. He used to suggest a *diminuendo* by crouching down more and more, and at a *pianissimo* he would almost creep under the desk. When the volume of sound grew he rose up almost as if out of a stage-trap, and with the entrance of the power of the band he would stand upon the tips of his toes almost as big as a giant, and waving his arms, seemed about to soar upwards to the skies.... When he observed that the players would enter into his intentions and play together with increasing ardour, inspired by the magical power of his creations, his face would be transfigured with joy... (Thayer, 1967, p. 371).

Seyfried gives the impression that Beethoven was an easy conductor to work with, showing consideration and patience, and likely to burst into laughter should something unexpected in his music cause the orchestra to break down. This view does not accord with other descriptions, or indeed with most depictions of his character. Ries refers to one occasion when the orchestra refused to allow him to conduct a rehearsal (Wegeler, 1987, p. 73), and another, on 22 December 1808, when the Choral Fantasia was performed for the first time. Beethoven became very angry when the clarinets made a wrong entry, even though his late completion of the work meant that it had scarcely been rehearsed (Wegeler, 1987, pp. 72–3).

The performance of *Die Weihe des Hauses* on 3 October 1822 marked Beethoven's last appearance as a conductor. According to Schindler (1966, pp. 235–6), who led the orchestra, Beethoven was unaware that he dragged the tempo, causing the orchestra and singers to be at odds with one another. Only one month later an attempt to conduct a dress rehearsal of *Fidelio* resulted in chaos. Beethoven never conducted again, although he set the beat at the first performance of his Ninth Symphony in 1824.

Teacher

Inevitably Beethoven was in demand as a piano teacher. He had given lessons since 1785 in Bonn, but he taught only reluctantly. According to Frau Breuning, 'From his earliest youth Beethoven had an extraordinary aversion to teaching.... He would set out, *ut iniquae mentis asellus*, ['like a bad-tempered little donkey'] because he knew he was being observed. However, he often turned round at the very door of the house, ran back, and promised he would teach for two hours the next day, it was simply not possible for him that day...' (Wegeler, 1987, p. 24).

During his early years in Vienna Beethoven taught numerous young ladies, usually from wealthy, aristocratic families, who would have paid him generously. Some, such as Princess Barbara Odescalchi (*née* Keglevics) and Baroness Dorothea Ertmann, were extremely able pianists. Very little is known of how the lessons were conducted or how often they took place. Apparently he taught Therese and Josephine Brunsvik on sixteen consecutive days when they visited Vienna in 1799, and stayed for not one, but four or five hours. It is quite likely that this was because Beethoven was in love with one or both of the girls. He frequently fell in love with his pupils, and his feelings were occasionally reciprocated. A close friendship developed between him and Josephine Brunsvik (see 'Personal relationships', p. 107), resulting in his being eager to teach and declining to accept payment. From Countess Guicciardi he would accept only linen, on the pretext that she had sewn it herself.

Only Archduke Rudolph (to whom he taught piano and composition) and Ferdinand Ries were formally acknowledged as Beethoven's pupils, and by 1805 he had ceased to give piano tuition. Rudolph's lessons in composition continued until at least 1824 (Letter 1322). Ries wrote:

> When Beethoven gave me lessons, I must say that contrary to his nature he was extraordinarily patient. I could only attribute this, and his almost unfailingly amicable behaviour toward me, mainly to his love and affection for my father. Thus he sometimes made me repeat a thing ten times or even more often. In the Variations in F major, dedicated to Princess Odescalchi (op. 34), I had to repeat the last Adagio variation entirely seventeen times. Still he was not satisfied with the expression in the little cadenza, even though I thought I played it just as well as he did. I received nearly two full hours of instruction that day. If I made a mistake somewhere in a passage, or struck wrong notes, or missed intervals – which he often wanted strongly emphasized – he rarely said anything. However, if I lacked expression in crescendos, etc. or in the character of a piece, he became angry because, he maintained, the first was accident, while the latter resulted from inadequate knowledge, feeling, or attention. (Wegeler, 1987, pp. 82–3)

Even for Ries, Beethoven could not be persuaded to teach figured bass and composition: 'He said it required a particular gift to explain them with clearness and precision, and, besides that,

Albrechtsberger was the acknowledged master of all composers...' (Thayer, 1967, p. 294).

Beethoven apparently had little sympathy for most of the piano methods in circulation. According to Schindler he disliked Hummel's, and he advised Stephan von Breuning not to practise Czerny's studies. Gerhard von Breuning wrote to Wegeler that Beethoven did not like him to use Pleyel's studies and had sent him Clementi's exercises instead. He had told him that he had intended, but never found the time, to write his own exercises: 'I would have written something quite unconventional, though.' (Wegeler, 1987, pp. 157–8) Beethoven himself kept Cramer's studies because he believed they contained all the fundamentals of good playing. According to Schindler, Beethoven marked some of them for his nephew to study, but the authenticity of his supposed annotations is highly suspect (Newman, 1988). He also advocated Karl's use of Clementi's sonatas.

Czerny's comment that Beethoven 'laid great stress on a correct position of the fingers (after the school of Emanuel Bach, which he used in teaching me)...' (Thayer, 1967, p. 368) is not very revealing. Therese von Brunsvik recorded that 'he never grew weary of holding down and bending my fingers, which I had been taught to lift high and hold straight' (Thayer, 1967, p. 235). This accords with the artist Mähler's description of Beethoven's playing in 1803: 'he played with his hands so very still...there was no tossing of them to and fro, up and down; they seemed to glide right and left over the keys, the fingers doing the work' (Thayer, 1967, p. 337). Countess Guicciardi supports Ries when she mentions that Beethoven insisted on the correct interpretation, right down to the last detail. It can be concluded that Beethoven was more concerned with interpretation than with matters of technique in both his teaching and performing.

Illnesses, deafness and death

BEETHOVEN WAS DOGGED by physical illness for much of his life, and also suffered bouts of depression. From the age of about twenty-seven his hearing began to fail, and during his last ten years he was almost totally deaf. But in spite of his poor health he appeared robust, at least in the early years, and his productivity was surprisingly little affected.

Apart from childhood smallpox, Beethoven's first serious illness was a fever in 1787 which left him with asthma and melancholia (depression). When he left Bonn in 1792 he was already suffering from a chronic abdominal disorder, as a letter to Wegeler in June 1801 reveals:

> But that jealous demon, my wretched health, has put a nasty spoke in my wheel; it amounts to this, that for the last three years my hearing has become weaker and weaker. The trouble is supposed to have been caused by the condition of my abdomen which, as you know, was wretched even before I left Bonn, but has become worse

in Vienna where I have been constantly afflicted with diarrhoea and have been suffering in consequence from an extraordinary debility (Letter 51).

This was his first reference to his deafness, which he attempted to conceal for as long as possible.

In 1797 (some reports give 1796) he contracted what Weissenbach called 'a terrible typhus', described in the Fischhof manuscript as 'a dangerous illness, which in his convalescence settled in his organs of hearing, after which his deafness steadily increased' (Thayer, 1967, pp. 252, 187–8). After this he suffered repeatedly from colds and catarrh, which on occasions developed into bronchitis or pneumonia, usually referred to as rheumatic attacks.

Over the years Beethoven consulted many doctors. He was understandably desperate to improve his health and cure his deafness, but he was also a difficult patient, unwilling to follow advice and intolerant when success was not immediately forthcoming. He told Wegeler that Dr Peter Frank had prescribed strengthening medicines to tone up his body and almond oil for his deafness, but to no avail. After a 'medical ass' had recommended cold baths, he consulted Dr Gerhard von Vering, who advised lukewarm baths in Danube water; pills, which gave his stomach some relief; and applied bark to his arms, which, although it did nothing to improve his hearing, alleviated the continual noises in his ears (Letter 54). After this he sought further help. Dr Johann Schmidt recommended that he rest his ears, so he spent the summer of 1802 in Heiligenstadt. There he considered suicide (see 'The Heiligenstadt Testament', pp. 169–72) before finding the strength, through music, to continue.

In 1804 Beethoven suffered another severe illness, following which he began to be plagued by headaches and became increasingly prone to infection: abscesses of the jaw and finger and a septic foot. Because his deafness had worsened, he consulted Father Weiss, who gave him daily infusions and ordered a strict diet and quiet, but he could not adhere to this and discontinued the treatment. Until 1810 Beethoven made few references to illness in his correspondence, but the more frequent mention of it from this time suggests that he was more often ill.

From 1815 Beethoven's health declined steadily. Colds were invariably accompanied by inflammation and fever, confining him to bed for weeks at a time. During the summer of 1817 he was prescribed medicinal powders, doses of tincture, and had to rub a healing ointment into his body. But he had little respite from illness. During this period he fell out with one doctor, Giovanni Malfatti, and developed a mistrust of another, Jakob Staudenheim. His hearing deteriorated to such an extent that by 1818 he could no longer hear most speech, and visitors had to communicate with him by writing in Conversation Books (see pp. 164–7). At the end of 1820 he suffered a serious feverish attack which confined him to bed for six weeks, and the following year he developed jaundice, the first sign of his fatal liver disorder. He sought relief at Baden, but had to leave prematurely because of severe diarrhoea.

In 1822 Beethoven finally accepted that nothing could be done for his deafness and never again sought help for it. The following year a new source of discomfort appeared: ophthalmia (or inflammation of the eye). Beset by so many ailments he wrote despairingly: 'I fear this trouble [catarrh] will soon cut the thread of my life or, worse still, will gradually gnaw it through...' (Letter 1230).

A grave illness occurred in 1825, and Dr Anton Braunhofer, who treated Beethoven after the refusal of Staudenheim to attend, feared that without the right precautions it could develop into inflammation of the bowel, a condition which would almost certainly have proved fatal in those days. The maintenance of a strict diet and the avoidance of alcohol brought about sufficient improvement for Beethoven to go to Baden. From there he wrote to Braunhofer that 'we are rather poorly – we still feel very weak and are belching and so forth ... my catarrhal condition is showing the following symptoms, I spit a good deal of blood, but probably only from my windpipe. But I have frequent nosebleeds ... and my stomach has become dreadfully weak, and so has, generally speaking, my whole constitution.' (Letter 1371) But the crisis had been avoided, and this was to be a productive year. Three string quartets were completed, and Beethoven acknowledged his recovery in the title of the third movement of the String Quartet in A minor, op. 132: 'Heiliger Dankgesang eines Genesenen an die Gottheit...' ('Sacred Song of Thanksgiving to the Deity by a Convalescent').

In September 1826 Beethoven went to stay with his brother Johann at Gneixendorf. He was a sick man, and Karl's attempted suicide had been a crushing blow. While there his appetite diminished, his thirst increased, and his abdomen and feet became swollen. He left for Vienna after a quarrel at the beginning of December, travelling in an open carriage in inclement weather. Overnight, in miserable lodgings, he developed a fever and a bad cough. On his arrival in Vienna he was seriously ill, but he received no medical attention until the third day, when Dr Andreas Wawruch arrived. He treated Beethoven for inflammation of the lungs (pneumonia), using herbs to induce sweating and lower his temperature. This was successful, but the fundamental problem remained. A few days later he took a turn for the worse. He had attacks of vomiting and diarrhoea, his liver and intestines gave him great pain, he was badly jaundiced, and the swelling, or dropsy, was increasing rapidly. Wawruch recommended an operation to relieve the pressure, and Staudenheim, who was now present, agreed. On 20 December 25 lb of fluid were drained at once and much more followed. The relief was only temporary and three more operations to drain abdominal fluid were carried out.

Beethoven, possibly encouraged by Schindler, disliked Wawruch, and insisted on Malfatti being called in. He, either because he knew from Beethoven's history that his case was hopeless or because of what he understood of Beethoven's nature, recommended something which would bring instant relief: iced punch. At first it seemed to be successful, but the respite was short-lived; Beethoven became delirious, the diarrhoea and abdominal pain worsened, and no longer able to eat he became very emaciated. On 23 March he signed his final will, and on 24 March he took the last sacrament before lapsing into unconsciousness. After four months' illness, he died on 26 March 1827.

An autopsy was performed by Dr Johann Wagner. Surprisingly, the lungs were found to be normal, but the abdominal cavity was filled with fluid, its organs showed abnormalities and the stomach and bowels were distended with air. The liver was shrunk and hardened, the spleen enlarged and the pancreas hardened. Regarding the ear, there was some evidence of inflammation, the auditory nerves were shrivelled and without nerve tissue, and their blood vessels dilated. With the benefits of modern medicine, Beethoven's condition can be summarized as follows: his stomach/ bowel disorder was undoubtedly ulcerative colitis, which can now be quite successfully treated with steroid drugs. This, together with the repeated feverish attacks, which particularly affected his chest, his low resistance to infection, ophthalmia, degeneration of arteries and cirrhosis of the liver (resulting from hepatitis or repeated inflammation), suggest that Beethoven suffered from connective tissue disease (Cooper, 1970, p. 439). The dropsy from which he was suffering at his death was probably a direct result of liver failure, although it could also indicate a weakening of the heart.

Beethoven's deafness has usually been attributed either to otosclerosis or to nerve damage. Otosclerosis is a progressive, often hereditary condition, which can be exacerbated by general ill-health, whereby the cartilage opening to the inner ear turns to bone. Although some of his symptoms – progression with periods of remission and pain in the face of loud noise – are in line with this, other common symptoms were not present and there was no evidence at the post-mortem. Nerve deafness usually manifests itself with the loss of high-pitched sounds first, accompanied by tinnitus. It is not normally progressive unless the original cause of the damage persists (Sorsby, 1930, pp. 539–40). If Beethoven was suffering from a connective tissue disorder it could have caused the damage to the blood vessels supplying the auditory nerves and nerve tissue, of which there was evidence at the autopsy.

This same disorder is now known to be able to affect a sufferer's mental health and could well account for Beethoven's highly-strung nature and the severe depression which afflicted him. Attempts to ascribe his symptoms to syphilis or alcoholism (London, 1964, pp. 442–8) are largely unfounded and can be dismissed. Some credit must be given to Wegeler, who wrote this astute summary: 'The seeds of his disorders, his hearing problem, and the dropsy which finally killed him, already lay within my friend's ailing body in 1796. The frequent interruptions of any regular regime were bound to aggravate this basic infirmity. However, Beethoven was also susceptible to other illnesses which could not be ascribed to the same source.' (Wegeler, 1987, pp. 150–51)

Beethoven's funeral took place on 29 March. An enormous crowd gathered, and amongst the procession were all the notable musicians in Vienna. After a service at St Stephen's Cathedral, the coffin was taken for burial at Währing Cemetery, where a moving funeral oration (Thayer, 1967, pp. 1057–8), written by Franz Grillparzer, was delivered by the actor Anschütz. In 1888 the remains were reburied in Vienna's Central Cemetery.

ANNE-LOUISE COLDICOTT

Section 7
BEETHOVEN'S BELIEFS AND OPINIONS

BEETHOVEN'S BELIEFS AND OPINIONS

MUCH OF WHAT WE KNOW about Beethoven as an individual comes from observations made by other people. But what a person says himself is often equally revealing about him, and Beethoven's utterances, whether in letters, notebooks or reliably reported conversations, are no exception. Here we provide a selection of his views on a variety of important subjects.

Philosophical ideas: ethics and art

BEETHOVEN WAS NO PHILOSOPHER, but he was very interested in the writings of some of the great philosophers, both ancient and recent, European and oriental. 'Socrates and Jesus were my models', he wrote in 1818 (Köhler, 1968, i.211); and his interest went back to his early years: 'I have tried since childhood to understand the meaning of the better and wiser people of every age' (Letter 228). He read widely and often underlined or copied down philosophical and proverbial sayings he came across; some were even set to music in the form of canons. A particularly large number of quotations, drawn from a great variety of sources, can be found in his *Tagebuch* of 1812–18 (see 'Diaries and other documents', p. 167).

Philosophy might be described as a search for truth, and Beethoven frequently expressed his love of truth. To Goethe he wrote: 'I love truth more than anything' (Letter 1136), and both here and in another letter he expressly contradicts the saying of Terence: 'Veritas odium parit' ('Truth begets hatred'). He also once wrote out a quotation from Schiller's *Don Carlos*: 'Truth is within the reach of a wise man. Beauty can be discerned by a sensitive heart. They belong to one another.' (Letter 21) Most of the time this love of truth is borne out in his dealings with other people; nevertheless he did not always quite live up to his ideals and was at times liable to mislead, as in his dealings with the *Missa Solemnis*, which was promised to several rival publishers at more or less the same time.

The moral law of doing good, acting nobly and seeking virtue was very dear to Beethoven's heart, right from the time of his childhood, and there are numerous places where he expressed a desire to help the needy and live for others. He was particularly glad when his art was able to be used in this way – for example through charity concerts: 'I count myself exceedingly fortunate when my art is turned to account for charitable purposes' (Letter 357). Hand in hand with the moral laws were the laws of nature, which he also loved to contemplate – whether the starry skies, the woods and fields, or the speculations of Immanuel Kant's *Allgemeine Naturgeschichte und Theorie des Himmels* (*General History of Nature and Theory of the Universe*). 'The moral law within us and the starry sky above us – Kant!!!' he wrote in a Conversation Book of 1820 (Köhler, 1968, i.235). (His preoccupation with Kant, however, was no greater than that of many educated people of the time, and he refused Wegeler's invitation to attend a series of lectures on Kant in the 1790s.)

To execute noble deeds it was essential in his mind to exert great effort and application in everything he did. His energetic legal battle with his sister-in-law, as he strove to protect his nephew from a mother whom he regarded as quite unworthy, is one of several examples (his action here was of course strongly motivated by irrational feelings, but he rationalized it as an effort to save his nephew). Another letter (Letter 373) refers to the pleasure he derived from overcoming the difficulties of a dangerous journey through a forest at night. The same attitude is reflected in his music, which compared with that of nearly all his contemporaries is learned, difficult, complex and noble. The great efforts he put into each composition in order to make it as excellent as possible are reflected in the extraordinary intensity of his sketching methods. To describe a work as 'difficult' was in his view 'the most lavish praise that can be bestowed', since 'what is difficult is also beautiful, good, great and so forth' (Letter 749). Music was for him a noble and elevating art and 'deserved to be studied' (Letter 767); 'only art and science can raise men to the level of gods' (Letter 376).

If, despite all efforts, the difficulties and hardships of life could not be overcome, then Beethoven regarded stoical acceptance of fate as the best course. 'Plutarch has shown me the path of resignation', he wrote in 1801 concerning his deafness (Letter 51); and in 1816 he jotted down similar sentiments in his *Tagebuch*: 'The chief characteristic of a distinguished man: endurance in adverse and harsh circumstances' (Solomon, 1982, no. 93a).

Connected with these ideas of elevation and distinction was the notion of an élite class of people, to which he, having been elevated by music, naturally belonged. He could therefore form friendships only with such people, for in his view 'true friendship can only be founded on the connection of similar natures' (Solomon, 1982, no. 127). And the rulers of the world ought also to be drawn from this noble and wise élite (see 'Politics' below).

Politics

AS THE LEADING COMPOSER of the period following the French Revolution, Beethoven has often been seen as having effected a similar revolution in music. It would be easy therefore to imagine that his sympathies were broadly in line with those of the French Revolution – liberty, equality and fraternity. In actual fact his political views were a great deal more complex and not entirely consistent; and although he took considerable interest in politics, he did not often express himself at any length on the subject (except, perhaps, in private conversations).

His most famous political comment occurred when he flew into a rage on hearing in 1804 that Napoleon had proclaimed himself emperor: 'So he too is nothing more than an ordinary man. Now he also will trample on all human rights and indulge only his own ambition. He will place himself above everyone and become a tyrant.' These are his words as recollected by Ferdinand Ries (Wegeler, 1987, p. 68, translation amended). Beethoven had long been opposed to tyranny (a fact reflected in such works as *Fidelio* and *Egmont*), and his idealized image of Napoleon as heroic champion of the poor was shattered not merely by the latter's 1804 proclamation but by the wars that followed, during which the French twice invaded Vienna. In these and later years Beethoven often expressed his detestation of the French. Yet his feelings towards Napoleon were somewhat ambivalent both before and after 1804. In 1802 he had refused a request to write a sonata on the revolution, whereas after 1804 his old admiration for Napoleon never completely vanished. As late as 1824 he said of Napoleon (according to Czerny): 'Earlier I couldn't have tolerated him. Now I think completely otherwise.' (Thayer, 1967, p. 920)

Beethoven's attitude to Britain was quite different. He held a lifelong admiration for the British people and their system of parliamentary democracy, and this admiration extended to every Briton with whom he came into contact, apart from one or two notable exceptions. One of the main reasons why he provided accompaniments for so many Scottish songs (not the most rewarding compositional task) was 'a certain very particular regard and affection I feel for the English nation and also for Scottish melody' (Letter 496).

As for his own adopted country, the Austria of the Habsburgs, he was sufficiently patriotic to compose nationalistic songs in the 1790s (WoO 121 and 122), plus some much more substantial works at the time of the overthrow of Napoleon in 1813–14: *Wellingtons Sieg* (the so-called 'Battle Symphony', op. 91) and the sizeable cantata *Der glorreiche Augenblick* (op. 136). His view of the Austrian people, however, was that they were more pleasure-loving than war-mongering or rebellious. In 1794, at the height of the French Revolution, when there was a possibility that revolution would spread to Austria and various repressive measures had been taken to prevent it (see 'Politics', pp. 60–61), Beethoven observed perceptively: 'I believe that so long as an Austrian can get his brown ale and his little sausages, he is not likely to revolt.' (Letter 12)

At times Beethoven expressed himself openly opposed to the repressive laws which were frequently in force in Vienna, notably after 1815. Such hostility ran the risk of imprisonment, but he was well known and not regarded as a subversive threat by the secret police, and so they left him alone. He once misquoted a line from Schiller's *An die Freude* in the form 'Princes are beggars', which has suggested to some that he was opposed to the ruling classes in general, but this does not seem to have been the case. He believed instead in a kind of meritocracy, in which those who were noble in spirit (including himself – see pp. 156–7) belonged to an élite class. Those who had power should then know how to use it wisely. The wise ruler is personified in several of Beethoven's works – not just the idealized Napoleon of the *Eroica* Symphony but also the minister Don Fernando in *Fidelio* and, at an earlier date, Joseph II in the 1790 Cantata mourning his death (WoO 87). Although he may never have expressly said so, Beethoven evidently believed that rulers on earth should be a reflection of the Divine Ruler.

He therefore cannot be seen as simply left-wing or right-wing, progressive or conservative, in the modern sense. Some of his views were strikingly progressive, such as his desire to embrace the world and bind distant peoples through art (Letter 1149); and he believed art itself should always be moving forward. But his disdain of the working classes was frequently evident: 'The common citizen should be excluded from higher men', he wrote in 1820 (Thayer, 1967, p. 712) – an attitude which seems somewhat strange today but was perfectly normal at the time. Thus in terms of the tenets of the French Revolution, he could be said to have supported Liberty wholeheartedly, Equality not at all, and Fraternity only in a limited way.

Religion

THE NATURE OF BEETHOVEN'S BELIEF in an all-powerful Divine Ruler was unorthodox and idiosyncratic but absolutely genuine. His image of God was not based solely on traditional Christian teaching but was drawn from a wide variety of influences including Classical antiquity and oriental religions. Although he was nominally a Roman Catholic his attitude to the church was lukewarm: we do not read of him going to church regularly, and only reluctantly did he agree to take the Last Rites shortly before his death.

His perception of the Divinity is perhaps best summed up in the words from Schiller's *An die Freude*, which was a powerful influence on his thinking: 'Brothers, above the canopy of stars, there must dwell a dear Father.' This 'dear Father' was to be approached and addressed directly, without any intermediary such as the church or even Christ himself, who is rarely mentioned by Beethoven except as a suffering fellow-human: in one letter he suggests that his 'most gracious master' (Archduke Rudolph?) should 'follow the example of Christ, i.e. suffer' (Letter 1316), and it is the earthly suffering of Christ, rather than his divinity, which is emphasized in the oratorio *Christus am Oelberge*.

Elsewhere, Christ is placed on the same level as Socrates (see 'Philosophical ideas', p. 142). Church leaders were not treated with any great respect. Beethoven's rather irreverent reference to Napoleon's Concordat with the Pope in 1802 is not untypical: 'Now that Buonaparte has concluded his Concordat with the Pope – to write a sonata of that kind? – If it were even a Missa pro Sancta Maria a tre voci, or a Vesper or something of that kind – In that case I would instantly take up my paint-brush – and with fat pound notes dash off a Credo in unum. But, good Heavens, such a sonata – in these newly developing Christian times – Ho ho – there you must leave me out.' (Letter 57)

The Father, however, was always held in a position of great awe, and Beethoven's perception of Him was in later years heavily influenced by oriental writings, which he became very interested in. Quoting from Georg Forster's translation of William Robertson's *An Historical Disquisition Concerning the Knowledge which the Ancients had of India*, Beethoven wrote in his *Tagebuch* in 1816 that God was 'eternal, omnipotent, omniscient, omnipresent' (Solomon, 1982, entry 93b). Another relevant quotation was taken from Schiller's account of ancient Egypt in *Die Sendung Moses*, in which the author quotes three well-known sentences from ancient Egyptian religion: 'I am that which is.' 'I am all, what is, what was, what will be; no mortal man has ever lifted my veil.' 'He is only and solely of Himself, and to this only One all things owe their existence.' Beethoven copied these sentences and kept them, framed in glass, on his table.

Elsewhere in his *Tagebuch*, Beethoven quoted at considerable length from translations by Johann Friedrich Kleuker and Georg Forster of various oriental writings about the nature of the Godhead (entries 61–5), such as the following, taken from a commentary on the *Rig-Veda*: 'Free from all passion and desire, that is the Mighty One. He alone. None is greater than He.' Beethoven even seems to have formulated some sentences of his own in the same style: 'All things flowed clear and pure from God. If I afterwards became darkened through passion for evil, I returned after manifold repentance and purification to the first sublime, pure source, to the Godhead.' In these passages God is being perceived as timeless and immutable, and the repeated 'I am' in the Egyptian sayings recalls God's statement to Moses (Exodus 3: 13–14): 'I am that I am', where God is beyond description in any terms less than Himself (Solomon, 1983, p. 115).

Beethoven was also greatly attracted by the *Betrachtungen über die Werke Gottes in Reiche der Natur* by the Lutheran clergyman Christian Sturm (1740–86). This work is a series of essays on the wonders of nature and how they lead to the praise of God their Creator; thus it combines several elements of particular appeal to Beethoven – creativity, love of nature, and the omnipotent Father – and he underlined many passages in his copy of the book.

Nevertheless, Beethoven was not simply a deist; he believed in a personal God who could be appealed to for help and comfort, and there is little doubt that he prayed frequently. (When his nephew was asked by the court in 1818 if Beethoven had instructed him to pray, he replied that the two of them prayed together every morning and evening.) Some of Beethoven's prayers have been written down. There is one in the middle of the Heiligenstadt Testament (see pp. 170–71) and several in the *Tagebuch*, for example: 'O God, give me strength to conquer myself'; 'O God, God, look down upon the unhappy B., do not let it continue like this any longer'; 'O hear, ever ineffable One, hear me, your unhappy, unhappiest of all mortals' (entries 1, 3, 160).

Beethoven also believed that some people were able, through contact with God, to spread religious sentiments to others. Thus Archduke Rudolph was able to do so by virtue of his position as archbishop: 'May Heaven bless me through Y[our] I[mperial] H[ighness] and may the Lord Himself ever watch over and guard Y.I.H. There is nothing higher than to approach the Godhead more nearly than other mortals and by means of that contact to spread the rays of the Godhead through the human race' (Letter 1248). Some other priests could do likewise; Haslinger was told: 'Go every Sunday to Father Werner [Zacharias Werner, 1768–1823, a popular preacher] who will tell you about the little book which will enable you to go straight to Heaven' (Letter 1058) – a remark that was clearly intended only half-seriously. Beethoven thought he himself could stir religion in others through his music, as is evident from a comment on the *Missa Solemnis*: 'My chief aim when I was composing this grand Mass was to awaken and permanently instil religious feelings not only into the singers but also into the listeners' (Letter 1307).

At certain periods of his life, Beethoven's religious impulses were rather in the background, and there is more than a hint of agnosticism in his 1813–14 setting of *An die Hoffnung* (op. 94), which begins 'Ob ein Gott sei?' ('Is there a God?') – a passage omitted in his 1805 setting of the song. But from about 1815 religion came very much more to the fore, along with his searches in eastern and Egyptian writings. *Tagebuch* entries begin referring to plans for religious works: 'A small chapel – in it the hymn written by me, performed for the glory of the Almighty, the Eternal, the Infinite' (entry 41, 1815); 'In order to write true church music go through all the plainchants of the monks' (entry 168, 1818). Soon the *Missa Solemnis* was being composed, and there were plans for two further masses (see Letters 1145 and 1153), one of which (in C♯ minor) was sketched briefly. Also planned were three additional movements (including a gradual and offertory) for the *Missa Solemnis*, a new oratorio and a requiem. Although these plans remained unfulfilled, religious elements began to permeate other works. The Ninth Symphony is an obvious example, and in 1818 he also made a sketch for a symphony with a 'pious song ... in the ancient modes – Lord God we praise Thee – alleluia' (Nottebohm, 1887, p. 163). Other works with religious connections are the song *Abendlied* (WoO 150) of 1820 and the chorale-like 'Heiliger Dankgesang' ('Sacred Song of Thanksgiving') in the op. 132 Quartet of 1825.

This turning towards religion may partly have been a reflection of a general religious revival that permeated Vienna after the Napoleonic Wars, but other elements were at work too. On the practical level, Beethoven's adoption of his nephew no doubt encouraged him to re-examine his faith, as he sought to impart to the boy sound moral and religious precepts such as he himself had learnt from his mother. Also he probably came to realize as he strove for the most elevated and lofty expression in his music, that the ultimate aim was music that somehow reached up 'above the canopy of stars' to the Godhead. And as he approached death, his anticipation of the next world would have grown stronger, as expressed in the final couplet of *Abendlied*: 'Ernte bald an Gottes Thron meines Leiden schönen Lohn.' ('Reaping soon on God's throne a fine recompense for my sufferings.')

Literature

'HE IS A GREAT ADMIRER of the ancients. Homer, particularly his *Odyssey*, and Plutarch he prefers to all the rest; and, of the native poets, he studies Schiller and Goethe, in preference to any other; this latter is his personal friend.' So wrote J. R. Schultz in *The Harmonicon* in January 1824; and although he derived his first-hand knowledge of Beethoven mainly from a single day spent in his company in September 1823, this statement is a very accurate assessment of Beethoven's literary tastes, being amply borne out by other evidence.

Beethoven himself painted a very similar picture in a letter to Breitkopf & Härtel of 8 August 1809 (Letter 224): 'Perhaps you could arrange for me to receive editions of Goethe's and Schiller's complete works.... These two poets are my favourites, as are also Ossian and Homer, though unfortunately I can read the latter only in translations.' His request for the works of Goethe and Schiller was repeated the following month, when he also added the name of Christoph Wieland. We do not hear much more about Ossian – perhaps Beethoven later heard reports that the writings attributed to this 3rd-century Irish bard were evidently the work of an 18th-century Scotsman, James Macpherson – nor about Wieland, none of whose texts was set by Beethoven; but Goethe, Schiller and Homer were quoted or mentioned by him on many other occasions.

Goethe he had admired from his youth, and set far more texts by this poet than by any other (see 'Who's Who of Beethoven's Contemporaries' and 'Songs', pp. 46–7 and 262). His admiration for Goethe was mentioned by several observers, and he himself expressed it repeatedly; *Wilhelm Meister* seems to have been a particular favourite. Schiller was mentioned less often and was rarely set to music, but Beethoven was fond of quoting from his works, including *Don Carlos*, *Die Jungfrau von Orleans*, *Die Braut von Messina* and *Wilhelm Tell*. There are many echoes of Schiller in Beethoven's writings, and eventually in 1824 he acquired a twenty-one volume set of Schiller's works for nephew Karl, an ardent admirer of Schiller.

Beethoven's interest in Homer is attested by occasional references in his letters and rather more in his Conversation Books; in addition, two passages from *The Iliad* and three from *The Odyssey* (in Johann Heinrich Voss's translation) were copied in his *Tagebuch*. On one occasion he wrote, 'I prefer to set to music the works of poets like Homer, Klopstock and Schiller' (Letter 1260), but the only Homer settings known are brief sketches such as those in the Scheide and Egerton Sketchbooks. His acquaintance with Plutarch, too, is evident from several of his letters, though the references to this writer are sometimes rather oblique.

The mention of Friedrich Klopstock suggests a great admiration for this poet, and on another occasion Beethoven asked Steiner to lend him the works of Klopstock (and Johann Gleim). He never set any of Klopstock's texts, however, and none were quoted in his *Tagebuch*. An oft-cited remark about Klopstock has been attributed to Beethoven: 'He leaps about so much and he begins at too lofty an elevation. Always *Maestoso*, D♮ major!' (Thayer, 1967, p. 802). But the reported comment is evidently spurious, invented by Rochlitz (Solomon, 1980b).

Beethoven was also familiar with many of Shakespeare's plays, in August von Schlegel's translation (Beethoven was able to read French fairly well and also some Latin and Italian, but he never learnt much English). In 1810 he recommended Shakespeare to Therese Malfatti and offered to lend her a copy (Letter 258). At one time he also began sketching an opera on *Macbeth* (as adapted by Collin from Shakespeare), and according to Amenda the slow movement of the Quartet op. 18 no. 1 was meant to depict the tomb scene in *Romeo and Juliet* – a claim supported by Beethoven's sketches. But Schindler's claim that Beethoven said the explanation for his D minor Sonata (op. 31 no. 2) could be found in Shakespeare's *Tempest* is almost certainly without foundation.

A good selection of Beethoven's literary interests in general is provided by the passages he quoted or referred to in his *Tagebuch*: apart from the conspicuous absence of Goethe, they provide a fair indication of his tastes in literature (further indication of his tastes can be gained from the literary titles occasionally noted in his Conversation Books). In addition to various philosophical and religious writings (see 'Philosophical ideas', pp. 142–3, and 'Religion', pp. 145–8), authors quoted or referred to in the *Tagebuch* include Count Vittorio Alfieri, Pedro Calderón, Homer, Amandus Müllner, Ovid, Pliny, Plutarch, Schiller, Shakespeare and Friedrich Werner. Although such a selection might seem strange today, it was perfectly normal at the time and very much in the mainstream of contemporary European literary taste.

What is most notable about the passages Beethoven quoted or copied out, however, is their frequent reference to fate, endurance, and the achievement of immortal fame through great deeds. Such passages say much about Beethoven's outlook on life, and suggest that he regarded himself as some latter-day successor to the heroes of ancient times, for they were clearly copied for their content rather than literary merit. Some examples are given below.

'"Pity my fate" I cry with Johanna.' (Schiller, *Die Jungfrau von Orleans,* V/2; Letter 296)

'Be more than your fate, love the hater, and seek the great good of self-completion in creating.' (Werner, *Die Söhne des Thals,* Part I, IV/2; *Tagebuch,* no. 60d)

'But now Fate catches me. Let me not sink into the dust inactive and inglorious, but first complete great things, of which future times also shall hear.' (Homer, *The Iliad,* XXII/303-5; *Tagebuch,* no. 49)

'For Fate gave man courage to endure.' (*ibid.,* XXIV/49; *Tagebuch,* no. 26)

'But he who is noble in thought and deed, his worthy fame is spread far and wide by strangers, to all men on earth, and everyone blesses the good man.' (Homer, *The Odyssey,* XIX/332-4; *Tagebuch,* no. 170)

'Sertorius...maintained that he would merely buy time, which is the most valuable thing for a man who wants to accomplish important things.' (Plutarch, *Sertorius; Tagebuch,* no. 150)

'Nevertheless, what greater thing can be given a man than fame and praise and immortality?' (Pliny, *Epistulae,* III/21, line 6; *Tagebuch,* no. 114)

Personal environment

BEETHOVEN'S RELATIONSHIPS AND BEHAVIOUR, as reported by his acquaintances, are discussed elsewhere (see 'Character and behaviour', pp. 103–6, and 'Personal relationships', pp. 106–10); here we look at his environment from his own point of view – how he perceived his friends and acquaintances, and his surroundings in general. Although he enjoyed the company of others, he had few very close friends. 'True friendship can only be founded on the connection of similar natures,' he wrote in 1817 (Solomon, 1982, no. 127), and so it is hardly surprising if such a brilliant, elevated and eccentric composer found few people with a 'similar nature'. In 1801 he wrote that Karl Amenda was one of only three people 'who have possessed all my affection' (Letter 52); the other two are thought to have been Stephan von Breuning and either Stephan's brother Lorenz or possibly Beethoven's own mother. Stephan von Breuning was described elsewhere as 'an excellent, splendid fellow, who...has his heart in the right place' (Letter 51). Before Beethoven fell out with his patron Prince Lichnowsky in 1806 he described him as 'one of my most loyal friends' (Letter 108); and in later years Archduke Rudolph was evidently regarded in a similar way, although he was sometimes felt to be too demanding in wanting long lessons in composition: 'After such lessons one is hardly able on the following day to think and, still less, to compose.' (Letter 1167)

Other people with whom Beethoven was on friendly terms were often not nearly so highly regarded. Zmeskall and Schuppanzigh were described as 'miserable egoists', who could 'never be noble witnesses to the fullest extent of my inward and outward activities' (Letter 53). But Beethoven reserved some of his worst invective for his sister-in-law Johanna and Schindler. The former he saw as lazy and slatternly, depraved, and devoid of moral worth. Schindler, meanwhile, was considered odious and contemptible; Beethoven was not openly hostile to him simply because, as he put it, Schindler was 'sufficiently punished by being what he is' (Letter 1233). And Beethoven's brother Johann was so far from being a kindred spirit that he was sometimes described as a 'pseudo-brother'.

Beethoven's hot temper and rough manners, and the potential jealousy of other musicians, made it easy for him to make enemies, though most of these were probably more imagined than real. As early as 1794 he perceived some of his rival pianists, who allegedly stole some of his best ideas for their own improvisations and compositions, as his sworn enemies, and in 1804 he told Rochlitz that he had 'a great number of enemies' (Letter 87a), which had resulted in several unfavourable reviews of Beethoven's compositions being sent to Rochlitz for publication in his *Allgemeine Musikalische Zeitung*. It is difficult to identify who these enemies were, but Beethoven mentioned the same year that the theatre manager Baron Braun had been 'persistently unfriendly' (Letter 88), and on another occasion he referred to Salieri as his 'most active opponent' (Letter 192). His suspicious nature sometimes also led him to identify, without strong reasons, others supposedly ill-disposed towards him, for example his tailor Joseph Lind and Prince Esterházy's courier Anton Wocher.

Beethoven customarily employed a domestic servant – occasionally two – but the relationships were never satisfactory and he often dismissed them after a short period. One, called Nanni, came in for particularly severe criticism; she was described by Beethoven variously as a 'disgusting beast', possessing 'extraordinary sauciness, wickedness and vulgarity', and belonging to a 'filthy tribe' (Letters 884 and 885). On other occasions he suspected his servants of having committed theft, and of possessing counterfeit keys. 'You always have to be suspicious with an inferior person around you.' (Solomon, 1982, no. 137) Added to this was their alleged immorality: 'As for the servants there is only one opinion everywhere on their immorality, to which all other misfortunes in this city can be ascribed.' (Letter 885) He felt extremely mortified at having to associate at all with such a class of people.

For a time his surroundings nearly drove him to leave Vienna altogether as he became increasingly exasperated. In about 1817 this exasperation was evidently having a profound effect on his output: he composed very little that year and seemed for a time unable to elevate himself above his everyday cares and concerns. 'There is no other way to save yourself except to leave here, only through this can you again lift yourself to the heights of your art, whereas here you are submerged in vulgarity,' he told himself in spring 1817 (Solomon, 1982, no. 119). Another occasion when he would have been glad to leave Vienna was during the French invasion in 1809: 'What a destructive and disorderly life I see and hear around me, nothing but drums, cannons, and human misery in every form.' (Letter 220)

The countryside, by contrast, was regarded as a haven of peace and tranquillity, in which he always delighted. In the letter just cited he speaks of the enjoyment of country life as indispensable to him (which is of course what might be expected of the composer of the *Pastoral* Symphony) and he spent most summers in the country around Vienna (see 'Residences and travel', pp. 125–9). One particularly effusive comment on his love of the country came in a letter to Therese Malfatti in 1810: 'How delighted I shall be to ramble for a while through bushes, woods, under trees, through grass and around rocks. No one can love the country as much as I do. For surely woods, trees and rocks produce the echo which man desires to hear' (Letter 258). But the country sometimes induced lethargy rather than activity, and bad weather there could also set him back. In town his dissatisfaction with his surroundings is reflected in frequent changes of lodgings (see 'Residences and travel', pp. 124–9), but even in the country his environment was often far from ideal. In 1825 he wrote from Baden: 'Really it is to be wondered at that I can compose here even tolerably well.' (Letter 1390)

As regards diet, Beethoven's preferences were not very different from those of the average Viennese citizen of the day, apart from an unusual predilection for fish. Types he preferred were freshwater fish such as carp, pike and pike-perch (zander). But he was in no sense a gourmet; his attitude seems to have been that enough is as good as a feast, and he rather disdained those who were too preoccupied with food: 'Man is but little above other animals if his chief pleasure is confined to the dinner-table', he is reported to have said (Thayer, 1967, p. 871). For drink he liked strong coffee and fine wines – especially those from his native Rhine and Moselle, which were difficult to obtain in Vienna. He also occasionally indulged in champagne but, as he observed after a particularly merry party in September 1825, this tended to be an impediment to his work (Letter 1427).

How far his environment had a significant effect on his musical output is an open question (see Cooper, 1990, pp. 42–58); but there was clearly some influence – an obvious example is the Piano Sonata *Das Lebewohl*, op. 81a, written to mark the departure, absence and return of his friend Archduke Rudolph. Despite Beethoven's aloofness, he was in many ways very sensitive to his surroundings, and rarely satisfied by them.

Other composers

BEETHOVEN HAD VERY DEFINITE VIEWS about the relative merits of the numerous composers whose music he had encountered; and although his views were by no means universally shared by others at the time, it is striking that the composers he regarded most highly are by and large the same as those 18th-century composers most widely admired today – Bach, Handel, Mozart and Haydn. Beethoven's 'greats' were the same as ours.

In his early years Beethoven had little opportunity to hear Handel's music, and Mozart was evidently his favourite composer. Indeed it was in order to study with Mozart that Beethoven made his first trip to Vienna in 1787, and for a long time he felt almost overawed by Mozart's greatness. On one occasion in 1799 while listening to Mozart's C minor Piano Concerto (K.491), Beethoven lamented that he himself would 'never be able to do anything like that' (Thayer, 1967, p. 209). Of Mozart's operas Beethoven preferred *The Magic Flute* – perhaps because it contained moral issues and elements of heroism that are largely absent in his three great comic operas. Ludwig Rellstab, who visited Beethoven in 1825, reports that Beethoven specifically condemned the plots of two of these three in the following words: 'I could not compose operas like *Don Giovanni* and *Figaro*. They are repugnant to me. I could not have chosen such subjects; they are too frivolous for me.' (Thayer, 1967, p. 947) This does not mean, however, that Beethoven had anything but the highest regard for Mozart's settings of them, and it was only when he became acquainted with Handel's music that Mozart's pre-eminence in Beethoven's eyes was lost. Even as late as 1826 Beethoven wrote, 'I have always counted myself amongst the greatest admirers of Mozart and shall remain so until my last breath.' (Letter 1468)

The change to Handel came gradually in the 1790s and early 1800s, after Beethoven had probably been introduced to Handel's vocal music by Baron van Swieten. According to Ries, whose knowledge was based primarily on acquaintance with Beethoven during 1801–5, Beethoven valued most highly Mozart and Handel, then Bach. But a decade later Handel was clearly the first preference: according to Cipriani Potter, who met Beethoven in 1817, Beethoven had early considered Mozart the best but since encountering Handel's music he had put him at the head. This is confirmed by what Beethoven told Schultz: 'Handel is the greatest composer that ever lived. I would uncover my head, and kneel down at his tomb!' (Thayer, 1967, p. 871) And when Stumpff asked him who was the greatest composer, his immediate reply was, 'Handel; to him I bow the knee.' (Thayer, 1967, p. 920)

Bach was not far behind Handel in Beethoven's estimation. He once said that among the older composers only Handel and Bach possessed genius (Letter 955), and elsewhere Bach was described as the 'patriarch of harmony' and even 'the immortal god of harmony' (Letters 44 and 48). In more poetic vein he said, according to Karl Freudenberg, 'His name ought not to be Bach (brook) but Ocean, because of his infinite and inexhaustible wealth of combinations and harmonies.' (Thayer, 1967, p. 956) Bach's son Emanuel was also highly regarded, especially his keyboard works: 'Some of them should certainly be in the possession of every true artist.' (Letter 220)

Beethoven's attitude to Haydn was somewhat more ambivalent, at least initially. 'Haydn seldom escaped without a few sly thrusts', said Ries (Thayer, 1967, p. 366), and Beethoven disapproved of frivolous word-painting as found in Haydn's *The Creation* and *The Seasons*. But he 'did recognize Haydn's greater achievements, especially the many choral works and certain other things for which he properly lavished praise on Haydn' (Wegeler, 1987, p. 68), and after Haydn's death Beethoven had nothing but praise for him. 'Do not rob Handel, Haydn and Mozart of their laurel wreaths', he wrote in 1812 (Letter 376), and in 1824 he referred to 'great men such as Haydn, Mozart and Cherubini' (Letter 1275). Likewise in 1815 he wrote in his *Tagebuch*, 'Portraits of Handel, Bach, Gluck, Mozart, and Haydn in my room. – – They can promote my capacity for endurance.' (Solomon, 1982, no. 43)

This is almost the only explicit indication of his admiration for Gluck, but Cherubini was mentioned on several occasions. Beethoven had been greatly impressed when Cherubini's operas first appeared in Vienna in 1802 and he admired Cherubini's Requiem more than Mozart's. When Potter asked him in 1817 who was the greatest living composer apart from Beethoven himself, the reply was Cherubini, and in 1823 Beethoven confirmed this in a letter to Schlösser: 'Of all our contemporaries I have the highest regard for him.' (Letter 1176) And to Cherubini himself Beethoven wrote in the same year: 'I value your works more highly than all other compositions for the theatre.' (Letter 1154)

Other composers also occasionally earned Beethoven's praise. Clementi, like C.P.E. Bach, was admired for his keyboard music; Spontini, like Cherubini, for his operas: 'There is much good in him; he understands theatrical effects and the musical noises of warfare thoroughly', Beethoven is reported to have said (Thayer, 1967, p. 956). He also came to have a very high opinion of Palestrina's church music, although he probably knew little of it. Beethoven was less receptive to the music of younger composers, however. He is said to have enjoyed some of Schubert's music, but much of the evidence for this is untrustworthy. As for Meyerbeer, Beethoven did not according to Tomášek think much of him either as man or as musician. Rossini he regarded as talented but his music too frivolous, while Spohr's music was 'too rich in dissonances' and too chromatic, according to Freudenberg's report (Thayer, 1967, p. 956). Beethoven's oft-quoted opinion of his one-time pupil Ries – 'he imitates me too much' – was allegedly made to Czerny, and it would certainly be valid; but Beethoven evidently liked some of Ries's music, notably a piano fantasia entitled *The Dream*. He also praised Weber's *Freischütz*, and Archduke Rudolph's 40 Variations on a theme Beethoven had given him.

When confronted with a performance of bad music, however, Beethoven was apt to laugh out loud, and he disdained performances that were mere displays of empty virtuosity, which were evidently not infrequent from pianists visiting Vienna and playing their own improvisations or compositions. Indeed there were few such pianists that Beethoven did admire, the notable exception being Johann Baptist Cramer. The rest were liable to be condemned as mere passage players who pranced up and down the keyboard playing music that signified nothing. And if bad music was disdained, bad performances sometimes induced extreme irritation, particularly in the case of *Fidelio*. In 1806 he wrote after a performance: 'All desire to compose anything more ceases completely if I have to have my work performed like that.' (Letter 130) When Potter told Beethoven in 1817 that he had heard *Fidelio*, Beethoven replied that Potter had not heard it since the singers were unable to sing it; and when in 1822 he heard the theme of his *Fidelio* overture played by a musical clock, he commented wrily: 'It plays it better than the orchestra in the Kärntnertor!' (Thayer, 1967, p. 809)

Beethoven preferred music that was elevated, serious and artful, and in later life his preferences tended to be towards older music – Bach, Handel, Palestrina and even plainsong. Perhaps the major surprise is that he preferred Handel to Bach; what seems to have particularly appealed was Handel's ability to build whole movements out of very simple ideas – an ability that was widely recognized even in his own day – and Beethoven imitated this technique in many of his own works. His lack of regard for the works of younger composers was partly due simply to the fact that so little great music was being written (except by Beethoven) during the first twenty years of the 19th century. Had he lived another fifteen years and been able to acquaint himself with not just the works of Schubert but also the masterpieces of such composers as Schumann, Chopin, Mendelssohn, Bellini, Wagner, Liszt and Berlioz, all of whom came to the fore during that period, he would doubtless have been more receptive to new music.

Himself

BEETHOVEN RARELY SAID MUCH about himself, but when he did it was often with considerable insight and a surprising amount of modesty for someone blessed with such exceptional gifts. 'It is a peculiar feeling to see and to hear oneself praised and at the same time to realize one's own inferiority as fully as I do.' (Letter 23) He tended to see himself as having wholly good and noble intentions and aspirations which were sometimes undermined by faults and inadequacies that he was only too willing to acknowledge. These faults sometimes led him to sudden breaks of friendship for which he would then apologize profusely and admit his faults (see 'Character and behaviour' and 'Personal relationships', pp. 103–10).

He was, for example, well aware of his irascibility: 'I am not wicked – Hot blood is my fault – my crime is that I am young.... Even though wildly surging emotions may betray my heart, yet my heart is good.' (Letter 4) And when he could no longer use youth as an excuse, the temperament remained the same: 'My sudden rage was merely an explosion resulting from several unpleasant incidents with him. I have the gift of being able to conceal and control my sensitivity about very many things. But if I happen to be irritated at a time when I am more liable to fly into a temper than usual, then I too erupt more violently than anyone else.' (Letter 94) This self-description certainly matches accounts related by his acquaintances.

Equally Beethoven was aware of his untidiness, carelessness and general disorderliness. To Zmeskall he wrote about 'our common lack of order, although each of us is untidy in a different way' (Letter 87); to Wegeler he mentioned 'my unpardonable carelessness' (Letter 51); and to Hoffmeister he wrote, 'Perhaps the only touch of genius which I possess is that my things are not always in very good order.' (Letter 47) Again these observations bear out those of his contemporaries.

Despite his faults, however, Beethoven believed himself to be essentially noble in mind and spirit, sometimes actually describing himself as noble-minded. To Wegeler he wrote in 1801: 'You will certainly see that I have become a first-rate fellow; not only as an artist but also as a man you will find me better and more fully developed.' (Letter 51) When he arrived in Vienna it was widely assumed that he was indeed of noble birth, for in Austria the prefix 'von' indicated as much and it was naturally presumed that the Dutch 'van' in Beethoven's name was equivalent, which it was not. Beethoven did nothing to contradict this assumption, since he believed that his unusual gifts entitled him to a place among the aristocracy (just as certain other commoners could be ennobled for their deeds). It has even been suggested that he fostered a 'nobility pretence' in which he fantasized about whether his true father were not someone more illustrious than the mediocre tenor singer and alcoholic from Bonn (Solomon, 1977).

But there were always bound to be suspicions about whether he was a genuine aristocrat, and the moment of truth came in 1818, during the battle for the guardianship of his nephew. Beethoven accidentally revealed that he was not of noble birth, and the case had to be transferred to a lower court. This infuriated him, for he continued to maintain that he was essentially noble by virtue of his character. The story that, when asked for proof of his nobility Beethoven simply pointed to his head and his heart, may be apocryphal, but it would be entirely characteristic. In a letter to Schindler in 1823 he wrote, 'As for the question of "being noble", I think I have given sufficient proof to you that I am so on principle.' (Letter 1194) None of this would, of course, convince a court of law, and Beethoven felt mortified at being assigned to a court suitable only for 'innkeepers, cobblers and tailors' (Letter 979), when he himself and by extension his nephew belonged to a higher class of person.

It was not only his talents but also his efforts which in his view entitled him to belong to this higher class. 'I can assure you that I have lived in a small unimportant town and – that entirely by my own efforts I achieved almost all that I have achieved both there and in Vienna', he wrote in 1804 (Letter 90). And it was through his own efforts that he had educated himself so extensively that he was able to cope with difficult and learned texts. 'There is hardly any treatise which could be too learned for me. I have not the slightest pretension to what is properly called erudition. Yet from my childhood I have striven to understand what the better and wiser people of every age were driving at in their works.' (Letter 228) His capacity for figures, however, was severely limited, as he readily acknowledged: 'I am really an incompetent business man who is bad at arithmetic.' (Letter 44) Many simple calculations survive in his handwriting, and his bad arithmetic is often in evidence. On one occasion he wanted to know the sum of eleven halves; not being able to multiply even whole numbers (let alone fractions), he wrote the figure $\frac{1}{2}$ eleven times in a column, added it up and wrote down his answer: $10\frac{1}{2}$ (*Jugendtagebuch*, f.7r).

Concerning his physical condition and bearing Beethoven rarely had much to say, apart from his numerous and sometimes detailed descriptions of his various illnesses (see 'Illnesses, deafness and death', pp. 136–40). Not fully aware that he had in some ways a very strong constitution, he sometimes maintained that he had always been a sickly type of person, with a weak abdomen, whereas it is likely that his environment was the cause of many of his maladies. He also made occasional passing references to other details about himself, such as an apparent allusion to having been born with a caul, and a mention of his well-documented habit of gazing upwards as he wandered through the streets of Vienna.

Socially he loved company, although this was not always evident on account of his deafness, especially during its early years when he felt obliged to cut himself off from society to conceal his affliction. 'I seemed to be a misanthrope and yet am far from being one', he wrote in 1801 (Letter 54), a sentiment echoed at the beginning of the Heiligenstadt Testament. Company of the wrong sort did not appeal at all, but where his friends were concerned he gained enormous pleasure from being with them: 'You can hardly conceive how depressed and sad I felt yesterday after you had all gone', he told his nephew in August 1825 (Letter 1414), while staying in Baden. 'It is too bad to be left alone again with this evil rabble who will never be reformed.' If Beethoven sometimes seemed aloof or remote, it was perhaps more through the weaknesses of others than any fault of his own, and it is likely that his deafness made him even more glad of company than he would have been otherwise.

His own music

BEETHOVEN'S VIEW of his own music was coloured by his perception of the function of art as an elevating force, and of his role as an artist attempting to raise men to the level of gods (see 'Philosophical ideas', pp. 142–3). He used the phrase 'true artist' on more than one occasion, implying that he either was or might become one by his efforts. The true artist 'has a vague awareness of how far he is from reaching his goal; and while others may perhaps be admiring him, he laments the fact that he has not yet reached the point whither his better genius only lights the way for him like a distant sun.' (Letter 376) Two important corollaries are inevitably generated by this attitude that the artist never achieves perfection: individual compositions can always be improved, no matter how good they are already; and new works can surpass earlier ones to create a sense of progress in art.

Beethoven subscribed to both these conclusions. His belief that works could always be improved is reflected in his obsessive sketching and revising, which frequently persisted almost up to the time of publication of a work (and occasionally even beyond). His autograph scores are often filled with messy corrections as he groped towards his artistic goals, and sometimes they still do not contain his final thoughts: the score of the Fifth Symphony was despatched to the publishers, only for Beethoven to supply them with a list of corrections and improvements some months later, after hearing the work. 'One should not want to be so like a god as not to have to correct something here and there in one's created works', he wrote to them (Letter 199). Another work that received an important last-minute revision was the slow movement of the 'Hammerklavier' Sonata, where Beethoven suddenly added an extra bar at the start, after having sent a copy of the rest to Ferdinand Ries; he simply told Ries, 'The first bar has still to be inserted.' (Letter 940) From time to time also he expressed a desire to reissue his earlier works in revised versions, as he became more and more aware of their defects, and it is likely that, had he carried out this plan, none of his works would have escaped alteration.

In fact in later life he became increasingly dismissive and contemptuous of his early works. According to J. R. Schultz in 1824, Beethoven could not bear to hear his earlier works praised, particularly his ever-popular Septet. 'I wish it were burned', he is reported to have said about it on another occasion (Thayer, 1967, p. 620). Even as early as 1803 he was lamenting the publication of 'so many wretched old things of mine' (Letter 81); and in 1809 his distaste for his early Sextet op. 71 is clearly evident beneath the rather restrained criticism: 'All that one can really say about it is that it was written by a composer who has produced at any rate a few better works.' (Letter 224)

On the whole, then, Beethoven preferred his later works to his earlier ones, and he felt obliged to be continually exploring new ideas that might surpass his earlier ones. 'Art demands of us that we shall not stand still', he once said to Holz (Thayer, 1967, p. 982), and to Archduke Rudolph he wrote: 'In the world of art, as in the whole of our great creation, freedom and progress are the main objectives.' (Letter 955) He is said to have remarked in about 1802 (the precise date is uncertain) that he was dissatisfied with what he had written up to then and intended to follow a 'new path'. On occasion he even drew attention to novel ideas in his works – notably the two sets of Variations opp. 34 and 35 – although he normally left it to others to point them out.

Artistic progress was not, however, a smooth continuum for him; not every work surpassed its immediate predecessor, as he was well aware, and sometimes a great work was followed by compositions of less significance before the next major leap forward. Thus he apparently considered his best symphonies to be the *Eroica* and the Ninth, though he also described the Seventh as 'one of the happiest products of my poor talents' (Letter 523). Of his piano sonatas he preferred the 'Appassionata', until he wrote the 'Hammerklavier', which he then regarded as his greatest; earlier he had also regarded the B♭ Sonata op. 22 very highly. Other works that gave him particular satisfaction include the song *Adelaide* (op. 46) and the Mass in C. Concerning the latter, Beethoven claimed that he had 'treated the text in a manner in which it has rarely been treated' (Letter 167), and described it as 'especially close to my heart' (Letter 169). Eventually, however, it was overshadowed by the Mass in D, which he then described as 'the greatest work which I have composed' (Letter 1079) and which he thought deserved to create a sensation in the musical world (Letter 1029). Of his quartets he inevitably preferred the late ones; but when asked which of the three Galitzin quartets (opp. 127, 130 and 132) was the greatest he replied evasively, 'Each in its own way'. Later he said that the op. 131 Quartet in C♯ minor was his greatest (Thayer, 1967, p. 982).

Some works, in contrast, were considered to be on a distinctly lower level. The Second Piano Concerto he described as not one of his best, and it was consequently sold at half price. Likewise he admitted that three overtures (*Ruinen von Athen*, *Namensfeier* and *König Stephan*) which had been performed unsuccessfully in London did 'not belong to my best and great works' (Letter 664).

A few years later he complained of having to write potboilers to support himself when he really wanted to write great operas, oratorios and church music. Thus he was well aware of the disparity between his best and his more mediocre works, but it is significant that the works he considered the best were usually the same as those most highly regarded today: the Second Piano Concerto is still considered his weakest, and the C♯ minor Quartet *primus inter pares*, while the potboilers he referred to are probably such works as the rarely heard Flute Variations opp. 105 and 107.

Concerning his compositional technique and methods, Beethoven was rather reticent. He rarely referred to his sketches and only made a few fairly general statements about such matters as keeping the whole in view when writing a work. The one extended description of his composing methods attributed to him, reported by Louis Schlösser and beginning, 'I carry my thoughts about with me for a long time, sometimes a very long time, before I set them down', was evidently invented by Schlösser (see Solomon, 1980b). Beethoven did indicate, however, that even in purely instrumental music the initial idea was sometimes sparked off by something non-musical. Examples known or at least claimed by others include the tomb scene in *Romeo and Juliet* (Quartet op. 18 no. 1, slow movement; confirmed by comments among the sketches), a galloping horse (Sonata op. 31 no. 2, finale), a starry sky (Quartet op. 59 no. 2, slow movement) and the call of the yellowhammer (Fifth Symphony, opening). But Czerny reports that Beethoven was not very communicative on this topic except occasionally, and that he believed anyway that music is not always so freely felt by listeners if they have been told beforehand of some specific image. Moreover Beethoven was of the view that 'all painting in instrumental music is lost if it is pushed too far' (Thayer, 1967, p. 436), and so it seems that musical syntax rather than extra-musical stimulus was the main determinant in shaping his instrumental works, even in the case of the *Pastoral* Symphony, to which these comments relate.

BARRY COOPER

Section 8

BIOGRAPHICAL AND MUSICAL SOURCE MATERIAL

BIOGRAPHICAL AND MUSICAL SOURCE MATERIAL

Letters

'I WOULD RATHER WRITE 10,000 notes than one letter of the alphabet', wrote Beethoven to Nikolaus Simrock on 28 November 1820. But somebody whose income depended largely on the marketing of his music could hardly avoid entering into lengthy and involved correspondence with publishers, patrons and performers; moreover, Beethoven's various handicaps – not just his deafness, but his clumsiness, his inability to cope with the most basic everyday tasks – made him unusually dependent on other people, with whom it was often necessary to communicate by letter. No doubt the conflict between his distaste for letter-writing and the impossibility of avoiding the task conditioned his epistolary style, which can hardly be described as elegant. Many of the letters are awkwardly expressed, poorly spelled and badly laid out, though there is evidence that he sometimes read through a letter before dispatching it: postscripts added at the head or foot of a page (or even in the margins), and additional words and phrases cued in at the appropriate points in the main text. But Beethoven clearly wrote in great haste on most occasions and had little concept of proper punctuation, a fact which often obscures the meaning of his prose and on occasion renders it unintelligible.

Exactly how many letters Beethoven wrote will never be known. The first attempt at a collected edition, by Nohl in 1865, included 411 documents in total. Just less than a century later, Emily Anderson's English translation of 1961 included over 1570 items; and previously unrecorded letters continue to appear at auction with some regularity. The earliest known letter is dated 15 September 1787; then there is a gap until 1792, and few letters survive between that year and 1799. The survival rate increases considerably from about 1809 onwards, and the last letters date from only days before Beethoven's death. The meaning of statistical comparisons like those above is obscured to some extent by one's definition of the term 'letter': should receipts and other documents like those discussed later in this section be included, for instance, or should a more restricted view be adopted? Moreover, the worldwide dispersal of the letters further contributes to the difficulty of assessing their total number. The richest and most important collection is the Bodmer Collection, now in the Beethovenhaus at Bonn. The national libraries in Berlin, London, Paris, Vienna and several other cities also have important holdings, and there is a large amount of material in private hands which is often inaccessible to scholars.

Most of Beethoven's letters are of course written in German and signed by the composer; but there are numerous exceptions. Letters to foreign correspondents were often written in another language (usually French, but sometimes Italian or English) by someone other than Beethoven, who merely signed them. Much of his correspondence with the publishers George Thomson and Robert Birchall was carried on in this way. On other occasions Beethoven himself attempted to write in a foreign language, with predictably poor results.

It was also necessary for Beethoven to use an amanuensis when he was too ill to write letters himself. His nephew Karl performed this duty, as did Schindler, who penned most of the letters from 1827. And in some cases a correspondence was carried on entirely on Beethoven's behalf by another person. There are, for example, nineteen letters written by Beethoven's brother Carl to Breitkopf & Härtel. Dating from 1802–5, they are mostly concerned with offers of new works by Beethoven and fully deserve to be considered 'Beethoven letters', yet they are not included in Anderson's edition. (They were published as an appendix to the second volume of Riemann's revision of Thayer's Beethoven biography (Thayer, 1917–23), and some were incorporated into the text of Forbes's subsequent revision of that work.)

The letters not only provide a great deal of factual information about Beethoven's life and activities but also reflect his character. The most famous letter of all is that to the 'Immortal Beloved'. It is now certain beyond all reasonable doubt that this was written in Teplitz in 1812, and that it was intended for a woman residing in Karlsbad at that time. Who that woman was has probably engendered more conjecture than any other aspect of Beethoven's life and work. Maynard Solomon's arguments in favour of Antonie Brentano are the most plausible yet published, but even they have not dampened further speculation (the Beloved's continued immortality seems well assured).

The letter to the 'Immortal Beloved' is a remarkable document, expressing by its passionate language and confused thought Beethoven's extreme emotional state at this time (see plate 30). It far surpasses his other love-letters, such as some of those to Josephine Deym. But at another extreme the letters also reflect the intense anger to which Beethoven could be roused: the inept copyist Ferdinand Wolanek received a stinging response to a letter in which he announced the withdrawal of his services in copying the *Missa Solemnis*. Beethoven scored through Wolanek's text and wrote 'stupid, conceited, asinine fellow' in huge letters across it (see plate 34) before writing his reply in the remaining spaces on the paper (Letter 1463; facsimile in Schmidt-Görg, 1970, p. 250). If this example shows how violently Beethoven could express his anger on paper, other letters reveal the extreme contrition of which he was capable.

However tiresome Beethoven may have claimed letter-writing to be, and however poor his control over the written word, there is little doubt that he obtained much satisfaction out of playing with language. Many letters reflect his wild sense of humour and his love of bad puns and double meanings. He delighted in exaggeratedly courteous and grandiloquent openings: Schindler is addressed as 'Most excellent Optimus Optime!' and 'Quite amazing and most excellent fellow!!', and on other occasions as the 'Samothracian Scoundrel', 'Most excellent Scoundrel of Epirus and not less of Brundisium and so forth!'. Bernard becomes 'Bernardus non Sanctus', and games are also played with Haslinger's name. Many letters to Holz would be unintelligible if the reader did not realize that in German *Holz* means 'wood'. Other letters contain serious messages or requests expressed almost entirely in terms of private jokes shared between Beethoven and the recipient. It is impossible to give more than an inkling of the range of Beethoven's humorous letters here: one might just add mention of some delightfully sarcastic examples from 1822 to his brother Johann and one, to Steiner, which shows that like Mozart (a far superior letter-writer) Beethoven was not averse to coarse language: 'With all my heart I embrace the L[ieutenant] G[eneral] and wish him the penis of a stallion.'

A number of the letters contain not only words but music also. Thus on 18 March 1820 Beethoven wrote out two folksongs with accompaniments in a letter to Nikolaus Simrock. Other letters contain canons or musical quips (see WoO 205 in Kinsky, 1955). Also of interest in connection with Beethoven's music are some passages in which he gives an idea of his method of composing: writing to Adolf Martin Schlesinger on 13 November 1821, for example, he remarked, 'now that my health appears to be better, I merely jot down certain ideas as I used to do, and when I have completed the whole in my head, everything is written down, but only once'.

Among the most interesting from a musical point of view are Beethoven's letters to his various publishers. They help to illustrate the difficulties and frustrations which often arose in the copying and engraving of new works: the letters to Steiner concerning the publication in 1816 of the Seventh Symphony are a case in point. Another letter to Steiner contains interesting information about the notation of the cello in Beethoven's manuscripts. Sometimes letters were also the vehicle for lists of corrections which needed to be made to scores: a long list of corrections for the English edition of the 'Hammerklavier' Sonata was sent to Ferdinand Ries in 1819, and a subsequent missive contains the newly-added first bar for the slow movement of that work. Other letters provide evidence for projected works which Beethoven never completed. For instance, the trio mentioned in a letter of 13 May 1816 to Countess Erdödy is presumably the Piano Trio in F minor which Beethoven began sketching around that time in the Scheide Sketchbook.

The mention of projected works may suitably introduce the topic of the reliability of Beethoven's letters and the proper critical approach to them (see especially Tyson, 1977a). It is well known that Beethoven was often not entirely honest in his dealings with publishers (see 'First editions and publishers', p. 192). He was also apt to exaggerate the progress he had made on works promised for publication; and since the testimony of the letters is often vital in establishing the chronology of a particular work, it is necessary to corroborate relevant statements wherever possible. Thus Beethoven's statement to Peters on 6 July 1822 that a promised string quartet 'is not yet quite finished' is considerably wide of the mark: no sketches for a string quartet survive from 1822, and even if there were some which are now lost, they can hardly have been very extensive.

Not only are the contents of numerous letters open to suspicion, but their dating also requires a cautious approach. In a number of cases Beethoven accidentally wrote the wrong date: a letter to the Countess Susanna Guicciardi (not in Anderson; see Tyson, 1973a) which most probably dates from 1802 is dated 1782, for example. But many more letters bear no date whatsoever. Either circumstance – an incorrect date or the lack of one – is sometimes compensated for by the fact that the recipient has noted the date of arrival, so that a fairly accurate date for the writing of the letter can be established. Otherwise one has to be guided where possible by the contents of the letter; in the worst cases the contents give no help at all, but in others it is possible to arrive at a date which is at least plausible. Unfortunately little help is to be obtained from watermark studies, which have proved so successful in establishing the chronology of the sketches, or from the study of Beethoven's handwriting.

Problems of dating and also of interpretation can sometimes be resolved if a letter is read not in isolation but in connection with other sources. Beethoven's *Tagebuch* of 1812–18 is useful in this respect, and for the years from 1818 onwards the Conversation Books (see pp. 164–7) provide a very rich background against which to set the letters. One example may serve to illustrate how the Conversation Books can serve both to date a letter and to illuminate its contents. Consider this letter from Beethoven to Steiner and Co:

> I am requesting Geh'bauer to let me have a few tickets (two), for some of my friends want to go to this *hole-and-corner musical performance* – Perhaps you yourselves have some of those *lavatory tickets*. If so, send me one or two.... The score belongs to the chorus [*Chor*], of which that *peasant* has the parts.

The letter is dated '[Vienna, 1821]' in Anderson's edition. The play on Gebauer's surname (*Bauer* means 'peasant') also occurs in a Conversation Book entry in Beethoven's hand that can be dated around 10 April 1820 (Köhler, 1968, ii.52). Directly below it Franz Oliva wrote: 'nevertheless I should like to hear this *choral work* [*Chor*]; I would be very pleased if you could perhaps get me a *ticket* for the *concert* at which it is to be performed'. The 'choral work' was probably *Meeresstille und glückliche Fahrt*, which was performed at two of Gebauer's Concerts Spirituels in April and May that year (Gebauer had visited Beethoven during March to discuss performances of his music in these concerts: see Köhler, 1968, i.342–3). Beethoven's letter to Steiner seems almost certain to have been written in response to Oliva's request for concert tickets, and it should therefore be redated to early April 1820.

That such redating and interpretation has still to be done (no doubt many more correspondences between letters and Conversation Books await discovery) is largely due to the fact that, at the time of writing, Anderson's remains the most complete and scholarly edition of Beethoven's letters available. Apart from its relative completeness, other merits of this edition were the fact that the letters had been newly translated from the original texts wherever possible, and that a brief commentary was provided where necessary. The location of the original text was also given wherever this was known. (Locations were given in Kastner, 1910, but then suppressed in Kastner-Kapp, 1923, which remains the most comprehensive German edition of the letters presently available; neither Kastner, Kastner-Kapp nor several other more selective collections of letters were provided with any commentary.) On the whole Anderson's translations were accurate, but she sometimes departed significantly from Beethoven's text. Thus, writing to Schlesinger on 20 September 1820 about the Sonatas opp. 109–11, Beethoven wrote: 'die erste [Sonate] ist fast bis zur *Correctur* ganz fertig', which Anderson translates as 'The first is quite ready save for correcting the copy'. The reference to a 'copy' of op. 109 is misleading.

Fortunately, a scholarly edition of the letters is presently in preparation by an international team of scholars, coordinated from the Beethovenhaus in Bonn. A pilot volume containing the correspondence with the publishers Schott has already appeared (the introductory material includes a useful summary of previous editions as well as an outline of the editorial principles underlying the new one). This new edition aims to be as complete and accurate as possible – accurate not only in textual matters but also in the chronological arrangement of the letters. Each letter will also be provided with a much more detailed commentary than hitherto. A very welcome feature is the decision to include in the new edition letters sent to Beethoven as well as those sent by him. This will help further to widen the context in which Beethoven's own letters can be read, and will sometimes clarify the meaning of obscure references. The letters sent to Beethoven may also shed light in other areas. For instance, the emergence some years ago (see Sotheby's, 9–10 May 1985, lot 6) of a letter-draft from Robert Birchall in reply to a letter from Beethoven dated 1 October 1816 makes clear that Birchall rejected Beethoven's offer of a piano trio. If this trio was the projected one in F minor referred to above, then Birchall's refusal to purchase it perhaps provides a motive for its abandonment by the composer.

NICHOLAS MARSTON

Conversation Books

(Note: Köhler, 1968 is the source for all quotations from the Conversation Books below. Volume and page references to this edition are given in brackets.)

ALTHOUGH BEETHOVEN HAD GOOD REASON to bemoan the tragic fate which rendered him almost totally deaf, posterity has good reason to be grateful for his affliction. Had Beethoven's hearing not been seriously impaired, there would have been no need for those who came into contact with him from about 1818 onwards to communicate with him in writing in many instances. Beethoven took to providing notebooks for this purpose. The Conversation Books, as these books are now called, are upright in format and usually measure about 18 × 12 cm. They contain varying numbers of leaves, but almost all are of immense interest both to Beethoven scholars and to anyone interested in daily life in Vienna in the 1820s.

The Conversation Books are primarily of biographical interest, and one of their most valuable characteristics is the sense of immediacy which they convey to the reader. Whereas biographers have to rely to a greater or lesser extent on memories and anecdotes which tend to become less trustworthy with the passing of time, the Conversation Books preserve the actual words 'spoken' to Beethoven during several of the most important phases of his last decade. There are lengthy discussions of the legal struggle for guardianship of his nephew Karl; a wealth of material concerning the preparations for and aftermath of the concert on 7 May 1824 at which the Ninth Symphony received its first performance (Ignaz Schuppanzigh remarks that the singers, rehearsing the finale for the first time, would like to take it more slowly: vi.124); and fascinating conversations from the years 1825–6 during which the late quartets were composed and Karl's attempted suicide took place. The last conversation dates from 5 March 1827, only three weeks before Beethoven's death.

What is not to be found in the Conversation Books in any great quantity is material relating to the actual composition of Beethoven's music; like many composers, Beethoven was reticent on this subject. However, there are occasional surprises, such as this remark of Franz Oliva, made some time between 22 and 24 April 1820: 'And perhaps you could use the little new piece in a sonata for *Schlesinger*' (ii. 87). Beethoven's letters and sketchbooks establish with some certainty that this 'little new piece' must have been the first movement of the Piano Sonata in E, op. 109. Accordingly, the implication of Oliva's remark is that the movement had been conceived as an independent composition, an interesting point in view of its unusual, fantasia-like quality. This example also indicates the extent to which the Conversation Books, like the letters (see pp. 162–4), need to be read in conjunction with other written sources to establish new facts or to clarify uncertain issues.

While the amount of conversation about the compositional process is small (and largely inauthentic, as explained below), there is much of interest concerning the practical aspects of getting new works performed and marketed: the case of the Ninth Symphony has already been referred to. There is also much talk of daily musical life in Vienna, and of other composers and their works. Mozart is often mentioned; a visit during April 1823 by the eleven-year-old Liszt is recorded (iii.168); and in October of that year Weber visited Beethoven prior to the first performance of his *Euryanthe* on the 25th. Following the premiere, Karl told Beethoven that the opera was 'full of horrible dissonances' and that the composer's presence was requested in the orchestra pit so that he could hear the nonsense of the notes for himself (iv.208).

Paradoxically, the greatest value of the Conversation Books may be thought to lie in the trivia which they preserve: everyday cares, gossip, malice and humour – all is presented with utter naturalness. In this respect the Conversation Books present a picture of Beethoven in his natural environment which no other documents can rival. Consider a conversation from early January 1820 (i.184) between Beethoven, Peters, Bernard and others. The location is an inn which Beethoven describes as 'for nobody but gourmets'. It is clearly a hard winter, for Bernard asks Beethoven how his lodgings are in the cold weather. Shortly before this, Peters makes a practical suggestion in view of the inclement season: 'Would you like to sleep with my wife? It's so cold'!

Despite their riches, the Conversation Books need to be used with some care. Their greatest drawback is that Beethoven is largely absent as a contributor to conversations: unless he did not wish to be overheard for any reason, he replied orally to his friends' written remarks. So reading a Conversation Book is very much like listening to one half of a telephone conversation: one has to reconstruct Beethoven's replies on the basis of the remarks made to him. This can sometimes be done with considerable confidence, but there are many other situations in which equally plausible but diametrically opposed statements can be put into Beethoven's mouth.

Nevertheless, Conversation Book entries in Beethoven's hand are by no means sparse. As well as using the books occasionally for purposes of communication, he also appropriated their pages for personal memoranda. Shopping lists appear frequently (not surprisingly, blotting paper is often listed), as do pages of accounts, drafts for letters and other documents, and transcriptions of advertisements from the newspapers. These often give details of newly-published books and so afford an insight into Beethoven's literary interests. There are also a number of short musical sketches (see, for instance, a sketch for the 'Freude' theme from the last movement of the Ninth Symphony: iv.299); since the Conversation Books can often be reliably dated (the copyings from newspapers are especially useful in this respect), these sketches are sometimes helpful in fixing the period during which corresponding sketches in the sketchbooks were made.

Obviously, the Conversation Books do not preserve every word spoken to Beethoven between 1818 and 1827. One reason for this is that some friends (the Archduke Rudolph, for instance) could make themselves understood orally. Also, it is clear that the Conversation Books were not the sole means of written communication with Beethoven; he also kept a slate which could be wiped clean after use, and no doubt the nearest available piece of paper was pressed into service when a Conversation Book was not immediately to hand. Furthermore, it is only to be expected that not all of the Conversation Books have survived, and that of those which have survived some are not intact. But these points bring us to consider the sinister role played by the first owner of the Conversation Books after Beethoven's death: Anton Schindler.

Exactly how many Conversation Books Schindler owned is unclear. Thayer mentioned a figure of 'about four hundred', and related Schindler's claim to have 'long preserved the books and papers intact, but not finding any person but himself who placed any value upon them, their weight and bulk had led him in the course of his long unsettled life by degrees to destroy those which he deemed to be of little or no importance' (Thayer, 1967, p. 730). In 1846 Schindler sold the remaining books to the Königliche Bibliothek (today the Deutsche Staatsbibliothek) in Berlin; there were 137 books and a number of loose leaves, and Schindler has accordingly been accused of an appalling act of vandalism ever since. But it has been suggested more recently that Thayer's figure of four hundred ('vierhundert') may have been a mishearing of the phrase 'well over one hundred' ('viel über hundert'), so Schindler may not have been quite as villainous as had been imagined; his claim to have destroyed any books at all has even been doubted.

Even if he can be acquitted on the charge of mass destruction, however, Schindler is nevertheless guilty of serious misconduct with respect to the Conversation Books. Whether or not he destroyed entire books, he appears to have suppressed passages which he felt would be damaging to Beethoven's posthumous reputation; and during the 1970s it became clear that he also invented a large number of conversations between himself and the 'master' which he entered into the Conversation Books long after Beethoven's death. These forged entries (all 'conversations' between Beethoven and Schindler for 1819 and 1820 are forged, for example), were intended to give an inflated picture of Schindler's own familiarity with Beethoven. Unfortunately, many of these entries are precisely those which scholars had valued for their revelations concerning Beethoven's compositional process and his attitude to his own music: there is mention, for instance, of the 'two principles' supposedly disputed in the Piano Sonatas op. 14 and of metronome markings for the Seventh Symphony. In addition to these false conversations, Schindler also annotated the books, identifying particular speakers and dating certain conversations. These annotations were often inaccurate, but at least they were not all intended to deceive.

Fortunately, the damage done by Schindler has been largely undone by scholarship during the last twenty-five years, with the forged entries all now identified. Attempts to launch an edition of the Conversation Books were made by Nohl in 1924 and by Schünemann, who published three volumes of a projected edition in 1941–3, but it was not until the early 1960s that the opportunity to prepare a really reliable and complete edition arose. Headed by Karl-Heinz Köhler, a team of scholars at the Deutsche Staatsbibliothek in Berlin is still working on a projected ten-volume edition which will in-clude not only the books preserved in that library's collection but the relatively small amount of material held elsewhere, such as in the Beethoven-haus, Bonn, and in private collections. Each volume provides not only an accurate text but also a very full critical apparatus. Particularly useful are the endnotes, which identify the speakers and persons referred to wherever possible and establish the context and amplify many details of the conversations. In many instances this helps to fix the dates of the conversations with considerable precision (but dating often remains speculative and caution is once again necessary). In those volumes published after the identification of Schindler's forged entries the relevant passages are marked by an asterisk in the text.

The following list gives a summary of the volumes published so far. Attention should be drawn to the irregular survival pattern of the Conversation Books. There is a gap of one year after March 1818, for example, and nothing has been preserved for the period between September 1820 and June 1822. Moreover, the size and scope of the books varies widely. Book 9 (i.319–65) contains 94 leaves covering a period of just over a week, while book 15 (ii.179–213) has 73 leaves devoted to a period of about six weeks. Other 'books' (for example, book 1: i.29–35) are no more than a gathering of a few leaves.

Vol. 1
Books 1–10
February–March 1818
March–May 1819
November 1819–March 1820

Vol. 2
Books 11–22
April–September 1820
June, November 1822
January–February 1823

Vol. 3
Books 23–37
February–July 1823

Vol. 4
Books 38–48
August–December 1823

Vol. 5
Books 49–60
December 1823–April 1824

Vol. 6
Books 61–76
April–September 1824

Vol. 7
Books 77–90
October 1824–July 1825

Vol. 8
Books 91–103
July–September 1825
November 1825–February 1826

Vol. 9
Books 104–13
February–June 1826

NICHOLAS MARSTON

Diaries and other documents

Diaries

BEETHOVEN IS NEVER KNOWN to have kept a diary as such, but during at least two periods of his life he kept a kind of memorandum book whose function sometimes resembled that of a diary or *Tagebuch*. The earlier one, known as the *Jugendtagebuch* and now in the British Library (Zweig MS 14, transcription and commentary in Busch-Weise, 1962), covers the period November 1792 to January 1794 or a little later. It is devoted largely to Beethoven's personal expenditure, beginning with the expenses of his journey from Bonn to Vienna. The initial part provides indications of his route as far as Würges, to where he had been accompanied by a companion, and hints at some of the dangers of long-distance travel in wartime: 'Tip because the chap drove us at the risk of a beating right through the Hessian army and drove like a devil'. The next few pages find Beethoven in Vienna, paying for such things as 'boots, shoes, piano desk, seal, wood, writing desk...', and noting down the cost of lessons with Haydn. Sometimes he noted down his principal monthly expenses, as for example (see 'Economics', pp. 68–70 for explanation of currency values):

house rent	14 fl.
piano [rent]	6 fl. 40 kr.
heating	12 kr. per day
meals with wine	16½ fl.

The names of certain acquaintances also appear, including Van Swieten, Schuppanzigh and Albrechtsberger, and at one point Beethoven wrote a note of self-encouragement, of the type that occurs several times in his later *Tagebuch*: 'Courage. Despite all weaknesses of body, my spirit shall rule. You have lived 25 [23?] years. This year must determine the complete man – nothing must remain undone.' This was probably written on New Year's Day 1794.

Beethoven's other *Tagebuch*, dating from 1812–18, was much more substantial. Although lost shortly after his death, a copy of it had by then been made by Anton Gräffer; and although this itself was lost for a time (it is now in the Stadtarchiv,

Iserlohn), copies made from it were known to Thayer and other biographers. A commentary, edition and translation of Gräffer's copy have been made by Maynard Solomon (Solomon, 1982). Three leaves in Beethoven's hand containing material from the *Tagebuch* do actually survive, and Clemens Brenneis has argued convincingly that two of them originally belonged in the *Tagebuch* itself; the third, however, has the material arranged differently from Gräffer's copy and therefore could not have belonged (Brenneis, 1984, pp. 86–7).

The *Tagebuch* contains an enormous variety of jottings. We find the mundane: 'Shoe-brushes for polishing when somebody comes'; the personal: 'Regard K[arl] as your own child...'; the musical: 'The best opening phrases in canons are built around harmonies'; the philosophical: 'All evil is mysterious and appears greater when viewed alone'; and the religious: 'O hear, ever ineffable One, hear me, your unhappy, unhappiest of all mortals.' There are also numerous quotations from literary sources, including oriental religious writings (see 'Religion' and 'Literature', pp. 145–50).

A few of the 171 entries can be dated precisely and from these the remainder can be dated approximately. Overall they provide enormous insights into Beethoven's emotional and mental turmoil during six crucial years of his life – the six years after the 'Immortal Beloved' affair of 1812, during which period he composed relatively little, although numerous works were begun. Two references to a certain 'A' and 'T' have been taken to refer to the 'Immortal Beloved' herself, assuming she was Antonie (Toni) Brentano, and the *Tagebuch* may even have been begun so as to provide an outlet for his pent-up stress from the events of 1812. Other entries show his concern to provide and care for his nephew Karl after the death of the boy's father, and his determination to accomplish great things in his art – if necessary by leaving Vienna. Such thoughts have an openness and integrity that come from having been written without any intention of being communicated to others. The *Tagebuch* also provides an excellent panorama of Beethoven's literary interests and some otherwise unobtainable insights into his religious beliefs. Without it, our understanding of him during these critical years would be immeasurably poorer.

Other documents

In addition to the Heiligenstadt Testament (see pp. 169–72) and the *Tagebücher*, many other documents survive pertaining to Beethoven's life. There has been no systematic attempt to provide a complete edition or list of them after the manner of documentary biographies for certain other composers, but most of the important ones were published by Thayer (see Thayer, 1917–23 and 1967). These documents include Beethoven's estate inventory and the 1827 auction catalogue of his musical effects, a number of contracts, many papers relating to the guardianship of his nephew, an album of 1792, memoirs written (with varying degrees of accuracy) by people who had come into contact with him, newspaper announcements, and various minor papers in or including his handwriting or referring to him by name.

The most significant of these is the auction catalogue. Five exemplars of this survive, plus a related list of prices and buyers. Three of the five are in the hand of Anton Gräffer, the auctioneer at the sale on 5 November 1827; two of these are now in the Stadt- und Landesarchiv, Vienna, and the remaining one is in the Beethovenhaus, Bonn, as is also the copy in the hand of Aloys Fuchs. The fifth copy is in the hand of Haslinger, while the list of prices and buyers was prepared by Hotschevar (the then guardian of Beethoven's nephew). An excellent edition of the first two sections of the catalogue has been published recently (Johnson, 1985, pp. 574–81), though it omits the prices paid. A complete but less accurate edition was issued earlier by Thayer (reprinted in Thayer, 1967, pp. 1062–70); it includes the appraised prices and the prices actually paid, but omits the names of the purchasers.

The catalogue is extremely useful for indicating the state of Beethoven's manuscripts at his death and it provides particularly invaluable information about the history of the sketchbooks and sketch-leaves. These formed the first two sections of the auction and comprised seventy items. Among them were many whole sketchbooks, a few of which can be identified precisely. Other items were given vague descriptions such as quartet sketches, mass sketches or simply 'Notirungen' when they could not be easily identified or described. Most items in these two sections, including whole sketchbooks, sold for between 1 and 3 fl. CM each – a price roughly comparable to the cost of a meal for two at a good inn. The third section of the auction consisted of autograph scores of works already published; most of the seventy-eight items sold for prices similar to those of the first two sections, though there were a few exceptions, notably the very popular Septet, which sold for 18 fl. CM. The fourth section included unpublished compositions, some of which attracted quite high prices; outstanding was a fragment of a new string quintet (WoO 62), for which Diabelli paid 30 fl. 30 kr. CM. The remaining three sections of the auction consisted mainly of: instrumental and vocal parts for a number of compositions; printed editions; and books on music. Also sold were a piano and two violins.

Related to the auction catalogue is Beethoven's estate inventory, which has also not been printed in a reliable edition; the version published by Thayer (see Thayer, 1967, pp. 1072–6) was based on only a copy of the original. The inventory provides a fascinating insight into Beethoven's personal possessions, for it gives details of all the furniture in each of his rooms, plus details of clothing, valuables (including a gold medallion and a silver watch), kitchenware and musical instruments. It also confirms paradoxically both Beethoven's view that he was in dire financial straits, and the posthumous view that he was not: before the arrival, shortly before his death, of the £100 gift from the Philharmonic Society of London, Beethoven's cash reserves amounted probably to less than what he owed his creditors, and he could see no way of changing that situation; but if the value of his possessions and especially the seven bank shares (each worth 1063 fl. CM at his death) that he had set aside as a legacy for his nephew are taken into account, he was better off than most Viennese of the period.

Among Beethoven's contracts are several with publishers, including Artaria, Traeg, Clementi, Breitkopf & Härtel, Steiner, and Thomson (see Anderson, 1961, pp. 1417–25), but his most important contract was that with his three patrons Kinsky, Lobkowitz and Archduke Rudolph (Thayer, 1967, p. 457), which is preserved in the Museum der Stadt Wien. The three undertook to pay Beethoven 4000 fl. per annum (see 'Beethoven's patrons and commissions', p. 95) until he received an appointment worth at least as much, which he never did; in return Beethoven merely undertook to reside in Vienna 'or in a city in one of the other hereditary countries of His Austrian Imperial Majesty'. He was not even obliged to compose anything, although it was implicitly assumed he would and the purpose of the contract was to enable him to do so 'in a position where the necessaries of life shall not cause him embarrassment'. A copy of the draft of the contract was also published by Thayer, but the original of this is not known to survive.

Many documents relate to Beethoven's litigation over the guardianship of his nephew (see Anderson, 1961, pp. 1360–1409). They include the longest known non-musical document in Beethoven's handwriting – a draft memorandum to the Court of Appeal dated 18 February 1820 that demonstrates the enormous effort he was putting into the matter at a time when he was supposed to be trying to work towards an imminent deadline for the *Missa Solemnis*. Beethoven's papers give a very clear picture of his side of the case, which he put forward very skilfully using a combination of persistence, repetition, exaggeration, innuendo and invective against his sister-in-law. Quite different are the minutes of the Landrecht court, which record in a matter-of-fact way interviews with the three persons concerned (Thayer, 1967, pp. 708–11).

A rather unusual document is the Fischhof Manuscript, in the Deutsche Staatsbibliothek,

Berlin. It consists of transcripts made by Joseph Fischhof (1804–57) of various papers relating to Beethoven, derived mainly from a collection assembled by Anton Gräffer in preparation for a projected (but abandoned) biography of the composer. Amongst these transcripts are Beethoven's *Tagebuch* and letters to and from him. The usefulness of the Fischhof Manuscript is limited since in most cases either the originals or earlier copies of the material survive; but there are a few items for which the Fischhof Manuscript is the only source. A detailed description and transcription of the entire contents (apart from the *Tagebuch*) have been published by Clemens Brenneis (1984).

Beethoven's album or *Stammbuch* was used by his friends in Bonn during the period 24 October–1 November 1792 (immediately before his departure for Vienna) for writing farewell greetings. There are fifteen entries altogether, the most notable contributors being Count Waldstein and members of the Koch and Breuning families (for a commentary and transcription, see Nottebohm, 1872, pp. 138–44). Although there is a surprising absence of the names of leading musicians, the album gives some indication of Beethoven's wide circle of friends and of the affection and admiration they had for him.

Many of Beethoven's acquaintances left accounts of their association with him, written after (or in a few cases before) his death. Apart from Schindler's biography and the reminiscences published jointly by Wegeler and Ries in 1838, the main ones include a lengthy series of recollections by Czerny (Czerny, 1970), and shorter accounts by such figures as Baron de Trémont, Seyfried, Schultz, Fischer and Treitschke. Some accounts were published at the time in periodicals such as *The Harmonicon*; others remained in manuscript (for example the Fischer Manuscript) before being published at a much later date. Although not all are equally reliable, between them they present a vivid picture of many aspects of the composer's life and his changing situation, and they are in general agreement about such matters as his eccentricity and the disorderliness of his rooms.

The newspaper announcements fall into two main categories – those of a relatively personal nature made by Beethoven himself, and those made by his publishers. Beethoven placed notices in the press on twelve occasions, all but two of them in the *Wiener Zeitung* (Anderson, 1961, pp. 1434–43). Several were to announce forthcoming concerts, or to thank publicly the performers who had taken part in one; most others were to warn the public about various unauthorized and incorrect editions or arrangements of his music. When new works were published, the publishers customarily placed an advertisement about them, usually also in the *Wiener Zeitung* (except for Schott's, who announced new works in their own musical journal *Caecilia*).

These announcements are extremely significant since they provide the prime evidence about the precise date of publication of nearly all of Beethoven's works.

Notices referring to Beethoven also sometimes appeared. The most important are the numerous reviews published in the Leipzig *Allgemeine Musikalische Zeitung* concerning his concerts or new compositions; E. T. A. Hoffmann's review of the Fifth Symphony has become particularly famous. Other newspaper references include, for example, a description of Maelzel's newly invented chronometer (later called a metronome) published in an article in the *Wiener Vaterländische Blätter* of 13 October 1813 (see 'Performance Practice in Beethoven's Day', p. 282).

Minor papers and documents that might also be mentioned include various correction lists, price lists, receipts, testimonials, pages from Beethoven's housekeeping books, his baptismal certificate, his annotations and underlinings in books from his library, references to him in the correspondence and diaries of his contemporaries, and archival records. All these and other such material help to extend our knowledge and understanding of the composer, and they provide an almost inexhaustible supply of information of potential use to the Beethoven biographer. Although they have been extensively examined, it will be many years before there is a complete list and transcription of all known material, and further discoveries, especially in obscure archives, can still be made at present.

BARRY COOPER

The Heiligenstadt Testament

BY FAR THE MOST FAMOUS literary document in Beethoven's hand is the so-called Heiligenstadt Testament of 1802, written in the depths of despair when he felt almost suicidal. It is a most moving, heartfelt plea for understanding and sympathy from his brothers, those around him and from the world at large. The Testament was found amongst his papers shortly after his death – probably by Schindler, who communicated the contents to Rochlitz. It then passed through the hands of the publishers Artaria & Co. and also Hotschevar (then guardian of Beethoven's nephew), and later Aloys Fuchs, Jenny Lind and her husband Otto Goldschmidt, who offered it in 1888 or 1890 to the Staats- und Universitätsbibliothek in Hamburg, where it now resides.

The background to the Testament began with the onset of Beethoven's hearing difficulty in about 1797. For a while he told nobody of the problem, but eventually in 1801 he confided in two close friends – Wegeler and Amenda – in letters dated

29 June and 1 July respectively. Others may have been informed (although the Testament implies that Beethoven's brothers still knew nothing) and he consulted doctors, who prescribed various remedies including strengthening medicines, almond oil, cold baths, tepid baths and an ear infusion. None was effective and finally, on the advice of Dr Schmidt, Beethoven resolved to spend six months away from the noise and activity of Vienna, in the quiet village of Heiligenstadt, in the hope that the tranquillity would enable his ears to recover. As the six months drew to a close in early October 1802, it became clear that this treatment, too, had been ineffective and he was going to have to live with his deafness permanently; his last hope of cure had gone. It was at this point, on 6 October, that the Testament was written, although it has been observed that the neatness of the document indicates a carefully prepared fair copy rather than a spur-of-the-moment outpouring (Solomon, 1977, p. 118; see plate 26). Since it is such an important statement it is given here in full, in a new translation:

FOR MY BROTHERS CARL AND [JOHANN] BEETHOVEN

O you men who think or say I am hostile, peevish, or misanthropic, how greatly you wrong me. You do not know the secret cause which makes me seem so to you. From childhood on, my heart and soul were full of the tender feeling of goodwill, and I was always inclined to accomplish great deeds. But just think, for six years now I have had an incurable condition, made worse by incompetent doctors, from year to year deceived with hopes of getting better, finally forced to face the prospect of a lasting infirmity (whose cure will perhaps take years or even be impossible). Though born with a fiery, lively temperament, susceptible to the diversions of society, I soon had to withdraw myself, to spend my life alone. And if I wished at times to ignore all this, oh how harshly was I pushed back by the doubly sad experience of my bad hearing; and yet it was impossible for me to say to people, 'Speak louder, shout, for I am deaf.' Ah, how could I possibly admit weakness of the *one sense* which should be more perfect in me than in others, a sense which I once possessed in the greatest perfection, a perfection such as few in my profession have or ever have had.

Oh I cannot do it; so forgive me if you see me draw back when I would gladly have mingled with you. My misfortune is doubly painful to me as I am bound to be misunderstood; for me there can be no relaxation in human company, no refined conversations, no mutual outpourings. I must live quite alone, like an outcast; I can enter society practically only as much as real necessity demands. If I approach people a burning anxiety comes over me, in that I fear being placed in danger of my condition being noticed.

It has also been like this during the last six months, which I have spent in the country. My understanding doctor, by ordering me to spare my hearing as much as possible, almost came to my own present natural disposition, although I sometimes let myself be drawn by my love of companionship. But what humiliation for me when someone standing near me heard a flute in the distance and *I heard nothing*, or someone heard the shepherd singing and again I heard nothing. Such incidents brought me almost to despair; a little more and I would have ended my life.

Only *my art* held me back. Ah, it seemed to me impossible to leave the world until I had produced all that I felt was within me; and so I spared this wretched life – truly wretched for so susceptible a body, which by a sudden change can reduce me from the best condition to the very worst.

Patience, they say, is what I must now choose for my guide, and I have done so – I hope my determination will firmly endure until it pleases the inexorable Parcae to break the thread. Perhaps I shall get better, perhaps not; I am ready.

Forced to become a philosopher already in my 28th year, it is not easy, and for the artist harder than for anyone else.

Divine One, thou lookest down on my inmost soul and knowest it; thou knowest that therein dwells the love of man and inclination to do good. O men, when at some point you read this, then consider that you have done me an injustice; and the unfortunate may console themselves to find a similar case to theirs, who despite all the limitations of nature yet did everything he could to be admitted to the ranks of worthy artists and men.

You, my brothers Carl and [Johann], as soon as I am dead, if Dr Schmidt is still alive, ask him in my name to describe my disease, and attach this written document to his account of my illness, so that at least as much as possible the world may be reconciled to me after my death.

At the same time, I here declare you two to be the heirs to my small fortune (if one can call it such); divide it fairly, and bear with and help each other. What you have done against me you know was long ago forgiven. You, brother Carl, I thank in particular for your recent proven attachment to me. My wish is that you have a better, more trouble-free life than I have had. Recommend *virtue* to your children; it alone, not money, can provide happiness. I speak from experience; virtue was what raised me in my distress. Thanks to it and to my art, I did not end my life by suicide.

Farewell and love each other.

I thank all my friends, particularly *Prince Lichnowsky* and *Professor Schmidt* – I want the instruments from Prince L. to be preserved by one of you, but not to cause strife between you; as soon as it is more useful to you, just sell them. How happy I am if I can still be of use to you in my grave – so let it be. With joy I hasten towards death. If it comes before I have had the chance to develop all my artistic abilities, then despite my harsh fate it will still be coming too soon and I should probably wish it later – yet even so I should be content, for would it not free me from a state of endless suffering? Come when thou wilt, I shall approach thee bravely.

Farewell, and do not completely forget me when I am dead. I have deserved this from you, since I often thought of you during my life, and of ways to make you happy; do be so.

Ludwig van Beethoven

Heiglnstadt
6 October 1802

For my brothers Carl and [Johann]
to be read and executed after my death.

Heiglnstadt, 10 October 1802, thus I take leave of
thee – and indeed sadly. Yes, the fond hope, which I
brought here with me, to be cured at least to some
degree – this I must now wholly abandon. As the
leaves of autumn fall and wither, so too has my hope
dried up; I go away almost as I came. Even the high
courage which often inspired me in the fine summer
days has disappeared.

O Providence – grant me some time a pure day of
joy. For so long now the heartfelt echo of true joy has
been strange to me. Oh when – oh when, oh Divine
One – can I feel it again in the temple of nature and
of mankind – Never? No – oh that would be too hard.

Several features in particular call for comment.
The first is the absence of the name of Beethoven's
brother Nikolaus Johann in all three places where
he is addressed personally: Beethoven simply left a
blank space each time, an omission that has resulted
in endless speculation on the relationship between
Beethoven and Johann at the time. Moreover, close
examination of the spacing in the manuscript makes
it almost certain that the names of both Carl and
Johann were originally omitted, with Carl's being
carefully inserted later (Solomon, 1977, p. 120).
This observation poses more problems than it
solves, however: was Beethoven almost incapable
of writing the names of his brothers, either because
he could not accept their independence (Solomon,
ibid.) or because he felt their relationship was so
special, just as a child rarely refers to its parents
by name? Or was it simply that he was undecided
which name to use in each case – the first, second
or both names?

Beethoven is of course addressing not just his
brothers but a wider audience. He asks the document to be made public, so that 'the world may be
reconciled to me', and there are places, including
the opening, where it is unclear whether just
the brothers or all people are being addressed.
Elsewhere he addresses the Godhead and Providence directly, offering a kind of prayer. And in
the postscript there is a curious remark to 'thee' in
the singular; this has puzzled some commentators,
but from the context it seems clear that he was
simply addressing Heiligenstadt itself, immediately
before his departure from the village.

Beethoven's description of an occasion when
someone standing beside him heard a distant flute
while he himself heard nothing is amplified by
Ferdinand Ries: 'I called his attention to a shepherd
in the forest who was playing most pleasantly on a
flute cut from lilac wood. For half an hour
Beethoven could not hear anything at all and
became extremely quiet and gloomy, even though
I repeatedly assured him that I did not hear
anything any longer either (which was, however,
not the case).' (Wegeler, 1987, pp. 86–7) It may
well be that Ries and Beethoven were referring to

the same occasion; alternatively, Ries's account,
published in 1838, may have been influenced
by him having by then read the Heiligenstadt
Testament.

Other passages echo Beethoven's own writings
elsewhere. He frequently expressed his love of
virtue, sometimes mentioning that this attitude had
been acquired at an early age (it seems that
his mother instilled virtuous precepts into him
throughout his childhood). His suicidal tendencies
were often not far below the surface (though they
were kept firmly in check), and were perhaps
inherited by his nephew, who attempted suicide in
1826. Beethoven's claim that he was saved from
suicide by his art is certainly credible, for his
deep devotion to music was frequently expressed
throughout his life. Thus instead of suicide he
resorted to patience and resignation to fate, as
indeed he indicated elsewhere: 'Plutarch has shown
me the path of resignation', he had written in 1801
(Letter 51), and a similar attitude emerged in his
setting of a poem *Resignation* (WoO 149), which he
sketched intermittently from *c.*1813 and finally
completed in 1817. Likewise his prayer for a pure
day of joy echoes Schiller's *An die Freude*, later set
to music in the Ninth Symphony; Beethoven had
also made an earlier setting of the text, according
to a letter by Ries in 1803, and so it is not surprising
to find an echo of it in the Heiligenstadt Testament.

The emotions that gave rise to the Testament
undoubtedly had a significant effect on Beethoven's
compositional output, but the effect has been
difficult to quantify and there has been much
confusion on the subject. Thayer asserted that the
brilliant and boisterous Second Symphony came
from the same period as the Heiligenstadt Testament despite being in utter contrast to it (Thayer,
1967, p. 306), thus implying that Beethoven's
personal and composing lives were quite independent. Thayer's assertion has been repeated many
times since, and even today visitors to the Beethoven
memorial house in Heiligenstadt are told that this
is where he wrote his Second Symphony. Yet in
truth the sketches for the Symphony were more or
less completed over a month before he began his
sojourn there; any work on it at Heiligenstadt
would therefore have been mere finishing touches
hardly likely to affect its overall mood of cheerful-
ness. The main compositions written during the
six-month stay were the three Piano Sonatas op.
31; these, too, embody little of the despair of the
Testament (except, perhaps, in parts of no. 2) and
seem rather to reflect the 'high courage' mentioned
in the postscript as having inspired Beethoven
during the summer.

This courage soon returned after Beethoven
had left Heiligenstadt, and the aftermath of the
Testament was marked by renewed determination;
it is as if by writing the document he set all
his anxiety behind him and was able to resume

composing almost without a break and with fresh energy. It was shortly after this time that works on an unprecedented scale began to appear – notably the *Eroica* but also such works as the 'Waldstein' and 'Kreutzer' Sonatas. More significantly, he began his oratorio *Christus am Oelberge* within a few months – indeed probably only a few weeks – of the Heiligenstadt Testament. The oratorio embodies many of the concepts of undeserved suffering, isolation, and universal love that had been expressed in the Testament, suggesting that he consciously resolved to write a work that treated his personal emotions and experiences in a general and universal way. The Heiligenstadt Testament therefore marks both a turning-point in his personal life and a major element in the background to his compositional output.

BARRY COOPER

Sketches

BEETHOVEN IS BY NO MEANS the only composer for whose works there survives a quantity of sketches; but it is his name that most readily comes to mind in connection with such documents. There are probably several reasons for this. Those who favour the image of Beethoven as Romantic hero, struggling to forge mighty works and to capture on paper some kind of perfect representation of the dictates of his inner genius, may see in the chaotic appearance of the sketches a welcome illustration of the notion that the art represents the man. More prosaically, one need only consider the enormous quantity of sketches by Beethoven which survive. The most authoritative examination to date lists thirty-three desk sketchbooks and thirty-seven pocketbooks (all these books are listed at the end of this section). With the loose sketchleaves and the score sketches also included, the total number of leaves stands at several thousand.

In addition to quantity, there is also what might be termed the 'quality' of Beethoven's sketches. The sketchbooks are not simply filled with work on those compositions which Beethoven completed and published. Rather than taking up a sketchbook when he felt the seeds of an *Eroica* or an 'Appassionata' stirring within him, Beethoven seems to have sketched compulsively, jotting down even the most trivial ideas which other composers would never have considered committing to paper. Thus the sketchbooks represent something more akin to a compositional diary rather than a series of workbooks linked to major projects. Nor did Beethoven discard a sketchbook when he had filled it. The major reason for the large surviving quantity of his sketches is that he himself preserved them very carefully. There is evidence, too, that he often

looked back through them, and sometimes took up and developed ideas that he had written but discarded years earlier. For instance, a fugue subject written in the Scheide Sketchbook of 1815–16 reappears in the Engelmann Sketchbook of 1823 among early sketches for the Ninth Symphony.

The distinction between sketch*leaves* and sketch*books* has already been drawn above; and although there exist numbers of loose leaves from all periods of Beethoven's life (the 'Hammerklavier' Sonata, for example, appears to have been sketched entirely without the support of a desk sketchbook), one large body of such leaves deserves special mention. These are the loose leaves and bifolia which Beethoven used prior to adopting bound sketchbooks in 1798; it is not surprising that a considerable quantity of these leaves appears to have gone missing, although around two hundred survive. Beethoven must already have amassed a large bundle of them by the time he arrived in Vienna in 1792. Today the surviving loose leaves are separated into two large miscellanies, named after two 19th-century collectors: the Kafka Miscellany is in the British Museum, London, and the Fischhof Miscellany in the Staatsbibliothek Preussischer Kulturbesitz, Berlin. Conceptually, however, the two Miscellanies belong together; in some cases a sketch on a Kafka leaf continues on a Fischhof leaf or vice versa. Moreover, these loose leaves also preserve technical exercises, autograph scores (such as that of WoO 32 in Kafka), and transcriptions of music by other composers as well as sketches in the strict sense of the term (see plates 22–4).

A similar variety of contents is also to be found in the sketchbooks, although it must not be thought that these are predominantly filled with anything other than what their name implies. First, however, we must distinguish between two types of sketchbook: desk sketchbooks, which were of oblong format and used for work indoors; and pocket sketchbooks, upright in format (they were usually made by folding a number of oblong leaves vertically) and small enough to fit into Beethoven's coat pocket when he went out. While the desk sketches are mostly written in ink, those in the pocketbooks are usually in pencil. Exactly when Beethoven began using pocketbooks is not entirely clear, but with the exception of a few leaves for op. 113 from 1811 (Artaria 205, bundle 2), the first surviving pocketbook is Mendelssohn 1, from 1815.

The sketches in the deskbooks can be divided into various types. There are the short, often fragmentary ideas which deal with a particular compositional problem: the exact shape of a theme or melodic line (the sketches for the song *Sehnsucht* WoO 146 in the Scheide Sketchbook are a good example), or some harmonic problem. Also familiar are the longer, single-voice sketches which map out either a whole movement or an individual section, such as an exposition or development: these sketches are generally known as 'continuity drafts', a term which captures what seems to have been their main function, that of charting the course of a long stretch of music and of regulating its inner proportions. Good examples of continuity drafts are to be found in Nottebohm's famous accounts of the Kessler and *Eroica* Sketchbooks (Nottebohm, 1865 and 1880). A third type of sketch was intended to fix the general shape of a movement, part of a movement or even an entire work. Usually such sketches (they are really series of sketches) fix the main points of articulation within a movement or provide a series of incipits for the movements of a multi-movement work. In the latter case one can often see that Beethoven tried out several different successions of keys and movement-types before fixing on the final one. Various names have been given to sketches of this type: 'concept sketch', 'tonal overview' and 'synopsis sketch' are three common terms. As might be expected, sketches of this kind are usually to be found in the early stages of work on a composition; Beethoven liked to get an idea of the whole before settling down to work in detail.

As well as sketches for works that were completed and published, the sketchbooks also contain many ideas for unfinished works, some of which were worked on in considerable detail before being abandoned. There are, for instance, a large number of sketches for the unfinished Piano Concerto in D of 1815 (Hess 15). In contrast to such extensive work on projects which Beethoven intended, initially at least, to complete, there are many doodlings which must have been no more than passing flights of fancy: ideas which came into his head and which he felt compelled to write down without ever intending to develop them further. Nor is it uncommon to find hastily scrawled memoranda – addresses, fragments of letters, sums – which Beethoven set down on the nearest piece of paper available. In some cases the sketchbook almost takes on the function of an autograph, and preserves the final version of part of a completed work: we should not assume that the passage from sketchbook to autograph score, from preliminary to final version, was invariably a one-way journey.

As might be expected, given their smaller dimensions and their outdoor function, the pocket sketchbooks are not as rich in continuity drafts as are the desk sketchbooks. Their main purpose seems to have been to capture temporarily ideas which could be expanded when Beethoven returned home to his desk. Not surprisingly, then, the pocket sketches for a work often run parallel to the desk sketches, and in some cases the correspondence between sketches in books of each kind is close enough to suggest direct copying from the pocketbook to the deskbook.

In addition to the desk- and pocketbooks there exists a third category of sketch manuscript, examples of which are most numerous among the sketches for the late quartets. Whereas in his sketchbooks Beethoven usually expressed his ideas in a single-line format, providing a *Hauptstimme* and sometimes brief indications of accompanimental figuration and other details, in his last years he made increasing use of 'score sketches'. These are sketches set out in full score, with a separate stave provided for each instrument (not every voice need be notated throughout, however). The predominance of score sketches for the late quartets testifies to the special textural problems which this medium posed for Beethoven, and also to his growing interest in matters of part-writing; the single-line continuity draft no longer sufficed to capture all the intricacies of this music and Beethoven had to resort to an additional sketching stage between work in the sketchbooks and the writing out of the autograph.

Earlier score sketches are also found in connection with the string trios and string quartets, but it would be wrong to assume that string chamber music was the only medium for which Beethoven needed this particular sketching aid: vocal score sketches for the Credo of the *Missa Solemnis* are to be found in the sketchbook Artaria 195. Moreover, there is clearly a degree of overlap between score sketches and the kind of 'composing score' that exists for the unfinished Piano Concerto and several other works. It is likely that further subtle but useful distinctions between Beethoven's sketch manuscripts will emerge as more material is made available in transcription.

This last point brings us to consideration of the history of Beethoven's sketches subsequent to the composer's death. At the *Nachlass* auction on 5 November 1827 almost two-thirds of the sketch manuscripts were bought very cheaply by Domenico Artaria. He and the other purchasers seem largely to have regarded the sketches as musically worthless but commercially valuable: after purchase, most of the sketchbooks were partially or totally dismembered and leaves sold off singly or in small groups to autograph collectors. This was the beginning of a process which led to the present-day situation in which the sketches are dispersed all over the world. Only two or three of the desk sketchbooks are still in the form in which Beethoven used them. Fortunately, the great majority of the sketches are today housed in major public collections (in Berlin, Bonn, Paris, Poland, London, Vienna and other locations), but many remain in private collections and are inaccessible. Previously lost or unknown manuscripts continue to turn up at auction, in a steady trickle.

The damage done to the sketchbooks in the 19th century has now been undone, at least conceptually, by the work on sketchbook reconstruction of Alan Tyson, Douglas Johnson, Robert Winter and others (see 'Sketch studies', p. 322), but it still remains the case that, for example, about two-thirds of the *Pastoral* Symphony Sketchbook is in London and most of the remainder is in Berlin. This problem would be alleviated to some extent if there existed an edition in facsimile of all the reconstructed sketchbooks. Earlier sketchbook editions, whether in facsimile or transcription, ignored missing leaves, even when these had been identified (such was the case with the transcription of the London portion of the *Pastoral* Symphony book). The edition (in transcription only) begun in 1952 by the Beethovenhaus in Bonn perpetuated this dubious tradition until a reaction by younger and largely non-German scholars brought about a reconsideration of aims and techniques.

Another target of this reaction was the standard of sketchbook transcription. It must be stressed that Beethoven's sketchbooks were private documents which needed to be intelligible only to the composer. As a rule he did not bother to notate clefs or key and time signatures, and even accidentals are not provided with any consistency. Added to all this, the notation of pitch is frequently approximate; the sketches are generally written in a kind of telegraphic style in which much is implied rather than being explicitly stated. A literal transcription of a sketchbook, then, usually results in a mass of apparently nonsensical musical ideas. To be at all useful, the transcription must interpret Beethoven's notation rather than reproduce it faithfully: and despite their frequently forbidding appearance, most pages of sketches are by no means undecipherable. Again, the early Beethovenhaus transcriptions were of the literal kind; transcriptions of the Wielhorsky Sketchbook and the Kafka Miscellany showed more regard for musical common sense, and a new standard was set by Sieghard Brandenburg in his edition of the Kessler Sketchbook, one of the few books which survives intact.

Finally, it may be pointed out that the often chaotic appearance of the sketches (and Beethoven's untidiness has perhaps been exaggerated in this connection) is very much at odds with Beethoven's orderly attitude towards them. His entire approach to the business of sketching – the purchase (or, increasingly in later years, the manufacture at home) of desk- and pocketbooks, the transfer of sketches from one format to the other or their expansion into score sketches and thence into autograph scores, the careful preservation of a growing pile of sketch manuscripts – suggests a tidy, even calculated approach to composition. Even if we can believe Schindler's description of an occasion during the composition of the *Missa Solemnis* when Beethoven was heard 'singing, yelling, stamping his feet' and eventually appeared, looking 'as though he had just engaged in a life and death struggle with the whole army of contrapuntists, his everlasting enemies' (Schindler, 1966, p. 229), we should not allow this alluring Romantic view to blind us to the spoils of those more private intellectual battles that were fought and won in the pages of the sketchbooks.

The remainder of this section is devoted to a list (pp. 185–7) of all the desk and pocket sketchbooks identified and reconstructed in Johnson, 1985. The name and location of each book are given first, followed by the approximate dates within which it appears to have been used. Next comes a summary of the main contents of the book and, finally, details of any modern edition, whether in facsimile or transcription.

It is worth drawing attention to some of the information that this list does *not* include: it does not indicate the size of the sketchbooks (for example, Mendelssohn 15 has 173 leaves while BH 110 has only two) nor their physical structure; it does not distinguish between professionally made books and homemade ones, such as the Mass in C Sketchbook; it does not give details of leaves which have been removed from the books, nor (with one exception to be dealt with below) does it deal with those bundles of leaves which transmit sketches for a single work (such as the 'Hammerklavier' Sonata) or group of works but which do not appear to represent all or part of a sketchbook; it does not list score sketches for the late quartets. On all these matters the reader is advised to consult Johnson, 1985. It must be stressed that in addition to the desk and pocket sketchbooks there exists a considerable number of loose leaves which seem never to have formed part of any book. These leaves are not dealt with in Johnson, 1985, and neither do they feature in the list below. The most comprehensive guide to them remains Schmidt, 1969, although this is by now considerably out of date; many new leaves have emerged from obscurity, others have changed hands, and the identification of contents given by Schmidt has proved unreliable in many cases. (See Albrecht, 1978 for an interim update on the leaves in American collections and Schmidt, 1971 for the Beethovenhaus collection.)

Finally, a word of warning about dating: many of the dates given below are tentative, and should by no means be regarded as watertight. Most are taken from Johnson, 1985, but in one or two instances an alternative is offered (and identified as such). Anyone working seriously with a sketchbook should examine the evidence for its dating as fully as possible and reach his or her own conclusions.

The one exception to the restriction of the list to sketch*books* is the inclusion below of the Kafka and Fischhof Miscellanies, which contain the major surviving portion of the loose leaves and bifolia on which Beethoven sketched before beginning to use sketchbooks. To omit these would be to leave a large and important period of Beethoven's career entirely unrepresented.

Plates 22–36

BEETHOVEN'S HAND

THE FOLLOWING SELECTION of illustrations provides specimens of Beethoven's handwriting ranging from his teens to the last week of his life. The first (plate 22, *c.* 1786), shows the first page of the autograph score of a Romance in E minor (Hess 13: see page 221), which is among the earliest confirmed specimens of his hand. Plate 23 shows a variety of harmonizations that Beethoven evidently used in Bonn during Holy Week to accompany the plainsong *Lamentations of Jeremiah*. The page (dating from *c.* 1791) corroborates Wegeler's story that Beethoven tried to throw the singer off the note by using strange harmonies, and succeeded all too well. The page is very worn (the right-hand edge has been clumsily repaired) and was probably used in successive years: the ink for the main score (staves 1–8) is different from that for the addenda that crowd into the rest of the page. The writing is more mature than in Hess 13; note in particular the more advanced treble clef (stave 15, centre).

During the 1790s Beethoven's hand evolved rapidly. Plate 24 (probably 1795) shows the beginning of a score of the unfinished Symphony in C (see p. 276), with the strings placed at the top above woodwind, brass and timpani. The treble clef has lost its central stem and dot, while the initial system brace is, unusually, a single barline. His system brace reached its final form about 1800 and is shown in plate 25, the start of the finale of the 'Moonlight' Sonata (1801). Noteworthy here is Beethoven's use of 'senza sordino' to indicate application of the sustaining pedal (cancelled by 'con sordino'); by 1804 he had adopted more modern signs for pedal markings (see p. 287).

Plate 26 shows the first page of the famous Heiligenstadt Testament of 6–10 October 1802, written in Beethoven's usual Gothic script (for translation see p. 170). The heading contains a conspicuous gap instead of the name of Beethoven's younger brother, although the gap is clearly too small to accommodate the necessary words 'Johann van' in the same size of writing.

The autograph score of the *Eroica* Symphony is lost but a copy survives with Beethoven's annotations. The title-page (plate 27) bears vivid testimony to Beethoven's anger on hearing that Napoleon had proclaimed himself Emperor (see p. 215), with the paper badly damaged where Napoleon's name had been. In the margins are Beethoven's instructions to a copyist, partly deleted, and immediately underneath Beethoven's name, in very faded pencil, are his words 'geschrieben auf Bonaparte'. The date 'August 1804' was inserted by neither Beethoven nor the copyist.

Plate 28 shows the birdcalls in the autograph score of the slow movement of the *Pastoral* Symphony (1808): the strings occupy the top three and bottom two staves of the score; the remaining staves are for woodwind and horns. At the foot is Beethoven's instruction to a copyist: 'NB: write the word Nightingale, Quail, Cuckoo, in the first flute, in the first oboe, in the first and second clarinets, exactly as here in the score'.

The popular *Für Elise* was composed in 1808 or 1810 but Beethoven amended his rough draft in 1822 in preparation for possible publication (plate 29). The difference between the relatively neat ink draft, and the messy pencil annotations characteristic of his late period, is quite striking.

Plate 30 shows the last page of his famous letter to his 'Immortal Beloved' (see p. 107), written in pencil on 6–7 July 1812. The passage reads: '[my] life — my all — farewell — oh love me continually — never misjudge the most faithful heart of your beloved /L. /ever yours /ever mine /ever us'.

Some of Beethoven's autograph scores are very heavily altered, and the *Missa Solemnis* (1819–23) is a prime example; plate 31 shows the last seven bars of the Kyrie, with every bar and almost every stave containing amendments, giving an overall impression of incredible untidiness. The sketches are in general even more difficult to decipher, and sometimes several works are jumbled together on a single page. Plate 32 shows an abandoned score for a military march or tattoo, with sketches for the Ninth and Tenth Symphonies (October 1822) in the empty spaces. By contrast some scores are surprisingly neat. That shown in plate 33, the start of the Bagatelle op. 126 no. 2, is only a rough draft (note the absence of tempo marks and slurs), yet it is practically clear enough to be used for performance.

Plate 34 shows Beethoven's angry response to Ferdinand Wolanek's attempt to defend himself as a copyist after previous criticism from Beethoven (cf. p. 163). Since Wolanek had probably been trying to copy pages like that in plate 31, it is hardly surprising that he made mistakes, and one cannot help feeling a certain sympathy for him.

The last page of music written by Beethoven before his death consists of sketches in his final pocket sketchbook (plate 35). Of the three fragments on the page, the middle one is for the String Quintet on which he was working shortly before his death (see p. 277); the top one may be for a possible scherzo for the same work, and contains prominent echoes of an early bagatelle; the final sketch seems unconnected with any known work. Contrary to some opinions, there is no reason to link any of these sketches to the Tenth Symphony.

Beethoven's final will (plate 36) is dated 23 March 1827, and is the last thing he wrote. The hand is unsteady and inaccurate — there are at least three *f*s in 'Neffe' and even 'Ludwig' is incorrect. The text reads: 'My nephew Karl shall be my sole heir; the capital from my estate shall however go to his natural or testamentary heirs. Vienna, 23 March 1827, Lu[d]wig van Beethoven'.

BARRY COOPER

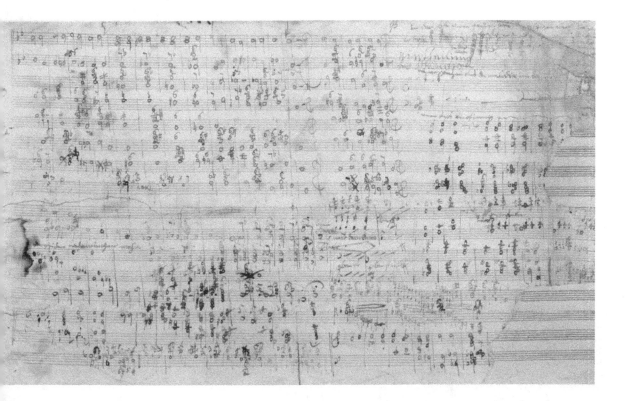

22   Romance in E minor, Hess 13 (*c.* 1786)

23   Harmonizations and sketches for the
Lamentations of Jeremiah, *c.* 1791–2

24   Draft for an unfinished Symphony in C, *c.* 1795

'Moonlight' Sonata, finale, autograph score, 1801
25

26 The Heiligenstadt Testament, 6 October 1802

27 *Eroica* Symphony, title-page of copyist's score, annotated by Beethoven, 1803–4

28 *Pastoral* Symphony, second movement, coda (autograph score), 1808

29   Draft for *Für Elise*, 1808–10, with annotations
of 1822

30   Last page of the letter to the 'Immortal
Beloved', 7 July 1812

31　Last page of the 'Kyrie' from the *Missa Solemnis*, 1819–23

32 Draft for a military tattoo, with sketches for Symphonies 9 and 10 (1822)

33 Draft for Bagatelle in G minor, op. 126 no. 2 (1824)

34 Letter from Ferdinand Wolanek, angrily annotated by Beethoven, 1825

35 Final page of Beethoven's last sketchbook, 1826–7

36 Beethoven's final will, 23 March 1827

LIST OF SKETCHBOOKS

Loose leaves and bifolia:

(italics indicate that the material includes a fair copy or autograph in addition to or in place of proper sketches)

Kafka Miscellany (Lbl); *c.*1786–1799
Opp. 1 nos *2*, 3; 5 nos 1, 2; 6; 7; 8; 9 no. 1; 10 nos 2, 3; 11; 13; 14 no. 1; 15; 16; *18 no. 5*; *19*; 21; 37; 46; 49 nos *1*, 2; 52 nos 2, 3; 65; 66; *71*; 75 no. 3; WoO 6; 8; 11; 13; 14; *32*; 43a–b; 44a–b; 53; *65*; 67; 71; 78; 88; 90; 92; *109*; *117*; 118; *119*; 126; Symphony in C
Facs. and trans., ed. Joseph Kerman, London, 1970

Fischhof Miscellany (B); *c.*1790–99
Opp. 1 nos 1–3; 2 nos 2, 3; 5 nos 1, 2; 7; 9 nos 1, 3; 10 nos 1–3; 12 nos 2, 3; 13; 14 no. 1; 15; 16; *19*; 20; 25; 37; 52 no. 2; 65; 75 no. 3; 81b; 103; WoO 25; 28; 29; 40; 42; 43a–b; 44a; 52; 53; 71; 72; 91 no. 2; *116*; 117; 118; Hess 149; Symphony in C; contrapuntal exercises
Trans. and commentary by Douglas Johnson, 1980a

Desk sketchbooks:

Grasnick 1 (Bds); summer or autumn 1798–February 1799
Opp. 18 nos 1, 3; 19; WoO 73

Grasnick 2 (B); February/March–late summer 1799
Opp. 18 nos 1, 2, 5; WoO 75
Facs. and trans., ed. Wilhelm Virneisel, Bonn, 1972–4

Autograph 19e, fols 12–31 (B); late spring and summer 1800
Opp. 17; 18 nos 1, 2, 6; 22; 23
Facs. and trans., ed. Richard Kramer, Bonn (forthcoming)

Landsberg 7 (B); summer/autumn 1800–March 1801
Opp. 23; 24; 26; 27 no. 1; 36; 43
Trans., ed. Karl Lothar Mikulicz, Leipzig, 1927 (repr. Hildesheim and New York, 1972)

Sauer (dispersed); April–November 1801?
Opp. 27 no. 2; 28; 29; 33

Kessler (Wgm); *c.* December 1801–*c.* June/July 1802
Opp. 30; 31 no. 1; 35; 36; WoO 92a
Facs. and trans., ed. Sieghard Brandenburg, Bonn, 1976–8

Wielhorsky (Mcm); autumn 1802–May 1803
Opp. 31 no. 3; 34; 35; 47; 85; 116; WoO 93
Facs., trans. and commentary, ed. Nathan L. Fishman, Moscow, 1962

Landsberg 6 or *Eroica* (Kj); *c.* June 1803–*c.* April 1804
Opp. 45; 53; 55; 56; 85; *Vestas Feuer; Leonore*

Mendelssohn 15 (B); May 1804–October 1805
Leonore; Opp. 32; 54; 56; 57
Discussion of chronology in Albrecht, 1989

Mass in C Sketchbook (Pn); *c.* July–August 1807
Op. 86

Sketchbook of *c.* September 1807–*c.* February 1808 (dispersed)
Opp. 67; 69; 138

***Pastoral* Symphony Sketchbook** (Lbl); *c.* January–September 1808
Opp. 68; 70 nos 1, 2
Trans., ed. Dagmar Weise, Bonn, 1961 (new facs. and trans., ed. Nicholas Marston, in preparation)

Grasnick 3 (Bds); *c.* early December 1808–early 1809
Opp. 73; 80
Trans., ed. Dagmar Weise, Bonn, 1957

Landsberg 5 (Bds); *c.* March–*c.* October 1809
Opp. 73; 74; 75; 76; 81a; 115

Landsberg 11 (Kj); winter 1809/10–autumn 1810
Opp. 83; 84; 95; 97

Sketchbook of late 1810–summer 1811 (dispersed)
Opp. 95; 97; 113; 117

Petter (BNba); September 1811–December 1812
Opp. 92; 93; 96; 113

***Meeresstille* Sketchbook** (dispersed); March 1813–early 1814
Opp. 94; 112; WoO 149
This book is identified as the 'Sketchbook of 1814–1815' in Johnson, 1985; but Barry Cooper (1990, pp. 217–18) has suggested that the dating (*c.* December 1814–*c.* February 1815) proposed there is too late.

Landsberg 9, pp. 17–68 (Bds); *c.* February–March 1814
Fidelio

Dessauer (Wgm); *c.* March–*c.* September 1814
Fidelio; Opp. 90; 115; 118; WoO 95; 103

Mendelssohn 6 (Kj); *c.* September 1814–
c. February 1815
Opp. 89; 136; Hess 15

Scheide (Princeton University); *c.* March 1815–
c. May 1816
Opp. 98; 101; 102 no. 2; WoO 24; 145; 146; Hess
15

Autograph 11/1 (B); June–November 1816
Op. 101
The dates refer only to the use of the surviving
leaves; the missing later portion of the book may
have been in use as late as 1818.

Wittgenstein (BNba); April/May 1819–
March/April 1820
Opp. 109; 120; 123
Facs. and trans., ed. Joseph Schmidt-Görg, Bonn,
1968–72
The date of May/June 1820 suggested for the end
of this book in Johnson, 1985, p. 258, seems too
late; compare the arguments in Marston, 1986.

Artaria 195 (B); April 1820–early 1821
Opp. 109; 119; 123

Artaria 197 (B); *c.* March–December 1821
Opp. 110; 111; 123

Artaria 201 (B); December 1821–October 1822?
(the book may have been in use as late as March
1823)
Opp. 111; 123; 124; WoO 98

Engelmann (BNba); *c.* February/March 1823
Opp. 120; 125
Facs., Leipzig, 1913

Landsberg 8/1 (Bds); *c.* April 1823
Opp. 120; 125

Landsberg 8/2 (Bds); *c.* May 1823–June 1824
Opp. 125; 126; 127

Autograph 11/2 (B); autumn 1824–January 1825
Opp. 121b; 122; 127; 132

De Roda (BNba); May–September 1825
Opp. 130; 132; 133

Kullak (B); October/November 1825–November
1826
Opp. 130; 131; 133; 135

Pocket sketchbooks:

Artaria 205/2 (Bds); August–September 1811
Op. 113

Mendelssohn 1 (Kj); *c.* February–
September/October 1815
Opp. 102 nos 1, 2; 112; 115; Hess 15; canons

Ms 78/103 (Pn); 1816
Op. 101/IV; WoO 147

Boldrini (lost); autumn 1817–April 1818
Op. 106/I–II

A 45 (Wgm); April–June/July 1818
Op. 106/III–IV

A 44 (Wgm); mid-summer 1818
Op. 106/IV

BH 110 (BNba); late spring/early summer 1819
Op. 123/I–III

Pocket Sketchbook of Summer 1819 (Bds)
Op. 123/II–III

Pocket Sketchbook of late Summer 1819
(dispersed)
Op. 123/II–III

BH 107 (BNba); *c.* November 1819–April 1820
Opp. 123/III; 109/I
Facs. and trans., ed. Joseph Schmidt-Görg, Bonn,
1952–68

BH 108 (BNba); April–June 1820
Op. 123/III
Facs. and trans., ed. Joseph Schmidt-Görg, Bonn,
1968–70

BH 109 (BNba); autumn 1820 (possibly
extending into 1821)
Op. 123/IV–V
Facs. and trans., ed. Joseph Schmidt-Görg, Bonn,
1968–70

Grasnick 5 (Bds); January–August 1821?
Op. 123/V

Pocket Sketchbook of *c.* August–November
1821 (Pn)
Opp. 123/III, V; 110/II–III; WoO 182

Ms 51 (Pn); December 1821–January/February
1822
Opp. 110/III; 111/I–II

Pocket Sketchbook of February/March 1822
(Pn and Bds)
Opp. 111/I–II; 123/V

Artaria 205/6a (Bds); March–August 1822
Op. 123/V

Artaria 205/1 (Bds); September 1822
Op. 124; WoO 98

Artaria 205/5 (Bds); April/May 1823
Op. 125/I–III

Rolland (BNba); *c.* September 1823
Op. 125/III

Autograph 8/1 (Kj); autumn 1823
Op. 125/III–IV

Autograph 8/2 (Kj); *c.* December 1823–
c. February 1824?
Op. 125/IV

Artaria 205/4 (Bds); *c.* February–September
1824
Opp. 125/IV; 127/I–III

Grasnick 4 (Kj); October–December 1824
Opp. 127/III–IV; 121b; Overture on B–A–C–H

Moscow (Mcm); May/June–July 1825
Opp. 132/III–V; 130/I
Facs. with commentary by M. Ivanov-Boretzky
in *Musikalische Bildung*, January–March 1927, pp.
9–91

Egerton 2795 (Lbl); July–August 1825
Op. 130/I–III, V

Autograph 9/5 (B); August–September 1825
Opp. 130/III–V; 133

Autograph 9/2 (B); September–October 1825
Opp. 130/V; 133; WoO 194

Autograph 9/1 (B); October–early November
1825
Op. 133; Tenth Symphony; Overture on
B–A–C–H

Autograph 9/1a (B); November 1825–early 1826
Opp. 133; 131/I–IV; WoO 195

BSk 22/Mh 96 (BNba); February–March 1826
Op. 131/I–IV

Autograph 9/3 (B); April/May 1826?
Op. 131/IV–V

Autograph 9/4 (B); late spring 1826
Op. 131/IV–VII

Autograph 10/1 (B); early summer 1826
Op. 131/IV–VII

Artaria 205/3 (Bds); late June/July–August 1826?
Opp. 131/IV–VII; 135/I–III

Ms 62/66 (Pn); autumn 1826
Opp. 135/II–IV; 130/VI

Autograph 10/2 (B); November 1826–March
1827?
String Quintet in C (WoO 62)

Library sigla

B	Berlin, Staatsbibliothek PreussischerKulturbesitz
Bds	Berlin, Deutsche Staatsbibliothek
BNba	Bonn, Beethoven-Archiv
Kj	Kraków, Biblioteka Jagiellońska
Lbl	London, British Library
Mcm	Moscow, Central (Glinka) Museum for Music Culture
Pn	Paris, Bibliothèque Nationale
Wgm	Vienna, Gesellschaft der Musikfreunde

NICHOLAS MARSTON

Autograph scores

DESPITE THE EXTENSIVE PRELIMINARY sketching
that took place for most, if not all, of Beethoven's
works, it was in the autograph score that each work
first came together on paper as a complete entity,
and so these scores are of fundamental importance
in any study of his music. It was always a major
step when he progressed from the private world of
his sketches, where he could make use of all kinds
of unorthodox signs and omit many details, to the
essentially public world of an autograph score that
would have to be read and copied by someone else;
and generally he took this step only when he had
formed a fairly clear idea in his head (with the aid
of his sketches) as to how the piece, or at least its
opening, was to sound.

One might imagine, therefore, that with all
the preparatory sketch work the autograph scores
would contain few alterations and be easily legible.
This was often not the case, however. The opening
is usually clear enough, with a heading (perhaps
even on a separate title-page), sometimes a date,
and usually a list of instruments in the left margin.
The first few pages then normally proceed with few
alterations, but further into the work changes
generally become more frequent; the crossings out
sometimes become so heavy that it is quite difficult

to make out the final version and even harder to establish the precise details of what was altered. The Cello Sonata op. 69 provides an excellent example.

In some scores the clarity degenerated so much that whole new pages had to be inserted, either as replacements or as supplements to the original score; such pages can often be distinguished as such by their different paper type. In a few cases not merely odd pages but a whole movement was written out afresh, as in the finale of the Piano Sonata op. 110 and the first movement of op. 111. Here, then, one can speak of a rough draft or composing score followed by a fair copy, but this was not Beethoven's usual practice: normally he tried to combine the functions of composing score and fair copy in a single manuscript. As he said himself: 'When I have completed the whole in my head, everything is written down, but only once.' (Letter 1060) Although one might assume from the messiness of the scores that he actually began writing them out well before he had 'completed the whole in his head', the main outlines of the works were hardly ever changed at this stage; nearly all the alterations are of small details such as texture, registration, orchestration and figuration.

Sometimes in the course of making such changes Beethoven would revert to his sketchbook to work out details; thus some sketches may postdate some stages of the autograph score. On other occasions sketches actually appear in the autograph itself, usually in blank staves at the foot of the page. In some works a continuous single-stave draft appears below the corresponding part of the score for several consecutive pages, forming what is sometimes known as a 'cue-staff' that functioned as a kind of final sketch before the full score was realized in detail. Such sketches, and the existence of many discarded pages from autograph scores, considerably blur the distinction between the concept of 'sketch' and 'autograph' (Lockwood, 1970b).

Once an autograph score was finished Beethoven generally passed it to a copyist to produce a fair copy for performance and/or publication (see 'Corrected copies and copyists', pp. 190–92). Occasionally no copyist was available, however, and he had to do the job himself; the results are perhaps surprisingly neat – his fair copies of cadenzas for his piano concertos, probably made in 1809 for Archduke Rudolph, are so clear that it is possible to perform direct from the facsimile (Hess, 1979) with little difficulty.

After publication of a work, Beethoven lost interest in the autograph score, according to Ries. 'Once they had been printed, they usually lay about in an adjoining room or scattered on the floor in the middle of his study with other pieces of music.... At any time I could have carried off all those originally autographed compositions that had been engraved already; he would also most

likely have given them to me without hesitation had I asked for them.' (Wegeler, 1987, p. 101) By the time he died Beethoven no longer possessed all his autographs; some had been given away and others lost. Most of those that remained were auctioned in November 1827, and many of these are now in various public libraries. Most of the early ones are lost while most of the later ones survive, but there are some notable exceptions (including the 'Moonlight' and 'Hammerklavier' Sonatas). The largest single collection was that in the Prussian State Library, but in 1945 this collection was split into three locations – East Berlin, West Berlin and Kraków; manuscripts in the last came to light only in 1977 and so hitherto there has been no complete list covering the current whereabouts of all known Beethoven autographs. Accordingly one is given here for all those works with opus numbers (which include all his major works). Manuscript numbers are given for the main collections (B, Bds, BNba and Kj; abbreviations and library sigla appear at the end of the list). Note that a few works have additional autograph material not listed here, such as instrumental parts or fragmentary early drafts.

op. 3	Pn (inc); Wc (IV only)
op. 15	B, aut. 12; BNba, SBH 521–3 (cads)
op. 19	B, aut. 13; BNba, SBH 524–5 (pf part and cad)
op. 20	Kj, Mend. 4
op. 24	Wn (I–III only)
op. 26	Kj, Gras. 12. Facs. Bonn 1895
op. 27/2	BNba, SBH 526. Facs. Vienna 1921 and Tokyo 1970
op. 28	BNba, SBH 527
op. 29	Kj, Mend. 5
op. 30/1	B, aut. 19d
op. 30/2	BNba, SBH 528
op. 30/3	Lbl. Facs. London 1980
op. 33	BNba, SBH 529
op. 34	BNba, SBH 530
op. 35	BNba, SBH 531
op. 37	Bds, aut. 14; Pn (cad)
op. 40	BNba, SBH 533
op. 47	BNba, SBH 534 (inc)
op. 48	BNba, SBH 535–6 (nos 5 and 6 only)
op. 50	Wc

op. 52/2	Wgm
op. 53	BNba, SBH 537. Facs. Bonn 1954
op. 57	Pn. Facs. Paris 1927 and Leipzig c. 1970
op. 58	BNba, SBH 538–543 (cads only)
op. 59/1	B, Mend. 10. Facs. London 1980
op. 59/2	B, aut. 21. Facs. London 1980
op. 59/3	BNba, SBH 544
op. 60	B, Mend. 12
op. 61	Wn; BNba (cad for pf version). Facs. (of score) Graz 1979
op. 62	BNba, SBH 548
op. 65	Pn (inc)
op. 67	B, Mend. 8. Facs. Berlin 1942
op. 68	BNba, SBH 549
op. 69	BNba (I only). Facs. New York 1970
op. 70/1	NYpm
op. 70/2	B, Art. 175
op. 72	B (several MSS, each inc) Bds, aut. 4 (no. 11 only). Facs. Leipzig 1976 BNba, SBH 550–52 (inc)
op. 73	Bds, aut. 15
op. 74	Kj, Mend. 14
op. 75	BNba, SBH 553 (no. 2); Bds, Art. 173 (nos 5 and 6)
op. 77	BNba, SBH 554
op. 78	BNba, SBH 555. Facs. Munich 1923
op. 79	BNba, SBH 556
op. 80	BNba, SBH 557 (inc)
op. 81a	Wgm (I only)
op. 82/1	Pn
op. 82/4	BNba, SBH 558
op. 83	Pn
op. 84	B, Art. 177 (nos 1–6)
op. 85	B, Art. 179 (inc)
op. 86	BNba, SBH 559 (I–II only)
op. 87	Bds, Art. 151
op. 90	BNba
op. 91	Bds, aut. 22
op. 92	Kj, Mend. 9

op. 93	aut. 20 split between B (I–II); Kj (III); Bds (IV)
op. 94	CA
op. 95	Wn
op. 96	NYpm. Facs. Munich 1976
op. 97	Kj, Mend. 3
op. 98	BNba, SBH 561. Facs. Munich 1970
op. 99	BNba, SBH 562
op. 101	Private coll, Germany (photocopy in BNba)
op. 102/1	B, aut. 18
op. 102/2	B, Art. 192
op. 103	B, Art. 132
op. 105	Lbl (inc)
op. 107	BNba, SBH 563 (inc); Lbl (inc)
op. 108	Bds, aut. 29 II (inc); NYpm (inc); Lsc (inc)
op. 109	Wc. Facs. New York 1965
op. 110	B, Art. 196; BNba, SBH 564 (finale only). Facs. (Art. 196) Stuttgart 1967
op. 111	Bds, Art. 198; BNba, SBH 565 (I only). Facs. (Art. 198) Munich 1922 and Leipzig 1969
op. 113	Bds, aut. 16 (except no. 5); Lbl (no. 5)
op. 114	Bds, aut. 16
op. 115	Wn
op. 117	Bds, aut. 65 (ov); B, Art. 162 (except ov)
op. 119	B, Art. 199 (nos 1–6); nos 7–11 split between private coll, Basle; BNba, SBH 566; and Pn
op. 120	Private coll, Germany (photocopy in BNba)
op. 121a	BNba, SBH 567
op. 121b	Wst
op. 122	Mbs
op. 123	B, aut. 1 (I); B, Art. 202 (III–VI). Facs. (Kyrie) Tutzing 1965
op. 124	Wst
op. 125	split between B and Bds (Art. 204 and aut. 2). Facs. Leipzig 1924 and 1975

op. 126	BNba, SBH 571. Facs. Bonn 1984
op. 127	split between Kj, Mend. 13 (I); Kj, Art. 207 (II); Smf (III); BNba, SBH 572 (IV)
op. 128	Lbl
op. 129	NYpm (on deposit)
op. 130	split between Kj (I); Wc (II); Pn (III); Bm (IV); B, Art. 208 (V); B, aut. 19c and Gras. 10 (VI)
op. 131	Kj, Art. 211 (except IV); Bds, Mend. 19 (IV only)
op. 132	B, Mend. 11
op. 133	Kj, Art. 215
op. 134	BNba, SBH 573 (inc)
op. 135	split between BNba, SBH 575 (I); Château de Mariemont, Belgium (III); B, aut. 19b (IV)
op. 136	Bds, aut. 17
op. 137	Pn

Abbreviations and library sigla

cad	cadenza
facs.	facsimile
inc	incomplete score
ov	overture
pf	pianoforte
B	Berlin, Staatsbibliothek Preussischer Kulturbesitz
Bds	Berlin, Deutsche Staatsbibliothek
Bm	Brno, Ústav Dějin Hudby Moravského Musea, Hudebněhistorické Oddělení
BNba	Bonn, Beethoven-Archiv
CA	Cambridge, Mass., Harvard University Music Libraries
Kj	Kraków, Biblioteka Jagiellońska
Lbl	London, British Library, Reference Division
Lsc	Leningrad (St Petersburg), Gosudarst-vennaya Publichnaya Biblioteka
Mbs	Munich, Bayerische Staatsbibliothek
NYpm	New York, Pierpont Morgan Library
Pn	Paris, Bibliothèque Nationale
Smf	Stockholm, Stiftelsen Musikkulturens Främjande
Wc	Washington, Library of Congress
Wgm	Vienna, Gesellschaft der Musikfreunde
Wn	Vienna, Nationalbibliothek, Musiksammlung
Wst	Vienna, Stadtbibliothek, Musiksammlung

BARRY COOPER

Corrected copies and copyists

MANY OF BEETHOVEN'S WORKS were copied by professional copyists before publication, either in score so that the publishers would receive a more legible copy than Beethoven's autograph, or as a set of parts in preparation for performance. Generally the copy was checked by Beethoven before use, and any errors were customarily corrected in red crayon (Beethoven's famous *Rötel*). While looking through the copy he would often make slight amendments or clarifications of the notation, such as additional dynamics or articulation marks; even the notes themselves were occasionally altered. Many such corrected copies, or *überprüfte Abschriften*, survive (see list below), and they are of great importance in helping to establish the best text of the work concerned. None, however, has been published complete in facsimile, unlike the sketch-books and autograph scores, and surprisingly little study has been made of the types of alterations most commonly found in them.

As regards the copyists themselves, there is no comprehensive picture of their activities or identities, and the main source of information on them is a single article by Alan Tyson (1970). The most important of the copyists was Wenzel Schlemmer (1760–1823), who was apparently doing work for Beethoven at least as early as 1799 and continued almost up to his death on 6 August 1823. Schlemmer was a very careful copyist and exceptionally good at deciphering Beethoven's difficult handwriting, but he did not himself copy a very large proportion of Beethoven's scores. He had a team of copyists working under him, and it was often they rather than he who wrote out the manuscripts, his role evidently being that of organizer and superviser, assisting with deciphering difficult passages and checking the copies of his assistants. One of these assistants was Wenzel Rampl, who was copying for Beethoven from as early as 1809 and who became his most important copyist after Schlemmer's death, copying three of the late quartets and a score of the Ninth Symphony. Beethoven made use of several other copyists after Schlemmer's death, including Peter Gläser, Ferdinand Wolanek, Paul Maschek, Mathias Wunderl and Karl Holz, but none appears to have matched Schlemmer.

Three more copyists distinguished by Tyson, all associated with Schlemmer, are still unidentified and simply labelled as copyists C, D and E (Schlemmer and Rampl are A and B respectively). Copyist C was active during 1803–5; his work includes the famous copy of the *Eroica* in which the phrase 'intitolata Bonaparte' has been heavily deleted. Copyist D copied several important scores around 1805–8; and Copyist E assisted about 1823. Four further copyists, labelled F–I, have since been distinguished by Tyson (Schmidt, 1971, p. XX), but many manuscripts have still not been scrutinized from this point of view.

Corrected copies of Beethoven's works:

Work	Location of Copies (inc = incomplete copy)	Copyist (if known)
Opus		
3	BNba	G
9/1, 3	Private coll. (photocopy in BNba)	
18/1	BNba (early version)	A
22	Bds	
39	Bds	
43	Wn (nos 4 and 5 missing)	F.X. Gebauer
47	Munich, Henle Verlag	partly A and C
48	Wgm	
51/2	B	
55	Wgm	C
56	1) B (inc);	1) D;
	2) Lbl (piano part)	2) partly A
58	Wgm (inc)	D
61	1) Lbl;	1) D
	2) Wgm (piano part)	
65	Wn	
67	Destroyed 1943 (inc photocopy in BNba)	D
68	Ljubljana, University Library	mostly D
72	1) B and Bds (inc);	1) partly C;
	2) Bds;	2) mainly B;
	3) BNba;	3) partly B;
	4) Prague, National Theatre;	
	5) Wgm (inc);	
	6) B (Leon. Ov. 2);	6) D
	7) BNba (Leon. Ov. 2)	
75	1) BNba (inc);	1) partly H
	2) Wgm (no. 4 only)	

Work	Location of Copies (inc = incomplete copy)	Copyist (if known)
Opus		
80	1) BNba (inc);	1) H
	2) Wgm (inc)	
81b	BNba	
84	1) BNba;	1) B and H
	2) Bds (inc);	
	3) Fmi (ov only);	
	4) Mbs (no. 4)	
85	1) B;	1) A;
	2) Lbl	2) partly C
86	Eisenstadt, Esterházy-Archiv	partly D
91	Bds (inc)	
92	1) BNba;	1) A. Diabelli
	2) Wgm	
93	Wgm (inc)	
95	BNba	N. Zmeskall
102	1) BNba;	1) B;
	2) Harvard Univ Lib. (no. 1 only);	2) B
	3) Pn (no. 2 only, inc)	
104	B	A and B
108	1) B and Bds (inc);	
	2) BNba	2) B
109	Wgm	
110	Wgm	B
111	BNba	B
112	BNba	B
113	1) BNba (inc);	1) partly A;
	2) Lbl (ov, on loan)	2) B
115	Lbl (on loan)	B
116	1) B;	1) B;
	2–4) BNba (3 copies)	2) G;
		3–4) B
117	1) Budapest, National Museum (inc);	
	2) BNba (inc);	2) A;
	3) Lbl (ov, on loan)	3) B
118	B	B
119/1–6	Bds	
120	BNba	mainly E, rest A
121b	MZsch	
122	MZsch	

Work	Location of Copies (inc = incomplete copy)	Copyist (if known)
Opus		
123	1–2) Wgm (2 copies); 3) MZsch; 4) BNba (inc); 5) Pn; 6) Dresden, Sächsische Landesbibl.; 7) Frankfurt, Stadt- und Universitätsbibl.	1) mainly B; 4) E
124	1) BNba; 2) MZsch; 3) Lbl (on loan)	3) partly B
125	1) Lbl (on loan); 2) MZsch; 3) Bds; 4) Wgm; 5) Aachen, Bibl. des städt. Konzerthauses	3) mainly B
127	MZsch	
128	MZsch	
130	BNba	B
131	MZsch	B
132	BNba	B
133	BNba	B
136	1) BNba; 2) Coburg, Veste Coll.	
138	BNba	
WoO		
2a	B	
3	Wgm	
4	B	
7	B	partly A
13	B	
18	1–2) Wgm (2 copies)	
19	1–2) Wgm (2 copies)	
92	Bds	
124	Wgm	
137	Bds	
139	Lbl	B
152–8	1) B (selections); 2) Bds (selections); 3) BNba (selections); 4) Darmstadt, Hessische Landesbibl. (selections)	

Library sigla

B	Berlin, Staatsbibliothek Preussischer Kulturbesitz
Bds	Berlin, Deutsche Staatsbibliothek
BNba	Bonn, Beethoven-Archiv
Fmi	Frankfurt, Musikwissentschaftliches Institut der Johann Wolfgang von Goethe Universität
Lbl	London, British Library, Reference Division
Mbs	Munich, Bayerische Staatsbibliothek
MZsch	Mainz, Musikverlag B. Schotts Söhne
Pn	Paris, Bibliothèque Nationale
Wgm	Vienna, Gesellschaft der Musikfreunde
Wn	Vienna, Nationalbibliothek, Musiksammlung

BARRY COOPER

First editions and publishers

IN BEETHOVEN'S DAY composers were normally paid a single lump sum by a publisher for a new work (see pp. 91–2). A composer's task was therefore to find the first publisher willing to pay the fee demanded for a work, or the publisher willing to pay the best fee. Consequently Beethoven frequently dealt with several publishers simultaneously over a single work. If some of his dealings might seem nowadays to border on the unethical (the *Missa Solemnis*, for example, was more or less promised to at least five publishers), this was almost inevitable in such a system, and many of the publishers themselves behaved no better.

With most types of works he seems to have had little difficulty in finding at least one publisher willing to print them, and often there were more. In 1801 he wrote, perhaps with slight exaggeration: 'For every composition I can count on six or seven publishers, and even more, if I want them.' (Letter 51) And in 1822: 'There is a general scramble to secure my works.' (Letter 1086) Most of his business with publishers was done locally in Vienna, where many of his works were first published by firms such as the Bureau des Arts et d'Industrie (or Kunst- und Industrie Comptoir), Domenico Artaria & Co., S. A. Steiner, and Giovanni Cappi. But as his reputation spread, firms from elsewhere began writing to him to ask for works (it would of course have been possible for him to offer works unsolicited to any part of Europe, but he preferred to wait for publishers to approach him, so that he could see how far his reputation had spread). Some publishers wrote initially just to enquire what works he had available, e.g. Breitkopf & Härtel of Leipzig in 1801, C. F. Peters of Leipzig in 1822 and Schott's Sons, of Mainz, in 1824. Others actually commissioned specific works, e.g. Nägeli of Zurich (op. 31 Piano Sonatas), Adolf Schlesinger of Berlin (opp. 109–11 Piano Sonatas) and George Thomson of Edinburgh (numerous folksong arrangements). Still others did business with Beethoven during visits to Vienna, e.g. Muzio Clementi in 1807 and Moritz (Maurice) Schlesinger (who had set up a Paris branch of his father Adolf's firm) in 1825.

The first editions themselves often contain many misprints. Sometimes Beethoven's corrections to the printed proofs were not fully incorporated into the first edition, and on occasion he was not even given an opportunity to proof-read at all before publication. Several of his letters include lists of errata for recently published works, for it was possible to amend the plates before reprinting (see 'Music copying and publishing', pp. 92–3), but the publishers rarely paid attention to these lists. Beethoven sometimes became exasperated by all the mistakes, and once wrote to Breitkopf & Härtel: 'Mistakes – mistakes – you yourself are a unique mistake.' (Letter 306) One of the worst offenders was Nägeli, whose edition of Op. 31 nos 1–2 managed to include four spurious bars in the first Sonata. Beethoven, furious, had the edition sent to Simrock of Bonn, along with a list of some eighty misprints, inviting him to publish an 'Edition très correcte'. The edition duly appeared shortly afterwards (though labelled rather unconvincingly 'Editiou tres Correcte'!) It is easy to assume that Beethoven's bad handwriting was the cause of many of the mistakes in first editions, but he once observed that 'the most correct engravings have been made of those compositions of mine which were written out in my own handwriting' (Letter 220), rather than those engraved from a copy of the autograph, where there was twice as much opportunity for mistakes to creep in.

Despite their faults, the first editions are essential source material for Beethoven's works. They sometimes incorporate last-minute changes that were never entered in the autograph score; and with some works, especially a number of the early ones, no autograph score or corrected copy survives, so that the printed edition forms the only source. (The same holds true even for a few works published posthumously – the bagatelle *Für Elise*, first published in 1867, is a well-known example.) Once a work was in print Beethoven hardly ever went back to revise it even if he could see ways of improving it (*Fidelio* is a notable exception), so that the published text represents a kind of official version of the work, superseding any earlier versions that may have existed.

Below is a list of the publishers of the First Editions that appeared during Beethoven's lifetime or immediately after his death. Of the remaining posthumous works, many first appeared in the Complete Edition or *Gesamtausgabe* (1862–88), or in the *Supplement zur Gesamtausgabe* ed. Willy Hess (1959–71), while others have appeared sporadically during the 19th and 20th centuries. A very small number of compositions (certain exercises, variant versions of known works, short items in sketchbooks, lost works etc.) have still not been published.

Continental publishers (Vienna unless otherwise stated)

Artaria & Co: opp. 1–8, 12, 43 (piano arr.), 46, 48, 51, 72 (1814 version), 87, 103–6. WoO 7, 8, 10, 11, 15, 40, 45, 68, 71, 73, 121–2, 138–9, 146

Artaria, M.: opp. 130, 133–4

Bossler, H. P. (Speyer): WoO 47–9, 107–8

Breitkopf & Härtel (Leipzig): opp. 29, 34–5, 67–71, 72 (1806 version), 73–80, 81a, 82–6. WoO 132, 136–7

Bureau des Arts et d'Industrie: opp. 14/1 (str qt version), 28, 30, 32, 33, 36–8, 45, 49–50, 52–62. WoO 55, 57, 74, 78–80, 82, 129, 134

Cappi, G.: opp. 25–7

Cappi & Czerny: WoO 24

Cappi & Diabelli: op. 120

Eder, J.: op. 10

Gerold, C.: WoO 142

Götz (Mannheim): WoO 63

Gombart & Co (Augsburg): WoO 140

Haslinger, T.: opp. 118, 137

Hoffmeister & Co (Vienna & Leipzig): opp. 13, 19–22. WoO 76

Hoffmeister & Kühnel (Leipzig): opp. 39–42, 43 (ov only), 44, 65

Hoftheatermusikverlag: WoO 94

Löschenkohl, H.: op. 88

Maisch, L.: WoO 42

Mechetti, P.: op. 89. WoO 143

Mollo, T.: opp. 11, 14–18, 23–4. WoO 14, 46, 75, 133

Müller, C. F.: WoO 84–6

Nägeli, J. G. (Zurich): op. 31

Riedl, J.: WoO 165

Schlesinger, A. (Berlin): opp. 108–11. WoO 18, 60

Schlesinger, M. (Paris): opp. 132, 135

Schott (Mainz): opp. 121b, 122–8, 131. WoO 65, 180, 187

Simrock, N. (Bonn): opp. 47, 81b, 102, 107. WoO 41, 64, 66–7, 117, 126–7, 140, 145, 148

Steiner, S. A.: opp. 90–101, 112–17, 121a. WoO 97

Starke, F.: op. 119/7–11

Strauss, A.: WoO 144, 185

Traeg, J.: opp. 9, 66. WoO 69–70, 72, 77, 83(?), 123–4

Wallishausser, I. B.: WoO 147

British publishers (London unless otherwise stated)

Birchall, R.: opp. 47, 96, 97
Broderip & Wilkinson: WoO 125
Chappell & Co.: op. 121a
Clementi & Co.: opp. 31/3, 59, 61 (original and arr. as piano conc), 73–80, 81a, 82, 110–11, 119. WoO 136–7, 139
Dale, J.: op. 33
Regent's Harmonic Institution: op. 106
Thomson, G. (Edinburgh): opp. 105, 107 (selection), 108. WoO 152–7 (selection)

Other publishers with whom Beethoven had unsuccessful dealings include Carl Lissner (St Petersburg), Antonio Pacini (Paris), Carl Friedrich Peters (Leipzig) and Heinrich Albert Probst (Leipzig).

BARRY COOPER

Manuscript paper and handwriting

SINCE ALL THE COMPOSITIONS on which Beethoven's fame rests first took concrete shape in the form of drafts on manuscript paper in his own handwriting, from which all subsequent editions, performances, recordings, commentaries and analyses are ultimately derived, a study of that paper and handwriting is of considerable interest in itself, as well as sometimes being able to provide new information about the works themselves – especially concerning their dating.

Systematic study of his manuscript paper is relatively new, having first been undertaken extensively in the 1960s and considerably refined in the 1970s, chiefly in connection with the sketchbooks. Two main characteristics of the manuscript paper itself have been of prime importance – the watermark and the stave-ruling. In Beethoven's day most paper was still handmade, and this was certainly true of all the paper he used (although in England the Industrial Revolution had resulted in much of the paper being machine-made by the early 19th century). It was usually made in large sheets which, when folded twice and cut, produced four leaves of manuscript paper; the positioning of the watermark design on the original sheet meant that part of it was usually visible on each of the four leaves eventually produced (see Johnson, 1985, pp. 46–8). Each type of watermark design (for example, three crescent moons, or a fleur-de-lys) tended to be used over quite a long period, but each individual variant of it had a very limited life – perhaps about six months to a year. As a result, each time Beethoven acquired a large batch of paper, it was liable to have a different watermark.

It has been demonstrated that he did not normally hoard large stocks of unused paper for any length of time, and so it can normally be assumed that all the paper with a particular watermark was used up within a fairly short period. This conclusion is demonstrable for works whose date is known by other means, and it can be used to date other works – whether sketches or autograph scores – fairly accurately.

Early work on these watermarks was less successful since it often did not take into account the slight differences in watermark pattern that could indicate very different dates (Schmidt-Görg, 1978), but the work of Douglas Johnson, Alan Tyson, Robert Winter and Sieghard Brandenburg has overcome this problem. Altogether fifty-seven different watermarks (or rather, pairs of watermarks, for in each case a pair of matching designs was used) have been distinguished in Beethoven's sketchbooks (1798–1826), plus a few others of infrequent occurrence (Johnson, 1985, pp. 544–63, illustrates all fifty-seven). Likewise, Johnson has identified about fifty different paper types from among Beethoven's papers (sketches and autograph scores) up to 1798; these fall into three readily distinguishable groups – paper used in Bonn (mainly from Holland and Switzerland), paper used in Vienna (made in north Italy), and paper used during Beethoven's tour of Prague and Berlin (made in Bohemia and Germany) in 1796 (see Johnson, 1980a). After about 1806, much of Beethoven's paper came from Austria and Bohemia rather than north Italy.

Most manuscript paper, unlike today, was in oblong format (breadth exceeding height), with a size of about 23 × 32 cm per leaf. Beethoven used paper with anything from 8 to 20 staves, but he generally preferred 16 staves for most purposes. The main reason for this choice is explained in an entry in his *Tagebuch*: 'Music paper is bought at Stadt Nürnberg [a Viennese shop] and a book costs 2 florins; from 10 to 16 staves is always the same price' (Solomon, 1982, no. 157, translation amended). A 'book' was probably 24 sheets, i.e. 96 leaves, and since 10-stave paper cost the same as 16-stave, the latter represented better value.

As with watermarks, individual stave patterns can be distinguished. In Beethoven's day virtually all staves were ruled by a machine, rather than by hand or being printed. This ruling was normally done much more locally than paper production, sometimes in the actual shop where the manuscript paper was sold. As with watermarks, each machine was slightly different and consequently produced its own 'signature' on the paper, usually in the form of slight but recurring irregularities at the ends of staves. Again, particular patterns did not normally last much more than about a year, and so there is a great variety of stave-rulings in Beethoven's paper; they can be distinguished by careful measurement. In most cases a new batch of paper would have a new watermark and stave-ruling, but sometimes a single pair of watermarks is found with more than one stave pattern, or conversely a single stave pattern occurs with more than one pair of watermarks. Thus the combination of watermark and stave-ruling can provide even more precise guides to dating undated works than either could on its own.

Beethoven's notoriously difficult handwriting combined general untidiness with certain special problems. Often the quill he was using was unsatisfactory, and in several letters he asked Zmeskall to provide him with fresh ones. Often there are blots on the paper, and he was not very systematic about using sand (the precursor of blotting paper) to mop them up. As was customary in his day, he used two different types of script, gothic for German words and italic for French, Italian or Latin; in the former, many of the letters are formed in a very different way from that familiar now – for example the letters 'r' and 'w' were very similar, while 'e' resembled the modern letter 'n'. Beethoven had his own particular variant of this script, thus compounding the problem of decipherment.

Early systematic study of his handwriting therefore concentrated on the problems of decipherment, and Max Unger's transcription (1926) of Beethoven's form of every letter of the alphabet in both capital and lower case, gothic and italic, has been of great benefit to successive generations of scholars.

Beethoven's musical script was equally idiosyncratic, with his treble clefs usually resembling a backwards 'S' and his quaver rests sometimes hard to distinguish from crotchets. More recent study by Douglas Johnson has refined Unger's observations and led to handwriting changes being used, like watermarks and stave-rulings, for establishing chronology (Johnson, 1980a). Unger had noted that Beethoven's early script did not conform to the standard pattern of later years, and Johnson was able to document several changes in such elements as clefs, system brace and the figure 4 (in time signatures) between 1785 and 1800. After this date Beethoven's handwriting changed very little, and it is therefore unreliable as a guide to precise dating.

The inks he used have a wide variety of different hues, ranging from light brown to black and sometimes with a tinge of orange, yellow, red, blue, grey or purple. Study of these inks is still in its infancy (Cooper, 1987b), but preliminary investigations suggest that a single type of ink usually lasted a period ranging from a few weeks to a few months, and that sometimes he was using more than one ink concurrently, though possibly for different purposes (e.g. one ink for correspondence and another for sketches). Further investigation of the subject, as well as refinement of studies in paper types and watermarks, is therefore still needed.

BARRY COOPER

Section 9

A CONSPECTUS OF BEETHOVEN'S MUSIC

A CONSPECTUS OF BEETHOVEN'S MUSIC

The stylistic periods

THE PARTITIONING OF BEETHOVEN'S MUSIC into various 'creative' or 'stylistic' periods is as old as Beethoven's music itself. Maynard Solomon (1988, pp. 116–25), charting the development of the ways in which writers have tried to express how his career as a composer went through various phases, noted that a three-period division was suggested as early as 1818, by an anonymous French writer; within a quarter-century of Beethoven's death, some half dozen variations on this theme had been proposed by a number of music scholars and Beethoven biographers, including F.-J. Fétis, Anton Schindler, and Wilhelm von Lenz.

Most early subdivisions are based on general stylistic criteria and use either opus numbers or dates of composition as the basis of grouping. Some used round numbers, which must seem extremely inaccurate given our refined sensitivity to Beethoven's stylistic development, e.g. the year 1800 dividing early from middle (Lenz), or op. 100 dividing middle from late (Schindler). Others saw specific pairs of works as straddling the boundary points, e.g. the 'Waldstein' and *Eroica*, and the Seventh and Eighth Symphonies (Fétis).

Later on, as the chronology of Beethoven's life and works became better known, thanks largely to the biographical researches of Thayer and the sketch studies of Nottebohm, attempts were made to link the stylistic periods with events in Beethoven's life, on the assumption that the composer's musical development was inextricably bound up with that of his life. A biographical 'event' might be as straightforward as a change of locality: thus Beethoven's move to Vienna in 1792 is thought to have important consequences for his outlook as an artist, and hence on his activity as a composer. It might be a financial circumstance: for instance, Beethoven's growth as a symphonist coincides largely with the period in which Prince Joseph von Lobkowitz was among his most important patrons. Or a personal crisis might be seen to foreshadow a change in style: for instance, the knowledge that Beethoven was going deaf (as expressed in the Heiligenstadt Testament in October 1802) has been seen as heralding a 'new manner' of composition.

Of course, not everyone agrees on which factors in Beethoven's biography have a crucial effect on the composer's musical language (if they affect it at all), nor is there a consensus about which pieces represent milestones in its development. The point is well illustrated by the various boundaries drawn between 'middle' and 'late' Beethoven. Some would see Beethoven's period of severe depression in 1813, following the 'Immortal Beloved' affair, as marking the beginning of the final period: the composer's physical and psychological deterioration leads to a period of withdrawal from society, the first artistic fruits of which are a series of highly 'intimate' sonatas such as op. 90 and op. 101 for piano and op. 102 for cello and piano, as well as the through-composed song cycle *An die ferne Geliebte*. Others would note the virtually total deterioration in Beethoven's hearing, marked biographically by the start of the Conversation Books in 1818 and musically by the commencement of the gigantic *Missa Solemnis* in early 1819; by this reasoning, the 'Hammerklavier' Sonata is viewed as a middle-period work, an *Eroica* for the piano and the only sonata composed after 1802 which comprises four substantial, independent movements (as is characteristic of most of the earlier sonatas). Some writers, like Alexandre Oulibicheff, go so far as to restrict the 'late period' to the last three years of the composer's life, after his final public appearances in the concerts of May 1824 (at which the Ninth Symphony and parts of the *Missa Solemnis* were first performed), when he occupied himself almost exclusively with the string quartet in an unprecedented (and, one could say, unequalled) series of musical experiments.

The tripartite division into 'early', 'middle' and 'late', though generally accepted by most Beethovenians, has not been without its critics. Liszt saw Beethoven's work developing in two phases, one in which Beethoven accepted the music of earlier composers as models for his own, another in which his musical invention required entirely new means of expression, resulting in new styles and forms. A similar thesis developed in a recent book (Broyles, 1987) views his development along two curves, which are seen to originate from a 'symphony style' and a 'sonata style' that behave dialectically in the late 18th century but may be seen to interact more competitively in Beethoven's mature work: here, the *Eroica* Symphony is the highpoint of the first phase, but at the same time it marks the beginning of a second phase which overtakes the first after the 'heroic' works of *c.*1803–8 and dominates what is more conventionally deemed the 'late' period.

Another alternative to the three-period division is the subdivision of one or more of them into sub-periods. Many writers, taking their cue from Beethoven's refusal to allow any of his juvenilia to be assigned an opus number, have divided the early work into two sub-periods, frequently designated geographically as 'Bonn' and 'early Viennese'. They would admit that, however much certain extracts from individual works look forward to the mature Beethoven (e.g. the Piano Quartets WoO 36 and the 'Joseph' Cantata), they lack the compositional finish to be allowed to stand beside such early masterpieces as the op. 2 Sonatas, or the *Pathétique*, or even the Second Piano Concerto in its revised form. That subdivisions in the later periods have been suggested is hardly surprising, given the wealth of biographical data and, above all, Beethoven's apparently unending search for new musical ideas and means of expressing them. The first part of the middle period is now frequently referred to as the 'heroic phase' (Tyson 1969), after the title of the Third Symphony and the underlying subject matter of near-contemporary works like the oratorio *Christus am Oelberge* and the opera *Leonore*. Many commentators now extend this concept to embrace the Fifth and Sixth Symphonies and the big concertos, i.e. virtually everything written up to the time of Beethoven's benefit concert of 22 December 1808. They note that a series of more intimate works beginning in 1809 marks a new phase: the Sonata in F♯ op. 78 may be taken to be the quintessential example of a more introspective style. For 'late' Beethoven, as already suggested, we are spoiled for choice of ways in which to demarcate sub-periods.

Now that we have lived with them for so long, it is difficult to disown the three stylistic periods. They provide a useful framework for explaining a musical development as varied and complex as Beethoven's. They work particularly well for the string quartets: the differences in scope and musical language between op. 18 (1800), op. 59 (1806) and the three 'Galitzin' Quartets (opp. 127, 132 and 130/133, 1824–6) are too obvious to be ignored, even if this means that a problematic work like the *Quartetto Serioso* op. 95 (1810) must be pigeonholed into the middle period. With the other major genres, the three periods work less well, either because a large number of works makes stylistic development too continuous (e.g. the piano sonatas), or because Beethoven did not follow a straight line of development in the genre (the symphonies). But so long as there are programme notes, essays written to accompany recordings, and all-Beethoven recitals, it is hard to imagine our ever giving up the notion of discrete stylistic periods.

Traditional elements of Beethoven's style

THE MUSICAL LANGUAGE of the late 18th century played a formative role in the shaping of Beethoven's musical personality, with far-reaching consequences not only for his compositional style but also for his choice of genres. It would not be an exaggeration to say that he 'inherited' a fully mature language, primarily from Mozart and Haydn, in the form of a seemingly inexhaustible repertory of masterworks, any one of which could serve either as a model for imitation or as a springboard for further development. His output strongly reflects both these possibilities.

In his youth, Beethoven was heavily exposed to the music of Mozart. The court Elector, Maximilian Franz, was a great admirer of Mozart and saw to it that his latest works were available to the musicians in his employment. The operas, symphonies, concertos and chamber music made a profound impression on the young Beethoven; and, as can be seen from a wide range of his compositions written in Bonn, he made rapid strides towards assimilating Mozart's style, gaining mastery of the principles of writing a sonata despite little formal supervision in original composition. Mozart's music remained the dominant influence on him until at least 1800.

The influence of Haydn is, on the whole, less well understood, partly because Haydn himself is today less well understood as a composer than Mozart, and partly because the relationship between Haydn and Beethoven has been clouded by myths which scholars have only recently begun to dispel (Webster, 1984). What Beethoven seems mainly to have learnt from Haydn's music was to be economical in the invention of themes and motifs, and to know how to develop them imaginatively. This was to be of utmost importance later, when problems of overall compositional unity were painstakingly worked out.

Beethoven's motivic economy should not be confused with Haydn's so-called 'monothematicism', whereby prominent themes of a sonata movement, stated in different keys, are nevertheless traceable to a common source. Beethoven generally followed Mozart's dualism by introducing a new key with something sounding like a new theme. In other words, in the external planning of his music he seems initially to have followed Mozart in the exposition of themes, and in recapitulating them; insofar as his development sections are freer, i.e. less predictable from one piece to the next, they bear a closer relationship to Haydn's compositional technique.

Harmony and tonality

IT IS DIFFICULT TO SINGLE OUT 'novel effects' in Beethoven's harmony without relating them to the design to which they belong. For instance, the famous move from C major to E major in the first movement of the 'Waldstein' Sonata (1804) has been rightly seen as an important step on Beethoven's way towards what Tovey called the 'crossing of the Rubicon'. (This relationship had in fact been used previously, in the Sonata in G op. 31 no. 1.) But it was not really a question of doing something different for the sake of being different: the modulation to the mediant major helps to create an entirely new relationship between the end of the exposition and the music which follows it, as well as having consequences for the tonal plan of the recapitulation and coda.

In certain later sonata-form movements, viz. the slow movement of the 'Ghost' Trio op. 70 no. 1 and the Scherzo of the Ninth Symphony, there is an even more 'daring' modulation, from D minor to C major, one which throws more weight on to the second key area because of the tonal dependence of D minor upon C, as its supertonic chord (i.e. as part of a ii-V-I progression in C major). By the late period, the 'standard' modulatory paths in sonata-form expositions of I-V in major keys, i-III in minor keys, are the exception rather than the rule: and each new tonal relationship brings with it a new set of possibilities for tonal development, and hence for formal planning.

Beethoven did not actually give up an essentially Classical, 18th-century harmonic language, however much he may have modified the traditional means of expressing it. It is often said, however, that in his mature music, motivic relationships begin to compete for power with tonality in the shaping of forms. This comes about not only by the avoidance of traditional tonic–dominant key relationships (as discussed above), but also by harmonic progressions not taking the route prescribed by the traditional 'laws' of tonality. In the finale of the Eighth Symphony, for instance, the F major chord at bars 88-90 is heard contextually as a subdominant of C major, and a transitional passage of several bars would normally be required for a return to the home key of F major; but Beethoven, disregarding the rules, simply proceeds to a recapitulation of the main theme in the home key without offering any harmonic 'explanation'. In the fifth movement of the Quartet in B♭ op. 130, the E♭ major chord at bar 49 functions as the dominant of A♭ minor; yet Beethoven uses this chord to bring back the beginning of the piece, without any modulatory passage. Such examples, however rare, indicate a change in attitude towards functional harmony which anticipates mid-19th-century practice.

Another way of relaxing the rules of 18th-century harmony is to use third-related progressions in place of dominant–tonic ones. Third-related harmonies occur throughout Beethoven's work, though invariably within a framework of traditional tonal relationships. In an exceptional passage (bars 89-108) from the third movement of the Piano Trio in E♭ op. 70 no. 2 (1809), the harmony is focused upon the relationship between A♭ major and E major; the enharmonic change (G♯ for A♭) needed to understand the passage, combined with the interplay between major and minor chords built on the same root (A♭ major, G♯ minor), imparts a very different sense of harmonic syntax to the passage, one which is more readily associated with the mature works of Schubert.

The occasions on which major–minor tonality is abandoned for a more archaic modality are few in number, and nearly all have programmatic connotations or occur in settings of a text. The 'Et incarnatus' from the Credo of the *Missa Solemnis* (1819–23) is cast in a kind of Dorian mode, which gives prominence to the relationship between D minor and C major (something which has been observed in other, non-modal contexts), and whose function is to provide an 'otherworldly' tonality based on D, to contrast with the ensuing D major 'Et homo factus est' and D minor 'Crucifixus'; it has been described, in other words, as a 'definite negation of major–minor tonality' (Dahlhaus, 1987). The 'Heiliger Dankgesang', the third movement of the Quartet in A minor op. 132, is described by the composer as being 'in the Lydian mode'; yet it is also possible to hear the chorale-based sections of the movement in C major, with a subdominant (rather than dominant) bias.

In the finale of the Quartet in F op. 135 (1826), a new trend may be discerned in the development of augmented triads (bars 1-4, 83-4, 243-6), but these can be clearly perceived as altered diatonic chords (e.g. the opening C–E–A♭ is a substitute for C–E–G, the dominant of F minor). Nowhere in Beethoven's oeuvre, however, can one identify true anticipations of such 'exotic' harmonies as the whole-tone experiments of mid-century Russians or the atonality of late Wagner and Liszt.

Counterpoint

FROM HIS TEACHER Christian Gottlob Neefe, Beethoven learned the Preludes and Fugues from Bach's *Well-Tempered Clavier* at an early age; from this experience he acquired a lifelong fascination with fugal and more general contrapuntal textures. The writing of intricate counterpoint did not come easily to him. His difficulties are testified to first of all by the numerous exercises in counterpoint undertaken at all stages of his career, for his Viennese teachers Haydn and Johann Georg Albrechtsberger, for himself, and for his own pupil the Archduke Rudolph. We can draw similar conclusions from the drafts of fugal textures that dominate many of the later sketchbooks: the 'Et vitam venturi' fugue from the *Missa Solemnis*, for instance, cost him more effort than all the rest of the Credo. A lifelong preoccupation with contrapuntal music of earlier composers (especially Bach and Handel) is also found in the sketchbooks, as well as copies of extracts from works such as Fux's *Gradus ad Parnassum* and Mattheson's *Der vollkommene Capellmeister*.

Although it is commonplace to say that Beethoven's late style is marked by a return to the severe contrapuntal disciplines of the High Baroque (as is witnessed by, for instance, the fugues of the 'Hammerklavier' and op. 110 sonatas, the Scherzo of the Ninth Symphony, and the late quartets, as well as by the chorale preludes from the 'Heiliger Dankgesang' in op. 132), it should be borne in mind that fugal textures appear frequently in the music from all periods. Fugue, it has been pointed out, has a 'flattening' effect in Beethoven's music (Kerman, 1983), creating expanses of dramatically undifferentiated time between more dynamic parts of a sonata form, yet rarely intended for a display of 'learnedness'. Alternatively, it can be used deliberately to evoke the style of an earlier age, e.g. in numerous subsections of the *Missa Solemnis* and the unabashedly Handelian overture *Die Weihe des Hauses* op. 124 (1822).

Orchestration

ALTHOUGH HE DID NOT COMPLETE his First Symphony until the age of twenty-nine, Beethoven's style of orchestral writing was close to that of his Viennese predecessors and did not change radically over the next quarter-century, certain famous passages and effects notwithstanding. The strings still dominate the texture, as they had done in Haydn's and Mozart's symphonies; and if the woodwind appear to be more prominent as early as the First Symphony, this can perhaps be traced to the orchestral textures of Mozart's mature piano concertos (a repertory Beethoven knew intimately), where the wind collectively contribute as much as the keyboard soloist to the concertante style. One notes an early interest in the cello (often doubled by the violas) as an important melodic voice; this too can be traced, via the string quartet tradition, back to Mozart. Perhaps the most important 'new' feature of Beethoven's orchestration lies in the designing of themes for instruments incapable of playing melodies: thus some of the most memorable moments in Beethoven's orchestral compositions feature instruments not normally given solo parts by Haydn and Mozart, viz. the horns (in virtually every symphony from the *Eroica* onwards) and the timpani (in exposed passages from the last three symphonies). Of course, improvements in wind instrument manufacture and playing technique in the 19th century meant that Beethoven could make his orchestral parts more taxing, and soloistically more challenging, as he developed as a symphonist; this is exemplified by the frantic passage-work for the bassoons in the Fourth Symphony and the Overture op. 124, the clarinet solo in the Trio of the Eighth Symphony, and the exposed fourth horn in the slow movement of the Ninth.

Musical form: innovations

ANY ATTEMPT TO PINPOINT Beethoven's innovations in harmony, melody, form, etc. can at best relate what may sound like a 'novel effect' to a musical structure of which that effect is an inseparable component. Whether it is the mournful oboe solo in the first movement of the Fifth Symphony, the bird-calls in the *Pastoral*, or the quotations from earlier movements in the finale of the Ninth, the effects themselves are not what make these works progressive, but rather the fact that they contribute to and hence become an integral element of the design of the work.

One element that makes Beethoven's music seem progressive, and to undergo an extraordinary development between about 1790 and 1826, is his changing conception of what a large-scale piece of music actually is: the shaping of works comprising a number of movements is a problem he faced up to in virtually every new major project. Solutions to the problem may be defined according to one or more of the following parameters: (i) the absolute size of the movements, (ii) tonal and/or thematic integration of the movements, and (iii) new definitions of what constitutes a movement, and of how works can be put together from formal elements of disparate sizes.

(i) A major advance in Beethoven's development occurs about 1803, with the increased size of movements, especially first movements in sonata form. Neither of the first two symphonies, nor any other work dating from the first decade in Vienna, prepares us for the Allegro con brio of the *Eroica*, whose awesome proportions have made it one of the most compelling subjects for analysis (for a summary of the literature on the *Eroica*, see Lockwood, 1982). The *Eroica* paved the way for works of comparable dimensions for piano (the 'Waldstein' Sonata, 1803–4), for piano and orchestra (Fourth Concerto, 1805–6), and for string quartet (op. 59 no. 1, 1806).

It is difficult to determine what motivated Beethoven to begin writing sonata movements on a vast scale: the longest 18th-century first-movement forms are found in the late piano concertos of Mozart, and also in some of his string quintets. Possibly Beethoven learnt something from both repertories: the quintets (especially K.515 in C major) for their breadth of phrasing, the concertos for their profusion of themes. The increased size of the exposition led to a proportional lengthening of the development section. Here, Beethoven seems to have found his own solution: to write not one but two discrete developments, which could then be joined by further transitional material. A glimpse of this process is provided by the first movement of the Quartet in F op. 59 no. 1, where there is a clear indication of an imminent return to the tonic at bar 152, barely forty bars after the exposition. But now the harmony veers away from the home key and eventually leads to a fugato, extending the development section by a further ninety bars. Similar composite development sections are found in the *Eroica* Symphony and the 'Waldstein', 'Appassionata' and 'Hammerklavier' Sonatas.

Though his monumental structures had a more profound influence on later generations, the miniaturizing of sonata forms was no less an achievement for Beethoven, whose later master-pieces include the Sonata in F♯ op. 78, the *Quartetto Serioso* in F minor op. 95 and the Eighth Symphony. As we shall see, one of the most interesting features of the late music is the way in which substantial pieces are fashioned from a selection of very long and very short movements.

(**ii**) From the start, Beethoven sought consciously to make the various parts of a multi-movement work fit together. He did this in many different ways: the following survey can only touch on a few of them. From the outset, he appears to have been conscious that many 18th-century instrumental works were somehow unified, despite being made up of a series of structurally independent movements. There was a particularly strong spiritual bond between the outer movements, and Beethoven sought to define this relationship more precisely by forging thematic links between them, e.g. by the emphasis on the interval C–E♭ in the main themes of the outer movements of the Trio op. 1 no. 3, or by the leap g′-b♭″ in the finale of the op. 1 no. 1, which recalls the arpeggio to b♭″ in the first movement. More subtly, the second movement of the Piano Sonata op. 2 no. 3 recalls the first by its sudden shift in harmony and development of theme. These examples may pale into insignificance when set beside similar procedures in the late quartets, e.g. the play on B♭-A in the first, third and final movements of op. 130 (with the *Grosse Fuge*) and a similar procedure using G♯-A in op. 132, but they show the composer's consciousness of these matters at an early stage.

Another integrative technique is the joining together of movements to make longer continuous stretches of music. This technique first comes to prominence about 1801, in the two sonatas 'quasi una fantasia'. In the first of these, the odd shapes of the movements make it difficult to understand any of them on its own, hence the connections result in a sonata that is 'greater than the sum of its movements', so to speak. In the second (the 'Moonlight'), however, the effect is psychologically more profound. Here the lowest note of the opening chord of the second movement (f') is higher than the highest note of the final chord of the first ($c\sharp'$); the effect is one of the rebirth of the music, after it has reached the point of expiration. (A similar effect may be observed between the slow movement and Minuet of the slightly earlier Sonata op. 10 no. 3, though Beethoven does not affirm the point by indicating *attacca*.)

In several works Beethoven joins the slow movement to the ensuing scherzo or finale by cutting off the final cadence at, or extending it to, an unstable chord, e.g. a diminished seventh or a dominant seventh. One of the earliest examples of this procedure occurs in the 'Appassionata' Sonata (1805); ten years later it had become almost a cliché, being used in the Violin Sonata in G op. 96, the 'Archduke' Trio op. 97, and the Cello Sonata in D op. 102 no. 2. Conversely, a finale might start quietly and/or harmonically off-centre, so that it appears to grow from the previous slow movement: examples of this include the Fourth Piano Concerto and the Quartet in B♭ op. 130 (with either finale). Beethoven also sometimes wrote a short transition linking the slow movement to the finale (Violin Concerto, 1806; Fifth Piano Concerto, 1809).

Related to this procedure is the reduction in the size of the slow movement, so that it behaves more like an introduction to the finale, and hence undermines the contrast a slow movement is intended to provide for works in the Classical style. Beethoven actually refashioned the 'Waldstein' Sonata in just this way at a late stage of the composition, suppressing the original, lengthy slow movement (later published as a separate piece, the *Andante favori*, WoO 57) and substituting for it a terse twenty-eight-bar 'Introduzione' to the final Rondo. In later sonatas, such as op. 69 for cello and piano, and op. 101 for piano solo, it is difficult to decide whether the short piece immediately preceding the finale is an introduction, or a much abbreviated slow movement.

Many of the techniques described above are related to another phenomenon which becomes an increasingly prominent feature of Beethoven's music: a tendency to push towards the final movement, and thus for the intellectual or psychological weight of the piece to be shifted from the beginning (where it lies in the vast majority of works by Haydn and Mozart) to the end. Perhaps the best-known illustration of this is the Fifth Symphony, whose finale ends in a blaze of glory in C major (with an extra complement of wind instruments), after three movements in which this key surfaces to provide a brief respite to the prevailing 'tragic' mood of C minor. The most extreme form of this technique is, of course, found in the Ninth Symphony, whose final-movement cantata apparently celebrates the end of serious, orchestral symphonic writing as exemplified by the first three movements (hence the mockingly self-critical proclamation 'O Freunde, nicht diese Töne!'). The Quartet op. 130 with the *Grosse Fuge* as finale was intended to have the same effect; but Beethoven substituted for the Fugue a much more conventional finale, realizing perhaps that larger performing forces, and not length alone, might be needed for a satisfactory realization of this plan.

Avoiding the difficulties involved in making the finale dwarf the previous movements, Beethoven nevertheless could convey movement towards the finale by the pacing of the previous movements. In the Sonata immediately preceding the 'quasi una fantasia' set, op. 26 in A♭, he began with a Theme and Variations, reserving the dramatic character of a full sonata movement until the finale. A very different arrangement of movements leading to a sonata-form finale in the home key is an important feature of the Quartet in C♯ minor op. 131, the planning of whose movements made up a large part of the creative process (see Winter, 1977). Elsewhere, Beethoven's music pushes towards the finale either because of the unusual shape of that movement (*Eroica* Symphony, Piano Sonata in A♭ op. 110) or because the entire work comprises only two movements (the Piano Sonatas opp. 54, 78 and 90, and especially the Sonata in C minor op. 111). A unique position is occupied by the Sixth Symphony (the *Pastoral*), whose dynamic traces a curve which climaxes in the fourth movement (the 'Storm'), and tails off in the final 'Shepherd's Song'.

(iii) We may finally consider Beethoven's use of musical 'chunks' of diverse size and scope to assemble larger compositions, a technique that had a profound effect upon Mahler and many 20th-century composers. Some of these have already been mentioned above, viz. sections of music which seem too short to be regarded as movements, too tuneful to be considered as introductions (op. 69, op. 101). Most examples of this practice, however, belong to the very last years of his life, which coincide with an interest in miniature forms (the Bagatelles published as op. 119 nos 7–11 and, more importantly, the 'cycle' of Bagatelles op. 126). In some respects, these experiments mark a return to the 18th-century divertimento, where weightier movements appear alongside marches and dances; this sense of 'divertimento' is well suited to the six-movement Quartet in B♭ op. 130 (with either finale). But now the intention is one of utmost seriousness: the short pieces provide a temporary escape from the 'intellectual' demands of the other movements. Moreover, the arrangement of material is different in each work.

In the Piano Sonata in A♭ op. 110 (1821–2) the role of slow movement is taken by a sixteen-bar tune, entitled 'Arioso dolente' (or 'Klagender Gesang'), preceded by seven bars of introduction and 'recitative'. As this material is too slender in relation to the previous fast movements and the subsequent fugal finale, Beethoven interrupts the fugue after eighty-eight bars to recall the 'Arioso dolente', though now in more anguished rhythms: in this way the slow movement and finale of a sonata have been fused into a single movement, with a perfect balance between the two components.

The most unusual arrangement in the late quartets is offered by op. 131 in C♯ minor, which Beethoven divides into seven numbered sections. The interior movements include a substantial set of variations (no. 4) and a scherzo (no. 5), but also a linking instrumental recitative (no. 3) and a twenty-eight-bar Adagio quasi un poco andante (no. 6) which, again, is too short for a slow movement but does not sound preparatory enough to be called an introduction to the finale. Even the second section of the piece, an Allegro molto vivace of almost two hundred bars, seems truncated, not quite a full movement. Moreover, in the tonal scheme of the Quartet, only the first and last movements are in the home key:

No.	1	2	3	4	5	6	7
	c♯	D	(b)	A	E	g♯	c♯

As the opening fugue is itself tonally unstable, it is difficult for any one movement to be perceived as an independent musical statement.

By a variety of techniques, then, Beethoven breaks down the concept of 'movement' in many of his works, and makes the work as a whole the artistic unit of measurement. This means taking in much larger stretches of music at a time: op. 131 does not appreciably exceed op. 18 no. 1 in clock time, yet it takes the listener on a long and varied journey through a variety of keys, moods and textures. This is a quality one senses in much of the best of Beethoven's mature works, even those which are morphologically more conventional: works like the *Eroica*, Fifth and *Pastoral* Symphonies, and the 'Hammerklavier' and late E major Piano Sonatas, to name just a few of the most obvious ones, are stories told in music.

WILLIAM DRABKIN

Section 10
THE MUSIC

THE MUSIC

Numerical list of works

THE INITIAL LIST BELOW presents all Beethoven's works in numerical order, followed by a reference to the page on which each work is documented in full. The list falls into three main sections – opus, WoO and Hess numbers. Most of the opus numbers were chosen by Beethoven himself; several letters survive in which he tells various publishers what opus numbers to assign to particular works. A few works, however, have at some time been known by a different opus number – for example, the op. 31 Sonatas were reprinted by Cappi in 1805 as 'op. 29', a number already used for a quintet; the Paris and Vienna editions of the Bagatelles op. 119 were issued as 'op. 112', and only acquired their present number in 1851. Other works that acquired their opus number posthumously include opp. 129 and 136–8.

Beethoven regarded many works as too slight to be given an opus number. They were classified as *Werke ohne Opuszahl* (works without opus number, usually abbreviated to WoO) in Kinsky, 1955. Meanwhile Willy Hess was at that time compiling a list of all works that had not been printed in the Complete Edition (1862–5 and 1888). Many of the works listed by Kinsky as WoO had appeared in this, but some had not and were published only later. Thus Hess's list (published in Hess, 1957) included many 'WoO' works plus many without even a WoO number – mainly variant versions, fragmentary works and trivia. Those that have no WoO number but are sufficiently significant are listed here with their Hess number. The present list also includes a few minor works with no number at all. In addition there are several unnumbered but more or less complete works (mostly short piano pieces) that have not been included since they could be thought to be too sketchy. Many were published in Kerman, 1970, while others are in Schmitz, 1924, and three are in Cooper, 1991; performing editions of twenty-one pieces from Kerman, 1970 are in Fecker, 1972. Doubtful and spurious works that had been attributed to Beethoven were listed by Kinsky in an Appendix (*Anhang*). Those for which there is still a reasonable possibility that Beethoven may have written them are included here with their Anh. number. Other works whose authenticity is now suspect but which were regarded by Kinsky as genuine are also listed, with a note about their authorship. Information about the manuscript sources (sketches, autographs and corrected copies) for all the main works is given in Section 8.

The numerical list is followed by classified lists with accompanying commentaries. Under each heading or subheading the works are listed in what is believed to be chronological order, except for the folksong arrangements, other arrangements and miscellaneous works, where a listing in numerical order was found to be preferable. The layout of individual entries varies slightly from genre to genre, but is basically as follows:

Opus no.
Title (with author of text if applicable), **key**.
Title of each movement (with key if different from that of work)
Scoring (with alternatives if applicable, as in Dance Music)
Date of composition; first performance (if known); publication (with publisher) if published during or just after Beethoven's lifetime
Dedication and special remarks (if any)

Abbreviations

A	alto, contralto
Anh.	Anhang (appendix)
B	bass (voice)
bd	bass drum
bhn	basset horn
bn	bassoon
cbn	contrabassoon
ch	chorus
cl	clarinet
cy	cymbal
db	double bass
ded.	dedicated
eng hn	english horn
fl	flute
Hess	no. in Hess, 1957
hn	horn
mand	mandolin
mil.	military
MS	manuscript
ob	oboe
orch	orchestra
org	organ
ov.	overture

perc	percussion
perf.	performed/performance
pf	piano
pic	piccolo
posth.	posthumous(ly)
publ.	published
qnt	quintet
qt	quartet
rev.	revised/revision
S	soprano
SATB	soprano, alto, tenor, bass
sd	side drum
serp	serpent
str	string(s)
T	tenor
tamb	tambourine
tbn	trombone
timp	timpani
tpt	trumpet
tri	triangle
v, vv	voice(s)
va	viola
vc	cello
vn	violin
WoO	Werk(e) ohne Opuszahl (see Kinsky, 1955)

BARRY COOPER

Symphonies

IT WOULD BE DIFFICULT to exaggerate the importance of Beethoven's nine completed symphonies, either in relation to the rest of his output or in relation to the subsequent history of music. For many listeners the symphonies represent the quintessential Beethoven; and although we should now shut the door firmly on Schindler's improbable claim about the knocking of fate in the Fifth Symphony, this work perhaps remains the quintessential symphony. Certainly, the nature of Beethoven's compositional thinking made it almost inevitable that he would excel in the genre and transform it radically.

Symphonic mastery was not easily won, however. At the beginning of his career Beethoven had to confront not only the legacy of Mozart but the continuing output of his teacher Haydn. Having already begun and abandoned a movement in C minor while at Bonn, he worked much more extensively on a symphony in C major during 1795–6. This piece, undoubtedly influenced by Haydn's Symphony no. 97, was also laid aside, although some material from it was later salvaged for the First Symphony (see 'Unfinished and projected works', p. 276, and Johnson, 1980a, pp. 461–9). (The 'Jena' Symphony, thought for some time to be another early Beethoven work, was identified over thirty years ago as the work of Friedrich Witt; see Landon, 1957.)

To dismiss the first two symphonies as purely derivative will not do. The 'wrong-key' opening of the First Symphony is often remarked upon, but this is perhaps less interesting in itself than in its effect on the rest of the work. The first two chords, with $e''' - f'''$ high up in the flute, present a kind of 'problem' which persists until it is 'resolved', again by the flute, as $f''' - e'''$ (now in C, the 'right' key) in the recapitulation of the last movement. This is an early but excellent example of the kind of long-range musical thinking which Beethoven developed much more powerfully in later works: consider, for example, the out-of-key C♯ near the beginning of the *Eroica* or the finale of the Eighth Symphony: in each case C♯ is absorbed and 'explained' by later events.

The Second Symphony already shows remarkable advances over the First. The slow introduction is much more substantial and foreshadows those of the Fourth and Seventh Symphonies; also, the finale already exhibits very clearly that sense of irresistible drive which is so characteristic of Beethoven (again, compare the finale of the Seventh Symphony). Prophetic too is the massive developmental coda of the finale: in scope it heralds that in the first movement of the *Eroica*, and its force is such that it grounds not only the last movement but the entire work. The sense of a psychological 'journey' from beginning to end which is thus created became an essential feature of Beethoven's symphonic style: the *locus classicus* is probably the Fifth Symphony, where the unbroken succession of the last two movements and the minor–major contrast add an almost spiritual dimension to the journey: in his famous review of the work, E. T. A. Hoffmann wrote of 'radiant, blinding sunlight which suddenly illuminates the dark night' (see Forbes, 1971, p. 161).

It was with the *Eroica*, however, that Beethoven changed the nature of the symphony once and for all. One of the first and most characteristic products of what has been termed Beethoven's 'heroic phase' (see Tyson, 1969) – a phase notable for the composition of uncompromising works on the largest scale, often bound up with extra-musical ideas – the *Eroica* was far longer and more complex than any symphony previously written. All this is certainly true of the huge first movement with its wealth of thematic material and remarkable tonal breadth (a theme which may be derived from the opening subject, but which is to all intents and purposes new, appears in the remote key of E minor in the development). Yet even the *Eroica* was to some extent derivative: the music owes not a little to the products of post-revolutionary composers in France; and Beethoven had already used the theme of the last movement in no fewer than three previous works – *Die Geschöpfe des Prometheus* op. 43, no. 7 of the Twelve Contredanses WoO 14 and the *Prometheus* (or 'Eroica') Variations op. 35.

The connection between the *Eroica* and Napoleon is well known and has been discussed by all major commentators. Beethoven's original intention was to dedicate the symphony to Napoleon, whose republican ideals he much admired; but subsequently he decided actually to entitle the work 'Bonaparte'. Ferdinand Ries recounted how he was the first to tell Beethoven that Bonaparte had proclaimed himself emperor, whereupon Beethoven flew into a rage, tore the title-page of the symphony in two and threw it to the ground (Wegeler, 1987, p. 68). This must have taken place in May 1804. According to Ries, the title-page which Beethoven mutilated bore the word 'Buonaparte' at the extreme top and 'Luigi van Beethoven' at the bottom. It probably belonged to the now lost autograph score. A different title-page survives in a copyist's score (see plate 27). The wording on this page originally read 'Sinfonia grande/intitolata Bonaparte/del Sigr/Louis van Beethoven'. The page is still in one piece; but the words 'intitolata Bonaparte' have been erased so heavily that the surface of the paper has been punctured where Beethoven's hero's name had been.

Nevertheless, the connection with Bonaparte did not end here, for the phrase 'geschrieben auf Bonaparte' was subsequently scrawled on the title-page of the copyist's score, underneath Beethoven's name; and in a letter to Breitkopf & Härtel dated 26 August 1804 (Letter 96) – that is, after the events described by Ries – Beethoven wrote that 'the title of the symphony is really *Bonaparte*'. But neither of these references need be taken to imply that Beethoven had decided to reinstate the title; it seems more likely that he was in each case referring more generally to the 'idea' behind the work: that idea was indeed expressed more generally on the title-page of the first edition as 'Sinfonia Eroica . . . per festeggiare il sovvenire di un grand Uomo' ('. . . to celebrate the memory of a great man').

In general, Beethoven did not alter the outward form of the symphony to any great degree. The symphonies were 'public' works, less suited to the kind of formal experimentation which increasingly characterized his output in the more intimate genres of the piano sonata and string quartet. He sometimes used a larger orchestra than Haydn – a third horn is required in the *Eroica*, for example, and piccolo, contrabassoon and trombones are added in the finale of the Fifth Symphony – but in other respects he adhered closely to the outward form of the older composer's works. The two symphonies which do depart significantly from the Haydn model are the *Pastoral* and the Ninth.

The *Pastoral* has five movements rather than the usual four, and each movement bears a descriptive title (although Beethoven described the work as 'more an expression of feeling than painting'). The last three movements follow one another without a break. The 'Storm' movement, which uses trombones and piccolo, is harmonically very unstable. It begins on D♭, the flattened sixth degree of the tonic key, and works its way through various tonal areas before settling back on the dominant in preparation for the final movement. The harmonic instability of the 'Storm' is thrown into relief by the corresponding stability of the other movements: the first movement particularly is devoid of harmonic tension and the symphony as a whole proceeds in a marvellously relaxed manner as a result of the emphasis placed on the subdominant throughout. In effect, the 'Storm' is a long interpolation between the third and fifth movements and its function within the symphony as a whole is akin to that of the development section of a sonata form. But to recognize this is to realize that the changed outward shape of the symphony is simply a consequence of its changed inner dynamic.

The most conspicuous 'outward' feature of the Ninth Symphony is of course the addition of chorus and soloists in the final movement. As in the Fifth Symphony, the entire work seems to move towards the finale: there can be no doubt of this when, at the beginning of the movement, fragments of the preceding movements are reintroduced, only to be abandoned in favour of the 'Freude' theme. The tonic major, which had earlier appeared at the recapitulation of the first movement, in the Trio of the second and even in the third, finally gains ascendancy over the minor here, as in the Fifth Symphony.

Whereas in the *Pastoral* Symphony Beethoven may be said to have projected a sonata-form design on to the entire work, in the finale of the Ninth he succeeded in condensing the overall dynamic of the Classical symphony into a single movement. The Turkish march section may be heard as a scherzo following the opening section; the Andante maestoso then represents a slow movement, and the finale (beginning 6/4, Allegro energico) brings a return to the tonic key and introduces the combination of the 'Freude' and 'Seid umschlungen' themes. But the finale of the Ninth is indebted to other formal models too: variation form (also used in the third movement) is perhaps the most obvious, but the principles of sonata and even concerto form are also clearly evident.

The blending of forms and genres exhibited by this gigantic movement, about which critical opinion has always been divided, is entirely typical of Beethoven's late period. Although the surviving sketch material for a Tenth Symphony has now been shown to be more substantial than had hitherto been suspected (see 'Unfinished and projected works', p. 277), it is by no means clear how this work would have unfolded. Thus the Ninth remains the pinnacle of Beethoven's achievement as a symphonist. A culminating work in every respect, it attempts to transform the public nature of the genre: 'all men become brothers', sings the chorus, making appeal to a universal public, mankind.

Mention has already been made of the *Eroica* finale and its connection with three earlier works. Recent sketch studies have shown that the connection between the symphony and the *Prometheus* Variations for piano is more significant than had previously been realized. Not only do the two works share thematic material, it now seems clear that the variations were the seed from which the first as well as the last movement of the symphony grew. The earliest sketches for the symphony date from 1802 and follow hard on the heels of the final sketches for the variations (see Lockwood, 1981).

The *Eroica* is not the only one of the symphonies for which Beethoven made preliminary sketches some time before beginning serious work. Although the Fifth and Sixth Symphonies were composed in 1807–8, the so-called *Eroica* Sketchbook of 1803–4 contains 'concept sketches' (see 'Sketches', p. 173) for both works. Moreover, it is clear that the first movement of the Eighth Symphony was originally planned as a piano concerto (see Brandenburg, 1979, pp. 135–41). But if the origins of the symphonies are compared it is again the Ninth which dwarfs the others in this as in so many other respects. Beethoven had conceived the idea of setting Schiller's *An die Freude*, albeit as a song rather than as the finale of a symphony, as early as 1792. Other sketches using Schiller's text are found in the Petter Sketchbook of 1811–12, in which there is also mention of a Symphony in D minor. Sketch material which relates directly to the symphony which we know today dates from as early as 1815/16, and the lost Boldrini Sketchbook reveals further progress in 1818; but the existence of so many early ideas does not in any way alter the fact that the serious, sustained composition of the work belongs to the years 1823–4.

It should be borne in mind that the first six symphonies were initially published in orchestral parts only. In the letter of 26 August 1804 mentioned above (Letter 96) Beethoven requested that the *Eroica* Symphony be published in score rather than in parts, but this was not to be the case. Only in 1809 was a score published, together with scores of the first two symphonies; the Fifth and Sixth were not published in this form until 1826. In the case of the last three symphonies, scores and parts were published simultaneously; and such was the popularity of the Seventh and Eighth that Steiner also published various chamber arrangements at the same time. In fact instrumental arrangements of all the symphonies except the Ninth abounded during Beethoven's lifetime and must have contributed in no small way to the dissemination of these works. Beethoven himself published an arrangement for piano trio of the Second Symphony in 1805 (see 'Arrangements', p. 273).

There is ample evidence from Beethoven's correspondence that the business of getting the symphonies published was an arduous one. Even today there is no scholarly edition of the symphonies available, and questions hang over even the most elemental issues; for instance, there has been much lively debate concerning the form of the third movement of the Fifth Symphony, specifically whether Beethoven intended a conventional three-part (ABA) form or a five-part (ABABA) one like that in the corresponding movement of the Fourth Symphony. The most substantial contribution to the debate is Brandenburg, 1984b, which argues that Beethoven failed to notice that the movement had been published as a three-part rather than a five-part form until it was too late to rectify the mistake. Brandenburg concludes that 'if we ask what is the "final version" ... one must answer that it is the three-part version. The one that corresponds to Beethoven's artistic intentions, however, is in five parts' (p. 198). Exactly the same formal issue has been raised in connection with a recent investigation of manuscript and printed sources for the *Eroica* (see Tusa, 1985).

In some cases there is evidence that Beethoven made modifications to the symphonies as a result of hearing them performed. Thus on 4 March 1809 he wrote to Breitkopf & Härtel: 'Tomorrow you will receive a notice about some small corrections which I made during the performance of the [Fifth and Sixth] symphonies – When I gave these works to you, I had not yet heard either of them performed – and one should not want to be so like a god as not to have to correct something here and there in one's created works' (Letter 199). Moreover, it has recently come to light that in the case of the *Eroica* Symphony Beethoven enjoyed the luxury of private rehearsals paid for by the work's dedicatee, Prince Lobkowitz (see Volek, 1986). No doubt these preliminary hearings played a part in the shaping of the definitive version.

The impact of Beethoven's symphonies, in particular the Ninth, on succeeding generations of composers has been enormous. Every symphonist, from Schubert onwards, has had to confront and come to terms with the seemingly inexhaustible legacy of these nine compositions. The opening, *in medias res*, of the Ninth had a profound influence on Bruckner, and the whole work seemed to Wagner to be a major staging-post between wordless instrumental music and his own conception of music drama. In Britain in the 20th century, Robert Simpson has repeatedly illustrated his debt to Beethoven, both in words and in the music of his own nine symphonies; and Tippett's Third Symphony not only makes use of the human voice in its final movement but also quotes and develops material from Beethoven's Ninth.

Op. 21
First Symphony, C
Adagio molto (4/4), Allegro con brio (2/2) –
Andante cantabile con moto (F, 3/8) – Menuetto:

Allegro molto e vivace (3/4) – Finale: Adagio
(2/4), Allegro molto e vivace (2/4)
2 fl, 2 ob, 2 cl, 2 bn, 2 hn, 2 tpt, timp, str
1799–1800; first perf. 2 April 1800; publ. 1801
(Hoffmeister, Leipzig)
Ded. to Baron van Swieten

Op. 36
Second Symphony, D
Adagio molto (3/4), Allegro con brio (4/4) –
Larghetto (A, 3/8) – Scherzo: Allegro (3/4) –
Allegro molto (2/2)
2 fl, 2 ob, 2 cl, 2 bn, 2 hn, 2 tpt, timp, str
1801–2; first perf. 5 April 1803; publ. 1804
(Bureau des Arts et d'Industrie, Vienna)
Ded. to Prince Lichnowsky

Op. 55
Third Symphony, *Eroica* E♭
Allegro con brio (3/4) – Marcia funebre: Adagio
assai (c, 2/4) – Scherzo: Allegro vivace (3/4) –
Finale: Allegro molto (2/4)
2 fl, 2 ob, 2 cl, 2 bn, 3 hn, 2 tpt, timp, str
1803; first perf. 7 April 1805; publ. 1806 (Bureau
des Arts et d'Industrie, Vienna)
Ded. to Prince Lobkowitz, although Napoleon
Bonaparte was originally intended as dedicatee

Op. 60
Fourth Symphony, B♭
Adagio, Allegro vivace (2/2) – Adagio (E♭, 3/4) –
Allegro vivace (3/4) – Allegro ma non troppo
(2/4)
fl, 2 ob, 2 cl, 2 bn, 2 hn, 2 tpt, timp, str
1806; first perf. March 1807; publ. 1808 (Bureau
des Arts et d'Industrie, Vienna)
Ded. to Count Oppersdorff

Op. 67
Fifth Symphony, c
Allegro con brio (2/4) – Andante con moto (A♭,
3/8) – Allegro (3/4) – Allegro (C, 4/4)
pic, 2 fl, 2 ob, 2 cl, 2 bn, cbn, 2 hn, 2 tpt, 3 tbn,
timp, str
1807–8; first perf. 22 December 1808; publ. 1809
(Breitkopf & Härtel, Leipzig)
Ded. to Prince Lobkowitz and Count
Razumovsky

Op. 68
Sixth Symphony, *Pastoral*, F
Allegro ma non troppo ('Erwachen heiterer
Empfindungen bei der Ankunft auf dem Lande'
['Awakening of happy feelings on arrival in the
country'], 2/4) – Andante molto moto ('Szene am
Bach' ['Scene by the brook'], B♭, 12/8) – Allegro
('Lustiges Zusammensein der Landleute' ['Joyous
gathering of country folk'], 3/4) – Allegro
('Gewitter, Sturm' ['Tempest, storm'], 4/4) –
Allegretto ('Hirtengesang: Frohe und dankbare

Gefühle nach dem Sturm' ['Shepherd's song:
happy and thankful feelings after the storm'], 6/8)
pic, 2 fl, 2 ob, 2 cl, 2 bn, 2 hn, 2 tpt, 2 tbn,
timp, str
1808; first perf. 22 December 1808; publ. 1809
(Breitkopf & Härtel, Leipzig)
Ded. to Prince Lobkowitz and Count
Razumovsky

Op. 92
Seventh Symphony, A
Poco sostenuto (4/4), Vivace (6/8) – Allegretto (a,
2/4) – Presto (F, 3/4) – Allegro con brio (2/4)
2 fl, 2 ob, 2 cl, 2 bn, 2 hn, 2 tpt, timp, str
1811–12; first perf. 8 December 1813; publ. 1816
(Steiner, Vienna)
Ded. to Count Fries; arr. for piano (2 and 4
hands) and two pianos ded. to Elisabeth
Alexiewna, Empress of Russia

Op. 93
Eighth Symphony, F
Allegro vivace e con brio (3/4) – Allegretto
scherzando (B♭, 2/4) – Tempo di Menuetto
(3/4) – Allegro vivace (2/2)
2 fl, 2 ob, 2 cl, 2 bn, 2 hn, 2 tpt, timp, str
1812; first perf. 27 February 1814; publ. 1817
(Steiner, Vienna)
No dedication. Schindler's claim that the second
movement was based on a canon for Maelzel
(WoO 162) is false.

Op. 91
Wellingtons Sieg (the 'Battle Symphony')
See 'Concertos and other orchestral music' (p.
222)

Op. 125
Ninth Symphony ('Choral'), d
Allegro ma non troppo, un poco maestoso (2/4) –
Molto vivace (3/4) – Adagio molto e cantabile
(B♭, 4/4) – Presto (d–D, 3/4), Allegro assai (D,
4/4), Presto (d–D, 3/4, 'O Freunde, nicht diese
Töne!'), Allegro assai (D, 4/4, 'Freude schöner
Götterfunken'), Allegro assai vivace: Alla marcia
(B♭–D, 6/8, 'Froh, wie seine Sonnen fliegen'),
Andante maestoso (G, 3/2, 'Seid umschlungen
Millionen'), Allegro energico, sempre ben
marcato (D, 6/4)
pic, 2 fl, 2 ob, 2 cl, 2 bn, cbn, 4 hn, 2 tpt, 3 tbn,
timp, tri, cy, bd, SATB soli, SATB ch
1823–4; first perf. 7 May 1824; publ. 1826
(Schott, Mainz)
Ded. to King Friedrich Wilhelm III of Prussia.
Only the main tonal and thematic regions of the
final movement are listed above.

NICHOLAS MARSTON

Concertos and other orchestral music

BEETHOVEN'S COMPLETED CONCERTOS ARE fairly small in number – five for piano, one for violin, and the Triple Concerto, plus the two Romances for violin and orchestra – and are all relatively early works, facts which belie his interest in the form. These, together with the lost and incomplete works, and sketches for numerous other works for soloist and orchestra, show that his interest actually spanned the period from the early E♭ Piano Concerto of the mid-1780s to as late as 1815, when he stopped work on what would have been his Sixth Piano Concerto (see 'Unfinished and projected works', p. 276).

The piano was a principal medium of expression for Beethoven, and his predilection for piano concertos confirms this. The increasing virtuosity of his writing for it is matched by his treatment of the orchestra: the orchestra itself is enlarged, its contributions are weightier, and the individual parts are more demanding than in previous concertos. In the Violin Concerto too, the technical demands on the soloist are such that at first it was considered virtually unplayable.

For whatever medium he was writing, Beethoven seems to have served an apprenticeship. The early Violin Concerto in C (WoO 5) and the two Romances were a preparation for the Violin Concerto in D; in the first two piano concertos he was attempting to master the formal problems of the genre; and the Triple Concerto was preceded by extensive sketches for an earlier Concertante in D. The earlier Classical orchestra of Piano Concerto no. 2 – 1 flute, 2 oboes, 2 bassoons, 2 horns and strings – is expanded in later concertos, and comprises 2 flutes, 2 oboes, 2 clarinets, 2 bassoons, 2 horns, 2 trumpets, timpani and strings in nos 3 and 5.

In nearly all Beethoven's works there is an unprecedented dynamism. The main theme of the finale of Piano Concerto no. 2 shows this element to have been important from the outset, although in fact the sketches reveal that Beethoven oscillated between notating the rhythm in the syncopated form in which we know it, and placing the barline after the first quaver. The peak of achievement in this respect is perhaps reached in the rondo theme of the Fifth Piano Concerto.

Much has been written in the past about how Beethoven inherited the concerto from Mozart, developed it, and introduced innovations, giving it a distinctive character. Within the limits of this description of the concertos, three aspects only will be considered in detail:

(i)   the treatment of the soloist's initial entry;
(ii) unity within and between movements;
(iii) tonal/harmonic expansion.

(i) Beethoven's opening tuttis, particularly from the Third Piano Concerto onwards, were longer and more symphonic than hitherto, thus forcing him to ensure that the solo entry be sufficiently imposing. He achieved this in a variety of ways. In the first two piano concertos the firm cadential endings of the orchestral expositions are followed by a new theme for the piano, introductory in character, before joint expositions of the main theme with the orchestra. The modulating opening tutti of the Third Piano Concerto has long been a source of discussion. Leaving that aside, the soloist's entry is noteworthy in that it is particularly dramatic in order to counterbalance the orchestral opening. The piano opens with three imposing scale passages which lead to a four-octave presentation of the principal theme. This flourish immediately attracts the listener's attention, and it establishes the virtuoso role of the piano. The ensuing unaccompanied rendering of the theme by the soloist also sets it apart. Furthermore, the scalic flourish is to be used twice more at significant points in the movement (the beginning of the development and the very end).

In Piano Concerto no. 4 there is an even more novel way of introducing the soloist. The piano opens the movement alone. This is not, of course, the first time the soloist has appeared at the start of a concerto, but in Mozart's Piano Concerto in E♭, K.271 the concept was different. There, the piano was treated as an extra dimension of the orchestra and was then reintroduced in its 'proper' place. Here, the solo part is more self-contained, and the piano then remains silent during the rest of the orchestral exposition. Its long withdrawal produces an element of suspense, and its silence is thereby positive. Its re-entry is improvisatory in character, perhaps anticipating the soloists' entries in the Violin and Fifth Piano Concertos. The violin's entry in op. 61 is virtuosic and almost cadenza-like, before leading to an elaboration of the main theme. In the 'Emperor' Concerto the innovations continue. Three orchestral chords punctuate a series of rhapsodic phrases by the soloist. This opening serves several purposes: it acts as an introduction to not only a long movement but a long work, it establishes the tonic key firmly before a number of wide-ranging modulations, and one is left in no doubt as to the virtuoso role of the soloist. Its re-entry is also dramatic: it reappears before the orchestral exposition has ended, and its presentation of the main theme in massive chords is in keeping with the scale of the work.

(ii) Interrelationships between (and within) movements form an important element throughout Beethoven's music, and the concertos are no exception. One of the most obvious methods is the physical linking of movements, as occurs in the Fourth and Fifth Piano Concertos, the Triple

Concerto and the Violin Concerto. However, Beethoven also employs other subtle and equally effective methods.

In Piano Concerto no. 1 in C the middle movement shows Beethoven's use of a broad tonal concept, being in the key of A♭ major. There are three reasons why the key does not sound foreign: the first movement ends on an unharmonized C, a note common to both tonic chords; the first note of the slow-movement theme *is* C; and the note A♭ has already been introduced in the development section of the first movement in a quite dramatic way. There is also unity within the first movement of this work. The octave leap figure of the opening permeates all elements of the exposition, and thus the whole movement; and the second theme of the orchestral exposition is incomplete, not heard in its entirety until it appears on the piano in the solo exposition.

Piano Concerto no. 3 shows considerable advances in many respects. In the first movement there is a definite attempt to produce a more integrated form. The orchestral exposition takes on symphonic proportions with three main themes, the second of which is introduced in the relative major, but the return of the opening theme in the tonic at the end retains the section's unity. The orchestral tutti following the solo exposition is unusually long because it not only rounds off what has gone before, but is also a preparation for what is to come. Because it does not draw on specifically cadential material it provides a seamless transition between the exposition and development sections. The Fourth and Fifth Piano Concertos show increased merging of sections. The slow movement of the Triple Concerto almost takes on the role of an introduction to the polonaise rondo finale. The slow movement of the Violin Concerto is extremely unusual in that it remains in the key of G until the very end, when there is dominant preparation for the finale. The unchanging tonality allows its beautiful themes to unfold in free variations, relying on orchestral colour and delicate embroidery, frequently in the upper register, by the soloist.

(iii) As in all his works Beethoven allows a wide tonal range between movements. In the concertos the middle movements are less closely related to the tonic key than had previously been the case. The use of the key of A♭ major for the slow movement of the First Piano Concerto has already been mentioned. A similar procedure recurs in the Triple and Fifth Piano Concertos, where the slow movements are also in the key of the flattened submediant. The relative frequency with which Beethoven used this relationship suggests that he saw it as an alternative to the use of the dominant key.

More surprising is the use of E major for the slow movement of Piano Concerto no. 3 in C minor.

Its effect is dramatic because it is so distant. Beethoven normally makes some sort of preparation for the juxtaposition of distant keys. In this case, however, the justification for E is retrospective, appearing only in the finale. Here the note A♭ (enharmonically G♯, the last note of the slow movement) is emphasized right at the start, and later in the movement, at bar 255, a bare A♭ is reiterated for six bars. It is then changed enharmonically to a G♯ and harmonized as the third of an E major chord, the key of the ensuing passage.

The tonal range within individual movements is expanded too, with unexpected turns of harmonic direction occurring on both large and small scales. An example of large-scale harmonic expansion takes place in the first movement of the 'Emperor', where the solo exposition modulates from E♭ to B♭ via B minor and C♭ major (in anticipation of the second movement). The major–minor ambivalence seen here had been apparent earlier, in the first and third movements of the Third Piano Concerto and in the first movement of the Violin Concerto.

The number of briefer but equally effective harmonic surprises is manifold, but a few examples will suffice to show that this was a feature of Beethoven's style throughout his creative life. Piano Concerto no. 2 – actually completed before no. 1 but bearing a higher opus number because it was published slightly later – caused Beethoven tremendous problems. Started before he left Bonn, it underwent a series of revisions (probably including the wholesale replacement of the original finale, the Rondo for piano and orchestra WoO 6) which continued even after the first performance right up to its publication in 1801. As Küthen (1977, p. 292) said: 'Publication made Proteus turn into a statue.' In the rondo finale the final return of the ritornello commences not as a resolution of what has gone before, but on the piano in G major, before finding its way back to the tonic, B♭, brought in by the full orchestra. In Piano Concerto no. 1 in C the second theme of the orchestral exposition (bar 49) enters in the distant key of E♭. To achieve this, the dominant chord at the end of the previous section had been 'emptied out', leaving only the bare G. Its function is then changed: a B♭ is added. Perhaps we are going to G minor? No; E♭ is then introduced in the bass, taking us to that key. A rather similar procedure occurs again at the beginning of the development section (bar 257). The G is once more left unharmonized and slips up to an A♭. We are left wondering what the role of the A♭ is to be. Two bars later its relevance is revealed: it is not a new tonic, but part of a dominant seventh chord leading to E♭ again. Perhaps most noteworthy in this movement is the link to the recapitulation (bars 335–54): over a pedal G in the horns there is a mysterious-sounding progression of diminished seventh chords in the piano. These chords, instead of resolving, repeatedly slip down a semitone, until one on B is reached, which is at last transformed into a dominant seventh, of C major. Even then tension is maintained as the resolution is delayed for a further four bars.

The finale of the Violin Concerto furnishes another excellent example. After the cadenza there is an unusually long coda, largely brought about by the unexpected turn of harmony immediately after the cadenza. Instead of the dominant (A) resolving to the tonic, there is a modulation to the remote key of A♭, which requires a long and complex series of harmonies to work back to the tonic. Mention must also be made of the link to the finale in the Fifth Piano Concerto. Its dramatic effect depends not only on the characteristic harmonic shift of a semitone, from the tonic B to B♭ which resolves to E♭ major, the key of the work, but on the piano phrase above which enigmatically foreshadows the rondo theme, without presaging any of its dynamism.

Of the two overtures referred to in this section, *Namensfeier* (*Name-day*) is unquestionably a concert overture. A rather dull piece, it is seldom heard. *Coriolan* is included here since, although it was written to precede a specific play, it is a self-sufficient work which has outlived the play which engendered it. In fact its first public performance was in a concert. Opening his review of it, E.T.A. Hoffmann said: 'Since it is now a custom, which is certainly not to be rejected, that each theatrical performance opens with music, every really significant play should have an overture which attunes the mind to the character of the piece.' Beethoven's *Coriolan*, written in 1807, certainly achieved this. The play by Collin depicts an irrational hero whose uncontrollable rage leads to his downfall. The music is violent in character, unable to settle, and eventually disintegrates, thus preparing the audience for the tragic events to follow.

Beethoven's 'Battle Symphony', more correctly entitled *Wellington's Victory or the Battle of Victoria* (op. 91), came into being as the result of an idea by Maelzel that Beethoven should write a work for his latest invention, the panharmonicon, a sort of mechanical orchestra. The timing coincided with Wellington's defeat of Napoleon in 1813, and Maelzel believed that a work depicting this would be sufficiently successful to finance a trip to England. He drew up a plan for the piece which Beethoven followed. Although Maelzel later decided that it would be more effective for a 'real' orchestra, he allowed Beethoven to retain his plan. The title 'symphony', which derives from the original English edition (1816) of the piano arrangement, is totally misplaced, but no doubt contributed to the work's popularity. Although it is probably one of Beethoven's most notorious compositions it

reaped immense financial rewards for him, both in Vienna and England. It is a programmatic piece for a large orchestra with a battery of military and Turkish percussion instruments, including cannons and muskets. The first section opens with an English bugle call followed by the patriotic tune *Rule, Britannia*, answered by a French bugle call and marching tune, known in Britain as *For he's a jolly good fellow*. Then comes a depiction of the battle. Part 2, called 'Victory Symphony', begins and ends with martial music but is otherwise based largely on the British national anthem, which is treated fugally.

I. Concertos

WoO 4
Piano Concerto, E♭
Allegro moderato (4/4) – Larghetto (B♭, 3/4) – Rondo (2/4)
1784; publ. posth.
Only the piano part, with orchestral cues, survives. A reconstruction by Willy Hess was published by Alkor-Edition in 1961.

WoO 5
Violin Concerto, C
Allegro con brio (4/4)
vn solo; fl, 2 ob, 2 bn, 2 hn, str
1790–92; publ. posth.
Ded. to Gerhard von Breuning. Only the first 259 bars of the autograph score survive, in a form which suggests there was once more. Three completions have been made, the most widely accepted by Willy Hess, publ. in Hess, 1959, vol. 3. Sketches from 1792/3 for a piano cadenza in G, based on the thematic material of this movement, exist.

Hess 12
Oboe Concerto, F
Allegro moderato (2/2) – II (B♭, 2/2) – Rondo: Allegretto (3/4)
1790–93(?)
Lost, but according to Thayer was in the possession of the publisher Diabelli in 1865

WoO 6
Rondo for piano and orchestra, B♭
Allegro (6/8)
pf solo; fl, 2 ob, 2 bn, 2 hn, str
1793; publ. posth. in 1829 (Diabelli, Vienna), the solo part completed by Czerny
The 1960 edition in Hess, 1959, vol. 3, is based more closely on the incomplete autograph score. This movement was probably the original finale to op. 19.

Op. 19
Piano Concerto no. 2, B♭

Allegro con brio (4/4) – Adagio (E♭, 3/4) –
Rondo: Molto allegro (6/8)
pf solo; fl, 2 ob, 2 bn, 2 hn, str
c.1788–1801; publ. 1801 (Hoffmeister, Leipzig)
Ded. to Carl Nicklas Edler von Nickelsberg.
Predates no. 1 (op. 15), which was published
first; was revised and rewritten over a long period
of time. Beethoven wrote a cadenza for the first
movement in 1809.

Op. 15
Piano Concerto no. 1, C

Allegro con brio (4/4) – Largo (A♭, 2/2) – Rondo:
Allegro scherzando (2/4)
pf solo; fl, 2 ob, 2 cl, 2 bn, 2 hn, 2 tpt, timp, str
1795 (revised 1800); first perf. 1795; publ. 1801
(Mollo, Vienna)
Ded. to Princess Barbara Odescalchi. Revisions
continued after the first performance until the
production of the autograph score for publication
in 1800. Beethoven made numerous sketches for
cadenzas, and autographs for three for the first
movement exist. Two, one of which is
incomplete, date from 1809, and the other is
slightly earlier.

Op. 37
Piano Concerto no. 3, c

Allegro con brio (2/2) – Largo (E, 3/8) – Rondo:
Allegro (2/4)
pf solo; 2 fl, 2 ob, 2 cl, 2 bn, 2 hn, 2 tpt, timp,
str
1800–03; first perf. 5 April 1803; publ. 1804
(Bureau des Arts et d'Industrie, Vienna)
Ded. to Prince Louis Ferdinand of Prussia.
Autograph score, with incomplete solo part, was
missing from World War II until rediscovery in
Poland in 1977. Beethoven composed a cadenza
for the first movement in 1809.

Op. 56
Triple Concerto for piano, violin and cello, C

Allegro (4/4) – Largo (A♭, 3/8) – Rondo alla
Polacca (3/4)
pf, vn, vc soli; fl, 2 ob, 2 cl, 2 bn, 2 hn, 2 tpt,
timp, str
1804–5; first perf. 1808; publ. 1807 (Bureau des
Arts et d'Industrie, Vienna)
Ded. to Archduke Rudolph

Op. 58
Piano Concerto no. 4, G

Allegro moderato (4/4) – Andante con moto (e,
2/4) – Rondo: Vivace (2/4)
pf solo; fl, 2 ob, 2 cl, 2 bn, 2 hn, 2 tpt, timp, str
1804–6/7; first perf. 22 December 1808; publ.
1808 (Bureau des Arts et d'Industrie, Vienna)

Ded. to Archduke Rudolph. Of the three
cadenzas for the first movement, one is
incomplete. One of the three for the finale is only
a fragment, and another, although incomplete,
resembles the one which appeared in the first
edition.

Op. 61
Violin Concerto, D

Allegro ma non troppo (4/4) – Larghetto (G,
4/4) – Rondo: Allegro (6/8)
vn solo; fl, 2 ob, 2 cl, 2 bn, 2 hn, 2 tpt, timp, str
1806; first perf. 23 December 1806; publ. 1808
(Bureau des Arts et d'Industrie, Vienna)
Ded. to Stephan von Breuning, although the
inscription on the autograph score is to Franz
Clement, the soloist at the first performance. The
autograph score is not the definitive version. The
first Viennese edition was based on a copy
annotated by Beethoven, and the first English
edition, by Clementi, was based on sets of parts
copied from the autograph, thereby producing
slight differences. Both editions reveal that
Beethoven considerably revised the solo part, but
no source exists. For the piano arrangement of
the Violin Concerto see 'Arrangements'
(pp. 272–3). Beethoven wrote four cadenzas for
this version, whereas none was written for the
violin version.

Op. 73
Piano Concerto no. 5 ('Emperor'), E♭

Allegro (4/4) – Adagio un poco moto (B, 4/4) –
Rondo: Allegro (6/8)
pf solo; 2 fl, 2 ob, 2 cl, 2 bn, 2 hn, 2 tpt, timp,
str
1809; first perf. 28 November 1811; publ. 1810
(Clementi, London)
Ded. to Archduke Rudolph

WoO 58
Two cadenzas

Mozart's Piano Concerto in D minor, K.466, first
and third movements
1809(?); publ. posth.
Written for pupil Ferdinand Ries

II. Other orchestral music

Hess 13
Romance for flute, bassoon, piano and orchestra, e

Romance cantabile (2/2)
fl, bn, pf soli; 2 ob, str
c.1786(?); publ. posth. in 1952, completed by
Willy Hess (Breitkopf & Härtel, Leipzig)
Its provenance suggests that this complete section
in e and one page of the *segue maggiore* section
was part of a once complete autograph of a slow
movement which may also have been part of a
complete concerto, the rest of which is now lost.

Op. 50
Romance for violin and orchestra, F
Adagio cantabile (4/4)
vn solo; fl, 2 ob, 2 bn, 2 hn, str
c. 1798; first perf. 1798(?); publ. 1805 (Bureau des Arts et d'Industrie, Vienna)

Op. 40
Romance for violin and orchestra, G
Andante (4/4)
vn solo; fl, 2 ob, 2 bn, 2 hn, str
1800–02; publ. 1803 (Hoffmeister, Leipzig)

Op. 62
Overture: *Coriolan*, c
Allegro con brio (4/4)
2 fl, 2 ob, 2 cl, 2 bn, 2 hn, 2 tpt, timp, str
1807; first perf. March 1807; publ. 1808 (Bureau des Arts et d'Industrie, Vienna)
Ded. to Heinrich Collin, author of the tragedy which it precedes

Op. 80
Choral Fantasia
See 'Choral music' (p. 258)

Op. 91
Wellingtons Sieg oder die Schlacht bei Vittoria ('Battle Symphony'), E♭
Section 1 (E♭–F♯, various time signatures) –
Section 2: Sieges-Symphonie (D, various time signatures)
pic, 2 fl, 2 ob, 2 cl, 2 bn, 4 hn, 4 tpt, 3 tbn, timp, perc, str
1813; first perf. 3 December 1813; publ. 1816 (Steiner, Vienna)
Ded. to Prince Regent (later King George IV) of England
Originally written for Maelzel's panharmonicon (see Hess 108, p. 274)

Op. 115
Overture: *Namensfeier*, C
2 fl, 2 ob, 2 cl, 2 bn, 4 hn, 2 tpt, timp, str
1814–15; first perf. 25 December 1815; publ. 1825 (Steiner, Vienna)
Ded. to Prince Radziwill

WoO 3
***Gratulations-Menuett*, E♭**
Tempo di Menuetto quasi Allegretto (3/4)
2 fl, 2 cl, 2 bn, 2 hn, 2 tpt, timp, str
1822; first perf. 3 November 1822; publ. 1832 (Artaria, Vienna)
Ded. by publisher to Karl Holz, but written as a tribute to Karl Hensler as part of a serenade programme

See also 'Stage music' (pp. 249–55)

ANNE-LOUISE COLDICOTT

Dance music and marches

THIS SECTION COMPRISES ALL those works intended to accompany ballroom dancing or marching – i.e. bodily movement in the abstract. It excludes music danced to on stage as ballet (see 'Stage music', pp. 249–55) and also those stylized dances that were intended as abstract pieces – whether independent works (e.g. the Polonaise, op. 89) or as parts of larger works (e.g. minuets in sonatas). With a few works, however, there is no clear distinction between pure dances and stylized ones, and cross-references have been used.

The works discussed here fall into two groups: sets of dances, all composed in 1806 or earlier; and music for military band, all composed in 1809 or later. The sets of dances were composed – and probably commissioned – for balls that were regularly held in Vienna during the winter months. An example is the ball held by the Gesellschaft der bildenden Künstler on 22 November 1795. This ball had been an annual event from 1792, when Haydn composed a set of 12 minuets and 12 German dances. The following year Kozeluch provided similar music, and in 1794 Dittersdorf wrote the music for the large Redoutensaal, while Eybler wrote it for the small Redoutensaal. In 1795 these eminent composers were followed by Süssmayr (large hall) and the twenty-four-year-old Beethoven (small hall), who wrote 12 Minuets (WoO 7) and 12 German Dances (WoO 8). For this grand occasion an orchestra was used, but it seems to have been more common for such dances to be performed at less extravagant affairs, and so composers frequently provided three versions of the music – for orchestra, for two violins and bass (which usually meant cello) and for piano solo. It is inappropriate to regard any version as being the main or original one, and so all three are listed here rather than under 'Arrangements'. Sometimes only the piano version was published, and even then only a small number of copies was generally issued, so that in a few cases no known copy of one or other version survives.

The Minuets are all in 3/4 with medium pace, but Beethoven is careful to maximize the contrast between successive dances by skilful choice of keys – often a third apart – and by varying the forces from one dance to the next. The same applies to his German Dances, also known as Deutsche, Allemandes or even Tedescas (compare the Tedesca in the op. 130 Quartet). These were also in 3/4 but somewhat faster, and in two of the three sets (WoO 8 and 13) Beethoven provides an extended coda to the final dance, giving eagerly exploited opportunities for development. The two sets of Ländler, also in a quick 3/4, are both entirely in D major (except for WoO 15 no. 4 in D minor), and again Beethoven provides an extended coda to the set. The unity of key suggests the dances were to be played consecutively without a break.

The Contredanses and Ecossaises are in 2/4, the former usually with a quaver upbeat and the latter normally without one. The set of Ecossaises is entirely in E♭, whereas the Contredanses are in contrasting keys, like the Minuets and German Dances. By far the best known of the dances is the Contredanse WoO 14 no. 7, the theme of which was later used in the *Eroica* Symphony. This theme and that of no. 11 were originally written in 1801 for the finale of the ballet *Prometheus*, the success of which perhaps induced Beethoven to include these two Contredanses in the published collection in 1802.

The music for military band consists of single movements written on a variety of different occasions. In some cases the origins are obscure, but in others we have some information. WoO 18 was written for the Böhmische Landwehr in 1809 and was rewritten the next year for performance, along with WoO 19 and perhaps other band pieces, at a tournament in Laxenburg in honour of the Empress's birthday. A letter from Beethoven to Archduke Rudolph seems to refer to this occasion: 'I see that Your Imperial Highness wants to have the effects of my music tried on horses as well. All right. But I must see whether the riders will thereby be enabled to make a few skilful somersaults.' (Letter 274) All the pieces are scored for wind (including piccolo and brass) and 'Turkish' percussion, with WoO 24 using a particularly large band including eight trumpets and a serpent. This piece is also the longest and best of the group, with some modulations to unexpected keys, and a recapitulation in D prepared by a passage in the unlikely key of C major.

In 1822, in response to a request from the publisher Peters, Beethoven offered amongst other things several marches and tattoos. These prove to be WoO 18–20 and 24. New autograph scores were written out for WoO 18–20, each now headed 'Zapfenstreich' (tattoo), numbered 1, 3 and 2 respectively, and each with a Trio added; Beethoven told Peters in September 1822: 'Among the marches there are a few for which I decided to compose new trios.' (Letter 1100) The original 1816 score of WoO 24, which already possessed a Trio, was simply annotated 'No. 4'. The four pieces were finally dispatched in February 1823, but Peters refused to publish them, implying they were of inferior quality. While they, and the sets of dances, cannot compare with Beethoven's greatest masterpieces, all are in fact very well written and, within the limited range possible in the genres, often highly imaginative.

WoO 9
Six Minuets: E♭, G, C, F, D, G
2 vn, bass

Before 1795?; publ. posth.
Since these Minuets are not known in any autograph version and were not published in Beethoven's lifetime, their authenticity cannot be fully confirmed. But Beethoven did have the sole surviving manuscript of them in his hands at one time, as is evident from his scrawled remark (probably 'grosse Stümperei' [great bungle]) on the first violin part (Kojima, 1978, p. 309). Other versions for orchestra and for piano may have existed at one time.

WoO 81
Allemande, A
see 'Piano music' (p. 247)

WoO 7
Twelve Minuets: D, B♭, G, E♭, C, A, D, B♭, G, E♭, C, F
a) pic, 2 fl, 2 ob, 2 cl, 2 bn, 2 hn, 2 tpt, timp, str; b) 2 vn, bass; c) pf
1795; publ. c) 1795 (Artaria, Vienna), b) 1802 (Mollo, Vienna), a) posth.

WoO 8
Twelve German Dances: C, A, F, B♭, E♭, G, C, A, F, D, G, C
a) pic, 2 fl, 2 ob, 2 cl, 2 bn, 2 hn, post horn, 2 tpt, timp, bd, str; b) 2 vn, bass; c) pf
1795; publ. c) 1795 (Artaria, Vienna), b) 1802 (Mollo?, Vienna; no copy known), a) posth.

WoO 10
Six Minuets: C, G, E♭, B♭, D, C
a) orch? (lost); b) pf
1795; publ. b) 1796 (Artaria, Vienna)
Only the piano version survives, but there is evidence that an orchestral version probably existed, and possibly also a version for two violins and bass.

WoO 42
Six German Dances: F, D, F, A, D, G
vn, pf
1796; publ. 1814 (Maisch, Vienna)
A copyist's score dated Prague, 1796, survives in the Nationalbibliothek, Vienna, with a dedication to 'the two Countesses Thun'. Which two Countesses is unclear: one Countess Thun was wife of Prince Lichnowsky, one of her two sisters was wife of Count Razumovsky, and their mother was a former patroness of Mozart and Haydn.

WoO 11
Seven Ländler: all in D
pf
1799; publ. 1799 (Artaria, Vienna)
A version for two violins and bass may also have been in existence. A sketch for the coda to the set dates from about February 1799 (see Brandenburg, 1977, p. 131).

WoO 12
Twelve Minuets (1799)
Spurious: by Beethoven's brother Carl (see
Kojima, 1978).

WoO 13
Twelve German Dances: D, B♭, G, D, F, B♭,
D, G, E♭, C, A, D
a) orch (lost); b) pf
c. 1792–7; publ. posth.
Some of the dances were sketched in 1792–3, and
a copyist's score of the piano version survives
from c. 1800.

WoO 14
Twelve Contredanses: C, A, D, B♭, E♭, C, E♭,
C, A, C, G, E♭
a) fl, 2 ob, 2 cl, 2 bn, 2 hn, tamb, str; b) 2 vn,
bass; c) pf
c. 1791–1801; publ. 1802 (Mollo, Vienna: all
three versions)
Sketches for nos 8 and 12 are found on Bonn
paper of c. 1791; nos 3, 4 and 6 were probably
composed in 1795; nos 2, 9 and 10 were
composed in late 1801; nos 7 and 11 derive from
the ballet music *Prometheus*, and the theme of no.
7 was later used in the *Eroica* Symphony. The
original edition of the piano version included
only six dances – nos 8, 7, 4, 10, 9, 1; but a
copyist's score contains additionally nos 2, 5 and
12.

WoO 15
Six Ländler: D, D, D, d, D, D
a) 2 vn, bass; b) pf
1802; publ. 1802 (Artaria, Vienna: both versions)

WoO 82
Minuet, E♭
See 'Piano music' (p. 248)

WoO 16
Twelve Ecossaises
pf; publ. 1806
Spurious. Advertised in 1807. The same applies to
a set of 12 waltzes advertised at the same time.
Seven of the waltzes are unauthentic
arrangements of Beethoven works (including the
Scherzo of the Second Symphony) and the other
five may be compositions by the arranger. A
similar situation holds for the Ecossaises, the first
of which is an unauthentic arrangement of part of
the First Symphony (Kojima, 1978). A copy
survives in Bonn.

WoO 83
Six Ecossaises: all in E♭
pf
c.1806; publ. 1807 (Traeg, Vienna)
A version for orchestra may also have existed. No
early source is known: the *Gesamtausgabe* is based
on Nottebohm's copy of Sonnleithner's
transcription of the first edition.

WoO 29
March, B♭
See 'Chamber music with wind' (p. 227)

WoO 18
March, F
mil. band (pic, 2 fl, 2 cl, 2 bn, cbn, 2 hn, 2 tpt,
perc)
1809, rev. 1810; publ. 1818–19 (Schlesinger,
Berlin)
Ded. to Archduke Anton. Beethoven added a
Trio in B♭, c. 1822.

WoO 19
March, F
mil. band (as WoO 18)
June 1810; publ. posth.
Ded. to Archduke Anton. Beethoven added a
Trio in f, c. 1822.

WoO 20
March, C
mil. band (pic, 2 ob, 2 cl, 2 bn, cbn, 2 hn, 2 tpt,
perc)
c. 1810?; publ. posth.
Beethoven added a Trio in F, c. 1822.

WoO 21
Polonaise, D
mil. band (pic, 2 ob, 2 cl, 2 bn, cbn, 2 hn, tpt,
perc)
1810; publ. posth.

WoO 22
Ecossaise, D
mil. band (as WoO 21)
1810; publ. posth.

WoO 23
Ecossaise, G
mil. band
c.1810
Lost, known only in Czerny's piano arrangement

WoO 24
March, D
mil. band (2 pic, 2 ob, 5 cl, 2 bn, cbn, 6 hn, 8
tpt, 2 tbn, serp, perc)
June 1816; publ. posth.

WoO 17
Eleven 'Mödling' Dances
Spurious. According to the extremely unreliable
Schindler, Beethoven wrote a set of waltzes for a
local band at an inn near Mödling during
summer 1819. In 1905 Hugo Riemann found in

Leipzig a set of parts for eleven dances and concluded that as they were well written they must be those referred to by Schindler. Since the set shows several differences from genuine Beethoven sets of dances (for example, in having a much less satisfactory key sequence), it can be dismissed on both internal and external grounds.

WoO 3
Gratulations-Menuett
See 'Concertos and other orchestral music' (p. 222)

WoO 84–6
Two Waltzes and Ecossaise for piano
See 'Piano Music' (pp. 248–9)

BARRY COOPER

Chamber music with wind

THE WORKS TO BE CONSIDERED in this section present a number of striking contrasts: while most of them belong to Beethoven's earliest period, the two sets of National Airs with Variations stem from the period of the 'Hammerklavier' Sonata; the 416-bar first movement of the op. 16 Quintet dwarfs the ten-bar Adagio for three horns, Hess 297; and while several pieces are hardly known at all, the popularity of the Septet op. 20 has never waned.

Beethoven virtually abandoned chamber music for wind ensemble after about 1801. Around 1803 he made an arrangement (op. 38) for piano trio of the Septet as a gesture of thanks and friendship to his doctor, Johann Adam Schmidt; and the Equali WoO 30 were the result of a request for music to be performed on All Souls' Day 1812 in Linz Cathedral (Beethoven was staying in Linz at the time). But many of the works written prior to 1801 were also simply *pièces d'occasion*: the Octet op. 103 was composed for the Elector Maximilian Franz, Beethoven's employer in Bonn; the Von Westerholt family, for whom the Trio WoO 37 was probably written, included a bassoon-playing father, a son who played the flute and a daughter, Maria Anna, who took piano lessons from Beethoven. Finally, the Horn Sonata op. 17 was inspired by a visit to Vienna by the virtuoso horn player Johann Wenzel Stich, known as Giovanni Punto. According to Ferdinand Ries, the Sonata was written only a day before its first performance, given by Punto and Beethoven; it pleased the audience so much on first hearing that it was repeated immediately.

It is difficult to date some of the wind music accurately (several pieces cannot even be ascribed to Beethoven with complete confidence); the most extensive and authoritative body of information concerning the sources and chronology of these and other early works is to be found in Johnson, 1980a. Several works that were eventually published separately were at one time interrelated. It seems that during 1793, his first year of study with Haydn in Vienna, Beethoven turned his hand to revising several works from his Bonn years rather than attempting any major new composition (Johnson, 1982, pp. 1–2). One such revised work was the Octet op. 103. When he prepared the new autograph score, Beethoven began writing out the Rondino WoO 25 as a finale. He quickly changed his mind, however, and substituted the present last movement, which may nevertheless have existed already in the original Bonn version (Johnson, 1980a, pp. 404–5).

The Octet and the Rondino, of course, are both scored for the same forces. This is also true of the Trio op. 87 and the Variations WoO 28 (both for two oboes and cor anglais) and it is possible that WoO 28 was originally intended as the finale of op. 87 (Johnson, 1973, p. 201, and 1980a, p. 411). If this was indeed so, it is worth observing that here, as in the Octet, Beethoven would have replaced an intended 'andante' finale by a 'presto' one.

It is not surprising that Beethoven should have abandoned chamber music with winds so early in his career. Despite the existence of Mozart's masterly serenades and divertimentos and the Quintet for piano and winds K. 452 (of which a little more later), the medium was not one in which a composer usually cast 'serious' works. Already by 1809 Beethoven could write rather apologetically to Breitkopf & Härtel that 'the sextet [op. 71] is one of my early works and, what is more, was composed in one night – All that one can really say about it is that it was written by a composer who has produced at any rate a few better works – Yet some people think that works of that type are the best.' (Letter 224) The work was certainly not written in such a short time, but Beethoven's attempt to belittle it in this way is significant. The great popularity of the Septet is said to have angered and embarrassed him in later life; and yet he did not scruple even as late as 1822 to try to sell the Variations WoO 28.

Admittedly, the chamber works for winds do not represent Beethoven's finest or most important music; but it would be unfair to disregard them entirely. They must have helped to develop the young composer's treatment of wind instruments in his orchestral works: it is ironic that a reviewer of the premiere on 2 April 1800 of the First Symphony and the Septet complained that in the Symphony 'the wind instruments were employed excessively, so that it was more military band than orchestral music' (quoted in Schmidt-Görg, 1970, p. 35).

More importantly, however, these chamber works provided a safe forum for the development of Beethoven's personal style. It has often been observed that he delayed confronting the serious genres of symphony and string quartet until he was sufficiently sure of himself: the acknowledged master, Haydn, was literally too close. But chamber music for wind ensemble was traditionally 'light', and by 1791 the acknowledged master, Mozart, was dead. The Octet op. 103 is something of a special case in relation to stylistic development: not only does its composition span the transition from Bonn to Vienna; Beethoven also substantially recomposed it as a string quintet (op. 4) in 1795. A comparison of the two versions provides valuable insights into Beethoven's handling of instrumental textures and remote key relationships.

The most adventurous of the works for wind ensemble is probably the Quintet op. 16. Although it is scored for the same forces as Mozart's K. 452, a work which Beethoven must surely have known, a comparison between the first movements of the two pieces serves mainly to highlight Mozart's extreme economy of material as opposed to Beethoven's over-extravagance. Here (as elsewhere in works from the mid-1790s) Beethoven is attempting to be symphonic in a non-symphonic medium. Op. 16 begins with a massive slow introduction, far more substantial than those in op. 20 and op. 71, and some attempt is made to integrate the material of the introduction with that of the development. The development section itself, although not as harmonically wide-ranging as some others, is connected more organically with the exposition, and the abrupt G–A♭ shift articulated by the rising scales with which it opens foreshadows later harmonic events. The slow movement of op. 16, too, is formally and harmonically more adventurous than those in the other works, with the possible exception of the Septet.

It may not be entirely coincidental that op. 16, in which winds are combined with Beethoven's own instrument, the piano, should be relatively so 'advanced'. Yet if the Quintet is compared with roughly contemporary works for other forces – notably the Cello Sonatas op. 5 and the Piano Sonatas op. 7 and op. 10 – it becomes clear that Beethoven reserved his boldest strokes for forces other than wind ensemble.

The two series of National Airs with Variations for piano with optional flute (or violin) were among the last products of Beethoven's long and not altogether happy relationship with the Scottish publisher George Thomson (see Oldman, 1951), an ardent admirer of folksong who persuaded several leading composers to set selected songs in technically undemanding arrangements, usually with piano trio accompaniment (see 'Folksong arrangements', p. 267). The idea for the sets of variations came from Thomson in a letter of June 1817, and in a further letter dated 28 December he warned Beethoven: 'You must write the vari-ations in a familiar, easy and slightly brilliant style; so that the greatest number of our ladies can play and enjoy them' (Willetts, 1970, pp. 21–2). Beethoven responded with a good deal more brilliance than ease: one wonders how many ladies could either play or enjoy the demanding keyboard part of op. 107 no. 5, for example.

While it is easy to regard opp. 105 and 107 as peripheral to Beethoven's other late works, they may be better understood as belonging to the compositional mainstream. In places the keyboard writing is not unlike that in the last piano sonatas. Moreover, these pieces directly reflect Beethoven's growing concern with variation technique; from such unpretentious, even unprepossessing themes, he built larger forms which exhibit much subtlety and invention. Two examples must suffice. Firstly, the final variation of op. 107 no. 7 incorporates an Andante passage which moves through the submediant and relative major before re-establishing the tonic for a thematic reprise. And the coda involves an abrupt juxtaposition of the tonic major and minor before concluding with a cadence which, with its contrasting dynamics and syncopated rhythm, is typically 'late' Beethoven. Secondly, op. 107 no. 1, in E♭, contains a 'minore' third variation which substitutes E minor for the more usual tonic minor. The abrupt manner in which Beethoven approaches and quits this new key is again very characteristic of his late style. The following, final variation also incorporates an abrupt tonal shift, this time to the subdominant, which disrupts the otherwise strict adherence to the structure of the theme.

Like some of the works for wind ensemble discussed earlier, opp. 105 and 107 are not among Beethoven's best-known music. But while he may have outgrown the 'light' genre of wind chamber music early in his career, he seems much later to have been drawn to produce works whose outwardly 'popular' trappings belie their much more personal contents: works, moreover, which probably had more than a negligible effect on his last keyboard masterpieces, not least the Diabelli Variations.

WoO 37
Trio, G
Allegro (4/4) – Adagio (g, 2/4) – Thema andante con Variazioni (2/4)
Pf, fl, bn
1786; publ. posth.
Probably written for the Von Westerholt-Gysenberg family. The autograph gives 'clavicembalo', not pf.

Anh. 4
Flute Sonata, B♭
[Allegro] (4/4) – Polonaise (3/4) – Largo (E♭, 2/2) – [Thema mit Variationen: Allegretto] (3/4)

pf, fl
?1790–92; publ. posth.
Spurious? Manuscript copy (not in Beethoven's hand) headed 'I Sonata...di Bethoe –' found among Beethoven's papers after his death

WoO 26
Duo, G
Allegro con brio (2/2) – Minuetto quasi Allegretto (3/4)
2 fl
August 1792; publ. posth.
Ded. to J. M. Degenhart; autograph dated '23 August, midnight', in another hand

Op. 103
Octet, E♭
Allegro (2/2) – Andante (B♭, 6/8) – Menuetto (3/4) – Finale: Presto (2/2)
2 ob, 2 cl, 2 hn, 2 bn
Before November 1792; publ. posth.
Written in Bonn, then rev. in Vienna in 1793. Later recomposed as a string quintet (op. 4)

WoO 25
Rondo (Rondino), E♭
Andante (2/4)
2 ob, 2 cl, 2 hn, 2bn
1793; publ. posth.
Intended at one time as finale to op. 103

Hess 19
Quintet, E♭
First movement ([4/4]; beginning missing) – Adagio mesto (2/4) – Menuetto Allegretto (3/4; incomplete)
ob, 3 hn, bn
?1793; publ. posth.

Op. 87
Trio, C
Allegro (4/4) – Adagio cantabile (F, 3/4) – Menuetto: Allegro molto. Scherzo (3/4) – Finale: Presto (2/4)
2 ob, eng hn
?1795; publ. 1806 (Artaria, Vienna)

WoO 28
Variations on 'Là ci darem la mano' from *Don Giovanni* (Mozart), C (2/4)
2 ob, eng hn
?1795; first perf. 23 December 1797; publ. posth.
Possibly associated originally with op. 87 (see Johnson, 1973, p. 201)

Op. 81b
Sextet, E♭
Allegro con brio (4/4) – Adagio (A♭, 2/4) – Rondo: Allegro (6/8)
2 hn, 2 vn, va, vc
?1795; publ. 1810 (Simrock, Bonn)

Op. 16
Quintet, E♭
Grave (4/4), Allegro ma non troppo (3/4) – Andante cantabile (B♭, 2/4) – Rondo: Allegro ma non troppo (6/8)
pf, ob, cl, hn, bn
1796; first perf. 6 April 1797; publ. 1801 (Mollo, Vienna)
Ded. to Prince Joseph Johann zu Schwarzenberg. The first edition also included parts for violin, viola and cello, replacing the wind instruments.

Op. 71
Sextet, E♭
Adagio (4/4), Allegro (3/4) – Adagio (B♭, 2/4) – Menuetto: Quasi Allegretto (3/4) – Rondo: Allegro (2/2)
2 cl, 2 hn, 2 bn
?1796; first perf. April 1805; publ. 1810 (Breitkopf & Härtel, Leipzig)
First two movements probably written before 1796

Op. 11
Trio B♭
Allegro con brio (4/4) – Adagio (E♭, 3/4) – Tema: 'Pria ch'io l'impegno': Allegretto (4/4)
pf, cl/vn, vc
1797(–8?); publ. 1798 (Mollo, Vienna)
Ded. to Countess Maria Wilhelmine von Thun

WoO 29
March, B♭ (2/2)
2 cl, 2 hn, 2 bn
1797–8; publ. posth.
See also Hess 107 (p. 275)

Op. 20
Septet, E♭
Adagio (3/4), Allegro con brio (2/2) – Adagio cantabile (A♭, 9/8) – Tempo di Menuetto (3/4) – Tema: Andante con Variazioni (B♭, 2/4) – Scherzo: Allegro molto e vivace (3/4) – Andante con moto alla Marcia (2/4), Presto (2/2)
cl, hn, bn, vn, va, vc, db
1799; first perf. 2 April 1800; publ. 1802 (Hoffmeister, Leipzig)
Ded. to Empress Maria Theresia. A private performance on 20 December 1799 is mentioned in Johnson, 1980a, p. 388. The theme of the Menuetto was taken from the Piano Sonata in G op. 49 no. 2.

Op. 17
Sonata, F
Allegro moderato (4/4) – Poco Adagio, quasi Andante (f, 2/4) – Rondo: Allegro moderato (2/2)
pf, hn
April 1800; first perf. 18 April 1800; publ. 1801 (Mollo, Vienna)
Ded. to Baroness Braun. Also arranged as cello sonata (see p. 273).

Op. 25
Serenade, D
Entrata: Allegro (4/4) – Tempo ordinario d'un Menuetto (3/4) – Allegro molto (d, 3/8) – Andante con Variazioni (G, 2/4) – Allegro scherzando e vivace (3/4) – Adagio (2/4) – Allegro vivace e disinvolto (2/4)

fl, vn, va

1801; publ. 1802 (Cappi, Vienna)

WoO 30
Three Equali
No. 1: Andante (d, 2/2). No. 2: Poco Adagio (D, 2/2). No. 3: Poco sostenuto (B♭, 3/2)

4 tbn

November 1812; publ. posth.

Written at the request of Franx Xaver Glöggl

WoO 27
Three Duos, C, F, B♭
No. 1: Allegro commodo (4/4) – Larghetto sostenuto (c, 3/4) – Rondo: Allegretto (4/4)

No. 2: Allegro affettuoso (4/4) – Aria: Larghetto (d, 3/4) – Rondo: Allegretto moderato (2/4)

No. 3: Allegro sostenuto (4/4) – Aria con Variazioni: Andantino con moto (2/4)

cl, bn

Date of composition unknown; publ. ?1810–15 (Paris)

Accepted as authentic in Kinsky, 1955, but listed as 'probably spurious' in Kerman, 1983

Hess 297
Adagio, A♭ (4/4)
3 hn

1815; publ. posth.

Occurs within a series of studies in instrumentation; headed 'Adagio f moll'

Op. 105
Six National Airs with Variations
1: *The Cottage Maid* (G, 2/4); 2: *Von edlem Geschlecht war Shinkin* (c, 4/4); 3: *A Schüsserl und a Reindl* (C, 2/4); 4: *The Last Rose of Summer* (E♭, 3/4); 5: *Chiling O'Guiry* (E♭, 6/8); 6: *Paddy Whack* (D, 6/8)

pf, fl/vn (ad lib.)

Nos 1–2, 4–6: 1818; no. 3: 1819; publ. 1819 (Preston, London; Thomson, Edinburgh; and Artaria, Vienna). The earlier, British edition also includes op. 107 nos 2, 6 and 7.

Op. 107
Ten National Airs with Variations
1: *I bin a Tiroler Bua* (E♭, 3/4); 2: *Bonny Laddie, Highland Laddie* (F, 2/4); 3: *Volkslied aus Kleinrussland* (G, 2/4); 4: *St Patrick's Day* (F, 6/8); 5: *A Madel, ja a Madel* (F, 3/4); 6: *Peggy's Daughter* (E♭, 6/8); 7: *Schöne Minka* (a, 2/4); 8: *O Mary, at thy Window be* (D, 2/4); 9: *Oh, Thou art the Lad of my Heart* (E♭, 6/8); 10: *The Highland Watch* (g, 2/4)

pf, fl/vn (ad lib.)

Nos 1–2, 4–5, 8–10: 1818; nos 3, 6–7: 1819; publ. 1819 (Preston, London; Thomson, Edinburgh); 1820 (Simrock, Bonn and Cologne). The 1819 edition contains only nos 2, 6 and 7 (see op. 105); the 1820 edition is complete.

See also 'Dance music and marches' (pp. 222–5) and 'Arrangements' (pp. 272–4)

NICHOLAS MARSTON

Chamber music for piano and strings

BEETHOVEN'S FIRST COMPOSITIONS in this medium were the three Piano Quartets WoO 36 of 1785. One is tempted to suggest that here was a case of Beethoven's receiving the spirit of Mozart without Haydn as an intermediary, for each of the Quartets is modelled on a Mozart violin sonata (Solomon, 1977, p. 47). Perhaps the most interesting of the three Quartets is the E♭ work, whose slow introductory movement leads directly into an Allegro con spirito in the unusual key of the tonic minor. The model here was Mozart's Sonata in G, K.379. Beethoven used a similar plan in two much more mature works to be considered below: the 'Kreutzer' Sonata, in which the minor-key Presto is preceded by a slow introduction in the major, and the Cello Sonata op. 102 no. 1, in which the tonal scheme is tonic–relative minor.

This drawing together of early and late works serves as a reminder of the extraordinary stylistic development represented by the chamber music for piano and strings. WoO 36 was an isolated experiment: after moving to Vienna Beethoven abandoned the piano quartet in favour of the piano trio. The third of the op. 1 Trios, in C minor, was one of the first in a long series of dramatic and turbulent compositions in this key and is generally regarded as the finest of the set. Much has been made of Ferdinand Ries's account of how Haydn advised Beethoven against publication of this Trio (see Wegeler, 1987, p. 74), but recent scholarship has decisively reinterpreted the evidence. It is now clear that the performance of these Trios which Haydn attended must have taken place after his return from London in August 1795, by which time it would have been too late to advise against publication (Johnson, 1980a, pp. 308–12).

The op. 1 Trios are uncharacteristic of the genre inasmuch as they each have four rather than three movements. This expansion of the total work is matched by a striving to expand and elaborate the content of individual movements in an attempt to give the music a symphonic breadth. At least one writer has described the results as 'pretentious' and has linked Beethoven's symphonic ambitions here with the achievements of Haydn's 'London' Symphonies, one of which (no. 95 in C minor) may have had a decisive influence on op. 1 no. 3 (Johnson, 1982, pp. 18–23).

The attempt to write symphonic chamber music was not limited to op. 1. The two Cello Sonatas op. 5 both contain main movements worked out on a grandiose scale, with weighty slow introductions giving way to massive sonata-form movements. The Violin Sonatas op. 12 were criticized for their 'learned' nature and unusual modulations: and while it might be difficult to sympathize readily with such criticisms today, one can perhaps still catch a certain sense of strain, of over-reaching, in gestures like the sudden deflection to E♭ major ten bars before the end of the slow movement in op. 12 no. 3.

Beethoven's middle-period works are especially noted for their symphonic qualities, and the 'Archduke' Trio is often taken to epitomize the successful transference of the composer's mature symphonic style to chamber music. But Sieghard Brandenburg's recent suggestion that the 'Archduke', as well as the Violin Sonata op. 96, was revised around 1814–15, prior to publication, should encourage us to regard these works as more significant for the development of Beethoven's late style than has hitherto been suspected. In this respect the prominence given to movements in variation form in both works is significant: the serene variation theme in the 'Archduke' is remarkably close in style and structure to that in the last movement of the Piano Sonata in E op. 109. Noteworthy also is the tendency to break down the barriers between individual movements, a tendency which is even more pronounced in the Cello Sonata op. 102 no. 1. This falls essentially into two distinct halves, each half comprising a slow introduction to a fast movement. What might be called the first movement proper (Allegro vivace) is notable for being in the relative minor rather than the tonic. The recall of the opening slow introduction before the final movement is a device which Beethoven also used in the Piano Sonata in A op. 101 of 1816, and is merely one of many unusual features of op. 102 no. 1 that fully justify Beethoven's description of it in the autograph score as a 'free' sonata.

In op. 102 no. 2 it is the final fugue which is perhaps most arresting. The sketches show that its composition cost Beethoven a good deal of effort; indeed, a sense of difficulty or strain seems to be part of the aesthetic aim of this movement – it is as if the music is not intended to sound easy or even attractive. Both in its uncompromising counterpoint and in its character, this fugue points ahead clearly to the finale of the 'Hammerklavier' Sonata and to the *Grosse Fuge*.

The fugue in op. 102 no. 2 is preceded by the only fully-fledged slow movement to be found in Beethoven's cello sonatas, a fact which may help to focus more clearly Beethoven's achievements with this instrumental duo. The cello sonatas are truly 'original' in that Beethoven had no models to follow: his op. 5 appear to have been the first to be provided with an obbligato (as opposed to continuo) keyboard accompaniment. His reluctance to write a full-length slow movement may be connected with the unconventionality of the genre and with the difficulty of achieving a satisfactory balance between the wide compass of the piano and a predominantly middle-register solo instrument. The compositional problems which this caused are illustrated particularly well in the autograph manuscript of the first movement of op. 69 (Lockwood, 1970a): Beethoven made massive alterations in the distribution of melodic material between the two instruments even at this very late compositional stage.

The two op. 5 Sonatas were written for the court of Friedrich Wilhelm II at Berlin. The King himself was an enthusiastic cellist, but it must have been his court player, Jean-Louis Duport, who was most influential in shaping the style of Beethoven's two Sonatas. Indeed, certain features of the cello writing in op. 5 were subsequently codified by Duport in a tutor for the instrument (Lockwood, 1978). Nor is this the only example of a performer's style affecting the style of a Beethoven composition. Two of the violin sonatas, the 'Kreutzer' and op. 96, make a contrasting pair in this respect. The prodigious size and virtuoso character of the 'Kreutzer' were largely inspired by the abilities of the mulatto violinist George Polgreen Bridgetower (a fragmentary autograph score of the work bears the description *Sonata mulattica*). Bridgetower left an interesting account of how he improvised, much to Beethoven's delight, a cadenza in bar 9 of the first movement to match that given to the piano in bar 18. On the other hand, op. 96 is largely devoid of opportunities for ostentation, and Beethoven himself revealed one reason for this in a letter of December 1812 to the Archduke Rudolph: 'In our Finales we like to have fairly noisy passages, but R[ode] does not care for them – and so I have been rather hampered.' (Letter 392) What he did not tell the Archduke was that several years earlier he had considered using the same finale theme for the Cello Sonata op. 69.

As is well known, the final movement of the 'Kreutzer' Sonata was originally intended for op. 30 no. 1 but Beethoven replaced it by a set of variations. The first two movements of the 'Kreutzer', then, were composed (very hastily) against the background of an existing finale. This accounts not only for the great length of the first movement but also, it has been claimed, for the emphasis placed there on D minor so as to balance the appearance of that key at the beginning of the coda in the finale.

Finally, let us clarify two prevalent misconceptions. It has been claimed by several writers that the 'Archduke' Trio was composed quickly, in three weeks during March 1811, using sketches made in the previous year. It is true that the autograph score is annotated 'Trio am 3ᵗᵉⁿ März 1811 … Geendigt am 26ᵗᵉⁿ März 1811'; but these dates, even if reliable, probably refer only to the writing of the autograph rather than to the total period of composition; moreover, the fact that the 'Archduke' was probably revised in 1814–15 means that the composition of the work as we know it can no longer be confined solely to the years 1810–11.

Another staple ingredient in accounts of the piano trios is the supposed connection of the slow movement of the so-called 'Ghost' Trio with plans for an opera, *Macbeth*. The sole basis for this is the presence of a short sketch in D minor headed 'Macbett', 'Ende' at the top of a page of sketches for the Trio movement (see Nottebohm, 1887, pp. 225–7, for the unsupported claim that the sketch can only be for a witches' chorus). The connection cannot be proved or disproved on such flimsy evidence. Perhaps it is more worthwhile to observe that the unusual key scheme (D minor–C major) in the first half of the slow movement of op. 70 no. 1 was to reappear many years later in the Scherzo of the Ninth Symphony: in this respect, at least, the Trio movement seems to have raised a 'ghost' of sorts.

Anh. 3
Piano Trio, D
Allegro (4/4) – Rondo: Allegretto (6/8)
Date?; publ. posth.
Spurious? The first movement is incomplete.

WoO 36
Three Piano Quartets, Eb, D, C
No. 1: Adagio assai (2/4), Allegro con spirito (eb, 3/4) – Thema: Cantabile (2/4)
No. 2: Allegro moderato (4/4) – Andante con moto (f♯, 3/4) – Rondo: Allegro (6/8)
No. 3: Allegro vivace (4/4) – Adagio con espressione (F, 3/4) – Rondo: Allegro (2/2)
pf, vn, va, vc
1785; publ. posth.
The autograph gives 'clave[c]in' and 'Basso' instead of piano and cello, and gives the order as C, Eb, D. Material from no. 3 was subsequently used in the Piano Sonatas op. 2 nos 1 and 3. The theme of the Allegro of no. 1 corresponds to a sketch for an early unfinished symphony in c (Hess 298).

WoO 38
Piano Trio, Eb
Allegro moderato (2/4) – Scherzo: Allegro ma non troppo (3/4) – Rondo: Allegretto (6/8)
?1791; publ. posth.

Date of composition is taken from Anton Gräffer's manuscript catalogue of Beethoven's works, according to which WoO 38 was originally intended for op. 1.

Hess 46
Violin Sonata, A
c. 1790–92; publ. posth.
Fragmentary: parts of a first movement (3/8) and a finale (4/4)

Hess 48
Allegretto, E♮ (3/4)
pf, vn, vc
c.1790–92; publ. posth.
Autograph in the 'Kafka' Miscellany, fol. 129, together with a fragment of a Trio section: see Kerman, 1970, ii, pp. 177–82, 291

WoO 40
Variations, F, on 'Se vuol ballare' from *The Marriage of Figaro* (Mozart)
Thema: Allegretto (3/4)
pf, vn
1792–3; publ. 1793 (Artaria, Vienna)
Ded. to Eleonore von Breuning

WoO 41
Rondo, G
Allegro (6/8)
pf, vn
1793–4; publ. 1808 (Simrock, Bonn)

Op. 1
Three Piano Trios, Eb, G, c
No. 1: Allegro (4/4) – Adagio cantabile (Ab, 3/4) – Scherzo: Allegro assai (3/4) – Finale: Presto (2/4)
No. 2: Adagio (3/4), Allegro vivace (2/4) – Largo con espressione (E, 6/8) – Scherzo: Allegro (3/4) – Finale: Presto (2/4)
No. 3: Allegro con brio (3/4) – Andante cantabile con variazioni (Eb, 2/4) – Menuetto: Quasi Allegro (3/4) – Finale: Prestissimo (2/2)
1794–5 (no. 1 was probably written earlier and revised at this time); publ. 1795 (Artaria, Vienna)
Ded. to Prince Lichnowsky. No. 3 was later arranged for string quintet as op. 104 (see 'Arrangements', p. 273).

WoO 42
Six German Dances
See 'Dance music and marches' (p. 223)

WoO 43a
Sonatina, c
Adagio (6/8)
pf, mand
1796; publ. posth.
Probably composed for Countess Josephine de Clary

WoO 43b
Adagio, E♭ (6/8)
pf, mand
1796; publ. posth.
Ded. to Countess Josephine de Clary; Hess 44 is a slightly variant version, headed 'Adagio ma non troppo'.

WoO 44a
Sonatina, C
Allegro (2/4)
pf, mand
1796; publ. posth.
Probably composed for Countess Josephine de Clary

WoO 44b
Andante con Variazioni, D (2/4)
pf, mand
1796; publ. posth.
Ded. to Countess Josephine de Clary

Op. 5
Two Cello Sonatas, F, g
No. 1: Adagio sostenuto (3/4), Allegro (4/4) – Allegro vivace (6/8)
No. 2: Adagio sostenuto e espressivo (4/4), Allegro molto più tosto presto (3/4) – Rondo: Allegro (G, 2/4)
1796; first perf. May or June 1796; publ. 1797 (Artaria, Vienna)
Ded. to Friedrich Wilhelm II of Prussia. Apparently first performed by Jean-Louis Duport rather than his brother Jean-Pierre (see Lockwood, 1978)

WoO 45
Variations, G, on 'See the conqu'ring hero comes' from _Judas Maccabaeus_ (Handel).
Thema: Allegretto (2/2)
pf, vc
1796; publ. 1797 (Artaria, Vienna)
Ded. to Princess Christiane von Lichnowsky

Op. 66
Variations, F, on 'Ein Mädchen oder Weibchen' from _The Magic Flute_ (Mozart)
Thema: Allegretto (2/4)
pf, vc
?1796; publ. 1798 (Traeg, Vienna)

Op. 12
Three Violin Sonatas, D, A, E♭
No. 1: Allegro con brio (4/4) – Tema con Variazioni: Andante con moto (A, 2/4) – Rondo: Allegro (6/8)
No. 2: Allegro vivace (6/8) – Andante più tosto Allegretto (2/4) – Allegro piacèvole (3/4)
No. 3: Allegro con spirito (4/4) – Adagio con molta espressione (C, 3/4) – Rondo: Allegro molto (2/4)
1797–8; publ. 1799 (Artaria, Vienna)
Ded. to Antonio Salieri. One of the sonatas was

probably performed by Beethoven and Schuppanzigh on 29 March 1798.

Op. 23
Violin Sonata, a
Presto (6/8) – Andante scherzoso più Allegretto (A, 2/4) – Allegro molto (2/2)
1800; publ. 1801 (Mollo, Vienna)
Ded. to Count Fries. Originally intended to be published together with op. 24

Op. 24
Violin Sonata, F ('Spring')
Allegro (4/4) – Adagio molto espressivo (B♭, 3/4) – Scherzo: Allegro molto (3/4) – Rondo: Allegro ma non troppo (2/2)
1800–1; publ. 1801 (Mollo, Vienna)
Ded. to Count Fries. Originally intended to be published together with op. 23

WoO 46
Variations, E♭, on 'Bei Männern, welche Liebe fühlen' from _The Magic Flute_ (Mozart)
Thema: Andante (6/8)
pf, vc
1801; publ. 1802 (Mollo, Vienna)
Ded. to Count Browne

Op. 30
Three Violin Sonatas, A, c, G
No. 1: Allegro (3/4) – Adagio molto espressivo (D, 2/4) – Allegretto con Variazioni (4/4)
No. 2: Allegro con brio (4/4) – Adagio cantabile (A♭, 4/4) – Scherzo: Allegro (C, 3/4) – Finale: Allegro (2/2)
No. 3: Allegro assai (6/8) – Tempo di Minuetto ma molto moderato e grazioso (E♭, 3/4) – Allegro vivace (2/4)
1801–2; publ. 1803 (Bureau des Arts et d'Industrie, Vienna)
Ded. to Czar Alexander I of Russia. See also op. 47 below.

Op. 44
Variations, E♭, on a theme from Dittersdorf's _Das rote Käppchen_, for piano trio
Thema: Andante (2/2)
Date of composition unknown; publ. 1804 (Hoffmeister, Leipzig)
Sketched in 1792, possibly as a finale for op. 1 no. 1 (Johnson, 1980a)

Op. 47
Violin Sonata, A ('Kreutzer')
Adagio sostenuto (3/4), Presto (a, 2/2) – Andante con Variazioni (F, 2/4) – Presto (6/8)
1802–3; first perf. 24 May 1803; publ. 1805 (Simrock, Bonn, and Birchall, London)
Ded. to Rodolphe Kreutzer, but the original dedicatee was George P. Bridgetower, who gave the first

performance. The finale was originally intended as the last movement of op. 30 no. 1. See Brandenburg, 1980.

Op. 121a
Variations, G, on 'Ich bin der Schneider Kakadu' from *Die Schwestern von Prag* (Müller)
Introduzione: Adagio assai (g, 4/4), Thema: Allegretto (2/4)
pf, vn, vc
?1803; rev. 1816; publ. 1824 (Steiner, Vienna, and Chappell, London). Probably offered for publication in 1803; the surviving autograph dates from c.1816–17. See Tyson, 1963c.

Op. 69
Cello Sonata, A
Allegro ma non tanto (2/2) – Scherzo: Allegro molto (a, 3/4) – Adagio cantabile (E, 2/4), Allegro vivace (2/2)
1807–8; publ. 1809 (Breitkopf & Härtel, Leipzig)
Ded. to Baron Gleichenstein

Op. 70
Two Piano Trios, D ('Ghost'), E♭
No. 1: Allegro vivace e con brio (3/4) – Largo assai e espressivo (d, 2/4) – Presto (4/4)
No. 2: Poco sostenuto (4/4), Allegro ma non troppo (6/8) – Allegretto (C, 2/4) – Allegretto ma non troppo (A♭, 3/4) – Finale: Allegro (2/4)
1808; publ. 1809 (Breitkopf & Härtel, Leipzig)
Ded. to Countess Marie Erdödy. Both works had been performed by the end of December 1808.

Op. 97
Piano Trio, B♭ ('Archduke')
Allegro moderato (4/4) – Scherzo: Allegro (3/4) – Andante cantabile (D, 3/4) – Allegro moderato (2/4)
1810–11; first perf. 11 April 1814; publ. 1816 (Steiner, Vienna, and Birchall, London)
Ded. to Archduke Rudolph. The surviving autograph dates from 1814–15 and presumably represents a revision of Beethoven's original conception: see Johnson, 1985, pp. 198–9, 237; Brandenburg, 1983, pp. 223–4.

Op. 96
Violin Sonata, G
Allegro moderato (3/4) – Adagio espressivo (E♭, 2/4) – Scherzo: Allegro (g-G, 3/4) – Poco Allegretto (2/4)
1812; first perf. 29 December 1812; publ. 1816 (Steiner, Vienna, and Birchall, London)
Ded. to Archduke Rudolph, but written for Pierre Rode. The first movement was probably written somewhat earlier than the others, and the entire work was probably revised in 1814–15, from which year the surviving autograph dates (Johnson, 1985, p. 214; Brandenburg, 1983, pp. 223–4).

WoO 39
Allegretto, B♭ (6/8)
pf, vn, vc
June 1812; publ. posth.
Ded. to Maximiliane Brentano

Op. 102
Two Cello Sonatas, C, D
No. 1: Andante (6/8), Allegro vivace (a, 2/2) – Adagio (4/4), Tempo d'Andante (6/8), Allegro vivace (2/4)
No. 2: Allegro con brio (4/4) – Adagio con molto sentimento d'affetto (d, 2/4) – Allegro, Allegro fugato (3/4)
1815; publ. 1817 (Simrock, Bonn)
Ded. to Countess Erdödy

See also 'Arrangements' (pp. 272–3)

NICHOLAS MARSTON

Chamber music for strings alone

BEETHOVEN'S CHAMBER MUSIC FOR STRINGS is of course dominated by the string quartets – and the quartets themselves are dominated, at least in many listeners' opinion, by the five late quartets (opp. 127, 130, 131, 132 and 135) and the *Grosse Fuge* op. 133. It is inevitable, then, that this account will reflect at least the first bias if not the second also. Inevitable, too, that in such a short space it will be hardly possible even to scratch the surface of the music at hand. Several books have been written about the string quartets, and an entire volume (Winter, 1982) has even been devoted to just one of them.

Beethoven's almost exclusive concentration on the string quartet in the last two years of his life might almost be regarded in retrospect as a compensation for his avoidance of it prior to 1798. While the early sketches reveal him trying his hand at a wide variety of genres including the symphony (see p. 214), there seems to be nothing for a full-scale string quartet. Beethoven's reticence in this respect is easy to explain: when he arrived in Vienna to study with Haydn, the older composer had already published a dazzling series of string quartets, the op. 64 set having appeared most recently in 1791. Opp. 71 and 74 were to be composed in 1793, Beethoven's first year of study with Haydn, and op. 77 would be finished before Beethoven began composing his own op. 18. In addition to Haydn's inspiring but doubtless inhibiting output there was also Mozart's legacy to be confronted. Not surprising, then, that Beethoven initially turned his attention elsewhere.

Beethoven's string trios should therefore not be regarded as in some sense a preparation for quartet writing: he turned to this medium precisely op. 18 Quartets to undergo such revision: the G major work, no. 2, also existed in an earlier version from 1799 and was radically revised in 1800 (see Brandenburg, 1977). It is even possible that a similar early version of no. 3 existed, but this cannot be demonstrated so convincingly.

Brandenburg's examination of the sketches has also shed light on the origins of the C minor Quartet, which has often been regarded as stylistically inferior to the rest of the set and presumed to have been composed earlier. The apparent absence of sketches for the work has been taken as evidence that it was not composed along with the others. But Brandenburg shows that sketches (dating from June 1799) do exist, and argues strongly for the unlikelihood of an earlier origin of the work.

One part of op. 18 no. 2 that underwent radical revision was the slow movement. In the 1799 version Beethoven apparently chose an ABA'B' + Coda form, the A sections being in the tonic and the B sections starting out from C minor and A♭ major respectively. The published version, however, was quite different. The overall scheme is simpler: ABA', with the A section consisting of an ornate melody which is treated even more sumptuously on its return. But the B section presents a total contrast: it picks up the closing motive from the A section and makes it the basis of a lighthearted dance-like section in a new key, tempo and metre. The return of the A section is as abrupt as Beethoven's rejection of it. It is difficult to think of a precedent for such a movement (the minor–major, Adagio–Allegro contrasts in the fourth movement of the Serenade op. 8 seem less wilful, more integrated) but easy to spot successors to it in later works. What matters here is less the precise formal design of the movement than the principle of dramatic emotional contrast. In a work such as the C♯ minor Quartet op. 131 the stark emotional leaps between the fourth or fifth and sixth movements, jammed together as these are, can seem almost grotesque.

Such grotesquerie is to be found even within op. 18. Nothing in the entire set prepares the listener for the slow movement bearing the title 'La Malinconia' ('Melancholy') which precedes the final movement of the B♭ Quartet op. 18 no. 6. Its emotional force is enormous (although Beethoven had already shown what he could do in this respect in the slow movement of op. 18 no. 1, a movement evidently inspired by the vault scene in *Romeo and Juliet*); and its labyrinthine harmonic scheme is extraordinary. 'La Malinconia' follows directly upon a Scherzo and Trio which is complicated only by the Scherzo's vacillation between a notated 3/4 and a perceived 6/8 metre; the Allegretto which follows is again very lightweight, a world apart from 'La Malinconia' which, however, intrudes twice upon this other world – and with devastating effect – before the Quartet closes. To insist upon thematic relationships between 'La Malinconia' and the Allegretto is to miss the point: these two parts of the Quartet are intended to sound mutually repellent.

Beethoven's next set of quartets, the three 'Razumovskys' op. 59, are a world apart from op. 18: they are 'post-*Eroica*' works and exhibit many aspects of that great deepening of Beethoven's musical style which the composition of the *Eroica* Symphony seems to have effected. Most obviously, it is the enormous size of the individual movements, the straining of the medium and the generally symphonic, orchestral character of the work which have led some writers to dub op. 59 no. 1 an *Eroica* for string quartet. Yet one might be tempted to hear an echo of the opening of the *Eroica* at the beginning of the E minor Quartet: two introductory chords followed by a thematic statement pushing up through the tonic triad to the fifth and falling back to the tonic note again. But it is the differences which are most telling: here there is none of the expansiveness of the *Eroica*, or of the first movement of op. 59 no. 1. The mood is taut, nervous, and the material is remarkably compressed. The immediate repetition on the Neapolitan degree (F) of the initial two-bar statement recalls the opening of the 'Appassionata' Sonata op. 57, which had been composed a year or so earlier, in 1804–5.

The slow movement of op. 59 no. 2, in the tonic major, is suggestive of the 'Heiliger Dankgesang' from op. 132 in its chorale-like opening and the *molto adagio* tempo; and the similarity of the subheading to that of 'La Malinconia' (op. 59 no. 2: 'this piece must be played with great feeling'; op. 18 no. 6: 'this piece must be played with the greatest delicacy') emphasizes the emotional depth that Beethoven associated with this movement, which, according to his friend and pupil Carl Czerny, 'occurred to him when contemplating the starry sky and thinking of the music of the spheres' (Thayer, 1967, pp. 408–9). It is worth mentioning that similar thoughts seem to have prompted him to choose E major as the key of the song *Abendlied unterm gestirnten Himmel* WoO 150, which he composed many years later, in 1820.

The inclusion of Russian themes in two of the 'Razumovsky' Quartets was an act of deference on Beethoven's part to their Russian dedicatee, Count Razumovsky. In the E minor Quartet the Russian theme appears in the Trio of the third movement, where it is given a relentless, almost parodistic quasi-fugal treatment that gives rise to some particularly gritty counterpoint – a foretaste, if not of parts of the *Grosse Fuge*, then certainly of the concluding fugue in the Cello Sonata op. 102 no. 2, and an idea taken up in the corresponding part of the 'Harp' Quartet op. 74.

The 'Razumovsky' Quartets were written quickly, probably between April and November 1806 (Tyson, 1982a, pp. 107–9). First reports of to avoid the string quartet. As Robert Simpson (1971, p. 243) has remarked: 'The quartet itself cannot by any stretch of the imagination be thought of as an enriched trio, or a proper trio as an impoverished quartet.' Even the E♭ Trio op. 3 already shows that Beethoven had fully mastered the problems of writing for this very lean instrumental combination and understood very well how to produce a wide variety of textures while rarely compromising the individuality of the three contributing parts. Comparing Beethoven's work with Mozart's Divertimento in E♭ for string trio, K. 563 (composed in 1788 and published in 1792), one is struck by the extent to which Beethoven was prepared to reduce the texture to a duo: see, for instance, the introduction of the second subject by violin and cello in the first movement, bars 41–8.

The number and combination of movements in op. 3 and in the Serenade op. 8 qualifies them both for the title 'divertimento' which Mozart gave to his K. 563. The three Trios op. 9, on the other hand, all adopt the four-movement form of the contemporary Haydn symphony. Indeed, the symphonic model is even more clearly evident in the slow introduction which opens op. 9 no. 1. As remarked elsewhere, Beethoven was not yet ready to take on Haydn as a symphonist but seems to have channelled what he learned from Haydn's symphonic style into other genres – the op. 1 Piano Trios and op. 2 Sonatas are also cast uncharacteristically as four-movement works, and symphonic slow introductions appear elsewhere, in the two Cello Sonatas op. 5 and the Quintet op. 16, for example.

Other traces of Haydn might be noted in op. 9 no. 1 – the off-tonic beginning of the first movement, which grows audibly from the figure $c''-d''-b'-a'$ in bars 3–4, and the surprising key (E major, the submediant major) of the slow movement: was Beethoven thinking here of Haydn's Quartet in G minor op. 74 no. 3? If so, he was also alluding strongly to an earlier work of his own, the Piano Trio op. 1 no. 2, which exhibits this and the other features of op. 9 no. 1 which have been mentioned. Consciousness of the op. 1 Trios is also clearly shown in the third of the op. 9 set which, like its op. 1 counterpart, is in C minor and begins with a unison thematic statement marked *piano* (even this may have had its origins in Haydn: for the best discussion of Beethoven's assimilation of Haydn's style in these and other works see Johnson, 1982).

How did Beethoven prepare for the composition of his first proper string quartets? He had tried his hand at the Minuet Hess 33 early in the 1790s. The string quartet version appears to have followed the piano one (Hess, 1959, vi.154) and it is tempting to speculate that this little piece was conceived by Beethoven as an exercise in scoring for quartet. There were also the Preludes and Fugues for string quartet (Hess 30–31), which were written as contrapuntal exercises for Albrechtsberger in about 1795.

It is worth pausing here to consider the relationship of counterpoint to Beethoven's quartet output. The importance to the quartet medium of a fluent contrapuntal technique, the ability to contrast and combine a number of polyphonic voices, needs little explanation. Beethoven's quartets contain several notable fugal movements – the finale of op. 59 no. 3, the first movement of op. 131 and of course the *Grosse Fuge* are the most obvious and thoroughgoing examples; among late works we should also note the Fugue for string quintet op. 137, written for a complete edition in manuscript of Beethoven's works which was begun by Tobias Haslinger. The fragmentary Prelude and Fugue Hess 40 was a forerunner of op. 137 and also of the second movement of the Ninth Symphony, which makes use of a slightly altered version of the Hess 40 fugue subject. As part of his preparation for Hess 40 Beethoven made a partial arrangement for string quartet of the Fugue in B minor from book 1 of Bach's '48'; back in 1801–2 he had made a similar arrangement, this time for string quintet, of the B♭ minor Fugue from the same book (the two Bach arrangements are Hess 35 and 38; see also Hess, 1972, pp. 54–63). Finally, the enormous number of score sketches (see pp. 173–4) which have survived for the late quartets testifies eloquently to Beethoven's intensive consideration of the problems of part-writing in this medium.

Copying of works by other composers was another means by which Beethoven flexed his muscles for the assault on the string quartet which resulted in op. 18. Especially noteworthy are his copyings of Haydn's op. 20 no. 1 in 1793–4 and two of Mozart's 'Haydn' Quartets, K. 387 and 464, at around the time that he began work on op. 18. (As is well known, Mozart's K. 464 was to act as a model for op. 18 no. 5.) It is also perhaps not coincidental that Beethoven's adoption of bound sketchbooks in preference to loose leaves and bifolia dates from precisely the period of composition of op. 18.

That Beethoven did not find the composition of his first string quartets easy has long been known, thanks to the existence of two versions of the F major work, op. 18 no. 1. The first version was written for Beethoven's friend Karl Amenda, to whom Beethoven wrote on 1 July 1801: 'Be sure not to pass on your quartet to anyone else, because I have substantially altered it. For only now have I learnt to write quartets properly – as you will surely see when you receive them.' (Letter 53) Indeed, a comparison of the two versions reveals just how thoroughly Beethoven overhauled his original conception, thinning out the texture, removing large-scale repeats and changing the harmonic direction of many passages (see Levy, 1982). However, no. 1 was not the only one of the performances date from the end of February the following year. The *Allgemeine Musikalische Zeitung* described them as 'long and difficult... profound and excellently wrought but not easily intelligible – except perhaps for the third, whose originality, melody and harmonic power will surely win over every educated music lover'. A curious verdict, and one that was to be decisively reversed.

Curious, because op. 59 no. 3 contains two of the strangest movements in the whole opus, perhaps even in Beethoven's career up to this point. What could have been less easily intelligible than the slow introduction with which the quartet begins? The initial attack on a diminished seventh built over F♯, the furthest point around the cycle of fifths from the tonic note, is only the first in a series of dissonant chords which are held together more by the gradually diverging outer voices, and particularly the stepwise descending bass, than by any sense of purposeful harmonic progression. The diminished seventh sonority returns again and again (bars 8–9, 15, 22–4) and when A♭ gives way to G in bars 26–9 there is little to suggest that here at last is the dominant of C major, the key of the movement. Even now all is not so straightforward, for the exposition opens with two cadenza-like passages for the first violin before the movement feels as though it has really got under way at bar 43. These passages will recur, always subtly altered, at the beginning of the development and recapitulation.

The Andante con moto which follows this first movement is also extraordinary. The first-violin solo passages in the previous movement are answered here by the cello, often playing pizzicato. The special treatment of this instrument, its frequent low pedal points and the chromatic nature of much of the melodic line (particularly the emphasis on the step G♯–F) all contribute to the remarkably bleak, brooding quality of the music. It has been suggested, quite plausibly, that Beethoven was attempting to emulate Russian folk melody here; certainly, the third 'Razumovsky' is the only one not to employ an actual Russian theme. And what about the form of this movement? The first sixty bars might suggest a sonata form, with a 'second subject' dutifully appearing in the relative major at bar 42. But the 'first subject' consists of two repeated halves plus a codetta: a strongly closed, independent section highly atypical of a sonata-form movement. This section (bars 1–25) will return intact towards the end of the movement – but not before the presumed second subject has returned, first in A major then immediately afterwards in E♭ (bars 101–22)!

Paradoxically, this second movement is probably the one which has worried modern critics the least, while the Minuet which follows it has seemed to many writers one of several weaknesses in the work when compared to its two companions. Op. 59 no.

3, it is claimed, is more conventional (it would be difficult not to think of Mozart's 'Dissonance' Quartet K. 465 in relation to the slow introduction, or of the finale of his K. 387 when confronted with the fugal opening of Beethoven's last movement); it exhibits inferior technique; it uses older material, and there is evidence that Beethoven was unsure about certain details, and even that he composed the work rather hastily. Perhaps it is the 'argument from tradition' that should be challenged most forcefully. For the bare fact of Beethoven's turning to traditional models (if it *is* a bare fact) is not enough to condemn the work; we need to ask why he turned to them, how he used them. In any case, one writer has argued convincingly that the other two 'Razumovsky' Quartets, along with many of Beethoven's middle-period works, display a similar debt to tradition (Webster, 1980); and Beethoven's very last quartet, op. 135, has been described, without censure, as the composer's 'most successful evocation of the style of Haydn and Mozart' (Kerman, 1967, p. 354). The traditional, retrospective elements in op. 59 no. 3 are not unique, then. We should also question carefully the idea that Mozart's 'Dissonance' Quartet served as a model for this piece: a model in what sense? Surely the composer of the *Eroica* Symphony would not have needed to depend on Mozart in 1806 in the way that he had used K. 464 when composing op. 18 no. 5?

One sense in which all three of the 'Razumovsky' Quartets may be considered traditional is in their publication together as a single opus. And this was a tradition from which Beethoven now departed in the remainder of his quartet output. The next work, the so-called 'Harp', has perhaps suffered from having to stand comparison with its close successor, the *Quartetto Serioso* in F minor. This title for op. 95 stems from Beethoven's autograph score and 'has had the unfortunate effect of suggesting that its immediate predecessor... does not have to be taken so seriously' (Griffiths, 1983, p. 92). But the 'Harp', whose nickname derives from the pizzicato effects in its first movement, is of course every bit as serious, in its own way, as any other Beethoven quartet. The final movement is, for the first and only time in Beethoven's quartets, a theme and variations. The six variations are organized most plainly into two interlocking sets, numbers 1, 3 and 5 being loud and (except for no. 5) contrapuntal, while numbers 2, 4 and 6 are softer and concentrate on a more lyrical treatment of the theme. Other unifying forces are also at work, however, and behind the elegant, unassuming surface of this movement there lurks an intellectual concern with the possibilities of variation form that is nothing if not *serioso* (Marston, 1989).

Just how seriously Beethoven took his op. 95 Quartet in F minor is shown not only by that autograph inscription but also by his delay in having it published, and his curious reticence about its performance: 'NB. The Quartet is written for a small circle of connoisseurs and is never to be performed in public', he warned Sir George Smart in 1816 (Letter 664). Perhaps he was aware of the work's extraordinary character, even dimly conscious that it was stylistically ahead of its time. Modern commentators have not failed to see it as a harbinger of the late quartets; and although proleptic characteristics are never spotted more easily than in retrospect, they are visible here with more than the usual clarity.

The characteristic most often associated with op. 95, and particularly with its first movement, is compression. The music exudes a sense of having been ruthlessly pared down until all that remains is the very essence of the musical material involved. The opening five bars are as good an example of this as any, but the sense of compression extends even to single notes or note-pairs: in the first movement, Db–C and C–Db come to bear a huge musical weight. Also noteworthy is Beethoven's avoidance of lengthy transitions: the establishment of Db major, the key of the second group, is brutally abrupt (bars 18–24).

Such compression is also to be observed in the first movement of Beethoven's last quartet, also in F although the mood here is completely different. And the smooth, introvert nature of the fugal section in the slow movement of op. 95 is not unlike the opening movement of op. 131. On a more technical level, one might compare the way in which, in op. 95, Beethoven whittles away his material to a bare octave D at the end of the slow movement and then transforms this note into the springboard for the next movement, with the transition between movements 1 and 2 or 2 and 3 in op. 131. Then there is the short Larghetto introduction to the last movement of op. 95: in its beginning on the dominant it suggests a passage like the Adagio ma non troppo con affetto in the Piano Sonata in A op. 101 (composed in 1816, the year that op. 95 was published), and the extremely expressive, almost vocal quality of the melody in both these passages was to give way to actual instrumental recitative in the introduction (Più allegro) to the finale of op. 132. Kerman (1967, pp. 183–4) also sees a parallel between the remarkable major-key Allegro section which brings op. 95 to a close and the Presto at the very end of op. 132. Certainly, the contrast of mood created here in the finale of op. 95 is to be encountered again and again in the late quartets.

It would be wrong, however, to set op. 95 apart simply as a kind of early late quartet. It is not as if the features described here as 'late' occur nowhere else. In the matter of dramatic compression, for example, one could find many similarities between op. 95 and op. 59 no. 2 (and both works also make much of the flattened second of the scale).

Moreover, we have already encountered violent, even grotesque contrast in op. 18 no. 6. Yet there is something about the overall tone of op. 95 that makes it difficult to avoid looking ahead into the mid-1820s.

Beethoven was talking of writing quartets again as early as June 1822, and in November of that year he received the commission from Prince Nikolas Galitzin which eventually produced the Eb, A minor and Bb Quartets opp. 127, 132 and 130. But although he promised to have the first quartet ready by mid-March 1823 at the latest, Beethoven had reckoned without the work yet to be done on the Ninth Symphony and Missa Solemnis: only in February 1825 was op. 127 completed.

Op. 127 has four movements: the slow movement, in the subdominant, is placed second (compare op. 74, also in Eb) and is a theme and variations; there is a scherzo with trio in the tonic minor, and a bright, tuneful finale. The scheme could hardly be more straightforward or conventional. But sketches for the work show that at one time Beethoven planned a six-movement work – a movement identified as 'La gaieté' was to stand second, and there was to be a mysterious Adagio in E preceding the finale (Brandenburg, 1983, pp. 273–4). Something approximating this plan for op. 127 was realized in the next quartet: in op. 132 an Allegro ma non tanto in A stands between the opening and slow movements, and the finale is introduced by the passage of recitative mentioned above. Further developments were yet to come: op. 130 has six movements in five different keys, while op. 131 has seven numbered sections with the key scheme c#–D–(b)–A–E–g#–c#.

By tabulating just these basic features we can already see how radically different were these quartets from any that had been written before, whether by Beethoven or by anyone else. But the number of different movements or keys matters less than the succession of forms and moods and the shape these impart to the work as a whole. Beethoven had long been experimenting with ways of shaping the total flow of a composition, and particularly with the means of shifting the main weight from the beginning to the end of a work. This is seen most clearly in op. 131, which opens very unusually with a slow fugue that eschews dramatic conflict. Such conflict is reserved for the very last movement, where a full-blown sonata form appears for the first time.

To dwell at any length on features of the individual movements of these quartets, several of which have already been alluded to in the discussion of earlier works, would simply be to present features of Beethoven's late style (see pp. 198–208 for a general stylistic discussion). We might mention merely the preoccupation with fugue, variation (even the Grosse Fuge is as much 'about' variation, or thematic transformation, as it is 'about' fugue), the combination and contrast of widely different moods (the first movements of opp. 127 and 130 both make use of material in contrasting tempi) and the unfailing ear for remarkable instrumental textures: listen, for example, to the 6/8 Adagio variation in the fourth movement of op. 131; or to the Adagio molto espressivo in the slow movement of op. 127. Beethoven's inventiveness in the use of register and chordal spacing in these works is truly astounding.

The ear that conceived those textures was, of course, an almost totally deaf one; and early opinion often considered the late quartets to be unfortunate aberrations on the part of a once-great composer who was now rapidly losing his touch. But music like this is bound to give rise to extreme critical positions. Counteracting the view just expressed is one common today that sees the late quartets as a quasi-mystical summary of Beethoven's life, art and philosophy. Thus all manner of interpretations have been placed on the 'difficult decision' – 'Must it be?' 'It must be!' – which stands at the head of the finale of op. 135, when all that can definitely be said about it is that it derives from Beethoven's humorous reply to Ignaz Dembscher, who wished to borrow the parts of op. 130 for a private performance and bemoaned the fact that Beethoven insisted on payment for them since Dembscher had not subscribed to the premiere of the work. Similarly, the 'Heiliger Dankgesang' from op. 132, with its double invocation of the Deity and the Lydian mode, may all too easily conjure up the picture of a sick and ageing composer reaching back through musical history for a 'purer' style in which to express some kind of religious conviction. A more dispassionate view (Brandenburg, 1982) has it that the archaic flavour of much of this wonderful movement has more to do with the 18th and early 19th century's stylized view of 16th-century sacred polyphony than with any direct engagement with that style.

Then there is the obviously shared thematic material of op. 131 (first and last movements), op. 132 (first movement) and the *Grosse Fuge*: hardly surprising that these and other thematic resemblances should have encouraged attempts to demonstrate an underlying unity embracing all of the late quartets. Cynics might suggest that the String Trio op. 9 no. 3 be included too, since its opening four notes (C–B–Ab–G) are a transposed interversion of the motive which features so prominently in Deryck Cooke's exhaustive analysis (1963). On the other hand, interrelationships between the quartets at a genetic level – the occurrence of the *Grosse Fuge* subject among sketches for opp. 127 and 132, the original intention to use the Alla danza tedesca in op. 132 rather than op. 130, the plan to conclude op. 131 with the slow-movement theme from op. 135 – speak eloquently for the kind of approach adopted by Cooke.

Questions of compositional intent and critical evaluation meet head-on when we consider the curious history of the *Grosse Fuge*, written as the finale to op. 130 and subsequently replaced by a movement of an altogether different character. Beethoven's behaviour in agreeing to replace the fugue, which had already been engraved with the rest of the quartet and performed to an unenthusiastic audience, seems extraordinary. Was he persuaded by the thought of the extra income to be gained by composing a new finale while publishing the old one separately, both in its original form and as an arrangement for piano duet? Or did he himself hold doubts about the viability of the *Grosse Fuge* as a finale for op. 130? Are both endings equally satisfying, or is one more appropriate, better than the other? This is a 'difficult decision' which each listener must make for him- or herself with each hearing. Nor is it easy to decide between the late quartets as individuals. Beethoven apparently came to regard op. 131 most highly; but when asked which of the three 'Galitzin' quartets was greatest, he replied: 'Each in its own way!' – an assessment which we might take more generally.

—
Duo, Eb (3/4)
vn, vc
Fragmentary; composed in Bonn; publ. in Kerman, 1970, ii.129 (see also *ibid.*, p. 287)

Hess 39
String Quintet, F
Lost; known only from posthumous writings. See Staehelin, 1980, p. 304 n. 11.

Hess 33
Minuet, Ab (3/4)
2 vn, va, vc
1790–92; publ. posth.
Also exists in piano version, Hess 88 (see 'Arrangements', p. 274)

Op. 3
String Trio, Eb
Allegro con brio (4/4) – Andante (Bb, 3/8) – Menuetto: Allegretto (3/4) – Adagio (Ab, 2/4) – Menuetto: Moderato (3/4) – Finale: Allegro (2/4)
Before 1794; publ. 1796 (Artaria, Vienna)
For the suggested date of composition see Thayer, 1967, pp. 166–9. The surviving autograph dates from 1795: Johnson, 1980a, pp. 138–40. Hess 25 probably does not represent an early version of the finale: see Platen, 1965, p. vii. An incomplete piano trio arrangement also exists (Hess 47).

Hess 29
Prelude and Fugue, e (3/4–[4/4])
2 vn, vc
1794–5; publ. posth.

Hess 30
Prelude and Fugue, F (3/4–4/4)
2 vn, va, vc
1794–5; publ. posth.

Hess 31
Prelude and Fugue, C (3/8–4/4)
2 vn, va, vc
1794–5; publ. posth.

Op. 4
String Quintet, E♭
Allegro con brio (4/4) – Andante (B♭, 6/8) –
Menuetto: Allegretto (3/4) – Finale: Presto (2/4)
2 vn, 2 va, vc
1795; publ. 1796 (Artaria, Vienna)
A recomposition of the Octet op. 103. See especially
Johnson, 1982, pp. 2–13.

Op. 8
Serenade, D
Marcia: Allegro (4/4) – Adagio (3/4) – Menuetto:
Allegretto (3/4) – Adagio (d, 2/4), Scherzo: Allegro
molto (2/4) – Allegretto alla Polacca (F, 3/4) –
Thema con Variazioni: Andante quasi Allegretto
(2/4) – Marcia: Allegro (4/4)
vn, va, vc
1796–7; publ. 1797 (Artaria, Vienna)

WoO 32
Duo, E♭, *Duett mit zwei obligaten Augengläsern*
([4/4]) – (C, 2/4) – Minuetto (3/4)
va, vc
1796–7; publ. posth.
Probably written for Nikolaus Zmeskall. The
second (slow) movement is fragmentary. See Kerman, 1970, ii. 78, 282.

Op. 9
Three String Trios, G, D, c
No. 1: Adagio (4/4), Allegro con brio (2/2) – Adagio,
ma non tanto, e cantabile (E, 3/4) – Scherzo:
Allegro (3/4) – Presto (2/2)
No. 2: Allegretto (2/4) – Andante quasi Allegretto
(d, 6/8) – Menuetto: Allegro (3/4) – Rondo: Allegro
(2/2)
No. 3: Allegro con spirito (6/8) – Adagio con
espressione (C, 4/4) – Scherzo: Allegro molto e
vivace (6/8) – Finale: Presto (2/2)
1797–8; publ. 1798 (Artaria, Vienna)
Ded. to Count Browne. Hess 28 is a second Trio
for the Scherzo of no. 1 which may subsequently
have been rejected from the autograph score:
Johnson, 1980a, pp. 327–8.

Op. 18
Six String Quartets, F, G, D, c, A, B♭
No. 1: Allegro con brio (3/4) – Adagio affettuoso

ed appassionato (d, 9/8) – Scherzo: Allegro molto
(3/4) – Allegro (2/4)
No. 2: Allegro (2/4) – Adagio cantabile (C, 3/4) –
Scherzo: Allegro (3/4) – Allegro molto, quasi Presto
(2/4)
No. 3: Allegro (2/2) – Andante con moto (B♭, 2/4) –
Allegro (3/4) – Presto (6/8)
No. 4: Allegro ma non tanto (4/4) – Andante
scherzoso quasi Allegretto (C, 3/8) – Menuetto:
Allegretto (3/4) – Allegro (2/2)
No. 5: Allegro (6/8) – Menuetto (3/4) – Andante
cantabile (D, 2/4) – Allegro (2/2)
No. 6: Allegro con brio (2/2) – Adagio ma non
troppo (E♭, 2/4) – Scherzo: Allegro (3/4) – Adagio,
'La Malinconia' (2/4), Allegretto quasi Allegro (3/8)
1798–1800; publ. 1801 (Mollo, Vienna)
Ded. to Prince Lobkowitz. According to Brandenburg, 1977, pp. 130–43, the order of composition
was nos 3, 1, 2, 5, 4, 6. Hess 32 is an early version
of no. 1 which was dedicated to Karl Amenda.

Op. 29
String Quintet, C
Allegro moderato (2/2) – Adagio molto espressivo
(F, 3/4) – Scherzo: Allegro (3/4) – Presto (6/8)
2 vn, 2 va, vc
1801; publ. 1802 (Breitkopf & Härtel, Leipzig)
Ded. to Count Fries

Op. 59
Three String Quartets, F, e, C ('Razumovsky')
No. 1: Allegro (4/4) – Allegretto vivace e sempre
scherzando (B♭, 3/8) – Adagio molto e mesto (f,
2/4) – Allegro (2/4)
No. 2: Allegro (6/8) – Molto adagio (E, 4/4) –
Allegretto (3/4) – Finale: Presto (2/2)
No. 3: Introduzione: Andante con moto (3/4);
Allegro vivace (4/4) – Andante con moto quasi
Allegretto (a, 6/8) – Menuetto grazioso (3/4) –
Allegro molto (2/2)
1806; publ. 1808 (Bureau des Arts et d'Industrie,
Vienna)
Ded. to Count Razumovsky, although Beethoven
changed the dedication in favour of Prince Lichnowsky for a short time

Op. 74
String Quartet, E♭ ('Harp')
Poco Adagio (2/2), Allegro (4/4) – Adagio ma non
troppo (A♭, 3/8) – Presto (c, 3/4) – Allegretto con
Variazioni (2/4)
1809; publ. 1810 (Breitkopf & Härtel, Leipzig;
Clementi, London)
Ded. to Prince Lobkowitz

Op. 95
String Quartet, f, *Serioso*
Allegro con brio (4/4) – Allegretto ma non troppo
(D, 2/4) – Allegro assai vivace ma serioso (3/4) –
Larghetto espressivo (2/4), Allegretto agitato (6/8)

1810–11; first perf. May 1814; publ. 1816 (Steiner, Vienna)

Ded. to Nikolaus Zmeskall. The autograph, which is dated October 1810, actually dates almost entirely from 1814. The quartet may have been revised at that time, prior to publication. See Brandenburg, 1983, pp. 221–2; Johnson, 1985, pp. 198, 206.

Op. 137
Fugue, D
Allegretto (3/8)

2 vn, 2 va, vc

November 1817; publ. posth.

Hess 40
Prelude and Fugue, d (2/4 – 3/8)

2 vn, 2 va, vc

1817; publ. posth.

Only the Prelude is complete; the Fugue breaks off after four bars.

WoO 34
Duet, A

2 vn

April 1822; publ. posth.

Ded. to Alexandre Boucher

Op. 127
String Quartet, E♭

Maestoso (2/4), Allegro (3/4) – Adagio, ma non troppo e molto cantabile (A♭, 12/8) – Scherzando vivace (3/4) – Finale (2/2)

1824–5; first perf. 6 March 1825; publ. 1826 (Schott, Mainz)

Ded. to Prince Nikolas Galitzin

Op. 132
String Quartet, a

Assai sostenuto (2/2), Allegro (4/4) – Allegro ma non tanto (A, 3/4) – Molto adagio ('Heiliger Dankgesang eines Genesenen an die Gottheit, in der lydischen Tonart' ['Sacred Song of Thanksgiving to the Deity from a Convalescent, in the Lydian Mode'], F, 4/4) – Alla Marcia, assai vivace (A, 4/4) – Più allegro (a, 4/4), Allegro appassionato (a – A, 3/4)

1825; first perf. 6 November 1825; publ. 1827 (Schlesinger, Paris)

Ded. to Prince Nikolas Galitzin. See also op. 130.

WoO 35
Duet, A (2 vn?)
See p. 261

Op. 130
String Quartet, B♭

Adagio ma non troppo (3/4), Allegro (4/4) – Presto (b♭, 2/2) – Andante con moto ma non troppo (D♭, 4/4) – Alla danza tedesca: Allegro assai (G, 3/8) – Cavatina: Adagio molto espressivo (E♭, 3/4) –

Finale: Allegro (2/4)

1825–6; first perf. 21 March 1826 (with op. 133 as finale), 22 April 1827 (with new finale); publ. 1827 (Mathias Artaria, Vienna)

Ded. to Prince Nikolas Galitzin. The Alla danza tedesca was originally intended for op. 132; the version with op. 133 as finale was completed by 9 January 1826; the replacement finale was completed by 22 November 1826.

Op. 133
Grosse Fuge for string quartet, B♭

Overtura: Allegro (6/8), Allegro, Fuga (4/4)

1825–6; first perf. (as finale of op. 130) 21 March 1826; publ. 1827 (Mathias Artaria, Vienna)

Ded. to Archduke Rudolph

Op. 131
String Quartet, c♯

No. 1: Adagio ma non troppo e molto espressivo (2/2), No. 2: Allegro molto vivace (D, 6/8), No. 3: Allegro moderato (b, 4/4), No. 4: Andante ma non troppo e molto cantabile (A, 2/4), No. 5: Presto (E, 2/2), No. 6: Adagio quasi un poco andante (g♯, 3/4), No. 7: Allegro (2/2)

1825–6; publ. 1827 (Schott, Mainz)

Ded. to Baron Joseph von Stutterheim. See also op. 135.

Op. 135
String Quartet, F

Allegretto (2/4) – Vivace (3/4) – Lento assai, cantante e tranquillo (D♭, 6/8) – Grave ma non troppo tratto (f, 3/2), Allegro (2/2)

1826; first perf. 23 March 1828; publ. 1827 (Schlesinger, Paris)

Ded. to Johann Wolfmayer. The theme of the third movement was originally associated with the finale of op. 131: Winter, 1977, pp. 124–5.

WoO 62
String Quintet in C
See 'Unfinished and projected works' (p. 277).

See also 'Arrangements' (pp. 272–5).

NICHOLAS MARSTON

Piano music

BEETHOVEN'S SOLO PIANO MUSIC is a central part of his output; spread throughout his career, it embraces not only the sonatas, but sets of variations and numerous shorter pieces. To some extent his achievement was dependent upon developments in the manufacture of instruments. The 'Hammerklavier' Sonata could not have been conceived for the piano for which he wrote his earliest works, but nonetheless the concept in some of his last works transcends the limitations of the instruments at his disposal.

Through his early teacher, Neefe, Beethoven was exposed to a wide variety of contemporary styles, and the influences of C.P.E. Bach, J.C. Bach, Dussek, Clementi, Haydn and Mozart are apparent in his early keyboard works. Beethoven's outstanding ability as a performer was another important factor in his development. In his teens and early twenties he wrote a considerable number of works for piano which he did not deem worthy of publishing with opus numbers. Some of these appeared later than the three Sonatas op. 2, indicating the particular importance Beethoven attached to the sonata.

Early variations

In the Ten Salieri Variations (WoO 73) of 1799, as in other early sets, ornamental melodic variation is the mainstay of the style. The execution is technically demanding, there are elements of contrast in the different tempo indications, and there is exploitation of the rhythmic and harmonic elements of the theme. In 1802 Beethoven wrote to the publishers Breitkopf & Härtel regarding the two sets of Variations opp. 34 and 35: 'Both sets are worked out in a quite new manner, and each in a separate and different way . . . ' (Letter 62). The two compositions do indeed display two different manifestations of variation form: the one 'improvisatory', the other formal or 'worked out'. The Six Variations on an Original Theme, op. 34, exude spontaneity and provide ample opportunity for brilliant pianistic display. They give the impression (perhaps wrongly, however) that Beethoven originally improvised them and only later committed them to paper. This is not to belittle them: based on a simple theme, the variations show organic growth, achieved on the simplest level by increasing their complexity towards the end, and on another level, by contrasting key, metre and tempo. Variation technique has moved some way from mere melodic decoration. In Variation 2 the original melody serves as little more than a skeletal framework, with interest concentrated on the 6/8 rhythm. Variation 4 moves further away and is perhaps the most improvisatory in character. The coda begins as a continuation of the final variation before leading to a return of the theme. For two bars it is in its original state, but then undergoes further variation. A slower tempo indication is necessary to accommodate the increasingly virtuosic treatment. A passage dominated by trills comes to rest on a high F which unleashes a cadenza-like flourish before the work comes to a peaceful end.

The *Prometheus* Variations, op. 35, stand midway in scope between the previous work and the Diabelli Variations. The character and volume of the sketches suggest that Beethoven approached this work with the seriousness reserved for major forms. The theme itself is not heard at the outset. It is preceded by an introduction in which its bass is heard four times, with the texture increasing on each repetition. The way has been paved for a plan in which the harmonic scheme takes precedence over the melodic material. The sketches reveal that Beethoven originally drafted a number of variations on the *Prometheus* theme, already used in two earlier works, without regard for sequence. That came later: those which were to be retained were grouped and regrouped, and would sometimes have to be revised to fit into their new environment. The last numbered variation is a Largo leading to the finale, which starts as a fugue, anticipating a similar procedure in the Diabelli Variations. The fugue recalls to prominence the bass theme, but two ensuing variations of the main theme settle any ambiguity as to which theme predominates.

The sonatas

The thirty-two piano sonatas not only chart Beethoven's development as a composer, but transform the genre beyond all recognition. Sheer number dictates that discussion must be selective, although they display such a variety of approach that almost every work is worthy of special mention. They can perhaps be best considered in three groups: those of opp. 2–22 and op. 49; opp. 26–31; and opp. 53–111.

In the first group the young composer appears consciously to be trying to come to terms with a major form. The majority do not adopt the three-movement pattern established by Haydn and Mozart, but comprise four movements. They were nearly all completed before the First Symphony and any of the string quartets, so Beethoven may have used the genre not only as his main vehicle of expression, but also as a sort of prototype for those forms. Their most obvious quality is the variety they encompass as regards expression, dynamic effects and their treatment of tonality and harmony.

The first three, op. 2, were written in 1793–5. No. 1 in F minor begins in a striking way with the momentum of the opening theme generating a compact, dramatic sonata-form movement. The slow movement of no. 2 in A fits well into the context of a work conceived on a broad scale. Its opening sustained chords, with a pizzicato-like bass, would have been possible only on the relatively new fortepianos of the time. The brilliance of no. 3 in C is emphasized by the cadenza passage in the coda of the first movement, and the finale is not immune from the influence of the concerto, a form which Beethoven was already addressing.

With Sonata no. 8 (*Pathétique*) a new path is forged. For the first time Beethoven employs a slow introduction. This Grave is more than a mere prologue; it introduces a new dimension of expression, and is integrated into the movement, returning in an abbreviated form at the beginning of both the development section and the coda. It is characterized by chords of the diminished seventh, an interval which appears melodically at the end of the introduction, resolving only at the start of the Allegro, into which it leads without a break. Its tentative final return is interrupted by the closing headlong dash of the Allegro, which leaves no doubt that this is the resolution of the poignant questioning of the Grave. The sustained lyricism of the slow movement calls for a simple rondo form. It is in Ab, a warm key in Beethoven's piano music, and one whose relationship with the tonic releases rather than admits tension.

In the next group Beethoven began to divert from the traditional form. It was this more flexible approach to the overall structure which was to pave the way for great diversity in the late works. In op. 26 Beethoven for the first time opened with a variation form movement. Mozart had begun his Sonata in A, K. 331, in this way, but with no evident attempt to disturb sonata tradition. Beethoven's work consists of four movements, with the Scherzo placed second so as to separate the slow variations from the funeral march. This slow movement exhibits a new kind of expression which lent itself readily to orchestration as part of the incidental music to *Leonore Prohaska*. It is in Ab minor, a key whose inherent psychological difficulties give it a particular intensity, emphasized by much use of enharmonic change to introduce distant keys. Rhythm is as much an element of the main theme as melody, and the effective use of a wide keyboard range helps to evoke muffled drum rolls and trumpet calls.

If in op. 26 Beethoven seemed to depart from the traditional sonata structure, this trend became all the more apparent in the next two sonatas. He showed his awareness of this by describing each of op. 27 nos 1 and 2 as *Sonata quasi una fantasia*. Neither first movement is in sonata form, and both are somewhat improvisatory in character: no. 1 alternates slow and fast sections, and in the famous Adagio sostenuto of no. 2, which gave the work its nickname ('Moonlight'), one mood and a slow speed are maintained throughout. The finales use sonata-rondo and sonata form; thus the drama and tension inherent in the sonata have been transferred from the beginning to the end of the works. Op. 28 and the three Sonatas of op. 31 are less experimental, although the first movement of op. 31 no. 2 integrates passages of Largo and Allegro in a novel way.

The 'Waldstein', op. 53, displays an unprecedented grandeur both in the technical demands of the keyboard writing and as regards its scale, which is in keeping with other works from this period. It is not on the huge time-scale first envisaged, since the original slow movement, now known as 'Andante favori' (WoO 57), was replaced by the Introduzione, Adagio molto, which acts as a slow introduction to the finale. A striking feature of the first movement is the juxtaposition of the tonalities of C and E for the first and second subjects, which is heightened by the contrast of mood: the restless quaver movement of the first subject and the simple chordal movement of the second. The mysterious, fragmented opening of the Introduzione looks forward to the later style. It is not until the end of bar 9 that the theme enters, in a low register, and only then is sense made of the broken phrases heard before. The spacious rondo theme of the finale is contrasted by two stormy minor episodes. The final return is the climax of the work, entering triumphantly and *fortissimo*. The trills are more than superficial embellishment and the triplet semiquaver movement gives the impression of a quickening of pace. Suddenly the momentum is lost. The music sinks to *ppp* and a pause. But this is only in order to gather breath before the theme returns, ever more brilliant, prestissimo.

The trend of extending boundaries, as regards the loosening of formal structure, expressive qualities and technique, continues in the 'Appassionata'. The sequence of the three movements is only outwardly conventional, and the finale is no resolution of the turmoil expressed at the outset. The prevailing mood of tragedy is portrayed immediately by the hushed presentation of the main theme. Although it is built on the notes of the tonic chord, its manner of articulation could be described as Romantic. It begins *pianissimo*, in a low register, and the rhythmic notation suggests tension. Furthermore, the emphasis on the F minor tonic is quickly undermined by a repetition of Gb. The unity of mood is reinforced by the close relationship between the first and second subjects. The slow movement temporarily suspends the overriding feeling of despair. Its Db tonality and simple harmonic progressions contribute to a lessening of tension and create a static impression. In the final variation the theme returns in its original condition, except that it is dislocated by changes of register, before collapsing on a diminished seventh chord. This is repeated *fortissimo* and leads directly into the finale, unleashing a torrent of semiquavers whose movement scarcely lets up. Again, one mood is maintained throughout. Unusually it is the second part of the movement which is directed to be repeated. The effect of this is to increase the tension by delaying the ever greater force of the presto coda. There is no escape from the mood of desperation, and the movement ends abruptly.

When Beethoven returned to the piano sonata after a lapse of four years, the intimacy of opp. 78 and 79 was in direct contrast to the style of the preceding works. The next sonata, op. 81a (*Das Lebewohl*) is also personal, having been written for Archduke Rudolph's departure from and return to Vienna in 1809–10, but is on a grander scale. Another four years passed before the composition of op. 90 in 1814. It stands on the brink of Beethoven's late style and foreshadows the last sonata with its two-movement structure, the first in the minor, the second in the major.

The last five sonatas, spread over a period of seven years, contain, like the late string quartets, a spiritual quality which transcends such considerations as form. Although they are considered as a group they differ greatly. All open with sonata-form movements, but they display a great diversity of expression: the strength and flamboyant defiance of the 'Hammerklavier' Sonata, op. 106, ranging through the anguish of op. 111, the warmth of op. 110 and the intimacy of op. 101. The presence of fugal elements is a common feature and is assimilated in varying degrees, from the fugal passages in the finale of op. 101 and the first movements of opp. 106 and 111, to a much more rigorous application in the finales of opp. 106 and 110. Albrechtsberger had believed in the fugue as a vehicle for serious and religious thought, and as a necessary means for producing 'the most elevating impression in vocal and instrumental music of Classic style' (Dickinson, 1955, p. 76).

The final movement of op. 110 is one of Beethoven's most original constructions, combining the function of slow and fast movements, and perhaps thereby solving the problem of abandoning the four-movement structure which he had been so reluctant to give up entirely. In the course of the opening eight bars which precede the first Arioso (slow) section, Beethoven has written nine tempo indications and numerous other directions so that his meaning should be clearly understood. Within a basically slow tempo he is attempting to achieve a spontaneity which musical notation cannot adequately express. The intensity of the communication of Beethoven's innermost thoughts in the Arioso ('Klagender Gesang') is released in the ensuing fugue. This is interrupted in mid-flow by the return of the Arioso, now in G minor, and introduced by the words 'ermattet, klagend' ('exhausted, plaintive'). It is fragmented, but gathers confidence to move to the major in preparation for the return of the fugue in inversion. The description now is 'Nach und nach wieder auflebend' ('gaining new life'), and it picks up from where it had left off. The voices enter one by one, reflecting the sentiments of a revival of strength. The slowing down of the basic tempo (meno allegro) paradoxically imparts the impression of greater speed by admitting more notes. When the recapitulation occurs (bar 168) there is an amazing revelation. The theme sounds out strongly, but it is not contrapuntal. Here Beethoven had achieved

total freedom, even within the fugue, that most intellectual of forms.

Op. 111 epitomizes Beethoven's late style. It is literally and figuratively a lifetime away from the op. 2 group. Words are inadequate to convey the range of emotions – the tension, the despair, the sublimity – expressed therein. Its two movements contrast with and complement each other; nothing else is required. The turbulent, intense desperation of the C minor sonata-form Allegro finds its resolution in the spacious variation form of the C major Arietta. Although ostensibly a slow movement, it encompasses a world of expression. Edwin Fischer (1959, p. 116) suggested that these two movements symbolize this world and the world to come: the relentless first movement portraying life's hard struggle, and the second representing the transcendental, in which details have become unimportant.

The opening gesture of the slow introduction immediately generates the tension which is to dominate the movement. This is not the defiant, 'heroic' figure of earlier works; the subsequent quiet, despairing journey through, but never resting on, distant keys, reveals it to be the tormented, confused questioning of the introvert. In the Allegro the restless character of the first subject derives from the chromatic intervals of the introduction and from variations of tempo typical of the late works. The compression of the development section is also characteristic of the late style, as is the opportunity for further variation in the recapitulation. The coda (bar 130) sees the disintegration of the force of the movement. A quiet passage reiterating IV–I progressions leads to the final resolution of the diminished seventh chords from the opening; it is a true reconciliation, and the soft major ending prepares the ear for the serenity of the Arietta theme.

The second movement comprises a theme, five variations and a coda. It is written in 9/16 metre, and the semiquaver notation ensures a slow speed. Variation 1 maintains the three groups of three semiquavers per bar, but seems faster because of the moving accompaniment. Variation 2, in spite of the 'L'istesso tempo' indication, seems faster still. The time signature is 6/16, but actually three groups of two semiquavers are implied. In Variation 3 there is a similar impression of an increase in speed with a 12/32 metre (three groups of four demisemiquavers). Here, syncopated accents and the use of the entire keyboard range contribute to a change of mood: one of energy, almost exuberance. The fourth variation reverts to the 9/16 metre but the nature of the accompaniment and the occurrences of the harmonies of the theme on weak beats give it a timeless feeling. The repeats here are written out, permitting further variation. The two 'extra' sections are extremely soft and are confined to the upper register, with the last section extended as if Beethoven were loth to leave these ecstatic heights. The harmony becomes increasingly static on C major, a cadenza-like passage emerges, and there is further extension before the fifth variation appears. The theme takes on greater breadth and richness without losing any of its simplicity. The coda (bar 161) is dominated by trills and the use of the upper register. The movement eventually dies away to the drooping intervals which define the theme.

Diabelli Variations

Beethoven was amongst a number of composers invited by Anton Diabelli in 1819 to write one variation on a waltz theme he had written. At first Beethoven is said to have dismissed the idea, scornfully mocking the theme for its 'Schusterfleck' ('cobbler's patch'), a term used to describe the sequential repetition of a little pattern. But his sketches show that by 1820 he had drafted about twenty variations, including the massive, fugal no. 32, and then added still more in 1823 (Kinderman, 1987).

Diabelli's theme is, as Tovey described it (1944a, p. 124), 'rich in musical facts'. It has a strong harmonic structure and its theme can be broken down into a number of rhythmic and melodic components. Taking these features as his starting-point, Beethoven extracts great variety without ever totally losing contact with the original, within a style typical of the late works, characterized by counterpoint, trills, intensive development of rhythmic figures, slow, meditative sections and mysterious-sounding passages. As Kinderman has written: 'The nature of their [the variations'] succession and of the large form that embraces the whole emerges from the cumulative effect of the individual variations and can be properly expressed only through examination of the entire massive edifice of variations.' (Kinderman, 1987, p. xix) This poses certain questions: how did Beethoven prevent the intrinsically simple theme from becoming a mere prelude to a work of this scope and intensity; how did he extract from it sufficient inspiration to produce such variety; and how did he balance unity and diversity over such a long time-span?

Beethoven's approach included recalling the theme as a point of reference, writing sections which are less variations than re-presentations with certain features grossly exaggerated. The scale of the work requires preparation, and this is achieved immediately after the statement of the theme. Variation 1 (Alla Marcia) has a grand air of anticipation but also parodies a particular aspect of the theme, the repeated G's. The harmonic structure remains basically intact and the point of the climax is retained, but the mood is entirely different. Thus the gulf between the character of the theme and the scale of the work is bridged. This paves the way for a series of variations in which different elements undergo change: the melodic line (Var. 3, 4), the static harmony of the opening (Var. 12), the texture (Var. 6), the harmonic scheme (Var. 9) and the rhythm (Var. 13, 14). Variation 15 is another supporting 'pillar', recapitulating the melodic contour of the theme at its original register. Its 'exaggerated' feature is the harmonic plan, which is static to the point that both halves end on the tonic. It comes at a psychologically important point, between variations which have moved some way from the theme. Variation 14 is on a large scale and its mood, metre and harmonic plan differ considerably from the theme. Variations 16 and 17 are linked and are imposing both in scale and in their brilliant, technically demanding style.

Variation 25 is the final deliberate point of reference. The theme's opening bass rhythm moves to the treble, assimilating the repeated G's from the melody. The trivial nature of the theme is emphasized by the rustic mood, but this does not disguise the recall of the interval of a fourth, the variation of the bass from bar 3, or the harmonic structure of the original. It precedes a succession of variations more closely linked than before. Nos 26 and 27 are linked by the similarity of their figuration, and nos 29–31 form a lyrical, meditative sequence, longer and more elaborate than anything yet heard. The harmonic plan of Variation 30 is particularly wide-ranging, although the striking move from C to D♭ had been foreshadowed in the previous variation. No. 31 accumulates still more tension and leads straight into the Fugue. Much has been said of the significance of the fugue in Beethoven's late works, and here, as elsewhere, it is a logical outcome. It breaks off suddenly to make way for a cadenza passage, after which there is a transition to Variation 33. This final variation gives the impression that the strife and energy of the preceding fugue have been spent, but its softness and rhythmic relaxation are deceptive. It is the apotheosis of all that has gone before, embracing all elements of the theme, with a new serenity. In its transcendental quality the long coda recalls the mood of the finale of the last sonata.

Other pieces

In the numerous shorter pieces which Beethoven produced throughout his career he showed himself to be a skilful miniaturist. The bagatelles particularly look forward to the Romantic character piece. Some works came into being as the result of their rejection from a sonata; others, such as the Fantasia, op. 77, of 1809, reflect Beethoven's predilection for improvising and variation form.

There are three sets of Bagatelles (opps. 33, 119 and 126). Only the last set was intended from the outset as an entity, as evidenced by the note 'Ciclus von Kleinigkeiten' in the sketches, but the first six of op. 119 form a kind of cycle too (Cooper, 1987a), and perhaps also the last five. The title means 'trifle', but this is not to be dismissive. They display a variety of rapidly painted moods; they can address themselves to a specific compositional problem or experiment with a particular technique. The eleven of op. 119 mainly use simple forms, but within these, no. 6, for example, introduces recitative-like writing, and no. 7 concentrates on trills. Those of op. 126 are on a slightly larger scale and not surprisingly assimilate the language of the late sonatas. Their unified conception is revealed in part by their key scheme, where after two pieces in G major and minor, the rest move through a sequence of descending major thirds. They provided the opportunity to experiment in a more relaxed setting than the sonata, where the whole must be kept in view.

I Sonatas; II Variations; III Other pieces; IV Works for four hands

I Sonatas

WoO 47
Three Sonatas ('Kurfürstensonaten'), E♭, f, D
No. 1: Allegro cantabile (4/4) – Andante (B♭, 2/4) – Rondo vivace (6/8)
No. 2: Larghetto maestoso (2/2)/Allegro assai (4/4) – Andante (A♭, 2/4) – Presto (2/4)
No. 3: Allegro (4/4) – Menuetto: Sostenuto (A, 3/4) – Scherzando: Allegro, ma non troppo (2/4)
1783(?); publ. 1783 (Bossler, Speyer)
Ded. to Archbishop Maximilian Friedrich

WoO 50
Two movements of a Sonata, F
I (4/4) – Allegretto (3/4)
c.1790–92; publ. posth.
Ded. to Franz Wegeler

Anh. 5
Two Sonatinas
G (Moderato, 4/4 – Romanze, 6/8); F (Allegro assai, 2/4 – Rondo: Allegro, 2/4)
c.1790–92? Probably spurious

Op. 2
Three Sonatas (nos 1–3), f, A, C
No. 1: Allegro (2/2) – Adagio (F, 3/4) – Menuetto: Allegretto (3/4) – Prestissimo (2/2)
No. 2: Allegro vivace (2/4) – Largo appassionato (D, 3/4) – Scherzo: Allegretto (3/4) – Rondo: Grazioso (4/4)
No. 3: Allegro con brio (4/4) – Adagio (E, 2/4) – Scherzo: Allegro (3/4) – Allegro assai (6/8)

1793–5; publ. 1796 (Artaria, Vienna)
Ded. to Haydn. Second movement of no. 1 uses material from Piano Quartet WoO 36 no. 3; first movement of no. 3 uses material from Piano Quartet WoO 36 no. 3.

Op. 49 no. 2
Sonata no. 20, G
Allegro ma non troppo (2/2) – Tempo di Menuetto (3/4)
1795–6; publ. 1805 (Bureau des Arts et d'Industrie, Vienna)

Op. 49 no. 1
Sonata no. 19, g
Andante (2/4) – Rondo: Allegro (G, 6/8)
1797(?); publ. 1805 (Bureau des Arts et d'Industrie, Vienna)

Op. 7
Sonata no. 4, E♭
Allegro molto e con brio (6/8) – Largo, con gran espressione (C, 3/4) – Allegro (3/4) – Rondo: Poco allegretto e grazioso (2/4)
1796–7; publ. 1797 (Artaria, Vienna)
Ded. to Countess Keglevics

Op. 10
Three Sonatas (nos. 5–7), c, F, D
No. 1: Allegro molto e con brio (3/4) – Adagio molto (A♭, 2/4) – Finale: Prestissimo (2/2)
No. 2: Allegro (2/4) – Allegretto (f, 3/4) – Presto (2/4)
No. 3: Presto (4/4) – Largo e mesto (d, 6/8) – Menuetto: Allegro (3/4) – Rondo: Allegro (4/4)
1795–8; publ. 1798 (Eder, Vienna)
Ded. to Countess Browne. See also WoO 52, WoO 53 and Hess 69 (below).

WoO 51
Sonata, C
Allegro (4/4) – Adagio (F, 3/4)
1791–8(?); publ. posth.
Ded. to Eleonore von Breuning. First edition completed by Ries, since small parts of the first two movements and the whole of the last movement are lost

Op. 13
Sonata no. 8, *Pathétique*, c
Grave (4/4)/Allegro di molto e con brio (2/2) – Adagio cantabile (A♭, 2/4) – Rondo: Allegro (2/2)
1797–8; publ. 1799 (Hoffmeister, Vienna)
Ded. to Prince Lichnowsky

Op. 14
Two Sonatas (nos. 9–10), E, G
No. 1: Allegro (4/4) – Allegretto (e, 3/4) – Rondo:

Allegro commodo (2/2)
No. 2: Allegro (2/4) – Andante (C, 4/4) –
Scherzo: Allegro assai (3/8)
1798–9; publ. 1799 (Mollo, Vienna)
Ded. to Baroness Braun. In 1801–2 Beethoven
arranged no. 1 for string quartet (see
'Arrangements', p. 273).

Op. 22
Sonata no. 11, B♭
Allegro con brio (4/4) – Adagio con molta
espressione (E♭, 9/8) – Menuetto (3/4) – Rondo:
Allegretto (2/4)
1800; publ. 1802 (Hoffmeister, Leipzig)
Ded. to Count Browne

Op. 26
Sonata no. 12, A♭
Andante con Variazioni (3/8) – Scherzo: Allegro
molto (3/4) – Marcia Funebre sulla morte d'un
Eroe: Maestoso andante (a[♭], 4/4) – Allegro (2/4)
1800–01; publ. 1802 (Cappi, Vienna)
Ded. to Prince Lichnowsky; third movement
arranged for no. 4 (Funeral March) of *Leonore
Prohaska* (WoO 96) (see 'Stage music', pp. 254–5)

Op. 27
Two Sonatas (nos. 13–14), E♭, c♯
No. 1, *Sonata quasi una fantasia*: Andante (2/2) –
Allegro molto e vivace (c, 3/4) – Adagio con
espressione (A♭, 3/4) – Allegro vivace (2/4)
No. 2, *Sonata quasi una fantasia* ('Moonlight'):
Adagio sostenuto (2/2) – Allegretto (D♭, 3/4) –
Presto agitato (4/4)
1801; publ. 1802 (Cappi, Vienna)
No. 1 ded. to Princess von Liechtenstein; no. 2 to
Countess Guicciardi

Op. 28
Sonata No. 15 ('Pastoral'), D
Allegro (3/4) – Andante (d, 2/4) – Scherzo:
Allegro vivace (3/4) – Rondo: Allegro ma non
troppo (6/8)
1801; publ. 1802 (Bureau des Arts et d'Industrie,
Vienna)
Ded. to Joseph Sonnenfels

Op. 31
Three Sonatas (nos 16–18), G, d, E♭
No. 1: Allegro vivace (2/4) – Adagio grazioso (C,
9/8) – Rondo: Allegretto (2/2)
No. 2: Largo/Allegro (2/2) – Adagio (B♭, 3/4) –
Allegretto (3/8)
No. 3: Allegro (3/4) – Scherzo: Allegretto vivace
(A♭, 2/4) – Menuetto: Moderato e grazioso
(3/4) – Presto con fuoco (6/8)
1802; nos 1 and 2 publ. 1803, no. 3 publ. 1804
(Nägeli, Zurich)
Commissioned by publisher

Op. 53
Sonata no. 21 ('Waldstein'), C
Allegro con brio (4/4) – Introduzione: Adagio
molto (F, 6/8) – Rondo: Allegretto moderato (2/4)
1803–4; publ. 1805 (Bureau des Arts et
d'Industrie, Vienna)
Ded. to Count Waldstein; see WoO 57 (p. 248)

Op. 54
Sonata no. 22, F
In tempo d'un Menuetto (3/4) – Allegretto (2/4)
1804; publ. 1806 (Bureau des Arts et d'Industrie,
Vienna)

Op. 57
Sonata no. 23 ('Appassionata'), f
Allegro assai (12/8) – Andante con moto (D♭,
2/4) – Allegro ma non troppo (2/4)
1804–5; publ. 1807 (Bureau des Arts et
d'Industrie, Vienna)
Ded. to Count Brunsvik

Op. 78
Sonata no. 24, F♯
Adagio cantabile (2/4)/Allegro ma non troppo
(4/4) – Allegro vivace (2/4)
1809; publ. 1810 (Clementi, London)
Ded. to Therese Brunsvik; commissioned by
Clementi

Op. 79
Sonata no. 25, G
Presto alla tedesca (3/4) – Andante (g, 9/8) –
Vivace (2/4)
1809; publ. 1810 (Clementi, London)
Commissioned by Clementi

Op. 81a
Sonata no. 26, *Das Lebewohl, Abwesenheit und Wiedersehn* ('Les Adieux'), E♭
Das Lebewohl [The Farewell]: Adagio
(2/4)/Allegro (2/2) – Abwesenheit [Absence]:
Andante espressivo (c, 2/4) – Das Wiedersehn
[The Return]: Vivacissimamente (6/8)
1809–10; publ. 1811 (Breitkopf & Härtel,
Leipzig)
Ded. to Archduke Rudolph

Op. 90
Sonata no. 27, e
Mit Lebhaftigkeit und durchaus mit Empfindung
und Ausdruck (3/4) – Nicht zu geschwind und
sehr singbar vorzutragen (E, 2/4)
1814; publ. 1815 (Steiner, Vienna)
Ded. to Count Lichnowsky

Op. 101
Sonata no. 28, A
Allegretto ma non troppo (6/8) – Vivace alla
Marcia (F, 4/4) – Adagio, ma non troppo, con

affetto (a, 2/4)/Tempo del primo pezzo
(6/8)/Allegro (2/4)
1816; publ. 1817 (Steiner, Vienna)
Ded. to Baroness Ertmann

Op. 106
Sonata no. 29, 'Hammerklavier', B♭
Allegro (2/2) – Scherzo: Assai vivace (3/4) –
Adagio sostenuto (f♯, 6/8) – Largo (F,
2/4)/Allegro risoluto (3/4)
1817–18; publ. 1819 (Artaria, Vienna)
Ded. to Archduke Rudolph

Op. 109
Sonata no. 30, E
Vivace ma non troppo (2/4) – Prestissimo (e,
6/8) – Andante molto cantabile ed espressivo (3/4)
1820; publ. 1821 (Schlesinger, Berlin)
Ded. to Maximiliane Brentano; commissioned by
publisher

Op. 110
Sonata no. 31, A♭
Moderato cantabile molto espressivo (3/4) –
Allegro molto (f, 2/4) – Adagio, ma non troppo
(b♭, 4/4)/Recitativo/Adagio, ma non troppo (a♭,
12/16) – Fuga: Allegro ma non troppo (6/8)
1821–2; publ. 1822 (Schlesinger, Berlin)
Commissioned by publisher

Op. 111
Sonata no. 32, c
Maestoso (4/4)/Allegro con brio ed appassionato –
Arietta: Adagio molto semplice e cantabile (C,
9/16)
1821–2; publ. 1823 (Schlesinger, Berlin)
Ded. to Archduke Rudolph (English edn ded. to
Antonie Brentano); commissioned by publisher

II Variations

WoO 63
Nine Variations on a March by Dressler, c
Maestoso (4/4)
1782; publ. 1782 (Götz, Mannheim)
Ded. to Countess Wolf-Metternich

WoO 65
Twenty-four Variations on Righini's Arietta
Venni amore, D
Allegretto (2/4)
c.1790–91; publ. 1791 (Schott, Mainz)
Ded. to Countess Hatzfeld. These remarkably
advanced variations were formerly thought to
exist only in a revised version of 1802, but recent
discovery of the original edition shows they
reached their final state as early as 1791
(Brandenburg, 1984c).

WoO 66
Thirteen Variations on 'Es war einmal ein
alter Mann' from Dittersdorf's *Das rote
Käppchen*, A
Allegretto (2/4)
1792; publ. 1793 (Simrock, Bonn)

WoO 64
Six Variations on a Swiss Song, F (for harp
or piano)
Andante con moto (4/4)
c.1790–92; publ. 1798(?) (Simrock, Bonn)

WoO 68
Twelve Variations on 'Menuett à la Vigano'
from Haibel's ballet *Le nozze disturbate*, C
Allegretto (4/4)
1795; publ. 1796 (Artaria, Vienna)

WoO 69
Nine Variations on 'Quant' è più bello'
from Paisiello's *La molinara*, C
Allegretto (2/4)
1795; publ. 1795 (Traeg, Vienna)
Ded. to Prince Lichnowsky

WoO 70
Six Variations on 'Nel cor più non mi sento'
from Paisiello's *La molinara*, G (6/8)
1795; publ. 1796 (Traeg, Vienna)

WoO 72
Eight Variations on 'Une fièvre brûlante'
from Grétry's *Richard Coeur de Lion*, C
Allegretto (3/4)
1795(?); publ. 1798 (Traeg, Vienna)

WoO 71
Twelve Variations on a Russian Dance
from Wranitzky's *Das Waldmädchen*, A
Allegretto (2/4)
1796–7; publ. 1797 (Artaria, Vienna)
Ded. to Countess Browne

WoO 73
Ten Variations on 'La stessa, la
stessissima' from Salieri's *Falstaff*, B♭
Andante con moto (2/2)
1799; publ. 1799 (Artaria, Vienna)
Ded. to Countess Keglevics

WoO 76
Six Variations on 'Tändeln und Scherzen'
from Süssmayr's *Soliman II*, F
Andante quasi Allegretto (3/8)
1799; publ. 1799 (Hoffmeister, Vienna)
Ded. to Countess Browne

WoO 75
Seven Variations on 'Kind, willst du ruhig

schlafen?' from Winter's *Das unterbrochene Opferfest*, F
Allegretto (2/4)
1799; publ. 1799 (Mollo, Vienna)

WoO 77
Six Variations on an Original Theme, G
Andante quasi Allegretto (2/4)
1800; publ. 1800 (Traeg, Vienna)

Op. 34
Six Variations on an Original Theme, F
Adagio (2/4)
1802; publ. 1803 (Breitkopf & Härtel, Leipzig)
Ded. to Princess Odescalchi (*née* Keglevics)

Op. 35
Fifteen Variations and a Fugue on an Original Theme (*Prometheus* Variations), E♭
Introduzione col Basso del Tema: Allegretto vivace (2/4)
1802; publ. 1803 (Breitkopf & Härtel, Leipzig)
Ded. to Prince Lichnowsky; theme from *Die Geschöpfe des Prometheus*, op. 43, and used also in Contredanse no. 7 from WoO 14 and in the *Eroica* Symphony. Commonly known as the 'Eroica' Variations, but Beethoven intended them to have a title referring to *Prometheus*.

WoO 78
Seven Variations on *God Save the King*, C
(3/4)
1802–3; publ. 1804 (Bureau des Arts et d'Industrie, Vienna)
Theme used again in *Wellingtons Sieg*, op. 91 (see p. 222)

WoO 79
Five Variations on 'Rule, Britannia' from *Alfred* (Thomas Arne), D
Tempo moderato (2/4)
1803; publ. 1804 (Bureau des Arts et d'Industrie, Vienna)
Theme used again in *Wellingtons Sieg*, op. 91 (see p. 222)

WoO 80
Thirty-two Variations on an Original Theme, c
Allegretto (3/4)
1806; publ. 1807 (Bureau des Arts et d'Industrie, Vienna)

Op. 76
Six Variations on an Original Theme, D
Allegro risoluto (2/4)
1809; publ. 1810 (Breitkopf & Härtel, Leipzig)
Ded. to Franz Oliva; theme used again for Turkish March (no. 4) in *Die Ruinen von Athen*, op. 113

Op. 120
Thirty-three Variations on a Waltz by Diabelli, C
Vivace (3/4)
1819 and 1823; publ. 1823 (Diabelli, Vienna)
Ded. to Antonie Brentano

III Other pieces

WoO 48
Rondo, C
Allegretto (3/8)
1783; publ. 1783 (Bossler, Speyer)

WoO 49
Rondo, A
Allegretto (2/4)
1783(?); publ. 1784 (Bossler, Speyer)

Op. 39
Two Preludes through all twelve major keys
No. 1: C (4/4)
No. 2: C (2/2)
1789(?); publ. 1803 (Hoffmeister, Leipzig)

WoO 81
Allemande, A (3/8)
c.1793, rev. 1822; publ. posth.

Op. 129
Rondo a capriccio ('The Rage over the Lost Penny'), G
Allegro vivace (2/4)
1795; publ. posth.
Incomplete; completed by an unknown editor (probably Diabelli)

Hess 64
Fugue, C (4/4)
1795; publ. posth.

WoO 52
Presto, c (3/4)
c.1795, rev. 1798 and 1822; publ. posth.
Originally intended for Piano Sonata op. 10 no. 1

Anh. 6
Rondo, B♭ (6/8)
c.1795–6? Probably spurious

Hess 69
Allegretto, c (3/4)
c.1795–6, rev. 1822; publ. posth.
Perhaps originally intended for Piano Sonata op. 10 no. 1

WoO 53
Allegretto, c (3/4)
1796–7; publ. posth.
Perhaps originally intended for Piano Sonata op.
10 no. 1

Op. 51, no. 1
Rondo, C
Moderato e grazioso (2/4)
c.1796–7; publ. 1797 (Artaria, Vienna)

Op. 51, no. 2
Rondo, G
Andante cantabile e grazioso (2/4)
c.1798; publ. 1802 (Artaria, Vienna)
Ded. to Countess Henriette Lichnowsky

Op. 33
Seven Bagatelles
1. E♭, Andante grazioso quasi Allegretto (6/8); 2.
C, Scherzo: Allegro (3/4); 3. F, Allegretto (6/8); 4.
A, Andante (2/4); 5. C, Allegro ma non troppo
(3/4); 6. D, Allegretto quasi andante (3/4); 7. A♭,
Presto (3/4)
1801–2; publ. 1803 (Bureau des Arts et
d'Industrie, Vienna)

WoO 54
Lustig-Traurig, **C**
Lustig (3/8) – Traurig (c, 3/8)
1802(?); publ. posth.

WoO 57
Andante ('Andante favori'), F
Andante grazioso con moto (3/8)
1803; publ. 1805 (Bureau des Arts et d'Industrie,
Vienna)
Originally intended as the slow movement for
Piano Sonata op. 53. According to Czerny, the
title 'Andante favori' (which is first found in an
1807 reprint) was given by Beethoven himself
when the work became popular.

WoO 56
Allegretto, C (3/4)
1803, rev. 1822; publ. posth.

WoO 55
Prelude, f (3/2)
c.1803; publ. 1805 (Bureau des Arts et
d'Industrie, Vienna)

WoO 82
Minuet, E♭
Moderato (3/4)
c.1803; publ. 1805 (Bureau des Arts et
d'Industrie, Vienna)

WoO 83
Six Ecossaises
See 'Dance music' (p. 224).

Op. 77
Fantasia, g
Allegro/Poco Adagio (4/4)
1809; publ. 1810 (Clementi, London)
Ded. to Count Brunsvik; commissioned by
Clementi

WoO 59
Bagatelle: *Für Elise*, a
Poco moto (3/8)
1808 or 1810; publ. posth.
Autograph missing, but 'Elise' probably denotes
Therese Malfatti. A revised but slightly
fragmentary version from 1822 also survives
(Cooper, 1984 and 1991).

Op. 89
Polonaise, C
Alla polacca, vivace (3/4)
1814; publ. 1815 (Mechetti, Vienna)
Ded. to Empress of Russia

WoO 60
Bagatelle, B♭
Ziemlich lebhaft (3/4)
1818; publ. 1824 (Schlesinger, Berlin)

Hess 65
See 'Arrangements' (p. 273)

WoO 61
Allegretto, b (2/2)
1821; publ. posth.
Ded. to Ferdinand Piringer

Op. 119
Eleven Bagatelles
1. g, Allegretto (3/4); 2. C, Andante con moto
(2/4); 3. D, à l'Allemande (3/8); 4. A, Andante
cantabile (4/4); 5. c, Risoluto (6/8); 6. G, Andante
(3/4); 7. C, Allegro ma non troppo (3/4); 8. C,
Moderato cantabile (3/4); 9. a, Vivace moderato
(3/4); 10. A, Allegramente (2/4); 11. B♭, Andante
ma non troppo (4/4)
1820–22; nos 7–11 publ. 1821 (Starke, Vienna)
in vol. 3 of F. Starke's *Wiener Piano-Forte-Schule*;
nos 1–11 publ. 1823 (Clementi, London)
Some pieces were started as early as c.1794.

Op. 126
Six Bagatelles
1. G, Andante con moto cantabile e
compiacevole (3/4); 2. g, Allegro (2/4); 3. E♭
Andante cantabile e grazioso (3/8); 4. b, Presto
(2/2); 5. G, Quasi Allegretto (6/8); 6. E♭, Presto
(2/2)/Andante amabile e con moto (3/8)
1824; publ. 1825 (Schott, Mainz)

WoO 84
Waltz, E♭ (3/4)

1824; publ. 1824 (Müller, Vienna)
Ded. by publisher to Friedrich Demmer

WoO 61a
Allegretto quasi andante, g (2/4)
1825; publ. posth.
Ded. to Sarah Burney Page

WoO 85
Waltz, D (3/8)
1825; publ. 1825 (Müller, Vienna)
Ded. by publisher to Duchess Sophie of Austria

WoO 86
Ecossaise, E♭ (2/4)
1825; publ. 1825 (Müller, Vienna)
Ded. by publisher to Duchess Sophie of Austria

See also 'Arrangements' (pp. 274–5).

IV   Works for four hands

WoO 67
Eight Variations on a Theme by Count Waldstein, C
Andante con moto (4/4)
1792(?); publ. 1794 (Simrock, Bonn)

Op. 6
Sonata, D
Allegro molto (3/4) – Rondo: Moderato (4/4)
1796–7; publ. 1797 (Artaria, Vienna)

WoO 74
Six Variations on *Ich denke dein*, D
Andantino cantabile (2/2)
1799; rev. 1803; publ. 1805 (Bureau des Arts et d'Industrie, Vienna)
Ded. to the sisters Therese von Brunsvik and Josephine Deym; Beethoven wrote the theme to the opening stanza of Goethe's poem *Ich denke dein*.

Op. 45
Three Marches
1. C, Allegro ma non troppo (4/4); 2. E♭, Vivace (2/4); 3. D, Vivace (2/2)
1803; publ. 1804 (Bureau des Arts et d'Industrie, Vienna)
Ded. to Princess Maria Esterházy; commissioned by Count Browne

Op. 134
Arrangement of *Grosse Fuge*, op. 133
See 'Arrangements' (p. 273)

ANNE-LOUISE COLDICOTT

Stage music

Prometheus

DIE GESCHÖPFE DES PROMETHEUS (*The Creatures of Prometheus*) was an important work for Beethoven in two respects. It was the first major stage work by a composer hitherto known for his chamber music, a symphony and two piano concertos; and with ballet highly regarded in Vienna at that time, it was a considerable honour for Beethoven to receive this commission. Secondly, the subject matter, concerned with heroic action, was close to Beethoven's heart. It is an allegorical story enacted by gods and a hero, the legendary Prometheus, demonstrating the goodness of Nature, the potential of man and the loftiness of his destiny.

Prometheus, a higher being and the bringer of fire, gives life to two statues and then attempts to civilize them through knowledge. At first his two creations seem to take on a life of their own and he is tempted to destroy them. Daybreak brings new inspiration, and he shows them freshly-picked flowers and fruits. The 'creatures' are tamed by the beauty of Nature and follow Prometheus to the Temple of Apollo on Mount Parnassus. Prometheus presents them to Apollo, who is surrounded by gods and demigods, and appeals to him to grant them reason and feelings. At Apollo's command their sensibilities are aroused by music from Orpheus and Euterpe (nos 5 and 6), and Apollo invites them to him to learn about war and peace. Military music (no. 8) heralds the procession of Mars, the bringer of war, followed by Death, in the guise of Melpomene (the Muse of Tragedy), who predicts the same fate for the creatures as for the dead warriors. She reproaches Prometheus for having given them life, and in spite of their attempt to protect him, she kills him. As night falls the creatures call on the gods for help. The spectre of death vanishes with the coming of dawn and the entry of a young couple. The creatures lift up Prometheus's body (no. 10), and minor deities enter and form a nuptial procession as the couple bind the creatures together. At a sign from Apollo, Prometheus is praised for his endeavours and takes his place at the feet of the gods in the finale (Lawrence, 1950).

The ballet, containing an Overture, Introduction and sixteen numbers, was favourably received, with sixteen performances in 1801 and nine in 1802, even though an anonymous review in the *Zeitung für die elegante Welt* (19 May 1801) was less than complimentary. After criticizing Vigano's choreography, it reads (Schmidt-Görg, 1970, p. 212): 'The music, too, did not completely come up to expectations, notwithstanding some uncommon virtues.' Perhaps the writer could have mentioned here some interesting features of orchestration, such as the effective depiction of a storm in the Introduction, the solo cello and harp in no. 5, or the bassethorn in no. 14. 'His writing is too learned for a ballet and pays too little regard to the dancing. Everything is on too large a scale for a divertissement, which is what a ballet ought to be, and in the absence of suitable situations it was bound to remain fragmentary rather than becoming a whole . . .'. It is true that the series of dances does not produce an integrated whole, and with the demise of the ballet itself, the music, with the exception of the Overture, has fallen into neglect. However, the theme of the finale was destined to live on in the seventh of the Twelve Contredanses (WoO 14), in the Piano Variations op. 35, and in the fourth movement of the *Eroica* Symphony. The Overture is conservative, and unlike the later *Coriolan* has little to do with the dramatic action which follows; nonetheless it is a good example of an 18th-century work of its kind and maintains limited popularity.

Fidelio

In 1799 Beethoven had become aware of the onset of deafness. By 1802 his acceptance and struggle to come to terms with it was eloquently expressed in his Heiligenstadt Testament in which he affirmed a deeply-held belief that worthwhile goals can be attained only through great effort (see pp. 169–72). It is possible that his reaction to his deafness may have caused Beethoven to identify himself with heroic figures, and it is surely not coincidental that the next few years, often referred to as his 'heroic phase', saw the production of the oratorio *Christus am Oelberge*, the early version of the opera *Leonore/Fidelio*, the *Eroica* Symphony and the 'Appassionata' Sonata. All four are suffused with heroic characteristics, and the first two overtly portray the victory of good over evil, liberty (moral and physical) over captivity.

Beethoven was originally commissioned to write an opera, *Vestas Feuer*, in 1803, by the librettist Schikaneder, at that time director of the Theater an der Wien. He completed only two scenes before abandoning the text (in about December 1803) in favour of Sonnleithner's German translation of Bouilly's *Léonore*, already set in French by Gaveaux and being set in Italian by Paer. It was to engender three different versions and four separate overtures, finally finding its form as *Fidelio*, with a revised libretto by Treitschke, only in 1814.

The 1804–5 version was performed three times with the Overture now known as *Leonore* no. 2. It was not well received, so Beethoven revised it. The three acts were reduced to two, with the content of the individual numbers drastically cut, and a new Overture, *Leonore* no. 3, was written. The reason for the revival in 1814 was the renewed popularity of Beethoven's music generally, and in its new form, *Fidelio*, it was greeted enthusiastically.

Its new-found success was in part due to the allegorical association with the recent victory of the rest of Europe over Napoleon.

The plot of *Fidelio* unfolds in and around the prison in Seville, Spain. Florestan (tenor), a nobleman, has been unjustly imprisoned by his political opponent Pizarro (bass), the prison governor. Florestan's wife, Leonore (soprano), refusing to believe reports that he is already dead, determines to save him. Having disguised herself as a man, Fidelio, she has persuaded the jailor, Rocco (bass), to employ her as his assistant. As Act I opens, Jaquino (tenor), the porter, is declaring his love for Rocco's daughter, Marzelline (soprano), but her thoughts are for Fidelio. This results in a canonic quartet, 'Mir ist so wunderbar' ('A wondrous feeling fills me'), in which Marzelline sings of Fidelio's interest in her, Leonore expresses pity for Marzelline's misguided love, Jaquino laments losing Marzelline to a rival, and Rocco gives his approval to the 'match'. Leonore is forced to go along with the situation, and uses it to her advantage, offering Rocco help with the prisoners in the dungeons. He is grateful for the offer and proposes to ask Pizarro's permission, but he warns that Fidelio must not go near one particular prisoner who is on the verge of death. Martial music announces the arrival of Pizarro, who hears that the Minister Don Fernando (baritone) is coming to make an inspection because he has heard that prisoners are being held unjustly. Pizarro declares that Florestan must be destroyed, and in 'Ha, welch ein Augenblick' ('Ha! What a moment'), he gloats over the imminence of his revenge, while a chorus of guards and soldiers comments on his wicked plans. Pizarro unsuccessfully attempts to bribe Rocco to murder Florestan and then announces he will do it himself. Terror and despair strike the heart of Leonore, but in the moving aria 'Komm, Hoffnung' ('Come, Hope') she vows that her everlasting love for Florestan will give her strength. She persuades Rocco to allow the prisoners to walk in the courtyard. In the finale to Act I the prisoners express their love of the fresh air, 'O welche Lust' ('Oh what delight'), Rocco asks Fidelio to help him dig the grave for the prisoner who is to be killed, and Pizarro's anger that the prisoners have been allowed outside is abated by Rocco's explanation that it was in honour of the King's name-day.

Florestan is seen for the first time in Act II. In the recitative 'Gott! Welch Dunkel hier' ('God! What darkness here'), he resigns himself to death, and in the ensuing aria 'In des Lebens Frühlingstagen' ('In the springtime of my life') he comforts himself that he has always done his duty, and imagines beside him an angel resembling Leonore. She and Rocco enter the cell to dig a grave in an old well. Only now does Florestan discover, from Rocco, who his captor is, and he begs in vain for a message to be sent to his wife. Pizarro arrives to kill Florestan. In the quartet 'Er sterbe! Doch er soll erst wissen' ('He shall die! But first he shall know') he reveals himself to Florestan in order to extract greater revenge, and then Leonore intervenes, revealing her true identity. She is threatening to shoot Pizarro when a trumpet call heralds the arrival of Don Fernando. The quartet ends with Leonore, Florestan and Rocco expressing relief and gladness, and Pizarro cursing with anger and fear. Leonore and Florestan are left alone and embrace each other, singing the ecstatic duet 'O namenlose Freude' ('Oh joy beyond expressing'). For the finale, the scene shifts to the parade ground outside the prison, where Don Fernando announces that he has been sent by the King to end tyranny and see that justice is done. He is surprised to see his old friend, Florestan, whom he believed dead, and hears from Rocco an account of what has taken place. Pizarro is led away and Leonore is given the key to unlock her husband's chains. The opera ends with a hymn of praise in which the townspeople, prisoners and all the principal characters, apart from Pizarro, praise the virtues of love and faith.

Fidelio has not always received the acclaim it deserves. This may be due more to the subject matter and to the necessity of gloomy staging than to the quality of the music. The atmosphere is one of human suffering, relieved only at the very end. The opera concludes with a simple hymn, a logical consequence of the relief from grief, passion and tension, but also one of several features which have led critics to say that Beethoven was unable to conceive the work in purely operatic terms. The hymn is in the key of C major, a key often symbolic of the triumph of hope over despair for Beethoven. Whereas all three *Leonore* Overtures were in that key, the new overture *Fidelio* is in E major. There is, however, a large-scale logic in this: it is a bright key, and anticipates the tonality of Leonore's aria of hope and heroism, 'Komm, Hoffnung'. In fact it is also prominent in *Leonore* Overtures 2 and 3 at the point where Florestan's main aria is foreshadowed. Strangely, the overture *Fidelio* does not allude to the musical content of the ensuing drama, as was the case with the other three overtures.

The problems which Beethoven encountered in the opera may have been due in part to the difficulty he had in keeping the whole in view because of his preoccupation with certain areas. For example, Florestan's recitative and aria at the beginning of Act II were radically reworked at both revisions. That they gave him particular trouble may have been because the sentiments reflected his own personal situation – his sense of isolation and his hope of rescue by a loving wife.

The opera is perhaps best summed up in the words of Thomas Love Peacock, writing in the *Examiner* (27 May 1832) after the first London performance:

Fidelio combined the profoundest harmony with melody that speaks to the soul. It carries to a pitch scarcely conceivable the true musical expression of the strongest passions and the gentlest emotions, in all their shades and contrasts. The playfulness of youthful hope, the heroism of devoted love, the rage of the tyrant, the despair of the captive, the bursting of the sunshine of liberty upon the gloom of the dungeons, which are the great outlines of the feelings successively developed in this opera, are portrayed in music, not merely with truth of expression, as that term might be applied to other works, but with a force and reality that make music an intelligible language, possessing an illimitable power of pouring forth thought in sound.

But what of the overture *Leonore* no. 1, op. 138? Firstly, its late opus number is misleading: it arises from the fact that the work came to light only at the auction of Beethoven's effects after his death. Secondly, it was long considered to be the earliest attempt because it cannot be associated with any of the three series of productions, and, indeed, when it was first published by Haslinger in 1838 he assigned it to 1805. Since then, however, Alan Tyson has conclusively proved that it was written in 1807, probably for a projected performance of the opera in Prague (Tyson, 1975, pp. 292–334). When that fell through, Beethoven laid the opera aside until 1814, when he composed the new overture *Fidelio*.

Egmont

That Beethoven found inspiration in Goethe's tragedy *Egmont* is hardly surprising. The theme of national liberation was one with which in 1809 he could easily identify, and the ideals embodied in the drama are similar to those in *Fidelio*, albeit with a different outcome. The story is set in the 16th century when Flanders was under Spanish rule. Count Egmont, a Flemish nobleman, is in love with Clärchen. He desires a more liberal treatment of his people, but although he adopts a moderate attitude in his attempts to mediate between the tyrannical Duke of Alba, the governor, and the extreme Calvinists in the Netherlands, he incurs Alba's enmity. He is captured and executed. This had been foreseen by Clärchen, who, after an unsuccessful attempt to rescue him, poisons herself. Egmont's death is both a tragedy and a triumph: a triumph because his spirit lives on to inspire the successful uprising of his people against their oppressors.

Beethoven's Overture is well known and popular. It opens in the dark key of F minor, with a dramatic, slow introduction which foreshadows the second subject. In the Allegro the agitated first subject, portraying conflict, consists of a descending cello phrase which does not settle and a short motif in the upper strings. The second-subject theme has been described as a 'destiny' figure. It could equally well be synonymous with Egmont or 'liberty'. In the recapitulation its rhythmic pattern becomes even stronger, and alternates with a quiet phrase implying that the cause of freedom has temporarily failed. The last time it breaks off dramatically. This point is usually associated with Egmont's execution. Suddenly the minor tonality changes to the major for a spirited coda signifying victory.

The ensuing numbers are less well known since away from the play they do not form a coherent whole. Only the final Victory Symphony recalls material from the Overture: the F major music from the coda. The seventh number, which describes Clärchen's death, is particularly noteworthy. Clärchen is depicted by a poignant oboe phrase and a chromatic figure in the violins, to the accompaniment of pulsating quavers. The music is very soft until there is a crescendo to a *sforzando* note at the point of her death, after which descending chromatic phrases become increasingly fragmentary, and the movement ends *ppp* with a string pizzicato chord.

Other stage works

It was decided to celebrate the opening of a new theatre in Pest, originally planned for 1811 but postponed until 1812, with a series of dramas based on subjects from Hungarian history. After Collin declined the invitation to write the plays, it went to Kotzebue. He wrote *König Stephan* (*King Stephen*) (or *Ungarns erster Wohltäter: Hungary's First Benefactor*) as the Prologue, and *Die Ruinen von Athen* (*The Ruins of Athens*) as the Epilogue. Beethoven, as the foremost composer, was invited to write the music for them, which he did rapidly during the summer of 1811. The themes of the plays were overtly nationalistic and intended to flatter the Emperor, but they did little to inspire Beethoven. *König Stephan*, op. 117, begins as a celebration of King Stephen but is transformed into a eulogy of the Emperor and his wife; and *Die Ruinen von Athen*, op. 113, glorifies Pest at the expense of Athens, which had been overrun by the Turks. Neither the text nor the music was of the highest standard. The music, scored for soloists, chorus and orchestra, is ceremonial and consists of a series of musical numbers separated by spoken dialogue, in the manner of a Singspiel. Only the overtures are occasionally played.

Die Weihe des Hauses (*The Consecration of the House*) was the play which marked the opening of the newly-built Josephstadt Theatre in Vienna in 1822. The director, Hensler, asked Carl Meisl to adapt the text of *The Ruins of Athens*, making it relevant to Vienna rather than Pest, and Beethoven was commissioned to adapt the music. He wrote a new Overture (op. 124) and a chorus with solo soprano

and violin (WoO 98). The adaptation of the March (no. 6) was to become known independently as op. 114. Beethoven's music, like that for opp. 113 and 117, was not his best, and only the Overture still receives occasional performances. It is a testimony to his high regard for Handel, with a grand, slow introduction and a fugal allegro. At the first performance Beethoven directed from the piano. Although his deafness made this an almost hopeless task, he received an enthusiastic reception from an audience who wished to pay tribute to a great composer.

WoO 1
Musik zu einem Ritterballett
Ballet
1. March; 2. German Song; 3. Hunting Song; 4. Love Song; 5. War Dance; 6. Drinking Song; 7. German Song; 8. Coda
pic, 2 cl, 2 hn, 2 tpt, timp, str
1790–91; first perf. 6 March 1791; publ. posth.
Originally thought to have been by Count Waldstein

WoO 91
Two arias: 'O welch ein Leben', F; 'Soll ein Schuh nicht drücken?', B♭
ST soli; fl, 2 ob, 2 bn, 2 hn, str
c.1795; first perf. *c*.1796; publ. posth.
Written for Umlauf's Singspiel *Die schöne Schusterin*. The theme of no. 1 was also used in the song *Maigesang*, op. 52 no. 4.

Op. 43
Die Geschöpfe des Prometheus
Ballet
Overture, C (Adagio – Allegro molto con brio); Introduction: La Tempesta; 1. Poco adagio – Allegro con brio; 2. Adagio – Allegro con brio; 3. Allegro vivace; 4. Maestoso – Andante; 5. Adagio – Andante quasi Allegretto; 6. Un poco Adagio – Allegro; 7. Grave; 8. Allegro con brio; 9. Adagio; 10. Pastorale; 11. Andante; 12. Solo di Gioja; 13. Allegro; 14. Solo della Cassentini; 15. Solo di Vigano; 16. Finale
2 fl, 2 ob, 2 cl/bhn, 2 bn, 2 hn, 2 tpt, timp, harp, str
1800–1; first perf. 28 March 1801; piano arr. publ. 1801 (see 'Arrangements', p. 274), Overture publ. 1804 (Hoffmeister, Leipzig), complete work publ. posth.
Ded. to Princess Christiane von Lichnowsky; commissioned by Salvatore Vigano, court ballet master

Hess 115
Vestas Feuer
See 'Unfinished and projected works' (p. 276)

Op. 72

(i) *Leonore* (Joseph Sonnleithner)
Opera, with overture *Leonore* no. 2
Overture, C (Andante con moto – Allegro con brio)

Act I	Aria (Marzelline) 'O, wär ich schon'
	2. Duet (Marzelline, Jaquino) 'Jetzt, Schätzen, jetzt'
	3. Trio (Marzelline, Jaquino, Rocco) 'Ein Mann ist bald genommen'
	4. Quartet (Marzelline, Leonore, Jaquino, Rocco) 'Mir is so wunderbar'
	5. Aria (Rocco) 'Hat man nicht auch Gold'
	6. Trio (Marzelline, Leonore, Rocco) 'Gut, Söhnchen, gut'
Act II	7. March
	8. Aria (Pizarro) with Chorus 'Ha, welch ein Augenblick'
	9. Duet (Pizarro, Rocco) 'Jetzt, Alter'
	10. Duet (Marzelline, Leonore) 'Um in der Ehe'
	11. Recit. and Aria (Leonore) 'Ach, brich noch nicht' – 'Komm, Hoffnung'
	12. Finale (Prisoners, Marzelline, Leonore, Pizarro, Rocco) 'O welche Lust'
Act III	13. Introduction, Recit. and Aria (Florestan) 'Gott, welch Dunkel' – 'In des Lebens Frühlingstagen'
	14. Duet (Leonore, Rocco) 'Nur hurtig fort'
	15. Trio (Leonore, Florestan, Rocco) 'Euch werde Lohn'
	16. Quartet (Leonore, Florestan, Pizarro, Rocco) 'Er sterbe!'
	17. Recit. and Duet (Leonore, Florestan) 'Ich kann mich noch nicht fassen' – 'O namenlose Freude'
	18. Finale (Prisoners, townspeople, Leonore, Marzelline, Florestan, Pizarro, Rocco, Don Fernando, Jaquino) 'Zur Rache'

1804–5; first perf. 20 November 1805; publ. posth.

(ii) *Leonore*
Opera (revised by Stephan von Breuning), with overture *Leonore* no. 3
Overture, C (Adagio – Allegro)

Act I	1. Aria (Marzelline) 'O wär ich schon'
	2. Duet (Marzelline, Jaquino) 'Jetzt, Schätzen, jetzt'
	3. Quartet (Leonore, Marzelline, Jaquino, Rocco) 'Mir ist so wunderbar'
	4. Trio (Marzelline, Leonore, Rocco) 'Gut, Söhnchen, gut'
	5. March
	6. Aria (Pizarro) with Chorus 'Ha, welch ein Augenblick'
	7. Duet (Pizarro, Rocco) 'Jetzt, Alter'
	8. Recit. and Aria (Leonore) 'Ach, brich noch nicht' – 'Komm, Hoffnung'
	9. Duet (Marzelline, Leonore) 'Um in der Ehe'
	10. Trio (Marzelline, Jaquino, Rocco) 'Ein Mann ist bald genommen'
	11. Finale (Prisoners, Marzelline, Leonore, Pizarro, Rocco) 'O welche Lust'
Act II	12. Introduction, Recit. and Aria (Florestan) 'Gott! welch Dunkel' – 'In des Lebens Frühlingstagen'
	13. Duet (Leonore, Rocco) 'Nur hurtig fort'
	14. Trio (Leonore, Florestan, Rocco) 'Euch werde Lohn'
	15. Quartet (Leonore, Florestan, Pizarro, Rocco) 'Er sterbe!'
	16. Recit. and Duet (Leonore, Florestan) 'Ich kann mich noch nicht fassen' – 'O namenlose Freude'
	17. Finale (Prisoners, townspeople, Leonore, Marzelline, Florestan, Pizarro, Rocco, Don Fernando, Jaquino) 'Zur Rache'

1805–6; first perf. 29 March 1806; vocal score (without Overture and finales) publ. 1810 (Breitkopf & Härtel, Leipzig), complete work publ. posth.

(iii) *Fidelio*
Opera (*Leonore* revised by Friedrich Treitschke), with overture *Fidelio*
Overture, E (Allegro)

Act I	1. Duet (Marzelline, Jaquino) 'Jetzt, Schätzen, jetzt'
	2. Aria (Marzelline) 'O wär ich schon'
	3. Quartet (Marzelline, Leonore, Jaquino, Rocco) 'Mir ist so wunderbar'
	4. Aria (Rocco) 'Hat man nicht auch Gold'
	5. Trio (Marzelline, Leonore, Rocco) 'Gut, Söhnchen, gut'
	6. March

7. Aria (Pizarro) with Chorus 'Ha, welch ein Augenblick'
8. Duet (Pizarro, Rocco) 'Jetzt, Alter'
9. Recit. and Aria (Leonore) 'Abscheulicher! Wo eilst du hin?' – 'Komm, Hoffnung'
10. Finale (Prisoners, Marzelline, Leonore, Jaquino, Pizarro, Rocco) 'O welche Lust'

Act II
11. Introduction, Recit. and Aria (Florestan) 'Gott! welch Dunkel' – 'In des Lebens Frühlingstagen'
12. Melodrama and duet (Leonore, Rocco) 'Wie kalt ist es' – 'Nur hurtig fort'
13. Trio (Leonore, Florestan, Rocco) 'Euch werde Lohn'
14. Quartet (Leonore, Florestan, Pizarro, Rocco) 'Er sterbe!'
15. Duet (Leonore, Florestan) 'O namelose Freude'
16. Finale (Prisoners, townspeople, Leonore, Marzelline, Florestan, Pizarro, Rocco, Don Fernando) 'Heil sei dem Tag'

SSTTBBB soli, SATTBB ch; pic, 2 fl, 2 ob, 2 cl, 2 bn, cbn, 4 hn, 2 tpt, 2 tbn (3 in *Leonore*), timp, str
1814; first perf. 23 May 1814 (ov. first perf. 26 May); publ. 1826 (Farrenc, Paris)
Originally commissioned by the Theater an der Wien

Op. 138
Overture: *Leonore* no. 1, C
(Andante con moto – Allegro con brio)
2 fl, 2 ob, 2 cl, 2 bn, 4 hn, 2 tpt, timp, str
1807; first perf. 7 Februrary 1828; publ. posth.

Op. 62
Overture: *Coriolan*
See 'Concertos and other orchestral music' (p. 222)

Op. 84
Egmont (Johann Wolfgang von Goethe)
Overture and incidental music
Overture, f (Sostenuto ma non troppo – Allegro); 1. Aria (Clärchen) 'Die Trommel gerühret'; 2. Zwischenakt I; 3. Zwischenakt II; 4. Aria (Clärchen) 'Freudvoll und leidvoll'; 5. Zwischenakt III; 6. Zwischenakt IV; 7. Musik, Clärchens Tod bezeichnend; 8. Melodrama (Egmont) 'Süsser Schlaf!'; 9. Siegessymphonie
S solo, male v (spoken); 2 fl/pic, 2 ob, 2 cl, 2 bn, 4 hn, 2 tpt, timp, sd, str
1809–10; first perf. 15 June 1810; Overture publ. 1810 (Breitkopf & Härtel, Leipzig), remainder publ. posth.

Op. 113
Die Ruinen von Athen (August von Kotzebue)
Singspiel
Overture, g–G (Andante con moto – Allegro ma non troppo); 1. Chorus 'Tochter des mächtigen Zeus!'; 2. Duet (Greek man and woman) 'Ohne Verschulden'; 3. Chorus (Dervishes) 'Du hast in deines Armels'; 4. Marcia alla Turca; 5. Musik hinter der Scene; 6. March, Chorus and Recit. (High Priest) 'Schmückt die Altäre' – 'Mit reger Freude'; 7. Chorus and Aria (High Priest) 'Wir tragen empfängliche Herzen' – 'Will unser Genius'; 8. Chorus 'Heil unserm König'
SB soli, SATB ch; pic, 2 fl, 2 ob, 2 cl, 2 bn, cbn, 4 hn, 2 tpt, 3 tbn, timp, perc. str
1811; first perf. 10 February 1812; Overture publ. 1823 (Steiner, Vienna), complete version publ. posth.
Complete version ded. by publisher (Artaria) to King Friedrich Wilhelm IV of Prussia.
Commissioned for the opening of the Hungarian Theatre at Pest

Op. 117
König Stephan (August von Kotzebue)
Singspiel
Overture, E♭ (Andante con moto – Presto); 1. Chorus (men) 'Ruhend von seinen Taten'; 2. Chorus (men) 'Auf dunklem Irrweg'; 3. Siegesmarsch; 4. Chorus (women) 'Wo die Unschuld'; 5. Melodrama (Stephan) 'Du hast dein Vaterland'; 6. Chorus 'Eine neue strahlende Sonne'; 7. Melodrama (Stephan) 'Ihr edlen Ungarn'; 8. March, Chorus and Melodrama (Stephan) 'Heil unserm Könige' – 'Ich schmücke ehrfurchtsvoll'; 9. Chorus 'Heil unsern Enkeln'
Male and female v (spoken), SSATTBB ch; pic, 2 fl, 2 ob, 2 cl, 2 bn, cbn, 4 hn, 2 tpt, 3 tbn, timp, str
1811; first perf. 10 February 1812; Overture publ. 1826 (Steiner, Vienna); complete work publ. posth.
Commissioned for the opening of the Hungarian Theatre at Pest

WoO 2
Two orchestral pieces for *Tarpeja* (tragedy by Christoph Kuffner)
Triumphmarsch (C, 4/4); Introduction to Act II (D, 4/4)
2 fl, 2 ob, 2 cl, 2 bn, 2/4 hn, 2 tpt, timp, str
1813; first perf. 26 March 1813; publ. posth.
The second piece was possibly written for Act II of a different work.

WoO 96
Leonore Prohaska (Friedrich Duncker)
Incidental music
1. Chorus (warriors) 'Wir bauen und sterben'; 2. Romanze (soprano) 'Es blüht eine Blume'; 3.

Melodrama 'Du, dem sie gewunden'; 4.
Trauermarsch
S solo, spoken v, TTBB ch; 2 fl, 2 cl, 2 bn, 4 hn,
timp, harp, armonica, str
1815; publ. posth.
Written for drama by Duncker. No. 4 arranged
from piano sonata op. 26

WoO 94
'Germania'
Aria, B♭
B solo, SATB ch; 2 fl, 2 ob, 2 cl, 2 bn, 2 hn, 2
tpt, timp, str
1814; first perf. 11 April 1814; vocal score publ.
1814 (Hoftheater Musik-Verlage, Vienna);
complete version publ. posth.
Written for Treitschke's Singspiel *Die gute
Nachricht*

WoO 97
'Es ist vollbracht'
Aria, D
B solo, SATB ch; 2 fl, 2 ob, 2 cl, 2 bn, 2 hn, 2
tpt, 2 tbn, timp, str
1815; first perf. 15 July 1815; vocal score publ.
1815 (Steiner, Vienna); complete version publ.
posth.
Written for Treitschke's Singspiel *Die Ehrenpforten*

Op. 124
Overture: *Die Weihe des Hauses*, C
Maestoso e sostenuto – Allegro con brio
2 fl, 2 ob, 2 cl, 2 bn, 4 hn, 2 tpt, 3 tbn, timp, str
1822; first perf. 3 October 1822; publ. 1825
(Schott, Mainz)
Ded. to Prince Galitzin; commissioned by
Hensler for the opening of the Josephstadt
Theatre, Vienna

WoO 98
Chorus 'Wo sich die Pulse' (Carl Meisl) for
Die Weihe des Hauses
S solo, SATB ch; 2 fl, 2 ob, 2 cl, 2 bn, 4 hn, 2
tpt, timp, str
1822; first perf. 3 October 1822; publ. posth.
See op. 124 above.

Op. 114
March with Chorus for *Die Weihe des Hauses*
SATB ch; pic, 2 fl, 2 ob, 2 cl, 2 bn, 2 hn, 2 tpt, 3
tbn, timp, str
1822 adaptation of no. 6 from *Die Ruinen von
Athen*; first perf. 3 October 1822; publ. 1826
(Steiner, Vienna)

Hess 118
Music for *Die Weihe des Hauses*
See 'Arrangements' (p. 274)

ANNE-LOUISE COLDICOTT

Choral music, vocal music with orchestra, canons

THE MUSIC LISTED in this section is very varied, ranging from the monumental *Missa Solemnis*, which was described by Beethoven in 1824 as 'my greatest work' (Letter 1270), to trivial and ephemeral canons only four bars long. In between there is a great variety of forms and genres, with much of the music having been written rapidly to suit particular sets of circumstances. Specifically excluded in the section are all stage works (whether or not they have chorus), and certain Lieder and folksongs that have simple choral refrains.

Major choral works

The three major large-scale choral works are the oratorio *Christus am Oelberge* (*Christ on the Mount of Olives*), the Mass in C and the Mass in D, commonly known as the *Missa Solemnis*. *Christus* was begun in late 1802 (or possibly early 1803), shortly after Beethoven's emotional crisis that had led to depths of despair and resulted in the Heiligenstadt Testament of 6–10 October 1802. Many of the ideas contained in the Heiligenstadt Testament are closely echoed in the oratorio, and Beethoven may have chosen this text deliberately as a means of expressing his personal suffering in a universal way. The oratorio was also written hard on the heels of Haydn's two great oratorios – *The Creation* and *The Seasons* (first performed in 1798 and 1801 respectively), which no doubt influenced Beethoven's decision to write a work of this kind. *Christus* was first performed on 5 April 1803 and was revised the following year, but it was not published until 1811. Opinion about its merits has remained divided. It was very popular during the 19th century, but more recently many writers have expressed reservations. Some describe it as uneven in quality, though there is no agreement about which are the weaker sections; others view it as all on a level, with nothing very outstanding. A contrasting and perhaps more correct view is that it is a very fine work containing some masterly passages. In the Seraph's aria, for instance, there is a wonderful sense of increasing tension after a gentle opening, with the entry of the choir halfway through, the addition of coloratura for the soloist, then the dramatic addition of the trombones as the speed increases for the second time, building up to a fearful climax on a prolonged diminished seventh at 'Verdammung ist ihr Los' ('damnation is their fate'). These and many other excellent ideas suggest the work deserves to be heard far more often.

The Mass in C was commissioned in 1807 by Prince Nikolaus Esterházy to celebrate the name-day of his wife (8 September). The event had been celebrated on several previous occasions by a newly commissioned mass by Haydn, and so Beethoven, perhaps in an effort to escape direct comparison with his former tutor, consciously set the text 'in a manner in which it has rarely been treated' (Letter 167). It certainly shows many highly original touches, even right from the outset, where it begins with unaccompanied chorus basses. As with *Christus am Oelberge*, opinions about its worth have differed. For Beethoven himself the work was 'especially dear to my heart', whereas Prince Esterházy, after hearing the first performance on 13 September 1807, described it as 'unbearably ridiculous and detestable'. It has since become overshadowed by the *Missa Solemnis*, but it has nevertheless won a regular place in the choral repertory and is widely loved and admired.

The *Missa Solemnis* is a monumental work in every sense, and stands beside Bach's B minor Mass as one of the two towering pinnacles in the whole history of the genre. It cost Beethoven more time and energy than any other work, with the possible exception of *Fidelio*, and took nearly four years from conception to completion. Begun at least as early as April 1819 (Winter, 1984), the Mass was originally intended to be used at the installation of Beethoven's friend and pupil Archduke Rudolph as Archbishop of Olmütz on 9 March 1820. Beethoven's hopes of completing the work in time persisted until early 1820, but in the event he had reached only as far as the Credo when the day arrived. Nevertheless he continued to work on the Mass for the rest of the year and it was nearly complete by the autumn, after which he worked on it more sporadically. A score was in existence by May 1822 at the latest, but minor revisions continued to be made, and not until 19 March 1823 did he finally present Rudolph with a fair copy. Meanwhile protracted negotations took place with several publishers, and at one stage he planned to write two further masses to satisfy all their interest; the work was eventually sold to Schott's for 1000 fl. Manuscript copies were also sold (at 50 ducats each) to ten subscribers: the Czar of Russia, the Kings of Prussia, France and Denmark, the Elector of Saxony, the Grand Dukes of Hesse-Darmstadt and Tuscany, Princes Galitzin and Radziwill, and the Caecilia Society of Frankfurt.

Beethoven's extensive – and intensive – sketching of the Mass in several sketchbooks resulted in a work of extreme complexity and subtlety, motivically, harmonically, tonally, and symbolically. Yet it is not a merely intellectual creation: it is also highly emotional in content. 'My chief aim when I was composing this grand Mass', he wrote, 'was to awaken and permanently instil religious feelings not only into the singers but also into the listeners.' (Letter 1307) The music is aimed to speak directly even to the uninitiated, as is indicated by the inscription at the head of the Kyrie: 'Vom Herzen – Möge es wieder – zu Herzen gehn!' ('From the heart – may it return to the heart').

Beethoven achieved this directness of expression by imbuing individual words with music of exceptional vividness and intensity. Right at the opening word, the massed voices of choir and orchestra present a picture of an almighty 'Kyrie' (Lord), set against the lone voice of a single suppliant begging for mercy. In the Credo, words such as 'omnipotens' and 'descendit' are set with the obvious pictorial devices stretched to the limits of what is musically possible. Other places with similar direct appeal include the evocation of deep burial at 'sepultus est', the dramatic contrast between life and death at 'vivos et mortuos', the almost absurd emphasis on 'non' at 'cujus regni non erit finis', the deliberately faulty accentuation at 'peccatorum', and the soaring to seemingly impossible heights for the resurrection of the dead at 'resurrectionem mortuorum'. Less obvious is Beethoven's setting of the little word 'et' ('and'). Out of thousands of settings of the Mass text, this is perhaps the only one to make something significant and motivic out of the numerous repetitions of this word, thereby emphasizing the many facets of Christian belief. Also notable is the representation of the Holy Spirit at 'Et incarnatus': in the visual arts the Holy Spirit is often represented by a dove, which Beethoven here transforms to bird-calls on the flute.

The Sanctus and Benedictus are set to continuous music, but are separated by a Praeludium. In long choral masses, it was common for the Consecration and Elevation of the Host, where the Divine presence enters the bread and wine, to take place between the Sanctus and Benedictus, usually accompanied by quiet organ improvisation (Kirkendale, 1970). Beethoven has therefore substituted organ-like music that serves the same purpose; the Divine presence then enters, like a ray of light, as a high solo violin above a dark orchestral background at the end of the Praeludium, and remains throughout the Benedictus.

The final section (Dona nobis) is headed by Beethoven: 'Bitte um innern und äussern Frieden' ('Prayer for inward and outward peace'). Peace is depicted by the lilting 6/8 rhythm of an Arcadian countryside during most of the movement, but there are two threats. The first is external – the threat of war, portrayed by trumpets and drums, military rhythms, and extraneous musical material, in a contrasting episode. The second danger is the loss of inner emotional peace, expressed in an even more terrifying episode where the main 'Dona nobis' theme is itself distorted and torn apart. Only after desperate invocations to the 'Lamb of God', and pounding heartbeats, is peace once more restored.

Beethoven retained or even resurrected many of the traditional features of mass settings, but infused the genre with a new power, genius and ardour that make his work seem totally new in conception.

Thus the *Missa Solemnis* as a whole, perhaps more than any other piece of music, is a magnificent blend of artful sophistication at the highest level, profound emotion, and simple, direct appeal.

Lesser choral works

Although Beethoven's other choral works do not match the scale and importance of the three major ones, a number of them are of excellent quality. Of the two early cantatas, on the death of Joseph II and the accession of Leopold II, the former is much more noteworthy; despite its early date (spring 1790) it contains a great many features typical of the mature Beethoven and is quite an extended work. An even more substantial cantata is *Der glorreiche Augenblick* (*The Glorious Moment*), written for the Congress of Vienna in 1814 to celebrate the defeat of Napoleon; but the banal text and bombastic music have meant that the work has proved ineffective outside its original context. Rather more successful is the Choral Fantasia, though it, too, has its detractors. Written very hastily in December 1808 to conclude a long and weighty concert, the work was revised and polished up the following year in preparation for publication. It is highly original in its overall conception, conveying a remarkable sense of progress from darkness to light, from chaos to order, and it contains many features reused and built upon by Beethoven years later in the finale of the Ninth Symphony.

Among the other choral works, *Meeresstille und glückliche Fahrt* (*Calm Sea and Prosperous Voyage*) must be singled out for its vivid pictorialism and the way Goethe's two poems are so excellently contrasted. The exquisite *Elegischer Gesang* (*Elegiac Song*) for four voices (perhaps solo voices, but they are treated as a chorus), and the *Opferlied* and *Bundeslied*, though rarely performed, are also very fine. Each is scored with an unusual accompaniment – string quartet (*Elegischer Gesang*), mixed ensemble or small orchestra (the two versions of *Opferlied*) and wind sextet (*Bundeslied*) – a fact which no doubt militates against more frequent performances. Beethoven's choral writing as a whole is sometimes very demanding for the voices, especially in the *Missa Solemnis* and the Ninth Symphony, but the demands are no greater than those made on instruments, and it must also be remembered that pitch in his day was in general slightly below that of today, so that the extremely high notes of these two works were not meant to strain the voice quite as much as they do now.

Solo voices with orchestra

The small group of works for solo voice(s) and orchestra dates entirely from Beethoven's early period, and only two of them were published during his lifetime. Three date from as early as his Bonn days, although one of them, *Primo amore*, is so long and impressive that for many years it was believed to date from the late 1790s. All seven works are in the Italian operatic style, and five of them have Italian texts; but although some of the texts derive from opera libretti, Beethoven's settings were evidently intended for concert performance rather than use on stage. The last three works in the group were apparently written as the culmination of Beethoven's studies with Salieri – studies that had begun with the partsongs of WoO 99. They include a soprano aria, a soprano and tenor duet and a trio for soprano, tenor and bass (a fourth similar work from the same period, *Grazie agl'inganni*, was left unfinished). It is significant that his next vocal work, *Christus am Oelberge*, included an aria, a duet and a trio scored for precisely the same combinations of voices, and there is even a melodic resemblance between *Tremate, empi, tremate* (op. 116) and the trio 'In meinen Adern' in the oratorio. Thus the three Italian pieces can be thought of as preliminary exercises to prepare him for writing a fully-fledged opera or oratorio.

Canons

Beethoven learnt the art of writing canons during his studies with Albrechtsberger in 1794–5, but he only really took an interest in the genre from 1813 onwards. (The so-called 'Maelzel' Canon, WoO 162, supposedly written in 1812 to celebrate Maelzel's invention of the metronome, appears now to have been composed by Anton Schindler in the 1840s and attributed by him to Beethoven (Howell, 1979; Goldschmidt, 1984).) Most of them were written as little gifts or mementos for friends and acquaintances. Some have humorous texts, usually written by Beethoven himself and sometimes including a pun on the recipient's name, for example *Kühl, nicht lau* (*Cool, not lukewarm*), written for the composer Kuhlau at a very merry dinner party on 2 September 1825. Other texts are more philosophical, such as *Ars longa, vita brevis* (*Art is long, life is short*), for which there are three settings (WoO 170, 192, 193), and *Wir irren allesamt, nur jeder irret anderst* (*We all make mistakes, but everybody does so differently*), which was Beethoven's last completed composition. Almost all the canons are very short pieces consisting of two or more voices in strict imitation; occasionally there is a non-canonic accompaniment. Several are puzzle canons, a genre where the composer writes out only one voice and leaves the reader to puzzle out where the other voice or voices should enter, and Beethoven's friends seem to have enjoyed trying to solve such puzzles. In some cases there is more than one solution, including one or two which may possibly not have occurred to the composer, so that one cannot say for certain how many voices were originally intended in such canons.

The first words of the piece are given after the title and author, if they differ from the title.

I Works with chorus

WoO 87
Cantata on the Death of Emperor Joseph II
(Severin Anton Averdonk)
1. 'Todt! Todt!' (ch); 2. 'Ein Ungeheuer' (recit.) –
'Da kam Joseph' (aria); 3. 'Da stiegen die Mensch-
en' (aria with ch); 4. 'Er schläft' (recit.) – 'Hier
schlummert' (aria); 5. 'Todt! Todt!' (ch)
SATB soli; SATB ch; 2 fl, 2 ob, 2 cl, 2 bn, 2 hn,
str
March 1790; publ. posth.

WoO 88
**Cantata on the Accession of Emperor Leopold
II** (Severin Anton Averdonk)
1. 'Er schlummert' (recit. with ch) – 'Fliesse,
Wonnezähre' (aria); 2. 'Ihr staunt' (recit.); 3. 'Wie
bebt mein Herz' (recit.) – 'Ihr, die Joseph ihren
Vater' (trio); 4. 'Heil' (ch) – 'Stürzet nieder,
Millionen' (ch)
SATB soli; SATB ch; 2 fl, 2 ob, 2 cl, 2 bn, 2 hn, 2
tpt, timp, str
September–October 1790; publ. posth.

WoO 99
Italian Partsongs (mostly Pietro Metastasio)
'Bei labbri'; 'Chi mai di questo core'; 'Fra tutte le
pene' (3 settings); 'Gia la notte' (2 settings); 'Giura
il nocchier' (2 settings); 'Ma tu tremi'; 'Nei campi'
(2 settings); 'O care selve'; 'Per te d'amico'; 'Quella
cetra' (3 settings); 'Scrivo in te'; 'Silvio amante'
2, 3 and 4 voices unaccompanied
1801–2; publ. posth.
Some of the songs also appear in earlier versions,
and there are a few additional partsongs not part
of WoO 99 (Hess 208–32).

WoO 100
Lob auf den Dicken: Musikalischer Scherz
(probably Beethoven)
'Schuppanzigh ist ein Lump'
TBB soli; SATB ch (unaccompanied)
Late 1801; publ. posth.
A short, humorous composition for the violinist
Ignaz Schuppanzigh

WoO 101
**Graf, Graf, liebster Graf: Musikalischer
Scherz** (Beethoven)
'Graf, Graf, Graf'
SAA (unaccompanied)
Autumn 1802; publ. posth.
A short, humorous composition for Beethoven's
friend Nikolaus Zmeskall

Op. 85
Christus am Oelberge (Franz Xaver Huber)
1. Introduction (orch) – 'Jehovah, du mein Vater'
(recit.) – 'Meine Seele ist erschüttert' (aria); 2.
'Erzittre, Erde' (recit.) – 'Preist des Erlösers Güte'
(aria with ch); 3. 'Verkündet, Seraph' (recit.) –
'So ruhe denn' (duet); 4. 'Wilkommen, Tod'
(recit.) – 'Wir haben ihn gesehen' (ch); 5. 'Die
mich zu fangen' (recit.) – 'Hier ist er' (ch); 6.
'Nicht ungestraft' (recit.) – 'In meinen Adern'
(trio) – 'Welten singen' (ch) – 'Preiset ihn' (ch)
STB soli; SATB ch; 2 fl 2 ob, 2 cl, 2 bn, 2 hn, 2
tpt, 3 tbn, timp, str
Early 1803, rev. 1804; first perf. 5 April 1803; publ.
1811 (Breitkopf & Härtel, Leipzig)

Op. 86
Mass in C
1. Kyrie; 2. Gloria; 3. Credo; 4. Sanctus – Osanna;
5. Benedictus – Osanna; 6. Agnus Dei – Dona
SATB soli; SATB ch; 2 fl, 2 ob, 2 cl, 2 bn, 2 hn, 2
tpt, timp, str, org
Summer 1807; first perf. 13 September 1807; publ.
1812 (Breitkopf & Härtel, Leipzig)
Ded. to Prince Kinsky

Op. 80
Choral Fantasia (Christoph Kuffner?)
'Schmeichelnd hold'
SSATTB soli; SATB ch; pf solo; 2 fl, 2 ob, 2 cl, 2
bn, 2 hn, 2 tpt, timp, str
December 1808, rev. 1809; first perf. 22 December
1808; publ. 1811 (Breitkopf & Härtel, Leipzig)
Ded. to King Maximilian Joseph of Bavaria

WoO 102
Abschiedsgesang (Joseph von Seyfried)
'Die Stunde schlägt'
TBB (unaccompanied)
May 1814; publ. posth.
Written for Leopold Weiss

WoO 103
Un lieto brindisi: Cantata campestre
(Clemente Bondi)
'Johannisfeier begehn wir heute'
STTB; pf
June 1814; first perf. 24 June 1814; publ. posth.
Written for Giovanni Malfatti, originally with
Italian words. The surviving source has only a
German text, but Harry Goldschmidt has recon-
structed a version with the original Italian
(Goldschmidt, 1975).

Op. 118
Elegischer Gesang (Ignaz Franz von Castelli?)
'Sanft wie du lebtest'
SATB (soli?); str qt
July 1814; first perf. (?) 5 August 1814; publ. 1826
(Haslinger, Vienna)

Ded. to Baron Pasqualati, and written to commemorate the third anniversary of the death of his wife

WoO 95
Chor auf die verbündeten Fürsten (Carl Bernard)
'Ihr weisen Gründer'
SATB ch; 2 fl, 2 ob, 2 cl, 2 bn, 2 hn, 2 tpt, timp, str
September 1814; publ. posth.

Op. 136
Der glorreiche Augenblick (Aloys Weissenbach)
1. 'Europa steht' (ch); 2. 'O seht sie nah' (recit.) – 'Vienna' (ch); 3. 'O Himmel' (recit.) – 'Alle die Herrscher' (aria with ch); 4. 'Das Auge schaut' (recit.) – 'Dem die erste Zähre (aria with ch); 5. 'Der den Bund' (recit.) – 'In meinen Mauern' (quartet); 6. 'Es treten hervor' (ch)
SSTB soli; SSATB ch; pic, 2 fl, 2 ob, 2 cl, 2 bn, 4 hn, 2 tpt, 3 tbn, timp, perc, str
Autumn 1814; first perf. 29 November 1814; publ. posth.

Op. 112
Meeresstille und glückliche Fahrt (Johann Wolfgang von Goethe)
'Tiefe Stille herrscht im Wasser' – 'Die Nebel zerreissen'
SATB ch; 2 fl, 2 ob, 2 cl, 2 bn, 4 hn, 2 tpt, timp, str
1814–15; first perf. 25 December 1815; publ. 1822 (Steiner, Vienna)
Ded. to Goethe

WoO 104
Gesang der Mönche (Friedrich von Schiller)
'Rasch tritt der Tod den Menschen an'
TTB (unaccompanied)
May 1817; publ. posth.

WoO 105
Hochzeitslied (Anton Joseph Stein)
'Auf, Freunde, singt dem Gott'
Solo v, ch, pf
January 1819; publ. posth.
Written for the wedding of Leopold Schmerling and Anna Giannatasio del Rio (6 February 1819), the work exists in two versions. The one in C is set for solo voice and unison chorus (probably all male), with piano accompaniment; the one in A, probably later, is set for male voice solo, SATB chorus and piano. It is uncertain which version was performed for the wedding.

Op. 123
Missa Solemnis, D
1. Kyrie; 2. Gloria; 3. Credo; 4. Sanctus – Osanna – Praeludium – Benedictus; 5. Agnus Dei – Dona
SATB soli; SATB ch; 2 fl, 2 ob, 2 cl, 2 bn, cbn, 4 hn, 2 tpt, 3 tbn, timp, str, org
1819–23; first perf. 18 April 1824, St Petersburg; publ. 1827 (Schott, Mainz)
Ded. to Archduke Rudolph; originally intended for his installation as Archbishop of Olmütz on 9 March 1820, but the Mass was not completed in time

Op. 121b
Opferlied (Friedrich von Matthisson)
'Die Flamme lodert'
1822, rev. 1824; first perf. 23 December 1822; publ. 1825 (Schott, Mainz)
Two versions of the work exist (as well as two earlier settings of the text – see WoO 126, p. 264). The 1822 version is set for SAT soli, SATB ch; 2 cl, hn, str (no vns). The 1824 version is for S solo, SATB ch; 2 cl, 2 bn, 2 hn, str. A piano accompaniment also exists (see Hess 91, p. 274).

WoO 106
Birthday Cantata for Prince Lobkowitz (Beethoven?)
'Es lebe unser teurer Fürst'
S solo, SATB ch, pf
April 1823; publ. posth.

Op. 122
Bundeslied (Johann Wolfgang von Goethe)
'In allen guten Stunden'
SA soli, SAA ch, 2 cl, 2 hn, 2 bn
1823–4; publ. 1825 (Schott, Mainz)
A piano accompaniment also exists (see Hess 92, p. 274).

Op. 125
Ninth Symphony
See 'Symphonies' (p. 217)

See also 'Stage music' and 'Songs'.

II Solo voice(s) with orchestra

WoO 92
Primo amore (author unknown)
S solo; fl, 2 ob, 2 bn, 2 hn, str
c.1790–92; publ. posth.

WoO 89
Prüfung des Küssens (author unknown)
'Meine weise Mutter spricht'
B solo; fl, 2 ob, 2 hn, str
c.1790–92; publ. posth.

WoO 90
Mit Mädeln sich vertragen (Johann Wolfgang von Goethe)
B solo; 2 ob, 2 hn, str
c.1791–2; publ. posth.

Op. 65
Ah! perfido (text partly by Pietro Metastasio, remainder unknown)
S solo; fl, 2 cl, 2 bn, 2 hn, str
Early 1796; publ. 1805 (Hoffmeister & Kühnel, Leipzig)
Composed for Countess Josephine de Clary

WoO 92a
No, non turbarti (Pietro Metastasio)
S solo; str orch
Early 1802; publ. posth.

Op. 116
Tremate, empi, tremate (Bettoni)
STB soli; 2 fl, 2 cl, 2 bn, 2 hn, 2 tpt, timp, str
1802, rev. 1814?; publ. 1826 (Steiner, Vienna)

WoO 93
Nei giorni tuoi felici (Pietro Metastasio)
ST soli; 2 fl, 2 ob, 2 bn, 2 hn, str
Late 1802; publ. posth.

III Canons

WoO 159
Im Arm der Liebe (3-pt)
c.1795; publ. posth.

WoO 160
Two Canons, untexted, in G and C (4-pt and 3-pt)
c.1795; publ. posth.

Hess 276
Herr Graf, ich komme zu fragen (3-pt)
c.1797?; publ. posth.

Hess 229
Languisco e moro (2-pt)
Early 1803; publ. posth.

Hess 274
Untexted canon in G (2-pt)
Early 1803; publ. posth.

Hess 275
Untexted canon in A♭ (2-pt)
c.November 1803; publ. posth.

WoO 161
Ewig dein (3-pt)
c.1811?; publ. posth.

WoO 162
Ta ta ta (4-pt)
Spurious: written by Anton Schindler

WoO 163
Kurz ist der Schmerz (3-pt, text by Friedrich von Schiller)
November 1813 (for Johann Friedrich Naue); publ. posth.

WoO 164
Freundschaft ist die Quelle (3-pt)
September 1814; publ. posth.

WoO 165
Glück zum neuen Jahr (4-pt)
January 1815 (for Baron von Pasqualati); publ. 1816 (Riedl, Vienna)

WoO 166
Kurz ist der Schmerz (3-pt)
March 1815 (for Louis Spohr); publ. posth.

WoO 167
Brauchle, Linke (3-pt)
c.1815 (probably for Joseph Brauchle and Joseph Linke); publ. posth.

WoO 168
Two Canons: *Das Schweigen* (puzzle canon); ***Das Reden*** (3-pt)
January 1816 (for Charles Neate); publ. posth.

WoO 169
Ich küsse Sie (puzzle canon)
January 1816 (for Anna Milder-Hauptmann); publ. posth.

WoO 170
Ars longa, vita brevis (2-pt)
April 1816 (for Johann Nepomuk Hummel); publ. posth.

WoO 171
Glück fehl' dir vor allem (4-pt)
1817 (for Anna Giannatasio del Rio); publ. posth.

WoO 172
Ich bitt' dich (3-pt)
c.1818? (for Vincent Hauschka); publ. posth.

WoO 173
Hol' euch der Teufel (puzzle canon)
Summer 1819 (for Sigmund Anton Steiner); publ. posth.

WoO 174
Glaube und hoffe (4-pt, not strict canon)
September 1819 (for Moritz Schlesinger); publ. posth.

WoO 176
Glück zum neuen Jahr (3-pt)
December 1819 (for Countess Erdödy); publ. posth.

WoO 179
Alles Gute (4-pt)
December 1819 (for Archduke Rudolph); publ.
posth.

WoO 175
Sankt Petrus war ein Fels (puzzle canon)
c. January 1820 (for Karl Peters and Carl Bernard);
publ. posth.

Hess 300
Liebe mich, werter Weissenbach (2-pt?)
c. January 1820 (for Aloys Weissenbach?); publ.
posth.

Hess 301
Wähner...es ist kein Wahn (2-pt?)
c. January 1820 (for Friedrich Wähner?); publ.
posth.

WoO 177
Bester Magistrat (4-pt plus bass)
*c.*1820; publ. posth.

WoO 178
Signor Abate (3-pt)
*c.*1820? (for Abbé Stadler?); publ. posth.

WoO 180
Hoffmann, sei ja kein Hofmann (2-pt)
March 1820; publ. 1825 (Schott, Mainz)

WoO 181
Three Canons: *Gedenket heute* (4-pt); *Gehabt
euch* (3-pt); *Tugend ist* (3-pt)
*c.*1820; publ. posth.

WoO 182
O Tobias (3-pt)
September 1821 (for Tobias Haslinger); publ.
posth.

WoO 183
Bester Herr Graf (4-pt)
February 1823 (for Count Lichnowsky); publ.
posth.

WoO 184
Falstafferel, lass' dich sehen (5-pt)
April 1823 (for Ignaz Schuppanzigh); publ. posth.

WoO 185
Edel sei der Mensch (6-pt): **two versions, in
E and E♭**
*c.*May 1823 (version in E♭ for Louis Schlösser);
version in E publ. 1823 (Strauss, Vienna)

WoO 186
Te solo adoro (2-pt)
June 1824 (for Carlo Soliva; there are also two

other similar settings of the same text, Hess 263–
4); publ. posth.

WoO 187
Schwenke dich ohne Schwänke (4-pt)
November 1824 (for Carl Schwencke); publ. 1825
(Schott, Mainz)

WoO 188
Gott ist eine feste Burg (2-pt)
January 1825; publ. posth.

WoO 189
Doktor, sperrt das Tor (4-pt)
May 1825 (for Anton Braunhofer); publ. posth.

WoO 190
Ich war hier, Doktor (2-pt)
June 1825 (for Anton Braunhofer); publ. posth.

WoO 35
Untexted Canon in A (2-pt, violins?)
August 1825 (for Otto de Boer); publ. posth.

WoO 191
Kühl, nicht lau (3-pt)
September 1825 (for Friedrich Kuhlau); publ.
posth.

WoO 192
Ars longa, vita brevis (puzzle canon)
September 1825 (for Sir George Smart); publ.
posth.

WoO 193
Ars longa, vita brevis (puzzle canon)
*c.*1825?; publ. posth.

WoO 194
Si non per portas (puzzle canon)
September 1825 (for Moritz Schlesinger); publ.
posth.

WoO 195
Freu' dich des Lebens (2-pt)
December 1825 (for Theodor Molt); publ. posth.

Bester Magistrat (3-pt)
*c.*April 1826 (in Kullak Sketchbook); unpubl.

WoO 196
Es muss sein (4-pt)
c. July 1826 (for Ignaz Dembscher); publ. posth.

WoO 197
Da ist das Werk (5-pt)
September 1826 (for Karl Holz): publ. posth.

Hess 277
Esel aller Esel (3-pt)
c. September 1826; publ. posth.

WoO 198
Wir irren allesamt (puzzle canon)
December 1826 (for Karl Holz); publ. posth.

BARRY COOPER

Songs

ALTHOUGH SCHUBERT IS OFTEN credited with the creation of the Romantic German Lied, the honour really belongs to Beethoven, who in this field as in so many forged a style that was to have a profound influence on his Romantic successors. As regards precedence, nearly all of Beethoven's songs were composed before any of Schubert's; and as regards song types, Beethoven used all the main ones employed by his successors, from simple strophic settings to elaborate through-composed works. This range contrasts with nearly all of his immediate predecessors, who generally preferred simple, folk-like settings where the piano had a purely subordinate role and often even incorporated the vocal line into the right-hand part of the accompaniment.

Beethoven chose his texts very carefully, with regard both to quality of poetry and to subject matter. He showed a marked preference for Goethe's texts, setting them far more often than those of any other poet. Others whose texts found favour include Matthisson, Bürger and Reissig, though with the latter it was partly through friendship that Beethoven set his texts so often. Schiller was set hardly at all (apart from in the Ninth Symphony): although Beethoven greatly admired his poetry, he found it very difficult to set to music as it was so elevated; Goethe was in this respect much easier to set. Nearly all the texts are German, but Beethoven set a handful of Italian ones (mostly Metastasio) as well as two in French and one in English.

The subject matter is very varied, but few of the poems give much opportunity for picturesque word-painting such as occurs in so many of Schubert's best-known songs. Indeed Beethoven once stated that pictorial description was more suitable for painters and poets than composers, and so his general avoidance of such texts was evidently deliberate. Several of the texts were probably chosen because of some autobiographical significance for him. *An die Hoffnung* (*To Hope*), op. 32, was written for Josephine Deym at a time when Beethoven's affections were turned towards her and he had hopes of fulfilment. *An die ferne Geliebte* (*To the Distant Beloved*) may have been written because his own beloved, the so-called 'Immortal Beloved', was by then living at a great distance from him (the poems may even have been written on this subject by Jeitteles at Beethoven's request). *Resignation* (1817) seems to embody some of the despair and helplessness that Beethoven felt at various times of his life, including the year of its composition. But it is unwise to speculate too far along these lines, since we know very little for certain about the motivation behind any of the songs.

The settings can be divided into three main types – strophic, varied strophic and through-composed; there are also a few borderline cases (e.g. where the variation between strophes is only very small) and a few songs with only a single strophe. Altogether there are almost equal numbers of strophic and through-composed songs, with varied strophic settings being rather less common. One might have expected Beethoven to progress from simple strophic settings in his early years, through varied strophic forms to through-composed songs towards the end, but in fact no such trend can be discerned. Strophic songs are easily in the majority before 1800, but after that date the three categories are much more nearly equal, and even some of his last songs (e.g. *Ruf vom Berge* and *So oder so*) are of the simple strophic variety.

For his strophic songs Beethoven devises music that is neutral enough to support the varying contents of the stanzas and yet evocative in capturing the mood of the whole poem. An excellent example is *An die Hoffnung* (op. 32), where the idea of Hope gently lifting and comforting the sad soul is conveyed by soaring broken chords and gentle harmonies in the piano part, while the contrast between sorrow and the arrival of Hope is reflected by a dramatic change of key at the appropriate point in each verse.

In the varied strophic settings Beethoven makes slight changes to the accompaniment or the vocal line from verse to verse, though the amount and type of variation differs in each song. This form provides much greater opportunities for individual word-painting, while still retaining echoes of the traditional folk-style settings. One of the loveliest examples is *Abendlied unterm gestirnten Himmel* (*Evening Song under the Starry Sky*), where the alterations in successive stanzas are minimal yet extremely telling, capturing every nuance in the text. The poet muses on the shimmering stars, which remind him that the troubles of his earthly pilgrimage are nearly over and that he will soon enjoy the rewards of Heaven (another subject with biographical significance for Beethoven). All these ideas are perfectly reflected in the piano part, which concludes with a very widely spaced chord that seems to sum up the contrast between earth and heaven. This was Beethoven's last real Lied composition: of the two later songs in the list below, *Der Kuss* was extensively sketched in 1798 and only touched up in 1822, while *Der edle Mensch* is just a short 'album leaf' of eleven bars, more on a par with some of his canons than his true Lieder.

The through-composed settings, with their still greater opportunities for expressing individual words, include many of Beethoven's finest songs. A notable early example is *Adelaide*, the composition of which gave Beethoven particular delight. Here the musical structure is quite independent of the poetic form, and the key scheme resembles that of sonata form, with a first section that modulates to the dominant, a middle section that wanders through various remote keys and a final section that stays mainly in the tonic. Another example from the same period is the song pair *Seufzer eines Ungeliebten* and *Gegenliebe* (*Sighs of an Unloved One; Love Returned*), conceived as a recitative and bipartite aria in which the contrasting emotions of the two songs are mirrored by a contrast between C minor and C major. Of the four settings of Goethe's poem *Nur wer die Sehnsucht kennt* (*Only He who Knows Yearning*), only the fourth is through-composed, and this is arguably the best of the four. It incorporates many of the best features of each of the other three, but the sense of the words is mirrored more closely and Beethoven follows the natural verbal rhythms of the two stanzas in a way impossible in a simple strophic setting.

Obtaining the right rhythm for the words was always a matter of major concern for him; his preliminary sketches for songs often show him experimenting with many different rhythms for the first phrase, while his latest alterations to the final version sometimes include minor improvements to the rhythm of the voice part. His concern for verbal accentuation sometimes led to unusual results, a remarkable example being the beginning of his second setting of *An die Hoffnung* (op. 94), where the music borders on declamatory recitative as well as being very chromatic and forward-looking harmonically.

Most of Beethoven's songs were written as individual items, but in two cases several were written as a group. The earlier one is the Gellert Lieder (op. 48), thought till recently to have been written in 1803 but now known to have been completed by March 1802. Since all six poems are by a single author and are on religious texts that are in some senses related, this group could be described as a song cycle; moreover the final song is much longer than any of the others and therefore functions well as a conclusion. But there is no musical coherence or overall structure in the group, and the sequence of keys shows no discernible pattern. Thus it is perhaps best to regard the six songs as a series or suite of contrasting bagatelle-like movements with only a tenuous connection between them, somewhat akin to the op. 33 Bagatelles, which are roughly contemporary.

In the second group, however, the songs form a definite cycle with an overall title, *An die ferne Geliebte*; indeed this work is sometimes described as the first ever song cycle. Whether this description is valid depends on the definition of a song cycle, but this was certainly the first time a major composer had organized a group of several solo songs with piano accompaniment into a coherent and unified whole – a practice that became widespread during the 19th century. Many features contribute to the musical unity of the cycle: the final song is in the same key as the first (E♭), the theme of the first returns at the end to emphasize the cyclic effect, and there are even definite joins between one song and the next (usually in the form of piano interludes), rather than clear breaks. The individual songs themselves, however, have almost artless, folklike melodies, so that the work as a whole is a perfect blend of apparent simplicity and great musical subtlety.

Although Beethoven's songs are performed relatively infrequently today, many of them are of the highest quality. They do not in general display the natural charm and flow of Schubert's melodies, but this is partly because Beethoven always strove to avoid anything that sounded too obvious or simple. Instead they tend to contain hidden beauties and subtleties that become apparent only after repeated hearings. Despite being overshadowed on the one side by Beethoven's own instrumental music and on the other by Schubert's prodigious output of songs, the Lieder deserve more attention than they generally receive.

In the following list the first words of the song are given after the title and author, if they differ from the title. Almost all the songs are scored for solo voice and piano.

WoO 107
Schilderung eines Mädchens (author unknown)
'Schildern, willst du Freund'
1783(?); publ. 1783 (H. P. Bossler, Speyer)

WoO 108
An einen Säugling (J. von Döhring)
'Noch weisst du nicht wess Kind du bist'
1784(?); publ. 1784 (H. P. Bossler, Speyer)

WoO 113
Klage (L. Hölty)
'Dein Silber schien durch Eichengrün'
c.1790; publ. posth.

WoO 110
Elegie auf den Tod eines Pudels (author unknown)
'Stirb immerhin'
c.1790?; publ. posth.

WoO 111
Punschlied (author unknown)
'Wer nicht, wenn warm' (with unison chorus)
*c.*1791; publ. posth.

WoO 109
Trinklied (author unknown)
'Erhebt das Glas' (with unison chorus)
*c.*1792; publ. posth.

WoO 112
An Laura (Friedrich von Matthisson)
'Freud' umblühe dich'
*c.*1792; publ. posth.

WoO 114
Selbstgespräch (J. W. L. Gleim)
'Ich, der mit flatterndem Sinn'
*c.*1792; publ. posth.

WoO 115
An Minna (author unknown)
'Nur bei dir, an deinem Herzen'
*c.*1792; publ. posth.

WoO 117
Der freie Mann (G. C. Pfeffel)
'Wer ist ein freier Mann?' (with unison chorus)
1792, rev. 1794; publ. 1808 (Simrock, Bonn)

WoO 116
Que le temps me dure (Jean-Jacques Rousseau)
c. early 1794; publ. posth.
Two versions exist, in c and C, neither fully notated.

WoO 119
O care selve (Pietro Metastasio) (with unison chorus)
*c.*1794; publ. posth.

WoO 126
Opferlied (Friedrich von Matthisson)
'Die Flamme lodert'
1794–5, rev. 1801–2; publ. 1808 (Simrock, Bonn)
For two later settings of the same text see op. 121b
(p. 259)

WoO 118
Seufzer eines Ungeliebten; Gegenliebe
(Gottfried August Bürger)
'Hast du nicht Liebe zugemessen'; 'Wüsst ich, dass du mich lieb'
1794–5; publ. posth.
The melody of *Gegenliebe* was later used in the Choral Fantasia, op. 80.

Op. 46
Adelaide (Friedrich von Matthisson)
'Einsam wandelt dein Freund'
*c.*1794–5; publ. 1797 (Artaria, Vienna)
Ded. to Matthisson

Hess 137
Ich wiege dich in meinem Arm (author unknown)
*c.*1795?; lost
This otherwise unknown song is referred to in a price list of 1822 compiled by Beethoven in preparation for possible publication (Tyson, 1984a; the title is incorrectly given by Hess as *Schwinge dich in meinen Dom*). The date suggested above is purely conjectural.

WoO 123
Zärtliche Liebe (Karl Friedrich Herrosee)
'Ich liebe dich'
*c.*1795; publ. 1803 (Traeg, Vienna)

WoO 124
La partenza (Pietro Metastasio)
'Ecco quel fiero istante'
*c.*1795–6; publ. 1803 (along with WoO 123, Traeg, Vienna)

WoO 121
Abschiedsgesang an Wiens Bürger (von Friedelberg)
'Keine Klage soll erschallen'
1796; publ. 1796 (Artaria, Vienna)
Ded. to Major von Kövesdy

WoO 122
Kriegslied der Oesterreicher (von Friedelberg)
'Ein grosses deutches Volk' (with unison chorus)
1797; publ. 1797 (Artaria, Vienna)

Hess 139
Minnesold von Bürger, in Tönen an Amenda ausbezahlt (Bürger?)
*c.*1798?; lost
The autograph of a song with this title was known in 1852, but it has since disappeared (see Hess, 1957).

WoO 127
Neue Liebe, neues Leben (Johann Wolfgang von Goethe)
'Herz, mein Herz'
1798–9; publ. 1808 (Simrock, Bonn)
For another setting of the same text, see op. 75 no. 2.

WoO 125
La tiranna (William Wennington)
'Ah grief to think'
1798–9; publ. 1799 (Broderip & Wilkinson, London)
Ded. (by Wennington) to Mrs Tschoffen. This was apparently Beethoven's first attempt at setting English words (see Tyson, 1971a).

WoO 128
Plaisir d'aimer (author unknown)
1798–9; publ. posth.

—
Meine Lebenszeit verstreicht (Christian Fürchtegott Gellert), in g
c.1798–1803?; lost
This otherwise unknown song is referred to in a price list of 1822 compiled by Beethoven in preparation for possible publication (cf. Hess 137 above). A setting of the text in f♯ was included in op. 48, but there are sketches for different settings in d and e dating from 1798 and 1803; some of these sketches may have developed into the lost setting (Tyson, 1984a).

Hess 143
An die Freude (Friedrich von Schiller)
'Freude, schöner Götterfunken'
c.1798–9; lost
This early setting of Schiller's famous poem *To Joy* is referred to by Ferdinand Ries in 1803. There is also a reference in 1793 to Beethoven's intention to set the text, and two brief sketches survive from 1798, but there is no trace of the complete song.

WoO 74
Ich denke dein (Johann Wolfgang von Goethe)
Song with variations for piano duet: see 'Piano music' (p. 249)

WoO 120
Man strebt die Flamme zu verhehlen (author unknown)
c.1802; publ. posth.
Written for Frau von Weissenthurn

Op. 48
Six Songs (Christian Fürchtegott Gellert)
1. *Bitten* ('Gott, deine Güte reicht so weit'); 2. *Die Liebe des Nächsten* ('So jemand spricht'); 3. *Vom Tode* ('Meine Lebenszeit verstreicht'); 4. *Die Ehre Gottes aus der Natur* ('Die Himmel rühmen'); 5. *Gottes Macht und Vorsehung* ('Gott ist mein Lied'); 6. *Busslied* ('An dir allein')
c.1801–early 1802; publ. 1803 (Artaria, Vienna)
Ded. to Count Browne

WoO 129
Der Wachtelschlag (S. F. Sauter)
'Ach, mir schallt's dorten'
1803; publ. 1804 (Bureau des Arts et d'Industrie, Vienna)
Written for Count Browne

Op. 88
Das Glück der Freundschaft (author unknown)
'Der lebt ein Leben wonniglich'
1803; publ. 1803 (Löschenkohl, Vienna)

Op. 52
Eight Songs
1. *Urians Reise um die Welt* (Matthias Claudius, 'Wenn jemand eine Reise tut'); 2. *Feuerfarb* (Sophie Mereau, 'Ich weiss eine Farbe'); 3. *Das Liedchen von der Ruhe* (Wilhelm Ueltzen, 'Im Arm der Liebe'); 4. *Maigesang* (Johann Wolfgang von Goethe, 'Wie herrlich leuchtet'); 5. *Mollys Abschied* (Gottfried August Bürger, 'Lebe wohl, du Mann'); 6. *Die Liebe* (Gotthold Ephraim Lessing, 'Ohne Liebe lebe'); 7. *Marmotte* (Goethe, 'Ich komme schon'); 8. *Das Blümchen Wunderhold* (Bürger, 'Es blüht ein Blümchen')
Compiled 1803–5; publ. 1805 (Bureau des Arts et d'Industrie, Vienna)
Most if not all of the songs were written in the 1790s, some even before Beethoven left Bonn, but they were probably revised shortly before publication.

Op. 32
An die Hoffnung (Christoph August Tiedge)
'Die du so gern'
Late 1804–early 1805; publ. 1805 (Bureau des Arts et d'Industrie, Vienna)
Written for Josephine Deym-Brunsvik. For a later setting of the text see op. 94 (1813–15) below.

WoO 132
Als die Geliebte sich trennen wollte (Stephan von Breuning, based on French text by Hoffmann)
'Der Hoffnung letzter Schimmer sinkt dahin'
1806; publ. 1809 (*Allgemeine Musikalische Zeitung*, Leipzig)
Also published with the title *Empfindungen bei Lydiens Untreue*

WoO 133
In questa tomba oscura (Giuseppe Carpani)
1806–7; publ. 1808 (Mollo, Vienna)
Written as a contribution to a collection of sixty-three settings of Carpani's text by a total of forty-six composers. The collection was dedicated (by Mollo) to Prince Lobkowitz.

WoO 134
Sehnsucht (Johann Wolfgang von Goethe)
'Nur wer die Sehnsucht kennt' (four settings)
Late 1807–early 1808; first setting publ. 1808 (Geistinger, Vienna), all four settings publ. 1810 (Bureau des Arts et d'Industrie, Vienna)
The autograph (facs., Bonn, 1986) bears the curious inscription: 'NB: I did not have enough time to produce a good one, so here are several attempts'.

WoO 136
Andenken (Friedrich von Matthisson)
'Ich denke dein'
1808; publ. 1810 (Breitkopf & Härtel, Leipzig; Clementi, London)

WoO 137
Lied aus der Ferne (Christian Ludwig Reissig)
'Als mir noch die Thräne'
1809; publ. 1810 (Breitkopf & Härtel, Leipzig;
Clementi, London)

WoO 138
Der Jüngling in der Fremde (Christian Ludwig
Reissig)
'Der Frühling entblühet'
1809; publ. 1810 (Artaria, Vienna)
Ded. (by Reissig) to Archduke Rudolph. The music
was originally written for the text of WoO 137 (see
above entry).

WoO 139
Der Liebende (Christian Ludwig Reissig)
'Welch ein wunderbares Leben'
1809; publ. 1810 (Artaria, Vienna; Clementi, Lon-
don)
Ded. (by Reissig) to Archduke Rudolph

Op. 75
Six Songs
1. *Mignon* (Johann Wolfgang von Goethe, 'Kennst
du das Land'); 2. *Neue Liebe, neues Leben* (Goethe,
'Herz, mein Herz'); 3. *Aus Goethes Faust* (Goethe,
'Es war einmal ein König', with unison chorus); 4.
Gretels Warnung (Gerhard Anton von Halem, 'Mit
Liebesblick und Spiel'); 5. *An den fernen Geliebten*
(Christian Ludwig Reissig, 'Einst wohnten süsse
Ruh'); 6. *Der Zufriedene* (Reissig, 'Zwar schuf das
Glück')
1809; publ. 1810 (Breitkopf & Härtel, Leipzig;
Clementi, London)
Ded. to Princess Kinsky. Text of no. 2 also set as
WoO 127 (see above). No. 3 originally drafted
c.1792–3

Op. 82
Four Ariettas and a Duet (for S, T)
1. *Hoffnung* (author unknown, 'Dimmi, ben mio');
2. *Liebes-Klage* (Pietro Metastasio, 'T'intendo, si,
mio cor'); 3. *L'amante impaziente* – arietta buffa
(Metastasio, 'Che fa il mio bene'); 4. *L'amante
impaziente* – arietta assai seriosa (Metastasio, 'Che
fa il mio bene'); 5. *Lebens-Genuss* (Metastasio, 'Odi
l'aura che dolci sospira')
1809 (?); publ. 1811 (Breitkopf & Härtel, Leipzig;
Clementi, London)
The original German edition included German
translations of the texts, by Christian Schreiber.

Op. 83
Three Songs (Johann Wolfgang von Goethe)
1. *Wonne der Wehmut* ('Trocknet nicht'); 2. *Sehnsucht*
('Was zieht mir das Herz'); 3. *Mit einem gemalten
Band* ('Kleine Blumen')
1810; publ. 1811 (Breitkopf & Härtel, Leipzig)
Ded. to Princess Kinsky

WoO 140
An die Geliebte (Johann Ludwig Stoll)
'O dass ich dir vom stillen Auge'
December 1811, rev. 1814; second version publ.
1814 (in journal *Friedensblätter*, Vienna), first version
publ. c.1826 (Gombart, Augsburg)
The first version is set for piano or guitar.

WoO 141
Der Gesang der Nachtigall (Johann Gottfried
Herder)
'Höre, die Nachtigall singt'
May 1813; publ. posth.

WoO 142
Der Bardengeist (Franz Rudolph Hermann)
'Dort auf dem hohen Felsen'
November 1813; publ. 1813 (*Musen-Almanach für
das Jahr 1814*, Vienna)

Op. 94
An die Hoffnung (Christoph August Tiedge)
'Ob ein Gott sei'
1813–15; publ. 1816 (Steiner, Vienna)
For an earlier setting of most of the text see op. 32
(1804–5) above.

WoO 143
Des Kriegers Abschied (Christian Ludwig
Reissig)
'Ich zieh' ins Feld'
Late 1814; publ. 1815 (Mechetti, Vienna)
Ded. (by Reissig) to Caroline Bernath

WoO 144
Merkenstein (Johann Baptist Rupprecht)
1814; publ. 1815 (in the almanac *Selam*, Vienna)
For another setting, see next entry.

Op. 100
Merkenstein (Johann Baptist Rupprecht)
For two voices (S, A)
1814; publ. 1816 (Steiner, Vienna)
Ded. (by Rupprecht) to Count Dietrichstein. For
another setting, see above entry.

WoO 135
Die laute Klage (Johann Gottfried Herder)
'Turteltaube, du klagest so laut'
c.1815?; publ. posth.

WoO 145
Das Geheimnis (Ignaz von Wessenberg)
'Wo blüht das Blümchen'
1815; publ. 1816 (in journal *Modenzeitung*, Vienna)

WoO 146
Sehnsucht (Christian Ludwig Reissig)
'Die stille Nacht umdunkelt'
Early 1816; publ. 1816 (Artaria, Vienna)

Op. 98
An die ferne Geliebte (song cycle, Alois Jeitteles)
1. 'Auf dem Hügel sitz ich spähend'; 2. 'Wo die Berge so blau'; 3. 'Leichte Segler in den Höhen'; 4. 'Diese Wolken in den Höhen'; 5. 'Es kehrt der Maien'; 6. 'Nimm sie hin denn diese Lieder'
April 1816; publ. 1816 (Steiner, Vienna)
Ded. to Prince Lobkowitz

Op. 99
Der Mann von Wort (Friedrich August Kleinschmid)
'Du sagtest, Freund'
c. May 1816; publ. 1816 (Steiner, Vienna)

WoO 147
Ruf vom Berge (Friedrich Treitschke)
'Wenn ich ein Vöglein wär'
December 1816; publ. 1817 (*Gedichte von Friedrich Treitschke*, Vienna)

WoO 148
So oder so (Carl Lappe)
'Nord oder Süd'
Early 1817; publ. 1817 (*Modenzeitung*, Vienna)

WoO 149
Resignation (Paul von Haugwitz)
'Lisch aus, mein Licht'
Early 1817 (some sketches date back to c.1814); publ. 1818 (*Modenzeitung*, Vienna)

WoO 200
O Hoffnung (Beethoven?)
Early 1818; publ. 1819 (Steiner, Vienna)
Written as a theme for Archduke Rudolph, who composed forty variations on it

WoO 130
Gedenke mein (author unknown)
c.1819–20 (originally drafted 1804–5?); publ. posth.

WoO 150
Abendlied unterm gestirnten Himmel (Heinrich Goeble)
'Wenn die Sonne nieder sinket'
March 1820; publ. 1820 (*Modenzeitung*, Vienna)

Op. 128
Der Kuss (Christian Felix Weisse)
'Ich war bei Chloen ganz allein'
November–December 1822 (sketched 1798); publ. 1825 (Schott, Mainz)

WoO 151
Der edle Mensch sei hülfreich und gut (Johann Wolfgang von Goethe)
January 1823; publ. posth.
Written for Baroness Cäcilie von Eskeles

BARRY COOPER

Folksong arrangements

BEETHOVEN'S FOLKSONG SETTINGS are among his least appreciated works. In general studies of his music, they are usually dismissed in a paragraph at most, and sometimes in as little as half a sentence. There is no agreement on how many there are (different books give widely differing figures) and the numbering system used in the standard reference works, though adopted here, leaves much to be desired. In the present list there are settings of 169 different melodies, counting WoO 156/6 and 157/9 separately (the two melodies have much in common, with the same text). Beethoven also made a second, completely different setting of ten of the melodies, for reasons explained below, bringing the total number of settings to 179. In addition, variant versions or abandoned drafts are known for some melodies (e.g. WoO 155 nos 7 and 14), but these are not counted here. Almost every setting is scored for solo voice in the treble clef (to be sung by either a soprano or tenor) with accompaniment, introduction and conclusion for piano, violin and cello. The string parts were designed to be optional (although this is not usually made clear in the published versions) and the voice is sometimes joined by a second or third voice or perhaps a chorus.

Beethoven was first asked to do the settings by the Edinburgh publisher George Thomson in 1809 (Haydn had earlier done some for him) and by November that year he had made a start on a set of forty-three melodies supplied by Thomson. Work was interrupted by the *Egmont* music, but by July 1810 he had completed the set of forty-three and also an additional ten. These fifty-three were despatched that month, and nine more were sent in February 1812. Thomson acknowledged that all sixty-two settings were 'marked with the stamp of genius, science and taste' but complained that nine of the accompaniments were too difficult, and asked Beethoven to simplify them. Beethoven, very angered, refused to change them at all, blaming Thomson for not specifying how easy they should be. Nevertheless he obligingly provided entirely new settings of the nine melodies, as follows:

No. in the 62 songs	Original setting	Replacement
4	Hess 206	WoO 155/20
28	WoO 152/5	Hess 192
37	Hess 196	WoO 153/12
43	Hess 203	Op. 108/20
44	Hess 197	WoO 153/15
52	Hess 194	WoO 153/5
57	WoO 152/25	WoO 154/2
60	WoO 152/22	WoO 154/7
61	Hess 198	WoO 154/9

These nine replacements were despatched in February 1813 with twenty-one new songs, which included one melody provided with two alternative settings (WoO 153/11 and Hess 195). After this, the picture is slightly less clear: the next set of fifteen songs is dated May 1815 in two Beethoven manuscripts, yet Thomson dated the copy he received '1814' – evidently incorrectly. By November 1818, 118 melodies were recorded as having been sent, and a few more were added in 1819 and 1820. Initially all the songs were British, but in 1816 Beethoven began setting continental ones too. It is generally stated that this was on his own initiative, yet the first mention of such settings in the Beethoven–Thomson correspondence is in a letter from Thomson on 1 January 1816 (Willetts, 1970, p. 21). Beethoven responded with twenty-seven continental settings, but despite Thomson's admiration for the lovely Sicilian air (WoO 157/4) he published none of them – apparently because of language and translation problems.

Altogether Thomson published 125 of Beethoven's British settings, but he omitted twenty-five others, including all ten duplicates. It is sometimes stated that Beethoven received £550 altogether for the settings, but he actually received much less. He was paid only 3 ducats per setting (or a bit less) up to 1814 and 4 ducats thereafter; even if he had been paid 4 ducats each for all 177 settings (two rather trivial ones, Hess 133–4, were not meant for Thomson), the total would have been barely £350.

It is widely assumed that all the texts were inserted by Thomson only after Beethoven had set the melodies. This is certainly true for the first set of fifty-three songs, but Beethoven complained that he needed the texts to make good settings and in 1812 he threatened to stop doing them if texts were not supplied. Thomson explained that he commissioned new poetry to add to old tunes after settings had been made; but this was not always the case, and it seems that, from 1813, some texts were sent: many of the titles are found in Beethoven's manuscripts thereafter, and in some cases a brief summary of the subject matter. Even then, however, the text supplied for Beethoven was not always retained: the manuscript of WoO 156/4 is headed 'My daddie is a canker'd Carle or Low down in the broom', but Thomson published it with a new text, 'The Lavrock shuns the palace gay', and later still the setting acquired its present text.

There is also internal evidence that Beethoven knew the subject of many of the songs. *Faithfu' Johnie* (op. 108/20) consists of a dialogue between a woman's question in the first half and her lover's reply in the second; Beethoven separates the two by a pause and two-bar interlude, whereas in his earlier setting (Hess 203) the music had been continuous. In *O Swiftly Glides the Bonny Boat* (op. 108/19) the words are depicted by semiquaver scale figures in the introduction; and *The Elfin Fairies* (WoO 154/1) has an extraordinarily light, wispy accompaniment ideally suited to the text.

Many of the melodies conform to the major–minor system, but there are four main types of irregularity: pentatonicism; double tonics; modality; and 'non-tonal' endings. Few melodies were purely pentatonic, for those that had been originally were usually modified in the 19th century, as in *Dim, Dim is my Eye* (op. 108/6), where the pentatonic melody is decorated by extraneous ornaments; in *Auld Lang Syne* (WoO 156/11) the pentatonicism has been corrupted in one place, probably by a scribal error. The modal melodies, many of which have a double tonic (i.e. one note functions as tonic in certain bars while another, usually a tone lower, does so in adjacent bars, as in *Highlander's Lament*, WoO 157/9), present problems for any harmonization, but Beethoven was far more sensitive to such modal inflections than most of his contemporaries. Although he eschewed the quasi-antique harmonies later employed by certain English composers, he equally tended to avoid the strong dominant–tonic progressions of his contemporaries in his modal settings. In *Sunset* (op. 108/2) his attempts to weaken the tonality even extend to harmonizing the end of the melody with a ♭VII–I cadence. With the melodies with 'non-tonal' endings, however, where the last note avoids the expected tonic, he harmonized the song more conventionally and resolved the unstable ending in the coda, as in *Bonny Laddie* (op. 108/7).

In all his settings Beethoven took considerable trouble to avoid the obvious and create something unexpected yet effective. The introductions and codas often show great skill in developing some prominent motif from the melody, as in *Could this Ill World* (op. 108/16), where the Scotch snap used for the crucial word 'woman' is developed, appropriately, at the head of the introduction. Likewise in the harmonies he often risked something primitive or awkward, or alternatively introduced some subtle chromaticism, rather than lapse into conventionality. Thomson's verdict on the settings, noted on the fly-leaf of a large volume of them, is entirely valid: 'Original and beautiful are these arrangements by this inimitable genius Beethoven' (Bartlitz, 1970, p. 67).

Index no.
Collection title
(publisher and date of first publication)

Song no.   *Song title* (text author or nationality); voices; date of completion

All the arrangements have piano accompaniment with optional violin and cello parts, except WoO 158/3 no. 4 and Hess 133-4, which have no string parts.

Op. 108
25 Scottish Songs
(Thomson, Edinburgh: 1818)

1 *Music, Love and Wine* (Smyth); S, SSA ch; February 1817
2 *Sunset* (Scott); S; February 1818
3 *Oh Sweet were the Hours* (Smyth); S; February 1817
4 *The Maid of Isla* (Scott); S; February 1817
5 *The Sweetest Lad was Jamie* (Smyth); S; May 1815
6 *Dim, Dim is my Eye* (Smyth); S; May 1815
7 *Bonny Laddie, Highland Laddie* (Hogg); S; May 1815
8 *The Lovely Lass of Inverness* (Burns); S; 1816
9 *Behold my Love how Green* (Burns); SA; February 1817
10 *Sympathy* (Smyth); S; May 1815
11 *Oh Thou art the Lad* (Smyth); S; October 1815
12 *Oh Had my Fate* (Byron); S; 1816
13 *Come Fill, Fill my Good Fellow* (Smyth); S, SAB ch; February 1817
14 *O How can I be Blithe* (Burns); S; 1816
15 *O Cruel was my Father* (Ballantyne); S; 1816
16 *Could this Ill World* (Hogg); S; 1816
17 *O Mary at thy Window be* (Burns); S; February 1817
18 *Enchantress, Farewell* (Scott); S; February 1818
19 *O Swiftly Glides the Bonny Boat* (Baillie); S, SATB ch; May 1815
20 *Faithfu' Johnie* (Grant); S; February 1813. See also Hess 203 below.
21 *Jeanie's Distress* (Smyth); S; February 1817
22 *The Highland Watch* (Hogg); S, STB ch; early 1817
23 *The Shepherd's Song* (Baillie); S; February 1818
24 *Again my Lyre* (Smyth); S; May 1815
25 *Sally in our Alley* (Carey); S; early 1817

The standard numbering is that of the first German edition (Schlesinger, Berlin: 1822), dedicated (by Schlesinger) to Prince Radziwill. The Scottish edition published the songs in a different order, interspersed with five by Haydn.

WoO 152
25 Irish Songs
(Thomson, Edinburgh: 1814)

1 *The Return to Ulster* (Scott); S; July 1810
2 *Sweet Power of Song* (Baillie); SA; July 1810
3 *Once more I Hail thee* (Burns); S; July 1810
4 *The Morning Air* (Baillie); S; July 1810
5 *On the Massacre of Glencoe* (Scott); S; July 1810. See also Hess 192 below.
6 *What shall I do* (Anon); SA; July 1810
7 *His Boat Comes* (Baillie); S; July 1810

8 *Come Draw we Round* (Baillie); S; July 1810
9 *The Soldier's Dream* (Campbell); S; July 1810
10 *The Deserter* (Curran); S, SA ch; February 1812
11 *Thou Emblem of Faith* (Curran); S; February 1812
12 *English Bulls* (Anon); S; July 1810
13 *Musing on the Roaring Ocean* (Burns); S; February 1812
14 *Dermot and Shelah* (Toms); S; July 1810
15 *Let Brain-spinning Swains* (Boswell); S; July 1810
16 *Hide not thy Anguish* (Smyth); S; July 1810
17 *In Vain to this Desert* (Grant and Burns); SA; July 1810
18 *They Bid me Slight* (Smyth); ST; July 1810
19 *Wife, Children and Friends* (Spencer); ST; February 1812
20 *Farewell Bliss* (Grant and Burns); SA, July 1810
21 *Morning a Cruel Turmoiler is* (Boswell); S; February 1812
22 *From Garyone* (Toms); S; February 1812. See also WoO 154 no. 7 below.
23 *A Wand'ring Gypsy* (Wolcot); S; July 1810
24 *The Traugh Welcome* (Anon); S; February 1812
25 *Oh Harp of Erin* (Thomson); S; February 1812. See also WoO 154 no. 2 below.

This group of songs was first published along with WoO 153 nos 1–4 (from which it has since become separated in the literature) and a Haydn setting, in March 1814.

WoO 153
20 Irish Songs
(Thomson, Edinburgh: 1814 (nos 1–4), 1816 (nos 5–20))

1 *When Eve's last Rays* (Thomson); SA; July 1810
2 *No Riches from his Scanty Store* (Williams); S; July 1810
3 *The British Light Dragoons* (Scott); S; July 1810
4 *Since Greybeards Inform us* (Toms); S; July 1810
5 *I Dream'd I Lay* (Burns); SA; February 1813. See also Hess 194 below.
6 *Sad and Luckless* (Smyth); S; May 1815
7 *O Soothe me, my Lyre* (Smyth); S; February 1813
8 *Norah of Balamagairy* (Boswell); S, STB ch; February 1813
9 *The Kiss, dear Maid* (Byron); S; February 1813
10 *Oh thou Hapless Soldier* (Smyth); SA; July 1810
11 *When Far from the Home* (Thomson); S; February 1813. See also Hess 195 below.

12 *I'll Praise the Saints* (Smyth); S; February 1813. See also Hess 196 below.

13 *'Tis Sunshine at Last* (Smyth); S (or ST); October 1815

14 *Paddy O'Rafferty* (Boswell); S; July 1810

15 *'Tis but in Vain* (Smyth); S; February 1813. See also Hess 197 below.

16 *O Might I but my Patrick Love* (Smyth); S; February 1813

17 *Come, Darby dear* (Smyth); S; February 1813

18 *No More, my Mary* (Smyth); S; February 1813

19 *Judy, Lovely, Matchless Creature* (Boswell); S; February 1813

20 *Thy Ship must Sail* (Smyth); S; February 1813

This is a factitious set, made up of the remaining four songs published in 1814 by Thomson along with WoO 152, and sixteen of the thirty songs published in Thomson's Volume 2 of 1816, selected from this volume on no particular basis.

WoO 154
12 Irish Songs

(Thomson, Edinburgh: 1816 (without nos 2 and 7))

1 *The Elfin Fairies* (Thomson); S, SA ch; February 1813

2 *Oh Harp of Erin* (Thomson); S; February 1813. See WoO 152 no. 25 above.

3 *The Farewell Song* (Smyth); S; February 1813

4 *The Pulse of an Irishman* (Boswell); S; February 1813

5 *Oh Who, my Dear Dermot* (Smyth); S; February 1813

6 *Put Round the Bright Wine* (Smyth); S; February 1813

7 *From Garyone* (Toms); S; February 1813. See WoO 152 no. 22 above.

8 *Save me from the Grave and Wise* (Smyth); S, STB ch; February 1813

9 *Oh Would I Were* (Smyth); ST; February 1813. See also Hess 198 below.

10 *The Hero may Perish* (Smyth); SA; February 1813

11 *The Soldier in a Foreign Land* (Baillie); ST; February 1813

12 *He Promised me at Parting* (Smyth); ST; February 1813

Like WoO 153, this is a factitious set; it was first put together in 1855 by Artaria & Co. (Vienna), with new words by Thomas Moore. It consists of ten of the remaining fourteen songs from Thomson's Volume 2, plus two settings not published by Thomson.

WoO 155
26 Welsh Songs

(Thomson, Edinburgh: 1817)

1 *Sion, the Son of Evan* (Grant); SA; July 1810

2 *The Monks of Bangor's March* (Scott); SA; July 1810

3 *The Cottage Maid* (Smyth); S; July 1810

4 *Love without Hope* (Richardson); S; July 1810

5 *The Golden Robe* (Hunter); S; July 1810

6 *The Fair Maid of Mona* (Smyth); S; July 1810

7 *Oh Let the Night* (Smyth); S; July 1810

8 *Farewell, thou Noisy Town* (Smyth); S; July 1810

9 *To the Aeolian Harp* (Hunter); S; July 1810

10 *Ned Pugh's Farewell* (Hunter); S; July 1810

11 *Merch Megan* (Hunter); S; July 1810

12 *Waken Lords and Ladies Gay* (Scott); S; July 1810

13 *Helpless Woman* (Burns); S; July 1810

14 *The Dream* (David ap Gwillim (Gwilym)); SS; July 1810

15 *When Mortals all to Rest Retire* (Smyth); S; February 1813

16 *The Damsels of Cardigan* (Jones); S; July 1810

17 *The Dairy House* (Hunter); S; July 1810

18 *Sweet Richard* (Opie); S; July 1810

19 *The Vale of Clwyd* (Opie); S; July 1810

20 *To the Blackbird* (David ap Gwillim (Gwilym)); S; February 1813. See also Hess 206 below.

21 *Cupid's Kindness* (Smyth); S; July 1810

22 *Constancy* (Burns); SS; July 1810

23 *The Old Strain* (Smyth); S; July 1810

24 *Three Hundred Pounds* (Litwyd); S; July 1810

25 *The Parting Kiss* (Smyth); S; May 1815

26 *Good Night* (Spencer); S; July 1810

These songs were first published, interspersed with four settings by Haydn, as a collection of thirty Welsh airs in 1817.

WoO 156
12 Scottish Songs

(Thomson, Edinburgh: 1822 (no. 1); 1824–5 (nos 2–4, 8, 9, 12); 1839 (nos 5, 6); 1841 (nos 7, 10, 11))

1 *The Banner of Buccleuch* (Scott); STB; 1819

2 *Duncan Gray* (Burns); STB; autumn 1818

3 *Up! Quit thy Bower* (Baillie); SSB; 1819

4 *Ye Shepherds of this Pleasant Vale* (Hamilton); STB; autumn 1818

5 *Cease your Funning* (Gay); S; early 1817

6 *Highland Harry* (Burns); S; May 1815

7 *Polly Stewart* (Burns); S; autumn 1818

8 *Womankind* (Smyth); STB; autumn 1818

9 *Lochnagar* (Byron); STB; autumn 1818

10 *Glencoe* (Scott); STB; 1819

11 *Auld Lang Syne* (Burns); STB, STB ch; autumn 1818

12 *The Quaker's Wife* (Hunter); STB; autumn 1818

This is a factitious set, containing most of Beethoven's Scottish songs other than those published in op. 108; no. 5, however, is not Scottish, being derived from *The Beggar's Opera*.

WoO 157
12 Assorted Folksongs
(Thomson, Edinburgh: 1816 (nos 2, 6, 8, 11); 1822 (no. 3); 1824–5 (no. 5); 1839 (no. 1))

1   *God Save the King* (English); S, STB ch; early 1817
2   *The Soldier* (Irish, Smyth); S; May 1815
3   *O Charlie is my Darling* (Scottish); SAB; early 1819
4   *O Sanctissima* (Sicilian); SSB; February 1817
5   *The Miller of Dee* (English); STB; 1819
6   *A Health to the Brave* (Irish, Dovaston); SA; May 1815
7   *Robin Adair* (Irish); STB; October 1815
8   *By the Side of the Shannon* (Irish, Smyth); S; May 1815
9   *Highlander's Lament* (Scottish, Burns); S, STB ch; 1820
10 *Sir Johnie Cope* (Scottish); S; February 1817
11 *The Wandering Minstrel* (Irish, Smyth); S, STB ch; May 1815
12 *La Gondoletta* (Venetian); S; 1816

Another factitious set, this one was first assembled for a German edition in 1860 by Peters from manuscripts which were by then in Berlin. The four Irish songs (nos 2, 6, 8 and 11) form a single group in the manuscript sources, but the remainder were written at various times.

WoO 158/1
23 Continental Folksongs
(publ. posth.)

1   *Ridder Stig tjener* (Danish); S, SATB ch; February 1817
2   *Horch auf, mein Liebchen* (German); S; 1816
3   *Wegen meiner bleib d'Fräula* (German); S; 1816
4   *Wann i in der Früh* (Tyrolean); S; 1816
5   *I bin a Tyroler Bua* (Tyrolean); S; 1816
6   *A Madel, ja a Madel* (Tyrolean); S; 1816
7   *Wer solche Buema* (Tyrolean); S; 1817
8   *Ih mag di nit* (Tyrolean); S; 1817
9   *Oj upiłem się w karczmie* (Polish); S; 1816
10 *Poszła baba po popiół* (Polish); S; 1816
11 *Yo no quiero embarcarme* (Iberian); S; 1816
12 *Seus lindos olhos* (Portuguese); SA; 1816
13 *Im Walde sind viele Mücklein* (Russian); S; 1816
14 *Ach Bächlein* (Russian); S; 1816
15 *Unsere Mädchen* (Russian); S; 1816
16 *Schöne Minka* (Ukrainian–Cossack); S; 1816
17 *Lilla Carl* (Swedish); S; 1817
18 *An ä Bergli bin i gesässe* (Swiss); SA; 1816
19 *Bolero a solo: Una paloma blanca* (Spanish); S; 1816
20 *Bolero a due; Como la mariposa* (Spanish); SA; 1816
21 *La tiranna se embarca* (Spanish); S; 1816
22 *Edes kinos emlékezet* (Hungarian); S; 1817
23 *Da brava, Catina* (Venetian); S; 1816

An earlier, slightly different version of no. 19 is also known (Hess 207, where it is wrongly described as an earlier version of no. 20).

WoO 158/2
7 British Folksongs
(publ. posth.)

1   *Adieu my Lov'd Harp* (Irish); S; February 1813
2   *Castle O'Neill* (Irish); STBar or STBarB; February 1813
3   *O Was not I a Weary Wight* (Scottish); S; February 1817
4   *Red Gleams the Sun* (Scottish); S; February 1817
5   *Erin! oh Erin!* (Scottish/Irish); S; May 1815. The melody was evidently known in both Scotland and Ireland.
6   *O Mary ye's be Clad in Silk* (Scottish); S; May 1815
7   *Lament for Owen Roe O'Neill* (Irish); S; July 1810

WoO 158/3
6 Assorted Folksongs
(publ. posth.)

1   *When my Hero in Court Appears* (Gay); S; early 1817
2   *Non, non, Colette* (Rousseau); S; early 1817
3   *Mark Yonder Pomp* (Burns); S; 1820
4   *Bonnie Wee Thing* (Burns); SSB; 1820
5   *From thee, Eliza I must Go* (Burns); STB; autumn 1818
6   (No text or title, Scottish); S; July 1810

Hess 133
Das liebe Kätzchen (Austrian)
S; March 1820

Hess 134
Der Knabe auf dem Berge (Austrian)
S; March 1820

Hess 168
(No text or title, French)
S; early 1817

Hess 192
On the Massacre of Glencoe (Scott)
S; February 1813. An intended replacement for WoO 152 no. 5 (see above)

Hess 194
I Dream'd I Lay (Burns)
SA; July 1810
Replaced by WoO 153 no. 5 (see above)

Hess 195
When Far from the Home (Thomson)
S; February 1813
An alternative to the setting listed as WoO 153
no. 11 above

Hess 196
I'll Praise the Saints (Smyth)
S; July 1810
Replaced by WoO 153 no. 12 (see above)

Hess 197
'Tis but in Vain (Smyth)
S; July 1810
Replaced by WoO 153 no. 15 (see above)

Hess 198
Oh Would I Were (Smyth)
ST; February 1812
Replaced by WoO 154 no. 9 (see above)

Hess 203
Faithfu' Johnie (Grant)
S; July 1810
Replaced by op. 108 no. 20 (see above)

Hess 206
To the Blackbird (David ap Gwillim
(Gwilym))
S; July 1810
Replaced by WoO 155 no. 20 (see above)

BARRY COOPER

Arrangements of his own music; miscellaneous works

DURING HIS LIFETIME many of Beethoven's compositions appeared in arrangements, a widely accepted method of making popular works more accessible. Most were not made by Beethoven himself, and it was not a practice which greatly interested him. In 1802 he published a disclaimer against quintet arrangements of his First Symphony and Septet: 'The making of transcriptions is on the whole a thing against which nowadays (in our prolific age of transcriptions) a composer would merely struggle in vain; but at least he is entitled to demand that the publishers shall mention the fact on the title-page, so that his honour as a composer may not be infringed nor the public deceived.' (Anderson, 1961, p. 1434) But he did not object to good arrangements. Ries claimed that he often made arrangements which Beethoven checked, and which

were sold under Beethoven's name. The arrangements of the Serenades opp. 8 and 25 are examples of Franz Kleinheinz's work, of which Beethoven wrote to his publishers in 1803: 'The *arrangements* were not made by me, but I have gone through them and made drastic corrections in some passages. So do not dare to state in writing that I have arranged them.... I could never have found the time, or even had the patience, to do work of that kind.' (Letter 82)

Beethoven's transcriptions of the Piano Sonata op. 14 no. 1, the Violin Concerto and the *Grosse Fuge* came about from specific requests. Nottebohm speculated that the Sonata may originally have been conceived for string quartet. The question has been explored in depth by Broyles (1970), who concludes that the hypothesis cannot be substantiated by the sketches; and Beethoven himself wrote: 'I have arranged only one of my sonatas for string quartet, because I was earnestly implored to do so' (Letter 59). In the same letter to Breitkopf & Härtel he divulged his feelings about transcribing piano works: 'The *unnatural mania*, now so prevalent, for transferring even *pianoforte compositions* to string instruments, instruments which in all respects are so different from one another, should really be checked. I firmly maintain that only *Mozart* could arrange for other instruments the works he composed for the pianoforte.'

Clementi commissioned the piano adaptation of the Violin Concerto op. 61. Beethoven's willingness to accept this is surprising, but there may have been a precedent: there is a piano cadenza in G which is thematically related to the existing fragment of the early Violin Concerto in C, WoO 5. This could signify that in 1790–92 Beethoven had considered adapting for piano a work conceived for the violin. There are very few alterations made to the solo line in op. 61, the left hand is given a predominantly accompanying part, and original cadenzas were written.

The piano four-hands arrangement of the *Grosse Fuge* was one result of the reaction to the String Quartet in B♭, op. 130, with the Fugue as its original finale. In response to inquiries for a piano arrangement of the Fugue, Beethoven authorized Anton Halm to make one; but he was not satisfied with the result and subsequently made his own.

The Quintet for piano and wind instruments op. 16 was published simultaneously with the arrangement for piano quartet (with strings). It was an external stimulus in 1817, however, which inspired Beethoven to rework the Piano Trio op. 1 no. 3, completed over twenty years earlier. An unknown composer, Kaufmann, presented him with an arrangement for string quintet. Although critical of it, Beethoven decided to use it as the basis for his own version. Kaufmann's arrangement was generally literal and unimaginative; Beethoven improved and vitalized it by altering sonorities, changing voice-leading and adding dynamics and phrasing. Surprisingly, he left some passages of inferior quality, and on occasions where Kaufmann had added new melodic material he retained it and even built on it. On the copyists' manuscript he wrote: 'Trio arranged as a three-part quintet by Mr Goodwill [Herr Kaufmann], and from a semblance of five parts brought to the light of day as five genuine parts, and at the same time raised from the most abject misery to some degree of respectability by Mr Wellwisher [himself] 14 August 1817.' (Tyson, 1973b)

The complete music for *Die Weihe des Hauses* was not so much an arrangement as a hastily assembled adaptation of music for *Die Ruinen von Athen* with a new overture and chorus.

Miscellaneous Beethoven works include one organ fugue, pieces for mechanical clock, musical jokes and mottos in letters, and the exercises he did for Haydn and Albrechtsberger. The pieces for mechanical clock were most likely written for Count Deym, who had a collection of mechanical instruments.

I Arrangements

Op. 16
Piano Quartet in E♭
Arranged from the Quintet for piano and wind (see p. 227)
1796; publ. March 1801 (Mollo, Vienna)
Ded. to Prince Schwarzenberg

Op. 17
Cello Sonata in F
Arranged from the Horn Sonata (see p. 227)
1801; publ. 1801 (Mollo, Vienna)

Op. 36
Piano Trio
Arrangement of Symphony no. 2 in D (see p. 217)
1805; publ. 1805 (Bureau des Arts et d'Industrie, Vienna)

Op. 38
Trio in E♭ for piano, clarinet or violin, and cello
Arranged from Septet, op. 20 (see p. 227)
1802–3; publ. 1805 (Bureau des Arts et d'Industrie, Vienna)
Ded. to J. A. Schmidt; first edition called Trio for pianoforte with accompaniment of clarinet or violin and cello

Op. 41
Serenade in D for flute/violin and piano
Arranged from Serenade op. 25 (see p. 228) 1803; publ. December 1803 (Hoffmeister & Kühnel, Leipzig)
Arranged by F. X. Kleinheinz, corrected and approved by Beethoven

Op. 42
Notturno in D for piano and viola
Arranged from Serenade op. 8 (see p. 238)
1803; publ. 1804 (Hoffmeister & Kühnel, Leipzig)
Arranged by F. X. Kleinheinz, corrected and approved by Beethoven

Op. 61
Piano Concerto in D
Arranged from Violin Concerto (see p. 221)
1807; publ. 1808 (Bureau des Arts et d'Industrie, Vienna)
Ded. to Julie von Breuning; new cadenzas composed for first and third movements

Op. 63
Trio in E♭ for piano, violin and cello
Arranged from String Quintet, op. 4 (see p. 238)
Publ. 1806 (Artaria, Vienna)
Arranged by someone else, possibly without Beethoven's knowledge

Op. 64
Sonata in E♭ for cello and piano
Arranged from String Trio op. 3 (see p. 237)
Publ. 1807 (Artaria, Vienna)
Arranged by someone else, possibly without Beethoven's knowledge

Op. 104
String Quintet in C minor
Arranged from Piano Trio op. 1 no. 3 (see p. 230)
1817; first perf. 10 December 1818; publ. 1819 (Artaria, Vienna)
Arranged by Kaufmann, corrected by Beethoven

Op. 134
Grosse Fuge in B♭ for piano duet
Arranged from String Quartet op. 133 (see p. 239)
1826; publ. 1827 (Artaria, Vienna)
Ded. to Archduke Rudolph

Hess 34
String Quartet in F
Arranged from Piano Sonata in E, op. 14, no. 1 (see p. 244)
1801–2; publ. May 1802 (Bureau des Arts et d'Industrie, Vienna)
Ded. to Baroness Josephine von Braun

Hess 65
Concert Finale, C
Piano arrangement of coda of finale of Third Piano Concerto, op. 37 (see p. 221)
1820–21; publ. 1821 (Starke, Vienna)

Hess 87
Piano arrangement of March in B♭ for six wind instruments, WoO 29 (see p. 227)
1797–8; publ. posth.

Hess 88
Piano arrangement of Minuet in A♭ for string quartet, Hess 33 (see p. 237)
1790–92; publ. posth.

Hess 89
Piano arrangement of *Ritterballett*, WoO 1
(see p. 252)
Publ. posth.

Hess 90
Piano arrangement of *Die Geschöpfe des Prometheus*, op. 43 (see p. 252)
1801; publ. 1801 (Artaria, Vienna)
Ded. to Princess Christiane Lichnowsky

Hess 91
***Opferlied* op. 121b** (see p. 259)
Arranged for soprano, choir and piano
Publ. 1825 (Schott, Mainz)

Hess 92
***Bundeslied* op. 122** (see p. 259)
Arranged for two soloists and piano
Publ. 1825 (Schott, Mainz)

Hess 93-5
A simplified setting and two keyboard versions of Clärchen's Lied, no. 4 of *Egmont*, op. 84 (see p. 254)
1810; publ. posth.

Hess 97
Piano arrangement of *Wellingtons Sieg*, op. 91 (see p. 222)
1816; publ. 1816 (Steiner, Vienna)

Hess 99
Piano arrangement of Military March in F, WoO 18 (see p. 224)
1809; publ. posth.

Hess 100-02
Piano versions of WoO 8, 7, 14: (see pp. 223–4)

Hess 108
Original version, for Maelzel's panharmonicon, of *Wellingtons Sieg*, op. 91, second part ('Siegessymphonie') (see p. 222)
1813; publ. posth.

Hess 118
Complete music for *Die Weihe des Hauses*, adapted from *Die Ruinen von Athen*, op. 113
(see p. 254)

Overture: see op. 124 (p. 255)
No. 1: op. 113 no. 1 with new text
Nos 2–4: same as op. 113 nos 2–4
No. 5: see WoO 98 (p. 255)
No. 6: see op. 114 (p. 255)
No. 7: op. 113 no. 5, text shortened
Nos 8–9: op. 113 nos 7–8, text altered
1822; publ. posth.

II Miscellaneous (none published in Beethoven's lifetime)

WoO 31
Fugue for organ, D
1783

WoO 33
5 Pieces for mechanical clock
No. 1 in F, 1799; no. 2 in G, 1799–1800; no. 3 in G, 1799(?); no. 4 in C, 1794(?); no. 5 in C, 1794(?)

WoO 199
Ich bin der Herr von zu (musical joke)
1814
Intended for Archduke Rudolph

WoO 201
Ich bin bereit! Amen (musical joke)
1818
In letter to Vincenz Hauschka (Letter 903)

WoO 202
Das Schöne zu dem Guten (musical motto)
1823; for Marie Pachler-Koschak

WoO 203
Das Schöne zu dem Guten (musical motto/puzzle canon)
1825, in letter to Rellstab (Letter 1366b)

WoO 204
Holz, Holz geigt die Quartette so (musical joke)
In Conversation Book of September 1825

WoO 205
Musical quips in letters

(a) *Baron, Baron*
In letter to Zmeskall, 1798 (Letter 29)

(b) *Allein, allein, allein*
To Count Lichnowsky, 1814 (Letter 498)

(c) *O Adjutant*
To Haslinger, 1817 (Letter 742)

(d) *Wo? Wo?*
To Nanette Streicher, 1817 (Letter 789 or 792)

(e) *Erfüllung, Erfüllung*
To Archduke Rudolph, 1819 (Letter 948)

(f) *Scheut euch nicht*
To Treitschke, *c.* 1822? (Letter 1068)

(g) *Tobias!*
To Haslinger, 1824 (Letter 1312)

(h) *Tobias Tobias*
To Haslinger, 1825 (Letter 1365)

(i) *Bester Tobias*
To Haslinger, 1826 (Letter 1534)

(k) *Erster aller Tobiasse*
To Haslinger, 1826 (Letter 1536)

—

Ach Tobias (musical quip)
To Haslinger, 1825 (Letter 1457)
Not listed under WoO 205 in Kinsky, 1955

Hess 36
String quartet arrangement of the fugue from the Overture to Handel's *Solomon*
*c.*1798

Hess 38
String quintet arrangement of Bach's Fugue in b♭ from Book 1 of the '48'
1801–2

Hess 107
***Grenadiermarsch* for mechanical clock, F**
Consists of a twenty-bar march by Haydn, an original transition and an arrangement of the March WoO 29 (see p. 227)

Hess 233–46
Exercises with Haydn and Albrechtsberger
1793–5
Hess 233: *c.*300 simple contrapuntal exercises on *cantus firmi*
Hess 234: *c.*125 exercises (strict counterpoint)
Hess 235: 26 exercises (free)
Hess 236: 18 simple 2-part fugues (strict) .
Hess 237: 7 simple 3-part-figures (strict)
Hess 238: 9 simple 4-part fugues (strict)
Hess 239: 3 chorale fugues
Hess 240: 4 2-part exercises in double counterpoint
Hess 241: 21 exercises in double counterpoint
Hess 242: 6 exercises in double counterpoint
Hess 243: 5 4-part fugues in double counterpoint
Hess 244: 2 4-part triple fugues
Hess 245: Fragment of a fugue in D minor for string quartet
Hess 246: Double fugue in F for 4-part choir

These exercises were not published in the *Gesamtausgabe* or in Hess, 1959; many can be found in Nottebohm, 1873.

ANNE-LOUISE COLDICOTT

Unfinished and projected works

IT IS NOT WIDELY appreciated that, if every independent scrap of Beethoven's music is counted separately, many more unfinished compositions survive than finished ones. In the Kafka Sketch Miscellany alone, for example, there are around six hundred unfinished fragments that could be counted as ideas for separate works; and, to take just one genre, Gustav Nottebohm estimated that Beethoven began at least fifty symphonies altogether (Nottebohm, 1887, p. 13).

Several factors make it impossible to produce anything like a comprehensive list of such unfinished works, most of which never progressed beyond a sketch of a few bars long. Often a sketch for an abandoned work will contain some elements in common with a completed one and therefore in a sense could be regarded as a sketch for that work. For example, an unfinished first movement of a projected sonata in C minor of *c.*1798 (Kafka Miscellany, f. 117r) has several features in common with the first movement of the *Pathétique* Sonata, which was composed very soon after, and so it might or might not be regarded as abandoned. Conversely a sketch clearly intended for a completed work may have virtually nothing in common with the final version; this often happened when Beethoven decided to write a movement quite different from the one originally planned – for example, he had several quite different ideas for a finale for his Quartet op. 130, each of which could be regarded as an unfinished quartet movement rather than a sketch for op. 130. Some abandoned sketches are so short – perhaps just a group of two or three chords – that they resemble passages in more than one finished work without being directly related to any of them.

There is also a problem with lost or partially lost works. Sometimes only a fragment survives of a work that is known to have been completed, as with an early Violin Concerto (WoO 5) and Oboe Concerto (Hess 12). For other works a fragmentary score survives that gives every impression of having once been complete, for example a Romance in E minor (Hess 13), or there is a reference that implies a work was completed, as with Ries's 1803 reference to an alleged Beethoven setting of Schiller's *An die Freude*; in each of these cases, however, it is possible that the work was not in fact ever completed. Furthermore, just as there are a few finished works known to be lost and it can be conjectured that there are a few others, equally it is certain that there must be many abandoned ideas sketched on pages now missing.

Large-scale works

The unfinished works can be divided into several categories, of which the principal one is the large-scale, major works for which substantial sketches survive. No major Beethoven works were left nearly complete, like Mahler's Tenth Symphony or Berg's *Lulu*, but Beethoven made significant progress on several before they were either abandoned or else interrupted by death – notably the following:

1795–6	Symphony in C
1802	Triple Concerto in D
1803	Opera *Vestas Feuer* (Hess 115)
1815	Piano Concerto no. 6 in D (Hess 15)
1816	Piano Trio in F minor
1817	String Quintet in D minor (Hess 40)
1823–4	Mass in C♯ minor
1822–5	Overture on B–A–C–H
1822–5	Symphony no. 10 in E♭
1826–7	String Quintet in C (WoO 62)

The Symphony in C was sketched extensively in 1795–6 – indeed more sketches survive for it than for most of Beethoven's completed works from before 1800. The sketches, and a brief fragment in score, relate mainly to the first movement, with only a few short ideas for possible later ones. The first movement contains a sizeable slow introduction of around thirty bars or more, drafted variously in 3/4 or 2/2 metre, and an Allegro with a theme eventually to be used in modified form in the finale of the First Symphony. In the latter context, however, the theme has a much more four-square, closed character typical of finale themes, whereas in the unfinished symphony the theme is more open-ended and is in most of the sketches subjected to development almost immediately. Why Beethoven abandoned the work after so much effort is unclear: perhaps it was intended for use on his tour to Prague and Berlin in 1796 and was simply not finished in time; or perhaps he became dissatisfied with some of the basic ideas and eventually had better ones for a new symphony in the same key.

Likewise the Triple Concerto in D was supplanted by a better one in C (op. 56). Both concertos are for violin, cello and piano, and the D major was sketched in early 1802, perhaps for a planned concert that spring. The concert was then cancelled by the theatre director, and Beethoven turned his attention to other works. But he still retained his intention to compose a triple concerto, for such a work was mentioned in a letter from his brother Carl to Breitkopf & Härtel on 14 October 1803 – several months before the earliest sketches

for op. 56. As with the Symphony in C, most of the sketches, and a fragmentary, largely empty 126-bar score, are for parts of the first movement, with only brief ideas for the later ones (Kramer, 1977).

In 1803 Beethoven was commissioned to write an opera, and he spent about six months working intermittently on *Vestas Feuer* (libretto by Schikaneder). By the end of that period he had made over twenty pages of sketches and written out a 275-bar first scene in full score, apart from a few gaps in the instrumental parts (see Hess, 1959, xiii.143–68). However, he became exasperated by the poor quality of the libretto and Schikaneder's refusal to have it improved. 'Just picture to yourself a Roman subject (of which I had been told neither the scheme nor anything else whatever) and language and verses such as could proceed only out of the mouths of our Viennese apple-women.' (Letter 87a) So he turned to *Leonore*.

Between 1813 and 1817 Beethoven sketched a great many works not brought to fruition. Most never progressed beyond a few bars, but in three of them substantial progress was made. The first was a Sixth Piano Concerto of 1815 (see Cook, 1989). The full score of this begins confidently, but contains increasingly large gaps before petering out altogether about halfway through the solo exposition. Sketches survive giving some indication of what might have followed, but the precise details can only be guessed at; a recent completion of the movement by Nicholas Cook has been performed but not published. Beethoven may have felt the work to be insufficiently striking or original, for it resembles the Violin Concerto in key, meter and certain other features.

The following year he sketched a Piano Trio in F minor, but again abandoned it about halfway through the first movement. Then in 1817 he began a String Quintet in D minor; the opening slow introduction or prelude was completed (see p. 239), but the ensuing fugue, whose theme resembles the Scherzo of the Ninth Symphony, was barely begun.

During the 1820s Beethoven made grandiose plans for many large-scale works, most of which never materialized; a few of those that did not, however, were sketched out in sufficient detail for us to obtain at least an inkling of what was intended. When the *Missa Solemnis* was written, so many publishers asked for it that Beethoven eventually resolved to write two further masses; the first was to have been in C♯ minor, but very few sketches exist – mainly for the 'Dona nobis'. Another work planned was an overture on B–A–C–H, which was intended to be 'very fugal with 3 trombones' and reflected Beethoven's great admiration for Bach's music. Several sketches were made during 1822–5 but all that emerged was a short B–A–C–H Canon (WoO 191) of September 1825 and the *Grosse Fuge* (op. 133) of September–December 1825; the latter has a theme incorporating a retrograde of B–A–

C–H, is highly contrapuntal and in the same key as the planned overture, which seems to have been abandoned after the completion of the *Grosse Fuge*.

Sketches for a Tenth Symphony cover almost the same period as those for the overture, but Beethoven definitely intended to complete the Symphony, for he indicated as much only eight days before his death. Recent investigation (Brandenburg, 1984a; Cooper, 1985) has resulted in the identification of about 350 bars of sketches for the work – mainly for the first movement; these sketches closely match a description of the movement, provided by Karl Holz, who claimed to have heard Beethoven play it on the piano. The movement is unusual, consisting of a gentle, lyrical Andante in E♭ major followed by a stormy Allegro in C minor and a return of the Andante theme. A conjectural reconstruction of the movement, based on the surviving sketches, has been made by Barry Cooper and was first performed in October 1988 (see Cooper, 1988; the score is published by Universal Edition, London).

The work being composed immediately before Beethoven's death, however, was a String Quintet in C, which had been requested by the publisher Diabelli. After Beethoven's death Diabelli purchased either a score or a score sketch of the first movement and published two arrangements of it – for solo piano and for piano duet – before apparently destroying the original manuscript. Attempts have been made to reconstruct the quintet version from these two arrangements, and there are also some sketches for the movement in Beethoven's last pocket sketchbook. These sketches are followed by some for another movement in C – presumably the second movement – implying that the first movement was complete or nearly so. Like the last Quartet, the work is very Classical in sound (Staehelin, 1980), and the first movement is, surprisingly, a short Polonaise in binary form with repeats. No attempt has yet been made to reconstruct what Beethoven had in mind for the second movement.

Other large-scale works were planned but scarcely started, if at all – especially towards the end of his life. These include numerous ideas for operas; *Macbeth* (text by Collin) was briefly sketched in 1808 and was still being considered in 1811; *Bradamante* (also by Collin) was discussed in 1808; in 1811 Beethoven expressed enthusiasm for a French text, *Les Ruines de Babylon*, which was to be adapted by Treitschke; the following year Karl Theodor Körner's *Ulysses Wiederkehr* was discussed, and in 1815 two libretti were considered – Amenda's *Bacchus* and Treitschke's *Romulus und Remus*. A few opera sketches from about December that year presumably relate to one of these two – probably the latter, which Beethoven asserted would have been composed had the theatre directors been able to offer him a slightly higher fee. In 1823 Grillparzer

was asked to write a libretto for Beethoven and he offered two subjects – *Die schöne Melusine* and *Drahomira*. The Conversation Books contain interesting discussions about both of them, with *Melusine* seeming the more likely to be taken up, but no sketches have been found. Meanwhile Beethoven indicated in 1823 that the work he most wanted to compose in any genre was *Faust* – whether as an opera or as incidental music to Goethe's play is unclear.

Several sacred works were also considered during Beethoven's last decade. An oratorio *Judith* is mentioned in discussions with Grillparzer, and for some time Beethoven was supposed to be setting Bernard's text *Der Sieg des Kreuzes* (*The Victory of the Cross*) for the Gesellschaft der Musikfreunde; a short sketch survives for this. In 1826 Beethoven turned his attention to *Saul*, inspired by Handel's model, and Kuffner prepared a text; Holz reports that Beethoven worked out some of the music in his head, but there are no known sketches. Beethoven also planned to write three additional movements (including a gradual and offertory) for the *Missa Solemnis*, and to write a full-length Requiem, but again nothing has been found.

Shorter works

Shorter works left unfinished consist mainly of piano pieces and songs (see Nottebohm, 1887, pp. 573–80; Schmidt, 1969, pp. 125–8). They range from those nearly complete to those where only the opening motif is sketched. The best known is the piano piece known as 'The Rage over the Lost Penny', which despite possessing an opus number (op. 129) was left unfinished; it was published posthumously in January 1828 by Diabelli, who was presumably responsible for the completion. Certain bagatelles planned for a collection in 1822 were left in an almost complete state, as were several early piano pieces in the Kafka Sketch Miscellany. A selection of many of those in the latter group has been published with suitable amplifications by Adolf Fecker (1972). One work omitted by Fecker is an interesting and lengthy piece in D, probably drafted in 1793 and revised in 1795 (Kerman, 1970, ii.110–125). It resembles a minuet with trio in the minor (but each section through-composed), followed by an extended version of the first section, leading to a slow movement in G. Perhaps it is an early attempt at a *sonata quasi una fantasia*.

Among the unfinished Lieder are several texts that were later to appear in famous settings by Schubert. These include *Erlkönig* (WoO 131), sketched in 1794 and 1796 and published in a completion by Reinhold Becker in 1897; *Rastlose Liebe* (Hess 149), which is found beside some of the *Erlkönig* sketches of 1796; *Heidenröslein* (Hess 150), sketched at various times including 1796, 1818 and

277

1822; and *Gretchen am Spinnrade*, sketched *c*.1793. Again the amount of detail varies from more or less complete melodic lines, as in *Traute Henriette* (Hess 151, published in a completion by Adolf Erler in 1949), to songs where only one or two phrases are set.

Shortage of time was perhaps the main reason why so many works were left unfinished. Beethoven's mind was so full of ideas for compositions that it would have been impossible for any composer – let alone one who devoted so much energy to refining his ideas – to develop them all into complete pieces. And although some of the abandoned works are relatively dull and uninspired, this is no more so than is the case with the early ideas for some of his greatest masterpieces. On the other hand certain abandoned ideas – especially some of the early, short ones that may have originated in improvisation sessions – are even more extraordinary than the finished works from the same period.

BARRY COOPER

Section 11

PERFORMANCE PRACTICE IN BEETHOVEN'S DAY

PERFORMANCE PRACTICE IN BEETHOVEN'S DAY

INFORMATION ABOUT PERFORMANCE practice in Beethoven's day is not only interesting from an historical point of view, but is also important to the present-day performer in order for him/her to reflect the composer's intentions faithfully (see 'Performance styles since Beethoven's day', pp. 298–302). The subject concerns the conditions under which performances took place (venues, programmes); the size, content and direction of orchestras; the types of instruments available; and information about the prevailing pitch and conventions regarding tempo, ornamentation, articulation, notation, etc. It quickly overlaps with, and leads to, the question of the composer's intentions. These have been divided by Randall Dipert into three categories: low-, middle-, and high-level intentions (Dipert, 1980, p. 206). The first, and one on which much information is readily available, concerns the types of instruments and ways of playing. The second concerns the actual sounds intended by the composer; in the general sense these are harder to understand because we can know little about what a composer heard in his head, or what he thought about instruments and performers in his day. High-level intentions concern the effect to be produced in the listener: on a technical level, the perception of tonal and formal relationships; on an aesthetic level, the ability of the music to inspire, entertain, move, etc. These are the most important to follow in order to capture the spirit of a work, but at the same time, the most difficult to understand. To be faithful to the first category may be to fall short here; but attaining these high-level intentions may be possible only by by-passing some of the low-level intentions.

The present discussion aims to suit the historian, the listener and the performer by pointing out the issues involved and providing the basis for more detailed study. Facts such as the conditions under which a performance took place are primarily of interest to the historian, while details of different contemporary keyboard instruments and their potential as regards volume, balance, articulation and pedalling are of interest primarily to the pianist. For the listener, the study of all aspects of a work's background leads to a heightened awareness of its aesthetic qualities. General matters such as pitch, tempo, expression marks, phrasing and articulation will be addressed first; a second section will deal with orchestral and instrumental music, including direction, cadenzas and improvisation; piano music will be considered separately, such is its importance in Beethoven's output and the wealth of material available; and finally the issue of ornamentation will be summarized.

Pitch, tempo and articulation

A variety of pitches prevailed in the late 18th/early 19th centuries. The size of the discrepancies can be appreciated from Wegeler's account of a rehearsal of Beethoven's First Piano Concerto in Vienna in the mid-1790s, at which the piano was found to be a semitone lower than the wind instruments. In order to remedy this, Beethoven transposed the solo part up a semitone. The determining factors were secular or sacred venues and locality. Although the variance was as much as a minor third, seemingly the most common pitches placed a' slightly lower than the so-called standard $a' = 440\,\mathrm{Hz}$ of today, with a tendency for pitch to rise during the first half of the 19th century.

The Classical style saw tempo determined largely by Italian directions, combined to a lesser extent with time signatures and note content. But whereas Haydn and Mozart contented themselves with a fairly limited number of terms, Beethoven's range of tempo directions was far wider, and increasingly incorporated qualifying terms or phrases to denote character and mood, thereby encroaching on the realms of expression markings (see below).

It is necessary to understand what is meant by the most commonly used terms, such as *allegro*. Before the invention of the metronome, Quantz in the 18th century used 80 human pulse beats to the minute as a guide. He grouped tempi as either fast or slow, with two subdivisions in each category. The fastest of the 'very fast' sub-group was denoted by *allegro assai*, which he estimated as $\jmath = 80$, and *allegretto* was the fastest of the 'moderately fast' group, measured as $\jmath = 80$. The slow category was considered to be half the speed, with *adagio cantabile* approximating to $\jmath = 40$, and *adagio assai* to $\jmath = 40$. He placed *allegro* and *vivace* in the middle of the fast category, giving them a speed of $\jmath = 120$. Marpurg also classified speed, and although he was more forward-looking in having three categories (fast, moderate and slow with their subdivisions), his system was less successful in that he did not take up Quantz's method of measurement, so he could not be precise.

Classical interpretation of speed grew out of these principles, and the writings of Türk and Koch are very informative. Türk tells us that an Allegro in the early 19th century was considerably faster than fifty years earlier, and that the rule that tempo was determined by the shortest note values was on the decline. However, it did continue to play a part because it was common for the tempo to change within a movement, depending on the note values of particular passages. Mozart and Beethoven both reportedly played Allegros faster than their predecessors, and the trend for fast movements to become faster is one which has continued. Rothschild quotes as an example the *Eroica* Symphony: a performance under Beethoven's direction lasted 'one full hour'; in Muller-Reuter's *Lexicon der deutschen Konzertliteratur* of 1921 it is timed at fifty-two minutes; and some modern recordings are as short as forty-six minutes (Rothschild, 1961, p. 9).

Beethoven reacted enthusiastically to Maelzel's invention of the metronome (or rather, its predecessor the chronometer) in 1813. A report in the *Wiener Vaterländische Blätter* on 13 October 1813 stated: 'Herr Beethoven looks upon this invention as a welcome means with which to secure the performance of his brilliant compositions in all places in the tempos conceived by him, which to his regret have so often been misunderstood.' (Thayer, 1967, p. 544) In 1817 he had a pamphlet published (by Steiner) giving metronome markings for his first eight symphonies and the Septet, op. 20; and another, soon after, for the string quartets to date (opp. 18, 59, 74 and 95). He provided metronome indications for the Piano Sonata op. 106, *Meeresstille* (op. 112), *Opferlied* (op. 121b) and the Ninth Symphony, and wrote frequently to Schott's of his intention, eventually unfulfilled, to send directions for the *Missa Solemnis*. As Kolisch states, the fact that Beethoven was prepared to adopt metronome indications for important works confirms that tempo is an essential part of the musical idea (1943, p. 174), as does Beethoven's letter of 1826 to Schott's: 'The metronome markings will be sent to you very soon. Do wait for them. In our century such indications are certainly necessary. Moreover, I have received letters from Berlin informing me that the first performance of the symphony [No. 9] was received with enthusiastic applause, which I ascribe largely to the metronome markings. We can scarcely have *tempi ordinari* any longer, since one must fall into line with the idea of unfettered genius.' (Letter 1545)

In spite of this, Beethoven's metronome markings have not been generally accepted. In part this can be ascribed to his alleged comment to Schindler: 'No more metronome! Anyone who can feel the music right does not need it; and for anyone who can't, nothing is of any use; he runs away with the whole orchestra anyway.' (Schindler, 1966, pp. 425–6) This remark should not be taken too seriously, since it may have been another of Schindler's inventions. The main objection is that the markings are generally believed to be too fast. But Beethoven is not alone in this; indeed, according to Willy Hess, music proceeds much quicker in the imagination than in reality, and the composer sitting at his desk is likely to ascribe quicker metronome markings to his music than he would adopt in performance (Hess, 1988, p. 17). This same point was acknowledged by Peter Stadlen when he investigated seemingly problematic metronome markings (1982, p. 54). The vast majority were on the fast side, but after he had taken numerous factors into account he concluded that most were 'within the realm of plausibility'. They become still more acceptable when tempered with flexibility. Newman defined this as follows: 'Like tempo itself, flexibility reflects the prevailing rhythmic character, though at a more local level. And, it similarly responds to changes in the harmonic rhythm, texture, articulation, ornamentation, and rhythmic progress.' (Newman, 1988, p. 110) There is plenty of evidence both in Beethoven's music and from contemporary reports to suggest that Beethoven favoured an underlying strict tempo into which a certain amount of flexibility could be introduced. These points must call into question the literalism which has been applied to some modern 'authentic' performances.

The additional qualifying terms used by Beethoven enabled him to indicate a degree of flexibility and to demand a more precise interpretation than hitherto, regulating sophisticated variations in speed. Reference has been made elsewhere to the finale of the Piano Sonata op. 110, where frequent adjustments of tempo are demanded within a short space of time (see 'Piano music', p. 242). Generally, the late works show a tendency for the directions to become more verbose: the third movement of the String Quartet op. 130 is marked 'Andante con moto, ma non troppo', with 'poco scherzando' below in parenthesis; likewise the slow movement of the 'Hammerklavier' Sonata has both 'Adagio sostenuto ($\musEighth = 80$)', and 'appassionato e con molto sentimento'. New words are added in Beethoven's quest for precision: in the fourth movement of String Quartet op. 131, 'Andante moderato e lusinghiero'. The effect of these painstaking directions adds to the intensity in performance. These qualifying marks for tempo and mood are closely related to the increased number of terms and signs used to express volume, attack and phrasing.

The questions of accentuation, articulation and phrasing can only be touched upon here. Accentuation, a tradition of the *style galant* and early Classical period, relied upon the subtle and uniform distribution of accents of varying strength depending on the time signature. With Haydn, Mozart and particularly Beethoven this underwent significant changes with a move towards melodic accentuation. Articulation in keyboard and stringed instruments has been well researched. Suffice it to say that the 'normal' articulation up to the early 19th century was something between legato and staccato. Beethoven adopted a more legato style in the manner of Clementi when playing the piano, and a similar change occurred in string playing along with the development of the modern Tourte bow. Slurs in Beethoven's day usually indicated legato playing rather than phrasing.

Orchestral and chamber music

A typical orchestral concert at the turn of the 19th century would include an overture, a concerto, a symphony, operatic arias and scenes, and the concerto soloist, usually a keyboard player, might improvise (see 'Beethoven's musical environment', pp. 87–91). They would normally take place in theatres; only later were there purpose-built concert halls. Beethoven did not always include operatic numbers, and would sometimes take the opportunity to introduce movements from religious choral works. The Gloria and Sanctus from the Mass in C were performed in a concert in December 1808, and the Kyrie, Credo and Agnus Dei from the *Missa Solemnis* were performed alongside an overture and the first performance of the 'Choral' Symphony in May 1824. Thus Beethoven broke early with the convention that church music was normally performed in churches. In fact the *Missa Solemnis* did not receive a liturgical performance until 1835 in Pressburg (Bratislava); in this respect he was anticipating present-day practice.

Performances in Beethoven's day, whether public or semiprivate, were far less polished affairs than they are today. It is clear from contemporary accounts that by today's standards they were very much under-rehearsed, and the physical conditions under which they took place were often far from ideal. Reichardt's diary for 1808 provides a valuable source of information on a variety of aspects of performance. He was present at the concert in the Theater an der Wien on 22 December 1808 at which Beethoven's Fifth and Sixth Symphonies, movements from the Mass in C, the Fourth Piano Concerto and the Choral Fantasia were performed. Apparently it had not been possible to arrange a full rehearsal of all the works and there was 'many a mishap in performance', with the Choral Fantasia being so disastrous that it had to be restarted. At another concert, with works by Romberg, Paer and Beethoven, the audience was crowded into three small rooms, totally unsuitable for Beethoven's 'gigantic and overpowering overture *Coriolan* – one was quite deafened by the noise of the trumpets, kettledrum, and wind instruments of all sorts.' Reichardt attended the series of concerts given by Schuppanzigh's String Quartet that same winter, and made interesting observations, particularly on Schuppanzigh's playing:

> The quartet is on the whole well-balanced.... Herr Schuppanzigh himself has an original, piquant style, more appropriate to the humorous quartets of Haydn, Mozart and Beethoven... he plays the most difficult passages clearly although not always quite in tune... he also accents very correctly and significantly, and his cantabile tone is often quite singing and affecting. He is likewise a good leader... though he disturbed me often with his accursed fashion, generally introduced here [Vienna] of beating time with his foot, even when there was no need for it, sometimes out of habit alone, at other times only to reinforce the *forte*... (Strunk, 1950, pp. 734–9).

The size and content of Beethoven's orchestras varied considerably. There was no official resident orchestra in Vienna until 1840 except those associated with the theatres, which would have formed the basis for concerts there. In 1808 the orchestra in the Theater an der Wien consisted of 12 violins, 4 violas, 3 cellos, 3 basses, 2 each of flutes, oboes, clarinets, bassoons, horns and trumpets, and timpani: a total of 35. But in 1815 in the Redoutensaal the strings comprised 36 violins, 14 violas, 12 cellos and 17 double basses. The private orchestra for a concert in Prince Schwarzenberg's house in 1792 consisted of 6, 6, 4, 3, 3, and single wind, but in the 1807–8 season Beethoven's first four symphonies were performed in the university hall by a much larger complement of strings – 13, 12, 7, 6, 4 – but still single wind. As time went on, large orchestras became increasingly normal; in 1817 the Tonkünstler-Societät performed *Christus am Oelberge* with 20, 20, 8, 7, 7, and woodwind parts doubled or trebled, and in 1824 the Ninth Symphony was performed by 24 violins, 10 violas, 12 cellos and 12 basses.

The sound and balance of the orchestra were different from today. Overall the wind were louder and more piercing than the strings; oboes were louder and more penetrative, bassoons produced a more vital sound, and only the flutes, made of wood, were softer than present-day instruments. The strings were softer due to their gut strings and the different manner of articulation dictated by contemporary bows.

The question of conducting is a difficult one in a period of transition where no hard and fast rules pertained. There are some reports of Beethoven as a conductor, and others of him directing from the piano in orchestral and choral works. In the latter case his main role would have been to maintain tempo and direct the voices, while the principal conductor, either the leader using his bow or a conductor with a baton, would set the speed and interpret the music. But although conductors with batons became increasingly common, they were not the norm for some time. This is apparent from the fact that Beethoven's first six symphonies were initially published without scores. Quite clearly a work of the complexity of the Ninth Symphony could not have been performed satisfactorily without a conductor.

Beethoven played and directed the first performance of his first four piano concertos. He would have played during the tutti passages and improvised cadenzas which are now lost to us. His attitude to the cadenza underwent a change: in the early years its precise form and character were less important to the concerto as a whole. Only in c.1809 did he decide to write out a number of cadenzas for the first four concertos, thus restricting a traditional freedom of the performer. In the third movement of the Fourth Concerto he was more specific than hitherto, with the remark 'La Cadenza sia corta' ('the cadenza is to be short'), and in the 'Emperor' Concerto nothing was left to chance: the first-movement cadenza is written out (unconventionally at the beginning), and at the point where a cadenza was customary he wrote 'no si fa una cadenza' ('do not play a cadenza').

Improvisation was not limited to cadenzas, nor to concertos. In keyboard music in particular it was conventional to embellish melodic lines in performance, and publishers would sometimes add these too. But Beethoven, generally speaking, was against such additions by others and made this clear to Ries (Wegeler, 1987, pp. 106–7), and in a letter to Czerny (Letter 610). In chamber music it was traditional to make short embellishments at pauses. There is a report of a notorious occasion in 1797, when

Beethoven, playing in the Quintet for piano and wind instruments, op. 16, made an unusually long cadenza; this was evidently not the norm.

Piano music

When we speak of Beethoven's pianos we are not speaking of one instrument but of a developing tradition where instruments differed from each other and from their present-day counterparts to an extent hardly found in any other instrument. The very construction of the modern pianoforte, with an iron frame supporting thick steel strings hit by large felt hammers, ensures a tone quality very different from that of the early 19th century instruments with wooden frames, lighter strings and small, leather-headed hammers, which produced notes with a sharper attack, quicker decay and more overtones. The early instruments displayed a greater tonal contrast between registers, and the balance was different: today's instruments have a much fuller bass which is proportionally much stronger than the treble. The differing tone qualities found amongst early instruments results from the two types of action in use. The Viennese action, used by Austrian and German manufacturers, was noted for its lightness of touch and the clear, gentle tone it produced, whilst the English action, used by English and French makers, was heavier and produced a stronger tone. In view of the reports of the power of Beethoven's playing it is perhaps surprising to find that he favoured the Viennese action. Although he occasionally requested greater resistance, he was certainly never entirely happy with the heavier action of the Erard and Broadwood instruments with which he was presented in 1803 and 1818 respectively, and he remained loyal to the work of the Stein/Streicher family throughout his life.

Although the extending range was an important aspect of keyboard development in the early 19th century, this has no bearing on a discussion of performance practice. The issues to be considered here are the sounds the instruments produced and how Beethoven's own style of playing exploited them. His virtuosity was mentioned in an earlier section (see pp. 132–3). The feature most often commented on was his legato or singing tone; to cite Czerny, 'But Beethoven's performance of slow and sustained passages produced an almost magical effect on every listener, and, so far as I know, was never surpassed.' (Thayer, 1967, p. 369) But seemingly Beethoven achieved this in spite of, rather than with the help of, the instruments at his disposal. In 1796 he wrote to Streicher: 'There is no doubt that so far as the manner of playing is concerned, the pianoforte is still the least studied and developed of all instruments; one often thinks one is merely listening to a harp. And I am delighted that you are one of the few who realize and perceive that provided that one can feel the music, one can also make the pianoforte sing.' (Letter 18) This is important in that it gives us a very clear clue as to the sound of the early instruments. But Beethoven's own style of playing was an important factor. The 'different' style of treating the instrument and the 'entirely new and daring' sounds (see p. 133) were unlike Mozart's playing, which although Beethoven praised, he found 'choppy' and developed from harpsichord style, and which Czerny described as having a 'brittle and short staccato touch' which was still the general style (Czerny, 1970, pp. 13 and 11). Two aspects of Beethoven's technique contributed to his cantabile style, and both are reflected in his piano compositions: his touch (method of tone production and fingering technique), and his use of the sustaining pedal. Indeed, his use of the pedals in general brought a new expressiveness to piano playing.

Reports of Beethoven's technique suggest that he played with rounded fingers, a 'gliding' style, and with his fingers constantly touching the keys; all of which point to an essentially legato style. Further evidence for this comes from the music itself, in which he marked an unusually large number of fingerings. Many were to facilitate particularly difficult passages, but others demonstrate a striving for legato effect: the thumb is used more frequently than hitherto and often on black keys; the thumb is often to be passed rapidly underneath the fingers to move the hand smoothly to a new position; and there are instances of a finger sliding between successive notes.

In his youth Beethoven would have been familiar with hand-, knee- and foot-operated devices which could alter keyboard tone. These could variously raise the dampers, providing a sustained tone (sometimes the two halves of the keyboard could be affected separately); shift the action sideways, enabling *una corda* and/or *due corde* effects; dampen the tone, by sliding material between the strings and the hammers; or produce special effects, such as lute or percussion. He only ever used two: the damper-raising and action-shifting devices.

From the early 1800s the devices were normally operated by foot pedals. Before *c*.1802, when a knee-operated damper-raising mechanism was often used, Beethoven indicated raised dampers by the term 'senza sordino' and cancelled it with 'con sordino' (see plate 25). The last major work in which this occurred was the Third Piano Concerto. After that he used the term 'Ped.' for raising the dampers by depressing the foot pedal, and 'O' for restoring them by releasing it. Pedalling indications do not appear uniformly throughout his works, but they are carefully marked where he obviously desired a particular effect. Czerny said of his playing that 'he used a lot of pedal, much more than is indicated in his works' (Czerny, 1970, p. 22), so it can be assumed that the use of the legato pedal would often be taken for granted.

Some of the sustaining pedal markings seem puzzling now. The most obvious examples are the opening of the slow movement of the Third Piano Concerto, where the pedal is directed to be depressed for several bars at a time over several changes of harmony, and, even more striking, the first movement of the

'Moonlight' Sonata, where the pianist is directed to play the whole movement delicately and without dampers. As far back as about 1840 Czerny wrote of the Third Piano Concerto: 'Beethoven (who played the concerto publicly in 1803) depressed the pedal throughout this whole theme, which worked very well on the weak-sounding pianos of that time, especially if the action-shifting pedal was used at the same time. But now, with a much stronger tone, we must advise that the damper pedal be reapplied with each significant change of harmony, yet so that no break in the tone can be noticed. For the whole theme must sound like a distant, holy, unearthly harmony' (Newman, 1988, pp. 247–8). The directions for the 'Moonlight' Sonata are not suited to the modern piano, but Newman believes that, since even performances on early pianos in the prescribed way produce a 'harmonic blur', this was an effect that Beethoven on occasions positively wanted (Newman, 1988, pp. 245–9).

Only 2 per cent of Beethoven's pedal indications refer to the action shifting or *una corda* pedal. They occur for the first time in the Fourth Piano Concerto and then in the last five sonatas. Its use was indicated by the terms 'una corda', 'tre corde' and 'tutte le corde'. The slow movement of the Concerto is directed to be played using the *una corda* pedal; but at one point there is the direction 'due e poi tre corde' and a little later 'due poi una corda'. This required a shift from one to two then three strings and back again. On certain contemporary triple-strung instruments it was possible to achieve this. It produced an extra gradation of both volume and tone colour between *una* and *tre corde* which is now lost to us on modern pianos. Other effects are likewise lost on the modern instrument. The result of a legato style of fingering and pedalling now differs considerably from the sound produced on 19th-century pianos. For the present-day performer on a modern instrument the problem is to decide on a balance between the imagined 19th-century sound and the potential of the modern piano. Perhaps Beethoven's comment to Holz in 1826 is proof that he had continually striven for a sound which he was never to achieve: 'It is and remains an inadequate instrument.' (Thayer, 1967, p. 984)

Ornamentation

One further aspect of performance practice which must be mentioned is ornamentation. This applies to all Beethoven's music, but occurs most frequently in the piano music. It has been the subject of several detailed studies (see, for example, Kullak, 1973, Badura-Skoda, 1980, and Newman, 1988), but there is still much scope for debate and conjecture.

Ornaments, and in particular trills, were used extensively, opening up new technical and expressive possibilities, but also, especially in the late works, becoming an organic part of the music. Beethoven's ornamentation may be indicated by conventional signs, may be written out (causing the fewest problems), or may be improvised in performance. This last category causes the most conjecture as to frequency and exact nature, but the first group causes the most problems in execution. The issue is further complicated by the fact that Beethoven was writing at a time of transition. The performance of trills, for example, poses several questions concerning the starting note, the content of the body of the trill, and its ending. In Beethoven's early years, trills normally began on the note above the written one, whereas by the end of his life it was becoming customary to begin on the written note itself. And in the one place where Beethoven wrote out an explanation of his trill sign (in the finale of the 'Waldstein' Sonata of 1803–4) he actually altered it from a written-note start to an upper-note start. Least problematic is the short *Schneller* trill comprising between three and six notes, its shortest manifestation being similar to the mordent or inverted mordent. In addition Beethoven introduced double and triple trills, and his own special trills where the same hand simultaneously plays a melodic line and executes a trill. Turns likewise usually began on the upper note when they were written directly above a note. Trills were often given a turn or suffix at the end, even if this was not notated, but again there is some uncertainty about the extent of this practice.

The problem of notation conventions in ornaments can perhaps be best exemplified by comparing the difference in notation between vocal and instrumental music. The instrumental recitative at the beginning of the finale of the Ninth Symphony is written as it is to be played, unlike the vocal recitative which imitates it later; here the singer, according to custom, would have been expected to add a long appoggiatura at the end of the phrase. Thus it is essential not merely to know what Beethoven wrote, but to understand what that notation implied to his contemporaries, if one is to achieve the goal of establishing precisely how his music was performed in his lifetime. Despite extensive research, we are still a long way from reaching that goal, and controversy continues to surround several issues discussed above.

ANNE-LOUISE COLDICOTT

Section 12

RECEPTION

RECEPTION

Contemporary assessments

BEETHOVEN'S GENIUS WAS widely recognized during his lifetime: contemporary writings have passed down an idea of the reception of his music by the general public, the impression it made on educated people outside music, and how it was perceived by professional musicians. The biographies of Wegeler, Ries, Schindler and Thayer are also important sources. *Beethoven. Impressions by his Contemporaries* (Sonneck, 1967) contains extracts from the writings of fellow-musicians and other prominent people: literary figures such as Goethe, Bettine von Arnim, Clemens Brentano, and travellers/historians such as Russell and Schultz. More 'immediate' were the brief newspaper reports and the more comprehensive reviews and extended essays in specialist music journals, although there has been no attempt to collate all these as yet.

In *Beethoven's Critics* Robin Wallace (1986) has summarized the attitudes of the principal critics in Germany, but very little primary material is reproduced and the most ready sources remain the extracts in Schindler and Thayer. Beethoven's music enjoyed great popularity in England, with articles appearing in *The Quarterly Musical Magazine and Review* and *The Harmonicon*, but these are poorly documented. In France it did not become very popular until after his death, but from Wallace, Schindler and Schrade (1942) we learn something of the initial reaction to it.

Beethoven's early music made an immediate impact, particularly on the young. Moscheles recalled the effect it had on him as a young student in spite of his teacher warning him against it; and Czerny wrote: 'He was always marvelled at and respected as an extraordinary being and his greatness was suspected even by those who did not understand him...' (Thayer, 1967, pp. 444–5). This was certainly true of the critics, who while complaining about the difficulties of his music did not fail to recognize his originality or technical ability. Early reviews in the Leipzig *Allgemeine Musikalische Zeitung (AMZ)* referred to 'the harshness of the modulations', and 'the unusual harmonic knowledge and love for serious composition'; the Violin Sonatas op. 12 were described as 'Learned, learned and always learned – nothing natural, no song'.

Gradually a new generation of critics emerged, better equipped to accept innovations. A reviewer of the Piano Sonatas opp. 26 and 27 wrote in 1802: 'Less educated musicians, and those who expect nothing more from music than a facile entertainment, will take up these works in vain...' (Wallace, 1986, p. 10). His piano and chamber music had by then been enthusiastically received by the public, but what was the reaction to his orchestral music? According to Wegeler, the first performances of major works were usually given before receptive, informal gatherings of musicians and music-lovers. Seemingly neither critics nor the general public were entirely enthusiastic about the large orchestral works, but reports from as far afield as Leipzig, Berlin, Mannheim and Prague over the next few years give an indication that they were widely performed, with only *Christus am Oelberge*, the Triple Concerto and *Fidelio* being consistently criticized. The reviewer of the Second Symphony in the *AMZ* complained of its length and other aspects, but ended his report: 'However, all of that is so outweighed by the powerful, fiery spirit alive in this colossal product, by the wealth of new ideas and by their almost entirely original treatment, as well as by the profundity of artistic learnedness, that one can prophesy for this work that it will endure and will always be heard with renewed pleasure long after a thousand fashionable ditties now being celebrated have been buried.' (Senner, 1986, p. 8) The *Eroica* Symphony produced the most reaction to date: the correspondent in the *Freymüthige* claimed that the audience found it much too long and difficult; Czerny recalled that at its first performance someone called out 'I'll give another kreuzer if the thing will but stop'; according to Schindler it was banned at the Prague Conservatoire as being 'morally corrupting'; and in the *AMZ* it was described as 'a tremendously expanded, daring and wild fantasia' but with 'too much that is glaring and bizarre' and an example of 'musical anarchy'.

The *AMZ* review of the Fifth Symphony in 1808 marked the introduction of the critic E.T.A. Hoffmann, an influential exponent of German Romanticism, who did much to contribute to the 19th-century conception of Beethoven as a heroic figure invested with magical powers. His style was new, incorporating general remarks on Beethoven and on musical aesthetics as well as a synthesis of analysis and interpretation in a new poetic literary style. Typical of his interpretative approach is the following excerpt:

> Beethoven's instrumental music opens to us the realm of the colossal and the immeasurable. Glowing beams of light shoot through the deep night of this realm and we perceive shadows surging back and forth, closer and closer around us...

But he could equally well describe *how* particular effects are achieved:

> The first Allegro... begins with a principal idea only two bars long, which reappears in many different guises in the course of the movement. In the second measure there is a fermata, followed by a repetition of the principal idea a tone lower, and by another fermata.... Not even the tonality is yet established; the listener expects E♭ major. The second violin begins again with the principal

idea, and in the following measure C, the fundamental note, is played by cellos and bassoons, while the viola and first violin, entering in imitation, establish C minor... (Wallace, 1986, pp. 21, 23)

Schindler wrote that at the end of Beethoven's second period (c.1814) he was 'at a height of fame never before achieved by a musician who was still in the midst of his artistic activity' (Schindler, 1966, p. 204). In later years Beethoven felt out of sympathy with the Viennese public; but this was not reflected by the serious critics, such as Amadeus Wendt, who had succeeded Hoffmann at the *AMZ*. Although he found Beethoven's works difficult to understand as far as their form was concerned, he acknowledged their invention and mastery. In his essay 'Beethoven's Musical Character' he wrote: 'For the true sign of great works is that they are repeatedly and increasingly enjoyed...' (Schindler, 1966, p. 185).

Some of Beethoven's music continued to find general acclaim – so much so that in 1818 Cipriani Potter wrote that 'it is now listened to with an attention and delight that his real friends and admirers could scarcely have anticipated...it is gratifying to witness the anxiety with which the uninitiated endeavour to comprehend what is termed classical writing...'. And in 1821 John Russell wrote: 'Beethoven is the most celebrated of living composers in Vienna, and in certain departments, the foremost of his day.' (Sonneck, 1967, pp. 108, 114)

In 1824, however, Beethoven still felt out of sympathy with the Viennese public (many of whom preferred Rossini) to such an extent that he considered holding the first performances of his two latest works, the *Missa Solemnis* and the Ninth Symphony, outside Vienna. His friends and admirers wrote to him assuring him of his standing and begging him not to withhold his latest masterpieces. As a result, the Symphony and three numbers from the Mass were performed in Vienna in May 1824. According to the critic in the *AMZ* the audience was deeply moved and their applause was 'enthusiastic to a degree'. But generally this was not the case with the Ninth Symphony. Neither the inclusion of voices in the finale nor its content were understood. The work received its first performance in England in 1825; whereas the earlier symphonies were popular, this one was not well received, being criticized for having 'no intelligible design' and for its 'noisy extravagance'.

Beethoven's late works received significantly less attention in the *AMZ*, but two relatively new publications, the Berlin journal of the same name and *Caecilia* in Mainz, upheld his music. A.B. Marx from the Berlin *AMZ* was one of the few critics sympathetic towards the Ninth Symphony's choral finale, and he sought to share his understanding of it with his readers:

Endless, as in a landscape or in immeasurable nature, are the possible shapes and combinations in instrumental music. Now the life of nature extends to human expression and song, and one tries to hear in it human meaning and song-speech; now that which is portrayed loses itself in its element, simple tone, and the simplest forgotten form shapes itself once again in many different combinations into a great, meaningful whole, as leaf upon leaf represents a tree. (Wallace, 1986, p. 56)

The first complete performance of the Mass was organized in St Petersburg by Prince Galitzin, who wrote of it to Beethoven: 'The effect of this music on the public cannot be described and I doubt if I exaggerate when I say that for my part I have never heard anything so sublime...it can be said that your genius has anticipated the centuries.' (Thayer, 1967, p. 925)

The late string quartets were perhaps surprisingly quickly accepted and admired by the public after initial difficulties with the first, op. 127 (mainly on account of it being under-rehearsed and consequently not understood by the performers or the audience). The chief stumbling block was the fugal finale to op. 130, which Beethoven was persuaded to replace and publish separately as the *Grosse Fuge*. The critics found it harder to come to terms with their overall structure, unprecedentedly long movements, and new level of dissonance.

Whereas Beethoven's music was readily accepted in England, in France there was much less interest. During his lifetime only the early symphonies, a few trios and quartets and the Septet were well known, and the perceived 'Germanism' in even these led to an initially hostile reaction. After a performance of the first two symphonies in 1811 Cambini wrote in *Tablettes de Polymnie*: 'The composer Beethoven, often bizarre and baroque, sometimes sparkles with extraordinary beauties. Now he takes the majestic flight of the eagle; then he creeps along grotesque paths. After penetrating the soul with a sweet melancholy he soon tears it by a mass of barbaric chords. He seems to harbour doves and crocodiles at the same time.' (Schrade, 1942, p. 3) The performance of the *Eroica* Symphony was abandoned after the audience was reduced to laughter on the grounds of it being too long and too serious. Not until 1820 was another symphony performed in Paris, when no. 5 was favourably received. That led the way for the others to be met with enthusiasm. The piano music was a different case; from 1815 it was encouraged at the Paris Conservatoire at a time when it was less popular in Germany.

Beethoven's fellow-musicians reflect the same spectrum of opinion as the critics and public, ranging from outright condemnation, through difficulty in understanding, to complete admiration, and it was the late works which presented the most problems.

ANNE-LOUISE COLDICOTT

Posthumous assessments: the 'Romantic hero'

THE ROMANTIC ERA in Germany was very receptive to the concept of an artist as a heroic figure. Beethoven was a perfect example, and even before his death, the 'Beethoven legend' was being established, in which his life story and descriptions of his appearance and behaviour played as important a part as his music. Particularly influential were the writings of Bettine von Arnim. She attributed certain qualities to Beethoven's music which contributed to its mystique. Arnold Schmitz (1927) later defined these as (i) child of nature, (ii) revolutionary, (iii) magician, (iv) religious leader and prophet. Some or all of these concepts were taken up by other commentators; and in some cases the music took second place, at the expense of portraying Beethoven as a typically Romantic figure.

Among those writing in the Romantic vein who did not lose sight of the actual music were E. T. A. Hoffmann, even though he took up the idea of magic in Beethoven's music; Schumann, who thought the element of David against the Philistines in the music reflected Beethoven's moral values; and Liszt, who wrote to Wilhelm von Lenz, 'For us musicians, Beethoven's work is like the pillar of cloud and fire which guided the Israelites through the desert.... His obscurity and his light trace for us equally the path we have to follow...' (Crofton, 1985, p. 16).

Wagner's reaction after hearing the Seventh Symphony in 1828 was typically Romantic, resulting from the combination of the music itself and the total impression: 'The effect on me was indescribable. To this must be added the impression produced on me by Beethoven's features, which I saw in the lithographs that were circulated everywhere at that time.... I soon conceived an image of him in my mind as a sublime and unique supernatural being...' (Wagner, 1963, p. 41). He did much to further the 19th-century image of Beethoven by public exposure and through his writings. He believed in the magic of Beethoven's 'inner world', evident particularly in the religious quality of the late quartets. In his *Das Kunstwerk der Zukunft* (1849) he claimed that in the Fifth Symphony Beethoven had succeeded in intensifying the expression of the music almost to the point of moral resolve; and that with the Ninth he released music from its own peculiar elements into the realm of universal art.

Sometimes the music itself appears to have been overlooked as Romantic artists used the popular concepts of Beethoven as springboards for their own imagination. This is true of the visual arts (see 'Monuments and memorials', pp. 302–4) and literature. For example, Beethoven was the inspiration for a poem by Ortlepp in 1831, another, *Walderszene*, by Grillparzer in 1844, and a play by Weise in 1836 entitled *Beethoven*; this was the first of several Beethoven dramas, which also included Müller's *Adelaide* of 1863.

In France, Beethoven's music was firmly accepted only after 1828, following the success of performances of his symphonies by Habeneck. Cherubini and Fétis, the conservative French historian and critic, remained opposed, but were in a minority. Berlioz was at the forefront of attempts to encourage acceptance of Beethoven's music by creating a complete image through his criticisms, which often took the form of poetic fantasies. He described the String Quartet op. 131 as 'a heavenly inspiration that took material shape' (Newman, 1983, p. 362). The religious element of the music was taken up by de Vigny, Lamartine and Hugo, who were drawn to the concept of the 'infinite' and felt they could identify with Beethoven. By the end of the 19th century their views led to Beethoven being perceived as the dispenser of salvation and the creator of a new moral universe.

The culmination of French thinking about Beethoven's music along these lines was reached with Romain Rolland at a time when there was an unprecedented number of performances, and many paintings and sculptures were being produced. In his *Life of Beethoven*, published at the turn of the century, he described Beethoven as the personification of liberty and heroism. The protagonist of his long novel *Jean-Christophe* of 1904–12 outwardly parallels Beethoven's life to some extent, but the inner man is strongly inspired by Beethoven's struggles against adversity and his faithfulness to his art.

The combination of anti-German feeling and a new rationality and objectivity prevailing after World War I brought the Beethoven cult in France to an abrupt end. Debussy was a prime deflator, not of the music, but of the verbiage it had inspired. He wrote that Beethoven 'hadn't two cents of literary worth in him, but loved music with a fierce pride' (Newman, 1983, p. 379).

England was less receptive to the Romantic image of Beethoven. His music had found early acceptance here, and continued to do so. John Lawrence Lambe's play *Beethoven Deaf* of 1911 is an exception. The 'mystique' extended more quickly and more vigorously in the USA, via the New England Transcendentalists, where in 1911 Nordling wrote the play *The Moonlight Sonata*. Literary examples from elsewhere also show both the gulf between fact and fiction and the inspiration of which Beethoven was capable. 1872 saw the Italian playwright Cossa's drama *Beethoven*, and 1889 Tolstoy's *The Kreutzer Sonata*, both of which have only tenuous links with the composer.

During the 19th century, Beethoven's music not only acted as an inspiration to the Romantics in general, but also directly influenced other composers (see 'Beethoven's place in music history', pp. 304–6). Furthermore, its intrinsic value led to the compilation of the Breitkopf & Härtel *Gesamtausgabe* (completed 1888), and inspired critical/analytical writings and a number of substantial scholarly studies, of which the most important are Thayer's biography (see pp. 310–11) and Nottebohm's sketch studies (see pp. 321–2).

The Romantic image of Beethoven had come about as a result of the impact of his music and personality on the imagination of a world ready to receive it. Attitudes changed in the 20th century.

The myth has evaporated, but the abiding popularity of the music *per se* has prevailed, and there has been an increase in the growth of all aspects of Beethoven scholarship.

ANNE-LOUISE COLDICOTT

Performance styles since Beethoven's day

SINCE BEETHOVEN'S DEATH, different styles of interpretation of his music have reflected changing musical taste. In the 1830s and 1840s Carl Czerny did much to ensure a continued interest in Beethoven's piano music. Although in performance he would depart from the text, adding upward transpositions, ornaments and pedalling, his serious writings (based partly on his own studies with Beethoven) advise against this: 'In the performance of all his works the player must by no means allow himself to alter the composition, nor to make any addition or abbreviation.' (Czerny, 1970, p. 22/32)

Liszt became an influential exponent of Beethoven's music as a conductor and pianist, transcribing the nine symphonies for piano and frequently performing the sonatas. In the early years he evidently took liberties (but apparently fewer than others), enriching the texture to display his virtuosity or to produce a fuller sonority. An observer wrote: 'Even where one might prove that Beethoven had wanted this or that different...there still always remains the energetic fire and the enthusiasm with which he carries out his concept as something much higher and much more powerful than the performance of the same works, perhaps faithful, but coldly calculated, that we find by many other pianists.' (Newman, 1972, p. 189) Berlioz wrote of two contrasting performances of the 'Moonlight' Sonata: in the earlier one Liszt added trills, tremolos and impassioned chords to the first movement and rushed and slowed the pace; but a few years later 'the noble elegy, the same that he had previously disfigured so curiously, stood out in all its sublime simplicity. Not one note, not one accent was now added to accents and notes supplied by the composer.' (*ibid.*, p. 194). Liszt's 1857 edition of the sonatas is surprisingly unrevealing about his interpretation, except in the last three works. His ideas are better transmitted in the 1871 edition by Lebert and von Bülow. Bülow had been a pupil of Liszt and was well able to reflect his intentions. This version is entirely uncontroversial in the facilitating of difficult passages by the redistribution of notes, renotation of rhythms and new fingerings. Considerably more questionable are the deliberate tempo changes; and it is flagrantly Romantic in the provision of programmatic suggestions. But it was made with great care and is a valuable record of the style of interpretation on which it is based.

The interpretation of the virtuoso pianist Ferruccio Busoni (1866–1924) can best be assessed from his comments about Beethoven's works in a letter of 1902: 'by cleaning them of the dust of tradition, I try to restore their youth, to present them as they sounded to people at the moment when they first sprang from the head and pen of the composer. The "Pathétique" was an almost revolutionary sonata in its own day, and ought to sound revolutionary now. One could never put enough passion into the "Appassionata", which was the culmination of passionate expression of its epoch' (Dent, 1933, p. 110).

Artur Schnabel (1882–1951) was the archetype of German pianists of his day, renowned for their integrity and scrupulous musicianship. He came to be regarded as a Beethoven specialist, partly because of his interpretations of the late works, to which he brought a visionary quality, and because in 1935 he published an edition of the sonatas and the Diabelli Variations. This contains his own fingerings, pedallings and phrasing. It remains very close to Beethoven, especially in the pedalling, but has been criticized for being too fussy and for not making fully clear what is Beethoven's and what is his. His views on modern instruments and the question of pedalling are particularly interesting: 'The effect of the pedalizations demanded by him [Beethoven] was exactly the same on the old instruments as on the new ones. The old piano is different from the modern piano in that you couldn't do...all that you can do on a modern piano. On that, however, you can do all that was possible on the old ones'. Beethoven's comparatively few pedal indications 'appear only in such places where he knew that the "normal" performer would have considered them sinful.... He simply created the unexpected, fantastic, adventurous.' Schnabel asserts that Beethoven's markings must be observed in all circumstances 'because they are an inseparable part of the music as such, and if one does not observe these pedal marks, the music is changed.' (Crankshaw, 1961, pp. 135–6)

Wilhelm Kempff (b 1895) is likewise renowned as a great Beethoven pianist. His two recorded cycles of the sonatas and the recordings of the piano concertos with Leo Blech still stand unequalled, marked by the singing quality of his tone and the clear textures. Very much in the same line is a more recent exponent, Alfred Brendel (b 1931). He respects the earlier Bülow and Schnabel editions, but in keeping with the times finds them outmoded, preferring Schenker's Urtext edition. He combines a very intellectual approach with great sensitivity to style. He prefers modern instruments, claiming that the modern concert grand has the volume of tone demanded by modern orchestras, halls, and, above all, ears. Other notable recordings have been made by, among others, Rudolf Serkin, Emil Gilels, Claudio Arrau, Daniel Barenboim and Vladimir Ashkenazy.

Over the last twenty years a number of executants have given performances of the keyboard music on fortepianos. Different tone qualities can be achieved, there are important implications for accompanying instruments, and also present is the psychological factor that the music stretches the instruments to the limits of their capabilities. Paul Badura-Skoda used a Graf for his excellent recordings of the sonatas, and Jörg Demus used both a Streicher and a Graf fortepiano. There are two recordings of the piano concerto cycle on period-style instruments accompanied by period-instrument orchestras: by Melvyn Tan with Roger Norrington and The London Classical Players, and by Steven Lubin with Christopher Hogwood and The Academy of Ancient Music. Such approaches have undoubtedly brought a new perspective to works already proved inexhaustible, and thereby widen the range of choice.

In spite of its immediate neglect, Beethoven's Violin Concerto found a firm place in the concerto repertoire after the young Joseph Joachim (1831–1907) performed it in London in 1844. He composed two cadenzas for it, but it is those by Fritz Kreisler (1875–1962) which are normally played now. Kreisler's recording is now available on record, revealing a performance which is perhaps unsurpassed. Zino Francescatti described the first-movement cadenza as 'three minutes of miracle, bewilderment, wonder, surprise and emotion', and the whole performance in 1912 as 'the greatest musical souvenir of my life' (Lochner, 1951, p. 367).

The 20th century has witnessed some monumental performances and recordings of the complete cycle of string quartets, notably by the Busch, Hungarian and Amadeus String Quartets. The Busch recording suffers from a few lapses of intonation, but these do not detract from their fervent but lucid renderings. The Hungarians brought a new standard of perfection which only the technically brilliant Amadeus, with its homogeneity of sound, and sensitive and polished interpretative style, has surpassed. Other notable recordings of the cycle are those by the Lindsay and Alban Berg Quartets and the Quartetto Italiano.

Beethoven's symphonies have been an irresistible challenge to conductors, inspiring some memorable performances. During the mid-19th century the large string sections used at the end of Beethoven's life became standard, and towards the end of the century orchestras increased still further in size. It may come as a surprise to learn that Wagner, one of Beethoven's most devoted admirers, took extensive liberties as a conductor, revising instrumentation and altering dynamics and tempi, in much the same way that Romantic pianists edited the keyboard works. He would vary the tempo within an allegro movement to reflect the different character of the various subjects and would use *ritardandi* for emphasis. In the Ninth Symphony he added brass to certain woodwind passages, thereby changing the tone quality.

Mahler, following the same tradition, had even fewer scruples about disregarding Beethoven's intentions. He said of the *Missa Solemnis* that if any work needed to be freely interpreted that one did, and he adopted this approach towards the symphonies. In the *Eroica* he apparently preceded the opening theme with a sustained pause. His revisions to the Fifth Symphony are anathema to modern thinking: in the first movement he strengthened the 'knocking' motif by adding timpani; in the Scherzo he called for muted horns at the beginning; and in the finale he frequently doubled bassoons with horns, adding an extra piccolo and an E♭ clarinet for greater penetration. In an 1895 performance of the Ninth Symphony the wind were doubled, trombones were added here and there, and a new horn part was written for the Trio section of the Scherzo. He even experimented with placing some of the wind players in the wings at the beginning of the Alla marcia section of the finale in order to achieve a huge crescendo. A performance in 1901 met with a mixed reception: the response from most of the audience was rapturous, but one critic described it as 'a transcription of Beethoven'.

Wilhelm Furtwängler (1886–1954) was one of the last of the Romantic school of conductors. In his recordings he showed himself capable of imposing overall unity on the works by bringing to them a great breadth which did not lose sight of clarity through precision of detail. But the somewhat improvisatory quality of his interpretations led to criticisms of too much rhythmic freedom. Otto Klemperer (1885–1973) is recognized as one of the most authoritative interpreters of Beethoven. Beginning his career when it was still commonplace to 'retouch', he resisted this practice except for some doubling of woodwind and horns to achieve a better balance, a practice now common where large string sections are used. In later years he became notorious for exceptionally slow tempi, but previously he achieved heroic dimensions and great power, resulting from his tremendous architectural grasp of a work. The Karajan performances of the 1960s have a special place for the new standards of orchestral playing he demanded from the Berlin Philharmonic Orchestra, and the energy, brilliance and commitment he brought to performances.

The 1980s were a period of striving towards historical accuracy in performance. In orchestral music this has manifested itself in the use of smaller forces and, more radically, of period instruments. Three such recordings of the symphonies have come out of Britain to date: from the Hanover Band (without a conductor), The London Classical Players under Roger Norrington, and The Academy of Ancient Music under Christopher Hogwood. One of the most interesting aspects is the question of tempo. In a desire to respect Beethoven's metronome markings these performances are generally faster than we have come to expect, and in apparent accordance with the practice of Beethoven's time there is much less flexibility, sometimes even rigidity. Between the three versions there are considerable variations in the size of the orchestra, the types of instruments used and the degree of control and sophistication imposed by the conductors. All display a refreshing transparency of texture and transmit a certain exhilaration. At their best, as Richard Taruskin wrote of Norrington's version of the Ninth Symphony, such performances are a 'restating rather than restoring of "literalism"' (Taruskin, 1989, pp. 240–56).

ANNE-LOUISE COLDICOTT

Monuments and memorials

DURING HIS LIFETIME Beethoven was a fashionable subject with artists. After his death it was more common to find sculptors producing busts and carvings of his head, such as those by Johannes Schilling and Antoine Bourdelle, now in the Beethovenhaus. Lyser, who had previously made lifelike sketches of Beethoven walking, was inspired to work on an ambitious engraving, Classical in style, of which the central area depicts the crowning of Beethoven, with smaller surrounding panels referring to specific works. Classical/allegorical settings were typical of the 19th century and reflect the myth-making process which was applied to Beethoven. A still more formal acknowledgement of Beethoven's reputation was the commissioning and erecting of statues in public places.

Plans to raise money for a monument in Bonn were under way for years before the necessary impetus was provided by an outsider, Liszt. In 1840 a competition to find a sculptor for a bronze statue was announced. The winner was Ernst Julius Hähnel of Dresden, whose statue was unveiled in Münsterplatz on 12 August 1845 (see plate 21). The occasion was marked by a festival with concerts of Beethoven's music. Prominent instrumentalists were drawn from all over Europe, and Liszt himself performed as both soloist and conductor, and wrote a special commemorative cantata. The entire event was entertainingly recorded by the English musician Sir George Smart, and his account has been published by Percy Young (1976). The cloaked figure of Beethoven stands erect, staring ahead, a pen in one hand and a notebook in the other, mounted on a pedestal whose four sides depict women, seemingly from classical mythology, playing musical instruments.

The first public monument to be erected in Austria was a larger-than-life bronze bust in Heiligenstadt in 1863. Some years later, in 1902, a marble 'walking' statue by Robert Weigl was erected there. Vienna was slow to honour Beethoven, but in 1871 the Gesellschaft der Musikfreunde set up a committee to organize a memorial. Kaspar Clemens Zumbusch (already famous for a bust of Ludwig II and a statue of Maria Theresa) was chosen as sculptor, and in 1877 a gala concert was held to raise money, with Liszt once again playing a prominent role. The monument was unveiled in the Beethovenplatz in May 1880 in the presence of Caroline (widow of Beethoven's nephew Karl) and her four daughters. It consists of a colossal bronze figure seated on a huge, twenty-two-foot-high granite pedestal surrounded by twelve smaller figures and angels and cherubs. Although seated, the Beethoven portrayed here is awesome: powerful, deep in concentration, and tense. He is clothed in contemporary garb, and the setting is not allegorical like the one in Bonn. He is depicted as a human hero rather than a god. The *Wiener Allgemeine Zeitung* described him as a citizen-hero who belonged to humanity but came from and returned to heaven.

Beethoven's birthplace is a different kind of memorial. In 1870, the centenary of his birth, a commemorative plaque was placed on the house in Bonngasse. In 1889, when it was to be sold, an appeal was made to enable it to be restored and run as a museum housing Beethoven memorabilia. Later the Beethoven-Archiv was established next door: this houses large manuscript collections and is an important research centre. Many of the houses where Beethoven lived or stayed have since been identified by commemorative plaques.

In 1902 Vienna staged a spectacular Beethoven exhibition, centred around Max Klinger's marble monument, which had taken seventeen years to complete and is one of the most distinguished examples. It was fashioned from a variety of materials: various coloured marbles, ivory, precious stones, polished gold and bronze. The figure of Beethoven, stripped to the waist, is unadorned and timeless. The face, in which lies its main strength, is based on Klein's life mask. The figure is seated on a throne with five angels' heads at the back, suggesting an enthroned and immortal genius. It is now in the Gewandhaus, Leipzig. In a desire to unite different art forms, a setting for the statue was provided by the artist Gustav Klimt, who provided a frieze, no longer in existence, a complex and somewhat mysterious depiction of scenes representing Beethoven's compositions, using a variety of media: stucco, mosaic, metal, glass, water and oil painting. The musical element of this *Gesamtkunstwerk* was Mahler's arrangement of the Ninth Symphony for the dedication ceremony, using brass bands and massed choirs. This marked the culmination of Romantic interpretations of the Beethoven myth.

In the 20th century, demythicization left Beethoven's reputation undiminished. The intrinsic quality of the music enabled it to come to the fore as it was addressed by the important theorists. Apart from the opening of the Beethovenhalle designed by S. Wolske, in Bonn in 1959, Beethoven has been honoured mainly by scholarly conferences, the most important of these being held in 1970, the bicentenary year, and 1977, 150 years after his death. A Beethoven Center has also been set up in San Jose, California.

Such is Beethoven's fame that he has been commemorated on postage stamps throughout the world. These depict either his head, places with which he was closely associated, or artifacts of his music, such as scores or instruments (Brilliant, 1988). A somewhat more unusual acknowledgment of his reputation was the inclusion of excerpts of his compositions on gold-coated copper records taken into space as possible means of communicating with other civilizations, by the American spacecrafts Voyagers 1 and 2 in 1977. Music from various cultures is represented: the Beethoven excerpts are the first movement of his Fifth Symphony and the Cavatina from the String Quartet op. 130.

ANNE-LOUISE COLDICOTT

Beethoven's place in music history

BEETHOVEN'S POSITION IN the history of music is absolutely central. For many, he is simply the greatest composer ever, and already in his own day some were rating him alongside such men as Shakespeare and Michelangelo as the finest exponent of his art (Solomon, 1982, no. 79). Even those who do not place him in such a superlative position accept almost universally that he at least is one of history's great composers.

But his central position does not derive just from the exceptional quality of his music. In terms of historical perspective as seen from today, he seems to fall more or less right in the middle of most people's view of music history – between those more remote composers whose works and performing styles have largely had to be rediscovered by music historians and recreated by 'Early Music' enthusiasts, and those more recent composers whose works have remained in the repertoire ever since their own lifetimes, and with whom we can in some sense still feel in touch (the instruments and orchestras they wrote for are not so very different from those of today).

In a more specific way, too, Beethoven's position is pivotal: his music looks both backwards to his predecessors and forward to his successors to an extent virtually unmatched by any other composer (perhaps only the great Renaissance master Josquin des Prez could claim to have such strong links to the two periods either side of him and to belong, like Beethoven, to both). Beethoven's connections with earlier composers have been discussed already (see 'Influences on Beethoven's style', pp. 78–87). He drew ideas and inspiration from all the major composers of the 18th century, apart from those whose music had meanwhile gone so out of fashion that they were scarcely known in his day (for example Vivaldi and Couperin). Conversely, his connections with later music are so widespread that few major composers of the next hundred years escaped his direct influence and none escaped his impact completely.

For Mendelssohn, the grandeur of the 'Choral' Symphony gave rise directly to the *Hymn of Praise* in his own Second Symphony. For Wagner, the necessity of adding voices in the finale of the 'Choral' confirmed his view of the supremacy of vocal music, while the rapid modulations in the Minuet of the First Symphony revealed unseen possibilities for tonality. For Brahms (whose First Symphony was impertinently dubbed 'Beethoven's Tenth'),

Bruckner, and others, Beethoven's symphonies were a model of pure instrumental music of the greatest kind, while Mahler took the cosmic breadth of the 'Choral' Symphony as a starting-point for many of his own. Other composers looked elsewhere in Beethoven's output. The poetic, Romantic quality of works such as the *Pastoral* Symphony and the descriptive overtures (especially *Leonore* no. 3, *Coriolan*, and *Egmont*) helped to generate the symphonic poems of Liszt and Richard Strauss as well as the poetic symphonies of Berlioz, Schumann, Tchaikovsky and others. Schumann also actually quoted a theme from Beethoven's *An die ferne Geliebte* in his C major Fantasy (op. 17). In contrast, it was the compression and concentration of the late bagatelles which attracted Webern, who produced his own bagatelles and other similarly concentrated works.

The one group of composers with whom Beethoven has very little connection is, paradoxically, his contemporaries. Indeed the development of music in general in the first quarter of the 19th century is perhaps best understood if Beethoven is ignored altogether (some of Schubert's music, for example, seems to follow on naturally from late Mozart, bypassing Beethoven completely). But Beethoven's aloofness and his reputed disdain of the music of his contemporaries was not entirely his own fault. During the first two decades of the 19th century, the composition of enduring works of art had reached something of a nadir. Few composers attempted to write great masterpieces and even fewer succeeded. Only a tiny handful of works written during these twenty years are today in the regular concert repertory, apart from those of Beethoven. It is all the more regrettable, therefore, that evidence of his connections with Schubert is so slender. How much of Schubert's music he knew and admired, and when, will perhaps never be fully known.

Beethoven stands, then, as the principal bridge between the Classical and Romantic eras, and arguments as to whether he belongs more in one or the other will be interminable. In terms of repertoire and genre he is best seen as the culmination of the Classical era, for most of the forms he used in his greatest works were those established as the primary ones by Haydn and Mozart – the four-movement symphony, the three-movement piano concerto, the string quartet and the piano sonata. In the *Répertoire international de la littérature musicale* (the main general music bibliography), where he had to be placed in one or other category for reference purposes, he has therefore been placed in the 'Classical' section (whereas Schubert, who died only a year later, is classified as 'Romantic').

Where it is a question of the more indefinable qualities of the spirit of his music, however, his connection with the Romantics is much stronger. He was often hailed by them, from E.T.A. Hoffmann onwards, as the original and archetypal Romantic (see 'Posthumous assessments', pp. 296–8). His music was seen as an embodiment of the Romantic spirit, with its grandiose gestures, heroic struggles, subjective emotion, larger-than-life structures and its reaching for the sublime. Its irregularities and contravention of Classical formal ideas also made Beethoven an inspiration for the Romantics, as the 'man who freed music' from the shackles of 18th-century formal conventionality. He was seen – and can still be seen – as the man who effected a revolution in music every bit as fundamental as the French Revolution in politics. His personal life as the lone artist, almost deaf and facing untold adversity, battling against all manner of convention to further the progress of art as he composed for posterity rather than immediate approval by wealthy patrons or the public at large, bound him still closer to the Romantic ideal. Such notions are in some ways a gross over-simplification of a very complex set of interrelationships, but they contain enough truth to place Beethoven in a unique position from quite a number of different points of view.

Thus although he was in some senses very much a man of his age, expanding the forms and genres he inherited and infusing them with the new *Zeitgeist*, he is also a man for every age. His music still influences the course of composition today, for some living composers have borrowed ideas or even actual material from it. Moreover its enormous intellectual strength and ingenuity are almost unfathomable, as has been shown by many recent scholars, who continue to discover hidden subtleties and delights wherever they look in his output. And it embodies the whole gamut of human emotions to such an intensity that it should find a ready response in audiences for all time.

BARRY COOPER

Section 13
BEETHOVEN LITERATURE

BEETHOVEN LITERATURE

Biography and biographers

Early history

THE STORY OF BEETHOVEN biography begins in the last decade of the composer's life. In 1820 a literary acquaintance, FRIEDRICH WÄHNER, asked Beethoven for an autobiographical sketch that he might fashion into an article about the composer for Brockhaus's encyclopedia in Leipzig, as a way of correcting the mis-statements of fact concerning his life. Beethoven turned Wähner down, but in the last years of his life became concerned to have an 'ungarbled' account of his life transmitted to posterity, and was persuaded by KARL HOLZ to assign such a task to him; despite having secured the composer's permission, Holz seems never to have taken any steps towards preparing his own Beethoven biography.

Shortly after Beethoven's death, however, two rival biographical projects were initiated by the composer's associates and friends in Vienna. One was organized by ANTON GRÄFFER, an employee of the Artaria publishing firm; he was supported in this by Jacob Hotschevar, who became the guardian of Beethoven's nephew after the untimely death of Stephan von Breuning in June 1827, and possibly by Holz. Gräffer copied and assembled a folder of material he believed to be useful for an official biography of the great composer, a project which was announced publicly in September 1827 as a kind of patriotic act ('since he [Beethoven] had lived in Vienna uninterruptedly for 35 years': Brenneis, 1984, p. 35) and, it was hoped, would be ready in time to mark the first anniversary of the composer's death in March of the following year. In the meantime, an extremely inaccurate biography, written by J.A. Schlosser, appeared in Prague. Lack of enthusiasm for Gräffer's project led to its cancellation early the following year.

Gräffer passed on his materials to a childhood friend, Ferdinand Simon Gassner (1798–1851). Holz, a rival of Anton Schindler's for Beethoven's attention in the late 1820s, also hoped that Gassner would write a biography 'whose facts would not be based on falsified or stolen conversation books' (Brenneis, 1979, p. 102: this is the earliest accusation of Schindler's underhand use of these manuscripts); but he, too, made no use of them. His widow lent the Gräffer collection to a later Beethoven biographer, Ludwig Nohl.

Along with Stephan von Breuning, SCHINDLER was closest to the composer during the four months of his final illness. A month after Breuning's death, Schindler wrote to Breuning's brother-in-law FRANZ WEGELER in Koblenz, saying that the dying composer had authorized Breuning and himself to write his biography, that he thought Wegeler could contribute something about his youth in Bonn, and that – as a result of Breuning's recent death – Wegeler's assistance was more urgent than ever.

Wegeler proved to be exceedingly cooperative at the start, furnishing Schindler with extensive notes about Beethoven's early life, letters, and other documents. But Schindler made little progress with these and, on account of his rivalry with Holz, was denied access to the materials assembled for the 'Viennese' biography. Wegeler, beginning to grow impatient with Schindler, who was appointed to musical posts at Münster in 1831 and Aachen in 1835 (and was thus further removed from important documents and personal contacts), proposed that FERDINAND RIES be included in the project. Ries, a devoted pupil of Beethoven's who was close to him during the 'middle period' (a grey area for both Wegeler and Schindler) had been co-opted early on by Wegeler to provide documents and any other useful 'Beethoveniana', but was reluctant to contribute to the writing of a biography, claiming that he lacked the necessary literary skills. Although he, too, initially cooperated with Schindler, personality clashes in 1836 led to a breakdown in the venture (see Tyson, 1984b).

Ries decided in the end to collaborate with Wegeler, and the two men spent the latter half of 1837 putting their materials into shape. Ries's death in January 1838, at the age of fifty-three, meant that the final compilation of the *Biographische Notizen über Ludwig van Beethoven* was left to Wegeler. It appeared in 1838. Seven years later Wegeler added a *Nachtrag* (supplement), including annotated letters from Beethoven to himself and to his wife Eleonore (Breuning's sister), as well as such records of the Beethoven family as were available from official registries. The enlarged text was reissued in 1906, with editorial notes by Alfred Kalischer (English translation in Wegeler, 1987; a thoroughly revised English edition/translation by Alan Tyson, announced in the early 1980s, has not yet appeared).

It seems clear that, from the outset, the *Notizen* were not to be a full-length biography, but merely a collection of faithfully recorded impressions, anecdotes and documents that might serve later biographers; and despite minor inaccuracies, they are widely believed to give the most faithful impression of Beethoven when his creative powers were at their height. It is to Ries that we owe our familiar portrait of a temperamental, moody Beethoven, thoroughly consumed by his art, but a basically good-hearted soul. He is also our source for many well-known and reliable anecdotes, such as those about the tearing-up of the *Eroica* title-page, and the third horn player's entry 'four bars early' in the first movement of that work.

Urged on, perhaps, by the appearance of his erstwhile collaborators' *Notizen*, SCHINDLER published the first version of his Beethoven biography in 1840. Unlike Wegeler and Ries, who sought to present an unbiased view of their subject, Schindler idealized Beethoven, and grossly exaggerated and idealized his own relation to the composer. Schindler claimed to have first met Beethoven in 1813; it is more probable that they did not meet until 1822, by which time he had given up his intended career in law and devoted himself entirely to music. Owing to a disagreement about the Akademien (benefit concerts) of May 1824 (Beethoven accused Schindler of cheating over the ticket receipts), the two men fell out and were not on speaking terms until the last year of Beethoven's life. Thus Schindler was close to Beethoven for perhaps only a few years; but because their periods of contact saw the composition of part of the *Missa Solemnis*, some of the late quartets, and above all the Ninth Symphony, they can claim a special importance. That Schindler was a constant visitor during the final illness meant that he had easy access to many Beethoven documents; today he is still suspected of having stolen the Conversation Books and other manuscripts; these he sold, shortly after completing his biography, to the Königliche Bibliothek in Berlin for a considerable sum of money plus a generous annuity.

Schindler's book is an important source of information about the composer, and is based on a large amount of documentation not available to other early biographers. But because of his allegedly dishonest dealings during Beethoven's lifetime, and patently dishonest behaviour after the composer's death (which included – most notoriously – the faking of conversations between Beethoven and himself: see 'Conversation Books', p. 166), every statement he made must now be checked against other sources. For instance, the claim that he advised Beethoven to choose a fugal, rather than a sonata-type, plan for the Overture op. 124 is corroborated by the presence of two strands of development in the relevant sketchbook (Artaria 201) and was therefore accepted by Nottebohm; but since the story is bolstered in one of the forged conversations, even its veracity must now be doubted.

Schindler's *Biographie* was translated into English by Ignaz Moscheles in 1841. Four years later a second edition appeared, with an extra chapter on Beethoven reception in France. A thorough overhauling of the book – billed as the third edition, but in effect a totally new biography – appeared in 1860.

Because of its reverent tone, Schindler's biography appealed to the Romantic age, having an enormous influence on such contemporary scholars as Wilhelm von Lenz and A. B. Marx. Its third edition was still regarded as a classic in 1966 when, for the first time, it was translated into English.

Thayer

Alexander Wheelock Thayer's multi-volume *Life of Beethoven* has often been compared to Spitta's *Bach*, Jahn's *Mozart*, and Pohl's *Haydn*; but it is only in its later completion and redaction by

Hermann Deiters and Hugo Riemann that it became a fully-fledged life-and-works study. An American by birth and (like Schindler) a lawyer by training, Thayer began his Beethoven studies with the aim of producing a reliable translation of Schindler; but as he compared Schindler's text with Wegeler and Ries's *Notizen*, he was struck by the discrepancies between them.

To resolve the problems caused by these differences became the basis of Thayer's research over the next half-century. In 1849 he embarked on the first of many trips to Europe to gather materials for a new Beethoven biography: court records, letters, diaries, recollections of Beethoven's acquaintances, the Conversation Books, the material assembled by Gräffer, and other documents. Thayer was also the first scholar to use the musical sketchbooks for the purpose of establishing a chronology of Beethoven's music; but he was quickly overtaken as a sketch scholar by Gustav Nottebohm, whose expertise in this capacity he readily admitted and frequently relied on.

From an early stage, Thayer intended his biography to be published in German: for this task he enlisted the help of Hermann Deiters who, working with him, edited and translated the first three volumes, taking Beethoven's life up to the year 1816. But constantly failing health prevented Thayer from bringing the project to a conclusion. After his death in 1897, his papers were forwarded to Deiters, who had drafted a fourth volume by 1907. Deiters died that same year, and it was now left to Hugo Riemann to see this volume, and the fifth, through the press. Riemann also re-edited the early volumes, and the definitive version of Thayer–Deiters–Riemann was finally completed in 1917.

In the meantime, the American critic HENRY KREHBIEL was undertaking the re-editing of Thayer's biography for the Beethoven Association of New York; this appeared in 1921. Since Krehbiel had Thayer's notes to go on for Beethoven's last decade, and was not bound to an authorized (German) text, he chose his own way of presenting the facts of Beethoven's final years; in doing so, for instance, he played down the matter of Beethoven's difficulties with his nephew. For this first English-language edition, Krehbiel also pruned much of Thayer's original documentation.

The need for an objective account of Beethoven's final decade was still wanting, and after Krehbiel's death (1923) Thayer's copious notes were passed on from one owner to the next. They were deemed lost by the time a new edition, by ELLIOT FORBES, was undertaken in the 1950s. Nonetheless, Forbes was able to make use of the most recent Beethoven research and produce a version of Thayer's *Life of Beethoven* which was up-to-date, which distinguished Thayer's original text from Forbes's editorial additions, and which was conceived in the original spirit of a project 'devoted to Beethoven the *man*'. To this day, Thayer–Forbes remains an indispensable reference work.

Later Beethoven biography

One important biographical project contemporary with Thayer is LUDWIG NOHL's three-volume *Beethovens Leben* (1864–77). Though far less meticulous a scholar than Thayer, Nohl had access to materials which Thayer did not see, and so – despite its shortcomings – his work is of documentary value. Nohl's work takes much greater account of the music, and is the first biography to make regular use of the sketchbooks in its discussion of the music, especially in volume III and in a separate book, *Beethoven, Liszt, Wagner* (1874).

After Thayer, biographical research concentrated on special topics. Numerous volumes were written, for instance, about the letter to the 'Immortal Beloved'. A popular type of publication was the collected reminiscences of Beethoven's contemporaries, some of whom had become illustrious musical figures in the 19th century. Among the most extensive books on a special topic is a full-length study of Beethoven's youth by LUDWIG SCHIEDER-MAIR (1925), which extensively documents life at the Palatinate court in Bonn under the Electors Maximilian Friedrich and Maximilian Franz, and of the musical environment in which Beethoven acquired his prodigious musical talents. Schiedermair, the first to investigate meticulously the influence of Mozart on the young Beethoven, was named director of the newly formed Beethoven-Archiv in Bonn in 1927, and was responsible for the assembly of microfilms, photocopies and (when they were bequested or put up for sale) original Beethoven documents to facilitate further research. A subsequent director of the Beethoven-haus, JOSEPH SCHMIDT-GÖRG, traced the genealogy of the Beethoven family back to Renaissance Flanders (1964).

Recent research

By far the most important contemporary biographical research, and interpretation of Beethoven's character, has appeared in the work of MAYNARD SOLOMON. His first major contribution was the amassing of an overwhelming body of evidence pointing to Antonie Brentano as the 'Immortal Beloved', an identification now accepted by most Beethoven scholars. Subsequent research included a thorough overhauling of the evidence concerning Beethoven's relationship to his nephew Karl, clearing away much mis-statement and misinterpretation of fact and, additionally, confronting the deeper sources of Beethoven's relation to his sister-in-law Johanna. Another core topic of Solomon's Beethoven research is the 'family romance', which concerns the composer's own uncertainty about his birth year, and consequently about his parentage.

A large number of Solomon's research papers were assembled to form the basis of a full-length biography, which appeared in 1977. Solomon continued to explore Beethoven's psyche, and its effect on his art, in a further series of writings; these were collected in a volume of *Beethoven Essays* (1988), and in a sense are a 'volume 2' of his biography. In an essay written expressly for this volume, on Beethoven's subconscious feelings towards his elder brother (Ludwig Maria, who died in infancy in 1769), Solomon ties together many of the threads of Beethoven's anguished life: the 'family romance', his attachment to Karl, and some important but never fully explained passages from documents such as the Heiligenstadt Testament. Here is Solomon's contribution to Beethoven biography in its classic, quintessential formulation.

Since the appearance of Solomon's biography, research into Beethoven's life has provided something of a clean-up operation. Rather than concentrate on new interpretations of the evidence, the 1970s and '80s have instead seen ambitious projects intended to make the primary documents more widely available in an authoritative form. As Solomon has remarked (1977, p. xi): 'The proper study of Beethoven is based on contemporary documents – on letters, diaries, Conversation Books, court and parish records, autograph manuscripts and sketches, music publications, reviews, concert programs, and similar materials.' The projects include Solomon's edition of the *Tagebuch* of 1812–18, the Deutsche Staatsbibliothek's edition of the Conversation Books (now nearing completion), and the Beethovenhaus edition of Beethoven's correspondence (in progress). Another important set of studies has concerned the history of important collections of Beethoven sources, e.g. the papers of Joseph Fischhof (Brenneis, 1984) and Ludwig Nohl's collection of Beethoveniana materials (Staehelin, 1983).

For the musical documents, the most significant publication of the 1980s was a complete listing, description, chronology and reconstruction of the Beethoven sketchbooks (Johnson, 1985); this work and other sketch studies have helped to record the story of Beethoven's creative life more precisely than ever before (see 'Sketch studies', pp. 321–3). It is entirely right to include them among the contributions to Beethoven's biography.

WILLIAM DRABKIN

Editions of the music

But what I have more at heart than anything else is the *publication of my collected works*, for I should like to arrange this during my lifetime. (Letter 1079)

THUS BEETHOVEN WROTE TO Carl Friedrich Peters on 5 June 1822. The idea of publishing a complete edition of his works was one which had long interested him, and which he had suggested to other publishers: to Breitkopf & Härtel in 1810 (Letter 273), and to Simrock in 1817 and 1820 (Letters 759, 1026, 1028 and 1029). Nor was the appeal to Peters the last of its kind, for in 1825

Beethoven took up the matter with Schott's (Letter 1345), who were at that time dealing with the publication of the *Missa Solemnis* and the Ninth Symphony.

Beethoven's desire to see a collected edition of his works during his lifetime was prompted largely by a concern for textual accuracy – this despite his own often reluctant and notoriously bad proof-reading – but also by a wish to make money. Yet despite his best efforts his plan never came to fruition. It seems that publishers were less interested in issuing correct editions of works that were already available, even if in unauthorized and inaccurate editions, than in selling new works from Beethoven's pen. Presumably it was in recognition of this that Beethoven eventually conceived the idea of distinguishing a complete edition by the composition of a new work for each category; this 'carrot' was offered first to Simrock in 1820 (Letter 1028) and remained a feature of the later offers to Peters and Schott's. In fact Beethoven's vision remains as yet unfulfilled; the following paragraphs will outline the course of subsequent attempts to publish a complete edition as well as highlighting the problems involved in such an undertaking.

Two editions, both of which remained incomplete, were begun shortly after Beethoven's death. The earlier one was that of TOBIAS HASLINGER. It was based on the handwritten edition which Haslinger had instigated around 1817, and for which Beethoven had composed the Fugue for string quintet, op. 137. (The sixty-two volumes of this edition, which is also incomplete, are today in the archives of the Gesellschaft der Musikfreunde in Vienna.) Haslinger's posthumous edition was published *c*.1828–45; a detailed discussion and list of contents may be found in Deutsch, 1930–31. The other early projected complete edition, which began publication around 1834, was that of Moscheles, who also (*c*.1858) issued a new edition of the piano sonatas (see Tyson, 1964).

In the event it was Breitkopf & Härtel who first realized something approaching Beethoven's conception, with the publication in 1862–5 of *Ludwig van Beethoven's Werke: vollständige kritisch durchgesehene überall berechtigte Ausgabe* (the GESAMTAUSGABE, hereafter *GA*). This edition contained 263 works arranged in twenty-four categories (or 'series'). A further forty-six compositions, many of them discovered by Nottebohm, were published in a supplementary volume in 1888. Among these newly published works were the two Cantatas of 1790, WoO 87–8.

The publication of the *GA* was a major event not only in Beethoven scholarship but in 19th-century musicology in general. Yet scholars were already pointing out its shortcomings in the early years of this century. Friedrich Spiro, in a paper delivered to the Fourth Congress of the International Musical Society held in London in 1911, called for a revision of the *GA* on the grounds that in its present form it was not sufficiently *kritisch*. There were numerous inaccuracies in the printed texts which needed correction; information concerning surviving manuscripts and early editions was necessary, as was some indication of those places where the *GA* text differed from the composer's autograph; 'biographical' information, such as dates of composition and first performance, ought to be included; and Beethoven's original title and dedication should be reproduced for each work. In short, Spiro was demanding many of those features which are considered indispensable in modern critical editions.

If the *GA* was insufficiently *kritisch*, even more so did it fail to convince on grounds of *completeness*. Spiro noted various works which had not been included even in the supplementary volume of 1888 (one was op. 134, Beethoven's piano duet arrangement of the *Grosse Fuge*). He went on to argue that a complete edition ought to aim to include every note which the composer wrote, including both finished and unfinished works, even pieces which did not proceed much further than the sketching stage. Perhaps it was this challenge laid down by Spiro which inspired the work of Willy Hess, who spent many years preparing a catalogue of works not included in the *GA*. When it was eventually published (Hess, 1957) this catalogue included no fewer than 335 items in its main section as well as details of a further sixty-six doubtful and wrongly attributed compositions (it should be recalled that the *GA* originally contained a mere 263 works!). Hess went on to make good Breitkopf & Härtel's omissions in the fourteen volumes of his *Supplemente zur Gesamtausgabe* (1959–71).

Like Spiro, Hess also seems to have believed that a 'complete' edition should aspire to publish every note which the composer wrote. Thus he argued for the inclusion of early or alternative versions of published works, or parts of such works. In volume 4 of the *Supplemente*, for example, there is a shortened version of the end of the first movement of the Eighth Symphony, while volume 6 contains the first version of the String Quartet in F op. 18 no. 1.

Hess also thought that unfinished works needed to be published, and it is thanks to his efforts that fragments such as the Violin Sonata Hess 46 were first made available for study. But a generous approach such as that of Hess or Spiro eventually calls into question the limits of the concept of the musical 'work'. While it seems reasonable to publish fragments which the composer may be thought to have intended to complete and publish himself, there is less justification for defining as 'works' musical passages which are basically working sketches or studies. A case in point is the ten-bar Adagio for three horns Hess 297. Hess culled this from a collection of loose sketchleaves mostly containing contrapuntal and instrumental studies. He himself acknowledged that it was basically a study (as opposed to a work intended for publication or performance), but argued for its inclusion in an edition on grounds of its completeness.

The publication in 1961 of the first volume of the *NEUE AUSGABE* (hereafter *NA*) of Beethoven's complete works required a standpoint to be adopted on such issues as this. Like the projected

Gesamtausgaben of the letters and sketchbooks, the *NA* was launched from the Beethovenhaus in Bonn under its then director, Joseph Schmidt-Görg. The editorial policy regarding alternative versions, which is stated in the general foreword printed in each volume of the *NA*, is that such versions will be published only if they are of particular interest, and if they are complete; this second condition accords with the more general policy of including in the *NA* only those works which Beethoven completed. However, the policy has not been adhered to entirely rigidly: Hess 40, an Introduction and fragmentary Fugue in D minor for string quintet, has been included on the grounds that the Introduction is 'largely complete in itself' ('weitgehend in sich abgeschlossen'), although it is harmonically 'open' and not performable as it stands. On the other hand, the fragmentary Violin Concerto WoO 5 has not been included. It is perhaps significant that the general foreword makes no mention of works included in Hess's catalogue; but whether or not the *NA* will rival Hess in its definition of 'works' largely remains to be seen, for the edition is as yet far from complete. Of the major genres, only the piano concertos up to no. 3 (and the Triple and Violin Concertos), the piano sonatas up to op. 57 and the string quartets up to op. 95 have as yet (1990) appeared; none of the symphonies has been published.

One reason for the slow progress of the *NA* is clearly the greater importance now attached to textual criticism. Not only are the methods more subtle and searching, but there are also many more sources to be consulted before a truly 'critical' edition can be published. And scholars today rightly demand that an editor give a proper account of the sources used, so that an informed assessment of his or her decisions may be made. To this end, it was announced that each volume of the *NA* would be accompanied by a critical report (*kritischer Bericht*). So far only one such report has been published (for the Piano Concertos nos 1–3), so that the majority of the *NA* texts have to be taken at face value. It appears that the reports will in future be bound in with the editions themselves; in the meantime, some of the textual issues involved can be gleaned from reviews of volumes which have appeared. A more general study of textual criticism in relation to Beethoven's works may be found in Unverricht, 1960.

This account has concentrated on the history of complete editions of Beethoven's works, but some reference to more specialized editions ought also to be made. Allied to the present-day concern for textual accuracy mentioned above in connection with the *NA* is the popularity of the so-called *Urtext* edition – one which aims to present the composer's intentions as clearly and faithfully as possible, with a minimum of editorial intervention; but earlier editors were by no means prepared to be so self-effacing. Because of their central importance to amateur pianists and students, Beethoven's piano sonatas have been issued in many editions which aim to provide more than just an accurate text.

The edition by Harold Craxton and Donald Tovey, first published in 1931 but still popular today, includes editorial phrasing and fingering as well as Tovey's perceptive (and often amusing) performance suggestions. Hugo Riemann's edition has an analytical bent, incorporating the notation which he devised to represent phrase structure. Celebrated pianists such as Schnabel and Von Bülow also prepared editions of the sonatas.

Textual, performance and analytical issues received their fullest attention in Schenker's individual *Erläuterungsausgaben* of four late sonatas: opp. 101 and 109–11, published between 1913 and 1921. These editions (like Schenker's later complete edition of the sonatas) were pioneering in their use of original sources (Schenker's claim to have been 'the true founder of the discipline of autograph-study' is not to be dismissed lightly: see Schenker, 1979, p. 7). Each volume presents Schenker's edition of the work accompanied by a lengthy analysis and a discussion of textual matters and performance suggestions. In addition, there is Schenker's characteristic dismissal of the work of most previous editors. The blend of contents in the *Erläuterungsausgaben* foreshadows the modern Norton Critical Scores, which include an edition of the Fifth Symphony incorporating Schenker's textual notes.

Among studies of the early textual history of Beethoven's music, Alan Tyson's work, in particular his elegant account of the authentic English editions (Tyson, 1963a), stands out most prominently. Finally, mention must be made of the growing number of facsimile editions of Beethoven's autographs. This trend further reflects the contemporary interest in the composer's unadulterated text. There is a certain irony in the fact that our own age publishes these documents, which in Beethoven's eyes were a mere preliminary to the publication of an accurate, printed edition; but there is no doubt that facsimile editions often illuminate important text-critical issues in a direct and forceful manner.

NICHOLAS MARSTON

Analytical studies

THE FOLLOWING SURVEY ATTEMPTS to give some idea of the enormously wide range of analytical studies of Beethoven's music available to the interested reader (Wenk, 1987 provides a useful guide to analyses written since 1940). So central is Beethoven's position in the history of music as seen from the latter end of the 20th century that his compositions feature extensively in any discussion of the musical language of the so-called Viennese Classical period: consider Charles Rosen's *The Classical Style: Haydn, Mozart, Beethoven* (1971, rev. 1976) or Leonard Ratner's *Classic Music: Expression, Form, and Style* (1979), to take just two excellent examples. Nor is there space to do more than mention some of the journals – *Music Analysis, Music Theory Spectrum,*

Journal of Music Theory, The Music Forum – in which many fascinating analyses of Beethoven works have been published in recent years. The three volumes of *Beethoven Studies* edited by Alan Tyson have also been an important vehicle for new analytical studies.

But if the sheer volume of analytical writing about Beethoven poses problems for the surveyor, so too does the very term 'analysis'. Ian Bent (1987, p. 1) has defined analysis as 'the resolution of a musical structure into relatively simpler constituent elements, and the investigation of the functions of those elements within that structure'; a good example of such an analysis might be Jonathan Dunsby's study of the *Klavierstück* WoO 60 (Dunsby, 1984) – although to the non-specialist it might seem that the 'constituent elements' of this analysis are a good deal less simple than the composition from which they are obtained. Two other features of Dunsby's study might also be identified as typical of contemporary analysis: the detailed concern with a single (and not necessarily lengthy or well-known) work; and the assumption that the analysis is an end in itself rather than a means to some other end.

If we now turn to earlier analytical studies of Beethoven's music we can see that these last two features are fairly recent developments. Indeed, the analysis of musical works as a self-sufficient and intrinsically worthwhile exercise is an essentially 20th-century trend. At the risk of some oversimplification, it may be helpful to divide 19th-century writings into two categories, each with its own largely non-analytical aim: analysis as an aid (or prerequisite) to the elucidation of some extramusical idea in the work, and the analysis of Beethoven's music as an aid to the teaching of composition.

Perhaps the most famous example of the former category is E.T.A. HOFFMANN's well-known review of the Fifth Symphony, first published in the *Allgemeine Musikalische Zeitung* for 1810 (the following quotations are taken from the translation in Forbes, 1971). Hoffmann's main concern was to emphasize the power of Beethoven's music to provide a vision of another world, 'the realm of the colossal and the immeasurable'; for him the whole Symphony induced a feeling of 'foreboding, indescribable longing' which he considered the essence of Romantic music. Nevertheless, in attempting to convey the musical means by which that feeling was induced Hoffmann did not shrink from copious musical quotation and a good deal of technical description which may fairly be called 'analysis' even if it seems superficial by today's standards: 'The first Allegro, in C minor and 2/4 meter, begins with the principal motive, which is stated completely in the first two measures and reappears again and again in many forms throughout the movement.'

It is worth mentioning that neither in this review nor in that of the Piano Trios op. 70 did Hoffmann use the term 'analysis' himself; he was a reviewer, and the most appropriate description of his writings might be 'criticism'. The same term could be applied to most of the other major 19th-century writings on Beethoven's music, among them Berlioz's 'Etude critique des symphonies de Beethoven', first published serially in 1837–8 and reprinted in *A travers chants* (1862); Wilhelm von Lenz's *Beethoven et ses trois styles* (1852–3); George Grove's *Beethoven and His Nine Symphonies* (1896); or Ernst von Elterlein's *Beethoven's Pianoforte Sonatas Explained for the Lovers of the Musical Art* (1856; Eng. trans., 1879), which represents the worst kind of 'analysis' intended for an amateur audience (the first movement of the 'Hammerklavier' Sonata 'is really constructed on two chief themes; the first displaying manly boldness . . . the second, womanly gentleness').

A prolific 19th-century writer was ADOLF BERNHARD MARX, the most important of whose work on Beethoven is contained in *Ludwig van Beethoven: Leben und Schaffen* (1859). Like Hoffmann, Marx was interested in elucidating the 'idea' behind the work (for an interesting comparison of Hoffmann's, Marx's and Berlioz's accounts of the Fifth Symphony, see Wallace, 1986), but if anything he had a finer ear for subtle motivic connections – for example, he identified a relationship between the first-violin motives at the beginning of the Poco Adagio and the Allegro in the first movement of the String Quartet op. 74.

Examples from Beethoven's music also feature prominently in Marx's composition treatise *Die Lehre von der musikalischen Komposition, praktisch-theoretisch* (1837–47). But probably more extensive use of Beethoven's music as a demonstration of compositional technique is to be found in treatises by CARL CZERNY (*School of Practical Composition*, ?1849) and JOHANN CHRISTIAN LOBE (*Lehrbuch der musikalischen Komposition*, especially volume 1 [1850]). Czerny reproduced complete compositions in order to illustrate various musical forms and their harmonic characteristics. Lobe, on the other hand, demonstrated a considerably more sophisticated analytical technique which involved the construction of a 'principal melodic strand' (*Hauptmelodiefaden*; see Bent, 1984 and 1987) for two movements from the op. 18 Quartets in order to show the various formal functions. He also carried out motivic analysis, isolating the main melodic ideas from which the first movement of op. 18 no. 2 was built up.

'One of the ghostliest things ever written': the language might be Hoffmann's, but this description of the return from the Trio to the Scherzo in the Fifth Symphony comes from DONALD TOVEY's unfinished book *Beethoven* (1944b, p. 17). Tovey was a major writer on music in the first half of this century, although compared with his contemporary Schenker his analytical skills seem meagre indeed. His *Essays in Musical Analysis* (1935–9) are really programme notes, which nevertheless contain many interesting observations; among Beethoven works dealt with in the *Essays* are all the symphonies, the piano concertos (except no. 2), the *Missa Solemnis* and the Diabelli Variations. Tovey's most genuinely analytical writing is largely contained in the still-useful

A Companion to Beethoven's Pianoforte Sonatas (Bar-to-Bar Analysis) of 1931, which was published in connection with the Tovey/Craxton edition of the sonatas (see 'Editions of the music', p. 317).

Tovey was concerned above all with the musical surface, and with those features that would be perceived most immediately by the 'naive listener'; he was mistrustful of long-range connections and hidden thematic relationships. Thus his approach to analysis was radically different from that of HEINRICH SCHENKER, whose work, in terms both of quantity and quality, remains the most impressive body of analytical writings on Beethoven's music yet published (for a complete index of Schenker's Beethoven analyses, see Laskowsky, 1978). Schenker gradually became convinced that every musical masterwork represented the 'composing-out' (*Auskomponierung*) of a simple diatonic 'fundamental structure' (*Ursatz*); and his extended analyses of the Ninth, Fifth and Third Symphonies (1912, 1925 and 1930), as well as the *Erläuterungsausgaben* of the Piano Sonatas opp. 101 and 109–11 (1913–21), repay the most careful study, as do the many Beethoven examples in his last work, *Free Composition (Der freie Satz*, 1935).

Tovey and Schenker were at least alike in the relative importance they accorded to harmonic or tonal features as opposed to melodic or thematic ones. RUDOLPH RETI, on the other hand, was convinced that the motive and motivic transformation were the basic sources of musical unity and development, a belief which he first expounded in *The Thematic Process in Music* (1951). The analysis of the 'thematic plan' of the Ninth Symphony which opens this book reaches the conclusion (p. 30) that ' one thematic idea permeates the whole work'. A second book, *Thematic Patterns in Sonatas of Beethoven* (1967), was prepared for publication after Reti's death by DERYCK COOKE, who had already taken up and extended Reti's ideas in his provocative study 'The Unity of Beethoven's Late Quartets' (Cooke, 1963).

Among other analytical approaches to Beethoven's music, Riemann's phrase-structure analyses of the string quartets (1903) and piano sonatas (1918–19) deserve special mention, if only because of the importance they accord to this relatively under-analysed musical feature. Various as the analytical techniques brought to bear on Beethoven's music may have been, however, they coincide in the premium which (in common with most music analysis) they place on demonstrating the unity of the work or works being analysed. Schenker's and Reti's concern for unity needs no further demonstration, but it perhaps needs to be pointed out that even the 19th-century writers discussed above recognized this feature of Beethoven's music. Thus Czerny on the opening of the Piano Concerto no. 3: 'This first tutti contains all the ideas and component parts, from which the whole...is formed.' (Czerny, ?1849, i, 764) A relatively isolated but nonetheless forceful attack on the present-day passion for unity and coherence is Hugh Macdonald's essay (1980) on the Fantasia op. 77.

Finally, there can be little doubt that as long as analysis is considered a worthwhile musical activity, analysts will continue to analyse Beethoven's music. It seems that even the most well-known works – the Fifth Symphony is an obvious case – contain an inexhaustible wealth of musical relationships which may be revealed or lie unnoticed, depending on the particular analytical technique employed. Voices, notably those of Joseph Kerman (1985) and Leo Treitler (1982), continue to be raised in warning at the self-imposed limits of most music analysis; but just as 'Beethoven has survived demythification' (Kerman, 1983, p. 156), so his music will not only survive but will continue to demand what the sceptical often regard as unnecessary 'mystification'.

NICHOLAS MARSTON

Sketch studies

IN THE TWO DECADES since the 1970 bicentenary of the composer's birth, sketch studies have probably advanced more rapidly than any other branch of Beethoven scholarship. The advances can be summarized under three main headings: sketchbook reconstruction; publication in facsimile and transcription; and analysis of the contents of the sketchbooks to yield new insights into the chronology and the structure of Beethoven's music. Yet all these advances would have been virtually unthinkable without the bedrock provided over a hundred years ago by the work of Gustav Nottebohm (1817–82), the first great sketch scholar.

Nottebohm's main publications are well known: extended studies of the Kessler and *Eroica* Sketchbooks, published in 1865 and 1880 respectively, and a host of shorter articles first published in the *Musikalisches Wochenblatt* but subsequently gathered into two anthologies, *Beethoveniana* (1872) and *Zweite Beethoveniana* (published posthumously in 1887). During his work on these publications Nottebohm became familiar with almost all the surviving sketchbooks. He was sensitive to the damage done to most of the books after Beethoven's death (see 'Sketches', pp. 173–4); indeed, his choice of the Kessler and *Eroica* Sketchbooks as the subjects of more extended discussions was dictated largely by the fact that they appeared to have survived more or less intact, for he realized the dangers of trying to trace the evolution of a composition in cases where the sources were defective.

Thus Nottebohm was aware of the relationship between the physical state of a sketchbook and the musical insights to be gained from it; and he would doubtless have applauded the elegant methods recently devised to test and restore the physical integrity of the many dismembered books. In his own work, however, he was often satisfied with tantalizingly brief descriptions of the physical characteristics of a sketchbook, although he usually noted the points at which leaves had been removed and estimated the number missing. The many transcriptions illustrating his articles also leave much to be desired in the way of editorial practice: locations within the sketchbook are often omitted, and additions, omissions or emendations are made silently. But to be fair, Nottebohm's main aims were to provide a general description of each book, to draw any necessary conclusions concerning the chronology of the works represented in it, and to draw attention to any sketches for unfinished works. The kind of rigorous description rightly insisted upon today was to some extent superfluous. And vague as they may be, Nottebohm's accounts are still invaluable in some cases; for instance, virtually all that is known of the lost Boldrini Pocketbook for the 'Hammerklavier' Sonata comes from Nottebohm's description.

Such was the seeming authority of Nottebohm's work that it was hardly called into question by succeeding generations of scholars. Paul Mies's attempt to analyse Beethoven's melodic style through a comparison of sketches and final versions was founded entirely on Nottebohm's transcriptions, which were about fifty years old when Mies's book was published in 1925. Schenker relied heavily on Nottebohm's transcriptions in his *Erläuterungsausgaben* of the late sonatas and his book on the Ninth Symphony (see 'Analytical studies', p. 320), but he was also one of the few to supplement Nottebohm's work to some extent. Perhaps the most progressive event in the early years of this century was the publication by Karl Mikulicz in 1927 of a transcription of the sketchbook Landsberg 7, along with what must have seemed at the time a rather utopian call for a *Gesamtausgabe* of the sketchbooks in facsimile and transcription.

Some of the subsequent stages in the publication of sketchbook editions have already been described (see 'Sketches', pp. 173–4). But this area of sketch research, like almost every other, was put on a different footing as a result of the work on reconstruction spearheaded by Alan Tyson and Douglas Johnson in the early 1970s. By careful scrutiny of watermarks, stave-rulings, inkblots and other physical characteristics, it became possible not only to discover with considerable accuracy where and in what quantities leaves had been removed from a sketchbook, but also to locate those leaves and conceptually 'restore' them to their original positions. The definitive account of these techniques of reconstruction and their results when applied to all the known sketchbooks is to be found in *The Beethoven Sketchbooks* (Johnson, 1985). It should be borne in mind, however, that in general this book does not deal with loose leaves that were not originally part of a sketchbook. The re-establishment of the original physical condition of the sketchbooks has in many cases entailed a revision of their internal chronology and contents, and this has brought fresh insights into the dating of individual works. Tyson and Sieghard Brandenburg have both contributed a number of important studies in this area.

We have seen that Nottebohm was alert to the dangers facing anyone trying to examine an incomplete series of sketches for a work. But Nottebohm also understood that all sketches, however complete in a physical sense, are incomplete in the sense that they do not record everything that went on in Beethoven's mind during the composition even of the most simple piece of music; least of all do they record the actual decision-making processes: 'The sketches do not reveal the law by which Beethoven was governed while creating.... They are superfluous to an understanding of a work of art, certainly – but not to the understanding of the artist.' (Nottebohm, 1887, pp. viii–ix) In a celebrated essay published in 1978 Douglas Johnson explored the development of sketch studies since Nottebohm and declared himself essentially in agreement with Nottebohm's views: in Johnson's terms, sketch studies have no role to play in the analysis of Beethoven's works; they afford only biographical information.

Johnson's article brought forth an immediate barrage of defensive replies. Most scholars are forced to admit that if Johnson's strict definition of musical analysis be accepted, there is no place in such an activity for the examination of sketches. Equally, however, publications focusing on the sketches for individual works continue to appear, and this suggests that there is some middle ground, however difficult to define, between the total rejection and the total acceptance of sketches as documents relevant to musical analysis. Much depends, no doubt, on the individual's view of the nature and aims of analysis; and a more general investigation of the relationship between a finished work of art and its genesis might at least offer some new viewpoints if not any definite answers. For the time being, however, we may simply note that Johnson's remains an isolated attack.

The future for Beethoven sketch studies looks bright, then. The fact that all the surviving sketchbooks have now been reconstructed (not entirely unproblematically, but very largely so) will allow analysis of their contents to proceed with a good deal more confidence. The single biggest drawback at present remains the unavailability in published form of most of the sources. The quality of transcriptions and facsimiles has improved enormously, but the pace of publication, especially of volumes in the Beethovenhaus *Skizzenausgabe*, needs to be accelerated if all the painstaking work of reconstruction is not to seem in vain. Admittedly, the sketches provide only a partial documentation of the entire creative process, and great care must be taken not to invest them with more significance than they can bear; nevertheless, there are few who would be willing to forgo the fascinating questions and answers of all kinds which these sources never cease to raise.

NICHOLAS MARSTON

Bibliographies, catalogues and indexes

RATHER LIKE DICTIONARIES, the kinds of publication being considered here are doomed to failure in the sense that they will inevitably be out of date by the time they appear; comprehensiveness and total accuracy must remain unattainable goals in this field. It is almost unthinkable, for instance, that any bibliography of writings about Beethoven – even one that was regularly updated – could record every article, every review, even if each new book which appeared could be noted. However, completeness is only one desirable goal: a bibliography also needs to be carefully ordered if it is to be a useful research tool.

Taking both these factors into account, the best Beethoven bibliographies are probably those which appear at the end of each issue of the *Beethoven-Jahrbuch* under the heading 'Beethoven-Schrifttum'. The most recent of these is divided into eight main sections, some of which contain as many as five or six subsections. A total of 623 items is listed, and the range of languages covered is wide. On the other hand, the chronological period covered is 1973–5, while the *Jahrbuch* (dated '1978/81') was published as recently as 1983. The continuing irregular publication of this 'yearbook' makes these bibliographies largely useless as a guide to recent research, despite their obvious value as a continuing guide to the vast literature on Beethoven. Among other specialist bibliographies, Donald MacArdle's *Beethoven Abstracts*, published posthumously in 1973, deserves mention. It deals only with literature in periodicals and provides brief descriptions and references for a huge number of articles. *The Music Index* has the advantage of relatively punctual publication, but it is devoted to the literature of music in general rather than to Beethoven alone.

While an accurate bibliography for a major composer is an important requirement, a thematic catalogue is indispensable. It is essential to have access to a list of the composer's works that is as complete and accurate as possible. The first such catalogue of Beethoven's works was published anonymously by Breitkopf & Härtel in 1851. It contained the 138 works with opus number, along with those works published without such number, although these were not presented in the sequence that has become standard today. In addition, the catalogue made reference to a few doubtful works and also contained a very short bibliography.

A second, enlarged edition of this catalogue was published in 1868, by which time publication of the *Gesamtausgabe* of Beethoven's works had been completed (see 'Editions of the music', pp. 314–15). Thayer had also published a catalogue in 1865; but it was the 1868 publication, edited by Nottebohm, which can be said to have laid the foundations for Kinsky's great work of the next century. While the 1851 catalogue had given only incipits and sparse details of publishers for each work, Nottebohm added a short commentary giving dates of composition, first performance and publication wherever possible, as well as information on surviving autograph and copyists' scores, original editions, arrangements and the like. A 1925 reissue of Nottebohm's catalogue also incorporated Kastner's bibliography *Bibliotheca Beethoveniana*, itself enlarged by Von Frimmel.

Thirty years after this reissue, Georg Kinsky's monumental catalogue appeared. Completed and edited by Hans Halm, it remains the standard thematic catalogue of Beethoven's works (Kinsky, 1955). Inevitably, the passing of time has revealed errors and refinements: to take one obvious example, the 'Jena' Symphony, which appeared in the list of doubtful works (Kinsky Anhang 1), can now be dropped altogether. As an interim measure pending a complete overhaul, a list of Addenda and Corrigenda appeared in 1978 together with a collection of bibliographical studies on various subjects (Dorfmüller, 1978). Willy Hess's catalogue of works which had been omitted from the *Gesamtausgabe* has been discussed above under 'Editions of the music' (p. 315). And while Kinsky, 1955 was expressly intended to document only Beethoven's completed works, Giovanni Biamonti's *Catalogo cronologico e tematico*, published in 1968, followed Hess in its broad definition of the 'work'; it includes complete and incomplete works as well as sketches, listing even those projects for which no music survives but which Beethoven is known to have been working on or planning. It differs further from Kinsky, 1955 in that it is arranged chronologically rather than by opus or WoO number, and in its inclusion of brief discussions of major works.

One area in which Kinsky, 1955 is particularly in need of revision is that of information on sketches and autograph manuscripts. The cataloguing of Beethoven's manuscripts may be said to have begun with the (handwritten) *Nachlass* catalogue prepared in 1827 by Anton Gräffer; later, in 1844, Gräffer catalogued the Artaria collection, which was to be catalogued twice more (by Adler in 1890 and by August Artaria in 1893) before the end of the century. As Douglas Johnson has shown (see Johnson, 1973 and 1985, especially chapter 1), these and other 19th-century catalogues – such as those of the Landsberg and Grasnick collections – are important in establishing the movements of the manuscripts prior to their arrival in their present-day locations.

In this century handsome catalogues of some private collections have been published. In particular, Kinsky's catalogue (1953) of the Koch collection deserves mention, since that collection, which contained some extremely important Beethoven items, is now dispersed. As for major public archives, the Beethovenhaus collection (autographs, sketches and letters) is well served by Schmidt, 1971. The Beethoven manuscripts in the Staatsbibliothek Preussischer Kulturbesitz have also been catalogued carefully (see Klein, 1975), while the highly important collection in the Deutsche Staatsbibliothek is only very sparsely documented in Bartlitz, 1970.

Despite these catalogues of individual holdings, there is still a need for a comprehensive listing of the sketches. Hans Schmidt's well-known catalogue (Schmidt, 1969) remains useful, but the contents of many manuscripts are wrongly identified (or not identified at all), and there is none of the bibliographical information concerning paper types and watermarks which has become a standard requirement today. While Johnson, 1985 may be used as a catalogue of the reconstructed sketchbooks, the large number of loose leaves that were apparently not part of any such book awaits similar treatment. Also useful would be a catalogue of Beethoven's autograph manuscripts, complete with details of paper types and structure.

If any general picture emerges from the foregoing brief account, it is that Beethoven bibliography – in the sense of bibliographical control of the sources for Beethoven's works – is in need of attention. A great deal of information is accessible, but only in a large number of diverse formats. There are some excellent specialized studies (Tyson's 1963 bibliography of authentic English Beethoven editions is a case in point); but the real need is for a central, authoritative reference work. One obvious solution is a wholly revised thematic catalogue. Details of autograph structure could be incorporated, for example, and Kinsky-Halm's 'Entstehungszeit' sections could be revised to take account of present-day knowledge concerning the sketches (although the inclusion of detailed bibliographical information would be impractical here). Similarly, the 'Briefbelege' would need to be revised in accordance with the findings of the new edition of the letters (see p. 164), and references to catalogues of individual archive holdings would require revision and expansion. The result would, of course, not be perfect; but even this imperfect service to Beethoven scholarship would be an important step forward.

NICHOLAS MARSTON

SELECT BIBLIOGRAPHY
LIST OF ILLUSTRATIONS
THE CONTRIBUTORS
INDEX

SELECT BIBLIOGRAPHY

It is believed that there is more literature on Beethoven than on any other composer except Wagner. Much of the older material has long since been superseded, but the present listing is still necessarily highly selective from the remainder. For a more extensive survey, especially of recent literature, see Albrecht, ?1992. Older periodical literature is systematically covered in MacArdle, 1973. A comprehensive list, but only for certain years, is provided in the *Beethoven-Jahrbuch*; meanwhile the Beethoven Center in San Jose, California, is planning to create a database that will provide an all-embracing Beethoven bibliography, including books, articles, scores and recordings.

The entries below are arranged alphabetically by author's surname, and chronologically under each surname. Where two or more publications by the same author appeared in the same year, the entries are distinguished by a letter suffixed to the year of publication.

Editions

Ludwig van Beethoven's Werke: Vollständige kritisch durchgesehene überall berechtigte Ausgabe, 25 vols, Leipzig, 1862–5, 1888. For 14-volume *Supplement* see Hess, 1959, below.
Ludwig van Beethoven: Werke: Neue Ausgabe sämtlicher Werke, Munich and Duisburg, 1961–

Facsimile editions of sketchbooks and autograph scores are listed on pp. 185–7 and 188–90 respectively (see also Hess, 1979, and Lühning, 1986, below). A facsimile reprint of the first editions of the 32 piano sonatas is in Jeffery, 1989. A few other notable editions of Beethoven's music are listed below, under the names of the editors.

Periodicals

The principal periodicals devoted specifically to Beethoven are as follows:

Beethovenjahrbuch, ed. Theodor Frimmel, 2 vols, Munich and Leipzig, 1908–9
Neues Beethoven-Jahrbuch, ed. Adolf Sandberger, 10 vols, 1924–42
Beethoven-Jahrbuch, ed. Joseph Schmidt-Görg and others, Bonn, 1953–
The Beethoven Newsletter, ed. William Meredith, San Jose, 1986–

The Beethoven-Haus in Bonn also issues several series of publications: Series 1–3 consist of sketchbooks, the *Beethoven-Jahrbuch* and manuscript facsimiles respectively; Series 4 is for books on specialized Beethoven topics (some are listed in the Bibliography below), and there is also a series of short *Jahresgaben*, as well as some individual publications. Other shorter series of Beethoven studies include Goldschmidt, 1979, 1984, 1988, and Tyson, 1973c, 1977b, 1982b. Individual articles from such periodical publications, as also from Beethoven symposia and congress reports, are normally listed separately below only if they have been cited in the main text.

Books, articles etc.

Abraham, G., ed., *The Age of Beethoven 1790–1830* (The New Oxford History of Music, viii), London, 1982

Albrecht, O. E., 'Beethoven Autographs in the United States', in Dorfmüller, 1978, pp. 1–11

Albrecht, T., 'Beethoven's *Leonore*: A New Compositional Chronology', *The Journal of Musicology*, vii (1989), 165–90

———, *Ludwig van Beethoven: A Guide to Research*, New York, ?1992

Anderson, E., trans. and ed., *The Letters of Beethoven*, 3 vols., London, 1961

———, trans. and ed., *The Letters of Mozart and his Family*, 3rd edn, London, 1985

Arnold, D., and Fortune, N., edd., *The Beethoven Companion*, London, 1971

Badura-Skoda, P., 'Eine wichtige Quelle zu Beethovens 4. Klavierkonzert', *Österreichische Musikzeitschrift*, xiii (1958), 418–26

Badura-Skoda, E., 'Performance Conventions in Beethoven's Early Works', in Winter, 1980, pp. 52–76

Barea, I., *Vienna*, New York, 1966

Barford, P., 'The Piano Music – II' in Arnold, 1971, pp. 126–93

Bartlitz, E., *Die Beethoven-Sammlung in der Musikabteilung der Deutschen Staatsbibliothek: Verzeichnis*, Berlin, 1970

Beahrs, V. O., 'Beethoven, Bonaparte, and the Republican Ideal – Exploring Alternative Perspectives', *The Beethoven Newsletter*, iv (1989), 25, 34–40

Beethoven-Haus Bonn [S. Brandenburg and

others], ed., *Ludwig van Beethoven: Der Briefwechsel mit dem Verlag Schott*, Munich, 1985

Bent, I., 'The Compositional Process in Music Theory 1713–1850', *Music Analysis*, iii (1984), 29–55

——, and Drabkin, W., *Analysis* (The New Grove Handbooks in Music), London, 1987

Bente, M., ed., *Musik-Edition Interpretation: Gedenkschrift Günter Henle*, Munich, 1980

Biamonti, G., *Catalogo cronologico e tematico delle opere di Beethoven*, Turin, 1968

Biba, O., 'Concert Life in Beethoven's Vienna', in Winter, 1980, pp. 77–93

Blume, F., *Classic and Romantic Music: A Comprehensive Survey*, trans. H. Norton, New York, 1970; London, 1972

Boettcher, H., *Beethoven als Liederkomponist*, Augsburg, 1928 (repr. 1974)

Brandenburg, S., 'The First Version of Beethoven's G major String Quartet op. 18 no. 2', *Music & Letters*, lviii (1977), 127–52

——, 'Ein Skizzenbuch Beethovens aus dem Jahre 1812: Zur Chronologie des Petterschen Skizzenbuches', in Goldschmidt, 1979, pp. 117–48

——, 'Zur Textgeschichte von Beethovens Violinsonate Opus 47', in Bente, 1980, pp. 111–24

——, 'The Historical Background to the *Heiliger Dankgesang* in Beethoven's A minor Quartet Op. 132', in Tyson, 1982b, pp. 161–91

——, 'Die Quellen zur Entstehungsgeschichte von Beethovens Streichquartett Es-dur Op. 127', *Beethoven-Jahrbuch*, x (1978–81), Bonn, 1983, 221–76

——, 'Die Skizzen zur Neunten Symphonie', 1984a, in Goldschmidt, 1984, pp. 88–129

——, 'Once Again: On the Question of the Repeat of the Scherzo and Trio in Beethoven's Fifth Symphony', 1984b, in Lockwood, 1984, pp. 146–98

——, and Staehelin, M., 'Die "erste Fassung" von Beethovens Righini-Variationen', in *Festschrift Albi Rosenthal*, ed. R. Elvers, Tutzing, 1984c, pp. 43–66

——, and Loos, H., edd., *Beiträge zu Beethovens Kammermusik: Symposion Bonn 1984*, Munich, 1987

——, and Gutiérrez-Denhoff, M., edd., *Beethoven und Böhmen: Beiträge zu Biographie und Wirkungsgeschichte Beethovens*, Bonn, 1988

Brenneis, C., 'Das Fischhof-Manuskript: Zur Frühgeschichte der Beethoven-Biographik', in Goldschmidt, 1979, pp. 90–116

——, 'Das Fischhof-Manuskript in der Deutschen Staatsbibliothek', in Goldschmidt, 1984, pp. 27–87

Breuning, G. von, *Aus dem Schwarzspanierhause, Erinnerungen an Ludwig van Beethoven aus meiner Jugendzeit*, Vienna, 1874; 2nd edn, ed. A. C. Kalischer, Berlin, 1907 (repr. Hildesheim, 1970)

Brilliant, R., 'Beethoven on Stamps', *The Beethoven Newsletter*, iii (1988), 12–13

Brion, M., *Daily Life in the Vienna of Mozart and Schubert*, trans. J. Stewart, New York, 1962

Broyles, M. E., 'Beethoven's Sonata op. 14 no. 1 – Originally for Strings?', *Journal of the American Musicological Society*, xxiii (1970), 405–19

——, *Beethoven: The Emergence and Evolution of Beethoven's Heroic Style*, New York, 1987

Busch-Weise, D. von, 'Beethovens Jugendtagebuch', *Studien zur Musikwissenschaft*, xxv (1962), 68–88

Carse, A., *The Orchestra from Beethoven to Berlioz*, Cambridge, 1948

Churgin, B., 'A New Edition of Beethoven's Fourth Symphony: Editorial Report', *Israel Studies in Musicology*, i (1978), 11–53

——, 'Beethoven and Mozart's Requiem: A New Connection', *The Journal of Musicology*, v (1987), 457–77

Comini, A., *The Changing Image of Beethoven*, New York, 1987

Cone, E. T., 'Beethoven's Experiments in Composition: The Late Bagatelles', in Tyson, 1977b, pp. 84–105

Cook, N., 'Beethoven's Unfinished Piano Concerto: a Case of Double Vision?' *Journal of the American Musicological Society*, xlii (1989), 338–74

Cooke, D., 'The Unity of Beethoven's Late Quartets', *The Music Review*, xxiv (1963), 30–49

Cooper, M., *Beethoven: The Last Decade*, Oxford, 1970

Cooper, B., 'Beethoven's Revisions to *Für Elise*', *The Musical Times*, cxxv (1984), 561–3

——, 'Newly Identified Sketches for Beethoven's Tenth Symphony', *Music & Letters*, lxvi (1985), 9–18

——, 'Beethoven's Portfolio of Bagatelles', *Journal of the Royal Musical Association*, cxii (1987a), 208–28

——, 'The Ink in Beethoven's "Kafka" Sketch Miscellany', *Music & Letters*, lxviii (1987b), 315–32

——, 'The Composition of "Und spür' ich" in Beethoven's *Fidelio*', *The Music Review*, xlvii (1987c), 231–7

——, 'The First Movement of Beethoven's Tenth Symphony: A Realization', *The Beethoven Newsletter*, iii (1988), 25–31

——, *Beethoven and the Creative Process*, Oxford, 1990

——, ed., *Beethoven: Three Bagatelles*, London, 1991

Crankshaw, E., ed., *Artur Schnabel: My Life and Music*, London, 1961

Crofton, I., and Fraser, D., *A Dictionary of Musical Quotations*, Sydney, 1985

Czerny, C., *School of Practical Composition*, London, ?1849 (originally published in German as *Schule der praktischen Tonsetzung*)

——, *On the Proper Performance of all Beethoven's Works for the Piano*, ed. P. Badura-Skoda, Vienna,

1970

Dahlhaus, C., and others, edd., *Bericht über den Internationalen Musikwissenschaftlichen Kongress Bonn 1970*, Kassel, 1971

——, *Ludwig van Beethoven und seine Zeit*, Laaber, 1987

——, *Nineteenth-Century Music*, trans. J. Bradford Robinson, Berkeley, 1989

De la Grange, H., *Mahler*, London, 1974

Dent, E. J., *Ferruccio Busoni*, London, 1933

De Roda, C., 'Un quaderno di autografi di Beethoven del 1825', *Rivista musicale italiana*, xii (1905), 63–108, 592–622, 734–67

Deutsch, O. E., 'Beethovens gesammelte Werke: des Meisters Plan und Haslingers Ausgabe', *Zeitschrift für Musikwissenschaft*, xiii (1930–31), 60–79

Dickinson, A. E. F., 'Beethoven's Early Fugal Style', *The Musical Times*, xcvi (1955), 76–9

Dipert, R., 'The Composer's Intentions: an Examination of their Relevance for Performance', *The Musical Quarterly*, lxvi (1980), 205–18

Dorfmüller, K., ed., *Beiträge zur Beethoven-Bibliographie*, Munich, 1978

Drabkin, W., 'Some Relationships between the Autographs of Beethoven's Sonata in C minor, Opus 111', *Current Musicology*, xiii (1972), 38–47

——, 'Beethoven's Sketches and the Thematic Process', *Proceedings of the Royal Musical Association*, cv (1978–9), 25–36

——, Review of *Beethoven Studies 3* (ed. Alan Tyson), *19th-Century Music*, vii (1983), 163–9

——, 'Beethoven and the Open String', *Music Analysis*, iv (1985a), 15–28

——, 'Building a Music Library, 1: The Beethoven Piano Sonatas', *The Musical Times*, cxxvi (1985b), 416–20

Dunsby, J., 'A Bagatelle on Beethoven's WoO 60', *Music Analysis*, iii (1984), 57–68

Eggebrecht, H. H., *Zur Geschichte der Beethoven-Rezeption*, Mainz, 1972

Enss, E., *Beethoven als Bearbeiter eigener Werke*, Taunusstein, 1988

Fecker, A., ed., *Ludwig van Beethoven: Unbekannte Klavierstücke*, Wolfenbüttel and Zurich, 1972

——, *Die Entstehung von Beethovens Musik zu Goethes Trauerspiel Egmont. Eine Abhandlung über die Skizzen*, Hamburg, 1978

Feder, G., 'Stilelemente Haydns in Beethovens Werken', in Dahlhaus, 1971, pp. 65–70

Finscher, L., ed., *Ludwig van Beethoven*, Darmstadt, 1983

Fischer, E., *Beethoven's Pianoforte Sonatas*, trans. S. Godman, London, 1959

Fischer, K. von, *Essays in Musicology*, New York, 1989

Fiske, R., *Beethoven's Missa Solemnis*, New York, 1979

Floros, C., *Beethovens Eroica und Prometheus-Musik*, Wilhelmshaven, 1978

Forbes, E., ed., *Ludwig van Beethoven: Symphony no. 5 in C minor*, New York, 1971

Fortune, N., 'The Chamber Music with Piano', in Arnold, 1971, pp. 197–240

Frimmel, T., *Beethoven-Handbuch*, 2 vols, Leipzig, 1926

Funk, A., *Vienna's Musical Sites and Landmarks*, Vienna, 1927

Geck, M., and Schleuning, P., 'Geschrieben auf Bonaparte': Beethovens 'Eroica' – Revolution, Reaktion, Rezeption*, Hamburg, 1989

Goldman, A., and Sprinchorn, E., edd., *Wagner on Music and Drama*, trans. W. A. Ellis, London, 1970

Goldschmidt, H., 'Un lieto brindisi: Cantata campestre', *Beethoven-Jahrbuch*, viii (1971–2), Bonn, 1975, 157–205

——, *Um die Unsterbliche Geliebte: Eine Bestandsaufnahme*, Leipzig, 1977

——, Köhler, K-H., and Niemann, K., edd., *Bericht über den Internationalen Beethoven-Kongress 20. bis 23. März 1977 in Berlin*, Leipzig, 1978

——, ed., *Zu Beethoven: Aufsätze und Annotationen*, Berlin, 1979

——, ed., *Zu Beethoven 2: Aufsätze und Dokumente*, Berlin, 1984

——, ed., *Zu Beethoven 3: Aufsätze und Dokumente*, Berlin, 1988

Gossett, P., 'Beethoven's Sixth Symphony: Sketches for the First Movement', *Journal of the American Musicological Society*, xxvii (1974), 248–84

Griffiths, P., *The String Quartet*, London, 1983

Gülke, P., *Zur Neuausgabe der Sinfonie Nr. 5 von Ludwig van Beethoven: Werk und Edition*, Leipzig, 1978

Hanson, A. M., 'Incomes and Outgoings in the Vienna of Beethoven and Schubert', *Music & Letters*, lxiv (1983), 173–82

——, *Musical Life in Biedermeier Vienna*, Cambridge, 1985

Hertzmann, E., 'The Newly Discovered Autograph of Beethoven's Rondo a capriccioso, Op. 129', *The Musical Quarterly*, xxxii (1946), 171–95

Hess, W., *Beethovens Oper Fidelio und ihre drei Fassungen*, Zurich, 1953

——, *Verzeichnis der nicht in der Gesamtausgabe veröffentlichte Werke Ludwig van Beethovens*, Wiesbaden, 1957

——, ed., *Ludwig van Beethoven: Supplement zur Gesamtausgabe*, 14 vols, Wiesbaden, 1959–71

——, *Beethovens Bühnenwerke*, Göttingen, 1962

——, *Beethoven-Studien*, Bonn, 1972

——, ed., *Ludwig van Beethoven, Sämtliche Kadenzen: The Complete Cadenzas* (facsimile edn), Zurich, 1979

——, 'The Right Tempo: Beethoven and the Metronome', *The Beethoven Newsletter*, iii (1988), 16–17

Hopkins, A., *The Nine Symphonies of Beethoven*, London, 1980

Hopkinson, C., and Oldman, C. B., 'Thomson's Collections of National Song, with Special Reference to the Contributions of Haydn and Beethoven', *Edinburgh Bibliographical Society Transactions*, ii (1938–45), 1–64; addenda and corrigenda, iii (1948–55), 121–4

Howell, S., 'Beethoven's Maelzel Canon: Another Schindler Forgery?', *The Musical Times*, cxx (1979), 987–90

Hutchings, A. J. B., *A Companion to Mozart's Piano Concertos*, London 1948

Jander, O., 'Exploring Sulzer's *Allgemeine Theorie* as a Source used by Beethoven', *The Beethoven Newsletter*, ii (1987), 1–7

Jeffery, B., ed., *Ludwig van Beethoven: The 32 Piano Sonatas in Reprints of the First and Early Editions*, London, 1989

Johnson, D., 'Beethoven's Sketches for the Scherzo of the Quartet Op. 18 No. 6', *Journal of the American Musicological Society*, xxiii (1970), 385–404

——, 'The Artaria Collection of Beethoven Manuscripts: A New Source', in Tyson, 1973c, pp. 174–236

——, 'Beethoven Scholars and Beethoven's Sketches', *19th-Century Music*, ii (1978), 3–17; see also *ibid.*, iii (1979), 270–79

——, *Beethoven's Early Sketches in the 'Fischhof Miscellany': Berlin Autograph 28*, 2 vols, Ann Arbor, 1980a

——, 'Music for Prague and Berlin: Beethoven's Concert Tour of 1796', 1980b, in Winter, 1980, pp. 24–40

——, '1794–1795: Decisive Years in Beethoven's Early Development', in Tyson, 1982b, pp. 1–28

——, Tyson, A., and Winter, R., *The Beethoven Sketchbooks: History, Reconstruction, Inventory*, ed. D. Johnson, Oxford, 1985

Jonas, O., 'Bemerkungen zu Beethovens op. 96', *Acta Musicologica*, xxxvii (1965), 87–9

Kagan, S., *Archduke Rudolph, Beethoven's Patron, Pupil, and Friend: His Life and Music*, Stuyvesant, 1988

Kastner, E., ed., *Ludwig van Beethovens sämtliche Briefe*, Leipzig, 1910; rev. J. Kapp, 1923

Kerman, J., 'Beethoven Sketchbooks in the British Museum', *Proceedings of the Royal Musical Association*, xciii (1966–7), 77–96

——, *The Beethoven Quartets*, Oxford, 1967

——, ed., *Ludwig van Beethoven: Autograph Miscellany from circa 1786 to 1799*, 2 vols, London, 1970

——, 'Tovey's Beethoven', in Tyson, 1977b, pp. 172–91

——, and Tyson, A., *The New Grove Beethoven*, London, 1983

——, *Musicology*, London, 1985

Kerst, F., ed., *Die Erinnerungen an Beethoven*, 2 vols, Stuttgart, 1913

——, *Beethoven, the Man and the Artist, as Revealed in his Own Words*, trans. H. E. Krehbiel, New York, R/1964

Kinderman, W., 'Beethoven's Symbol for the Deity in the *Missa solemnis* and the Ninth Symphony', *19th-Century Music*, ix (1985), 102–18

——, *Beethoven's Diabelli Variations*, Oxford, 1987

Kinsky, G., *Manuskripte, Briefe, Dokumente von Scarlatti bis Stravinsky: Katalog der Musikautographen-Sammlung Louis Koch*, Stuttgart, 1953

——, *Das Werk Beethovens: Thematisch-bibliographisches Verzeichnis seiner sämtlichen vollendeten Kompositionen*, completed/ed. H. Halm, Munich, 1955

Kirkendale, W., 'New Roads to Old Ideas in Beethoven's *Missa Solemnis*', *The Musical Quarterly*, lvi (1970), 665–701 (reprinted in Lang, 1971)

Klein, H-G., *Ludwig van Beethoven: Autographe und Abschriften*, Berlin, 1975

Klein, R., ed., *Beethoven-Kolloquium 1977: Dokumentation und Aufführungspraxis*, Kassel, 1978

Knight, F., *Beethoven and the Age of Revolution*, London, 1973

Köhler, K-H., and others, *Ludwig van Beethovens Konversationshefte*, 10 vols, Leipzig, 1968–

Kojima, S-A., 'Die Solovioline-Fassungen und -Varianten von Beethovens Violinkonzert op. 61–ihre Entstehung und Bedeutung', *Beethoven-Jahrbuch*, viii (1971–2), Bonn, 1975, 97–145

——, 'Zweifelhafte Authentizität einiger Beethoven zugeschriebener Orchestertänze', in Goldschmidt, 1978, pp. 307–22

Kolisch, R., 'Tempo and Character in Beethoven's Music', *The Musical Quarterly*, xxix (1943), 169–87, 291–312

Kramer, R., *The Sketches for Beethoven's Violin Sonatas, Op. 30*, Ph.D. diss., Princeton University, 1974

——, 'Notes to Beethoven's Education', *Journal of the American Musicological Society*, xxviii (1975), 72–101

——, 'An Unfinished Concertante of 1802', in Tyson, 1977b, pp. 33–65

——, '"Das Organische der Fuge": On the Autograph of Beethoven's String Quartet in F major, Opus 59 No. 1', in Wolff, 1980, pp. 223–65

Kullak, F., *Beethoven's Piano-Playing*, trans. T. Baker, New York, 1973

Küthen, H-W., *Klavierkonzerte I: Kritischer Bericht* (Neue Ausgabe, III/2), Munich, 1984

——, 'Probleme der Chronologie in den Skizzen und Autographen zu Beethovens Klavierkonzert Op.19', *Beethoven-Jahrbuch*, ix (1973–7), Bonn, 1977, 263–92

La Mara (pseud. of M. Lipsius), *Beethoven und die Brunsviks*, Leipzig, 1920

Landon, H. C. R., and Mitchell, D., edd., *The Mozart Companion*, London, 1956

Landon, H. C. R. 'The *Jena* Symphony', *The Music Review*, xviii (1957), 109–13

——, *Beethoven: A Documentary Study*, London, 1970; abridged edn, 1974

——, *Haydn: Chronicle and Works: Haydn at Esterhaza 1766–1790*, London, 1978

Landon, C., and Weinmann, A., 'Beethovens

Sonate op. 111: Eigenhändiges Korrekturexemplar der Wiener Ausgabe von Cappi & Diabelli. Eine neu aufgefundene Quelle', *Fontes artis musicae*, xxvi (1979), 281–94

Lang, P. H., ed., *The Creative World of Beethoven*, New York, 1971 (reprint of *The Musical Quarterly*, lvi (1970), 515–793, here numbered as pp. 13–291)

Larsen, J. P., and Feder, G., *The New Grove Haydn*, London, 1982

Laskowsky, L., *Heinrich Schenker: An Annotated Index to his Analyses of Musical Works*, New York, 1978

Lawrence, R., *Ballets and Ballet Music*, New York, 1950

Le Huray, P., and Day, J., *Music and Aesthetics in the Eighteenth and Early-Nineteenth Centuries*, Cambridge, 1981

Lenz, W. von, *Beethoven et ses trois styles*, St Petersburg, 1852–3

Lester, J., 'Revisions in the Autograph of the *Missa Solemnis Kyrie*', *Journal of the American Musicological Society*, xxiii (1970), 420–38

Levy, J. M., *Beethoven's Compositional Choices: The Two Versions of Opus 18, No. 1, First Movement*, Philadelphia, 1982

Lochner, L., *Fritz Kreisler*, New York, 2nd edn, 1951

Lockwood, L., 'The Autograph of the First Movement of Beethoven's Sonata for Violoncello and Pianoforte, Opus 69', *The Music Forum*, ii (1970a), 1–109

——, 'On Beethoven's Sketches and Autographs: Some Problems of Definition and Interpretation', *Acta Musicologica*, xlii (1970b), 32–47

——, 'Beethoven's Early Works for Violoncello and Contemporary Violoncello Technique', in Klein, 1978, pp. 174–82

——, 'Beethoven's Earliest Sketches for the *Eroica* Symphony', *The Musical Quarterly*, lxvii (1981), 457–78

——, '"Eroica" Perspectives: Strategy and Design in the First Movement', in Tyson, 1982b, pp. 85–105

——, and Benjamin, P., edd., *Beethoven Essays: Studies in Honor of Elliot Forbes*, Cambridge, Mass., 1984

London, S. J., 'Beethoven, Case Report of a Titan's Last Crisis', *Archives of Internal Medicine*, cxiii (1964), 442–8

Lühning, H., *Beethoven. 'Nur wer die Sehnsucht kennt' WoO 134* (with facsimile edn), ed. S. Brandenburg, Bonn, 1986

MacArdle, D., 'Beethoven and George Thomson', *Music & Letters*, xxxvii (1956), 27–49

——, 'Beethoven and the Czernys', *Monthly Musical Record*, lxxxviii (1958), 124–35

——, 'Beethoven and Grillparzer', *Music & Letters*, xl (1959), 44–55

——, 'Beethoven and Handel', *Music & Letters*, xli (1960), 33–7

——, 'Beethoven and Ferdinand Ries', *Music & Letters*, xlvi (1965), 23–34

——, 'Beethoven und Karl Holz', *Die Musikforschung*, xx (1967), 19–29

——, *Beethoven Abstracts*, Detroit, 1973

Macdonald, H., 'Fantasy and Order in Beethoven's Phantasie Op. 77', *Modern Musical Scholarship*, ed. Edward Olleson, Stocksfield, 1980, pp. 141–50

Mamatey, V. S., *Rise of the Habsburg Empire 1526–1815*, New York, 1971

Marmorek, E., 'On Listening to Beethoven's Last Piano Sonata', *The Beethoven Newsletter*, iii (1988), 14–15

Marston, N., 'The Origins of Beethoven's Op. 109: Further Thoughts', *The Musical Times*, cxxvii (1986), 199–201

——, 'Schenker and Forte Reconsidered: Beethoven's Sketches for the Piano Sonata in E, Op. 109', *19th-Century Music*, x (1986–7), 24–42

——, 'Analysing Variations: The Final Movement of Beethoven's String Quartet, Op. 74', *Music Analysis*, viii (1989), 303–24

——, 'Beethoven's "Anti-Organicism"? The Origins of the Slow Movement of the Ninth Symphony', in *Studies in the History of Music 3: The Compositional Process*, New York, ?1991

Marx, A. B., *Ludwig van Beethoven: Leben und Schaffen* (Berlin, 1859)

Matthews, D., *Beethoven Piano Sonatas*, London, 1967

——, *Beethoven*, London, 1985

Meredith, W., 'The Origins of Beethoven's Op. 109', *The Musical Times*, cxxvi (1985), 713–6

——, 'Beethoven's Creativity', *The Beethoven Newsletter*, i (1986a), 25–8, 37, 39–44

——, 'The Cavatina in Space', *The Beethoven Newsletter*, i (1986b), 29–30

Mies, P., *Die Bedeutung der Skizzen Beethovens zur Erkenntnis seines Stiles*, Leipzig, 1925; trans. D. L. Mackinnon as *Beethoven's Sketches*, New York, 1929, R/1974

——, *Textkritische Untersuchungen bei Beethoven*, Bonn, 1957

Misch, L., *Die Faktoren der Einheit in der Mehrsätzigkeit der Werke Beethovens*, Munich and Duisburg, 1958

——, *Neue Beethoven-Studien und andere Themen*, Munich and Duisburg, 1967

Mitchell, W. J., 'Beethoven's La Malinconia from the String Quartet, Opus 18, No. 6', *The Music Forum*, iii (1973), 269–80

Moore, J., *Beethoven and Musical Economics*, Ph.D. diss., University of Urbana, Illinois, 1987

Morrow, M. S., *Concert Life in Haydn's Vienna*, New York, 1987

Münster, A., *Studien zu Beethovens Diabelli-Variationen*, Munich, 1982

Nettl, P., *Beethoven Encyclopedia*, New York, 1956; London, 1957

Newman, E., *The Unconscious Beethoven*, London, 1927 (rev. edn, 2/1969)

Newman, W. S., 'Liszt's Interpreting of Beethoven's

Piano Sonatas', *The Musical Quarterly*, lviii (1972), 185–209

——, 'Beethoven's Fingerings as Interpretive Clues', *The Journal of Musicology*, i (1982), 171–97

——, 'The Beethoven Mystique in Romantic Art, Literature and Music', *The Musical Quarterly*, lxix (1983), 345–87

——, *Beethoven on Beethoven: Playing His Piano Music His Way*, New York, 1988

Nohl, L., *Beethovens Leben*, 3 vols, Vienna, 1864; Leipzig, 1867 and 1877

——, *Beethoven, Liszt, Wagner*, Vienna, 1874

Nottebohm, G., *Ein Skizzenbuch von Beethoven*, Leipzig, 1865 (repr. New York, 1970)

——, *Beethoveniana*, Leipzig, 1872 (repr. New York, 1970)

——, *Beethoven's Studien*, Leipzig and Winterthur, 1873

——, *Ein Skizzenbuch von Beethoven aus dem Jahre 1803*, Leipzig, 1880 (repr. New York, 1970)

——, *Zweite Beethoveniana*, Leipzig, 1887 (repr. New York, 1970)

Obelkevich, M. R., 'The Growth of a Musical Idea – Beethoven's Op. 96', *Current Musicology*, xi (1971), 91–114

Oldman, C. B., 'Beethoven's *Variations on National Themes*: Their Composition and First Publication', *The Music Review*, xii (1951), 45–51

Peake, L. E., 'The Antecedents of Beethoven's *Liederkreis*', *Music & Letters*, lxiii (1982), 242–60

Plantinga, L., *Muzio Clementi: His Life and Music*, London, 1976

——, 'When did Beethoven Compose his Third Piano Concerto?', *The Journal of Musicology*, vii (1989), 275–307

Platen, E., ed., *Streichtrios und Streichduo* (Neue Ausgabe, VI/6), Munich, 1965

Radcliffe, P., *Beethoven's String Quartets*, London, 1965

Ramm, A., *Germany 1789–1919: A Political History*, London, 1967

Ratner, L., *Classic Music: Expression, Form, and Style*, New York, 1979

Reti, R., *The Thematic Process in Music*, New York, 1951

——, *Thematic Patterns in Sonatas of Beethoven*, London, 1967

Reynolds, C., 'Ends and Means in the Second Finale to Beethoven's Op. 30, no. 1', in Lockwood, 1984, pp. 127–45

Ringer, A. L., 'Clementi and the *Eroica*', *The Musical Quarterly*, xlvii (1961), 454–68

——, 'Beethoven and the London Pianoforte School', *The Musical Quarterly*, lvi (1970), 742–58 (reprinted in Lang, 1971)

Rivera, B. V., 'Rhythmic Organisation in Beethoven's Seventh Symphony: A Study of Cancelled Measures in the Autograph', *19th-Century Music*, vi (1982–3), 241–51

Rolland, R., *Les grands époques créatrices*, Paris, 1928–57 (vol. i. trans. E. Newman as *Beethoven the Creator*, London, 1929, New York, 2/1964; vol. ii as *Goethe and Beethoven*, 1931)

Rosen, C., *The Classical Style: Haydn, Mozart, Beethoven*, rev. edn, London, 1976

Rothschild, F., *Musical Performance in the Times of Mozart and Beethoven*, London, 1961

Rushton, J., *Classical Music: A Concise History from Gluck to Beethoven*, London, 1986

Russell, J., *A Tour in Germany, and some of the Southern Provinces of the Austrian Empire, in 1820, 1821, 1822*, Edinburgh, 1828

Schenk, E., ed., *Beethoven Symposion Wien 1970*, Vienna, 1971

Schenker, H., *Beethovens Neunte Sinfonie*, Vienna, 1912 (repr. 1969)

——, *Die letzten Sonaten von Beethoven: kritische Ausgabe mit Einführung und Erläuterung*, Vienna, 1913–21

——, *Beethovens Fünfte Sinfonie*, Vienna, 1925 (repr. 1969)

——, *Der freie Satz*, Vienna, 1935; rev. O. Jonas, 1956; trans. E. Oster as *Free Composition*, 2 vols, New York and London, 1979

Schiedermair, L., *Der junge Beethoven*, Leipzig, 1925

Schindler, A., *Biographie von Ludwig van Beethoven*, Münster, 1840; English trans. as *The Life of Beethoven*, ed. I. Moscheles, London, 1841; 2nd edn with supplementary chapter 'Beethoven in Paris', Münster, 1845; 3rd edn, 2 vols., Münster, 1860, trans. C. S. Jolly as *Beethoven as I Knew Him*, ed. D. W. MacArdle, London, 1966

Schleuning, P., 'Beethoven in alter Deutung: Der "neue Weg" mit der "Sinfonia eroica"', *Archiv für Musikwissenschaft*, xliv (1987), 165–94

Schmidt, H., 'Verzeichnis der Skizzen Beethovens', *Beethoven-Jahrbuch*, vi (1965–8), Bonn, 1969, 7-128

——, 'Die Beethovenhandschriften des Beethovenhauses in Bonn', *Beethoven-Jahrbuch*, vii (1969–70), Bonn, 1971, vii–xxiv, 1–443; addenda and corrigenda in *Beethoven-Jahrbuch*, viii (1971–2), Bonn, 1975, 207–20

Schmidt-Görg, J., *Beethoven: die Geschichte seiner Familie*, Bonn, 1964

——, and Schmidt, H., edd., *Ludwig van Beethoven*, Bonn and Hamburg, 1970

——, ed., *Des Bonner Bäckermeisters Gottfried Fischer Aufzeichnungen über Beethovens Jugend*, Bonn and Munich, 1971

——, 'Die Wasserzeichen in Beethovens Notenpapieren', in Dorfmüller, 1978, pp. 167–95

Schmitz, A., *Beethoven: Unbekannte Skizzen und Entwürfe*, Bonn, 1924

——, *Das romantische Beethovenbild*, Berlin and Bonn, 1927

Schneider, H., *Ludwig van Beethoven: 8. Sinfonie F-Dur, op. 93*, Mainz, 1989

Schrade, L., *Beethoven in France*, New Haven, 1942

Schuler, M., 'Zwei unbekannte "Fidelio"-Partitur-abschriften aus dem Jahre 1814', *Archiv für Musikwissenschaft*, xxxix (1982), 151–67

Schürmann, K., *Beethoven Texte*, Münster, 1980

Schwarz, B., 'Beethoven and the French Violin School', *The Musical Quarterly*, xliv (1958), 431–47

Senner, W. M., 'The Reception of Beethoven's Musical Compositions by His Contemporaries', *The Beethoven Newsletter*, i (1986), 7–9

Seyfried, I. von, *Ludwig van Beethovens Studien im Generalbass, Contrapunkt und in der Compositionslehre*, Vienna, 1832

Simpson, R., 'The Chamber Music for Strings', in Arnold, 1971, pp. 241–78

Smolle, K., *Wohnstätten Ludwig van Beethovens von 1792 bis zu seinem Tod*, Bonn, 1970

Solomon, M., *Beethoven*, New York, 1977

——, 'Beethoven and Schiller', 1980a, in Winter, 1980, pp. 162–75 (rev. version in Solomon, 1988)

——, 'On Beethoven's Creative Process: a Two-Part Invention', *Music & Letters*, lxi (1980b), 272–83 (rev. version in Solomon, 1988)

——, 'Beethoven's Tagebuch of 1812–1818', in Tyson, 1982b, pp. 193–288 (rev. version in Solomon, 1988; see also Solomon, 1990)

——, 'Beethoven: the Quest for Faith', *Beethoven-Jahrbuch*, x (1978–81), Bonn, 1983, 101–19 (rev. version in Solomon, 1988)

——, *Beethoven Essays*, Cambridge, Mass., 1988

——, *Beethovens Tagebuch* (facsimile, transcription and commentary), ed. Sieghard Brandenburg, Bonn, 1990

Sonneck, O. G., ed., *Beethoven: Impressions of Contemporaries*, New York, 1926, R/1967

Sorsby, M., 'Beethoven's Deafness', *Journal of Laryngology and Otology*, xlv (1930), 529–44

Stadlen, P., 'Schindler's Beethoven Forgeries', *The Musical Times*, cxviii (1977), 549–52

——, 'Schindler and the Conversation Books', *Soundings*, vii (1978), 2–18

——, 'Beethoven and the Metronome', *Soundings*, ix (1982), 38–73

Staehelin, M., 'Another Approach to Beethoven's Last String Quartet Oeuvre: The Unfinished String Quintet of 1826/27', in Wolff, 1980, pp. 302–23

——, 'Die Beethoven-Materialien im Nachlass von Ludwig Nohl', *Beethoven-Jahrbuch*, x (1978–81), Bonn, 1983, 201–19

Sterba, E. and R., *Beethoven and his Nephew*, New York, 1954

Sternfeld, F. W., 'Goethe and Beethoven', in Dahlhaus, 1971, pp. 587–90

Stowell, R., *Violin Technique and Performance Practice in the Late 18th and Early 19th Centuries*, Cambridge, England, 1985

Strunk, O., *Source Readings in Music History*, New York, 1950

Taruskin, R., 'Performers and Instruments', *19th-Century Music*, xii (1989), 240–56

Tellenbach, M-E., *Beethoven und seine 'unsterbliche Geliebte' Josephine Brunswick*, Zurich, 1983

Thayer, A. W., *Ludwig van Beethovens Leben*, 3 vols, Berlin, 1866–79; vol. i rev. H. Deiters, Berlin, 1901, rev. H. Riemann, Leipzig, 1917; vols ii–iii rev. H. Riemann, Leipzig, 1910–11; vols iv–v continued and completed by H. Deiters and H. Riemann, rev. Riemann, Leipzig, 1907–8; vols ii–v reissued, Leipzig, 1922–3; English version, ed. and rev. H. Krehbiel, New York, 1921; rev. E. Forbes as *Thayer's Life of Beethoven*, Princeton, 1964, 2/1967

Timbrell, C., 'Notes on the Sources of Beethoven's Op. 111', *Music & Letters*, lviii (1977), 204–15

Tovey, D. F., *A Companion to Beethoven's Pianoforte Sonatas*, London, 1931

——, *Essays in Musical Analysis*, 6 vols, London, 1935–9

——, *Essays in Musical Analysis: Chamber Music*, ed. H. J. Foss, London, 1944a

——, *Beethoven*, London, 1944b

Treitler, L., ' "To Worship that Celestial Sound": Motives for Analysis', *Journal of Musicology*, i (1982), 153–70

Truscott, H., 'The Piano Music – I', in Arnold, 1971, pp. 68–125

Tusa, M. C., 'Die authentischen Quellen der "Eroica" ', *Archiv für Musikwissenschaft*, xlii (1985), 121–50

Tyson, A., 'Beethoven in Steiner's Shop', *The Music Review*, xxiii (1962), 119–27

——, *The Authentic English Editions of Beethoven*, London, 1963a

——, 'The First Edition of Beethoven's Op. 119 Bagatelles', *The Musical Quarterly*, xlix (1963b), 331–8

——, 'Beethoven's *Kakadu* Variations and their English History', *The Musical Times*, civ (1963c), 108–10

——, 'Moscheles and his "Complete Edition" of Beethoven', *The Music Review*, xxv (1964), 136–41

——, 'The Textual Problems of Beethoven's Violin Concerto', *The Musical Quarterly*, liii (1967), 482–502

——, 'Beethoven's Heroic Phase', *The Musical Times*, cx (1969), 139–41

——, 'Notes on Five of Beethoven's Copyists', *Journal of the American Musicological Society*, xxiii (1970), 439–71

——, 'Stages in the Composition of Beethoven's Piano Trio Op. 70, No. 1', *Proceedings of the Royal Musical Association*, xcvii (1970–71), 1–19

——, 'Beethoven's English Canzonetta', *The Musical Times*, cxii (1971a), 122–5

——, 'Steps to Publication – and Beyond', 1971b, in Arnold, 1971, pp. 459–89

——, 'Beethoven to the Countess Susanna Guicciardi: A New Letter', 1973a, in Tyson, 1973c, pp. 1–17

———, 'The Authors of the Op. 104 String Quintet', 1973b, in Tyson, 1973c, pp. 158–73

———, ed., *Beethoven Studies* [vol. i], New York, 1973c; London, 1974

———, 'The Problem of Beethoven's "First" *Leonore* Overture', *Journal of the American Musicological Society*, xxviii (1975), 292–334

———, 'Prolegomena to a Future Edition of Beethoven's Letters', 1977a, in Tyson, 1977b, pp. 1–19

———, ed., *Beethoven Studies 2*, London, 1977b

———, 'Yet Another "Leonore" Overture?', *Music & Letters*, lviii (1977c), 192–204

———, 'The "Razumovsky" Quartets: Some Aspects of the Sources', 1982a, in Tyson, 1982b, pp. 107–40

———, ed., *Beethoven Studies 3*, Cambridge, 1982b

———, 'A Beethoven Price List of 1822', 1984a, in Lockwood, 1984, pp. 53–65

———, 'Ferdinand Ries (1784–1838): the History of his Contribution to Beethoven Biography', *19th-Century Music*, vii (1984b), 209–21

Unger, M., *Beethovens Handschrift*, Bonn, 1926

———, 'Die Beethovenhandschriften der Pariser Konservatoriumsbibliothek', *Neues Beethoven-Jahrbuch*, vi (1935), 87–123

———, 'From Beethoven's Workshop', *The Musical Quarterly*, xxiv (1938), 323–40

Unverricht, H., *Die Eigenschriften und die Originalausgaben von Werken Beethovens in ihrer Bedeutung für die moderne Textkritik*, Basel, 1960

Volek, T., and Macek, J., 'Beethoven's Rehearsals at the Lobkowitz's', *The Musical Times*, cxxvii (1986), 75–80

Wade, R., 'Beethoven's Eroica Sketchbook', *Fontes artis musicae*, xxiv (1977), 254–89

Wagner, R., *Mein Leben*, 2 vols, Munich, 1963

Wallace, R., *Beethoven's Critics: Aesthetic Dilemmas and Resolutions during the Composer's Lifetime*, Cambridge, 1986

———, 'Background and Expression in the First Movement of Beethoven's Op. 132', *The Journal of Musicology*, vii (1989), 3–20

Walz, M., 'Kontrastierende Werkpaare in Beethovens Symphonien', *Archiv für Musikwissenschaft*, xlvi (1989), 271–93

Watson, J. A., 'Beethoven's Debt to Mozart', *Music & Letters*, xviii (1937), 248–58

Webster, J., 'Traditional Elements in Beethoven's Middle-Period String Quartets', in Winter, 1980, pp. 94–133

———, 'The Falling-Out between Haydn and Beethoven: the Evidence of the Sources', in Lockwood, 1984, pp. 3–45

Wegeler, F. G., and Ries, F., *Biographische Notizen über Ludwig van Beethoven*, Koblenz, 1838; 2nd edn (with 'Nachtrag' by Wegeler), Koblenz, 1845; rev. A. Kalischer, Berlin, 1906; trans. F. Noonan as *Remembering Beethoven*, Arlington, 1987

Wendel, T., 'Beethoven Recordings on the Fortepiano', *The Beethoven Newsletter*, i (1986), pp. 10–12

Wenk, A., *Analyses of Nineteenth- and Twentieth-Century Music: 1940–1985*, Boston, 1987

Westphal, K., *Vom Einfall zur Symphonie: Einblick in Beethovens Schaffensweise*, Berlin, 1965

Wheeler, K. M., ed., *German Aesthetic and Literary Criticism: The Romantic Ironists and Goethe*, Cambridge, England, 1984

Willetts, P. J., *Beethoven and England: An Account of Sources in the British Musueum*, London, 1970

Winter, R., 'Plans for the Structure of the String Quartet in C sharp minor, Op. 131', in Tyson, 1977b, pp. 106–37

———, and Carr, B., edd., *Beethoven, Performers, and Critics: The International Beethoven Congress Detroit 1977*, Detroit, 1980

———, *Compositional Origins of Beethoven's Opus 131*, Ann Arbor, 1982

———, 'Reconstructing Riddles: The Sources for Beethoven's *Missa Solemnis*', in Lockwood, 1984, pp. 217–50

Wolff, C., ed., *The String Quartets of Haydn, Mozart, and Beethoven: Studies of the Autograph Manuscripts* (Isham Library Papers, iii), Cambridge, Mass., 1980

Young, P. M., *Beethoven: A Victorian Tribute*, London, 1976

Zenck, M., *Die Bach-Rezeption des späten Beethoven*, Stuttgart, 1986

Zickenheiner, O., *Untersuchungen zur Credo-Fuge der Missa Solemnis von Ludwig van Beethoven*, Munich, 1984

LIST OF ILLUSTRATIONS

THE CONTRIBUTORS

Dr Barry Cooper is a Senior Lecturer in Music at Manchester University, having moved from Aberdeen University in 1990. He has written articles and reviews on Beethoven and other subjects for *Music & Letters, The Musical Times, The Beethoven Newsletter* and many other journals. His book *Beethoven and the Creative Process* was published to wide acclaim, and more recently he has published *Beethoven's Folksong Settings*, a book which grew out of work for *The Beethoven Compendium*. His identification of some sketches for what would have been Beethoven's Tenth Symphony, and his subsequent realization and completion of the first movement in 1988, attracted great international attention: the work has been recorded by three different companies and received live performances in many countries. He has also published books on English Baroque keyboard music and on music theory in Britain in the 17th and 18th centuries.

Dr Anne-Louise Coldicott was formerly a Lecturer in Music at Salford University. She wrote a Ph.D. dissertation on the sources of Beethoven's concertos, and is preparing some of the material for publication. She combines the continuation of her research on Beethoven with violin teaching and performing and work for a publishing firm.

Dr Nicholas Marston is a Lecturer in Music at Oxford University. His research into Beethoven's sketch material and compositional processes has resulted in a number of articles and reviews in *Music Analysis, 19th-Century Music* and other periodicals. He has recently published a book on Beethoven's Piano Sonata op.109, and his edition of the sketchbook for the *Pastoral* Symphony is due to be published shortly.

Dr William Drabkin completed his doctoral thesis, on the sketches for Beethoven's Piano Sonata op.111, at Princeton University in 1977 and has taught since then at the University of Southampton. His writings include a book on the *Missa Solemnis*, essays on Beethoven's compositional process and other Classical topics, writings on Heinrich Schenker, and analytical studies of Italian operas. He is a member of the editorial board of *Music Analysis* and the new *Beethoven Forum*.

INDEX

Page numbers in *italic* refer to illustrations.
Page numbers in **bold** indicate the principal references.

CPSIA information can be obtained
at www.ICGtesting.com
Printed in the USA
FSHW011011190820
73105FS